Guyanese Achievers USA & Canada

A CELEBRATION

A collection of profiles
compiled by

VIDUR DINDAYAL

Order this book online at www.trafford.com
or email orders@trafford.com

Most Trafford titles are also available at major online book retailers.

© Copyright 2011 Vidur Dindayal.
All rights reserved. No part of this publication may be reproduced, stored in a retrieval system, or transmitted, in any form or by any means, electronic, mechanical, photocopying, recording, or otherwise, without the written prior permission of the author.

Printed in the United States of America.

ISBN: 978-1-4269-5861-8 (sc)
ISBN: 978-1-4269-5860-1 (hc)
ISBN: 978-1-4269-5862-5 (e)

Library of Congress Control Number: 2011902946

Trafford rev. 04/07/2011

 www.trafford.com

North America & international
toll-free: 1 888 232 4444 (USA & Canada)
phone: 250 383 6864 ♦ fax: 812 355 4082

A message from His Excellency Bayney Karran

Ambassador of Guyana to the USA

Guyanese are a migratory people. For decades they have departed their native shores in large numbers to find increased opportunities for their families. In North America and beyond, the ranks of the Guyanese diaspora is steadily swollen by new immigrants out of Guyana and those born of them. Overseas Guyanese communities, sometimes referred to as Little Guyanas, have facilitated the spread of the culture and the traditions of their homeland in foreign metropoles.

Virtually every entry in this volume represents a triumph of achievement, often in the face of adversity, solitude, and sacrifice. Yet with a well-earned reputation as an industrious and talented people, Guyanese have ascended inexorably within the fabric of their host societies. Many have distinguished themselves professionally in fields as diverse as the arts, the sciences, culture, politics, and entertainment. Guyanese have often been welcomed and recognized among overseas communities for their contributions.

Many among them who maintain linkages with Guyana contribute in good measure to our country's progress and development. This is evident in areas such as commercial and technological development, as well as in the general globalization of our society. The development of Guyana's diaspora reflects a process of pollination among cultures and is an example of fraternity among peoples.

As individuals and families from such a small nation emigrate to far-flung places, human bonds are frayed. The extensiveness of the diaspora leads to a yearning for contact and connectivity that are the lifeblood of human interaction. This worthwhile compilation of biographies by Vidur Dindayal helps address this need and is a significant source of information about overseas Guyanese who have done their compatriots proud.

Bayney Karran
Ambassador of Guyana to the
United States of America

Message from His Excellency Rajnarine Singh

High Commissioner for Guyana to Canada

I commend Mr. Vidur Dindayal for his work in compiling the material for this book. Guyana is a small country, but the contribution it has made to the international community is immense.

Not many people around the world know of this, and Vidur's work would surely help to improve the knowledge of those who are not familiar with our country or its people. His book highlights the work the diaspora is doing in helping to make the world a better place.

Documenting the achievements of Guyanese abroad also could help to encourage the younger generation to aspire to greatness. Having seen the accomplishments of those before them, the younger generation would have role models to emulate.

This piece of work by Vidur Dindayal is highly praiseworthy.

Rajnarine Singh
High Commissioner

Foreword

Vibert C. Cambridge, PhD

Professor, School of Media Arts and Studies
Scripps College of Communication, Ohio University
Athens, Ohio

Vidur Dindayal must be congratulated for his commitment to celebrating and promoting the achievements of Guyanese living around the world. In 2007, he published *Guyanese Achievers UK*, which celebrated the achievements of members of the Guyanese diaspora in the United Kingdom. In 2010, he focused on Guyanese achievers in North America. *Guyanese Achievers, USA & Canada* is the result of collaboration between Vidur and the Guyanese diaspora, who shared with him its recommendations on whom to identify as exemplars of achievement.

In this volume we meet Guyanese from all of Guyana's regions and who reflect the nation's rich multi-ethnic heritage. These personalities demonstrate that Guyanese have been successful in North America for a long time. For example, Sir James Douglas became the governor of the colony of Vancouver Island and later the colony of British Columbia in the 1850s. Today, he is considered the "father of British Columbia." For Guyanese, he is Guyana's "first gift to Canada." A statue of Sir James Douglas was unveiled in 2008 at his birthplace in Belmont, Mahaica. At the end of the first decade of the twenty-first century, the list of Guyanese who have been gifts to the United States and Canada is impressive.

This volume is an important step in recognizing and celebrating them. These include academics, actors, cultural leaders, doctors, educators, entrepreneurs, folklorists, lawyers, judges, musicians, scientists, and others who, by demonstrating inventiveness and persistence, have been recognized as exemplars of Guyanese achievement in North America.

The people celebrated in this volume are indicative of the Guyanese tradition of attaining excellence. There are many others who are not mentioned in this volume, and a new generation is building upon the foundations laid by the achievers celebrated in this volume. I am confident that Vidur's commitment to this project will result in updated editions to include those who are not mentioned.

The achievements of Guyanese in North America are impressive. Guyanese have made manifest Reverend Hawley Bryant's appeal to Guyana's children to purposefully move "onward and upward." These achievers have shown what Guyana's "sons and daughters can be." Their achievements will inspire the current generation of Guyanese at home and abroad.

> Vibert C. Cambridge
> Athens, OH
> September 27, 2010

Contents

Preface XV
Acknowledgements XIX
Guyana, formerly British Guiana 1
Villages and Towns 4
Vincent Adams 7
Jaleel Ali 15
Fareed Amin 18
Bertie Bacchus 20
M. Kazim Bacchus 32
Ivor J. Benjamin 39
Frank Birbalsingh 43
Gowkarran Budhu 47
Vibert Cambridge 58
Hazel Campayne 68
Frederick Case 70
Henry Chan 80
Deviekha Chetram 85
Nesbit Chhangur 92
Brian A. Chin 97
Godfrey Chin 101
Laurence Clarke 117
Valerie G. Coddett 125
Ken Corsbie 133
Cyril Dabydeen 139
Desmond and Joan deBarros 143
M. Jamal Deen 145
Budhendranauth Doobay 149
Danny Doobay 154
James Douglas 157
Clyde Duncan 171
Ghansham K. Dutt 175
Shaykh Faisal 177
John Farley 180

Frank Fernandes 182
Milton and Lena Ganpatsingh 185
Ulric P. Gibson 187
Ivelaw Lloyd Griffith 194
Marva Gullins 197
Sewack Gurdin 202
Peter Halder 205
Melanie Fiona Hallim 212
Harry Harakh 214
Mohamed N. Hassan 216
Arthur Ingram Hazlewood 226
Paula Matthews Hazlewood 232
Walter Hewick 236
Percy C. Hintzen 243
George E. Hopkinson 248
Dhaman Kissoon 257
V. Chris Lakhan 262
Vibert A. R. Lampkin 266
Jolyon A. Lamwatt 281
Vivian Lee 284
Geeta Leo 291
Ray Luck 299
Alli B. Majeed 302
A. Shakoor Manraj 309
Heytram Maraj 318
Wordsworth McAndrew 322
Clifton Ancel H. McDonald 324
Shirley McDonald 334
Chris Mohan 337
Janet Naidu 339
Suresh Narine 343
Richard Outram 346
Michael Anthony Patterson 354
Birendra (Don) Persaud 360
Dwarka Persaud 363
Kavita Persaud 366
Parmanand (George) Poonai 370

Premsukh Poonai	373
CCH Pounder	378
Lisa Punit	380
Gloria Rajkumar	382
Vivian Rambihar	384
Bram Ramjiawan	392
Harry Ramkhelawan	394
Pandit Ramlall	396
Mohabir L. Ramnarine	403
Dindial Ramotar	408
Ashook Ramsaran	410
John R. Rickford	422
Shyraz Riyasat	433
John Rodriguez	438
Hugh Sam	440
Terry B. Sawh	448
Joseph Schuler	450
Gail S. Seeram	451
Ishwar Sharma	455
Roop Narine Sharma	457
Shakir Sheikh	462
Joy Simon	467
Chet Singh	469
Chetram Singh	473
Cyril Patraj Singh	480
Ken Singh	486
Onkar Singh	493
Ramraj Singh	498
Samuel Sewpersad Singh	501
Vernon Singhroy	508
George Subraj	510
Ken Subraj	516
Trev Sue-A-Quan	521
Margaret S. D. Sukhram	526
Satyanand Sukul	531
Albert Sweetnam	535
Pauline Thomas	537

Rampersaud Tiwari 539
Alissa Trotz 549
Belle Patricia Tyndall 556
Michael Van Cooten 567
Ivan G. Van Sertima 569
Jennifer Welshman 580
Leslie Wight 584
Geoffrey E. Woo-Ming...587
Michael O. Woo-Ming...588
Map of Guyana 603

Preface

I am inspired by stories of the achievements of people who often come from humble origins, and I expect so would the young. I feel this compilation of pen portraits of achievers will meet a need for examples of those who have done well and successfully navigated the turbulence of life.

Role models for the young are invariably people who make the headlines, often limited to pop, sports, and TV celebrities. Surely we should also know about the achievers in other fields, such as in public service, community service, the uniformed services, teaching, nursing, transport, academic life, industry, trade, and the arts.

Guyanese immigrants, by and large, have done well wherever they have settled, whether in the United States of America, Canada, the UK, or elsewhere. This book, which contains only a small collection of mini-biographies of a cross section of Guyanese who are a credit to their origins, is particularly aimed at celebrating the achievements of Guyanese who have settled in the United States and Canada.

I offer my sincere apologies for the limited number of names in this book. After I started on this project early in 2008, I received a large volume of material, which may lead to a follow-up to this edition at some point in the future.

In this collection I have sought to record shining examples of Guyanese achievers and to capture something of their fine qualities as an illustration and inspiration to others—especially to those just beginning to face life's challenges—of what can be done. Longfellow reminds us of the value of the lives of people who have achieved in his poem "A Psalm of Life."

> Lives of great men all remind us
> We can make our lives sublime,
> And, departing, leave behind us
> Footprints on the sands of time.

This work also aims to share more widely the experiences of those few whose inspirational lives and achievements are little known outside their immediate circle, as Thomas Gray's "Elegy Written in a Country Churchyard" so eloquently explains.

> Full many a gem of purest ray serene,
> The dark unfathomed caves of ocean bear;
> Full many a flower is born to blush unseen,
> And waste its sweetness on the desert air.

In these pages I have recorded success achieved through hard work. Longfellow, in his "The Ladder of Saint Augustine, expressed it thus:

> The heights by great men reached and kept
> Were not attained by sudden flight,
> But they, while their companions slept,
> Were toiling upward in the night.

What makes an achiever? Is there an "achievement gene" and a link with the country of Guyana, a microcosm of the world, with all the ingredients of the world's heritage and culture, in all its rich variety, confluent in Guyana's small cosmopolitan population?

Factors that perhaps contribute to the drive to achieve are that most Guyanese share a common background of modest means; an education system with strict discipline, in which they are expected to obtain top marks; where achievers are highly valued, as is respect for elders in the family and in the community; and a strong sense of belonging to the larger community, be it a village, the sugar plantation, or a part of town.

Achievers' DNA appears to contain components best described in the following quote from a speech given by Sir Arthur Lewis, the internationally renowned economist and Nobel Laureate, at his installation as Chancellor of the University of Guyana, on January 25, 1967.

> Excellence is achieved not only by intellect; it derives even more from character. As the old saying goes, "genius is an infinite capacity for taking pains." To achieve excellence, one must

have self-discipline; to practice the same thing over and over again, while others are enjoying themselves; to push oneself from the easy part to the hard part; to listen to criticism and use it; to reject one's own work and try again. Only the humble achieve excellence, since only the humble can learn. Excellence also implies reliability; whatever you do is well done, so that others coming after you can rely on what you have done. In the university we build character no less than brain; since brain without character achieves nothing.

Perhaps a significant component of Guyanese achievers' DNA is to be found right at home—the subliminal driving force in these stirring, uplifting, and inspiring words of the "The Song of Guyana's Children," which all sing as school children:

> Born in the land of the mighty Roraima,
> Land of great rivers and far stretching sea;
> So like the mountain, the sea and the river
> Great, wide and deep in our lives would we be;
> Onward, upward, may we ever go
> Day by day in strength and beauty grow,
> Till at length we each of us may show,
> What Guyana's sons and daughters can be.

I would like to share some of the rewarding experiences that occurred during the preparation for producing this book—this is the other half of the story of Guyanese achievement in the United States, Canada, and the UK.

My first book, *Guyanese Achievers UK*, was published in 2007. The seed of the idea was planted in a conversation with my good friend, the late Jerry Singh, a distinguished Guyanese UK lawyer and tribunal judge. I turned to Ansari Ramjohn, law lecturer, for advice and guidance as I progressed with the book. Professor Eric Midwinter, OBE, prolific writer, social historian, and cricket historian, gave me self-belief and guidance, and Guyanese writer and broadcaster John Mair was unstinting in his support and encouragement.

I am very pleased to see the stellar achievements of our fellow Guyanese, the distinguished Baroness Valerie Amos, who wrote the foreword to *Guyanese Achievers UK*. She was then leader of the House of Lords. She has since been UK High Commissioner to Australia and recently was appointed head of the UN's Office of the Coordination of Humanitarian Affairs, to become the most senior Briton in the UN.

Guyanese Achievers, USA & Canada has been a very rewarding and often exciting experience. It has been a joy to learn of Guyanese, everywhere in the United States and Canada, who have excelled and done us proud.

I am pleased to record here my deepest gratitude to many who have helped me to make this book a reality. For their support and very kind messages, I am most grateful to His Excellency Bayney Karran, Ambassador of Guyana to the United States; and to His Excellency Rajnarine Singh, High Commissioner of Guyana to Canada.

I am grateful to our distinguished Guyanese media scholar Vibert C. Cambridge, PhD, professor at the School of Media Arts and Studies, Scripps College of Communication, Ohio University, who has been gracious in writing the foreword to this book.

To all who have encouraged me and helped me with information toward producing this book, I am eternally indebted. This book would not have been possible without help from Samuel Singh, Clyde Duncan, and Ram Tiwari, among others who have spent valuable time and energy in assisting with my research.

I am grateful to everyone whose profile appears in this book and for a rewarding journey of learning about the rich and varied experiences in their lives. Everyone to whom I have spoken about this book has showered me with kind words of praise and encouragement.

Finally, for most of us our birthplace is sacred and our attachment spiritual. As Guyanese say, we are attached to it by our navel string. This book would not be complete without paying respect to the place where we were born. I have, therefore, included a list of villages and townships on Guyana's coastal belt, where most Guyanese live. I have also included a sketch of aspects of Guyana to provide a context for this work.

Vidur Dindayal

Acknowledgements

I acknowledge with grateful thanks the following for use of material from their websites and publications:

Canadian Cardiovascular Society
Canadian Immigrant
City University of New York
County Court Courier, Florida
Daily Chronicle
Guyana Consulate Toronto (Canada), Guyana Awards
Guyana Folk Festival
Guyana Journal
Hibiscus magazine
Indo-Caribbean Times
McMaster University
Indo-Caribbean World
Islamic Forum of Canada
Journal of African Civilizations, Ltd., Inc.
Kaieteur News
Life Illustrated
ML Brampton Guardian
New College, University of Toronto
Newsweek
St. Stanislaus College Alumni Association Toronto
Stabroek News
Sunday Chronicle
Sunday Stabroek

Trent University
University of Alberta
University of Minnesota
University of Utah
West Indian Medical Journal

I acknowledge with grateful thanks the following distinguished writers for the use of their material and publications:

John Adams
Jerry Adler
Ronald Austin
David Clandfield
Orin Davidson
Adit Kumar
Ian McDonald
Janet Naidu
K. Persaud
Iana Seales
Jacqueline L. P. Van Sertima

Guyana, formerly British Guiana

Guyana was known formerly as British Guiana. It was the only British colony in South America. It is bounded by the Atlantic Ocean on the north, Venezuela on the West, Suriname on the East, and Brazil on the south and southwest.

In Guyana's sparsely populated hinterland, nature flourishes in its near pristine beauty, with rain forest, rivers and rapids, mountains and savannahs, lakes and waterfalls. Kaieteur, one of the most majestic of waterfalls in the world, five times higher than Niagara, is in the heart of Guyana. Nearby are the great rivers of South America, Amazon to the south, and Orinoco to the west.

Guyana is a tropical paradise, weather-wise. Evenly hot throughout the year, the heat is tempered by a constant sea breeze. There is a rainy season. The landscape is predominantly bright green. The capital, Georgetown, has a reputation of being the garden city of South America.

Most people work in the sugar industry, on rice cultivation, small-scale farming, fishing, and in cattle rearing. Mining of bauxite, gold, diamond, and minerals, and lumbering are significant industries. Greenheart, reputed to be the hardest wood in the world, comes from Guyana. Resistant to termites, it thrives in water and is widely used for structures such as wharves. Guyana boasts the highest wooden building in the world, St. George's Cathedral.

In sport, Guyana together with the former British West Indian Islands, makes up the West Indies Cricket team. Prominent Guyanese players have included, among others, Robert Christiani, Lance Gibbs, Rohan Kanhai, Joe Solomon, Kallicharan, Roy Fredericks, Clive Lloyd, Roger Harper, Chanderpaul, and Sarwan.

Bookers, of the Booker Prize, had been the biggest industrial and commercial business in the colony. Guyana's economic and political life had been closely bound to the fortunes of this company.

The country was first sighted by Christopher Columbus in 1498 and settled by the Dutch, around 1580. It was also sighted by Sir Walter Raleigh searching for El Dorado, "the country of gold" in 1595. The British took over part of the colony in 1814 and the whole country in 1831, and named it British Guiana. The early Dutch occupation accounts for Dutch names of most of the villages and townships.

Most of Guyana's population live on the flat coastal belt facing the Atlantic. In area, Guyana is about as large as the United Kingdom, but the population is just under a million.

Guyana is called the land of six peoples, people of African, East Indian, Amerindian, Chinese, Portuguese, and other European descent. The early European settlers cultivated sugar cane using slave labor. After the abolition of slavery they obtained laborers from Europe, particularly Portuguese from Madeira, East Indians from India, and Chinese laborers. This accounts for the cosmopolitan population.

Culturally, Guyanese are a microcosm of the world, reflecting the cultures of Europe, Africa, Asia, and the indigenous Amerindians. Indian music, European music and Caribbean music are all played everywhere. Churches, Hindu temples, and mosques have pride of place everywhere, and Christian, Hindu, and Muslim festivals are, for the most part, celebrated by all.

English is the language of Guyanese. The colloquial language is a rich blend of accents, words, and phrases derived from colonial sugar planters, from England, Scotland, Wales, and Holland, and from the early Africans, East Indians, and Chinese. During the early years of uncompromising colonial rule, the Indians, Africans, and Chinese lost their languages, yet the core values of their cultures have survived, a testimony to the indomitable nature of humans.

The innate survival kit in humankind everywhere, to survive, to adjust, adapt and grow stronger, to remove obstacles and thrive in their new world has made Guyanese build up traditions of excellence in virtually every field of activity that people anywhere would be proud of. Patterned on the old British systems, their schools and colleges have been second to none, so too their legal system, administration system, and standards set by professionals and business people.

Every one of the achievers has inspired many who followed them. They have set benchmarks and records, which will continue to be set higher and higher. That is the stuff of achievers, the march to improve, to do well, to attain excellence in whatever we do.

Villages and Towns

Our birthplace is very dear to us. For some, it is sacred, the attachment spiritual. We say we are tied to it by our navel string. As a mark of respect, the following list is included, of the villages and towns on the Guyana coastal belt where most of us were born, from Charity on the Essequibo Coast to Orealla on the Corentyne River—with sincere apologies for inadvertent errors and omissions.

The Essequibo Coast: Charity, New Road, Somerset and Berks, Evergreen, Opposite, Maria's Delight, La Resource, Better Hope, Andrews, Better Success, Bounty Hall, Dartmouth, Perth, Dunkeld, Lisa, Paradise, Walton Hall, Devonshire Castle, Hampton Court, Sparta, Danielstown, Coffee Grove, Lima, Henrietta, Anna Regina, Cotton Field, Bushlot, Reliance, Land of Plenty, Three Friends, Aberdeen, Affiance, Taymouth Manor, Queenstown, La Union, Tapacuma, Perseverence, Golden Fleece, Cullen, Zorg, Joanna Cicelia, Maria's Lodge, Suddie, Onderneeming, Adventure, Airy Hall, Riverstown, Huis T'Dieren, Middlesex, Fairfield, Blegezeight, Aurora, Supernaam, Bartica, Adventure.

Wakenaam, Leguan, Hog Island, Great Truli Island, Fort Island.

West Coast Demerara: Parika, Hydronie, Farm, Bushy Park, Greenwich Park, Vergenoegen, Tuschen, Boeraserie, Met-en-meer-zorg, De Willem, De Kendren, Zeeburg, De Groot and Klyne, Uitvlugt, Stewartville, Leonora, Groenveldt, Anna Chatherina, Cornelia Ida, Hague, Den Amstel, Blankenburg, La Jalouise, Windsor Forest, Riumzigt, Harlem, Rotterdam, La Union, Best Village, Vreed-en-Hoop.

West Bank Demerara. Vreed-en-Hoop, Plantain Walk, Coglan Bush, Phoenix Park Pouderoyen, Versailles, Goed Fortuin, Schoon Ord, La Grange, Canal No 1 Polder, Bagotville, Nismes, Zoevlugt, La Retraite,

Stanley Town, Canal No 2 Polder, Belle Vue, Goed-in-Tent, Sisters, Wales, Patentia, Potosi, Wismar.

East Bank Demerara: Georgetown, Albuoystown, Alexander Village, La Penitence, Ruimveldt, Houston, Agricola, Rome, Eccles, Bagotstown, Republic Park, Mc Doom Village, Mocha, Peter's Hall, Nandy Park Providence, Ramsburg, Herstelling, Farm, Vreed-en-Rust, Covent Garden, Prospect, Little Diamond, Diamond, Golden Grove, Good Success, Craig, Hutsonville, New Hope, Friendship, Garden of Eden, Brickery, Supply, Support, Relief, Land of Canaan, Sarah Johanna, Pearl, Caledonia, Huist Coverden, Den Heuvel, Soesdyke, CBJ International Airport Timehri, Linden.

East Coast Demerara: Georgetown, Sophia, Kitty, Prashad Nagar, Lamaha Gardens,Bel Air, Subryan Ville, Campbellville, Newtown,Liliendaal, Pattensen, Bel Air Park,Turkeyen, Cummings Lodge, Oleander Gardens, Plaisance, Industry, Ogle, Success, Courida Park, Mon Repos, Goedverwagting, Sparendaam, Plaisance, Better Hope, Vryheid Lust, Brothers, Montrose, Felicity, Le Ressouvenir, Success, Chateau Margot, La Bonne Intention, Beterverwagting, Triumph, Mon Repos, De Endragt, Good Hope, Two Friends, Nog Eens, Lusignan, Annandale, La Reconaissance, Buxton, Friendship, Vigilance, Bladen Hall, Strathspey, Coldingen, Non Pareil, Enterprise, Melanie Damishana, Bachelor's Adventure, Paradise, Foulis, Hope, Enmore, Haslington, Golden Grove, Nabaclis, Cove & John, Craig Milne, Victoria, Belfield, Nootenzuil, Lowlands, Hope, Dochfour, Two Friends, Anns Grove, Clonbrook, Bee Hive, Greenfield, Orange Nassau, Grove, Unity, Lancaster, Mahaica.

Mahaica Creek: Mahaica, Hand-en-Veldt, Good Hope, Helena 1 & 2, Belmont, Supply, Vereeniging, La Bonne Mere, Cane Grove, Handsome Tree.

Mahaicony Creek: Mahaicony, Washclothes, Champagne, Gover, Yarrow Creek, Bora Point, Pine Grounds, Gordon Table, Savannah.

Mahaica to Abary: Mahaica, Essex, Belvedere, High Dam, Broomhall, Fairfield, Bath, Strangroen, De Kendren, Zeland, Bushy Park, Cottage, Sarah, Drill, Mahaicony, Huntley, Airey Hall, Novar, Burma, Good Faith, Recess, Dundee,Little Abary.

West Coast Berbice: Profit, Foulis, Eldorado, Belladrum, Paradise, Golden Fleece, Weldaad, Rising Sun, Washington, Numbers 42, 41, and 40, BelleVue, Lichfield, Number 37, Cottage, Phoenix, Kingelly, Brahn, Ross, Yeoville, Chester, Britannia, Tempi, Numbers 30, 29, 28, and 27, Lovely Lass, Golden Grove, Onverwagt, Bush Lot, Armadale, Hopetown,

Fort Wellington, Rodborugh, Bath, Bath Settlement, Woodley Park, Numbers 12 to 2, Cotton Tree, D'Edwards, Rosignol.

West Bank Berbice: Rosignol, Plantain Walk, Shields Town, Number 43, Blairmont, Blairmont Settlement, Ithaca.

East Bank Berbice: News Amsterdam, Stanleytown, Vryheid's Lust, Providence, Friends, Edinburgh, Rotterdam, Mara.

Canje: Cumberland, Cane Field, Neulear Compound, Park Lane, Rose Hall, Reliance, Adelphi, Goed Bananen Land, Betsy Ground, Gold Stone Hall, Gangaram, Enterprise, Speculation, Good Hand, Volkert's Hast, Bachelor's Adventure, Zorg, New Forest.

New Amsterdam to Orealla: New Amsterdam, Queenstown, Voorburg, Sheet Anchor, Number 2, Palmyra, Bramfield, Industry, Gibraltar, Courtland, Nineteen, Fyrish, Kilkoy, Bohemia, Lothian, Chesney, Albion Front, Albion, Nigg, Belvedere, Williamsburg, Rosehall Town, Port Mourant, Ankerville, Haswell, Resource, MissPhoebe, Tain, Bloomfield, Letterkenny, Auchlyne, Lancaster, Manchester, Ulverston, Whim, Hampshire, Alness, Hoggstye, Adventure, Limlair, Friendship, Nurney, Kildonan, Maida, Kilmarnock, Cromarty, Wellington Park, Tarlogie, Haversham, Bushlot, Phillipi, Brighton, Kiltern, Eversham, Epsom, Goed Hope, Leeds, Bengal, Union, Dead Tree Farm, Nemes, Maida, Numbers 60 and 63, Benab, New Market, Numbers 66 to 77, Springlands, Eliza and Mary, Numbers 78 and 79, Queenstown, Kingston, Skeldon, Crabwood Creek, Jackson Creek, Orealla.

Dr. Vincent Adams

BSc, MS, PhD
Environmental Scientist
Office Director, US Department of Energy

Dr. Vincent Adams is a senior executive service (SES) official of the United States federal government. This SES corps comprises the highest level of civilian career professionals in the government and is equivalent of general in the ranks of the army. The corps of professionals runs the day-to-day operations of the government while working alongside the political appointees, who come and go with changes in the administration.

Since his swearing-in in July 2007, Dr. Adams has headed several key areas of responsibility in the US Department of Energy's (DOE) $6–8 billion per year environmental management's (EM) massive decommissioning, decontamination, dismantlement (DDD) and cleanup of the nation's nuclear weapons complex, built and operated during the fighting of the cold war.

In June 2010, he relocated to Ohio to head the estimated $16 billion operations at the Portsmouth, Ohio, site, formerly used to enrich uranium for the manufacture of nuclear weapons and fuels for commercial nuclear reactors. The Portsmouth complex is only one of three such facilities built in the United States for enriching uranium and is the second to undergo DDD and cleaned up. Dr. Adams was also responsible for the DDD and cleanup of the first complex in Oak Ridge, Tennessee, during the tail end of his nineteen years in Oak Ridge. In addition to the DDD and cleanup, other important missions at the Portsmouth site include the development of the next generation of uranium enrichment technologies and the conversion of the facilities and real estate, as appropriate, to an industrial complex for long-term economic sustenance to the community.

From March 2009 to the time of his moving to Portsmouth in 2010, Dr. Adams was called upon to serve as the deputy director for standing up and managing the Department of Energy's $6 billion stimulus allocation. His efforts led the way in creating and saving thousands of jobs, while accelerating the completion of many cleanup projects throughout the United States. During this period, he was urgently dispatched to the DOE's largest nuclear site, occupying 320 square miles (twice the size of Barbados) at Savannah River, South Carolina, where he spent six months successfully rectifying some major issues concerning the mismanagement of projects related to the $1.7 billion in stimulus funds allocated to the site.

During his first year as an SES in Washington DC, Dr. Adams headed the development of new science and technologies that will enhance and accelerate the cleanup of the groundwater and soils and protect some of the largest groundwater reservoirs and rivers that form the lifeline of the United States from further contamination and risk to the nation's economy, health, and the environment.

In June 2010, the Linden Fund's website featured a glowing report on Dr. Adams's sterling achievements, both in his profession as a scientist and in his limitless support of the Linden Fund. The Linden Fund is an umbrella organization that mobilizes the overseas diaspora and residents of the Linden community in the economic and social redevelopment of the town of Linden, in Guyana. The following profile is based on and contains excerpts from that report, titled "Congratulations to Dr. Vincent Adams!"

Vincent Adams was born and bred at Christianburg, Linden. He excelled in sports in his young days and played on the Guyana national cricket team while only a teenager. Unfortunately, at the age of nineteen, his promising cricketing career was cut short by an automobile accident.

This prompted him to pursue academics. Vincent was among the first class of engineers graduating from the University of Guyana (UG) in 1973. After receiving his bachelor's degree in civil and public health engineering from UG, he spent his first two years with the Guyana Water Authority as the Guyana government's counterpart engineer on the United Nations Development Program project, conducting feasibility studies for the design and construction of sewerage, water supply, and storm water systems for Guyana. In his second two years with the Water Authority, Vincent was the lead engineer responsible for the planning, design, and construction of all water wells in Guyana, east of the Demerara River.

He afterwards emigrated to the United States, where he obtained two master's degrees in groundwater hydrology, and geological and petroleum engineering, and a PhD in environmental engineering.

Dr. Adams has specialized in environmental cleanup, petroleum reservoir engineering, and technology development. He has spent the past thirty years working for the Department of Energy and Amoco Oil Company, dedicating himself to solving problems in these fields.

In the past twenty-four years with the Department of Energy, he has headed many highly visible and critical—sometimes very controversial—projects, including transforming nuclear weapons technologies into applications for medicines and medical procedures, curtailing greenhouse gases, fuel cell development to reduce dependency on fossil energy, and improvement to petroleum refining efficiency; developing the science and technologies for safe underground storage of wastes from nuclear power plants; designing, constructing, and operating the only incinerator in the United States licensed to treat any form and type of waste; and developing the science and technologies for homeland security to protect commerce across ports and highways from terrorists attacks.

Dr. Adams also developed the theory and the first set of mathematical equations that describe the operation and performance of the internationally renowned state-of-the-art ionizing wet scrubber, used for cleaning effluents from stack emissions. While at Amoco for five years as a petroleum reservoir engineer, Dr. Adams pioneered work in the use of carbon dioxide flooding for the tertiary recovery of oil, a technology that has now become state of the art for oil recovery within the petroleum industry.

Highly regarded nationally and internationally among his peers of scientists and engineers, Dr. Adams serves in leadership roles on various national and international technical committees.

He currently represents the DOE as a consultant to the International Atomic Energy Agency (IAEA) based in Vienna, Austria, the United Nations' arm responsible for monitoring and overseeing all nuclear materials and weapons throughout the world. He was chairman of the 2nd IAEA international conference, held in Kazakhstan in 2009, on the remediation of land, air, and water contaminated by nuclear operations throughout the world. The conference was attended by over fifty nations.

He was the chairman of the Southern Section of the Air & Waste Management Association, governing the states of Alabama, Georgia, Mississippi, and Tennessee. The association is a preeminent professional organization with a membership of over nine thousand environmental professionals in sixty-five countries.

He led a US technical team to Germany and was cochair for the international conference on developing technologies and strategies for the safe recycling and reuse of radioactive materials. He has the unique distinction of being an expert in contaminant transport and behavior in all three media (air, water, and soil) of the environment.

Dr. Adams's accomplishments at the highest levels in the United States government is matched, with equal drive and commitment, by his support of the Linden Fund. In acknowledging his many accomplishments, Dr. Adams, without hesitation, acclaimed that his biggest contribution to mankind is being chairman of the Linden Fund for the past nine years. He sees this voluntary service as his obligation and a way to pay back the community and country that raised and molded him into what he is today. He is driven by the passion of his beliefs that no child should be denied an education, health care, food, or shelter because of the lack of means.

He holds great love and passion for the Linden community and Guyana. He is in constant contact with people there, and he makes frequent trips home. As chairman of the Linden Fund, USA, Dr. Adams plays a key leadership role in revitalizing the Linden community. He has been a driving force behind the strategic five-year development plan for Linden and Region 10, the brainchild of Regional Chairman Mortimer Mingo. This plan charts the social and economic future of this area.

The Linden Fund has provided several scholarships; medical supplies and equipment to the area, including several medical teams that provide surgeries and other critical-care needs to the hospitals; and furniture for the schools. The Linden Fund is engaged in a revitalization program to create new job opportunities for the area. The fund sponsors the Adopt-a-Child (AAC) program, in partnership with the Linden Care Foundation. In the

AAC program, individuals are allowed to "adopt" a child or children by providing a monthly donation that covers the cost of nutrition, education, and life skills. Additionally, the Linden Fund has ensured the graduation of students from various institutions, including University of Guyana, through their sponsorship of tuition and other costs for eleven students. The fund led the way in partnering with the Region 10 chairman and the mayor, along with private entities, in establishing the now-popular annual Linden Town Week that injects millions of dollars on an annual basis into the community. The fund continues to comanage this annual event, which has become the largest carnival and festival in Guyana.

Mortimer Mingo, the chairman of Region 10, has paid a tribute to Dr. Adams's accomplishments. He said that Dr. Adams has always demonstrated his love for and commitment to the development of Linden and Region 10 in very tangible ways. He has held up this "distinguished gentleman as a role model for all of our residents, and indeed all of Guyana. He never strays far from his roots and has always held Linden dear to his heart in thought and deed, especially through his work with the Linden Fund, and for this our residents will surely be equally proud of his achievements, and I extend best wishes to Dr. Adams on their behalf as well."

Ronald Austin, freelance journalist, captain of the first Guyana under-nineteen cricket team in 1977, academic, and a former Guyana ambassador to China, wrote a glowing tribute to Vincent, the stellar achiever, scientist, cricketer, philanthropist, and the man. In his article "Dr. Vincent Adams—A Model of Excellence," Ronald wrote, among other things:

> I have always been fascinated by the fact that … Guyanese continue to excel in different parts of the world. It doesn't matter where you go, whether it is Canada, the United States, or Europe, you will always find a Guyanese who is a renowned and recognized professional. …
>
> Dr. Adams's achievement is an example of application, persistence, and a dedication to a life of the mind—and not narrowly so. He is a rounded individual who has retained a capacity for compassion and charity which ensures that he spends long hours and days in trying to give back to the Linden community what it gave him as an individual. And I must hasten to add that Dr. Adams's professional distinction is adorned by a personality which is characterized by an

engaging sense of humor and a becoming modesty. You see, like all gifted people, he allows his achievements to speak for themselves. ...

Vincent Adams, like most young men in Guyana, had grown up at a time when the suffocating colonial system was coming to an end and the first shoots of an emerging meritocracy were becoming evident. This was one of the blessings of independence. The society was moving from one where individuals could ascend the social ladder on the basis of their pigmentation and social connections, to one where talent mattered. Cricket was one of the first areas where a system based on merit was emerging with some clarity. And it is no accident that it was here that Vincent first tested his mettle. But to make my point the greater force, it must be understood that cricket was not divorced from education as a means of making one's way in a meritocratic society. Let us remember that by the 1960s, "muscular learning," as Professor Seecharan has described this phenomenon (i.e., cricket and education) was firmly entrenched in our society. It was no surprise to me, therefore, when I learned in later years [that] Vincent had gone on to the University of Guyana and [had become] qualified as an engineer. Whether the young Dr. Adams knew it then or not, he was in the coils of forces which were driving him in the direction of excellence and accomplishments. And coming as he did from a family that wanted to see him scale the heights, the young Adams could do nothing but respond and fulfill its wishes.

Ronald ended his tribute thus: "Dr. Vincent Adams's accomplishments do not stand by themselves. They serve as a powerful symbol and motivating factor for other young Guyanese, whether at home or in the diaspora. For his life and his professional career are testimony to the fact that poverty is no barrier to reaching goals and ambitions. Now that Vincent Adams has become a senior executive service official of the United States government, every young man and woman in the Linden community must feel that they have a chance in life. Knowing Vincent as well as I do, I am sure he would like to know, in the years to come, that he led the way for many young Guyanese from Linden and the rest of the country."

Orin Davidson, a writer of renown, penned an article, published in the *Stabroek News*, September 30, 2010, in which he captured inspiring moments of Vince's career and revealed how deeply Vince feels about Guyana. Orin writes:

> A motor accident several years ago may have cut short a promising cricketing career; life, however, is full of ironies, and when one door was closed to Vincent Adams, another threw itself open for him to step in ... and today he is one of the most respected engineers employed by the United States government....
>
> When you engage Vincent Adams, you are unlikely to think of him as a key player in the most vital sub-sector of the United States energy sector. Vince, as he is known to his friends, is an enduringly humble man, whose retention of both the mannerisms and accent of a Guyanese appears deliberate. ...
>
> A typical month in Dr. Adams's schedule includes travels around the world from Europe to South America and around the United States. Remarkably, he still finds the time to visit Guyana every year in his capacity as chairman of Linden Fund. ...
>
> Adams concedes that his enduringly Guyanese accent baffles those influential US and international executives with whom he interfaces in the course of his work. "But they all respect authority. Once you are capable enough to attain top positions, they view you for what you are and where you are from," he explains. ...
>
> Many years ago Jamaican reggae star Jimmy Cliff made a hit tune titled "Hard Road to Travel." He may well have been reflecting on Adams's rags-to-riches story, his progress from poor Linden boy to top technocrat in the United States government. Apart from not being born with a "silver spoon in mouth," Adams had no role models in academia where he lived in Christianburg ward. ... His mother had never had the opportunity to master the basic skills of reading and writing. ... He recalls that once he was soundly whipped by a teacher for not managing to place better than third in his class. ...

Discipline has been a watchword in his distinguished career. He jogged every day, rain or shine. It was that discipline that enabled him to strike a balance between his social and his professional lives.

He maintains an abiding interest in Guyana. "Guyana has the potential to become the richest country on the planet," Dr. Adams says. "There are resources and talent and a small population to maintain." He is highly enthused about plans to develop hydroelectric power in Guyana, an undertaking he feels is long overdue. "The advantage hydropower has is a lesser cost factor compared to oil drilling. You don't have to conduct expensive feasibility studies, which most times lead to nothing. With hydropower knowledge already established, the cost information is known."

Dr. Adams is also a firm believer in renewable energy and cites Brazil as a country which remains largely unaffected by energy crises because they were wise enough to invest in ethanol production. The road to Brazil, he says, holds much promise for his own hometown, Linden, as it does for Guyana as a whole.

When asked in a telephone interview about his greatest disappointment, Vincent said, with a smile. "Being robbed the opportunity to play cricket for the West Indies by that accident, but then, would I want to trade what I have accomplished with those of many of my good pals who became famous cricketers? I don't think so. My biggest disappointment and frustration is not being able to do more for the younger generation, but I still have great hope for them, for if I did it, you bet they can."

Vincent described how he became so emotional at the swearing-in ceremony (on his appointment as SES official of the United States), when he realized "how far this little boy from the alleys of Christianburg had come" and how much he "owed the little village of Lindeners that raised him." He said, "It is now my turn and the Linden Fund's turn to do our part and be that village for raising the generations for the future of Linden and Guyana."

October 9, 2010

Dr. Jaleel Ali

BSc, PhD
Professor of Chemistry
Dawson College, Montreal

Jaleel has been professor of chemistry at Dawson College, Montreal, for over eighteen years, and is currently chair in the Department of Chemistry & Chemical Technology.

He was recipient in his early years of the university scholarship for graduating in the top 10 percent of all students in McGill University's Faculty of Arts & Sciences in 1979. He received the T. Sterry-Hunt Award in 1980 for excellence as a teaching assistant and in 1982 for excellence as the senior teaching assistant responsible for conducting tutorials as well as various administrative tasks in the general chemistry courses at McGill University.

Jaleel Ahmad Ali was born on February 5, 1957, at Number 5 Village, West Coast Berbice, British Guiana. His late father was Rafiq Ali, a senior welfare officer with Bookers Sugar Estates. His mother is Yaswanti Ali, a retired teacher.

Jaleel attended Dawson College, and in 1976 he obtained the Diploma of College Studies- DEC (Health Science). He followed this in 1979 with a bachelor's degree in chemistry (with honors) at McGill University. His thesis was titled "Heat Capacities of Solute Transfer into n-Hexadecane." His supervisor was Prof. Donald Patterson. In 1984 Jaleel obtained his PhD in chemistry from McGill University. The title of his thesis was "Some Deductions from the Kinetic Theory of Gases for Chemically Reacting Systems and Semiconductors." His supervisor was Prof. Byung C. Eu.

He started on a teaching career in September 1979, when he was appointed as a teaching assistant at McGill University in the Department of Chemistry. His supervisors were Prof. James Hogan and Prof. Arthur Grosser. In November 1984, he was appointed a postdoctoral fellow, University of British Columbia, Department of Chemistry. His supervisor was Prof. Robert Snider. From January 1987 to August 1987, he was research associate, McGill University, Department of Chemistry, under the supervision of Prof. Byung C. Eu. He was appointed assistant professor (as a leave replacement), University of Guelph, Department of Chemistry & Biochemistry, in 1990 until 1991, and in the same period he was senior scientist, Hypercube Inc., Waterloo, Ontario. In 1992, Jaleel was appointed a professor at Dawson College, Montreal.

Jaleel has played an active role at Dawson College. He was a member of the Executive Council from 1997 to 1998 and was the returning officer of the Dawson Teachers Union from 2003 to 2004. He was on the Budget Consultation Committee from 1998 to 2005 and a senator from 1998 to 2004, and from 2007 to the present.

As a member of the Academic Planning Committee (APC), from 2000 to the present, he reviewed every program evaluation, program revision, and AEC program as part of the senate approval process. On the senate's instructions, in 2001 he helped complete the report on the re-evaluation of Dawson College's social science program that was submitted to the Commission d'évaluation d'enseignement collégiale.

On curriculum improvements at the college, he has been, from 1997 to the present, Dawson Research Journal of Experimental Science (DrJes) faculty advisor, and member of a team of science faculty that was awarded an NTIC grant of $106,000 to integrate computer technology in Dawson College's science program in 1998. He conceived and coauthored the *Science Students' Handbook*.

Jaleel has made a number of contributions to the Dawson College science program. He was a member of a team of science faculty that began developing the science program's comprehensive assessment (1996–1997) and was a member of a team that developed and implemented integrative activities in the science program (1997–1998). He was chair of the Writing Committee that revised Dawson College's science program (1998–1999).

He was first choice science program coordinator (2000–2003), chair of the Writing Committee that evaluated Dawson College's science program (2001–2003), and the science program coordinator (1998–2004).In the period from 2003 until 2005, Jaleel, as a member of the Institutional Program Evaluation Committee, actively participated in the revision of the college policy.

In the Chemistry Department, he has been chair, Department of Chemistry & Chemical Technology Dawson College (2007–present), as well as chair of the department's Health and Safety Committee (2004–2007). He has redesigned Dawson's chemistry laboratory experiments for computer-assisted data acquisition; trained chemistry faculty in the use of the computer technology; revised and rewritten four of Dawson College's laboratory manuals on behalf of the Department of Chemistry and Chemical Technology (*Physical Science, Introduction to College Chemistry, General Chemistry,* and *Chemistry of Solutions*). He was frequently course coordinator for courses offered by the department.

Jaleel has coauthored the following publications:

- *Irreversible Thermodynamics and Nonlinear Transport Processes and Instability: Application to Current Fluctuation Phenomena in Semiconductors.* Jaleel Ali and Byung C. Eu.1984.
- *Current Instability, Limit Cycles and the Entropy Production Surface.* Jaleel Ali and Byung C. Eu 1984.
- *Molecular Structure and Orientational Order Effects in Enthalpies and Heat Capacities in Solute Transfer into n-Hexadecane: Part II—Cyclic and Aromatic Solutes.* Jaleel Ali, Lina Andreoli-Ball, Sailendra Bhattacharya, Bengt Kronberg and Donald Patterson. 1985.
- *Equations of Change with Dimer Formation and Decay.* P. K. I. Tse, Jaleel Ali and Robert Snider.1988.

October 17, 2008

Fareed Amin

BA, MA
Ontario Deputy Minister

Fareed Amin is a public-sector leader in Canada with over twenty years of experience. He was winner of the Guyana Awards (Canada) 2009 Leadership Award.

The citation of the Award contains the following information, among other things:

Fareed Amin was appointed deputy minister of the Ministry of Municipal Affairs and Housing, effective December 8, 2008.

He was, prior to his recent appointment, deputy minister of the Ministry of Economic Development and the Ministry of International Trade and Investment, where he guided the conception, development, and implementation of an ambitious $1.15 billion program designed to foster innovative businesses and create well-paying, sustainable jobs. The program supports the establishment of "green" products, efficient technologies, health cures and treatments. It provides companies and businesses with a single point of contact and a service delivery guarantee.

He had served for twenty years in the Ontario Public Service. Previously, he was deputy minister in five ministries or portfolios, including

Citizenship and Immigration; Intergovernmental Affairs; Small Business and Entrepreneurship; and as deputy minister responsible for seniors and for women's issues.

When he was deputy city manager for the city of Toronto, Fareed Amin was responsible for corporate oversight, administrative governance, and coordinating the collective expertise on major citywide initiatives and projects. His portfolio at the city included building, city planning, and the waterfront secretariat.

Fareed has a master's degree in public administration from Queen's University in Kingston, Ontario, a certificate in public administration from the University of Toronto, and an undergraduate degree in applied geography and planning from the University of Guyana.

He is president of the Islamic Institute of Toronto and is married with three children.

Sources: Websites accessed May 27, 2010, on Guyana Consulate Toronto, Guyana Awards (Canada), 2009

May 27, 2010

Bertie Bacchus

BComm, CGA, MPA
Guyana and Ontario Civil Servant and College Professor

He grew up in the poor home of his mother and stepfather. His mother imparted in him a love for learning. In his teens he worked as a postman, delivering and collecting mail, for which he cycled fifty miles a day. He has traveled far since. As a college professor and World Bank finance consultant, dearest to his heart are the annual scholarships he gives to students of his village alma mater so they may study at university.

In this mini-biography, this man of quiet dignity cites the lessons he learned in his life's journey, which was full of hard blows of disappointment and despair, tempered in good measure with joys of achieving and his nestling in the sublime love, care, and support of his dear, loving family.

Bertie Glasford Bacchus was born on November 4, 1935, at Number 4 Village, West Coast Berbice, British Guiana, South America, the son of Edwin Bacchus and Clara Tim. Edwin was a wealthy businessman who lived at Number 6 Village called Belair. He owned a coconut estate and a rice mill and had acres of rice land leased to rice farmers.

Clara Tim was a domestic who married a villager named John when Bertie was a young boy. John was a worker in the seasonal balata industry in Guyana's northwest district and on the off-season, like other balata bleeders in the community, was a small-scale rice farmer, mainly for domestic consumption.

Bertie grew up in the poor but nurturing home environment of his mother and stepfather, whom he referred to as Uncle John. Uncle John was always keen in taking him around. He would take Bertie to the back dam to pick coconuts and mangoes, reap provisions from his maternal grandfather's farm, and to monitor the growth and development of the rice plant.

They would also help "mash" the rice after it had grown and was cut. They would separate the rice paddy from the stalk by using cows to repeatedly walk on the cut paddy that was placed on a very dry part of the dam. For Bertie and other boys of his age, participating in mashing rice was an enjoyable experience, because they could actively participate in harvesting and be involved with the cows. During these early years, Uncle John also taught him to play the guitar.

One of the most pivotal memories of his preteen upbringing was his mother, Clara's, influence on his life and the way she imparted her love for his learning. Her interest in his learning was boundless. Every day after school she would review with him what he'd learned and instill in him the importance of studying. What most impressed him was at the time when he was writing "school leaving," which was an exit exam for primary school students, she had already made arrangements for him to write a test for a partial scholarship to attend Wray High School in Georgetown.

Bertie passed both exams and was soon sent to stay in Lodge, a suburb of Georgetown, with a helpful and kind relative named Aunt Ella in order to attend Wray High School. His mother's hunch and belief in him paid off. Wray High recognized his lust for learning and fast-tracked him to be among its students who had started at Wray the year before, to write the final year of the Junior Cambridge Examination in 1950. Bertie passed all the seven subjects he had taken at that examination.

During those early years, Bertie kept up steady positive contacts with his father; paternal grandfather, Matbarally whom he called Bap; the housekeeper, Leisha; and his paternal aunt Jaitoon Khan and her family. Bertie's father also had relatives who lived at Numbers 4 and 3 Villages, so his family connection on both sides extended throughout the villages from Numbers 3 to 6. Although communication with his father was sometimes through relatives on both sides who worked at the estate, Bertie always felt welcomed at Number 6 Village.

On Fridays, Bap would look out for Bertie on his way to the mosque at Cotton Tree Village, which was farther away, and would regularly stop his oversized donkey-driven cart in front of Clara's house to give Bertie money. Bap was over six feet tall and carried a cane of similar length and hardiness over his shoulder as he walked on the public road that ran through the estate. He would chase off the boys from Bertie's school who came to the estate to steal tamarind and fruits.

Bap lived to be one hundred years old, by which time Bertie had returned to the community as a schoolteacher. As Bap lay dying, he reminded Bertie not to stand over him but to sit on the chair beside his bed. This closeness with his paternal family led Bertie's father to pick him up early on the morning of Bap's death so they could travel to Cotton Tree and Rosignol to arrange for his funeral.

Grandpa Bap Matbarally

Bertie says of these formative years: "They gave me a sense of purpose in succeeding academically and a sense of family, generosity, kindness, and sharing. It is truly a reflection that it takes a village—or in my case, villages—to raise a child."

Bertie returned to the village after his successful stint at Wray High. He secured a temporary job as a postal apprentice at the Rosignol Post Office. After a week of training from the postmaster and letter carriers, he date stamped, sorted, and delivered the mail daily from Cotton Tree to Number 12 Village, carried stamps for sale to villagers, and cleared the mail boxes on his return trip to the post office.

For his work at the post office, he rode his bicycle about fifty miles a day. He enjoyed the responsibilities and the dependence and the appreciation of local villagers when the mail was delivered at their doorstep. His mother Clara, however, had other plans for him. Her brother, Anthony Tim, also called Bishun, had been working for several years at Mackenzie, the mining town now known as Linden. Clara arranged for Bertie to join his uncle Tim at Mackenzie.

Uncle Tim took Bertie to stay with him at Mackenzie. Bertie felt that he was sent to join his uncle to find a better job as a clerk in one of the bauxite company offices. His uncle soon set him straight—his mother had sent him to Mackenzie to finish high school, and he was registered the following week at the Echol's High School, later renamed Mackenzie High School. Bertie joined the class to write the Senior Cambridge Examination the next year.

In terms of living accommodation, Uncle Tim lived in bachelor quarters. That is where Bertie had to live as well. Each bachelor quarter had about twenty rooms on each side of a common hallway and with common areas for bath and toilet at one end of the building. Each room accommodated two company employees. It was furnished with a closet, cooking area, and a single bed on either side of a circulation space in the center of the room. Bertie learned to share the limited space, plus the shopping and cooking, with his uncle.

While at Echol's High School and preparing to write the Senior Cambridge examination, Bertie learned that his mother had suffered a stroke. Before long, she was discharged from New Amsterdam Hospital and returned home to the village to continue her recuperation. She corresponded regularly with Bertie. On June 15, 1951, he received a letter from his mother. That night, coincidentally, he received news through the 9:00 p.m. radio announcements that his mother had passed away. She was only thirty-five years old, and Bertie was not yet sixteen years old.

At that time, the only way of traveling the sixty-five miles from Mackenzie to Georgetown was by steamer. The steamer, the *RH Carr*, made the journey in seven hours. The next one to Georgetown was on Sunday. Bertie and his uncle traveled on the Sunday, but because the steamer arrived after 4:00 p.m., they could not get transportation to Berbice until Monday. The result was that they missed his mother's funeral, which occurred on Sunday. In those days, there was no facility in most rural areas to keep the dead without burial beyond a day or so.

Bertie and Uncle Tim were very disappointed. Bertie said, "Indeed, it has been a very negative and disappointing part of my life. However, Uncle Tim and I returned to Mackenzie to try to continue with our respective pursuits. I continued my preparation for the Senior Cambridge Examination and wrote it a few months after my mother's passing." He obtained a distinction in economics and a Grade II pass. In those days passes were graded I, II, and III. Grade I was the best, and Grade II above average.

Bertie returned to his village in Berbice before receiving the examination results. In Berbice, Bertie, just over sixteen years old, was offered a job as a third-year pupil teacher at his village school. He accepted the job and very soon afterward passed the fourth-year pupil teacher's examination.

But Bertie was restless about the limited opportunity for educational advancement outside of Georgetown. He was easily persuaded to seek a job in the civil service by Rafiq Ali, a community development officer, who was engaged to be married to a fellow teacher from the village. He applied to the civil service and was appointed a clerk at the Department of Education, just after reaching his twenty-first birthday. He lived with his Aunt Ella, as he did during his early high school days.

Although Bertie was now in a respectable job with good prospects in the civil service, he was still restless. The seed of his quest for higher learning that his mother, Clara, had planted in him had rooted firmly and was growing healthily. Bertie continued with self-study for the Cambridge University Higher School Certificate and the London University Advanced Level Certificate and joined study groups with individuals with similar pursuits and subject interest.

His self-study enabled him to pass history and economics examinations for the Cambridge University Higher School Certificate, and the economics examination for the London University Advanced Level Certificate. In addition, he connected with Samuel Singh, a senior colleague and fellow Berbician, to assist a few students in evening classes who needed help in preparing for the London University GCE Ordinary Level Examinations.

Bertie's quest for continuing his education yielded two great benefits: "First, I applied in 1961 and gained admission as a new student at the University of the West Indies (UWI). Second, in the same year, I was successful at a civil service examination."

The Guyana Public Service Commission had held an examination to select administrative cadets for on-the-job and university training within a two-year period. The successful candidates would be promoted to senior administrative positions and ultimately move into the highest administrative rank of the civil service. Bertie was successful at this examination and interview and chose to continue his civil service career, rather than leave for UWI.

The lesson that Bertie says continually becomes reinforced is: "Planning for and taking self-improvement actions almost always lead to successful outcomes."

In 1961 Bertie was one of a select group of twelve administrative cadets. His training included several postings. One was in the interior, working in the Rupununi District under the district commissioner. Others were at the Ministry of Works and Hydraulics and the Ministry of Education and Training, shadowing the permanent secretaries and principal assistant secretaries, and with different professionals in various roles in those ministries.

Bertie's ministry postings were very beneficial, rewarding, and successful. "These postings taught me that to learn and move ahead in one's career development, one must learn to adapt and learn from different people who have made it through their careers."

In December 1961 Bertie became engaged to Rita Glasgow, a colleague at the Ministry of Education, who lived at La Bonne Intention (LBI) Sugar Estate. Her father, Lionel, was secretary accountant at the estate.

The government arranged for a UN management expert to work in Guyana, and the twelve cadets met with him on a weekly basis to identify, research, discuss, and write reports on topical issues in the public service. At the end of this program, the cadets who had successfully completed their training, including Bertie, attended an American International Development (USAID) four-months program in public administration at the University of Puerto Rico, beginning August 1962. A number of middle-management public servants who also joined the cadet group attended the program.

Bertie and Rita got married on August 11, 1962, a few days before the group left for Puerto Rico. Rita joined Bertie in Puerto Rico shortly thereafter. At the end of the program, Bertie obtained a University of Puerto Rico certificate in public administration.

On their return from Puerto Rico, Bertie and Rita made their home in Georgetown, and Bertie returned to work as an administrative assistant at the Ministry of Education and Training. Their first daughter, Sandra, was born on July 18, 1963.

In November 1963, Bertie was selected with about twenty other Guyanese public servants and attended a six-weeks Caribbean Regional UN Diplomatic Training program in Barbados, with attendees from Guyana, Trinidad, Barbados, and Jamaica.

Bertie says of the program: "The purpose of the program was to prepare for the establishment of diplomatic offices in the various Caribbean countries and a Caribbean diplomatic core. This was before Guyana's independence. Included in the Guyanese contingent was Rasleigh Jackson, who later became Guyana's Minister of Foreign Affairs, and Rudy Insanally, who for several years was Guyana's UN ambassador and is currently Guyana's Minister of Foreign Affairs."

From 1963, the Ministry of Education and Training looked to returning Guyanese with degrees for information and policy advice. Rudy Grant, fresh with a BA from UWI, had joined the minister's office as an advisor, and MK (Kazim) Bacchus, with an MEd and MPH, was appointed Assistant Director of Education.

The minister sought out the views of the new technical staff to ensure he obtained maximum advice from the professional/administrative staff. This, along with urgings from Rudy Grant, impressed upon Bertie the importance of obtaining a university degree. His remarkable achievements thus far in the civil service had not quenched his thirst for higher learning. Bertie decided he must have a university degree and explained how he worked toward that goal:

> I had a cordial relationship with Minister Nunes and discussed my intention with him. The minister suggested that I consider a university accounting degree, as the minister knew a few friends who had done well as accountants in the United States. I had already applied to the universities of Toronto, British Columbia (BC), and Manitoba, and the minister offered me a letter to take to the Canadian High Commissioner for a university placement in September 1964.
>
> I received acceptance letters from Manitoba and from BC. I decided on registering at the University of Manitoba, as they were the first to respond. I, [along with] Rita and one-year-old Sandra, arrived in Winnipeg, Manitoba, on September 6, 1964, and [we] were met at the airport by the president and a few members of the Caribbean Student Council, who accommodated us at the house they were sharing until my family and I could find our own accommodation.
>
> The house was owned by Professor Barry Hammond and his family. Barry was interested in working at the University of Guyana, and when he and his family moved to Guyana, Rita and I introduced him and his wife, Lois, to our family circle in Guyana. They became good friends with Rita's parents and with Aunt Ella (from my high school and pre-marriage days).

This proves that helpfulness and kindness know no boundaries and should be meted out as much as possible to anyone needing assistance.

Life was challenging as a university student with a family and with the coldness of the Canadian winter. Bertie and Rita moved into an apartment in downtown Winnipeg, Manitoba, while they waited for the birth of their second child. Bertie took the bus to attend the Faculty of Commerce at the Fort Garry campus, as well as to study at the university or at the Faculty of Commerce library on Saturdays and/or Sundays. To help maintain themselves, Rita found a babysitter for Sandra and took a temporary job at the University School of Nursing at the Fort Garry campus; her parents sent parcels whenever they could. Their son, Colin, was born on December 28, 1964. Bertie finished the 1964-65 school year after taking a couple of courses in the summer of 1965.

For summer employment, like other Caribbean students, Bertie worked on the passenger railway from Winnipeg to Vancouver (through western Canadian provinces and capital cities), a journey that took about five days away from home—and from Rita and the two young children. In between work availability on the railway, Bertie would find—sometimes with much difficulty—other employment through general employment agency work. This was a period of great sacrifice, perseverance, and determination to finish university. He graduated with a commerce degree in 1967, the only Caribbean student in his graduating class.

Failing to find a placement with any of the Canadian accounting firms that held campus interviews for graduating commerce students, Bertie journeyed to Toronto to find a job with a Toronto accounting firm. He secured a job with an owner-run accounting firm.

> I soon learned that the emphasis in a small accounting firm is not to train students for professional designation but to get as much work done by them [as possible]. This was learned through bitter experience, as I was not given the promised time off [that was given to other employed Canadian students] to study for examinations. The specious excuse was that their work experience and contributions were not significant and would not be missed.
>
> I was soon forced to shift to pursuing the less rigorous accounting programs—CGA (certified general accountant)

and/or CMA (certified management accountant)—because of the focus of passing one or two subjects at a time, rather than the CA (chartered accountant) intermediate and final levels, which each contained groups of subjects to be passed at one time. In 1973, I obtained my CGA designation.

The lesson here is that many employers/management do not practice a level playing field for certain employees' advancement, and one should not be discouraged but resolve to pursue an acceptable alternative for self advancement.

Bertie's employment with the Ontario government began in January 1974 at the Ministry of Treasury, Economics & Intergovernmental Affairs. From 1976 to 1979, he enjoyed two promotions at the Ministry of Community and Social Services (MCSS), the second being to middle management as Regional Manager of Finance and Administration.

In 1980 he enrolled in Queen's University's in-service program for the master's in public administration. He used his entitled vacation to attend the program, as his assistant deputy minister (ADM) refused him the customary time off and traveling expenses. After his success in securing the MPA, the vacation he had used was restored by the same ADM.

Bertie's lesson from this experience was:

> This was another example that determination and success in pursuing one's goals engender respect and admiration from erstwhile detractors and non-supporters.

> To be closer to home and family in 1981, I left the MCSS on promotion to the Ministry of Health & Long-Term Care, as senior financial coordinator, with financial oversight for forty-three hospitals in southwest Ontario. I worked with senior management at these hospitals. I received additional promotions as district manager for Northern Ontario Hospitals and for Eastern Ontario Hospitals, in each case managing a team of consultants. Also, I acted as regional director in the absence of the regional director.

> The lesson to impart from these achievements is that being a conscientious and hard worker and practicing good interpersonal skills are good habits for recognition and promotion.

Bertie progressed to secure appointments as an international consultant. Through the recommendation of Chetram Singh, former chief operating officer of St. Joseph's Hospital in London, Ontario (one of the hospitals at which Bertie served as the Ministry of Health financial coordinator), Bertie was appointed as financial management consultant to the Guyana Ministry of Health/Inter-American Development Bank (IADB), on a fifteen-month project in Guyana (1993–1994).

He directed the design and implementation of the hospital management information system (MIS) to improve financial management of Georgetown Hospital. He negotiated with the ministries of Health and Finance in designing and implementing revamped payment schemes and developed the cost-accounting system. He was a member of Guyana's National Health Plan Committee (NHPC), chaired by the Minister of Health. With other members of the NHPC, he liaised between public and private health institutions in the development of Guyana's five-year national health plan until 2000, in the setting up of hospital boards, in the training of senior and management staff in financial management, and in the development of self-motivation and team building.

In the same capacity, he was again in Guyana in 2003 on a three-month project, adapting the Vote Book introduced by Canadian International Development Agency (CIDA) for monthly ministry financial reporting to the treasury/central agency to the Georgetown Hospital, Chart of Accounts, so as to provide a seamless turnkey reporting system that was faster and more reliable information and to improve workload efficiencies.

On invitation from the World Bank, Bertie joined the Resources Management Consultant team in reviewing hospital operations in Albania and assisted in the preparation of proposals for hospital operational enhancements for Albania.

Bertie had now acquired valuable experience and recognition for his expertise in financial management.

He attended and presented a paper at the World Bank-sponsored conference on hospital-based management information systems (MIS) in Budapest, Hungary, in October 1977. In 1994 he attended the World Bank workshop on "Poverty in the Social Sector in Guyana" and led a group workshop on health-care financing in Guyana. In the same year, at the UNICEF conference on the Bamako Initiative in Guyana, he attended the workshop on implementing the Pan American Health Organization's (PAHO's) management information system.

Bertie has been a college instructor/professor at Seneca College in the Continuing Education Department, for CGA and CMA diplomas (1986–1993). He lectured in management accounting, management macro-economics, intermediate financial accounting, and marker for management accounting. He also has been a CGA certification lecturer (1995–2003, and 2004 to present) in financial accounting.

He also runs his own business, Berit Consultants Inc., as an income tax and financial consultant.

The lesson Bertie has learned in these various undertakings is "to always practice the best possible interpersonal skills, to be as much help to others who rely on you for assistance, but to always remember not to be distracted from achieving the results you set out to accomplish."

Bertie's deep involvement in the diaspora include student education and community affairs.

For several years, Bertie has sponsored two student scholarship programs. The Bertie Bacchus Scholarship Fund (BBSF) has offered scholarships to students from Number 5 Primary School, his alma mater and where he was a primary school teacher. The scholarships have been granted for students to receive secondary education and university education. To date, among thirty recipients, some have attended the President's College and some have graduated from the University of Guyana.

In 2007, he established a school library and is currently sending computers for postsecondary computer graduates (original awardees from BBSF) to train primary schoolers in the use of the computer.

The other scholarship program is at the Christianburg–Wismar Multilateral School. The Anthony Tim Award, which Bertie started in 2003, is dedicated to the memory of his uncle, who spent his adult life working in the bauxite industry and who was responsible for Bertie's completing his secondary education in the community. About sixteen recipients have received the scholarship.

In community affairs, Bertie has played a lead role in the Guyana Berbice Association (GBA)–Toronto Inc. He was past president for six years (three two-year terms) and president for another two-year term (2008-09). The GBA is international, with chapters also in the United States and in England. Bertie was a member of the GBA Toronto Group that visited England to help set up the UK chapter in 1988.

Bertie's service to the diaspora has been duly recognized. In 1990, he and fellow GBA presidents from England, New York, and Washington traveled to Guyana to receive from the president of Guyana the Guyana

Medal of Service award for GBA contributions to Guyana. For the 2007 Guyana Community award, he received nominations from two sources, with six supporting recommendations.

His other community and public service roles have included:

- Auditor of the Guyana Independence Republic Day Celebrations, the Guyana Awards Canada, the Guyana Flood Relief Committee
- Linden Fund Association—USA and Canada, member. Auditor of LFA—Canada.
- Guyana Canada Chamber of Commerce (GCCC). One of the group of founding members, executive member, and current GCCC treasurer.

He represented the GCCC in England (November 2007) on a two-week Canada/UK program for Canada to learn UK approaches in the development of diaspora programs in Africa, India, etc., for adaptation to the Guyana diaspora, and GCCC participation for the training of young adults in business development and management.

Bertie and Rita have four grown children, three of whom became university graduates after graduating from high school with distinctions as Ontario scholars. Sandra, with a master's in law, is a criminal lawyer and a senior crown prosecutor. She is married with two daughters, ages eight and four. Colin (unmarried) is a high school graduate and a factory worker. Wendy is an elementary school vice principal. She is married with three children, ages eight, five, and two. Alyssa, a university graduate in French and political science, is an Ontario government executive assistant, is married, and is pursuing advanced professional studies.

Bertie is not one to forget where he came from. Doing something for his village alma mater has given Bertie the greatest satisfaction. He says: "The lesson I learned from the scholarship programs and community participation is that the greatest happiness one can have is to help and inspire others in attaining their fullest potential, with the hope that this would set an example for the beneficiaries and others in providing a cycle of improvements, so that the community can be a better place for all."

January 31, 2009

Dr. M. Kazim Bacchus

DipEd, MPH, BA, BSc (Soc), MA (Dist), PhD, DLitt
Professor Emeritus
University of Alberta

Dr. M. Kazim Bacchus, renowned worldwide scholar, was the most qualified and experienced Guyanese in the field of education. He was possibly the most highly qualified in the world in his particular field, education in developing countries. He was the founder and first director of the Center for International Education and Development, University of Alberta. Dr. Bacchus was also founding director of the Institute for Educational Development, Aga Khan University, Pakistan. In his esteemed career, he was also the Assistant Director of Education in Guyana.

M. Kazim Bacchus was born on October 11, 1929, at Queenstown in Essequibo. His father, George Bacchus, was a businessman who died when Kazim was just eight years old. His mother, Jaitoon (later Ally), was a homemaker who actually never had the opportunities to attend school herself but supported Kazim's zest for education. The first school he attended was Queenstown Primary School in Essequibo.

Kazim was the fourth of nine siblings: Clement, Ghani, Zabeeda (married name: Usman), Kazim, Naseer, Raymond (Buds), Shad, Fazal, and Farina (married name: Gafoor). He married Shamsun Nehar (nee Jabbar) of Leguan in 1951. They had three children: Nari (born in Leguan, 1952), Zeeda (born in London, 1956) and Fahiem (born in London, 1957).

His illustrious career started as a humble school teacher in Guyana. In 1951 he went to London to further his studies in education. In 1952-53 he obtained the Professional Certificate of Education and Academic Diploma in Education from the Institute of Education, London University. He also qualified with a graduate diploma of the Institute of Personnel Management (UK). He furthered his studies at the London School of Economics (LSE), where he obtained the a bachelor's degree (with honors) in sociology (with economics), and also won the prestigious Leverhulme Scholarship.

He returned to Guyana in 1958 and worked at the Ministry of Health. In December 1960 he attended Berkeley College, University of California, and obtained a master's degree in public health education (MPH).

In 1963 he returned to Guyana and was appointed Assistant Director of Education. He returned to London in 1964 and, in early 1965, he achieved his master's degree (with distinction), having majored in the social psychology of education, from the Institute of Education, London University. After a brief return home in 1965, he left Guyana (in a move that was to be his permanent departure from his homeland) for an appointment as lecturer at the University of the West Indies, Mona Campus, Kingston, Jamaica. While working in Jamaica he returned to London and achieved his PhD in education in 1968, again from the Institute of Education, London University.

Dr. Bacchus joined the University of Alberta (Edmonton, Canada) in 1969. He was granted tenure as associate professor in 1971 and moved to full professor in 1974. At the time he was serving as visiting scholar at University of Chicago's Comparative Education Center. He also served as principal at the College of the Bahamas (1976–1978). He was academic visitor, London School of Economics, in 1981–82, and acting chair, Department of International and Comparative Education, University of London Institute of Education, 1984–85.

In his career Kazim Bacchus taught in the UK—in special schools in London and at a boys school in Essex. He lectured at Regent Street Polytechnic (now the University of Westminster), at the University of

Guyana (part-time), and at the Institute of Education, London. Dr. Bacchus was a visiting professor/scholar: at the Institute of Development Studies, Sussex (UK); at Stanford University's International Development Education Center (USA); at Monash University in Australia; and Osmania University in India.

Dr. Bacchus was a consultant on educational projects worldwide to the CIDA (Canadian International Development Agency), CFTC (Commonwealth Fund for Technical Cooperation), USAID, the World Bank, the British Council, the UK Ministry of Overseas Development (now DFID), the Commonwealth Secretariat, UNESCO, and the United Nations University International Leadership Academy.

Dr. Bacchus was also consulted on various educational projects in the Caribbean, Tanzania, Uganda, Brunei, Namibia, Fiji, Papua and New Guinea, Malaysia, South Korea, Nepal, the Philippines, Sri Lanka, Thailand, Pakistan, Bangladesh, and Jordan.

Nearer his retirement from the University of Alberta, he was "head hunted" by the Aga Khan University in Karachi, Pakistan. He was recruited in 1993 to establish a new Institute of Educational Development at the university. He accepted the appointment and became the founding director of the Institute of Education of the Aga Khan University.

The Aga Khan, Prince Karim Al Husseini, would write to Dr. Bacchus after his retirement, crediting him with being instrumental in putting the institute on a firm footing. The Aga Khan, who is the leader of Nizari Ismaili Muslims and one of the world's wealthiest philanthropists, praised Dr. Bacchus's "practical approach to problem solving" and his "ability to attract, recruit, and mentor faculty."

Dr. Bacchus worked on a plan to develop a Center for Education in Small Nation States, with headquarters at the University of Darussalam, Brunei. He worked on the early stages of a cooperative program with Southeast Asian Ministers of Education Organization (SEAMEO) to train rural school principals in the Association of Southeast Asian Nations (ASEAN) countries. He went to Nepal in 1988 to assess needs of the Center for Education Research and Innovation in Tribhuvan University, and he has been asked by Sri Lanka and the United Nations Development Program (UNDP) to help the National Institute of Education. He was involved with developing a link between the Alberta School for the Deaf and the School for the Deaf in Malaysia (in staff training) and a cooperative research project with University of Santo Thomas in the Philippines. He has made numerous travels worldwide, providing guidance on education.

Over the years, he was invited to deliver lectures at many international venues. He wrote several books on education, even after retiring from the University of Alberta.

In 1992, he was awarded a doctor of literature degree (DLitt) by the University of London for his work in the area of education in developing countries. This degree is only granted to scholars with an exceptional record of research and publication over many years, and it ranks above a PhD. It was the university's first such degree in the field of education. This prestigious degree is an unprecedented achievement and is usually presented to recipients by the British royalty. Kazim was the first Guyanese to receive such an award and, in doing so, also became the first professor in the world to be granted a DLitt in the field of education in developing countries.

Kazim has authored over one hundred works on education in developing countries, as books, chapters in books, and refereed articles in journals. These include, in part:

- "Education in the Third World: Present Realities and Future Prospects,"
- "Key Issues in the Provision of Higher Education in Small Nation States."
- "Decentralization of Education within the Context of Small Nation States."
- "Educational Policy and Development Strategy in the Third World."
- "Comparative Review of Nation Studies."
- "International Educational Cooperation within the North South Context."
- "Education for Development or Underdevelopment."

He was a "truly remarkable Guyanese whose life and work has made the world a much better place," wrote Daoud Yamin, a friend of Kazim's for over fifty-five years.

Dr. Terry Carson, University of Alberta, Department of Secondary Education, wrote in his tribute to Kazim on the university's website:

> Kazim was an incredibly productive scholar, a much-loved teacher, a respected colleague, an administrator and a true citizen of the world. He was mentor to literally hundreds of students, many of them international students. Dr. Bacchus's distinguished alumni can be found around the

world in academia, in government ministries, on the staff of international organizations, with nongovernmental agencies and in school classrooms everywhere.

A symposium held in his honor on his retirement from the University of Alberta in 1995 … attended by scholars from around the world, many of them former students of Dr. Bacchus … spoke warmly of their association with him … of the energy that surrounded Kazim's return from one of his many travels, bringing news of other projects and fresh opportunities that awaited in some quarter of the developing world. … Like many others in the Faculty of Education, I owe the origins of my own international work to initiatives begun by Dr. Bacchus.

Dr. Bacchus was unflagging in his commitment to international educational development, founded upon this abiding belief in equity among the nations, and his deep faith in realizing human potential through education. He tirelessly recruited colleagues to this life project and traveled the world, teaching, writing, establishing, and supporting new institutions.

Dr. Bacchus … in demand as a consultant, advisor, and as a mentor to new ventures … [was] recruited … to establish a new Institute for Educational Development at the Aga Khan University in Karachi. This was to be a lighthouse institution for educational reform and teacher development, not only in Pakistan but also for all of the schools of south Asia, central Asia, and east Africa served by the Aga Khan Educational Services. … Kazim consulted widely with colleagues here at the U of A and elsewhere in shaping this new institute. … Our faculty continues to have close links with Aga Khan University … a lasting legacy of goodwill with Dr. Bacchus's institutional contacts and former students around the world.

Dr. Bacchus enjoyed many honors … including a University of Alberta McCalla professorship. … But probably the greatest honor lives on in the work of those he inspired through his vision and unwavering support.

The University of Alberta, Faculty of Graduate Studies and Research, has been endowed with a special scholarship, the Bacchus Graduate Scholarship award, for international and first nation students.

This jewel of Guyana, whose unparalleled life as an international educationist was surpassed only by his remarkable humility and unassuming caring nature, has adorned the crown of Guyanese in the hallowed halls of knowledge and learning in universities the world over. Sadly, this very special mortal passed away in 2007, leaving a void impossible ever to fill.

Zeeda Bacchus, in a message to friends and colleagues informing of her dad's demise, stated, in part:

> My dear friends and colleagues, my father, M. Kazim Bacchus, passed away on Thursday, March 22, of idiopathic pulmonary fibrosis. He was born Oct. 11, 1929, and was seventy-seven at the time of his passing. His funeral was last Tuesday and it's been such a sad time for my entire family. My dad was a wonderfully warm and loving man who left a legacy to the world in his extensive work in the developing countries.
>
> He was a great father, husband, grandpa, uncle, cousin to all of his family and extended family, and a great friend, colleague, scholar, and educator to countless others. We will all miss him tremendously.
>
> Part of his obituary stated: "A key factor in his achievements, both personal and professional, was his ability to foster great love and deep friendship. He developed lifelong friendships with innumerable people in many parts of the world. He also inspired many of those around him that there are no limits to what they could accomplish, and through his vision and unwavering support, they were often able to achieve much more than they had thought possible."
>
> He was a humble, decent, and loving man and father who will be missed greatly. [He was someone] I was proud to call Dad. ... On his funeral program we chose to add one of his favorite pieces [from John Donne's "Meditation XVII"], which he also used in one of his books. It truly defines my father's belief about life:

Vidur Dindayal

No man is an island, entire of itself;
Every man is a piece of the continent, a part of the main;
If a clod be washed away by the sea, Europe is the less,
As well as if a promontory were,
As well as if a manor of thy friend's or of thine own were;
Any man's death diminishes me, because I am involved in mankind,
And therefore never send to know for whom the bell tolls;
It tolls for thee.

October 4, 2010

Ivor J. Benjamin

BA, MD
Professor of Biochemistry and of Medicine
University of Utah School of Medicine

In 2009, cardiologist Ivor J. Benjamin was awarded one of the National Institutes of Health's (NIH) most prestigious honors, a $2.5 million Pioneer Award, for furtherance of his research work on the prevention of heart disease.

Ivor J. Benjamin, MD, professor of internal medicine and biochemistry and the Christi T. Smith Endowed Chair of Cardiovascular Research at the University of Utah School of Medicine, believes that one of the body's most powerful antioxidants—molecules generally believed to protect the heart—actually might lead to disease in the heart and other organs when a gene mutation causes the body to overproduce the molecule.

Ivor Benjamin was born and grew up in Beterverwagting, East Coast Demerara. He was schooled at Central High School in Smyth Street, Georgetown, as was his sister, Edris.

He received his bachelor's degree in 1978 from Hunter College at the City University of New York, and his MD in 1982 from Johns

Hopkins University School of Medicine. He completed a residency in internal medicine at Yale–New Haven Hospital, Yale University School of Medicine, in 1985, and a cardiology fellowship at the Cardiovascular Institute, Michael Reese Hospital and Medical Center, University of Chicago, in 1988.

Dr. Benjamin completed an AHA-Bugher Fellowship (1990–92) in molecular cardiology and was promoted in 2002 to professor of medicine *with tenure* at the University of Texas Southwestern Medical Center at Dallas. A recipient of the Established Investigator award from the American Heart Association, Dr. Benjamin has been honored for his scientific contributions and received the Ken Bowman Research Achievement Award from the University of Manitoba. In 1999, Dr. Benjamin was elected into the American Society of Clinical Investigation and, in 2005, into the Association of American Physicians. At the University of Utah, he served as professor of medicine and division chief of cardiology from 2003 through 2009.

After a highly competitive and critical review process, the NIH chose Benjamin to further investigate his idea, as one of only eighteen researchers to receive a Pioneer Award.

NIH Director Francis Collins, MD, PhD, presented Benjamin and the other recipients with their awards in a ceremony at the agency's headquarters in Bethesda, Maryland.

Benjamin received $500,000 annually for five years to pursue his research. Much of the Pioneer Award program's appeal is that it encourages researchers to think outside the box while receiving substantial funds to test their ideas, according to Collins. "The fact that we continue to receive such strong proposals for funding through the program attests to the wealth of creative ideas in so many fields of science today," he said.

An estimated three million Americans suffer from heart failure, with 500,000 new cases diagnosed annually. Disease that leads to heart failure long has been associated with oxidative stress, the process in which the body produces "free radical" molecules in response to oxygen intake. Once they are produced, free radicals roam the body, creating chemical reactions that damage organs and other tissue.

To protect cells from free radicals, the body makes antioxidants. Benjamin's work focuses on a particular antioxidant, reduced glutathione. This is produced when a protein called alpha B-crystallin unfolds inside of cells, leading in turn to excessive production of reduced glutathione and heart damage. Benjamin terms this condition "reductive stress."

Until recently, reductive stress has not been looked at in the context of disease. But Benjamin showed that too much reduced glutathione is linked to increased heart failure rates, while normal levels of the antioxidant is not. Given the role of antioxidants, the theory is counterintuitive, Benjamin acknowledges. But if he is correct, it could lead to developing an entirely new class of antireductant drugs to treat or even prevent heart disease caused by reductive stress.

"Our findings show that the potential for reductive stress causing heart disease definitely warrants more investigation," Benjamin says. "The Pioneer Award will enable us the freedom to investigate the consequences and mechanisms of reductive stress and, hopefully, do the kind of work that can be transformative."

Benjamin's research represents the kind of imaginative and searching science that the University of Utah values in its faculty, according to Lorris Betz, MD, PhD, the University of Utah's senior vice president for health sciences. "As a research university, we want our investigators to expand the bounds of science, even when that means questioning or contradicting conventional theories and wisdom. Ivor Benjamin does just that. On behalf of the entire University of Utah health sciences community, I congratulate and applaud Dr. Benjamin for being recognized with this tremendous honor."

The Benjamin Laboratory provides research opportunities for graduate, medical, and MD/PhD students and postdoctoral trainees. Among diverse yet complementary projects, the laboratory focuses on the genetics of heritable cardiomyopathies, transcriptional regulation of stress response pathways, molecular mechanisms of left ventricular remodeling, and the role of molecular chaperones (i.e., heat shock proteins) in protein aggregation diseases.

From Utah's unique history in genealogy, the discipline of human genetics has propelled the University of Utah into international acclaim, with notable firsts in numerous fields, especially cardiovascular genetics. The campus now sports its first Nobel Laureate, Dr. Mario Capecchi, who was awarded the 2007 Nobel Prize for Physiology and Medicine for his pioneering work on gene targeting in knockout mice.

Although the Pioneer Award is in his name, Dr. Benjamin is quick to credit his laboratory team and colleagues with making the award possible. "I am honored and humbled to have been chosen for the award," he says. "But the real story is my multidisciplinary team. They deserve a lot of credit, too."

Sources:
Websites accessed November 9, 2010
www.utah.edu/http
http://healthcare.utah.edu/publicaffairs/news/archive/2009/IvorBenjaminNIHAward.html
http://www.bioscience.utah.edu/mb/mbFaculty/benjamin/benjamin.html

November 9, 2010

Dr. Frank Birbalsingh

BA Hons, MA, PhD (London University)
Professor Emeritus

Frank Mahabal Birbalsingh is currently professor emeritus of English at York University in Toronto, Canada.

He was born on February 11, 1938, at Sister's Village, East Bank Berbice, Guyana, and grew up at Better Hope, East Coast Demerara, where his father, Ezrom S. Birbalsingh, was headmaster of the Better Hope Canadian Mission School. Frank's mother died when he was six years old, and his father only remarried after his children had all grown up and left home. Frank grew up as the second to last child in a family of four brothers and three sisters. Two brothers and one sister are already deceased, and the remaining brother and two sisters, like him, live in Toronto.

Frank's family was closely associated with the Canadian Presbyterian Church in Guyana. They are from an Indo-Guyanese Presbyterian background. Frank attended the Better Hope Canadian Mission School from 1947 to 1949, when he won a government county scholarship to attend Queen's College, the leading government secondary school for boys in Guyana.

At Queen's, Frank passed his GCE Ordinary Level in 1954, and his GCE Advanced Level in 1956. He then taught at St. Stanislaus College, a Catholic boys school in Georgetown, before proceeding to the University College of the West Indies in Jamaica in 1957. He graduated in 1961 with a bachelor's degree (with honors) in English and taught at Queen's College for one year.

Frank then took up a commonwealth scholarship to India to complete his master's degree. His plans, however, did not work out in India, and he went on to London, England, where he completed his MA (London) studies in 1966, while working as a supply teacher in various secondary schools in London and Birmingham. His master's thesis was on West Indian novels from 1940 to 1963.

In 1967, opportunities for employment and higher studies in Canada seemed to be better than in England, so Frank emigrated to Toronto, where he studied for his PhD in Canadian literature. Again, he worked as a supply teacher while doing research on the subject, "National Identity in the Canadian Novel." He began teaching at York University as a lecturer in 1970, and he completed his PhD (London) in 1972.

Dr. Frank Birbalsingh was then appointed as assistant professor at York University, where for nine years he consolidated his position. He was granted tenure in 1976, and he was appointed associate professor, York University, in 1981.

Associate professor Birbalsingh established himself over the next fifteen years as a highly respected member of the staff at York University, and in 1996, he was duly elevated to professor. He held this position with distinction from 1996 to 2003, and in 2003 Frank was awarded the signal honor of the title professor emeritus, Department of English, York University, Toronto, Canada.

Frank took a keen interest in the work of colleagues in his field worldwide, and he was suitably rewarded with honors from various countries. As early as 1962, Frank secured an appointment as a research fellow at the University of New Delhi, India, under the Commonwealth Scholarship and Fellowships plan. In 1973–74, he was appointed post-doctoral research fellow at University of Auckland, New Zealand.

In 1976–77 he was Canada Council leave fellow and visiting fellow at the University of Ibadan, Nigeria. In 1983–84 he was Professeur Associe de Recherche, Universite de Rouen, France. In 1989–90, Dr. Birbalsingh was a visiting fellow, Center for Caribbean Studies, University of Warwick, England.

A professor is not merely a teacher of very high rank but one who is a leader and at the forefront of knowledge in his field. He writes books and papers and contributes to journals and publications; he speaks on his subject. Prof. Birbalsingh does it all, and his writings cover a wide range of subjects.

During his career Frank has written or edited twelve books, three monographs, several chapters in books, and numerous articles and reviews. His most recent books are *The People's Progressive Party of Guyana 1950: An Oral History* and *Neil Bissondath: The Indo-Caribbean-Canadian Diaspora*. His writings are an impressive handful. This prodigious writer also writes occasional book reviews for *Indo-Caribbean World*.

What drew Frank Birbalsingh to study and major in the subject English for his first degree and later to spend the better part of his life ascending the stairways to the highest reaches in academia, lecturing and writing on the subject English? He explains it this way: "When I began my research in the early 1960s, commonwealth literature was just beginning to appear; that is to say, literature in English produced outside Britain or the United States. It was a new field, and I have spent my life exploring it because my colonial experience in the Caribbean is part of it. The exploration helped me to understand myself, my history, and my culture. Today, the field is called post-colonial literature."

In his exploration he traveled widely and received many honors. He touches briefly on some of the highlights: "Going to India was interesting because it is my ancestral homeland. Nigeria was similarly interesting because I grew up among Guyanese friends descended from Africans. France gave me a chance to visit most Western European countries, and New Zealand opened my eyes to the Pacific."

Prof. Birbalsingh found time in what has been a full diary of commitments to contribute significantly to community activities where he lives in Canada. In 1986 he founded the Ontario Society for Studies in Indo-Caribbean Culture (OSSICC), an organization that flourished for twelve years in Toronto, Canada. OSSICC was the first organization in Canada to explore the Indian presence in the Caribbean. It served as forerunner to numerous Indo-Caribbean organizations that now exist in Canada.

On his significant achievements, Prof. Birbalsingh says, "My achievement is mainly academic. That's all."

About his interests in life, he says, "My writing is the chief interest in my life."

He says he has had no life-changing experiences. "I suppose the best decision I made was to leave England and emigrate to Canada in 1967. There were more opportunities in Canada, both for further study and for employment."

He attributes his success to hard work. Reflecting on his career, he says, "Perhaps, the lowest point was my supply teaching in English schools in the 1960s, which was hard going because of problems in maintaining discipline." Probably the most satisfying, however, was "writing my cricket book, *The Rise of West Indian Cricket*, which has sold better than my other books."

In 1967, soon after emigrating to Toronto, Frank was married to Norma. They have two daughters: Katharine, former assistant head of Dunraven School in London, England; and Christine, who is a closed captions editor in Toronto.

This is a very modest man. Where he lives and works, people ask themselves, "Where is this man from?" Prof. Frank Birbalsingh, professor emeritus, Department of English, University of York, Toronto, Canada, avid writer, is a true star in his profession. In his achievement as a Guyanese, he is a beacon that throws its beams on all who know him. He has set a gold standard for all who shall come after him.

October 7, 2010

Dr. Gowkarran Budhu

DipTech, MICE, CE, MS, PhD
Civil Engineer
Associate Professor Transportation Engineering

Dr. Gowkarran Budhu, an expert in transport engineering, was associate professor, Department of Civil Engineering, Louisiana Tech University; coordinator of the International Roads Federation Fellowship program; and former head of the Roads Division, Ministry of Works, Guyana.

He has traveled the world over and made presentations on transport engineering in cities in the United States, Canada, the UK, Egypt, the Netherlands, South Korea, and Australia. He was appointed a member of a review team for the awarding of the International Road Federation scholarships around the world.

Gowkarran Budhu was born on April 8, 1937, at Cornelia Ida, West Coast Demerara, British Guiana. He received his early education at Cornelia Ida Primary School and at Central High School in Georgetown. After obtaining his GCEs, he went to London to study engineering.

In London, Gowkarran obtained admission to the Brixton School of Building, Engineering Department, where he studied for a diploma in engineering. He obtained his professional diploma (DipTech) and became a fully qualified civil engineer in 1965, also gaining membership in the learned Institution of Civil Engineering, London. For his diploma he majored in structural engineering.

Undergraduate training, arranged by the Brixton School of Building, included the following jobs:

- Summer 1962. Northwestern Regional Hospital Board. Assisted in surveying of proposed hospital sites for the northern region of England.
- Summer 1963. Messrs. Cubbitts and Green. Assisted in setting out of "interchange" section of the M4 Motorway, Langley, England.
- Summer 1964. Assistant site engineer, Hyde Reinforced Concrete Ltd. In charge of setting out and placing of steel bar reinforcement and concrete for an eight-story commercial assurance building, Leicester, England.

After he qualified, Gowkarran wasted no time in enlisting in the service of Guyana in 1966, where he returned to take up a position as project engineer in the Roads Division of the Ministry of Works, Guyana, with offices at Fort Street, Kingston, Georgetown. From that office, Gowkarran laid the foundations of a glittering career in roads engineering, culminating in his becoming an expert of international standing in the field of transport engineering and a leading figure in the International Roads Federation.

In 1970 he was awarded an International Roads Federation (IRF) scholarship to pursue graduate studies in highway engineering at Ohio State University, Columbus, Ohio. His studies involved traveling in the United States, observing road and airport construction in five states. In 1971, he obtained the higher highway engineering degree of Civil Engineer -CE. That experience at Ohio whet Gowkarran's appetite for learning and specializing.

Now in a position of considerable experience and authority,\ in the Roads Division of the Ministry of Works, Guyana, Gowkarran was selected as one of Guyana's representatives for nation-to-nation exchanges and other visits to:

- Brazil, in 1972, in a three-man delegation, by invitation of the Brazilian government, to observe construction techniques on the Trans-Amazon Highway. He also attended the International Roads Federation Conference in Brasilia.

- Jamaica, in 1972, for a multidisciplinary conference sponsored by Pan American Health Organization / World Health Organization (PAHO/WHO) on highway accident prevention and safety. In the same year, he went to Montserrat, West Indies, as a member of six-man delegation, by invitation of the Montserrat government, to advise on road and runway construction.

- India, in 1973, in a three-man delegation, by invitation of the Indian government, to observe mountainous road construction in the Himalayas between Kashmir and Jammu.

- Costa Rica, Colombia, Venezuela, and Trinidad in 1975, to discuss with highway officials the possibility of using rapid-erection steel bridges for highway crossings.

Gowkarran and family later emigrated to the United States. He chose to enhance his knowledge by attending Virginia Polytechnic Institute and State University, where in 1978 he obtained his master of science (MS) degree. For his MS he majored in transportation engineering .His thesis was titled "Prioritization of Developmental Roads—Case Study of Guyana, South America."

He later studied for his PhD, which he obtained from Virginia Polytechnic Institute and State University in 1981. For his PhD, he majored in transportation engineering, with a minor in systems engineering. His dissertation was titled "A System Dynamics Approach to Rural Transportation Planning in Less Developed Countries."

Dr. Budhu's rise to prominence in his profession as an engineer and specialization in the field of transport engineering is catalogued under many headings below. The following lists provide a sample of the wide range of his activities in numerous parts of America, Canada, and cities the world over, as well as his appointments, international visits, presentations at conferences, publications, honors, and awards.

Academic appointments

1975–1977. Lecturer, Department of Civil Engineering, University of Guyana. One of a team of five members involved in setting up the first bachelor of science programs in civil engineering at University of Guyana.

1977–1981. Graduate teaching/research assistant in the College of Engineering, Department of Civil Engineering, Virginia Polytechnic Institute and State University.

1981–1984. Assistant professor, Department of Civil Engineering, University of North Carolina at Charlotte.

1984–2000. James F. Naylor Jr. endowed associate professor, Department of Civil Engineering, Louisiana Tech University, Ruston, Louisiana; faculty advisor, Institute of Transportation Engineers Student Chapter; coordinator of the IRF fellowship program; coordinator of the summer internship program within the Department of Civil Engineering, College of Engineering and Science.

Courses taught at:
Louisiana Tech University, Ruston, Louisiana, at graduate level, include:

- Pavement Design Procedures
- Airport Planning and Design
- Systems Analysis for Civil Engineers
- Microcomputer Applications in Traffic Engineering
- Transportation Systems Planning
- Advanced Traffic Engineering
- Soils and Foundation Engineering
- Transportation Engineering
- Geometric Design of Transportation Facilities
- Construction Equipment and Methods
- Capstone Design
- Soils in Engineering

University of North Carolina, Charlotte:
- Engineering—Urban Traffic
- Urban Transportation
- Systems and Design
- Airport Design

University of Guyana, Georgetown, Guyana: Senior course in construction planning

Professional experience:

1965. Structural engineer, Helical Bar and Reinforced Concrete, Ltd., London, England; preparing designs and estimates for multistoried structures from architects' drawings.

1966. Structural engineer, Lowe and Rodin, London, England; responsible for the design of reinforced concrete raft and pile foundations for multistoried structures.

1967. Project engineer, Roads Division, Ministry of Works and Hydraulics, Guyana; responsible for construction of forty miles of highway (including Georgetown to Rosignol), and shipping wharf.

1971. Assistant chief engineer, Roads Division, Ministry of Works and Hydraulics, Guyana; responsible for coordination of design aspects of roads and airport.

1974. Acting chief engineer, Roads Division, Ministry of Works and Hydraulics. Guyana; responsible for long-term planning and consultant services.

1975. Director, Consulting Engineering Associates, and consultant to the engineering firm ENECON, SA., Brazil, with responsibility for the feasibility study of 140 miles of roads in Guyana, a World Bank-funded project.

1987. Consultant to the engineering firm of Design and Construction Services, Ltd., Georgetown, Guyana.

1989. Consultant on the research study for transit needs for the cities of Monroe, Ruston, and Grambling, Louisiana.

1991. Consultant to the law firm of Barnes, Jefferson & Robertson, Monroe, Louisiana, "State of Louisiana, Dom vs. Thomas H. Fields," #88-4014; Potential Impacts on Sales Volume Due to the Redesign of the Intersection at LA 616 and LA 143, West Monroe, Louisiana.

1993. Consultant to Grambling State University on project titled "Student Training and Educational Program." US DOT grant for educational opportunities in transportation engineering areas.

International visits:

1987. Caribbean Development Bank, Barbados, West Indies, to discuss with bank officials (Transportation section) the possibility of developing a "post-investment model for transportation funding."

1987. The University of the West Indies, Trinidad, to discuss with the head, Department of Civil Engineering, the possibility of offering "training seminars and short courses" in the areas of road and airport planning and design.

1990. The University of the West Indies, Trinidad, to discuss with the faculty of the Department of Civil Engineering the possibility of collaboration on Neighbourhood Support Fund –NSF funded projects in the Caribbean Basin.

1990. Barbados, West Indies, Ministry of Works, to discuss training seminars on construction management and microtunneling.

1990. England, invited guest lecturer at the University of Newcastle upon Tyne, on "Urban Transportation System Planning."

1997. 'People to People, USA,' in national delegation of twenty-two experts in transportation engineering to the People's Republic of China.

Thirty presentations in different cities in the United States and worldwide include:
- "Evaluation of Transport Investment in Less Developed Countries—A Linear Programming Approach," presented at the 59th Annual Meeting of the Transportation Research Board, Washington DC, January 1980.

- "Possible Solutions to Close the Gap between US Production and Demand for Petroleum," presented at the Conference on Transportation and Energy Conservation Workshop, Blacksburg, Virginia, August 1981.

- "Comprehensive Rural Investment Planning at the National Level in an Agri-Based Less-Developed Country—A System Concept," VI IRF Conference, Cairo, Egypt, 1986.

- "A Microcomputer Generic System Dynamics Model for Transportation Planning in Less-Developed Countries—An Aid to Decision Making in Agricultural Based Economies," University of Guyana, 1987.

- "A Systems Model with Post-Investment Monitoring Capabilities for Transportation and Related Infrastructure Planning in Developing Countries," University of California, Berkeley, 1987.

- "A Historical Review of the Civil Engineering Profession and Probable Directions in the 21st Century," two-lecture series presented to Department of Technology, Grambling State University, May 1990.

- "An Integrated Approach to Human Transportation Services Using the Urban Transportation Planning Process and Linear Programming—A Case Study of Monroe, Louisiana," presented at the 22nd Annual Pittsburgh Conference on Modeling and Simulation, Pittsburgh, Pennsylvania, 1991.

- "A Policy-Based Infrastructure Planning for Urbanized Regions Using System Dynamics and the Urban Transportation Planning Process: A Conceptual View for the Study of Shreveport/Bossier, Louisiana," presented to IRF/ARF 1992 Road Conference on Efficient Roads and the Quality of Life, Queensland, Australia, 1992.

- "The Need for Comprehensive Analysis of Urban at-Grade-Intersection Redesign—Case Study of the Intersection of LA 616 and LA 143, West Monroe, Louisiana," presented to the 1st International Conference on Managing Traffic and Transportation, Amsterdam, the Netherlands, 1992.

- "Identification and Evaluation of Transportation Control Measures (TCM) for Air Quality Improvements—Case Study of Baton Rouge, Louisiana," presented to the l2th IRF World Meeting, Madrid, Spain, May 1993.

- "The Economics of Trenchless Technology V8, Traditional Cut-and-Fill in High-Density Activity Urban Corridors—A Research Concept in a Real World Environment," North American NO-DIG '94 Conference, 1994, Dallas, Texas.

- "The Incorporation of Social Cost Impacts of Trenchless Technology for Contract Awards in High Density Urban Corridors," international conference sponsored by CERIU of Canada, 1994, Montreal, Canada.

- "The Incorporation of Safety in the Economic Analysis of Highway Improvements in Developing Countries—Guidelines from a Developed Country," Proceedings, IRF Regional Conference, Taipei, Taiwan, ROC, 1996.

- "A 5-Step Approach to the Incorporation of Fixed Object Accidents in Economic Analysis and Prioritization of Highway Projects," Proceedings, ASCE Conference on Traffic Congestion and Traffic Safety in the 21st Century, Chicago, Illinois, 1997.

He also has prepared twenty-seven research proposals, fourteen refereed publications, eight conference publications, and two contributions to texts. He has headed a number of funded and nonfunded projects at Louisiana Tech University.

Professional registration and memberships include:
- 1970 MICE. Member, Institution of Civil Engineers, England
- 1972 Member, Guyana Association of Professional Engineers
- 1984 Sigma Chi, Scientific Research Society
- 1985 Member, American Society for Engineering Education
- 1987 Member, Institute of Transportation Engineers

Honors and awards received include:

1970. International Roads Federation (IRF) Scholarship, to pursue graduate studies in highway engineering at Ohio State University, Columbus.

1984. Crying Towel Award for Teaching, ASCE, Student Chapter, Department of Civil Engineering, Louisiana Tech University, Ruston, Louisiana.

1991. Outstanding Service Award with check for $750, College of Engineering, Louisiana Tech University, Ruston, Louisiana.

1994. Outstanding Research Award with check for $750, College of Engineering, Louisiana Tech University.

1995. James F. Naylor Jr. endowed associate professor.

His last great service

At the peak of his career, Dr. Budhu, an international expert in transport engineering, fulfilled yet another dream, which is in the hearts of many Guyanese abroad—to return to serve the motherland in the field in which he acquired expertise. He seized the opportunity to head a project funded by the Inter-American Development Bank (IDB), organized by the Guyana Ministry of Public Works, in collaboration with the Police Traffic Department. The project was to review current engineering designs on the country's major roadways and do necessary corrective works to ensure that the high rate of accidents was significantly reduced.

A report on the appointment and the background to it was carried in the *Guyana Chronicle*, September 2, 2001. The report, "IDB funding project to make major roadways safer," read in part:

> Data on road fatalities collected over the past three years established that the Georgetown-to-Buxton section of the East Coast Demerara highway accounted for the most deaths during that period.
>
> Most of those accidents involved public transport, Budhu said, noting that analysis on the impact of such mishaps on other main thoroughfares has not yet been properly compiled.
>
> He announced plans to do some design corrections on the Georgetown-to-Buxton route, based on an analysis that was part of his ongoing study.

Dr. Budhu criticized the concrete medians that blocked some main turnoff points on East Coast Demerara. He attributed them to bad design and noted they caused an increase in fuel consumption and time loss, among other costs, which ordinary people had to bear. He said that roads must not only be designed for vehicular traffic but also for cyclists and pedestrians.

He said a highway safety unit would be established within the Public Works Ministry, but it must be supported by a highway safety code, which was enforced to help minimize the results of accidents.

Dr. Budhu's analysis of the problems on the high rate of accidents reached the conclusion that speeding accounted for 21 percent of all cases of road fatalities countrywide. His analysis identified the need for remedial engineering work to make roads safer. Under the Road Safety Engineering Program, efforts were made to improve road safety through clearer road signs and markings, pedestrian crossings and sidewalks, reflectorized spikes, and street lights in selected areas, all of which were necessary.

Dr. Budhu also advised that in designing and constructing roads, engineers must take into account how their use would affect people's day-to-day lives. He remarked, "Road safety is no accident; it can be achieved only by deliberate planning and greater collaboration between the two ministries—Home Affairs and Transport and Hydraulics—responsible for traffic regulation and road construction, respectively." He had also recommended the establishment of a highway safety unit supported by a highway safety code to help to minimize accidents.

Dr. Budhu was about to complete his contract in Guyana and resume his work on the world stage when tragedy struck. After a short illness, he passed away. Fate dealt him, his family, and Guyana a terrible blow. The suddenness of his death was shocking news.

He had won the admiration, respect, and hearts of many who got to know him, and after his death, newspapers featured many tributes. One of the tributes in the *Guyana Chronicle* on July 4, 2003, was written in a letter to the editor by Denise Dias, of Mothers in Black. She wrote that she was "stunned to learn of the recent and untimely passing of Dr. Gowkarran Budhu ... a petite Guyanese with the heart and soul of a giant." She wrote that she'd learned of Dr. Budhu when he phoned to introduce himself in response to a call she'd placed to him on behalf of Mothers in Black. He assured her that he and his colleagues would stop the carnage on our roads, and afterward she was invited to his many road safety engineering presentations.

She said, "Dr. Budhu's expertise in engineering and road safety rehabilitation throughout Guyana cannot be described in words. Like the veins on one's hand, he knew every street, every road, every village, every bridge throughout Guyana. Dr. Budhu returned home to share his knowledge, and despite the many adverse challenges he encountered, he left us a masterpiece … volumes upon volumes of road safety data. I, along with the Alicea Foundation and Mothers in Black, wish to convey our deepest sympathy to Dr. Budhu's family and friends and sincerely hope that the IDB Road Project will be expedited."

That letter epitomized the many tributes to Dr. Budhu, an indication of his outstanding qualities and his commitment to his work. Like so many life stories we know, his achievement exceeded well beyond the normal expectations in any profession. His personal gifts and expertise in the field of transport engineering reached far beyond the boundaries of our beloved Guyana.

Dr. Budhu is survived by his loving wife, Shanti, and their son, Jitendra, and his wife, Leena, and their two children.

Sources:
Websites accessed August 26, 2009.
Guyana Chronicle. Archive for September 2, 2001.
Guyana Chronicle online. Archive of July 4, 2003.
Stabroek News. Archive. June 22, 2007.

September 7, 2009

Professor Vibert Cambridge

MA, PhD
Media Scholar

Dr. Vibert C. Cambridge is a professor, School of Media Arts and Studies (formerly School of Telecommunications), Scripps College of Communication, Ohio University. He is a former communication coordinator, Guyana National Service; program director and member of the board of directors, Guyana Broadcasting Corporation; and a member of the Advisory Committee to the Minister of Information, Guyana.

He has over thirty years of experience as an administrator, educator, and designer of public communication and media education programs in developed and developing countries.

Vibert C. Cambridge was born on July 31, 1944, in Georgetown, Guyana. His father was Cecil Cambridge, a trade unionist. His mother was Lennie Cambridge (nee Simmons), a seamstress.

He is the eldest of three children. His two brothers are Dr. Richard Cambridge, a senior economist with the World Bank in Washington DC, and Dr. Charles Cambridge, a professor at Chico State University, Chico, California.

Vibert attended Comenius Moravian Primary School in Queenstown, Georgetown, from 1947 to 1955. His headmaster was Mr. Basil McGowan. He then attended Queen's College, Georgetown, from 1955 to 1961.

He proceeded to London, England, for higher education. He attended South West London College, and in 1969 he obtained the intermediate and part II final diploma in public administration.

His professional career started with his appointment as public relations officer, National Insurance Scheme, Guyana, in 1969. He was then appointed personnel and industrial relations officer, Guyana Airways Corporation. He spent the early 1970s in Canada, where he was employed as the associate director of personnel, St. Michael's Hospital, Toronto, and was program host for *Statements in Black* on Metro Cable Television, Toronto.

From 1976 to1981 he held a number of appointments in Guyana. These included communication coordinator, Guyana National Service; planning officer, National Television Development Office, Ministry of Information; program director, Guyana Broadcasting Corporation; member of select committee on the media, Office of the President of Guyana; member, board of directors, Guyana Broadcasting Corporation; and executive secretary, Guyana Commemoration Commission. From 1985 to1986 he was a member of the Advisory Committee to the Minister of Information, Guyana.

In 1986 he headed for Ohio University, Athens, Ohio, for graduate studies. As a graduate student he was employed as an instructor at the Center for Afro-American Studies and later as a research associate at the School of Telecommunications. In 1988 he obtained his master's degree in international relations (communication and development), and in 1989 he was awarded his PhD in mass communication.

Immediately after receiving his PhD, Dr. Cambridge joined the faculty of the School of Telecommunications as an assistant professor. This was the beginning of his career as a scholar and academic administrator. Among his early academic administration positions were liaison, Technical Cooperation Program between the College of Communication, Ohio University, and the Caribbean Broadcasting Union, Bridgetown, Barbados; chair, Caribbean Advisory Committee, Center for International Studies; acting director, Communication and Development Studies program, Center for International Studies; and associate director, School of Telecommunications.

As associate director, School of Telecommunications, his responsibilities included managing the undergraduate curriculum and chairing the Planning Committee that coordinated the formulation of the school's five-year plan.

In 1995, Vibert was promoted to associate professor, School of Telecommunications. In the fall of 1996, he was appointed as interim director for the Communication and Development Studies program in the Center for International Studies and was confirmed in that position in 1997. Among his accomplishments as director were increasing the recruitment of international students, establishing the broadcasting for a development laboratory, and organizing the Second International Conference on Entertainment-Education and Social Change.

He held this position until 2001, when he was seconded to the College of Arts and Sciences to serve as the chair of the Department of African American Studies. He held that position until 2007.

A sampling of his accomplishments in this role include revitalizing the department; establishing the African American Studies Research and Service Institute; establishing *Black Praxis*, the journal of the Department of African American Studies; and organizing annual conferences on various aspects of the African diaspora in the Americas.

Between 2001 and 2007, he was a member of the university's task force on diversity; the Task Force of Inclusiveness and Equality; Presidential Search and Screening Committee; Expert Advisory Group on Diversity, Strategic Planning Team; and of the Honorary Degree Committee. He was chair of the seven-year evaluation committee of the Institute for Telecommunications Studies, School of Telecommunications; the Interdisciplinary Initiatives Implementation Team of VISION OHIO (the university's strategic plan), and in the years 2004 to 2006 he was president of the Caucus of Educators and Staff of African Descent (COESAD).

In 2006 Vibert was promoted to professor, School of Telecommunications, Ohio University.

Vibert has deployed his knowledge and experience across the United States, the Caribbean, and other parts of the world, variously as a consultant or organizer, on numerous projects, including:

- Consultant to the Broadcast Organization of Non-Aligned Countries (BONAC). Executed UNESCO-sponsored survey in the Caribbean on the establishment of a regional program bank (1983).

- Television producer of *In Living Color,* a television program showcasing the international community at Ohio University (1987–1988).

- Co-organizer, Voice of America, and Ohio University conference and workshop on radio drama in the Caribbean (1988).

- Special invitee and participant, First International Conference on Entertainment-E`ducation, sponsored by the Population Communication Services of Johns Hopkins University and the University of Southern California, held at the University of Southern California (1988).

- Special invitee and participant, UNICEF-sponsored Inter-Agency Technical Advisory Group (INTAG) meeting at UNICEF's headquarters in New York, to examine communication strategies for implementing the Basic Education for All program (1991).

- Consultant to UNESCO's regional communication advisor to the Caribbean. Conducted impact evaluation of UNESCO's International Program for the Development of Communication's (IPDC) investments in the Caribbean Institute for Mass Communication (CARIMAC), University of the West Indies (1995).

- Designing with the United States Agency for International Development (USAID) and the Voice of America, *A Song for Wangu*, a multi-genre broadcast intervention to support child survival in Africa (spring 1998).

- Special invitee, international conference "Strengthening Lifeline Media in Regions of Conflict," sponsored by the International Center for Humanitarian Reporting and Ubuntu Productions, Cape Town, Republic of South Africa (December 1998).

- Director, UNESCO-sponsored workshop on entertainment-education radio drama serials for reproductive health for broadcasters from Central Asia, Turkmenistan (November 1999).

- Cochair, Third International Conference on Entertainment-Education and Social Change, Amsterdam, Netherlands (2000).

- Keynote presenter at the United Nations Education, Scientific, and Cultural Organization (UNESCO), International Telecommunications Union (ITU), Friedrich Ebert Stiftung (FES), and the Caribbean Broadcasting Union (CBU)-sponsored conference on media education and the twenty-first century in the Caribbean, Bridgetown, Barbados (2000).

- Keynote speaker to the conference "Developing a Research Agenda for Entertainment-Education and Multicultural Audiences," funded by Centers for Disease Control and Prevention and organized by the Norman Lear Center's Hollywood, Health & Society program at the University of Southern California (2003).

- External examiner, Caribbean Institute for Mass Communication, University of the West Indies, Mona, Jamaica (since 2005).

- Member of the jury, Guyana Prize for Literature (2005).

- Convener of the conference "The African Diaspora in the Americas: Current Research," Ohio University, Athens, Ohio, April, 2003..

- Coconvener (with the University of the West Indies, Cave Hill, Barbados) of "Soundscapes: Reflections on Caribbean Oral and Aural Traditions," Barbados (2005).

- Co-organizer of the Guyana Folk Festival Symposium, "Folk, Identity, and National Cohesiveness" at the International Convention Center, Liliendaal, East Coast Demerara, Guyana (2008).

- Coordinator of the three-year USAID/HED/Ohio University/University of Guyana partnership to upgrade journalism and mass communication in Guyana (since 2008).

- Coordinator of TV production workshops, Georgetown and New Amsterdam, Guyana (2009).

He has presented more than fifty papers at conferences in the United States and countries as far afield as Singapore and Estonia. These include:

- "Caribbean Christians and human development: A study of the communication strategies of the Caribbean Conference of Churches (1971–1986)." The Annual Meeting of the Canadian Association for Latin American & Caribbean Studies, Windsor, Ontario. 1987.

- "Radio soap operas: Implications for global Africa." The Howard University Nineteenth Annual Communication Conference, Washington DC. 1990.

- "Twenty-five years later: A popular culture record of post-independence culture in Guyana." The Symposium on the Twenty-Fifth Anniversary of Guyana's Independence, Washington DC. 1991.

- "Immigration, race and ethnicity in US broadcasting." The International Conference on Immigration and Communication, Tallinn, Estonia. 1993.

- "The Caribbean diaspora and Caribbean broadcasting." The first annual meeting of the Caribbean Association for Communication Research (CACR), University of the West Indies, Mona, Jamaica. 1994.

- "The rehabilitation of 'failed states': Eritrea as a beta-site for distance education technologies." The Educational Technology 2000 Conference organized by the Commonwealth of Learning and the Asian Mass Communication Research and Information Center, Singapore. 1996.

- "Developing human resources for the Caribbean broadcast industry in the age of convergence." Regional seminar on challenges to broadcasting in the Caribbean, sponsored by the International Telecommunications Union, UNESCO, Caribbean Broadcasting Union, and the Frederich Ebert Stiftung, Accra Beach Hotel, Bridgetown, Barbados. 2000.

- "Entertainment-education for peace and reconciliation: The Guyanese sitcom *Agree to Disagree*—an intuitive

- entertainment-education product from Guyana." The Fiftieth Annual Conference of the International Communication Association, Acapulco, Mexico. 2000.

- "Think big, start small, act now: New technologies and the rehabilitation of the African-Guyanese child." Keynote address to the Ninth Anniversary Scholarship Awards Banquet of the Guyana Association of Georgia, Atlanta, Georgia. 2000.

- "New media technologies: Impact on human communication." The Thirty-First Annual General Assembly of the Caribbean Broadcasting Union, Havana, Cuba. 2001.

- "Jacob Lawrence, global Africa, and *The Cosby Show*." Colloquium on Jacob Lawrence at the Kennedy Museum, Ohio University, Athens, Ohio. 2003.

- "Music and the construction of race in the Guyanese diaspora in North America: Chutney in Richmond Hill." The symposium "The African Diaspora in the Americas: Current Research," Ohio University, Athens, Ohio. 2003.

- "Bird song and the Guyanese diaspora." Soundscapes: Reflections on Caribbean Oral and Aural Traditions, University of the West Indies, Cave Hill, Barbados. 2005.

- "Ghana's independence and the West Indies." Conference on the fiftieth anniversary of Ghana's independence, Ohio University, Athens, Ohio. 2007.

- "Music and Working People in Guyana during the twentieth century." Critchlow Lecture Series, Critchlow Labor College, Georgetown, Guyana. 2007.

- "Ved Vatuk & Indo-Guyanese folk music." Paper presented to the Guyana Folk Festival Symposium, National Convention Center, Lilendaal, Guyana (2008).

Selected Publications: books and book chapters:

Immigration, Diversity and Broadcasting in the United States, 1990–2001. Ohio University Press.

With J. P. Jeter, K. R. Ramphal, and C. Pratt. *International Afro Mass Media*. Westport, CT.

Excuse Me! May I Offer Some Interpretations? Toronto.

"Evolution of mass communication: Mass communication and sustainable futures." *The Encyclopedia of Life Support Systems*. Paris: UNESCO.

"Writings on Guyanese Music 2003–2004." *Black Praxis* (special edition). Ohio.

"The Third Temptation." In Charlotte Williams and Evelyn Williams (eds.), *Denis Williams: A Life in Works—New and Collected Essays*. Amsterdam.

"Milestones in Communication and National Development." In Y. Kamalipour (ed.), *Global Communication* (2nd ed.). Belmont, CA.

Vibert has edited a number of articles on celebrities in the Guyana newspaper *Sunday Stabroek*. He has been the editor of "Celebrating Our Creative Personalities," a fortnightly series published in *Sunday Stabroek* (Guyana), 2003–2006. The list of personalities he has featured include Hilton Hemerding, Derry Etkins, George Simmons, James Ingram, Rannie Hart, Frank Holder, David Campbell, Michael Currica, Winston Ewart (Sir Wins), W. Herbert L. Allsopp, Joyce Ferdinand-Saunders, Rudy Seymour, Rudolph Dunbar, Wilfred Robert Adams, Hubert (Bert) and Edward (Eddie)—the Rogers brothers, Tony Phillips, Aubrey Cummings, Stanley Greaves, and Al Seales. Other celebrities include Valerie Rodway, James "Jimmy" Woodrow Weekes, Kim Clark, Bertram DeVarell—the father of steel band in Guyana, Charwin Burnham, Winston Edgar Beckles, Andrew Watson, Alan Bush, the Valz family, Billy Moore, Dave Martins, Dorothy Taitt, Percy A. Braithwaite, John "Bagpipe" Fredericks, Dr. Joycelynne Loncke, Charles Knights LRSM, ARCM, Vesta Lowe, Monica Chopperfield, Vincent De Abreu, the Mootoo Brothers, Eusi Kwyana, James Alexander Phoenix and the British Guiana Police Male Voice Choir, Nesbit Chhanghur, and Ken "Snakehips" Johnson.

Vibert has found the time for community service. He was cofounder of Drums Three—a performing arts group based at Ohio University, dedicated to the promotion of international understanding through the performance of global African and other international literatures. He was a member of the executive committee for the Guyana Folk Festival—an annual festival of Guyana's multicultural heritage and scholarship. The festival is held in Brooklyn, New York. He established Community and Campus Days at Ohio University, and he is a member of the Leadership and Governance Committee of the Foundation for Appalachia.

In recognition of his sterling work, Vibert has received numerous honors and awards, including:

- The Anthony Trisolini Fellowship for distinguished achievement as a doctoral student at Ohio University (1989).

- Eighth Annual Carlos and Guillermo Vigil Prize for the best article to appear in Volume 11, 1992, of *Studies in Latin American Popular Culture* (1993).

- Academic Specialist Award by the United States Information Agency to conduct formative research with the University of Asmara, Eritrea, to support the development of a distance education system for Eritrea (1995).

- Award for service to the field of entertainment-education by the Netherlands Entertainment-Education Foundation (NEEF), Amsterdam, the Netherlands (2000).

- The Friends of the Libraries of Ohio University Honor in 2005 for the publication of *Immigration, Diversity, and Broadcasting in the United States, 1990-2001*.

- Image Award, National Association for the Advancement of Colored People (NAACP), Ohio University Chapter (2005).

- The Guyana Folk Festival Award for outstanding contribution to Guyana's culture and heritage (2005).

Vibert is particularly committed to his role as vice president of the Guyana Cultural Association, the organizers of the annual Guyana Folk Festival. This not-for-profit organization is dedicated to preserving, promoting, and perpetuating Guyana's folk heritage.

From where does he draw his inspiration? What drives him to do well? In a single word:– communication. "Communication," he asserts with deep conviction, "is essential for human understanding and social change." Finding cultural similarities across human cultures is his passion.

A significant part of Vibert's work is associated with field research—collecting and documenting folk life, especially Guyanese musical expressions. He is very thankful to Peter Kempadoo and Marc Matthews for introducing him to this research method during 1971 and 1972 in Guyana.

Vibert's spouse is Dr. Patricia Cambridge, a Guyanese achiever in her own right. She is a former Bishops' High School student, accomplished pianist, and professor in the School of Journalism, Ohio University. They have two children, Nadine and Nigel. Nadine studied sociology and African American studies at Ohio University. As of this writing, Nigel is a freshman at Ohio University, where he is majoring in political science, with special emphasis on international relations.

September 27, 2010

Sister Hazel Campayne

BA, MA, PhD
Educator and Social Justice Reformer

Sister Hazel Campayne was winner of the Guyana Awards (Canada) 2007 Lifetime Achievement Award. The citation of the award contains the following information, among other things:

Dr. Hazel Campayne has dedicated her life as a tireless advocate of social justice, human rights, peace, and democracy in Guyana, the Caribbean, Canada, and internationally. She has earned the reputation of being a true patriot of Guyana with an indomitable spirit, who made great sacrifices—at the risk of her own personal security—to promote peace, justice, and democracy in Guyana.

She never faltered in her commitment to these principles, even after she left Guyana in 1980 to join the Guyanese community in Canada, where she was a founding member of the Canada Guyana Forum, which champions the cause of social justice for Guyanese in Guyana and in Canada.

Dr. Campayne's career in Guyana as an educator can only be described in superlatives. As the headmistress of St. Rose's High School, Sister Hazel (as she was fondly known) was highly respected as a strict disciplinarian and talented educator who inspired her students to strive not only for academic excellence but also for the highest levels of achievement in other aspects of life, including community service, sports, and culture.

In the 1990s, through the Canada Guyana Forum, Dr. Campayne was instrumental in implementing the Education Renewal Project that established an educational program for youth in the Tiger Bay area of Georgetown.

In Canada, Dr. Campayne was recently appointed by the Ontario government to the new Ontario Bicentenary Commemorative Committee on the Abolition of the Slave Trade.

She is a member of the National Diversity Committee and the coordinator for the local parish group of the Canadian Catholic Organization for Development and Peace, an international organization promoting development and social justice. Dr. Campayne is a member of the Ontario Black History Society, the Women's Inter-Church Council of Canada and the Ecumenical Network for Women's Justice, and was a member of the delegations that monitored the historic 1992 elections in Guyana and the 1994 elections in South Africa.

An accomplished academic with a doctorate in theology, two master's degrees, two postgraduate certificates, and a bachelor's degree obtained in Canada, England, and Jamaica, Dr. Campayne has been awarded several national and international scholarships and other accolades.

In 1975, the United Nations International Year of Women, she was honored as Woman of the Year by the Rotary Club for her work in education, especially with youth.

An alumnus of Bishops' High School, Dr. Campayne is originally from Port Mourant, Berbice, Guyana.

Source:
Websites accessed May 27, 2010, on Guyana Consulate Toronto, Guyana Awards (Canada).

May 27, 2010.

Frederick Case

BA, MA, PhD
Linguist French Master
Professor Emeritus
University of Toronto

He was the chair of the Department of French at the University of Toronto. He was the principal of New College, University of Toronto. He is a linguist and a French master. He was Vice-President of the Association of Directors of the Departments of French Studies of Universities and Colleges of Canada and President, (ADDÉFUCC).

Frederick Ivor Case obtained a teachers certificate in 1960 at the De La Salle College of Education, University of Manchester, England. He studied the theory, history, and methods of education, English literature, and French language and literature. In 1965 he obtained his bachelor's degree from the University of Hull. His special subjects were French and Spanish. In 1968 Fred obtained his master's degree from the University of Leicester. He majored in political science—European political studies. His dissertation was "Charles de Gaulle and the Constitution of the Fifth French Republic."

In 1970, he was awarded the The Doctorate of the University, Faculty of Humanities, University of Lille, France; Mention: Right Honourable unanimously. The title of His thesis was: Socialism and Social Structure in Work of Emile Zola.

Fred Case was born on September 19, 1939, at Georgetown. His father, Edward Case, a postman and reporter, joined the army and later became a staff sergeant. Fred's mother, Honora, was a housewife. Fred was one of nine siblings.

Fred's teaching career started with his appointment in 1960 as assistant master for French at the Cardinal Wiseman Boys School in Coventry, England. After inspection and a successful probationary period, he was granted certification to teach in England and in France in 1961 and 1968, respectively. From 1967 to 1968 he was Professor of English at The Professional Institute Roubaix, Roubaix, France, and at Industrial and Commercial School in Tourcoing, France (Section: Technical High School).

He moved to Canada in 1968, where he secured the appointment as lecturer in the Department of French at the University of Toronto. His career progressed rapidly at the University of Toronto. He was assistant professor from 1971 to 1974, and then became associate professor, Department of French.

In addition, Fred employed his gifts as a specialist in French in other universities. In 1974–1975, he did volunteer teaching at the Center (Dominicain) Lebret, Dakar, Sénégal, in African literature to classes First and Final. In 1975 and 1976 he taught African, Caribbean and African American literature during the summer session at the Department of Humanities, Atkinson College, York University. He taught African and Caribbean literature in French at the Department of Romance Languages and Literatures at McMaster University, Hamilton, Canada, in the fall term, and in the spring term he taught an upper-level seminar on Aimé Césaire.

In 1980 Fred was appointed a full professor in the Department of French, University of Toronto. Between 1981 and 1984 he was external examiner in French, African, and Caribbean literatures at the Department of French, University of the West Indies, Jamaica, Barbados, and Trinidad. In 1984–85 and since 2005 he has been associate chair, Graduate Studies, University of Toronto, and from 1985 to 1990 he was chair, Department of French, University of Toronto.

In 1991 Fred was appointed principal of New College, University of Toronto. He held this post until 1996. During this period he took on extra responsibilities. In 1990–91 he did volunteer teaching at the Center (Dominican) Lebret, Dakar, Sénégal, English, Terminal, and in 1997–98 he was international coordinator, Institut Universitaire du Boeny, Madagascar. From 1998 to 2001, he was consultant to the Canadian International Development Agency/Aga Khan Development Network CIDA/AKDN Project to establish the Institute for [Teachers'] Professional Development, Khorog, Tajikistan, and in 2002–2003, he was senior administrator, Institute for [Teachers'] Professional Development.

In 2005, while in retirement, Fred Case was honored by the University of Toronto with the title professor emeritus. In 2006, he accepted an appointment as professor at the University of Guyana.

Fred's professional affiliations and activities from 1997 to date include Fellow, Center for Research in Latin American and Caribbean Studies, York University, Toronto; and from 2003, executive committee member, Ryerson University Caribbean Research Center.

Professor Case's scholarly and professional works include books, refereed and non-refereed publications, chapters in books, presentations and papers, pedagogical materials and texts, translations, and manuscripts in print and in preparation. Altogether, they total over three hundred separate pieces of work.

His books include:
- *Aimé Césaire: Bibliographie,* Toronto, Manna, 1973.
- *La Cité ideale dans Travail d'Emile Zola*, Toronto, University of Toronto Press, 1974.
- *Racism and National Consciousness*, Toronto, Plowshare, 1979. Revised and republished. Toronto, Othereye, 2002.
- *The Crisis of Identity: Studies in the Guadeloupean and Martiniquan Novel.* Sherbrooke, Naaman, 1985.

His refereed publications, numbering over seventy since 1970, include the following articles in publications:
- "Aimé Césaire et l'Occident chrétien," *L'Esprit Créateur..*
- "Culture nègre et idéologie dans Kotia-Nima de Boubou Hama," *Présence Francophone.*
- "The socio-cultural functions of women in the Senegalese novel," *Cultures et Développement.*
- *Dictionnaire des Oeuvres littéraires négro-africaines de Langue française.* (Éd. Ambroise Kom) Sherbrooke, Naaman.
- "Eléments des civilisations égyptienne, grecque et romaine dans Et les chiens se taisaient," in *Le Soleil éclaté: Mélanges offerts à Aimé Césaire à l'occasion de son soixante-dixième anniversaire.*
- "School-University Partnerships: The Challenges of Educating African Canadians," in K. Brathwaite & C. E. James (eds.) *Educating African Canadians*, Toronto, James Lorimer & Co., 1996. 205–215.
- "Caribbean novel: Francophone" in P. Schellinger (ed.) *Encyclopedia of the Novel.*
- "The Intersemiotics of Obeah and Kali Mai in Guyana," in P. Taylor (ed) *Nation Dance.*
- "Dimensions of Access to Transition," in K. S. Brathwaite (ed.) *Access & Equity in the University.*

His non-refereed publications include:
- "Le Ghetto des travailleurs de couleur," *Tribune Socialiste*.
- "Racial Minorities in Canada," *Communist Viewpoint*.
- "South African Liberation and the Rebirth of Pan-African Consciousnes in Canada," *Southern Africa Report*.
- "How we made plans for FESPAC in Dakar, " *Contrast*.
- "Follow the North Star," in Henry Chase (ed.) *In Their Footsteps*.

His pedagogical materials and texts include:
- *Black Cultural Heritage Curriculum*. In collaboration with D. Melville and E. Lynch-Richards. Toronto, Toronto Board of Education, 1989.
- *Concise Bibliography of the English-Speaking Caribbean*, Toronto, Learning Resources Kit on the W. I. (Xerox), 1979.
- *Études Afro-Canadiennes: Guide pédagogique—Cycle intermédiaire*. Coordonnateur du projet. En collaboration avec S. Crosta, M. Gagbegnon et B. Moitt. Toronto, Ministère de l'Éducation, 1988.
- *Excellence et équité*, Ministère de l'Education, Ontario, 1995.

Fred has translated Pathé Diagne, *Cheikh Anta Diop and World History in 1997*. He has written "The Orange," a collection of ten short stories, and "Hungry Eyes," a long poem in four parts.

His manuscripts include:
- Teacher education in a difficult environment. The case of Guyana (monograph).
- Encyclopedia of Caribbean Religions (coeditor with P. Taylor, York U.) One thousand pages to be published by University of Illinois Press.
- Entries on the works of Ramabai Espinet and Arnold Harrichand Itwaru, respectively, in *Border Crossings: Caribbean-Canadian Writing*—a bio-bibliographical critical sourcebook. (Eds. Frank Birbalsingh and Hyacinth Simpson). Caribbean Studies Press.

Papers presented at his own request include:
- "Aimé Césaire et Frantz Fanon: théoriciens de la littérature révolutionnaire." Modern Languages Association, New York.

- "Santo oba ko so." Modern Languages Association, New York.
- "Family and Marriage in the Senegalese Novel." Canadian Association of African Studies, York University.
- "Revolutionary Optimism and Resignation in African Poetry in Portuguese." College Language Association, Washington DC.
- "L'Université face au Dévélopement," AUPELF, New Delhi. December 15, 1988.

Papers presented by invitation, over fifty papers from 1970, include:
- Videotaped discussion with H. Mitterand, B. Bakker, and H. Weinberg on Emile Zola. Scarborough College, University of Toronto.
- "Revolt and Ideology in the Works of Aimé Césaire," Department of French and Italian, University of California, Irvine.
- "Analyse phonostylistique de la parole du griot Mamadou Kouyaté dans Soundjata de Djibril Tamsir Niane," African Studies Association (of the United States), Boston.
- "L'esthétique poétique d'Edouard Glissant," Festival européen de Poésie, Université de Louvain.
- "Le discours islamique dans l'oeuvre d'Aminata Sow Fall," Buffalo State College.
- "Les Africain(e)s du Canada," FESPAC, Dakar, Sénégal.
- "Esthétique et révolte: analyse de la poétique de Léon-Gontran Damas," Colloque Léon-Gontran Damas, Paris.
- "L'enseignement des littératures africaine et caribéenne," Conseil International d'Études francophones, Nouvelle-Orléans.
- "La cura de enfermedades mentales y la aplicacion de los principios de la espiritualidad Africana," Congreso: Migraciones y sincretismo cultural, Casa del Caribe, Santiago de Cuba.
- Congrès africain d'Éducation à la Paix: Enseignants pour la Paix, Université Cheikh Anta Diop, Dakar.

Invited lectures and seminars, over ninety presentations from 1971, include:
- "Négritude and Utopianism." La Société Champlain. "Culture et Société des Caraibes," Cercle d'Etudes françaises.

- "L'Aventure ambigue de l'écrivain." Département de français, Trent University, Peterborough.
- "L'Intention poétique d'Aimé Césaire." Faculté des Arts, Université de Sherbrooke.
- Keynote lecture: Black Parents' Conference, Oakwood Collegiate Institute, Toronto.
- Seminar on political and socio-economic factors in Haiti following projection of the film "La Langue française dans la littérature africaine," Department of Romance Languages, Oberlin College, Ohio.
- "Post-Secondary Education in Guyana: the Challenge of Partnerships," State visit of His Excellency President Cheddi Jagan of Guyana, Education Center, Toronto.
- "Analyse du Discours et Exégèse du Texte sacré," Faculté de Théologie. Tananarivo, Madagascar. Série de 12 séminaires.
- "Forms of Spirituality in the Caribbean," Institute for Professional Development, Khorog, Tajikistan.
- Three-day workshop to teachers, university students, and community leaders, Pan-Africanism. National Library, Georgetown, Guyana.
- "The interface of Islam and traditional spirituality in Africa," Black Students Association and Varsity Christian Fellowship, University of Toronto.
- "Sequels of Soviet Colonialism in Central Asia: the Case of Tajikistan," World Events Forum, Fairfield Seniors' Center, Etobicoke.
- Series of seminars to sixth-form students at New Amsterdam Multilateral School, Berbice, on Jane Austen, Roger Mais, Ngugi wa Thiong'o, Arthur Miller, Ernest Hemingway, and William Shakespeare.
- Upper -year class on drama, University of Guyana. Seminar to fifth-form students at St. Stanislaus School, Georgetown, on Merle Hodge, Michael Anthony, John Knowles, and John Steinbeck.

Since 1972 Professor Case has supervised, over thirty students reading for their master's degrees and PhDs. In addition, he was examiner, variously as internal appraiser or external examiner of candidates' submissions for PhD, from 1975 to 2006 at various universities, including Ontario

Institute for Studies in Education, Toronto; University of British Columbia; University of Toronto; Université de Sherbrooke; York University; Institute of Social Studies, the Hague; McGill University; University of Western Australia; and Université d'Ottawa.

Fred has been an assessor of manuscripts submitted to the Canadian Federation for the Humanities; Canadian Journal of African Studies; Présence Francophone; Proceedings of the Modern Language Association; Research in African Literatures,- Journal of the University of Moncton – Liaison; 1994 Adjudication Committee, Writing and Publication Program, Canadian Heritage.

He was evaluator of curricula and textbooks for the Ontario Ministry of Education, Ministère de l'Education, Toronto Board of Education; and Learning Resources Kit, North York Board of Education. He was advisor to the board of directors, Artists and Books for Children; Evaluation Committee: Batista Graduate Essay Competition, Centre for Research on Latin America and the Caribbean (CERLAC), York University; and Undergraduate Essay Competition 2005.

He has held a number of administrative positions at the University of Toronto. These include chair of the Department of French (1985–1990); principal of New College (1991–96); cochair, Center for the Study of Race, Ethnicity, Culture, and Power (1992–94); director, Language Learning Research Center (1993–96); director, Caribbean Studies Program; chairman, Policy Committee, Transitional Year Program; executive member, African Studies Committee, Center for International Studies (1995–96).

He has been a member of a number of administrative bodies at the University of Toronto, including the President's Consultative Council, Dean's Advisory Committee on College Programs, Academic Board of the Governing Council, President's Advisory Committee, Provost's Advisory Group, and President's Advisory Committee on Race Relations. He was chair of the West Indies Student Exchange Selection Committee.

Fred's Other activities related to University Work include: - Vice-President of the Association of Heads of Departments of French Studies of Universities and Colleges of Canada President; Member: Regional Committee for North America - Canada Association of Partially or Wholly French; Member: Interdisciplinary and International Association for the Promotion of African Archaeology; Member, Executive Committee, Ryerson Centre for Research on the Caribbean; Evaluator of applications for research awards and grants conference in the Fields of African and Caribbean literatures.

Outside the university, Fred's roles have included: president of the Black Education Project and chairman of the board of directors; a member of the selection committee for initial hiring procedures, race relations and multiculturalism, Toronto Board of Education; Member: International Planning Committee, Festival Pan African Arts and Culture, Dakar, Sénégal; member, the evaluation committee, Department of French and Italian, University of Massachusetts, Amherst; trustee, Royal Ontario Museum; the board of directors, Canadian Center for Victims of Torture, chair of its International Committee. He was chair of the evaluation committee, MEd, class of 2002, the Aga Khan University, Institute of Educational Development, Karachi.

Very sadly, Fred passed away in May 2008. A glowing tribute was paid to Fred's sterling humanity and his achievements in an article by Prof. David Clandfield, which appeared on the New College, University of Toronto website on May 2008.

Titled "Remembering Professor Fred Case, Principal of New College (1991–1996)," the touching tribute about Fred's dedication and commitment to noble works, which are an inspiration to all, states, among other things:-

> Fred's career as a professor of French would be enough for most people. An excellent undergraduate teacher, an inspirational graduate thesis supervisor (primary supervisor of thirty-three doctoral students; cosupervisor and examiner of countless more), a conscientious administrator and natural leader (graduate secretary, associate chair and then chair of the Department of French), an active researcher (five books, scores of articles, countless conference papers and invitational lectures), he also did much to ensure that a significant place was found within the French programs of the University of Toronto for the literature and culture of la francophonie (most notably of north and west Africa and the Caribbean).
>
> But Fred went well beyond the confines of French studies to become a pioneer of interdisciplinary studies in New College where he played a predominant role in the founding of two programs: African Studies in the 1970s and Caribbean Studies in the 1990s ... but also lay the groundwork for two other

New College programs (sponsoring Bengali courses in the undergraduate South Asian Studies, now sponsored entirely by New College; and Jungian psychology courses, later to receive the largest ever endowment at the college) …

He was an influential participant in the founding and development of the Transitional Year Program, designed to make it easier for marginalized people with non-typical educational backgrounds to get into university. He worked to bring students of poor and immigrant backgrounds into contact with the university, both at the elementary and secondary levels (mentoring many of them personally), in order to help them break out of the cycle of low expectations that is so often their lot. He was frequently called upon to advise senior university administrators on race relations, employment equity, Native students, and overseas exchanges …

Some examples are his work on black education with the Toronto Board of Education, on human rights education at the Ministry of Education, on Native students' access to higher education at the Ministry of Colleges and Universities, as a trustee of the Royal Ontario Museum (in the wake of the controversial "Out of Africa" exhibit), and his active role on the board of directors of the Canadian Center for Victims of Torture.

He was particularly anxious to work in countries of the South, visiting and lecturing in the University of the West Indies and Senegal, contributing to the development of university programs in Madagascar and Tajikistan and to education policy in Guyana…

As principal of New College, the stresses that he subjected himself to were already affecting his health, until he was forced to undergo bypass surgery and end his term of office two years earlier than anticipated. Even as he recovered from the surgery, he returned to the principal's office for nine more months to oversee the transfer of control of the New College residence and food services from central control to the college, a change that would bring an additional income stream from summer business and enable the college to develop its programs and services significantly over the ensuing decade.

At the end of his principalship ... he left to work on a three-year project—a teachers' training institute in Tajikistan (on the border with Afghanistan), before returning to spend much of his time in Guyana. It was on a return trip to Toronto to attend the thesis defense of two more graduate students that he finally succumbed to the heart attack that took him from us.

Fred Case was not the longest-serving principal of New College, nor is the full extent of his contribution as widely known as that of others. But in a college that proclaims as its mission the study, pursuit, and advocacy of equity and diversity in all our activities, his work stands as an inspiration to all who share those principles, as it has been for the countless young people whose lives were touched and enriched by his deep compassion and commitment to their cause.

Sources:

http://www.newcollege.utoronto.ca/aboutnew/news/Remembering_Professor_Fred_Case.htm

September 29, 2008

Reverend Dr. Henry Chan

BS, MBA, DPA, Dmin STM, PhD, PsyD
Anglican Priest

The Reverend Dr. Henry Chan was a parish priest in the diocese of Long Island, New York, for twenty-five years. In his early years, he was tutored by the Anglican Archbishop of the West Indies and Bishop of Guyana, the Most Reverend Dr. Alan John Knight.

Henry Albert Chan was born at Grove, East Bank, Demerara, on January 7, 1946, to Clarence and Ruby Chan. He is the eldest of eight children. After living in New Amsterdam and Canje, Berbice, his father was able to secure a job at Plantation Versailles sugar estate on the West Bank, Demerara. The family moved to Plantation Schoon Ord, which was connected with Plantation Versailles.

Henry attended St. Mary's Anglican School at Goed Fortuin and was awarded a Booker's Scholarship in 1957 to attend Queen's College (QC) in Georgetown. While at QC, Henry embarked on an intense and restless search for wisdom and truth. This exploration resulted in a deep interest in philosophy. He spent more time on this personal quest than on his academic studies

During his years at QC, Henry faithfully followed in the footsteps of his ancestors, who were either Anglicans when they left China in the 1860s or became Anglicans soon after their arrival in British Guiana—he is a fourth generation Chinese who was born in British Guiana. His parents were staunch Anglicans at St. Swithin's Church at Vreed-en-Hoop. His paternal grandfather, Henry Chan, or "Mr. Daniel," as he was familiarly known in the village, was a leading member among a small number of Anglicans who built the first Anglican church, St. Peter's, at Rosignol, West Cost Berbice, in the early '50s. Prior to that, church services were held in Mr. Daniel's living room on Sundays, and Henry remembers helping to set up the chairs whenever he visited his grandfather as a little boy.

One day, the parish priest, at Vreed-en-Hoop, the Venerable Lewis John Rowe, told his parents that he believed that Henry had a vocation for the priesthood. Archdeacon Rowe also communicated this observation to Archbishop Alan John Knight, who was Archbishop of the West Indies as well as Bishop of British Guiana. Thereupon, Archbishop Knight took Henry "under his wing" and tutored him for about five years in preparation for the ministry of the church.

During this time, Henry recalls, Archbishop Knight told him that he considered himself as a "father in God" and saw Henry as a "son in Christ." Henry remembers that after weekly classes at Austin House, the official residence of the Bishop of British Guiana, Archbishop Knight would invite him for tea. During this time, they would spend another half an hour or so, talking about philosophy, theology, and psychology, among other things.

When Henry graduated from QC in 1964, Archbishop Knight told Henry that he wanted him to gain experience in the world by working for the next four years, after which he would attend Codrington College in Barbados for academic preparation for ordination to the priesthood, and then he would go on to further his studies at Durham University in England. For the next three years, Henry taught in schools at the primary and secondary school levels and worked in a few positions at the Demerara Bauxite Company (DEMBA) at McKenzie, Demerara River.

In 1967, Archbishop Knight wanted Henry to work for one more year, but Henry's spirit yearned to do something more challenging in life. In September 1967, with three other coworkers from DEMBA, he emigrated to New York to further his studies. While working in computer programming, systems analysis and design, and long-range planning, Henry obtained a bachelor of science degree in computer and information science from Empire State College, State University of New York; a master of business administration degree from Dowling College, New York; and a doctor of public administration degree from Nova Southeastern University, Florida. This was his academic preparation for a career path in business or government.

During this time, Henry met Jean Langdon, a Trinidadian, in New York, and they were married on April 26, 1969. They have three children: Anthony, who was born March 23, 1970, and is a graduate of the Wharton School of Business, University of Pennsylvania; Andre, who was born on November 5, 1972, and is a graduate of the School of Engineering, Columbia University, as well as the University of California, Berkeley; and Natasha, who was born on September 6, 1978, and is a graduate of the Georgia Institute of Technology as well as Rutgers University. Their son, Anthony, and his wife, Gloria, have three children: Justin, Jordan, and Victoria.

After marriage, all was going well for Henry—he had a good job, a new house, and two cars. Later on, Jean was able to leave her job so that she could stay home to personally take care of their children. Then, there was a life-changing occurrence on October 21, 1975, as Henry commuted from his job in New York City to his home out on Long Island, New York. This led him to test his vocation again in the Episcopal Church, the United States of America's branch of the worldwide Anglican Communion. This was most pleasing to Archbishop Knight, who wanted to know when Henry would be returning to what was now Guyana. Unfortunately, the archbishop died in 1979 before Henry would complete his theological studies. Henry was ordained as a deacon in 1982 and a priest in 1983 in Long Island, New York.

The fire from the quest for wisdom and truth still burned within, so Henry went on to earn a doctor of ministry degree from the University of the South, Sewanee, Tennessee, in 1987; a master of sacred theology degree from the General Theological Seminary in New York City, New York; and a doctor of philosophy in pastoral psychology, as well as a doctor of psychology degree from the Graduate Theological Foundation in Indiana.

A diplomate of the Viktor Frankl Institute, Henry holds memberships in the American Psychological Association, the American Society for Public Administration, and the New York State Dispute Resolution Association. He has published two books through Wyndham Hall Press, Lima, Ohio, on mediation and psychology: *The Mediator as Human Being: From a Study of the Major Concepts of Sigmund Freud, Carl Jung, Erik Erikson and*

Abraham Maslow (2005); and *The Humanity of Mediators: From a Study of the Major Concepts of Viktor E. Frankl* (2007).

He is also listed in *Marquis Who's Who in the East, 1999–2000* and *Marquis Who's who in America, 2000*. Additionally, he is listed in the *USA Congressional Record* as "A Point of Light for All Americans," June 22, 2001. He was awarded the Dorothy Day Prize in Pastoral Care and Counseling by the Graduate Theological Foundation, Mishawaka, Indiana, on May 6, 2005.

Henry is currently retired after serving in the ordained ministry for twenty-five years in the diocese of Long Island, New York. He has not retired, however, from the rest of life, and so his restless spirit is now searching for opportunities to use the gifts and skills that God has given him to make the lives of people better ... somewhere, somehow.

July 27, 2009

Deviekha Chetram

Deviekha Chetram

Indian Classical Kathak Dancer
Artistic Director, Tarana Dance Center, Toronto

Deviekha Chetram is a celebrated Indian classical dancer and dance teacher. With over thirty years' experience teaching classical Indian dance, Deviekha is the artistic director of the Tarana Dance Center in Toronto. She and her sister Geeta were the first West Indians to establish a teaching institution for Indian dance in Canada. Deviekha is a recipient of many awards from the South Asian and Indo-Caribbean community for her contribution to the arts in Canada.

She specialized in Kathak, a classical dance form of northern India. Kathak is known for its fancy footwork, fast spins, and geometric hand movements—the expressions and choreography tell a story in dance. The three major schools and traditions of Kathak are drawn from three major cities in India—Lucknow, Jaipur, and Varanasi in northern India.

Deviekha Chetram, nee Singh, the youngest of fourteen children, was born on May 24, 1957, in Alexander Village, East Bank Demerara, Guyana. Her parents were the late Radhay Janki Singh and Jai Narain Singh of Alexander Village. Her father, known as Uncle Gully, was overseer for Ruimveldt Sugar Estate. Her mother, affectionately known as Aunty Radhay, was a businesswoman.

Deviekha comes from a very artistic family; both of her parents loved to sing, and her mother played the harmonium and sang bhajans (hindu hymns) and kirtans (singing) at temples. They instilled a strong value for Indian culture in all their children. They taught their children to be proud of their religion, culture, and heritage. Her mother was an organizer of many melas (fairs) for the temple in the village and Christmas parties for handicapped children through the Red Cross.

The family home was a wonderful staging ground for the children's achievements in the field of Indian culture music and dance. Deviekha's eldest sister, Indra, is married to Pandit Reepu Daman Persaud and has focused on promoting Indian culture through the work of the Guyana Hindu Dharmic Sabha in Guyana. Sister Geeta is an accomplished Odissi dancer and teacher of Indian classical dance. Brother Onkar was an accomplished tabla player, sitarist, teacher of Indian classical music, and philanthropist. Brother Vickram is an excellent tabla player. Sister Looma is a reputable singer of bhajans and kirtans. Sister Ronica (Jaipershad-Boni) is very talented; even though she did not have formal training, she plays the dholak, harmonium, and keyboard and is involved in promoting Indian culture in Tampa, Florida.

Deviekha and several members of her family were very much involved in cultural presentations in Guyana. Sisters Vijai, Looma, Ronica, and Geeta all participated in cultural presentations for the Maha Sabha, Gandhi Youth, and Dharmic Sabha, until they emigrated overseas.

Deviekha received her primary school education from 1963 to 1969 at Sacred Heart Roman Catholic School in Georgetown and then proceeded to St. Joseph's High School, where she graduated with five GCE "O" levels in 1974. She attended Mrs. Singh's Commercial School in Georgetown from 1973 to '74.

After high school, Deviekha worked for various financial institutions; first, the Bank of Nova Scotia, Georgetown, until 1979, when she emigrated to Canada. In 1984 she joined the Chase Manhattan Bank, New York, and from 1987 to1988 she worked at the Royal Bank of Canada, Toronto. From 1988 to 1998, she was accounting supervisor at Amcu/Hepcoe Credit Union, and from 1998 to 2001, she worked at SLM Software.

Deviekha developed her love and passion for dance from her early years. Since age six she has performed at various Diwali and Phagwah concerts at the temple in her village. Later, she received formal training in classical Indian dance at the Indian Cultural Center (ICC) in Georgetown, where she studied Kathak under the guidance of Guru Pratap Pawar and the late Pandit Durgalall, whom she accompanied in several dance performances and concerts

When she emigrated to Canada in 1979, she felt there was a void—even though there were religious organizations, there was not much happening for dance and music. Responding to numerous requests and needs from the Indo-Caribbean community, she started performing and teaching dances for local charitable and religious organizations. One of Deviekha's first performances was for Vishnu Mandir at the first Diwali dinner held at the Royal York Hotel in Toronto in 1979.

Deviekha started the Tarana Dance School in May 1989 from the basement of her home; she had only five students. Her sister Geeta Leo joined her in 1990. Deviekha saw the Tarana Dance School as a way of preserving her culture and heritage and imparting the knowledge to the younger generation. Their premier concert in 1989 was at the Ontario

Science Center, where both sisters were introduced by their brother, Onkar, who played the sitar. Sister Looma Doodnauth sang melodious tunes from old Hindi films, and the emcee for the evening was another sister, Ronica, one of the founders of the Indo-Caribbean Golden Age Association.

The Tarana Dance School became very popular. It was known as a dance school that produced dances with a touch of class. Many cultural and religious organizations requested performances by the students of the Tarana Dance School. The school has seen a tremendous growth, and both Deviekha and Geeta have established their own schools and a niche within the South Asian and Indo-Caribbean communities in Canada and abroad. Deviekha opened the Tarana Dance Center in 2001; Geeta is the owner of Geetika—Indian Dance Company in Ajax, Ontario. It was not easy in the beginning, as many of the established Indian dance gurus were not very accepting in the initial stage of Deviekha's and Geeta's dance schools, but today both sisters are recognized as dance teachers who impart quality training to their students.

Deviekha invites Kathak dancers and teachers from India to work with her senior students, many of whom have gone on to make a name for themselves and perform with other dance companies. Several of her students have pursued dance as a career. Her students have been featured on several TV programs. Deviekha has produced many successful shows in Canada and the United States.

She served on the board of directors for Markham Arts Council and has judicated several local dance competitions and pageants. Deviekha was recently appointed as artistic director for Natya Arts Productions Inc., an organization for the promotion of classical Indian dance and music. In 2006 she brought the legendary Kathak master Pandit Birju Maharaj to Canada, along with his disciple Saswati Sen, to conduct Kathak workshops for her students and other Kathak students from Canada and abroad. Two of her students have traveled to India to study under Pandit Birju Maharaj. In June 2008, Deviekha again sponsored this workshop, and young professional and emerging artistes of Kathak performed for Pandit Maharaj. The show, "Rhythm of the Ghungroos," was a resounding success, thus creating an alliance between her Tarana Dance Center and Kalashram (dance academy) New Delhi. Kalashram is the dream of Kathak maestro Pandit Birju Maharaj. It focuses on imparting training mainly in the field of Kathak.

Highlights of Deviekha's accomplishments include performances in:

- *Anmol Bandhan*, the first locally produced movie
- Various Hindu societies' Phagwah and Diwali events
- Dharmic Sabha annual presentations
- Holi celebrations at Magistrate Prem Persaud's residence
- Guyana Hindu Dharmic Sabha Holi Mela at Farnum Fairground
- Indian Cultural Center annual events

She performed with Pratap and Priya Pawar in several programs and venues in Guyana, including the Theater Guild, Queen's College. She performed with Pandit Durgalall at the University of Guyana, Queen's College, Town Hall, Georgetown, and she represented Guyana in Cuba in 1977. She performed in Progressive Youth Organization (PYO) and People's Progressive Party (PPP) annual presentations and choreographed and taught Indian dance from 1976 through 1979 for the Guyana Hindu Dharmic Sabha.

Her work in Canada also includes her students' performances, as well as the Vishnu Mandir Diwali Dinner at Royal York Hotel in 1979. She taught and choreographed dances for Vishnu Mandir Diwali Concert in 1980, and presented various performances in the Greater Toronto Area for several temples (1981–83). The 1989 premier concert at the Ontario Science Center was attended by the Minister of Culture.

From 1990 to the present, Deviekha has produced her own concerts at several theaters in the GTA, including Markham Theater, Leah Poslun Theater, City Playhouse Theater, Minkler Auditorium, Yorkwoods Library Theater, Isabel Bader Theater, Vishnu Mandir, Toronto Arya Samaj—Vedic Cultural Center, Devi Mandir—Pickering, TINTS—the Interacting Nations Society, OSSICC—Ontario Society for Studies in Indo-Caribbean Culture, Indo-Caribbean Golden Age Association, Voice of Dharma, University of Toronto Saffron Ball—2005/2006/2007, AWIC—Association of Indian Women in Canada, Panorama India, Guyana Embassy events, Canada Wonderland, Annual Guyana independence celebrations.

Other venues of her concerts have included "The Many Faces of Markham," Federation of Hindus premier Diwali program at the Air Canada Center, CIBC—multicultural festival 2007–2008, Coca-Cola Black—2006, Caravan and Carissauga, Trillium Health Diwali Celebrations 2004, Caribana—2007, Ghanna Khanna Masti—2006–

2007, Harbor Front World Routes Festival—2007, Last Lap Lime—2008, St. Joseph's Brunch—2007-2008, Queen's College Brunch—2006-2007, Harbor Front Luminateau Festival—2008, The Pranav Hindu Mandir Annual Awards Dinner—2008, EKTAA—2008.

Deviekha was the adjudicator for several dance competitions, including SAAYA and the Mallyallam community in 2006, the Bollywood dance challenge in 2007, and Nach Baliye— Tarana Dance in 2007.

Between 1984 and 1987, Deviekha performed in the United States and taught several students in performances throughout New York. In 2008 Deviekha established the Tarana Dance Academy in Tampa, Florida, and her students have performed for the India Festival in Tampa in November 2008. She now travels between Canada and the United States to conduct dance classes.

Deviekha's students have been making their own mark over the years. Several of her students have performed for festivals and established dance companies, as well as being back-up dancers for Indian Film stars in a variety of shows. Some of her students are teaching dance in the GTA and some have started their own dance schools. One a professional Kathak dancer, has choreographed dances for the Miss World Canada organization and a movie.

Deviekha's consummate performances and her accomplishments have been duly recognized and reflected in the numerous awards she has received. These include:

- 1990, Pegasus Cricket Club, support for fundraising activities
- 1990, OSSICC, participation in Annual Heritage Day
- 1993, OSSICC, outstanding contribution to the Indo-Caribbean community
- 2002, Vedic Cultural Center, Toronto Arya Samaj. Recognition award to the Tarana Dance School for outstanding contribution in the field of dance and promotion of Indian cultural heritage
- 2005, Vision TV, commitment to the promotion of arts and culture in a multifaith community
- 2005, Gwalior Children's Hospital Charity, Saffron Ball
- 2006, Bollywood Dance Challenge, outstanding contribution to dance and culture

She has received several participation awards from the Indo-Caribbean Golden Age Association and the Guyana Consulate.

Recognition and plaudits for her achievements have also received wide media coverage on TV and in the press, including West Indians United TV, ATN, Badhai Ho, Bollywood Blvd., Guyana Beat, *Toronto Star*, Share newspapers, the *Scarborough Mirror*, the *Economist*, *Caribbean Camera*, and *Indo-Caribbean News*.

Deviekha is always looking for more opportunities to promote the arts and to build bridges between the West Indian and South Asian culture, and she always upgrades her skills through dance workshops in Toronto and New Delhi, India. Deviekha is dedicated to dance and believes in the words of Persian Dervish poet, Rumi: *Whosoever knoweth the power of the dance, dwelleth in God.*

She says this about her passion: "Classical Indian dance originated in the temples of India, and God is worshipped through dance. I feel dance instills discipline, giving spiritual upliftment and freedom through movement. It gives me a sense of contentment to know that I can impart this wonderful art, develop the talent, and bring out the best in my students at Tarana Dance Center. It truly is a wonderful feeling when I see my students perform." Today, Deviekha feels proud to know that she has contributed to the cultural mosaic of Canada, and she continues to keep her traditions and culture alive by offering many programs and classes in Kathak, Bollywood, Bhajans and chants, and Tabla.

Deviekha is married to Dilip Chetram of Number 47 Village, Corentyne, Berbice. He runs his own accounting company, Ledgers Scarborough. They have two children: their son, Arun Yogendra, who is pursuing a degree in marketing at York University; and their daughter, Reshmi, who is following in Deviekha's footsteps by pursuing a career as a professional classical Indian dancer.

November 24, 2008

Nesbit Chhangur

Nesbit Chhangur

Guyana's Singing Cowboy

Nesbit Chhangur—singer, songwriter, broadcaster, youth leader, family man, teacher, and community worker—has made history. Starting in the 1940s in British Guiana, he became Guyana's "singing cowboy" and truly is a living legend

His renditions of such songs as *My Darling Clementine*, *Home on the Range*, and *Deep in the Heart of Texas* lifted the hearts of listeners and got their feet tapping. When Nesbit Chhangur strapped on his guitar to entertain, his music—and his dress style—held his audience spellbound.

While gramophones and radios throughout what was then British Guiana seemed to play nonstop such selections as Vera Lynn's *The White Cliffs of Dover* or Bing Crosby's *I'm Dreaming of a White Christmas*, the cowboy songs of Gene Autry and Roy Rogers also were as popular—and so was our own yodeling "cowboy" Nesbit Chhangur.

His imitation of Hank Williams in songs like *Wedding Bells*, *Your Cheating Heart*, *I Can't Help It (If I'm Still in Love with You)*, *Cold Cold Heart,* and *Lovesick Blues,* as well as his rendition of Hank Thompson's *Blackboard of My Heart* left many of his fans believing that he was the original singer of these songs.

He learned his craft during his early teen years after becoming smitten with the melodies broadcast over the radio. From the barely audible broadcasts from American stations, he learned whatever he could—music, lyrics, yodeling. By the early 1950s, Nesbit was a household name as singer and guitarist and was featured regularly on radio.

Born at Fyrish on the lower Corentyne coast in the county of Berbice, British Guiana, he was the son of Russell Chhangur and Christina (nee Parvatan) Chhangur. His brothers are Jeffrey, former headmaster at Number 48 Primary School and later a lawyer; Shallson, teacher and later an Anglican priest in Barbados and Jamaica; and Sherlock, also a teacher. His sisters are Joy, Candy, Evangeline, and Saintaline. Evangeline and Saintaline are former deaconesses on the Corentyne coast.

He attended the Fyrish and Albion primary schools and Corentyne High School at Rosehall.

Nesbit inherited his talent from his musical parents—his father sang and played the sitar. Nesbit liked singing. At age eight, he sang "The Rose of Tralee" at school, with his brother Shallson accompanying him on the piano accordion.

He got his first lesson on the guitar, when he was about ten years old, from Buddy Hector, an elderly villager from Fyrish. A couple of years later, when he was good at playing, his parents bought him a guitar, and he became a regular singer at concerts, at school, at his church, and on stage.

In the early 1940s, he won a talent contest on the radio. It was the *Gong Show* on radio station ZFY in Georgetown. He also appeared as a guest artist with other local bands on radio. Later, the legendary Olga Lopes Seale, broadcast doyen of British Guiana, featured Nesbit on her weekly programs. She broadcast two programs from New Amsterdam: *Berbice Calling* on Tuesdays, and *Olga Lopes Sings* on Thursdays. On both shows, Nesbit was the guest artist every week.

After the war years, when goods from abroad were scarce, including American records, his only option for hearing new music was to tune in to American radio stations and learn all he could of cowboy music that way. He was an avid listener of the *Grand Ole Opry*, broadcast from station WSM in Nashville on Saturday nights, as well as similar programs from station WWVA 1170, Wheeling, West Virginia, and other stations in Ohio and Kentucky. Later, he was able to visit all of these places.

Nesbit got married in April 1952 to Greta Leila Mungalsingh of New Amsterdam. A major role for Greta in the couple's early years was building up Nesbit's repertoire as singing cowboy. How? Religiously, they would listen to songs on the American radio stations. He would concentrate on memorizing the tunes; she would write down the words in shorthand—tape recorders were nonexistent at the time.

In those early years, during the war, there was a shortage of guitar strings. Nesbit cites the story of how he got around this problem:

"I used to play at Providence on the East Bank of the Berbice River. It is near Everton, where they loaded boats with bauxite for America. American sailors from those boats came to Providence and came to one of the radio broadcast shows in New Amsterdam and heard me singing. They were so pleased to hear their own cowboy songs so far away from their home that they offered to help me out. On their next trip back to Everton, they brought me guitar strings, and a country-and-western music song book."

Nesbit cut his first records in Guyana in the 1950s. This was a historic event, as records were virtually all imported from abroad at that time. It was produced at ACE Records, a business set up by the enterprising, well-known broadcaster and impresario, Vivian Lee.

Nesbit recorded his composition, *Sunny Corentyne*, as well as other popular songs, such as *There's No Room in My Heart for Another*; *Bring Back My Daddy*; *Mother, the Queen of My Heart*; *Starry Waltz*; and *I'm So Lonesome I Could Cry*. He recorded *Santa Samba* and *Rock around the Moon* on 78s in Guyana and then sent them to a record producer in Trinidad, where they were manufactured into 45s

Nesbit's version of *There's No Room in My Heart for Another* is used in a BBC documentary on Guyana called *Roraima, The Lost World*. In 1964, he recorded *Guianese Lament* and *Call to Guiana*. He donated the money raised from the record *Guianese Lament* to the Red Cross disaster fund.

Although widely known for singing and music, Nesbit has had another career as a teacher, and he has served Guyana well in numerous community activities and in charities.

He was a primary school teacher at Albion, Albion Front, and West Coast Bushlot schools. Then, in 1950, he was appointed as one of the first teachers of the newly established Berbice Educational Institute (BEI), the second high school in New Amsterdam, founded by Alfred Ramlochand. The premises, originally at the corner of Main and Pilot Streets, moved later to Vryheid, New Amsterdam. Nesbit later became vice principal of BEI. Nesbit's singing at the school will forever be a highlight in the life of the students and fellow staff members of the day.

He was the country's first Guianese YMCA executive director and general secretary. In this role he had the opportunity to travel around the world.

In 1961, when Dr. Jagan was elected as prime minister of Guyana, he invited Nesbit to sing at his inauguration. In 1965, on the occasion of the Catholic Standard Diamond Jubilee, Nesbit composed and sang *A Jubilee Song* on the Catholic Broadcast program. He was invited to sing at the Miss Guyana competition, hosted by the celebrated Sarah Lou Carter.

In 1966, during Nesbit's travels in the United States, an attorney who had interests in the recording business spotted Nesbit in Nashville, Tennessee, The man signed Nesbit to a two-year contract to sing and play in Nashville. Although Nesbit signed the contract, he later had to rescind it to return to Guyana because he was on a Youth Leaders Study scholarship in the United States. Before he returned, however, he made his debut as a singer in Canada when he entered the Take a Bow contest and won first prize. A year later, he emigrated to Canada.

Although Nesbit enjoyed playing music, his first love, it did not provide a steady income, so he found work, first as a salesman, then decided to return to teaching. After all he had teaching experience in Guyana, as Primary School teacher and later as Vice Principal of the Berbice Educational Institute, in New Amsterdam.

He entered the Ottawa Teacher's College in 1970 for training, and in 1971, he became a qualified and certified teacher in Canada. He has since worked at Hillcrest High School and several other high schools in adult education evening classes with the Ottawa (Ontario) Board of Education. He has been part of the Ottawa-Carleton District School Board for over twenty-eight years. Nesbit also has served as a member of: the Visiting Committee to Prisons, Oxfam, the Duke of Edinburgh Award Scheme, the National Youth Association, the Badminton Association, and the Swimming Association. In 1975 he retired from teaching, and started working for the Canadian federal government and is now a retired civil servant from the federal government in Ottawa, Ontario. In 1987 Nesbit was featured in a CBC TV series, *It's About Time*. This program featured individuals who had a hobby or dream and never gave up.

But, Nesbit is, first and foremost, a singer musician. He continues to perform whenever and wherever he can. He plays with bands all over Ottawa and has sung at many senior citizen homes and lodges for the sick, as well as in hospitals, nursing homes, and other institutions, free of charge—his way of saying thanks to Canada and Canadians.

He has a warm place in his heart for Canada, where he has lived for over forty years. He wrote the song *Canadians We Will Always Be* in 1979 as his tribute to Canada.

He has released a number of recordings:

- *Joanne* (1980)
- *You'll Always be There*—a collection of sixteen of his compositions (2000)
- *Tropical Haven*—a tribute to Guyana (2002). This song was used in the film *Buscando*.
- *The Best of Nez* (2007)

In addition to his singing, his expertise on the guitar has provided him with two other part-time jobs. He qualified as a guitar technician and has been teaching the guitar for over twenty-nine years for the Continuing Education program with the Ottawa Board of Education. He is widely known as "Nez, the guitar teacher."

In Orleans, Ontario, where he has lived for over fourteen years, he was the guitar instructor for the beginners and intermediate evening classes at Cairine Wilson Secondary School. The course included learning to tune the guitar, play guitar chords, learn finger picking, singing and strumming techniques, chord progressions, and playing tabs. He was also a string instrument technician and repaired string instruments for music shops and musicians in Ottawa.

He has received numerous awards and honors for his music and his charitable work. In New York, he received the Guyana Folk Festival 2002 Wordsworth McAndrew Award for his contribution to the musical heritage of Guyana. He was honored in November 2004 with a special award from the Berbice Educational Institute, where he was a teacher and vice-principal.

Nesbit continues to play and record. He has a registered business called Gretnes Productions and has a recording studio at home. He is a well-known name in the Caribbean music world and is quite content with his legendary musical achievements.

Nesbit and Greta celebrated their fiftieth wedding anniversary in 2002. Greta has been the consultant, critic, cowriter and financier of their music enterprise for nearly forty years.

They have been blessed with six children—four boys and two girls—and six grandchildren. Their sons Rohan and Brian lead their own bands, and Sean is a pianist of jazz and funk. Anthony plays the drums, Sandra the guitar, and Arlene the piano and flute.

Nesbit and his sons also formed a band, Nesbit Chhangur & Sons, that has played at nightclubs and private functions throughout the Ottawa area, as well as playing on Nesbit's LP and CDs

During a visit to Fort Worth, Texas, in the 1980s, Nesbit and Greta went with some friends to a nightclub. His friends asked the house band if they would let Nesbit sing a song because he was a country singer in Canada. After the first song, the audience called for an encore and then another encore. The next day, the owners of the club asked Nesbit if he would appear as a guest with the band that night. After Nesbit returned to Canada, he wrote the song *Fort Worth, I Love You*.

Long may his music live on. Long may he entertain. For many, the name Nesbit Chhangur *is* music.

October 6, 2010

Colonel Brian A. Chin

United States Marine Corps (Ret.)

Colonel Brian Chin, USMC, is a twenty-four-year veteran of the US Marines, with both active and reserve service. He served as an artillery officer, with additional specialties as Latin American Foreign Area Officer and Civil Affairs Officer. He has extensive experience, serving in the counter-narco-terrorism (CNT) field in South America and the Caribbean. He is a recipient of the US Defense Meritorious Service medal for combat operations in Iraq. His other awards include commendations from both the US Coast Guard and the marines for participation in a US-sponsored Riverine Operations Seminar to the Guyana Defense Force.

Brian's military career includes service in Korea and Japan He was the first US military officer assigned to serve as a liaison to the command element of the post-Sandinista Nicaraguan military. He also served in Peru, Bolivia, Colombia, and Mexico, where he advised local security forces to combat the drug trade. In Iraq he was responsible for escorting the currency shipments for the Central Bank of Iraq.

His civilian career includes service as the general manager of Securicor Guyana Incorporated, a security services company jointly owned by the UK-based Securicor PLC, and Neal and Massy, Guyana.

Brian was born in Georgetown. He spent his early childhood days in the suburb of Charlestown and his high school days at Belvoir Court, Bel Air. His father, Godfrey Chin, is the well-known writer, social commentator, and impresario, the author of *Nostalgias*—a collection of writings that record the aspects of life in the Guyana of yesteryear. Brian's mother is Shirley (nee Gibson), and his siblings are two well-known personalities in Caribbean squash: Gary and Richard.

Brian attended St. John's Boys School (now defunct) and later, St. Stanislaus College (class of 1980). Brian is very proud to be one of the St. John's students who went on to St. Stanislaus after passing the common entrance examinations. Brian fondly remembers Mr. Mike Christophe (former Guyana table tennis champion) as a particularly memorable teacher/mentor to a generation of those St. John's students.

After St. Stanislaus, Brian emigrated to the United States and attended Syracuse University, from which he obtained his bachelor's degree in economics in 1986. In the same year, he was commissioned as a marine officer.

Why did he want to be a US Marine? He has said, "I was driven by a strong sense to serve my adopted country and was drawn to the adventures offered by a military career." He was primarily inspired by the achievements of his parents, and he harbors a strong commitment to help Guyana and perhaps to relocate there in the future.

His fondest memories are of his teens and the camaraderie of St. Stanislaus College. That era, he says, "left an indelible mark on my life, and I remain very nostalgic about my days in scouting with Troop 24, St. Stanislaus's own, and intramural field hockey." His counts as his most pensive moments the times when he was driving an SUV through downtown Baghdad while escorting up to $700,000 (US) at a time.

Brain enjoys Guyanese reunions. "Every year that I attend Carabana in Toronto. I look out over that mass of the Guyanese diasporas and the talent pool, and I wonder if there's a way to harness some of it for Guyana's future. I would like to retire to Guyana and to contribute in some way to make it a better country."

Sources:

Photo. Website accessed May 31.2010.
www.torontosaints.gy-saints.com/member-news.

September 11, 2010

Godfrey Chin's Nostalgias

Golden Memories of Guyana 1940 to 1980

Godfrey Chin

Chronicler, Social Commentator, Graphic Artist, Costume Designer, Set Decorator, Dancer, DJ

Godfrey Chin's *Nostalgias* and photo collection are a national treasure. They bring to life our beloved Guyana, with profuse images of Guyana in the twentieth century (1940s through 1980s). They make rich, pleasant moments for many who knew Guyana at that time, and satisfy the hunger of the young for glimpses of Guyana in the "good old days."

His passion is Guyana, its history, its music, arts, people, sites, celebrities, folklore, nancy stories, and stories on any subject. His writings are legendary. He has been described as a "nationally recognized icon, son of the soil, and Guyanese to the bone!"

From his base in Florida and blessed with boundless energy, Godfrey is in perpetual motion, as costume designer, set decorator, graphic artist, writer and social commentator, ballroom dancer, DJ, and more. He is often referred to in his homeland as the "local Cecil B. DeMille."

His writings are widely known, from Guyana to the USA, to Canada, to the UK and the Caribbean—wherever Guyanese happen to be. His book *Nostalgias: Golden Memories of Guyana, 1940 to 1980* is a collection of some of his best writings, a window to view delights of Guyanese society in the recent past from his unique perspective.

The book includes such topics (totaling fifty in all) as "Christmas 1944, In Memory of My Father"; "Growing Up in Tenement Yards"; "Movies in Guyana, 1945 to 1982"; "Gaiety Cinema, Silent Days"; "Remembering the Coast Railways, 1846 to 1970"; "Chinese in Sports, Guyana, Yesteryear"; "My Last Kite-Flying Experience in Guyana"; "Georgetown, the Garden City"; " Olga Lopes-Seales, Our Darling Valentine"; "Guyana Rum Shops"; "Discos - Saturday Night Fever"; "Guyana's Blackest Friday, 16 Feb 1962"; "Ken Kingston, Sea Wall 1950 to Stadium 2007"; "Tributes to Robert Christiani"; "60 Years of Social Dancing in Guyana, 1945 – 2005"; "Golden Age of British Movies in Guyana"; "Remembering Theatre Guild"; "Comic Books in Guyana"; "Cook-shop-fly in Jail!"; "Steel bands, Festivals and Mashramani"; "The Public Buildings & Public Service"; "Toys for Tots"; "Decorating the Christmas Tree"; "The True Guyanese Christmas Spirit"; and "Creolese Glossary of Common Words."

Distinguished Guyanese professor, and media scholar Dr. Vibert Cambridge of Ohio University has written a commentary about Godfrey's *Nostalgia* series that is included on Godfrey's website. It reads, in part:

> Godfrey Chin, a true Guyanese "son of the soil," is a "man of all seasons." Since 2001 he has documented and preserved his many memories of our "Oh Beautiful Guyana"—yesteryear—with witty sarcasm and self-deprecating humor.
>
> He refers to himself as a "regular cook-shop fly," involved in every spectrum of life in Guyana, and uses these vantage points along with his outstanding athletic career, corporate executive, and the eye of a social scientist, to comment on all aspects of Guyanese social life in his *Nostalgia* series.
>
> He is also blessed with an outstanding photographic memory. The result is that his *Nostalgias* are important records of Guyana's social history.
>
> His *Nostalgias* have also been flavored by his school days, his life in sports, his influential creative roles in Guyana's national celebrations, such as festivals, Mashramani, steel band competitions, and a plethora of fund-raisers.
>
> His *Nostalgia* series, now numbering over three hundred, enjoys wide circulation and have been published in the local and overseas press, in *Guyfolkfest* magazine, and on the Internet. His piece on Guyana fashion was a subject of a lecture in Canada.
>
> His *Nostalgias* are participatory in that they trigger memories from his readers, and sets in train conversation and debate that is invigorating and invaluable.
>
> Godfrey's contribution to the preservation and perpetuation of our culture and heritage was recognized with the award to him in 2005 of the prestigious Wordsworth McAndrew Award. In October 2005, his presentation of "Social Dancing in Guyana after WWII" at the borough of Manhattan Community College was received with raves by the students and staff.

Winfield Godfrey Chin was born on May 7, 1937, in Georgetown, Guyana, and his career is truly reflective of a Guyanese to the bone. Educated at Smith Church Congregational and Central High School, he worked in the civil service from 1955 to 1963 and as an assistant circulation and publications manager at Guyana Graphic until April 1967. He was then the operations sales supervisor at ESSO for fifteen years before he emigrated to the United States in September 1982.

In Orlando, Florida, he qualified as an accomplished calligrapher/graphic artist and was owner/operator of Godfrey's Graphics. Continuing his effervescent creative enthusiasm, he also operated Godfrey's Music with Feeling, as well as Theme Party Décor and Balloon Pageantry. Recently, his specialty has included conventions, tradeshows, and exhibition setup.

A sportsman "ball buridee," Godfrey represented Guyana in hockey for over sixteen years, enabling Guyana to retain the Caribbean championship title from 1961 to 1972. He also played cricket, football, badminton, table tennis, and squash at the local competitive club level. He was responsible for instituting the first junior squash program in 1977 and is proud that Guyana's squash championship status started then.

He has won Costume Band of the Year on three occasions and has produced many prize-winning floats and queens at Guyana's Festival and Mashramani celebrations. His credo is "Volunteer and get involved," and he is ever ready to roll up his sleeves and pitch in with his expertise in a plethora of activities, fund-raising, or cultural activities, whether in Toronto, New York, Florida, or back home in his native Guyana. His expertise in ballroom and salsa dancing is legend.

Hailed as a "regular cook-shop [café] fly," involved in every aspect of the Guyana landscape, his *Nostalgia* series is his attempt to record for posterity the glorious days of his Guyana, -El Dorado, for all to reminisce. Below are excerpts from Godfrey's *Nostalgias*.

Central High School, 1948–55

Rites of Spring. The "Rites of Spring" of Central were a milestone, as bewildering as Lewis Carroll's *Alice in Wonderland*. At eleven plus, you were faced with a new breed of authority figures—the teaching staff: Caleb, Collins, Smith-Green, Persaud, Munroe. Senior Prefects were Stanley and Donald Luck, and Robert Moore, all of whom were substitute teachers, much to our relief. New subjects included Latin (*amo, amas, amat*), French (*Je suis le garcon*), history from the first Jacobite

Rebellion against King George I, the theorems of geometry, and the hierolyphics of minuses and pluses placed between letters, that needed the Enigma Decoder to decipher. That was Algebra—taught only to make my school days miserable … The only consolation was that this was our first close contact with beautiful girls our own age, and our subsequent crushes did keep us on track with school studies, and inspired us to be more than the class idiot.

Top Grades. All our teachers must have received salary increases at the end of our first term—December '48—as the grade average of every student in the three Remove forms was 85 plus. The miracle was that the spoiled Roneoed test papers had been inadvertently dumped behind the toilets at the back, and obviously, that first-term test was a piece of cake. Thereafter, my term grades diminished in harmonic progression … Our favorite subject was then Girlometry and Boyology, and my assured 'A' grade each term was for being talkative, troublesome, and terrible.

Survival in high school required augmented skills, especially if you were not one of the gifted ones and was study-impaired. So instead of wasting time studying, I honed other skills, which caused me to wear spectacles in later years.

I bettered Clarke Kent's x-ray vision by mastering the art of "seeing in a curve and around corners." Sitting behind the bright ones, I could copy all their answers from the exercise books before them. On one occasion, I even copied Vasil Persaud's name on my test paper, much to the amusement of the entire class. History teacher Hope solved the problem, by seating me alone at the back of the class. What an honor, to have a whole desk and special space for yourself. When my test paper recorded "This battle will be dealt with more fully in the preceding chapters," that was the final straw. Back in the principal's office, Stella, with a smug smile, immediately reached for the cane. No questions asked—guilty without representation. Isn't that why the colonies rebelled? J. C. was in stitches; he ordered Stella to make a note of this scholastic misdemeanor for the school's yearbook, and immediately

> promoted me to prefect. Thereafter, I walked the corridors with a halo around my head, and became Saint Godfrey. The principal and I were henceforth bosom buddies. ...
>
> I was the school's Don Corleone, settling underdesk disputes and having my own numbers game by soliciting bets on the West Indies cricket team mesmerizing England 1950 with the three WWWs—Ram and Val, Robert Christiani, Stollmeyer and Goddard. With the six-hour time difference, I picked up the daily cricket scores from Mount Eagle by the Astor during the school lunch break, and gave betting odds accordingly, thereby relieving students of their pocket money.

All work and no play? Not so for Godfrey. He played and did well at Central High at cricket and other sports. When the time came for serious studies, he was there at the rostrum with the best of them.

> The next year (1954), I became tired of shenanigans—had tried, done all the high school tricks, and actually reformed. I became a model student, and left school with honors—Prelim BSc. Top grades in econ/econ history, English/Eng literature, British/European history and supplementary French.
>
> *Movies in Guyana, 1945 to 1982*
>
> My earliest movie experience was limited to magic-lantern shows at St. George's, and penny-film shows every Wednesday at CYO on Robb Street. I even recall, vividly, viewing John Wayne's *Flying Tigers* (16mm) upstairs at Booker's Drug Store, Main Street, next to the Chronicle. ...
>
> For young Guyanese, the first major movie cinema experience was *Passion Play*, a black-and-white version of the life of Christ with narration and subtitles. I swear this movie was made before talkies came in 1927. The grainy film was stored at the vaults in Lodge, brought out, dusted for one day, Holy Thursday, and doubled with either a Tom Keene or a Johnny Mack Brown 'B' western. This annual ritual I likened to the US Groundhog Day, but more memorable, because the next day was Good Friday, when we dared not leave the house, except to go to church. All businesses were shut tight. ...

Astor, which opened in 1940 with William Holden's *Golden Boy*, was my favorite cinema. ... In those days, new film releases usually started on Thursday and later on Fridays. Additional features to single releases included a cartoon, a two-week-old Pathe world newsreel, a sing-along with a ball bouncing on the words, or a two-reeler big band musical concert. World Championship fights, featured on screen, one week later, included slow-motion highlights and were doubled with a Tarzan feature plus a Leon Errol two-reel comedy...

My personal collection of the original pamphlets of Rudolph Valentino's *Son of the Sheik* and other classic—*Ben Hur* with Ramon Navarro, the first *Tarzan* film starring Elmo Lincoln, *King Kong*, and *Spoilers*, Gary Cooper vs. William Boyd, would now be worth a fortune as collectors items. ... Midweek features were B film doubles, detective Boston Blackie plus a Charles Starrett western. Our movie bonanzas were, of course, the action serials—the *Masked Marvel*, *Spy Smasher*, *Desert Agent*, and *Drums of Fu Manchu*.

Around 1952 the old London was replaced by the Plaza with the eagerly awaited Dennis Morgan musical, *Painting the Clouds with Sunshine* followed by Errol Flynn's *Adventures of Don Juan*. ... Other big hits, included Disney's *Cinderella*, Cecil B. De Mille's *Samson and Delilah* and the world's intro to rock and roll, *Blackboard Jungle* and later, *Rock around the Clock*. ... In 1952 the new kid on the block, Globe, opened with the biblical epic *David and Bathsheba*, Gregory Peck and Susan Hayward on a magnificent floating screen with surround sound. ...

The Strand was the first fully air-conditioned cinema. Their starry lighted roof matched Radio City Music Hall (excuse the hyperbole) and opening night with Marlon Brando's *Sayonara* received rave reviews, even though we froze our butts. ... Even earlier, Hollywood in Kitty opened with *Christmas Carol*, and the Doren replaced the Rialto on Vlissengen Road. The Capitol cinema, Punt Trench, Albouystown, together with the Olympic were closed shortly after.

Starlite Drive-In on the east coast opened around Easter 1964 with Elvis Presley in *Blue Hawaii*. Our first and only passion pit, facilitating a family picnic-style outing every Sunday at dusk. Pajamas were allowed so the kids could be put straight to bed later. ...

In addition to being our entertainment mecca, the Guyanese cinemas were the venue of live shows for the masses, our own Coliseum. From the earliest vaudeville shows of Madame O'Lindy, Sam Chase, and Jack Mello comedies, Len Houston and Young Joe Louis purse fights, to Vivian Lee's talent shows, the movie houses' accommodation allowed us, the wretched poor, the opportunity to enjoy and support our local talent. International artists later included the illusionist Cleopatra, Johnny Mathis, Byron Lee and his Dragonnaires, and the Mighty Sparrow, plus fashion and Miss Guyana contests. Doubles have always been the mainstay of the Guyanese box office. A good cinema manager was judged by the excellent double programs he presented ... In the fifties, the Empire was the doubles stronghold, offering contrasting programs (e.g., a musical plus an action flick). Johnny Weissmuller's debut as *Tarzan the Apeman* and Howard Keel/Kathryn Grayson in *Showboat*. Classic pairings to match Gable and Leigh were *Count of Monte Cristo* and *Corsican Brothers*, and for adventure, *King Solomon's Mines* plus *Scaramouche*. ...

If you liked tear-jerkers you took a towel or two boxes of Kleenex to see Lana Turner's unforgettable *Madame X* plus *Imitation of Life*. ... When ... *Lawrence of Arabia* [was paired with] *Lion of the Desert*, I left the cinema drenched from desert-heat exhaustion and drank water like a camel for a week This was the nadir of my movie experience.

Godfrey's mastery as a storyteller is equally matched by his talent as a sports commentator. He paints the backdrop, then proceeds to a roll call of the good, the very good, and the superb of sports stars whose glittering achievements continue to give pleasure and inspire.

Chinese in Sports – Guyana, Yesteryear

The cliché "All work and no play, makes Jack a dull boy" certainly does not apply to the Guyana Chinese community. By WWII, eighty-six years after the first shipment of Chinese indentured laborers arrived [Jan. 1853] ... They had entrenched themselves as an integral part of the colony, excelling in enterprises of commerce and trade [Yong Hing], education [J. C. Luck at Central High], medicine [Dr. Hugh], and law [Fung-a-Fat].

Their children, grandchildren and great-grands were now ready to "come out to play" and also devote themselves to the other social, cultural aspects of life as available, in the colony then.

In cricket, the outstanding past Chinese performances included P. W. Lee—138 [1937], C. V. Too-Chung—106 not out, E. S. Gillette—101, W. R. Luck—127 [1939], J. Ho-A-Shoo—148, L. Ching—103 not out [1949], and George Fung-On—118 [1952]. James Chin, Clement Choo-See-Nam, William Lieu, Trevor Lee, Billy Fung-a-Fat, Bud Lee, who could have been a West Indies Sobers.

When Bud Lee, Walter Chin, Arnold Gibbons [the Guyanese Trio] finished batting, the captain often declared, as the score was 300 odd for three ... Another great batsman, the Chinese Vivian Richards, was Albert Choy ... Add Gary Lee, and Chinese Sports Club ... became as fearsome an opponent, as the Boxers in their Rebellion in China [1900]. ...

Other outstanding cricketers included Rudy Low, Milton Wong, Hilton Quan, Michael Chung ... there was a Chinese umpire at Bourda, Wing Gillette ... Other outstanding cricket assets included Tuni Low-a-Chee, Michael Akai, Jerry Manson-Hing, Terry Solomon, Richard Chung, Arthur Chang-Yen, Randolph Choo-See-Nam, and Roddy Too-Chung. Should I mention myself?

In hockey by 1960, they were unbeaten in local competition. Past hockey stars included Ted Loquan, Walter Fung, Joe

Chin, and Henry Lee. Five of the members of that team, plus V. P. Chung and Billy Lee [GFC], were the nucleus of the Guyana team that won the first Caribbean Quadrangular Hockey Championship in Trinidad, June 1961.

Godfrey Chin in goal, Walter Chin [Capt.] and V. P. Chung, wing halves with Cha-Cha John Embleton, center half, forming a maginot line. The attack of the brothers, Rollo and Gary Lee inside forwards, Gerald Wong, outside left, with the nippy Eddie Caetano at center-forward and Norman Wight, right wing. This team was the equivalent of the USA basketball dream team of the '80s Olympics. Must record that Skip Roberts and Ian Leal were the backs, and the team was unchanged for the six-test series.

Other national Chinese hockey stars were Jeffrey Lee, Sydney Wong, William Lieu, David Cho-Chu, Roger Dyaljee, Dennis Fung, Frankie Chin, Trevor Chang, Jackie Chin, and Lindsay Lee.

In 1972, Godfrey Chin, Gary Lee, nephew Lindsay Lee, Dennis Fung, and Frankie Chin paved the way for the Republic to retain the Caribbean hockey title at GFC, under floodlights … justifying the German captain's query, "Are we playing Guyana or Chinatown?"

Cassian Mittleholzer and Maurice Pollard then, Hockey Sportscasters, were in a tizzy that afternoon, with Chin, Chin, Chin, Chin, Lee, Lee, Lee, and Fung. To put a handle to this Chinese crossword, it would read, starting in goal, Godfrey, Walter, Jackie, Frankie, Gary, Rollo, Lindsay, and Dennis, and adding to this Chinese fried rice, Billy Lee was coach …

Yours truly, Godfrey Chin from 1961 to 1976, represented Guyana, 26 occasions, the President's XI - 19 times - two PanAm Games - unbeaten in three Caribbean Championships - let in 49 goals, while his team-mates, up front scored 56. At no time in my career - as custodian were there less than four Chinese up front…

In Women's hockey, Patty Fung-on [capt.] and Center Half - Donna Tiam-Fook forward - Joy Lee and the sisters Merle and Sandra Choo-Wee-Nam, also led the Women's hockey team to major Caribbean victories.

In basketball, the Chinese called themselves the Clowns, with Gary Lee, Roy Wong and James Chin-Pac-Hon. They even had two ladies teams, the Candies and Clownettes, with Sarah Lou Carter playing.

In the club's pavilion Doreen Chow-wah was mastering table tennis to emerge a national champion, and teaming up with Denise Osman, reigning Caribbean doubles champion. Christopher Chung-Wee was also a national male champion.

In badminton, Bud Lee made the national team with Laurie Lewis, and the Holder's clan. Candy Lee, Gary's niece, was also a national star.

In 1975, with a scarcity of badminton shuttlecocks, Chinese racquet wielders took up squash. Bud Lee, Walter Chin, and Godfrey Chin truly joined the national squad to Trinidad the next year, and Bud became the first permanent Chinese fixture then, on the national squash team.

Godfrey, as manager of the squad to the first Caribbean Squash Championship in Nassau, Bahamas, 1977, undertook introducing and supervising a Junior Squash program on return home!

I am proud that Guyana's squash supremacy today, started with that initial Junior Squad, formed at a time in 1977, when the thought of school-agers at the aristocratic Georgetown Club, repulsed the adults. ... In 1977, I had to plead with Richard Lee's father, Bud, for Richard at QC, preparing for GCE O level, to be a reserve on the Guyana team to the First Caribbean Squash Games in Nassau, Bahamas. Two years later in Jamaica, Richard was runner-up to Orville Haslam for the Caribbean champion title.

A sixteen-year-old Gary Chin won the Junior Caribbean title for Guyana on that tour. Richard Lee later became Southern Caribbean squash champion.

The next year, 1980, Richard Chin, at ten, our first prodigy of the promising youths, snatched the under-fourteen boys title at the first Junior Games in St. Vincent, and went on to win biannually the under-sixteen and under-nineteen Caribbean Junior games title. Diane Lee followed like a true Lee to win the local and Southern Caribbean titles. Combining the boys and girls, Guyana won its first Junior Team title. Our Junior program was paying dividends! Bless the kids!

Gary Chin, in 1981, then eighteen, defended successfully his Junior [under twenty-one] Caribbean title at the Games in Barbados, and was runner-up to Clive Lloyd as Guyana's Sportsman of the Year, a supreme first achievement for squash and the Chinese … The Guyanese Ladies Squad was strengthened by Luana Choo-See-Nam …

In 1986, I took Richard/Garfield Wiltshire and Roger Arjoon to Houston, Texas, to win the US Open Team Championship. Richard Chin continued to fly his country's flag in the United States, sweeping titles at their junior level.

He was a member of the Cornell squash team 1987–1991 … cocaptained the team in his senior year. In addition Richard was a four time All-American, earning first team honors in '88, '90, and '91, second team honors, 1989. He received the John Skilman Award in 1991 and represented the United States at the bi-annual World Games [including PanAm Games] continuously since 1992. He was the US National Finalist 2000, and in November 2002, was inducted in the Cornell's Athletic Hall of Fame. Richard resumed playing for Guyana in 2010 and won the Caribbean title at the recent games in the Cayman Islands. He also won the St. Lucia Open this year and the Barbados Open 2009.

> [In lawn tennis], Derek Phang was singles and doubles champion in the 1950s and '60s. Michael Tang reached national level in tennis, as did Joe Chin, an excellent doubles player.

On women's tennis, Godfrey states:

> I must thank Trevor Sue-a-Quan, author of the definitive work *Cane Reapers*, and the sequel *Cane Ripples*, which records efficiently the history of Chinese indentured immigrants in Guyana, for apprising me of this next "good news" gem Cynthia Hoahing, daughter of New Amsterdam merchant, represented Great Britain at Wimbledon, 1937–1938, before reaching the age of eighteen.

> In rifle shooting Maurice Yong and Cyril were excellent sharp-shooters. I recall with pride one Chinese footballer Vivian Lee, who played for BG vs. Surinam … Bud Lee, immediately after QC, was the left-wing of the BGCC 1949 football champion team!

> The sole Chinese track and field athlete would be Leslie Chin, who hurdled for BG, in the late fifties … Elson and Errol Ten-Pow, Colin and Stanley Ming relished horse-power, and excelled in their respective class at the Dakota motor racing. Other successful Chinese motor enthusiasts, included Keith Corsbie, William and Dennis Shim-ping, Patrick-Tong, and Clive Ng-a-Keen

> Must not forget our own Bruce Lee, Charles Woon-a-Tai, martial arts black belt, who reached also a world standard …

> Without prejudice, my choice of nomination for any Guyanese Chinese Sport Hall of Fame would be Irwin 'Bud' Lee, Gary Lee, and Richard Chin. For the Chinese ladies, Doreen Chow-Wah, Patti-Fung-On, and Amanda Lee, a champion swimmer …

That was a brief sample of Godfrey's talents as sports writer. What exciting days!. Where are those celebrated names of Chinese in Guyanese sports now?

Godfrey held an exhibition of his collection of photos and pictures of scouting in Guyana. *Stabroek News,* August 9, 2009, featured a report on the event. The report, headed "Godfrey Chin launches pictorial Nostalgia," read:

> Godfrey Chin teamed up with corporate sponsors, GT&T and Banks DIH Ltd to launch his Nostalgia Pictorial History of 20th Century Guyana exhibition. The first showing of the exhibition, a pictorial history of scouting in Guyana 1909 to 2009, will be during the 14th Caribbean Jamboree in the Main Auditorium at the Sophia Exhibition Center.
>
> The exhibits feature pictures of the first Jamboree held locally and showcases contingents at World Jamboree at Arrowpoint, UK 1929, INDABA, and Greece 1963 plus previous thirteen Caribbean Jamborees. Highlights of the exhibit include the third Caribbean Jamboree held at the Queen Elizabeth Park as well as "Scouting today in Guyana."
>
> Subsequent exhibitions will be held at the Centennial Celebrations of the National Library, the St. Stanislaus and Queen's College reunions, and at GuyExpo in September.

Godfrey now has an exhibition of over three thousand pictures that have been on display in cities in the United States, Canada, and Guyana. It is currently updated to depict "Glimpses of Guyana in the Twentieth Century."

What started in 2006 as his attempt to procure a few pictures for his book *Nostalgias* is now a "Traveling exhibition of 1001 Guyana delights," ideal for nostalgic reminisces wherever Guyanese meet.

Following displays in Vancouver, Washington DC, Orlando, Brooklyn, Fort Lauderdale, Toronto, Last Lap Lime and Georgetown, the traveling exhibit, with its companion, the newly released *Comprehensive Chronological History of Guyana in the Twentieth Century,* is the ideal showcase for Guyanese.

The exhibit includes categories such as:
- From Whence We Came
- Origins
- Our Garden City
- Georgetown during World Cup 2007

- Guyana Sports Stars
- Feast, Festivities and Mash—Hinterland
- Guyana
- Shrines & Monuments
- Schools, Churches, and Cinemas
- Vending in Guyana
- Historic Guyana.

Also added for the republic celebrations of the GCACF in Orlando, Florida, 2009, was the new "Guyana Flower" in five colors.

Dr. Ian McDonald, celebrated literary critic, writer, and columnist, paid a glowing tribute to Godfrey's book *Nostalgias* in an article in *Stabroek News* of December 16, 2007, titled "History—A Perspective: Godfrey Chin's Nostalgias."

The article read, in part:

> The book is subtitled *Golden Memories of Guyana 1940 to 1980*. It is a remarkable book … a distillation of just forty-eight memories out of more than three hundred such pieces written down by the author since 2000. And Godfrey, at seventy years of age, continues to write these wonderful sketches with endless industry and unrivalled panache, springing them off every page at us with matchless freshness and fervor.

Dr. McDonald, a doyen of commentators on Guyana, placed the book at its rightful place in Guyana's literary works and stated the book was truly a classic of its kind, a recapturing of vivid memories, bringing the past astonishingly to life again in a way that will delight those who knew those days, instruct future generations, and also enlighten serious scholars of social history and preserve forever the wonderful days and exploits and fun and excitement and humor and games and more of a whole era in a country's life. He complimented Godfrey, saying that he had done a great service, that he deserved praise and thanks and honors. Further, that it was good to think that there are other volumes of *Nostalgias* waiting to be published in the future, that they will be Godfrey's life's masterpiece, a five-volume remembrance of things past.

Ian McDonald listed six points about Godfrey's *Nostalgias* that make them truly compelling:

- They are wonderfully entertaining. Here we see the art of living in all its glorious variety thrown onto Godfrey's own special canvas.
- This is an extraordinary feat of memory and creative recall. Very few people have the gift of photographic memory which delves deeply into the past and even fewer have the wonderful gift of making recollection come so vibrantly alive.
- These *Nostalgias* of Godfrey's are remarkable in their rich profusion. The subject list is as long as life itself in all its variety and the detail is astonishing. The never-ending profusion of exact memories crowding Godfrey's gallery again and again amazes me and they are never-ending. Anyone could suggest a subject to Godfrey, sweeties, say, or seawall or sugar estates or dominoes or the old D'Urban racetrack or anything you like and, hardly pausing, Godfrey could produce a nostalgia which will make you laugh and wonder and say yes that is how it was.
- These *Nostalgias* marvelously enhance and enrich our lives by bringing to vivid life again events, people, ways of enjoying ourselves, sports, festivities, food, frolic and a thousand and one things which had faded from our memories and our lives and now live again as fresh as ever.
- Godfrey's style is all his very own and it is immediately recognizable and perfectly suited to its purpose. Godfrey has a wonderful knack for joyous storytelling prose which is robust, carefree, optimistic, racy, and memorably written in lovely easy sentences of great impact.
- Finally, I believe Godfrey's *Nostalgias* make a truly remarkable, even unique, contribution to our social, cultural, sporting, and general history. This is valuable, priceless material for historians. I think what a treasure these *Nostalgias* will be not only to ordinary readers but also to historians and scholars decades and more into the future. These *Nostalgias* delight us now and in future they will provide a wonderful fund of knowledge for those who research and look into how we once lived.

Ian McDonald extolled Godfrey's achievement with these words: "So it is that an ordinary 'cook-shop fly,' as Godfrey describes himself, is in the process of creating an immensely rich panorama of Guyana's past which constantly keeps us stimulated and in high good humor in the present, and which will endure as an infinitely varied, vivid, unforgettable portrait of pastimes, traditions, places and people in a bygone era. I cannot think of an achievement in living history to match this in Guyana or, indeed, in the Caribbean."

This son of Guyana has left for posterity in his *Nostalgias* and other works permanent records of Guyana in the old days, for enjoyment, for enriching our lives with sweet satisfying reminiscences, and for enhancing our knowledge, be we young or old.

Godfrey retired to his homeland in July 2009 and continues his research and writings, at the same time continuing to offer his fifty-five years' experience in event coordination to add, he says, 'pizazz to local events. Ya think it easy!'

Sources:
Websites accessed. January 20.2010
http://godfreychin.com/themes/index.php
http://www.guyana.org/special/central_school.html
http://www.sdnp.org.gy/chinese/docs/ChineseinGuyaneseSports.doc.
http://www.sweetsoca.com/bmp/think/godfreychins_nostalgias.htm

September 10, 2010

Dr. Laurence Clarke

BScEcon, BBA, MBA, PhD, ACIB, FCIB, DipEMT
Finance Advisor–World Bank

Dr. Laurence Clarke is the manager of World Bank Southern Sudan Program and Juba Office, Juba, Southern Sudan. He was the head of Africa Enterprise Fund (Washington and Kenya), International Finance Corporation. He was financial analyst at the World Bank. He was economic advisor to the president of Liberia; deputy governor of Central Bank of Botswana, and executive director at the Caribbean Center for Monetary Studies, University of the West Indies.

His sterling achievements have been recognized at the highest levels. He won recognition for his overall central banking effort by Nobel Laureate in economics Prof. Joseph Stiglitz in his best-selling book *Globalization and Its Discontents*, published in 2000. Dr. Clarke was cited for his successful work as deputy governor at the Bank of Botswana (1991–95). He received the award of Honorary Member of Botswana Institute of Bankers in 1993.

Dr. Clarke was the founding chairman of the World Bank/IMF Staff Caribbean Association from 1982 through 1986. In 1969 he was chairman of the Royal Bank of Canada Staff Men's Forum. In 1970 he was leader of Guyana's five-person youth delegation to the World Assembly of Youth at the UN in New York. From 1972 to 75 he was chairman of the Guyana National Cooperative Bank Staff Activities Committee. In 1974 he received the Government of Canada Graduate Scholarship Award, and in 1976 he was winner of the Financial Post Investment Award—Best Graduate Finance Student, University of Windsor, Canada.

He has worked is most countries in Africa—Angola, Botswana, Cote d'Ivoire, Gambia, Kenya, Lesotho, Liberia, Malawi, Mauritania, Mauritius, Nigeria, Somalia, Sudan, Tanzania, Zambia, and Zimbabwe. He also has worked in the Philippines, Malaysia, Singapore, Thailand, Vietnam, Guyana, Belize, Cuba, OECS (Organization of East Caribbean States), Suriname, Trinidad and Tobago, Venezuela, and the United States.

He is a linguist—apart from his native English, he has a command of French, Portuguese, and Spanish.

Laurence Clairmonte Clarke was born in Plaisance, British Guiana, on January 26, 1952. His mother was Daphne Petronnella Clarke of Plaisance, and his father Vivian Slowe of Beterverwagting. He attended St. Paul's Anglican School in Plaisance, and Comenius Moravian School in Georgetown. He passed the common entrance examination, which gained him a place at Queen's College (QC) in 1962.

He was one of the youngest in his class at QC. Consistently placed among the top three academically in his class, he passed his GCE O levels in eight subjects, and in 1969 he passed his GCE A levels in three subjects.

Laurence was an all-round student. He was school prefect, head of Austin House, sergeant of the Cadet Corps, editor of the *Lictor* (the QC school magazine), and secretary of the Historical Society.

He was a very good all-rounder in sports. He was in the QC Wight Cup cricket team and was the under-seventeen track-and-field champion and senior track-and-field champion; the under-seventeen Triple Jump school record holder; and senior Triple Jump school record holder. He also was runner-up in the 1964 Junior Table Tennis Championship and 1968 Table Tennis Senior Championship. He won school colors in table tennis and was the 1968 Queen's College Sportsman of the Year. Laurence represented QC at secondary school track-and-field championships. He held the school colors in track-and-field

In 1969, Laurence started on his career in banking when he joined the Guyana National Cooperative Bank (GNCB). In the period from 1969 to

1976, Laurence laid sound foundations for his outstanding career. He was a senior manager at GNCB (international, credit and bank training) and loan accounts clerk at the Royal Bank of Canada, Georgetown, (processing of credit and credit arrears transactions).

Laurence was one of the youngest managers in the GNCB at a time when the indigenous national bank was being set up and with branches throughout Guyana. He was also the youngest Guyanese to have completed the professional banking exam for associateship of the UK Institute of Bankers in 1976.

While at GNCB, Laurence studied economics at the University of Guyana and, in 1974, obtained his bachelor of science degree in economics. He then proceeded to further banking-related studies and obtained from the University of Windsor, Canada, the degree of bachelor of business Administration in 1975 (with special honors in finance), and in 1976, obtained his masters of business administration (finance and international business, first-class standing) at the University of Windsor.

In 1978 the World Bank welcomed Laurence into its fold. He was appointed a financial analyst at the World Bank, a post he held until 1984. He was on the Young Professionals Program from April 1978 to June1979. He has been with the World Bank from 1978 to1991; 1998 to 2006; and again from 2008.

In 1984, Laurence was appointed the senior investment officer and head of the Africa Enterprise Fund (Washington—Kenya). This was the start of a significant career for Laurence in Africa. He moved to Kenya.

In 1998, he was appointed country manager/resident representative (Zambia) and from 2002 to 2005 he was country manager/resident representative (Angola). In March 2008 he was appointed senior manager, Southern Sudan Program and Juba Office, Government of Southern Sudan. He is working with the Southern Sudanese government in anticipation of the referendum on the independence of the Southern Sudan that is scheduled for January 2011.

At the World Bank, his key accomplishments for over twenty years are:

He led the preparation of numerous developmental projects in some twenty countries in Africa, Asia, and the Caribbean; managed the World Bank's operations in five of these countries, and supported its operations in another fifteen, with portfolios ranging from $500 million in post-conflict Sudan to $200 million in post-conflict Angola. His work covered projects and programs in the provision of infrastructure, health, education, transport, tourism, private sector development, public sector management and governance. He laid the basis in Zambia and Malawi for massive debt relief involving billions of dollars in these countries, as well as the formulation of national economic policy and strategies of poverty reduction and post-war reconstruction in many countries. He played a leadership role in the creation of myriad private sector financial and other institutions, such as leasing, development finance, debt swaps, etc., in Trinidad, Philippines, Malawi, Zimbabwe, and Mauritius, catalyzing strong private/public partnerships.

During his service at the World Bank, Laurence was made a fellow of the Chartered Institute of Bankers, FCIB (UK)—Commercial Banking in 1982, and in 1986 he was awarded his doctorate in monetary economics from the University of the West Indies, Jamaica. His thesis was "Banking Distortions in Global Financial Structures." In 1998 he was awarded the executive management training diploma from Harvard University.

Laurence carried out a number of consultancy and advisory roles on leave from the World Bank. These included being economic advisor to the president of Liberia, Mrs. Ellen Johnson Sirleaf (Jan. 1, 2006–Feb. 29, 2008). His key accomplishments were actively supporting and providing technical and policy advice to Africa's first female president and her national economic team, including the preparation of Liberia's first interim and full poverty reduction and national reconstruction strategy documents for its three million people. He also aided in development of coordination processes with the country's public and private donors and actively supported Liberia's movement towards relief of its $4.5 billion external debt.

As deputy governor of Central Bank of Botswana (1991–1995), his key achievements include:

- Under IMF Tech Assistance Program, he ran the operations of one of Africa's most efficient central banks and globally managed an investment portfolio of some $5 billion (US) of the nation's foreign reserves.
- He laid the conceptual basis for Botswana's regional financial center of today.
- He was a key factor in setting up Botswana's Institute of Bankers as founding director.

As executive director, Caribbean Center for Monetary Studies, University of the West Indies, Trinidad (1995–1998), his key achievements there include:

- Under IMF Tech., Assistance Program, he worked closely with the eight central banks of the Caribbean.
- He led and grew the regional Monetary Research Center based at UWI St. Augustine, that was researching the establishment of a single Caribbean currency.
- He oversaw the publication of some two dozen Caribbean academic and professional writings in the area of money and finance.
- He personally edited and published three pieces of research on the financial development of the Caribbean.
- He worked closely with eight central banks of the Caribbean and the establishment of a single Caribbean currency.

His other key awards and achievements include:

- 1966–1969. Leadership in various youth organizations in Plaisance/Sparendaam villages.
- 1980–2000. Professional publications: Several papers and books on banking, finance, and monetary economics on Africa and the Caribbean.
- 1989. Award of Recognition for Outstanding Service, QC Alumni Association, Washington chapter.
- 1994. Publication of *QC Records of a Tradition of Excellence (Book of Records)*. The book chronicles Queen's College from 1844 to 1994 and has become the reference on historical Queen's College facts.
- He was a principal player in the birth of the Washington chapter of the QC Alumni Association and is an honorary member of the London chapter.

Laurence was the honoree at the Queen's College Alumni Association (New York), Vernley Ward Memorial 2008 Benefit Dinner and Dance. In the illuminating introductory remarks by Karen Wharton, assistant secretary, the audience listened with rapture to Dr. Clarke's inspiring résumé. Karen said, in part:

> When we look to recognize achievers, we generally recognize the person with the impressive resume. The Guyana scholar. The Rhodes scholar. The Fulbright scholar. The Yale or Harvard graduate. Obviously, these are qualities that need to be recognized. But there are other qualities what we need to focus on with the same intensity. We need to focus on a person's ability to inspire, to motivate and his fellowship with his community. Does she give back to the community from whence she came? Is he a good ancestor? Does she possess a sense of social consciousness, social justice? Laurence possesses the résumé and the sense of responsibility that make him a good citizen of the world. …
>
> I learned that Laurence spent his formative years in what he has described as "abject poverty." His experience has led him on his lifelong fight against poverty, banking is his weapon. Laurence's war against poverty is not restricted to his professional life. His philanthropy, quiet as it is, frequently reaches all the way back to his place of birth, Guyana and particularly, Plaisance.

At Plaisance, Laurence had sponsored a Mother's Day event. When asked why he did this, he responded:

> In material terms, it's a tiny little to share occasionally with a community that has so generously given so much to me and my family over so many years, and which we can really never ever fully repay. In spiritual terms, it's about maintaining connections with one's humble beginnings and roots, staying anchored in the one place one can truly call home, without which we are adrift.

The international banker and all-round sportsman lists his hobbies as philately, numismatics (stamps and coin collecting) and ping pong (table tennis).

Laurence is married to Ingrid Clarke (nee Baker). They have two children: son Ayinde Nkosi and daughter Tawina Ashanti.

One of his heroes is Booker T. Washington, whose profound comment on success has been the guiding light in Laurence's life of achievement. It is this: "Success is to be measured not so much by the position that one has reached in life .... [but] by the obstacles that he has overcome while trying to succeed."

October 1, 2008

Valerie G. Coddett

Valerie G. Coddett

Art Collector and Art Exhibitor

Valerie G. Coddett, art collector and art exhibitor, was a young talented pianist in New Amsterdam, Berbice, Guyana. She worked as a clerical assistant in the Guyana Civil Service and later in New York at the United Nations Secretariat, Kenya Mission to the United Nations, and in a New York law firm for many years.

Her father, Kingsley Coddett, was headmaster at Blairmont Government School, West Bank, Berbice. Her mother, Olga Martin Coddett, homemaker, was a violinist who studied with Mr. Francis P. Loncke, a member of an outstanding musical family in Georgetown. Before marriage, Olga regularly took part in concerts at the New Amsterdam Town Hall and the Mission Chapel Congregational Church.

Born in New Amsterdam in 1942, Valerie attended All Saints Anglican Primary School. The headmaster was Mr. Robert Anderson Charles. She then attended Berbice High School, where she passed GCE O levels in six subjects; she also spent one year at Bishops' High School, gaining music at O level.

Valerie was skilled at the piano at a young age. At the 1954 British Guiana Music Festival, where music students from all over the country participate, she placed second in the under-fourteen piano solo competition. She continued with music, studying for the London Royal Schools of Music examinations, both theory and practical, as far as grade seven, gaining many distinctions.

In 1960 Valerie started work as a clerical assistant in the government of Guyana civil service. She worked in various departments; the last position held was that of secretary to Dr. Balwant Singh, senior government bacteriologist and pathologist at the Central Medical Laboratory, Georgetown.

In 1964 she emigrated to the United States and attended Albany Business College, Albany, New York. There, she obtained a diploma that prepared her for her journey in the world of business. She then set off on her career: first at the United Nations Secretariat as a typist of speeches made in the General Assembly, followed by an appointment as secretary to the education attaché responsible for the welfare of Kenyan students in North America, and then she was upgraded to work for the ambassador at the Kenya Mission to the United Nations. Years later, she found herself working at UNICEF (United Nations International Children's Emergency Fund), spending a total of seven years in the UN arena.

For twenty-one years she was employed at a New York corporate and real estate law firm, working for partners and associates on highly sensitive legal documentation, including acquisitions, mergers, trusts and estates, and litigation matters. Five years were also spent in a marketing firm as secretary to the president. She retired in 2002.

Her hobbies include playing the piano, reading, writing poetry and short stories, traveling, and collecting art.

How and when did she become interested in art and become a collector?

She responds to this often-asked question by saying, "By accident." But her dear friend Spencer Richards has reminded her, "It is not by accident; think of all the exposure you've had!"

This is what Valerie says about her journey that took her into the realm of art collecting:

> Well, I knew that it began with "music" and that goes back to New Amsterdam to the time when I was doing those London Royal Schools of Music examinations every year, both theory and practical. Or possibly it began even long before that. My mother played the violin, and I remember as a child waking up to strains of music on Christmas mornings; only then would she play the violin. And at weekends my father would play Mozart symphonies, borrowing records from friends. As the music flowed, he would conduct. It was strange to behold! I would watch.
>
> I immigrated to the United States in 1964, and my exposure to music fueled my interest in other art forms. I found myself attending concerts at Lincoln Center and Carnegie Hall and Broadway productions. And on vacations I went to Europe and would visit the great museums: the Prado in Madrid, the Uffizi in Florence, the Louvre in Paris, the Tate in London, the Vatican in Rome to see the Michelangelos; the Forbidden City, Beijing; and in 2008, a visit to the Hermitage Museum in St. Petersburg, Russia, represented the sine qua non for me.

It was music to art—art to hang over her grand piano, followed by an awakening when she was bowled over by an exhibition of Haitian artists, some of whose works can be found in the collection of the Museum of Modern Art, and the Metropolitan Museum in New York City. Valerie continues the story of her journey:

> When I left home, I was twenty-two years old. In Guyana I learned music under the tutelage of Edith V. Pieters. She was my godmother and head librarian at the New Amsterdam Public Library. Later, she became a music educator at Bishops' High School, a period in which she made her most significant contributions to music education in Guyana. She influenced me a great deal, and her input expanded my life experience immensely. I lived in her home during my teenage years and was her first student to take the General Certificate of Education music examination at Bishops' High School. I knew nothing about artists and paintings then. (As a parallel, in literature classes at Berbice High School, we were taught works by European writers—no books by our own writers that I can remember—and it was from Aunt Edith's shelves that I read many books).
>
> In 1987 when I obtained a grand piano, I decided I needed a work of art to hang over it. Only then did I start looking at work by artists of color and discovered a Pandora's box! And only then did I realize that as a result of going to exhibitions at museums that I had absorbed art!
>
> A gallery exhibition by Haitian artists was the first that I attended. Bowled over by what came out of Haiti, art and art at different levels, numerous visits to other galleries followed and works by artists whom I liked were selected, having observed their track record. Soon I discovered my fellow Guyanese and incorporated them—Phillip Moore, Aubrey Williams, Stanley Greaves, Donald Locke, Leila Locke, Dudley Charles, Hazel Shury, Marjorie Broodhagen, Matthew French Young, an historian and artist, et al. They all converse from neighboring walls!

> I believe the artist and collector share a symbiotic relationship. Artists need you to buy their work to gain entry into prestigious collections—museums, public institutions, or private buyers—and the collector needs them to enhance and bring greater value to his collection.

In 1998 Valerie had attended the Aubrey Williams Retrospective at White Chapel Gallery in London, England. She also attended the Freda Kahlo, and Cezanne and Beyond exhibitions at the Philadelphia Museum and recently, the Francis Bacon Retrospective at the J. M. W. Turner exhibition at the Metropolitan Museum, New York, and the Yinka Shonibare OBE exhibition at the Brooklyn Museum.

On the question "What is art?" Valerie says: "If someone has the ability to fashion a work that speaks to me and draws me in ... but perhaps Laura Esquivel describes it best in her novel, *The Law of Love*:

> It's easy enough to detect disorder in the real world; what's difficult is to discover the hidden order in things that cannot be seen. Few have this power, and among them are artists, who are supreme reconcilers. With their special perception they decide where on the canvas to place the yellow, blue and red; where the notes and silences fall; what the first word of the poem should be. They go along fitting these pieces together, guided only by that inner voice telling them: "This goes here," or "That doesn't go there," until the last piece falls into place. This predetermined ordering of colors, sounds of words, means that a work of art achieves a purpose beyond the simple satisfaction of its creator. It means that even before it is made it already has been assigned a unique place in the human soul.

Valerie put together an exhibition for Black History Month for the community in which she lived in New York. Historic lithographs, executed by Elizabeth Catlett, a prominent African American artist, were depicted—"Black is Beautiful"; "Harriet Tubman Leading Slaves to Freedom"; and "Supreme Court Justice Thurgood Marshall." "The Lovers" (Ku Klux Klan) executed by well-known artist Ernest Critchlow was also part of the presentation.

She also organized another exhibition for Caribbean Week at Queen's College. Thirty paintings from the collection were displayed, along with biographies researched for each painter. Some students were required to choose a painting and write about it.

Valerie continues with fervor:

> The collection is still a work in progress, featuring works by artists from the Caribbean, United States, and Africa. Eventually, I hope to take it to the next level when I am satisfied that I have a collection that can be displayed in New York and elsewhere. This will combine my craft with my other passions.
>
> Currently my focus is writing poetry and short stories. My ultimate goal is to have my work published and combine literary products with art collection/displays. In 2009, I hosted a 'dialogue' with friends on the Internet; the topic was my hometown, New Amsterdam, which used to be a vibrant community, brimming over with the arts. At the 1952 British Guiana Music Festival, the town gained three of the four championship cups offered at the Music Festival:
> 1) NAMS (New Amsterdam Musicians' Society) Choir—best adult choir
> 2) Soprano Annie Rambarran—best vocal soloist, NA
> 3) Pianist Norma Romalho—best adult instrumental soloist. She gained the highest points in the entire festival. A joyous, festive occasion it was, and the town celebrated!
> 4) Georgetown's Maranatha Quartet—best adult vocal ensemble.
>
> And again at the 1954 Music Festival, having gained ten firsts, New Amsterdam had cause to celebrate.

When asked to expound on the New Amsterdam 'dialogue', Valerie said:

> The tone of the 'dialogue' shifted from music to include other "art" forms. I chose excerpts to be read from works by authors from Berbice:

> (1) Jan Lowe Shinebourne, in "The Last English Plantation," contains an excellent description of a girl riding her bicycle from Canje to Berbice High School, my alma mater.
> (2) Edgar Mittelholzer, in "A Swarthy Boy," describes Ms. Doris Glasgow-Cooper, his teacher at Berbice High School in the mid-1920s. (She was also my teacher many years later in the 1950s).
> (3) Bernard Heydorn, in "Walk Good, Guyana Boy," portrays the hustle and bustle of Pitt Street, New Amsterdam, with much humor.
> (4) David Dabydeen, in "The Intended," narrates the story of a madman playing the guitar and the fascination it held for him as a child in New Amsterdam.
>
> In my own short story, "Living with the Masters," the paintings were fighting among themselves. I shared the collection with this group of friends5. And if I may add, Frank Bowling, OBE, RA, whose work hangs in the Tate Museum in London and in both the Metropolitan Museum and Museum of Modern Art in New York City, hails from New Amsterdam. In 2005 he was elected a member of Britain's Royal Academy of Art and was among about a dozen artists proposed to fill one of two vacancies in the eighty-member academy. He is the first black British artist to be elected a Royal academician in the history of the institution.

What is it about art and art collecting that got into Valerie's soul? She lets us into her thoughts:

> Part of the enjoyment of art collecting is meeting with fellow collectors and artists from various parts of the world, including Guyana. I am a member of the Brooklyn Museum and a member of the Haitian Art Society. Once a year, members of the Society meet to rekindle and promote interest, understanding and value of Haitian art. We view art works of collectors in the group, a learning experience in itself. Seminars are held where an expert lectures to encourage and educate attendees about the history of art and other related dimensions. I do not paint, but I have a very deep appreciation for works of

art, even something as simple as embroidery on a cushion. My mother made beautiful embroidery designs via the Singer sewing machine.

Valerie has gone to exhibitions around the world. Peregrinations took root, bearing fruit in this manner. What she does is different! She asks herself whether she has been successful in the exercise, and she reflects:

> I continued to pursue the arts more vigorously, not just collecting! One art form inspires another to a certain level. For me, success is defined in the satisfaction I derive from the collection, music, and writing. Satisfaction is a necessary ingredient for success, in one's own mind at least. And I receive great pleasure in knowing that some friends and acquaintances, of whom I am aware, have been drawn into the sphere.
>
> Success is not about the size of one's house or bank account. It is about the life one has lived by giving and sharing and optimizing one's talents.

The following was written by one of Valerie's acquaintances when recommending her participation in this book:

> To Valerie, success comes from the happiness art brings. Val has written several short stories and hopes to have her writings published eventually. Val also enjoys cooking and entertaining. She is a classic example that success takes many forms and means different things to each individual. She inspires those around her to be creative and seek enjoyment in the arts. She is one of those ladies who can accommodate you at any level. For example, when one of our friends passed away, she said she soothed herself by playing the *Moonlight Sonata* on her piano. This placed me in a mood of serenity at a time when I was in deep shock at our friend's demise. Whenever we visited Val, she would play a piece on her piano to entertain us and set the tone for a wonderful time together.

In an interview in July 2010, conducted by Dr. Patricia A. Banks of the W.E.B. DuBois Institute for African and African American Research,

Vidur Dindayal

Harvard University, Valerie had the opportunity to discuss her odyssey in the art world. On art collecting, Valerie has said, "Some folk regard collecting art as an obsession. For me, it is a magnificent obsession that takes me places above so many spheres of normal existence."

October 3, 2010

Ken Corsbie

Theater Icon

Ken Corsbie is the "authentic and complete Caribbean storyteller, standup comic, poetry performer, workshop leader, teller of folk tales, literary and personal stories. He brings the sound, the sun, and the songs of the islands; he brings the rivers of the rainforest; he brings the rhymes and rhythms; he brings the voices and variety of the Caribbean … and gives them all to you with joy," states Lee Pennington, the director of the Corn Island Storytelling Festival in Louisville, Kentucky.

Von Martin, producer of the annual Caribbean Comedy Festival in Washington DC, calls Ken "a true Caribbean humorist," and Henry Muttoo, artistic director of the Cayman Islands Cultural Foundation, agrees. "Ken is a Caribbean theater icon with a unique sense of humor and drama."

Ken Corsbie is a name now synonymous with Guyanese and Caribbean performing arts, theater, drama, and radio. He is the recipient of nine awards and has produced four CDs with various aspects of his stage performances.

Born in Georgetown on July 25, 1930, Ken Corsbie is the second child of Ivan D'Wight Corsbie of San Fernando, Trinidad, who worked at Cable and Wireless until he retired. Ken's mother was Louise Maude (nee Begg, of Tobago), a housewife, mother, and nurturer.

With parents from Trinidad and Tobago, Ken says he is one-third Chinese, one-sixth Scottish, one-fourth African, two-sevenths Amerindian, one seventh Welsh, half Trinidadian, one-tenth Barbadian, four-fifths Guyanese, and therefore, a "true true full-blooded West Indian stereotype."

His brother Percy, three years older, owned his own chicken farm at Soesdyke, twenty-three miles upriver of Georgetown, with a high reputation for his "Corsbie chickens." Sister Joyce married Trinidadian Leary McComie, and they lived in Trinidad with stints in other islands, as he was an engineer for oil companies. She now lives in Tobago. Deryck, Ken's younger brother, married Joan Martins, and they moved to Jamaica, where they had their own business. Sadly, he was killed by burglars at his hobby fruit farm.

During his primary school days, Ken lived in Waterloo Street, Georgetown. Afterward, the family moved to 310 East Street, Georgetown, where they lived for ten years. Ken was at Main Street RC Primary School from 1935 to 1942. Mr. Hope was the sixth standard teacher. Ken relates that Mr. Hope used the "wild cane" ruthlessly on small hands. The entire school was very eclectic, comprising the supposedly seven races of Guyana. "The rough playing field at the back of the school was the basis of my later athletic careers," Ken has said.

He attended St. Stanislaus College from 1942 to 1947, then the Rose Bruford College for Speech and Drama (UK) from 1965 to 1968, where he studied stage/lighting design and directing, with a stint at the BBC Radio and Television School. On returning to Guyana, he was radio producer/announcer with the Guyana Broadcasting Service radio station and liaison officer throughout the islands for the then-fledgling Caribbean Broadcasting Union. It was during these visits, Ken says, that "like Columbus I discovered the Caribbean," and ever since has been a "die-hard Caribbeanist."

In 1971, Ken saw Guyanese actor Slade Hopkinson perform a solo show at the Theater Guild in Georgetown. It was in three parts: his poetry, Shakespeare bits, and Caribbean story (Sam Selvon, Caribbean writer and novelist, for example). The audience response to the Caribbean section was the most enthusiastic. This brought out Ken's latent gifts. Less than a year later, he did his own solo HE ONE, which was an instant success. He was the producer/performer of a two- and four-person theater group (DEM TWO and ALL AH WE), and for the next thirty years, he was back to his one-man shows of personal stories, folk and literary tales, performable poetry, and comedy routines. His fellow actors in the DEM TWO and ALL AH WE were Marc Matthews, Henry Muttoo, and John Agard; they are all still very active theater and literary figures.

Ken had a very active life and was an outstanding high school athlete (he eventually won the "old boys" race five times). In his teenage years he played in Murray Street, Georgetown, where he honed his athletic skills and where basketball began to eventually become the third most played sport in Guyana. He was player, coach, and manager of the national basketball team.

He emigrated to Barbados in 1979 and for the next seventeen years worked throughout the island chain, from Guyana to Belize, as a solo entertainer, educator, journalist, storyteller, poetry performer, stand-up comedian, theater designer, and director. Finally, in 1996 he came with his wife, Elizabeth Barnum, to live in America, becoming a US citizen in 2003. Elizabeth is an anthropologist and assistant dean for International Services at StonyBrook University in Long Island.

Ken continues to perform in the Caribbean and North America, where he runs workshops, designs, directs, and storytells at festivals, cafes, schools, universities, libraries, after dinners, anniversaries, conferences, and special events. He has been a specially invited guest performer to all ten of the Cayman Islands GIMISTORY Festivals, where his long-time theater friend, Henry Muttoo, is artistic director of the islands' Cultural Foundation.

Along the way, Ken received nine awards for contribution to the arts in the Caribbean, including the Arrow of Achievement from the Guyana government, the Caribbean Cacique Award from the Trinidad & Tobago Drama Association, several for stage design and directing, and a special award from the Long Island Traditions Organization.

Ken's repertoire spans folk, literary, and personal stories; performance poetry; and song, all from the English-speaking Caribbean, from Guyana in the South to Belize via the entire island chain. His personal stories are of living in and leaving the Caribbean and arriving and adapting (or not) to North America. Literary tales come from short stories of island writers while the poetry he performs are narrative and dramatic by the very best regional poets. He is also a recognized stand-up comedian in the Caribbean and the North American diaspora.

He reconstructs Caribbean folk tales and designs his personal stories to suit his style that has been formed and honed by fifty years in radio and theater, three years formal training at an English theater school and his dance training background.

A collection of Ken's numerous works include:

Theater in the Caribbean (Hodder and Staughton, 1983), is a slim book designed for early high schoolers with an introduction to the themes, styles, and sources of theater in the islands at that time.

CDs:
- *This Mango Sweeet, Singing in the Rain*, and *My Mummy* Personal stories of growing up and living in Guyana and the Caribbean memories of family, arriving and (mal)adjusting in America.
- *Monkey Liver Soup* and *Quetzy the Savior*. Four folk and literary tales of wonder. An action adventure of four young boys, the passing and resurrection of the Amerindian village patriarch.
- *Walls of Jericho*. The best of his stand-up comedy routines recorded at on stage in the Caribbean and North America.
- *11 O'Clock Goods Train*. With Marc Matthews, Henry Muttoo, John Agard, and Ken Corsbie. During the 1970s these four artists almost revolutionized the way we hear and see Caribbean poetry. They chose the most performable "action and riddim" poetry from the widest cross-section of the region's best poets and songwriters.

42 episodes of *ARTS CARIBBEAN* - 15 minutes radio programs for the *CARIBBEAN NEWS AGENCY (CANA). 1993.*

Centre Stage - a series of columns written for The *Nation* newspaper, Barbados. Focus on things theatre/drama. 1992.

On-camera presenter of 13 half-hour television programs - CARIBBEAN EYE - of the arts/cultures of the region. Producer BANYAN STUDIO of Trinidad.

Paper written for CARIFESTA St.KITTS symposium on storytelling as an alternative and legitimate theatre art.

Paper written for Conference on MOON ON A RAINBOW SHAWL, Cayman Islands. His theme was THE YARD NEXT DOOR (that boys growing up in Tenement Yards, of Georgetown, Guyana, had a totally different and exciting/adventurous perspective than the adults shown in the play).

Theatre Spaces. a booklet illustrating alternative shapes, styles, configurations, architecture of venues and spaces that are theatrical and point to different ways of creating theatre. (1978 Guyana).

A scale model of a flexible THEATRE IN THE ROUND in collaboration with Henry Muttoo, one of the best designers/directors of theatre in the Caribbean.

Participated in three CARIFESTA'S, in the prestigious "Shakespeare-in-Paradise" theatre festival in the Bahamas.

From where does Ken draw inspiration He reveals: "Over the past twelve years, I've been drawing my themes, inspirations, whatever from everyday living. I think becoming part of the Caribbean Comedy Festivals back in the '90s made me having to draw references from everyday life around me. Since then I've written and performed several stories centered around personal experiences—growing up in Guyana, leaving it, and arriving in America, adjusting or not—most of my work is heavily tinged with humor."

Ken was married to Daphne Pendleton of the Taitt's Yard - she was a first cousin of the Taitts. They have three children: Len, who is a video producer in Georgetown, Guyana; Kim, who lives and works in Barbados with her husband, Mark Trotman, the chief agricultural officer; and Nigel, a music arranger/producer in London.

Ken's goal is to make a DVD of his performances over the past eighteen years, as well as writing a book of his life stories. This will be his eightieth birthday year, and he plans to tour some of the islands with his signature one-man show of personal, folk, and literary tales; Caribbean poetry; and his best stand-up routines. He says these performances may be his "swan

Vidur Dindayal

songs" ...but then again, very likely not. The word "retirement" is not in his vocabulary.

As of this writing, Ken has an active website, kcorsbie.com, and many of his videos can be found at YouTube.com.

Sources.

Website accessed August 15, 2008, www.kcorsbie.com

January 5, 2010

Cyril Dabydeen

Writer, Poet, Novelist, Literary Critic, Educator
Race Relations Advisor

Cyril Dabydeen was the winner of the Lifetime Achievement Award of the Guyana (Canada) Awards 2010. He is a prolific writer and educator. He was the official Poet Laureate of Ottawa from 1984 to 1987. He is included in Canada's *Who's Who*. He was recently nominated for an Order of Canada

Cyril Dabydeen was born in Berbice, Guyana, where he received teacher training and taught at St Patrick's Anglican School at Canje Rose Hall throughout the sixties. He won the Sandbach Parker Gold Medal for Poetry in 1964, then Guyana's highest poetry prize, and the first A. J. Seymour Lyric Poetry Prize in 1967. In Canada he pursued higher education and holds postgraduate degrees in English and in public administration from Queen's University, Ontario.

He has written twenty books, including three anthologies of Black and Asian, Caribbean-born writers, published in Canada and the UK. He has written over one hundred book reviews, numerous op-ed articles and essays, and has done hundreds of public readings across Canada and worldwide. His poetry and short fiction have been published for over thirty years and featured in over sixty literary magazines and anthologized in over a dozen countries.

Cyril Dabydeen's novel *Drums of My Flesh* (TSAR Publications) won the Guyana Prize for Literature 2006–07. He was nominated for the prestigious IMPAC/Dublin Literary Prize and was a finalist for the city of Ottawa Book Prize. He is recipient of Ottawa's first Heritage Award for Writing and Publishing (2000), a certificate of merit from the government of Canada (1988), the prestigious Ontario Arts Council and Canada Council of the Arts Awards, among others.

Cyril has taught in Canada for about twenty years and won the 2007 Part-Time Professor of the Year Award from the University of Ottawa, where he currently teaches writing.

Cyril Dabydeen is the only Guyanese to have twice juried for Canada's prestigious Governor General's Award. He also adjudicated the renowned Neustadt International Prize for Literature (University of Oklahoma).

Cyril served as administrator to the city of Ottawa, Ontario, and in the Canadian federal government, and he subsequently managed the Federation of Canadian Municipalities (FCM) Race Relations Program (1990–99), traveling to over thirty towns and cities to advance diversity and equity causes while liaising with mayors and ethnocultural communities and other institutions, such as boards of trade, chiefs of police associations, and human rights commissions. He also coordinated the FCM's National Action Committee on Race Relations, fostering racial equality.

Cyril Dabydeen's work is frequently studied in schools, colleges, and universities. Academic papers have been presented on his work in Canada, the United States, the UK, and Europe, Australia, the Caribbean, and Asia. He is known as "Canada's most popular post-colonial writer" (*Danforth Review*), and that his reading style has been called "Stravinsky's rhythms" (*Ottawa Citizen*).

One of Cyril's poems from *Unanimous Night* (Black Moss Press, Ontario, Canada, 2009) is offered below:

COSMIC DANCE

>The way we've come to it with
>one breath, heaving in with more
>than the lotus flower, or what we

contrive because of longings of
the spirit with mystics of old,
rishies at our doorstep, or what's
conceived of only in the Vedas.

Going beyond an ashram in Rishikesh,
or somewhere like it, it's the cowherd girls,
gopies, with choreography in their eyebrows,
that I think about, their foreheads arched,
hands & feet filigreed–as I will imagine
Britney Spears, Paris Hilton, or Shakira
belly-dancing, when the god Shiva appears,
preserver & destroyer--
celestial fires burning; and I will want
to do penance or make sacrifices,
if just pretending I've been singular
   —over the years.

Shiva's presence with his consort Parvati
(in the guise of fearsome Kali, tongue
stretched out), and nothing will be the same
again because of what keeps occurring
down through the years; indeed,
I will want to be before an altar
wrestling with faith, which upstarts
like Hitchens or Dawkins will never
acknowledge or know about–as I aim
to be an avatar of sorts seeking
enlightenment in Canada
   —in ice & cold.

Yoga in me, I subject myself to rebirth
one last time and stare into the waters
of the Ganges (I imagine), even if it's
only a lotus flower blossoming, or
my seeing the St Lawrence: a miracle again–
that I twist & twirl, one foot pressed down,
Nataraja-like, on a dwarf (ignorance, see),

and drums beating; and fire: oh fire,
as I seek escape from illusion,
non-attachment really
 —nirvana in the offing.

Sources:
Websites accessed May 27, 2010, on Guyana Consulate Toronto, Guyana Awards (Canada)

November 24, 2010

Desmond and Joan deBarros

Desmond and Joan deBarros were winners of the Guyana Awards (Canada) 2008, Community Service (Individual) Award. The citation of the award contains the following information, in part:

Desmond was the driving force behind the formation of the Guyana Christian Charities (Canada) Inc. (GCC) in the mid-1970s. He played a significant role in getting the organization incorporated and achieving its charitable status.

Desmond and Joan emigrated to Canada in 1963 but have never turned their backs on the people of Guyana. Desmond has held several offices within the GCC, including a lengthy period as president. At age eighty-three he is still very active in the organization.

Joan is a former director and officer and has been a pillar in the GCC. She has visited Guyana to ascertain specific charities in need of assistance, in particular those serving children, the sick, the aged, and the poor, regardless of political or religious affiliation. Joan also pioneered GCC's flagship fund-raising event, the annual fall bake sale, which raises $20,000 annually.

Both Desmond and Joan have actively assisted in the formation of the Guyana Burn and Healthcare Charitable Foundation (GBHCF), with Desmond holding the post of board member and Joan contributing her considerable fund-raising skills for the benefit of the Burn Care Unit.

Desmond and Joan deBarros have dedicated their lives in Canada to helping Guyanese. Their active community service and commitment to Guyana has inspired other Guyanese-Canadians to do likewise.

Sources:

Websites accessed May 27.2010, on Guyana Consulate Toronto, Guyana Awards (Canada), 2008.

May 27, 2010

Professor M. Jamal Deen

PhD, FRSC, FCAE, FINAE, FIEEE, FAPS, FECS, FAAAS, FEIC
Engineering Scientist

Professor M. Jamal Deen is one of the most distinguished engineering scientists to emerge from Guyana, the Caribbean and South America. Prof. Deen attended Queen's College where he was a regular prizewinner. Later, at the University of Guyana, he won the Chancellor's Medal as the second ranking student in the university and the Dr. Irving Adler's Prize as the first-ranked mathematics student. For his graduate work, he attended Case Western Reserve University in Cleveland, Ohio, USA, as a Fulbright Scholar (under the Latin American program) and an American vacuum Society Scholar. He obtained his PhD for his research work on the design and modeling of a new CARS (Coherent Anti-Stokes Raman Scattering) spectrometer for dynamic temperature measurements and combustion optimization in rocket and jet engines that was sponsored and used by NASA, Cleveland, USA.

From extremely humble beginnings in Guyana, Dr. Deen has risen to become a major contributor and world leader in micro/nano-electronics and optoelectronics and their engineering applications. His research productivity and impact in these fields have been truly exceptional, not only for their originality and rigour, but also for their blend of theory and practice. He is the world's foremost authority in modeling and noise of electronic and optoelectronic devices, particularly silicon transistors and high-speed photodetectors for application in communication systems. He has successfully transferred powerful engineering and circuit models for the accurate analysis and design of high-performance semiconductor devices and circuits to numerous companies. His models for the accurate prediction of noise in semiconductor devices and circuits have solved a major signal-to-noise ratio bottleneck in wireless communication systems today. His practical models for high-performance optical detectors and experimental innovations to predict their reliability have contributed to the design and manufacture of reliable photodetectors in fiber communication systems

Because of his exceptional research credentials, he is also a highly sought-after invited, plenary and keynote speaker at international conferences and as editor of several prestigious international conference proceedings. Dr. Deen is a founding Executive Editor of Fluctuations and Noise Letters; and a Member of the Editorial Boards of the following journals – Nanotechnology; Journal of Semiconductor Technology and Science; The Journal of Nanoelectronics and Optoelectronics; the International Journal of High Speed Electronics and Systems, the Microelectronics Journal; Nanoscience & Nanotechnology-Asia; Research Letters in Electronics; and the Open Journal of Applied Physics. He also served as the Solid-State Editor of the Institute of Electrical and Electronics Engineers (IEEE) Transactions on Electron Devices for 9 years and the Regional Editor for Canada and Central USA of the IEEE Electron Devices Society Newsletter for 6 years. Because of his research accomplishments and international stature, Dr. Deen serves or has served as the technical chair, general chair, principal organizer, member of the technical committee or member of the international steering committee of numerous conferences in his fields of research interest.

Dr. Deen's professional and volunteer work has been recognized by his peers through numerous awards and honors, a few of which are highlighted below. First, is his winning of the Guyana Awards (Canada) 2008, Academic Excellence Award for his exceptional research work and his contributions in education, to Guyana and the Caribbean. Second is his Technology Achievement of the Indo-Canada Chamber of Commerce (ICCC) in 2009 in recognition of his world-class standing as a scholar and his contributions to Indian science and technology through leading roles in international conferences, mentorship of Indian students and researchers and other professional and societal volunteer activities. Third is the 2010 New Pioneers Science and Technology Award that primarily recognizes his rise to become one of the world's highest ranked engineering scientist and his community service.

Dr. Deen was also a Natural Sciences and Engineering Research Council (NSERC) Senior Industrial Fellow in 1993 and is a Distinguished Lecturer of the IEEE Electron Device Society since 2001. His other awards and honors include the 2002 Thomas D. Callinan Award from the Electrochemical Society; the Distinguished Researcher Award, Province of Ontario in 2001; a Humboldt Research Award from the Alexander von Humboldt Foundation in 2006; an IBM Faculty Award in 2006; the Eadie Medal from the Royal Society of Canada in 2008; the 2011 Electronics and Photonics Division Award from the Electrochemical Society; the 2011 Fessenden Medal from IEEE Canada; and the degree Doctor of Engineering honoris causa from University of Waterloo in 2011.

Dr. Deen's peers have elected him to Fellow status in an impressive eight national academies and professional organizations, including election as Fellow of the Royal Society of Canada (FRSC), the highest academic accolade in Canada that is available to scientists and scholars; and Fellow of the Canadian Academy of Engineering (FCAE) – this highest honor for engineers in Canada. This FCAE citation reads "Professor M. Jamal Deen, McMaster University, is internationally recognized for his outstanding and seminal contributions to the analysis, modeling and applications of microelectronic and optoelectronic devices. He has developed powerful models for the accurate analysis and design of high-performance semiconductor devices and circuits. These contributions build on his innovative experimental techniques to study important device properties. A highly accomplished researcher, inventor and a prolific scholar, his device models and experimental innovations are used worldwide. He is also noted for his mentoring of engineers and scientists, his competency and proficiency as a teacher, and his effectiveness in technology transfer to industry."

Prof. Deen holds a variety of senior academic roles within Canada, serving as the Senior Canada Research Chair in Information Technology, Director of Micro- and Nano-Systems Laboratory, and Professor of Electrical and Computer Engineering at McMaster University. Dr. Deen was also a Visiting Scientist at the Herzberg Institute of Astrophysics, National Research Council, Ottawa in summer 1986, and he spent his sabbatical leave as a Visiting Scientist at Northern Telecom, Ottawa in 1992-1993. He was a Visiting Professor in the Faculty of Electrical Engineering, Delft University of Technology, in summer 1997.He was a CNRS Directeur de Recherche at the Physics of Semiconductor Devices Laboratory, Grenoble, France in summer 1998 and at the Université de Montpellier II, France in 2002-2003, and an Invited Professor at the Technische Universitaet Berlin, Fachgebiet Mikrowellentechnik from January to July 2007.

Dr. Deen also has a prolific research record of more than 430 peer-reviewed articles, has won seven best paper awards for his research work, was awarded six patents that have been used in industry, written sixteen invited book chapters and was co-editor of fifteen books and conference proceedings. These accomplishments and achievements have helped McMaster University and Canada become a major center for innovative and cutting-edge research in micro-, nano-, and opto-electronics.

Professor Jamal Deen has had a significant impact in micro-electronics, nano-electronics and opto-electronics research at collaborating institutions in many countries and remains involved in the social development of Guyana. He is an exceptional role model for the people of Guyana and the Caribbean and is very proud of his heritage.

Sources:

Websites accessed May 27.2010, on Guyana Consulate Toronto, Guyana Awards (Canada), 2008.
Personal Communications, Professor Jamal Deen, February 1,2011.
http://en.wikipedia.org/wiki/M._Jamal_Deen
http://www.ventusfund.com/news/Canadian_Study_Aug_Sept.pdf
http://www.ece.mcmaster.ca/~jamal/
http://www.worldscibooks.com/engineering/4921.html
http://www.elsevier.com/wps/find/bookdescription.editors/675545/description#description
http://www.irpel.org/phpfiles/speakers/M.%20JAMAL%20DEEN.php
http://ieeexplore.ieee.org/stamp/stamp.jsp?arnumber=04218980
http://www.bentham.org/nanoasia/EBM.htm
http://www-elec.inaoep.mx/portalfiles/file/LiMEMS_Opening_WCA.pdf

February 1, 2011

Dr. Budhendranauth Doobay

MB, BS (LOND), FRCS (ENG), FRCS (C)
Order of Ontario
Cardiologist and Religious Teacher

Dr. Doobay is a cardiologist and religious teacher. He is one of the most highly respected leaders and philanthropists of the South Asian community of the Greater Toronto Area. In his medical field and as a community leader, Dr. Doobay has enriched the lives of many. He has gained the trust and respect of people through his various voluntary community service roles in Canada and other parts of the world.

Budhendranauth entered the University of the West Indies to study medicine in 1965. In 1970, he qualified as a doctor, obtaining distinction in surgery and his degrees of MB BS with Honors (London). In the same year he passed the highly exacting examinations to be awarded his fellowship—FRCS (Edin.), Fellow of the Royal College of Surgeons of Edinburgh, and FRCS (Eng.), Fellow of the Royal College of Surgeons of England.

Dr. Doobay moved to Canada in 1975. There, he studied for and obtained the Canadian specialist qualifications of Fellow of the Royal

College of Surgeons, General Surgery, Canada in 1977, and Fellow of the Royal College Cardiovascular and Thoracic Surgery in 1978. He is a member of the International Society of Endovascular Specialists.

Dr. Doobay has been assistant clinical professor in surgery for over twenty-five years. He interviews and teaches medical students and was head of vascular surgery from 1980 to 1986 at Hamilton Hospital, Greater Toronto. He has been assistant clinical professor in surgery at McMaster.

He has been a consultant attached to the Hamilton Health Sciences Corporation: St Joseph's Hospital in Hamilton, Joseph Brant Hospital in Burlington, and Oakville Trafalgar Hospital in Oakville.

Dr. Doobay's community activities are now legend. He has long devoted his life to his community wherever he has lived. He does so through providing spiritual and medical guidance.

When he arrived in Canada, he saw the need for Hindus to have a place for worship and for celebrating their culture. With a few members of the community, he started a place of worship at the David and Mary Thompson Collegiate in Scarborough.

In 1976 he started a television program on Hinduism. He hosted the program on Vision TV for a number of years, and it continues now on CTS, where he discusses controversial topics on Hinduism. This program is the only one of its kind in North America. Through the organization's website, Dr. Doobay answers many questions on spirituality and Hinduism to worldwide viewers. He shares his thoughts and ideas, with a monthly message to viewers.

He is a founding member of the Vishnu Temple and currently is the president of the Voice of the Vedas Cultural Sabha Inc. in Richmond Hill, Ontario. This organization has drawn crowds from all parts of the world, including the West Indies, Africa, and India. People have been attracted to Dr. Doobay's teachings on spirituality; on Sundays, an audience of around eight hundred devotees attends his services. His ability to explain the Hindu scriptures in simple terms and the emphasis on day-to-day life has been one of his strengths.

Dr. Doobay has led numerous groups to the forefront of life in Canada with his intention of integrating and encouraging the communities to be part of mainstream Canada. In 1999 he organized the first Grand Diwali celebration at the Air Canada Center. For two consecutive years, 2000 and 2001, he led over 30,000 Canadians, from Queens Park to Nathan Phillips Square, in celebrating the festival of lights and helping Canadians to understand and be part of this festival. People from all backgrounds participated to make these occasions successful.

In 2004 Dr. Doobay founded and now chairs the first of its kind Canadian Museum of Hindu Civilization in North America. This museum adjoins the temple. He hopes that this museum will provide many Canadians with the opportunity to understand and share the ancient South Asian culture. Canadians will be able to integrate and share the Vedic thought process.

With his vision of trying to extend knowledge to all ages, he opened the first Montessori School, VOV Academy of Learning, in September 2005, for children 2½ years to 5 years old.

In 2006 he opened a musical school to encourage children and adults to participate in music, dancing, and playing of musical instruments. Dr. Doobay had a vision of a "Wall of Peace" at the museum; this was made a reality. It was inaugurated on May 27, 2007, by Dr. Deepak Chopra, who also became its patron.

Dr. Doobay is also the president of India Heritage Foundation (IHRF), which is in the process of publishing an encyclopedia on Hinduism.

Dr. Doobay is also known and recognized worldwide for his hard work and dedication to the teachings of Hinduism. He has traveled throughout Canada to meet with leaders to help raise awareness of spirituality among young people.

He was the founding chairman of the Federation of Hindu Temples of Canada and the president for the Canadian Council of Hindus. These organizations were formed to give Hindus in Canada a common voice in political, social, and economic matters.

Through his leadership, he has set up many groups dedicated to serving the South Asian community of the Greater Toronto Area, its neighboring communities, and various international aid organizations.

Under his guidance at the temple, a women's group, youth group, and seniors group were formed. As a cardiologist and a teacher in the medical field, Dr. Doobay arranges for many knowledgeable speakers to provide lectures and guidance to the community. He actively participates in these seminars, translating medical jargon into layman's terms for the benefit of the immigrants and seniors. He uses his medical experience and teaching skills to make sure those individuals who attend the seminars benefit from them.

Dr. Doobay has helped many seniors by guiding and providing support as needed. Hundreds of seniors from different parts of the world have settled in Canada without prior knowledge of what to expect. He has filled the void in the lives of many such seniors and makes a point of spending time with them, guiding them to the right channels so they can settle easily in Canada without frustration or loneliness. He visits them regularly to make sure they are comfortable and not in any kind of need, financial or otherwise. Many seniors consider this organization as their second home because of their involvement in the activities of the temple and, as such, have a sense of belonging. Dr. Doobay's vision was to build a seniors home near to the temple. He feels that the atmosphere in a seniors home will assist in recovery of elderly patients.

Many youths seek Dr. Doobay's help in guiding them through their education planning. He makes sure they get help in completion of applications and financial support, if needed. He holds and arranges seminars, youth conferences, and forums for youths so as to encourage and guide them in their applications to universities and colleges.

Through Dr. Doobay's initiatives, the temple had awarded bursaries to first-year university students over the past fifteen years. He has made a difference in many young people's lives in communicating to them the way to deal with their parents who immigrated from other cultures to live in Canada. He makes it simple for parents and children to adjust to a Canadian lifestyle. His interaction in family lives has saved many relationships with youths and parents, as he defines each role in simple terms to make the parents understand the benefits of living in Canada.

Dr. Doobay has headed many fund-raising events to provide disaster relief throughout the world. He spearheaded fund-raising events for the tsunami and Pakistani disaster and raised funds for the flood victims of Guyana. He also headed the disaster relief group for the Gujarat earthquake and raised funds to build more than two hundred homes there. Through his generous nature, he's raised funds to build an orphanage for young girls in Orissa, India, after the monsoon had wreaked havoc in that province. He continues to maintain the orphanage and to educate the girls and in some cases, he has assisted in their marriages.

Dr. Doobay's fund-raising efforts have extended to heading fund-raising events for the vision impaired and providing medical supplies for those who cannot afford them.

He was responsible for opening a medical clinic in Guyana. In this clinic, patients were examined at no charge, and medication was provided free of charge. This effort was to help the poor receive proper medical care. During his vacation, Dr. Doobay has gone to Guyana to give medical care to patients. Medical supplies are sent from Canada to help thousands of patients from all parts of Guyana.

In addition, Dr. Doobay opened the first IT school in Guyana in August 2005, where children can have the benefit and use of computers. Over twenty-five computers were sent and trained teachers were hired.

Because of his dynamic leadership and accomplishments, Dr. Doobay was the first South Asian to be awarded the Order of Ontario for his contributions to Canadian society.

He was honored in 2002 with the Golden Jubilee Medal, which was created to commemorate the Golden Jubilee of Queen Elizabeth. This medal is awarded to distinguished Canadians who have made a significant achievement to their fellow citizens, their communities, or to Canada. On February 7, 2006, Dr. Doobay was awarded the Good Citizenship award by the Governor General.

Dr. Doobay has been honored with many other awards, including:

- Brahman Samaj Award, 2002
- Toronto Police Service Award from the province of Ontario for contribution and participation for the September 11, 2001/2002 memorial service
- AGRA award for volunteerism
- Guyana Award for Leadership, May 2004
- Lifetime Outstanding Achievement by Indo-Canada Chamber of Commerce, June 2007

Dr. Doobay holds positions on many boards, whether business, medical, or community involvement. His activities in the community and in Canada are quite extensive and diverse. With his many activities and inspiration, Dr. Doobay generates a fusion to assist many Canadians around him to better achieve their potential in their personal and professional lives.

July 28, 2008

Danny Doobay

BA, MA
Former Honorary Consul of Guyana in Toronto, Canada

Danny Doobay has been at the forefront and has been an active participant in Guyanese community activities in Canada ever since his appointment as honorary consul of Guyana. After serving in this role for twelve years, he resigned in October 2010 to further his interest in technology. He has since founded Baylaan Technologies, a software development company with offices in Canada, Guyana, and India.

The website of Guyana's consulate in Toronto contains an account of Danny Doobay, the honorary consul, his work and achievements. It is headed "Biographical Summary of Hon. Consul Danny Doobay, Honorary Consul of Guyana to Canada."

The following is part of the information found there:

> Hon. Consul Danny Doobay was appointed to his…post as the honorary consul general of Guyana to Canada in October 1998, with jurisdictional responsibilities for the

Greater Toronto area, western Ontario, and western Canada. He previously worked as the general manager of the Guyana Television Corporation (GTV). Prior to his appointment at GTV, he worked in Toronto with Tomahdia Associates, a company which he co-owned, as the vice president for marketing and design,

Since his appointment as honorary consul, Danny Doobay has represented Guyana at numerous meetings, forums, and assemblies, including a diaspora conference in Mexico in 2004. In Guyana, he served as a member of the Advisory Council to the Minister of Information.

Danny Doobay has actively participated in the Guyanese community in Canada since 1978. He served as director of the Association of Concerned Guyanese (ACG) from 1978 to 1996; as president of Superstars Sports Club (1984–86); director of Guyana Canadian Association (1990–91); president of the Association of Concerned Guyanese (1992–1995); editor of Guyana Current (1992–1996); cochair of the Guyana Independence Committee (1994–95); president of Bushlot High School Alumni Association (1993–1996); and director of St. John Ambulance (Toronto).

Hon. Consul Doobay serves as the honorary chair of the Guyana Festival Committee and the Guyana Awards Committee. In addition, he chairs Global Partnership for Literacy, which is implementing the SchoolNet program in Guyana. The program, which Doobay authored, seeks to computerize 120 secondary schools in Guyana.

Hon. Consul Doobay was instrumental in setting up the Guyana independence celebrations in Toronto and pioneered its rebranding as the Guyana Festival. He also spearheaded the establishment of the Guyana Awards program, the Cross-Canada Celebration and the Guyana Canada Chamber of Commerce.

Danny holds a master's degree in business administration from the University of Toronto, and a bachelor's degree (with honors) in public administration. He is married and has two children, Rejhan and Ashaya.

Sources:

Website accessed November 1, 2010
www.guyanaconsulate.com/bio_doobay.html

November 19, 2010

Sir James Douglas, KCB

First Governor of British Columbia

Sir James Douglas, the first Governor of British Columbia, Canada, was born in Guyana. He worked his way up from teenage apprentice clerk with the Hudson's Bay Company in the fur trade to chief trader, through hardships and tragedies, to building Fort Victoria, to be appointed Governor.

His mother was of mixed race (black and white), his father white. His wife was also of mixed race (white and Cree, of the First Nation indigenous people). They have made an indelible stamp on the rich multicultural heritage of British Columbia, the theme of the province's 150th anniversary celebrations in 2008.

Historian and heritage enthusiast John Adams wrote a book, *Old Square Toes and His Lady: The Life of James and Amelia Douglas*, which is replete with details on the background of the families, the social economic and physical environment in which they lived, their struggles, tragedies, disappointments, and achievements. This excellent book by John Adams is the source of much of this mini biography, and the quoted material in the paragraphs that follow.

James Douglas was born in 1803 in British Guiana. His mother was Martha Ann. She had been residing with her mother, Rebecca Ritchie, in New Amsterdam, Berbice, from the late 1790s until 1812, when they moved to Georgetown. Martha Ann and her mother were described as "free colored women." Until recently, the word "colored" generally referred to people of mixed (white and black) race, irrespective of the proportion of white or black ancestry.

James's father was John Douglas, a sugar merchant, who owned sugar plantations in Guyana. At that time, Guyana was three separate colonies: Berbice, Demerara, and Essequibo. These later became one colony, British Guiana, and on independence was renamed Guyana.

John Douglas came from a prosperous Scottish business family. He and his two brothers, Thomas and Archibald, set up the firm of J, T & A Douglas & Company, based in Glasgow. They were merchants and owned plantations in British Guiana and the West Indies.

John Douglas and Martha Ann had three children, all born in Guyana. Alexander, the eldest child, was born in 1801, James in 1803, and daughter, Cecilia, in 1812.

In 1812, John Douglas brought his two sons to Scotland. Nine-year-old James had apparently a Guianese accent, a darker complexion than the usual pallid one found in Glasgow, and a lingering memory of the "land of the mountains and the flood"—the tropical world in which he was born and raised.

John Douglas sent his sons to the Lanark Grammar School, which was near to their aunt's estate. At this boarding school, established in 1150, the subjects taught were standard at the time: Latin, Greek, French, mathematics, geography, and bookkeeping. James and his brother were not boarders but lived with a family nearby. School life was tough for James. Having to fight his way with all sorts of boys must have strengthened his character and his determination to do well. He is reputed to have been strong and bright.

When his sons had completed their education, John Douglas sent the young men west, to Canada, to make their own way in life. It must have been very brave of the two teenagers to travel so far away to work in a country that was vastly different from Scotland where they grew up.

James Douglas set sail for Quebec on the brig *Matthew*. The trip lasted six weeks. From Quebec, he proceeded by steamer up river to his destination, Montreal. At Montreal, James joined the North West Company to work in the fur trading business as an apprentice clerk.

North West Company's rival was Hudson's Bay Company. There was hatred between them, squabbling and fighting, even massacre. Stockades and bastions were built to safeguard their posts. This was the backdrop to James's life and work in the fur trade.

The fifteen-year-old apprentice clerk was described as a tall, powerfully built young man, with a good education. His first task was to travel up to Fort William, where he would see the fur trading business at its peak, in the height of the summer, with brigades descending from far-flung posts, to deliver the previous year's harvest of furs and oversee the loading of canoes heading back to their posts with trade goods.

His journey to Fort William, lasting about a month, partly overland and partly by boat, started at Montreal, along the St. Lawrence and Ottawa rivers, to Georgian Bay, across Lake Huron, then along the north shore of Lake Superior to Fort William.

Traveling across Canada, its vast expanses of rough terrain, lakes, and rivers, all with hazards, was an essential part of the work in the fur trade. Over the years James would make these journeys, lasting weeks and sometimes months, often more than once a year. After a while at Fort William, James was posted to Ile a la Crosse, in present-day northern Saskatchewan. There he spent the next five years.

In 1821, the North West Company merged with Hudson's Bay Company (HBC). HBC was managed by people in England, but the hierarchy for running the company in Canada was the governor, then the chief factor, then chief trader, and the rest. George Simpson, the governor at the time of the merger, was now in charge of a much larger organization, the Northern Department, a vast region stretching from the Great Lakes to the Rocky Mountains.

Governor Simpson familiarized himself with the detailed workings of the organization under his command and visited the posts. James was still learning his job, when Simpson personally examined his accounts and must have been impressed with the work James showed him. When Simpson made drastic cuts to staff in the new organization, he kept James on.

The chief factor at Ile a la Crosse, George Keith, was also impressed with James's work. Keith believed that James was a "very sensible, steady young man," whose experience in the fur country had prepared him to be a good Indian trader.

In January 1823, when Keith had to go away on a two-week trip, he put James in charge of Ile a la Crosse. Later, James was put in charge of two other posts, where he increased the trade. He was given more responsibility and sent on fur trading expeditions, which were successful. He was making a good name for himself with the top brass.

When George Keith learned that clerks were needed at Fort Vermillion in what is now northern Alberta, he dispatched James there in April 1825. James was successful there.

Governor Simpson had big plans for expansion of the business in the fur rich region west of the Rockies in the New Caledonia District (present-day northern British Columbia). He planned to establish new trading posts to supply the posts by sea from England around Cape Horn, and to find effective routes from the company's trading depots west of the Rockies to Fort Vancouver.

Needing the right people to make his plan work, Governor Simpson appointed William Connolly as the chief factor for New Caledonia and James to accompany him as clerk. They were posted at Fort St. James, the HBC's headquarters in New Caledonia.

James worked hard, and when his contract of indenture had expired on May 31, 1826, after seven years, he was signed to a new contract—Connolly wrote a glowing report which read, in part:

> James Douglas is a strong young man, able to execute any difficult duty … His knowledge of the general character of Indians … added to a readiness and particular attention to his duty, qualify him in a high degree for this part of the country. … He has served six years of apprenticeship under able masters, acquiring good knowledge of the trade, general Indian character, business methods, good education and sound sense, good mental and bodily capacity to bridge any difficulty qualifying him for promotion.

Furs were now to be taken to Fort Vancouver instead of to York Factory on Hudson's Bay. The journey from Fort St. James to Fort Vancouver was difficult. Connolly wanted experienced men to accompany him, but none was available. He decided to take James.

The party of canoes, loaded up with furs, arrived at Fort Vancouver after six weeks. Their return journey to Fort St. James, however, was fraught with numerous difficulties. It took about ten weeks. At one stage, James was put in command and was sent ahead with some men to make the way clear, building bridges and clearing fallen trees.

James was dispatched to other posts on fur trading expeditions and trading for salmon, among other duties. He spent most of the winter of 1826–27 at Fort Fraser, taking turns with another clerk in being in charge of the post. His success in the summer of 1827 in trading and fishing was particularly beneficial, as it averted starvation at Fort St. James and worries that New Caledonia was unable to support its population.

James, now twenty-four years old, had grown into adulthood in Canada, working in the fur trade. In a world of survival of the fittest, he learned fast. He was intellectually able and physically strong and powerful in build. He had applied himself diligently to his work. The fur trade was the only business he knew. He survived his baptismal of fire in that crucible of the Wild West, which tested brain and brawn to the fullest, in numerous challenges and on a few near-death experiences.

John Adams wrote that James thought seriously of leaving the country, but his boss Connolly was, "determined not to lose the able clerk who had proven so useful since he had arrived in New Caledonia … [he] knew that if he lost Douglas, he would have to close one of the forts in the district, so there was tremendous incentive for him to deploy whatever means were necessary to keep him. It is quite possible, that Connolly's trump card was his daughter, Amelia."

James Douglas and Amelia were married on April 27, 1828. John Adams described the couple in his book, *Old Square-Toes and His Lady*. James was "literally tall, dark, and handsome, standing several inches over six feet, with broad shoulders and an erect muscular frame. His hair was black and wavy … Amelia was petite, standing not much over five feet and had delicate features. Her hair was black and straight."

In 1830 James was appointed accountant. Governor Simpson sent orders for him to go without delay to Fort Vancouver "to take up the vacant post of accountant." Fort Vancouver was the headquarters of the Columbia department under chief factor Dr. John McLoughlin.

James's work as accountant at Fort Vancouver included the arduous job of taking the Columbia Department's accounts to York Factory—HBC's administrative center—for the meeting of HBC Northern Council. The job entailed waiting for the council meeting to end, then returning to Fort Vancouver with instructions for the next season. The journey from Fort Vancouver to York factory lasted nearly three months and covered about 2,500 miles. James was asked to repeat the journey the next year and the year after.

His work and his ability were more widely recognized and in 1835, when he went for the Northern Council meeting, a surprise awaited him. James Douglas was appointed chief trader and was invited to participate in the council's deliberations.

Chief Trader James Douglas, at age thirty-two, had reached a position at HBC of considerable authority and with it, a big rise in income. As clerk and as accountant, his earnings had been £100 per year, now it was to be based on the actual profits of the company. This, in 1834, worked out at about £400 plus.

James Douglas had been chief trader for six years when chief factor Dr. McLoughlin had to visit England. In his absence James was asked to take charge of the Columbia Department. McLoughlin wrote to James expressing his confidence in him: "I am sensible of the ability and zeal with which you have always exerted yourself to promote the interest of the company and … I will always remember with pleasure the valuable support and assistance you afforded me."

James was now placed "in the most responsible position of his career and he intended to impress McLoughlin and those above him." Securing food for the posts was always a concern. James started a farm, clearing land and raising cattle and cultivating wheat and other crops.

When Dr. McLoughlin returned in October 1839, after an absence of about two years, he was so impressed with James's achievements that he wrote to London that he'd "found every branch of the business in the most correct order and going on in the most prosperous manner, which reflects much credit on the judicious management and zealous conduct of Chief Trader Douglas."

Fort Vancouver had become the center of political controversy. Although the Treaty of Ghent had established the 49th parallel as the boundary between British and American territory, there was no agreement as to the boundary west of the Rockies. A Convention of Joint Occupancy gave equal right to both parties over the states now known as Oregon, Washington, and Idaho and much of British Columbia. Not surprisingly, rivalry and tensions were high between the American and HBC fur traders in these areas.

Chief Trader James Douglas pursued several key assignments that took him away frequently from Fort Vancouver. In April 1840 he went on a long trip, which included inspection of the company's posts and diplomatic negotiations with a Russian American Company in Alaska.

On his return from Alaska, James was greeted with "momentous news ... he had been made a chief factor, a rank attained by only a small number of men in the company. Financially, James was now a big earner, with income nearly double that of the chief trader."

On the political front, the boundary issue in the Oregon country was still unresolved. There was increasing pressure from the Americans to annex all of Oregon, as American settlers were moving into the area.

To confirm Britain's claim to all of Vancouver Island, Governor Simpson decided on the need to set up a new post at the southern end of Vancouver Island. He dispatched Chief Factor James Douglas to survey the area. James found the perfect place, which he likened to a perfect Eden. They decided to build the post there, to be called Fort Victoria, without delay. In March 1843, James and a party of fifteen men started construction. The post was nearly complete by year end.

HBC was the de facto government in the area, but as pressure from the Americans on the boundary issue grew, Governor Simpson grew worried about the outcome of boundary negotiations. In 1845, the HBC decided that the affairs of their Columbia Department should be governed by a three man board of management, instead of solely by the Chief Factor Dr. McLoughlin. James Douglas was appointed one the three-man group.

The scope of James Douglas's work as a fur trader now expanded to include activities associated with diplomacy and negotiations with American settlers.

In June 1846, the Treaty of Washington settled the boundary matter, giving the United States all the territory south of the 49th parallel, except for the southern tip of Vancouver Island and the Gulf Islands. The die was now cast for the formal establishment of a new British colony.

In 1848, HBC decided upon receipt of an important letter from London to transfer James Douglas to Fort Victoria and appoint him governor pro tempore of the proposed new colony of Vancouver Island. James was ordered to transfer the company's headquarters from Fort Vancouver to Fort Victoria. The transfer took place in 1849.

The next year, a Richard Blanshard arrived at Fort Victoria to take up the post of governor. He did not stay long. He resigned after only a few months in office, and in August 1851, James Douglas was officially confirmed as the governor.

James Douglas, the forty-eight-year-old fur trader, had now moved into the establishment. He was "impressed by [the official documents of the commission], the magnificent parchment with its massive seal, informing him that he was now Governor, Commander-in-Chief and Vice Admiral 'in and over the Island of Vancouver and its dependencies.' He recognized that it was a great honor to have reached this position and he was determined to succeed."…

One of his priorities as governor was to improve the condition of the First Nations of Vancouver Island, whom he considered "a highly interesting people … worthy of attention." Another key decision was to take matters into his own hands in dealing with the gold rush along the Thompson River. He had a reputation for autocratic behavior and on December 29, 1857, he issued a proclamation declaring the rights of the Crown over gold found in the Fraser and Thompson rivers and forbidding all persons "to dig or disturb the soil in search of gold until authorized on that behalf by Her Majesty's colonial government." He believed the Colonial Office would approve his action. It did approve his action retroactively.

Under his governorship, "members of the black community were able to purchase land, start businesses, and vote (if they were British subjects). … Douglas officially countered discrimination by appointing blacks to Victoria's first police force and offering rifles to the all-black Victoria Pioneer Rifle corps (commonly known as the African Rifles)."

James Douglas, in seven years, had consolidated his position as governor and personified British presence and authority in the region, when the British government decided to create a new colony: British Columbia. On November 19, 1858, the colony was officially formed, comprising the Queen Charlotte Islands and all of what is now mainland British Columbia. Vancouver Island was included in 1866.

James was appointed governor of British Columbia, while he retained the governorship of the colony of Vancouver Island. He had to sever all connections with Hudson's Bay Company and the Puget Sound Agricultural Company, which he was happy to do. "I place my humble services unhesitatingly at the disposal of Her Majesty's government." On November 19, 1858, James was sworn in as governor of the new colony of British Columbia.

In 1863, when James was sixty years old, he decided to retire. He was financially well off; he had a large farm in Victoria. He had been governor of Vancouver for two six-year terms and his governorship of British Columbia was due to end in 1864.

In October 1863 the news reached Victoria and New Westminster that James had been made a Knight Commander of the Bath by Queen

Victoria. It was a major honor. He was to be called Sir James Douglas, KCB.

Sir James retired from the two governorships in 1864. On March 10, 1864, the citizens of Victoria gave a grand retirement banquet in honor of their governor, and on April 8, a banquet was held to honor Sir James in New Westminster, the capital of British Columbia. The highlight of the evening was a testimonial in praise of James Douglas, with nine hundred signatures.

Sir James Douglas, now retired, set off on a Grand Tour of Europe. The fifteen-year-old, who crossed the Atlantic from England to Quebec on a sailing ship, was now a sixty-year-old on a journey in a vastly changed world, on routes of discovery. He traveled by steamer to San Francisco, by another steamer to Panama, by train across the isthmus, then on to a boat for the final voyage across the Atlantic to the Azores, and on to England. His tour lasted over a year. He returned to Victoria in June 1865.

In retirement Sir James was now the elder statesman, regarded as the "father of British Columbia." Free from official duties, he was "still a figure of note … [who] played the role of retired statesman when duty called, such as during the visit of the Governor General of Canada and his wife, Lord and Lady Dufferin, in August 1876." Lord Dufferin, impressed at meeting James, remarked, "Douglas's manner is exquisite. Where can he have got it?"

Family meant a great deal to James. He and his wife, Amelia, were doting parents. They had suffered tragedy many times. Despite their status, life was still hard by many standards—near starvation, sickness, living in harsh climates, and making frequent moves. Of their thirteen children, only five had survived at the time when James died. Amelia bore her children over a period of twenty-five years without the benefit of modern medicine or hospitals. They buried seven children in infancy and two in adulthood.

Cecilia, James's sister, who was born in British Guiana, was eighteen years old in 1830. James had not seen his sister and mother since he left Guyana in 1812, but "he still remembered them in a very generous way … after he reached Fort Vancouver in 1830, he sent £50—half of his annual salary—to Cecilia, probably as a wedding present."

James helped support his sister after his mother's death. Cecilia's husband, David Cameron, a Scotsman, had a plantation in Essequibo, Guyana. His business ran into difficulties, and they came to settle in Vancouver Island in 1853, where James Douglas and his sister, Cecilia

Cameron, were reunited after forty-one years. She had a lifetime of family news and gossip to share, as Douglas was only nine years old when he last saw his mother and grandmother in British Guiana.

His steady rise to the very top must be attributable to his innate abilities and from spending some of his formative years in British Guiana. It seems James was one to keep his head down, do his work, and was focused. He learned all about the business and the people around him, especially the culture of the Indians. He spoke French well. He seemed to have had a strong faith. His humanitarian qualities endeared him to the people.

Sir James Douglas died two weeks before his seventy-fourth birthday, in the evening of August 2, 1877. The people of Victoria organized "a fitting farewell to the man who had already become legendary as the father of British Columbia and who had lived in Victoria longer than almost anyone else."

It was a state funeral. Sir James was laid out for viewing in an ornate metal and rosewood coffin, in the front parlor at James Bay House. On August 6, at 2:30 p.m., most businesses were closed, flags were at half-mast, buildings were draped in mourning, and many people on the street had black crepe bands on their left arms. Marines and sailors from HMS *Rocket* in Victoria Harbor, joined the waiting militia company, then marched to the Douglas home, led by the band of the HMS *Shah*. They formed a military escort to accompany the body to the church. People lined the streets.

The coffin was carried out and placed in the hearse by pallbearers, who represented political leaders of the province and James's oldest colleagues from his days with Hudson's Bay Company.

"At the church, the procession was joined by about a hundred representatives of the aboriginal population ... The church was filled to overflowing ... A large crowd of spectators formed outside. The day was warm and the doors were left open so the strains of the organ could be heard as it led the choir in the Ninetieth Psalm ... the coffin was carried back out to the waiting hearse as the bells of the fire department, Christ Church Cathedral and all the other churches in the downtown area began to toll, and the guns of HMS *Rocket* boomed out at one minute intervals.

"The procession included sixty-three carriages ... At the underground vault the sailors were on one side and the marines and militia on the other ... At the end, the choir sang ... "Praise God from Whom all

Blessings Flow," and the marines and militia fired three rounds of blank cartridges. The procession then headed back to town and dispersed."

Guyanese-born Sir James Douglas, father of British Columbia, made history.

In 2008, there were celebrations throughout the province to commemorate the 150th anniversary of the founding of the Crown Colony of British Columbia.

The highlight of the celebrations for the CARICOM community in British Columbia was a gala banquet and multicultural entertainment program, hosted by the Guyanese Canadian Cultural Association of British Columbia, in collaboration with the British Columbia Organization of Caribbean Cultural Associations. It was held on Saturday, July 12, 2008; the venue was the Sheraton Vancouver Guildford Hotel in Surrey.

A memento of the joyous event, titled "Celebrating the Multi-Cultural Origins of British Columbia 1858–2008." was published by the organizers. It included these congratulatory messages:

The Lieutenant Governor of British Columbia, the Honorable Steven L. Point, OBC, wrote: "British Columbia has always been a truly multi-cultural place. Born in Guyana, of Scottish and Creole descent, schooled in England and fluent in French, Sir James Douglas was the embodiment of multi-culturalism. I am honored to represent the Crown, as Douglas did 150 years ago."

Prime Minister of Canada, the Right Honorable Stephen Harper, PC, MP, wrote: "Considered the founding father of British Columbia, Sir James Douglas [was born] in … British Guiana in 1803 and educated in Scotland. … [He] rose through the ranks of the Hudson's Bay Company before being appointed governor of the colony of Vancouver Island in 1851. In 1858 he was inaugurated as the Governor of the colony of British Columbia…"

The Premier of British Columbia, Gordon Campbell, said in his message, in part: "I am pleased to join with the British Columbia Organization of Caribbean Cultural Associations and the Guyanese Canadian Cultural Association of British Columbia … to celebrate the proclamation of the first Governor of British Columbia, Sir James Douglas…"

Guyana's High Commissioner to Canada, His Excellency Rajnarine Singh, in his warm greetings, stated, in part: "With a sense of pride, knowing that the first Governor of British Columbia, Sir James Douglas, was a son of Guyana … As events would unfold British Columbia could lay claim that it is the birthplace of multi-culturalism in Canada…"

Clyde Duncan, president of the Guyanese Canadian Cultural Association of British Columbia wrote his tribute. His letter read, in part:

> In 1858, multiculturalism took root in British Columbia with the proclamation of the first governor, Guyanese-born Sir James Douglas … father of British Columbia. His wife, Lady Amelia Douglas, was of First Nations ancestry. Together, they represented our multicultural origins. In 1871, British Columbia joined the Confederation of Canada.
>
> In 1971, Canada was the first country in the world to adopt a multiculturalism policy.
>
> As the Song of Guyana's Children goes:
>
> *Onward, Upward, May we ever go*
> *Day by Day in strength and beauty grow,*
> *Till at Length we each of us may show,*
> *What Guyana's sons and daughters can be.*
>
> Sir James is the epitome of what Guyana's sons and daughters can be. We believe his success is a result of the influence of his formative years spent in Demerara, Guyana.
>
> We are sending a duplicate of the statue of Sir James Douglas to Guyana, to be unveiled by a prominent Canadian during Carifesta 2008. Canada Post will be issuing a postage stamp on August 1, 2008, to commemorate BC 150 years.
>
> We are glad to be celebrating, alongside First Nations and other communities, the 150th anniversary of the multicultural origins of British Columbia, the first Governor and First Lady Douglas.

The sterling efforts of Clyde Duncan and colleagues of the Guyanese Canadian Cultural Association of British Columbia were amply rewarded when at Carifesta X (Caribbean Festival of Arts) 2008, a commemorative stamp to honor Sir James was issued at a formal launch in Guyana on

August 25, 2008, and the statue of Sir James was unveiled at a formal ceremony in Mahaica, Guyana, on August 27, 2008.

GINA, the Guyana Information Agency, reported on the two events. The launch and unveiling were performed by Prime Minister Samuel Hinds in the presence of Canadian High Commissioner Charles Court; Minister of Culture, Youth, and Sport Dr. Frank Anthony; Chairman of the Guyana Post Office Corporation, Bishop Juan Edghill; and president of the Guyanese Canadian Cultural Association of British Columbia, Clyde Duncan, among others.

At the launch of the commemorative stamp, His Excellency Charles Court, the Canadian High Commissioner, said that the story of Sir James Douglas was "an important link in the chain of relationships between Canada and Guyana … today's launching also coincides with British Columbia celebrating its 150th anniversary this year. … We became a colony following the discovery of gold in 1857, and James Douglas was said to have set up this colony on Fort Victoria in Vancouver Island and because he had the power to handle these matters."

The high commissioner praised the president and members of the Guyanese Canadian Cultural Association of British Columbia for their efforts in honoring Guyanese-born Sir James Douglas, the first Governor of British Columbia, with the commemorative stamp and the statue at Mahaica.

The Sir James Douglas commemorative stamp was also issued around the world through the Inter-Governmental Philatelic Corporation of New York.

Prime Minister Samuel Hinds, unveiling the statue, located in front of the Helena Nursery School at Mahaica, said that recognition given to Sir James was timely, and he extended his appreciation to the many Guyanese in British Columbia who contributed to the symbolic statue. "It is important that we draw lessons from history to help us today and into the future … [The] life and achievements of Sir James Douglas is a challenge to all Guyanese born who have migrated or are planning to migrate elsewhere."

Dr. Frank Anthony, the culture minister, said that unveiling the monument was the best example of paying tribute to local heroes, noting that it would be beneficial to Guyanese youths. He added that the unveiling was also a symbol of the bond which existed between Guyana and British Columbia.

Minister Dr. Desrey Fox said, "I think sometimes we forget that we do have a lot of other invisible Guyanese heroes, and this statue is reminding us that there are many more that were born on this soil that we do not know about."

Clyde Duncan said he was interested in honoring Sir James because he felt there was need "to educate people about historic heroes who came from the Guyanese soil and the many contributions they have made to the world." He said the Guyanese Canadian Cultural Association of British Columbia had plans "in the areas of education, culture and sports and the establishment of a Sir James Douglas Foundation."

An interesting footnote: the statue at Mahaica, Demerara, was cast from the same mold as the statue of Sir James Douglas at the historic site of Fort Langley, the birthplace of British Columbia. Clyde Duncan paid for the statue and presented it as a gift to the government of Guyana. Assistance for purchasing a bronze plaque to identify the statue, and shipping the statue to Guyana from British Columbia, was received from Canadian National Railways, LaParkan-Canada, and Fort Langley Legacy Foundation.

Sir James Douglas, was a gifted man in many ways. He started as a teenage clerk in the fur trade. Ahead of him in his life's journey were obstacles—physical, social, and cultural. He rose above all these to become the leader in his business, to head the province of British Columbia and become its first Governor.

Sources:

Book: *Old Square-Toes and His Family. The Life of James and Amelia Douglas* by John Adams. Horsdal & Schubart Publications Ltd. Victoria, BC, Canada. 2001. (text and photo).
Brochure. "Celebrating the Multicultural Origins of British Columbia, 1858–2008." Designed and printed by Bluetree Graphics, Toronto: Rajiv Persaud & Clyde Duncan.
Clyde Duncan. president of the Guyanese Canadian Cultural Association of British Columbia.

August 30, 2010

Clyde Duncan

Sir James Douglas Promoter

    Clyde Duncan works in British Columbia with Canadian National Railways (CN). He emigrated to Toronto, Canada, in 1967, and in 1973, he relocated to British Columbia. He attended the British Columbia Institute of Technology (BCIT), obtaining certification in the mechanical trades. He later achieved certification in administrative and human resource management. Clyde also attained his diploma in safety and loss control from the Industrial Accident Prevention Association of Ontario.

    He was born in British Guiana and attended Sacred Heart R. C. School, Wedgewood Junior, Central High School, and the Government Technical Institute. He grew up in Alberttown, Demerara (a Georgetown boy).

    Clyde is the son of Percy E. A. Duncan, retired sergeant of the British Guiana Police and British Guiana sprint champion in the 1940s. In Canada, Percy Duncan was the personal coach and trainer of the late Charlie Francis who, as a young sprinter, represented Canada at the Canadian Track-and-Field Championships and the 1972 Olympic Games held in Munich, Germany. Percy later coached Ben Johnson. Charlie Francis and Ben Johnson are two of only six athletes to be Canadian champions in both 100 meter and 200 meter events at the same championships. Charlie Francis wrote about Percy in his book, *Speed Trap*, in the chapter titled "Mentor." In fact, Percy Duncan is still the holder of the Canadian Masters 100m sprint record for the age sixty category.

After moving to British Columbia, Clyde soon became interested and active in the trade union movement. He attended local union meetings and ultimately was elected to several positions, including local recording secretary, local chairperson, and local president with the Canadian Brotherhood of Railway, Transport, and General Workers Union, which merged with the Canadian Auto Workers (CAW) union in 1994. Clyde is still active in CAW. He is also active in other organizations within the community.

Clyde became a member of the Guyanese Canadian Cultural Association of British Columbia in 1990. He was elected president in 2007, a position he still holds. He was also elected chairperson of the Advisory Committee to the Council for the City of Vancouver on Diversity Issues. In 2008, he resigned the position of chair and the committee entirely because of time constraints.

In 2007, Clyde was invited to the unveiling of the statue of Sir James Douglas at the birthplace of British Columbia, the historic site of the fort at Fort Langley, BC. At that time, Clyde felt strongly that a duplicate statue should be erected at the birthplace of James Douglas in Mahaica, Demerara, Guyana.

In 2008, as British Columbia celebrated its 150th anniversary of the proclamation of the colony of British Columbia and the first governor, Guyanese-born Sir James Douglas, Clyde still felt strongly that the opportunity must be seized to give prominence to the Guyanese connection and its contribution, in particular, to British Columbia, as well as contributions made nationally within Canada. He proposed to the association that they should get this done.

Roger Farrier, founding member and currently the treasurer of the association, offered some advice and accompanied Clyde to a meeting with Bays Blackhall and Grant Rawstron of the Fort Langley Legacy Foundation, as well as the sculptor, Lois Hannah.

Dr. Bert Allsopp was supportive and gracious in arranging a meeting with the prime minister of Guyana, Hon. Sam Hinds, and Dr. James Rose, chair of the National Trust of Guyana.

Dr. Rose referred Clyde to Nirvana Persaud, national conservation officer at the National Trust in Guyana. Danny Doobay, honorary consul general for Guyana in Toronto, arranged a meeting with His Excellency Charles Court, Canadian high commissioner in Guyana. The office of the Canadian high commissioner played a huge part in arranging for the statue to be placed at Mahaica and later, translating the wording for the bronze plaque into French.

CN Rail arranged for the statue to be shipped from BC to Toronto, and Dr. Jerald LaRose of Laparkan arranged its shipment from Toronto to Guyana. Bays Blackhall and the Fort Langley Legacy Foundation organized the ceremony for the departure of the statue. Included in the honor guard was the now-retired, longest serving African Guyanese member of the Royal Canadian Mounted Police in British Columbia, Officer Aubrey Bacchus.

The statue was unveiled in August 2008 at Mahaica, Demerara, by the prime minister of Guyana and the Canadian high commissioner to Guyana, during Carifesta X celebrations.

In 2009, final approval of the wording for a bronze plaque (to identify the statue) was received. At the time of this writing, the plaque is with the office of the prime minister of Guyana, awaiting a suitable time for installation, as well as a formal celebration.

The only problem in this seemingly seamless transition from sculptor to final destination at Mahaica, Demerara, was how to pay for it. Clyde certainly did not have the time to organize fund-raising events, and it seemed as though he was abandoned by everyone else. Clyde reflected upon the inspiration he drew from, among others, a distinguished Guyanese-born, former realtor in British Columbia, the late Gerald (Gerry) DeCarmo. Gerry had emigrated to British Columbia from British Guiana around 1949 but clung to the Guyana he left behind. He enjoyed success in his career and was generous to a fault with regard to anything related to Guyana. Clyde knew that, had Gerry been alive, he likely would have paid for the statue. Ultimately Clyde paid for the statue and it has been declared a gift to the Government of Guyana.

Clyde feels that British Columbia and British Guiana have a number of commonalities. He has highlighted a few examples for celebration: Driving Regulations in both British Columbia and British Guiana deemed that motorists drive on the left-hand side of the road; Gold attracted American miners to BC and Gold attracted explorers to El Dorado, BG; the Sandpiper has been flying from the mud flats in BC to the Corentyne area of BG for centuries; Sir James Douglas worked for HBC – Hudson's Bay Company. The colors of the HBC blanket are identical to the colors

Vidur Dindayal

of the Golden Arrowhead, the national flag of Guyana. Clyde hopes to use this list as a basis to expand on the similarities in both cultures, educational activities and economic enterprises.

October 19, 2010

Ghansham K. Dutt

BME, BSMET, AASMET
Design Mechanical Aerospace Engineer, NASA

He is a design engineer, in the applied structural mechanics branch of the National Aeronautics and Space Administration (NASA) at the John H. Glenn Research Center in Cleveland, Ohio.

Ghansham Krishna Dutt (nicknamed Shammi) was born at Cotton Tree Village, West Coast Berbice, Guyana. He is the eldest of three children born to Krishna Dutt Jaikissoon and Radica. He attended Cotton Tree Primary and Rosignol Primary Schools, and at age eleven, in 1979, his family moved to the United States. He grew up in Cleveland, Ohio, and went to Cleveland State University. At the university he earned two engineering degrees—a bachelor's in mechanical engineering (BME) and a bachelor of science in mechanical engineering technology (BSMET), at which point he was recruited by NASA.

At NASA he designs and analyzes such things as new space vehicles and ion engine thrusters for deep-space probes to other planets and their moons, as well as researching and testing new emerging cutting-edge technologies. He also holds an associate of applied science in mechanical engineering technology degree (AASMET) from a local college. He is currently in a master's in mechanical engineering program.

Ghansham is a member of the American Society of Mechanical Engineers and NASA's Scientist and Engineers Society. He has received many awards while working on many different NASA projects and missions throughout his nineteen-year career with NASA.

Why did Ghansham choose to join NASA? What is it about aerospace that interests him? He reveals briefly: "I was always interested in aerospace. I like to set a good example to my younger relatives and friends and work to develop new technologies to benefit all mankind."

October 7, 2010

Imam Shaykh Faisal Hamid Abdur-Razak

Shaykh Faisal Hamid Abdur-Razak is an internationally renowned scholar of Islam. He is an imam and the founder and president of the Islamic Forum of Canada.

The Islamic Forum of Canada is a community-based Islamic organization, in Brampton, Ontario. Its activities are spread far and wide. In addition to education, the organization is dedicated to helping Muslims in all facets of their lives. The forum helps the needy and the poor, and it provides counseling for individuals and families in need. It also has the authority to perform *nikkah* (Islamic marriages) and make arrangements for *janazah* (Islamic funerals). It provides for the religious and social needs of the community.

Imam Shaykh Faisal lives in Toronto, Ontario. He was born in Better Hope, East Coast Demerara, Guyana.

He has received *ijaaza* (certificate in traditional Islamic learning) in many sacred Islamic sciences. He is an *ameer* (spiritual leader) of the CCAS (Canadian Council of Ahlus Sunnah Organizations, and is Shaykh-ul Islam (spiritual leader) of the Anjuman Sunnatul Jamaat Association of Trinidad and Tobago.

From 1977 to 1986 he studied in Saudi Arabia, first at Umm Al-Qurra University in Makkah, then at King Abdulaziz University in Jeddah. He also studied at York University, Toronto. While in Saudi Arabia, in addition to university studies, he studied under many highly regarded scholars and shaykhs.

After completing his studies in Saudi Arabia in 1986, he returned to Canada, where he became actively involved in Islamic Da'wah (the preaching of Islam) and education. He served as imam/khateeb of several Masjids and Islamic centers, including the Islamic Society of Peel, the Islamic Center of Brampton, and the Toronto and Region Islamic Center.

Shaykh Faisal has been actively involved in interfaith activities to build bridges with all the different faith communities. He served on the Government of Canada Interfaith Committee, the Province of Ontario Multifaith Council, and the City of Brampton Multifaith Committee.

He is also the president of the Sunni Council of Canada, former vice-president of the Islamic Council of Imams of Canada, and a member of the Coalition of Muslim Organizations.

He has lectured on a wide range of Islamic topics to gatherings in many countries, including Canada, the United States, England, Germany, Norway, Pakistan, India, Saudi Arabia, Jordan, Palestine, Turkey, Syria, the United Arab Emirates, Guyana, Barbados, and Trinidad and Tobago.

He has recorded hundreds of titles on audio and video media. Many of his lectures are available on YouTube. Shaykh Faisal appears regularly on television, radio, and in the print media, where he conveys the message and spirit of Islam in a language and style appropriate to the time in which we live. He has weekly television programs broadcasted in many countries.

Shaykh Faisal is a prolific writer. When he is not teaching, counseling, and doing Da'wah locally and internationally, he spends a great deal of time writing practical books for the benefit of ordinary Muslims, teachers, and workers in the Muslim community.

His published works include *Quran, Hadith, Gems of Prophetic Wisdom, Arabic Language, Teach Yourself Arabic Reading, Teach Yourself Arabic Calligraphy, Arabic Language for Beginners, Family Life, Love & Marriage, Fiqh—Islamic Jurisprudence, Kitab as Siyam –A Manual of Fasting, Kitab as*

Salah—A Manual of Prayer, Kitab al Hajj—A Manual of Hajj and Umrah, Islamic Spirituality, Ramadan Companion—Spiritual Reflections, Miraaj Un Nabi, Islamic Studies, and many more.

Sources include:

Website: IslamicForumOnline.com, accessed October 15, 2010

October 15, 2010

Dr. John Farley

BSc (Hons), MBBS, FRCP
British Columbia Epidemiologist
HIV/AIDS Treatment Specialist

Dr. John Farley was the winner of the Guyana Awards (Canada) 2009 Special Achievement Award. The citation of the award contains, in part, the following information:

Dr. Farley has had a distinguished career in medicine and communicable diseases control, with many publications in peer-reviewed journals, and is a clinical assistant professor in the Department of Medicine at the University of British Columbia. In 1987, as provincial epidemiologist at the British Colombia Center for Disease Control, he spearheaded a campaign to have all grade six students in the province vaccinated for hepatitis B, which led to the Universal Hepatitis B Vaccine Program in the province.

John Farley was born in Rose Hall Town, Corentyne, Berbice. He received his undergraduate degree in biology (with honors) from the University of Waterloo in 1974, and his bachelor of medicine and surgery degree (MB BS) from the University of Lagos, Nigeria, in 1979. He did specialty training in internal medicine and infectious diseases at the

University of Alberta in 1984, then trained as an epidemiologist through the Health Canada Field Epidemiology Program.

In 1990, because of his desire to give back to his region, Dr. Farley accepted a position in the Caribbean as head of a special project on HIV/AIDS with the World Health Organization/Pan American Health Organization. There, he used his expertise in epidemiology to assist local authorities in the control the spread of HIV throughout the Caribbean and Guyana.

He subsequently held the post of Chief of Surveillance for HIV/AIDS at the Bureau of HIV/Aids, Ottawa, Ontario, where he was responsible for setting up a Canada-wide electronic based surveillance system for HIV/AIDS. Dr. Farley was also one of the doctors involved in controlling the 1998 SARS outbreak in Canada.

Dr. Farley now has his own busy medical clinics in Vancouver and Abbotsford, British Columbia, where he treats mainly infectious diseases such as hepatitis B and C and HIV/AIDS.

For the past eight years, he has done tremendous work as the infectious diseases consultant for Corrections Canada and in the Pacific Region, treating and raising awareness and prevention of hepatitis B and C and coinfection with HIV/AIDS.

Through the Canadian Society for International Health (CSIH), he traveled to and from Guyana to assist in an HIV-control program and assisted in enhancing the diseases surveillance system at the Ministry of Health.

Married, with a nine-year-old son, Dr. John Farley is a founding member and the first president of the Guyanese Canadian Cultural Association of British Columbia.

Sources:

Websites accessed May 27, 2010, on Guyana Consulate Toronto, Guyana Awards (Canada).

May 27, 2010

Frank Fernandes

Chair, Board of Directors, St. John Ambulance
Auxiliary Superintendent Toronto Police

Frank Fernandes was winner of the Guyana Awards (Canada) 2007 Leadership Award. The citation of the award contains, in part, the following information:

Frank Fernandes is a successful entrepreneur who owns and operates two businesses and yet has effectively managed to play a leading role in community life, winning several awards in recognition of his leadership, innovation, and service to his community.

Born in Georgetown, he is an alumnus of St. Stanislaus College. He emigrated to Canada in 1966.

His leadership qualities are amply demonstrated in the many senior positions he has held: chair of the board of directors of St. John Ambulance, Toronto; former president of the Rotary Clubs of Vaughan and Scarborough Bluffs; cochair of the Scarborough Community Safety Audit Committee; chair of the Blue Knights Law Enforcement Motorcycle Club Toy Ride; member of the Scarborough/Toronto Community Safety Council; and cofounder of the Motorcycle Ride for the Prevention of Child Abuse.

As auxiliary superintendent of the Toronto Police, Frank, a volunteer in the Toronto Police Auxiliary since 1971, is its second highest-ranking auxiliary officer. Through his positions as auxiliary superintendent and in the St. John Ambulance, he has been instrumental in organizing the services of volunteers of the auxiliary police and St. John Ambulance at several Guyanese community events, particularly the annual Guyana Independence Festival.

As a highly respected community leader, Frank has successfully built bridges between the local communities and the police service and is a role model for high standards of excellence in volunteerism and community service.

The patron of the Alliance of Guyanese Canadian Organizations (ACGO), Frank Fernandes tangibly demonstrated his dedication to Guyana during the 2005 flood crisis.

Frank has been honored with numerous awards: the Queen's Golden Jubilee medal; the Bicentennial Award: Order of Merit, Scarborough; the 2003 Ontario Volunteer Service Award; Order of St. John medal; Ontario Auxiliary Police Medal for Good Conduct and Loyal Support to the Community; Paul Harris Fellowship Award by Rotary International; Scarborough Chamber of Commerce Special Community Service Award; City of Toronto/Scarborough Race Relations Committee Award for the promotion of racial harmony; Leadership Award, Toronto Police Service; Community Leadership Award from the ACGO; and, Roots—Humanitarian Community Service Award of Excellence for promoting racial harmony and community service.

Sources:

Websites accessed May 27, 2010, on Guyana Consulate Toronto, Guyana Awards (Canada).

May 27, 2010

Milton and Lena Ganpatsingh

Milton and Lena Ganpatsingh Nonagenarians

Milton and Lena Ganpatsingh have been married for seventy years. She was twenty-one and he was twenty-six when they tied the knot.

He has been a chemist and druggist for over seventy years. He was a businessman in New Amsterdam for over sixty years. He has given long service to the RSPCA, the Berbice Chamber of Commerce, the Guyana and Canada Lyons Club, and as a trustee of the Anglican Diocese of Guyana. He was deputy mayor of New Amsterdam.

Milton R. D. Ganpatsingh was born in Cotton Tree, West Coast Berbice, British Guyana, on March 16, 1913.

His father was Tooly Ganpatsingh, who used to supply wood to Sprostons for the steam engine ferry boat which plied up the Berbice River. Tooly sold and distributed milk that he received from the Corentyne through Richard James. Milton's mother was Sumintra Rugibance. She was involved in the milk business.

Milton is the third of four siblings. The eldest was brother Robert, then came a sister, Pearl, then Milton, and the last was Beverley. Robert, Pearl, and Beverley have passed away.

In 1914, when Milton was just a year old, the family moved to New Amsterdam. He attended Central Wesleyan Primary School. The Headmaster was Mr Harper. He then went to Berbice High School for Boys in New Amsterdam. The Principal was Mr J.A. Scrimgeor. One teacher at Berbice High School was the well-known Mr. J. I. Ramphal, who later became Guyana's Commissioner of Labor. He is the father of former Commonwealth Secretary General Sir S.S. Ramphal.

Milton worked at Georgetown Hospital as a sick-nurse and dispenser-student from 1932 to 1935 and qualified in 1936 as a sick-nurse and dispenser.

He then attended Queens College, Georgetown, in extramural classes as a student in chemistry and physics for the pharmacy examination. He qualified in 1938 as a pharmacist (then known as chemist and druggist).

Milton worked at Davson's Pharmacy for two years, then founded Ganpatsingh Drug Store in 1940, with his mother as proprietrix at 15 the Strand, New Amsterdam.

He left Ganpatsingh Drug Store in 1951 and set up Milton's Drug Store at Lancaster, Corentyne, Berbice. In 1953 he returned to New Amsterdam and established the Milton's Drug Store at 18 Strand, New Amsterdam. On January 1, 1962, he moved Milton's Drug Store to 16 New Street, New Amsterdam.

In addition to his successful career in his business as a pharmacist, Milton has provided voluntary service for over forty years to his community in a number of organizations, including the church and the local municipality.

He was the government-nominated member of New Amsterdam municipality for nine years from 1955 to 1964. He served for two years (1963, and 1964) as deputy mayor. He was treasurer for Berbice Chamber of Commerce and Development Association from 1958 to 1960 and president in 1968. He was chairman of the Discharged Prisoners Committee Berbice from 1962 to 1964.

He was president of the New Amsterdam Lions Club in 1963, and he was appointed deputy district governor for the Lions Club in Guyana from 1964 to 1965. He was treasurer for the RSPCA Berbice branch.

An active member of his church for many years, Milton was treasurer of All Saints Church, New Amsterdam, from 1969 to 1975, He was the warden and member of Vestry and Synod and of the Diocesan Council from 1969 to 1985. He was appointed as one of the trustees of the diocese from 1976 to 1985. He was elected a member of the Provincial Synod of Antigua and St. Vincent. He resigned from all of these when he emigrated to Canada.

In Toronto he is currently a Life Member of the Toronto Kaieteur Club.

Milton's "better half" is Lena. She is the daughter of Duncan McGregor Stuart, who was a school master of the Central Wesleyan School and also Caribbean Cycle Champion. Milton and Lena were married in 1939.

They have seven children, all of whom were educated in Guyana and the United Kingdom. Their eldest, Louis, is a judge in Guyana; Sumintra is a nurse midwife and health visitor; Desmond, a computer technician; Bernice, administrative secretary at Blue Cross; Rohini Ann, state enrolled nurse; Doris Nalini, dentist; and Elizabeth, executive secretary.

December 15, 2008

Ulric P. Gibson

BSc, MS, PhD, FICE, PE, CPG
Environmental Health Engineer
Water Resources Engineer Hydrogeologist

Ulric Gibson is the recipient of the University of Minnesota's School of Public Health highest alumni honor, the Outstanding Achievement Award in recognition of his contributions to world health. He is the primary author of *Water Well Manual*, which the award citation states is "an instructional book that for the first time offered simple, easy-to-understand directions on how to build sources of safe drinking water for families and communities. Published in 1969, the international best-seller is still used throughout the world today, and it is widely regarded as directly improving the health of millions of people worldwide."

Ulric Gibson has had an extensive and illustrious career in the United States, holding senior positions in several environmental consulting firms, with responsibility for many important national and international projects. He was the founder and former general manager/deputy chairman of the Guyana Water Authority.

He was a member of the 1992 US Environmental Business Technology Delegation to Russia and Ukraine, and a member of the World Bank's Gambia (water) Utilities Corporation Supervision Mission. He directed multidisciplinary teams in environmental assessments of USAID projects in Africa as the environmental specialist for International Health Programs of the American Public Health Association (APHA).

Ulric Gibson holds the following degrees: BSc. (with honors) in civil engineering, University of Edinburgh, Scotland; master's in public health engineering, University of Minnesota; and PhD in environmental health engineering/water resources from the University of Minnesota.

He is registered as a professional engineer (PE) in the District of Columbia and Maryland; a fellow and corporate engineer with the Institution of Civil Engineers (FICE), Great Britain and British Commonwealth; certified professional geologist (CPG) from the American Institute of Professional Geologists; and certified AHERA project designer, Maryland.

The eldest of three children (including sister Megan and brother Ivelaw), Ulric was born on December 16, 1934, at Charlestown, Georgetown, British Guiana. His father, Adolphus Theophilus Gibson, carpenter and trade unionist, was founder/president/secretary of the British Guiana Building Trade Workers Union; and founder/president of the British Guiana Trades Union Congress, the umbrella organization for all trade unions in the country. He was honored by Queen Elizabeth II with a gold medal for his services to trade unionism in British Guiana/Guyana. Ulric's mother was a housewife.

Ulric received his schooling in Georgetown. He attended St. Barnabas Anglican School from 1938 to 1945. There he passed the common entrance examination and went to Enterprise High School from 1945 to 1950. He passed the Junior Cambridge certificate at the young age of twelve, and the Senior Cambridge certificate at age thirteen. He passed a second Junior Cambridge certificate at age fourteen and won a government Junior Scholarship to Queen's College (QC). He obtained his general certificate of education (GCE) ordinary levels in 1951, and advanced levels in 1953.

On leaving QC, Ulric decided he wanted to be an engineer. However, his first available job was at Bookers Universal Laboratory in 1953, doing experimental studies on the sugar cane plant. He later got a job as an engineering apprentice at the Public Works Department, British Guiana government, Ministry of Works, where he won a scholarship that took him to the University of Edinburgh in 1955. He graduated in three years with a bachelor of science degree (with honors) in civil engineering in 1958 and returned to Guyana.

Ulric's professional career started in 1958 as assistant engineer in the Pure Water Supply Division of the Ministry of Works, Hydraulics, and Supply in British Guiana. He was promoted in 1962 to engineer and then to executive engineer. In this post, Ulric was responsible for development and implementation of potable water supplies throughout Guyana. He managed a staff of six hundred, working on a $400 million plan for sixty water systems.

In 1966, he secured the appointment as assistant professor, candidate for doctorate in Environmental Health and Water Resources at the University of Minnesota, School of Public Health. There, he organized and lectured in an annual international course on ground water development, sponsored by the World Health Organization (WHO) and USAID. He was a member of a task force for development of a comprehensive water resources management plan for the state of Minnesota.

Ulric returned to Guyana in 1970 to take up the post of water resources advisor, Ministry of Works, Hydraulics, and Supply, with responsibility for the planning and establishment of the Guyana Water Authority. He also prepared the feasibility study for a $3 million water supply project.

He held the post of general manager and deputy chairman, Guyana Water Authority, from 1972 to 1976. His responsibilities included the management of water supply and wastewater disposal systems throughout Guyana, implementation of programs worth $500 million, through a staff of 1,200 members countrywide. He served as comanager of a joint United Nations/Guyana $200 million project to provide improved water, sewerage, and storm drainage services to more than one-third of Guyana's 800,000 population by 1980. He was consultant to the World Health Organization. He organized and lectured on the University of Guyana bachelor of technology course in public health engineering.

In 1976 Ulric was a consultant to the Pan American Health Organization/World Health Organization (PAHO/WHO) in the provision of ground water development services to the Jamaican government, and he advised on the hydraulic characteristics of alluvium and limestone aquifers; lectured on ground water hydrology, well design, construction, and operation. He developed an operation and maintenance manual for the country's water supply systems.

He was environmental specialist for International Health Programs, American Public Health Association (APHA) from 1976 to 1977 on environmental and health sector assessments in the Sahel and other African countries on behalf of USAID. He directed multidisciplinary teams in environmental assessments of USAID projects in Africa, and performed literature research of major endemic parasitic diseases in African countries.

As senior environmental engineer/manager at Wapora Inc., from 1977 to 1980, he conducted environmental impact studies for federal, state, local, and private agencies throughout the United States. Ulric directed multidisciplinary teams on studies related to the National Environmental Policy Act, Clean Water Act, Resource Conservation and Recovery Act, Energy Supply and Energy Conservation Act, and other major legislation. He directed Wapora's international services to the World Bank, World Health Organization, and USAID, and was a member of the World Bank's Gambia Utilities Corporation Supervision Mission.

Ulric moved to CC Johnson & Malhotra, PC, where as director and senior environmental engineer/hydrologist from 1980 to 1989, he played a major role in the growth of the firm, from a staff of four persons in 1980 to more than 120 in 1989. As the deputy quality assurance director for the EPA REM II contract, he established and managed the quality assurance program, nationwide. He also managed plans for the major Wastewater Treatment Plants (WWTP) in Baltimore, Montgomery, and Prince George's counties in Maryland, the Blue Plains WWTP in Washington DC, and the Adams Field WWTP in Little Rock, Arkansas.

From 1989 to 1991 he was program manager at Williams-Russell and Johnson, Inc. There he managed the multimillion dollar US Environmental Protection Agency's (EPA) REM V program. He was site manager for technical oversight of the Department of Energy's (DOE) remedial activities at facilities containing radioactive wastes to be remediated under the Superfund program.

Ulric was appointed vice president at Marcor Environmental, Inc., where, from 1991 to 1993, he was responsible for MEI's environmental operations. Clients included Fortune 500 industrial and petroleum companies, and federal, state, and local government agencies. He won awards of multimillion dollar contracts by the state of Maryland for emergency spill response; and US Postal Service underground storage tank management services throughout Delaware, Maryland, and West Virginia.

He was instrumental in the successful proposal for desalination water supply projects in Senegal, West Africa. In 1992 he was a member of the US Environmental Business Technology delegation to Russia and Ukraine under the People-to-People Citizen Ambassador program, founded by President Eisenhower.

As Senior environmental engineer/hydrogeologist for the KEVRIC Company, Inc., from 1994 to 1997, he was responsible for the management and development of KEVRIC's environmental engineering and hazardous wastes management programs, nationally and internationally. He was project manager on a variety of projects including:

- Martin Marietta Energy Systems/Environmental Restoration and Waste Management programs' regulatory compliance support "niche" contract for the Department of Energy's facilities in Oak Ridge, Tennessee; Portsmouth, Ohio, and Paducah, Kentucky
- United States Coast Guard Vessel Response Plans project, on the management of oil spill response plans for vessels carrying oil in bulk in US waters
- USCG Telecommunications Information Systems Command contract for architectural and engineering services
- Washington Suburban Sanitary Commission Hazardous Waste Technical Support program
- Montgomery County Department of Transportation Engineering Services for storm drain analysis and design

Dr. Gibson had been a member of these professional societies:

- New York Academy of Science
- American Society of Civil Engineers—president, National Capital Section/Water
- Resources Engineering Committee
- American Public Health Association
- American Association for the Advancement of Science
- British Institution of Civil Engineers, fellow
- Guyana Association of Professional Engineers, fellow
- National Water Well Association
- American Institute of Professional Geologists—vice president, national capital section

He is in *Who's Who in Health Care, Who's Who in America, Dictionary of International Biography*, and *Personalities Caribbean*. He was a member of the American Public Health Association Committee on International Health.

Ulric is the author of numerous publications on potable water supply, water quality management, and waste water disposal, and manuals on water wells. Among the publications are:

> *Small Wells Manual.* Department of State, Agency for International Development (AID), Washington DC, 1969.
>
> "Pollution," Background Information for Framework Statewide Water and Related Land Resources Planning in Minnesota. Minnesota State Planning Agency, St. Paul, MN, 1969.
>
> *Water Well Manual.* Premier Press, Berkeley, CA, 1971.
>
> *Manual De Los Pozos Peguenos.* Centro Regional De Ayuda Technica Para El Desarollo Internacional (AID), Mexico/Buenos Aires. 1971.
>
> Water Resources Management in Guyana. Ministry of Works and Hydraulics, Government of Guyana, Georgetown, Guyana, 1971.
>
> "Water Resources Management in Guyana." Proceedings of United Nations Inter-Regional Seminar On Water Resources Administration. New Delhi. India, 1971.
>
> "Integrating Water Quality Management into Total Water Resources Management," CRC Critical Reviews in Environmental Control. Vol. 2. Issue 1. pp. 1–55.
>
> CRC Press Reviewer, "Hygienic and Technical Guidelines for Water Supply and Wastewater Systems in Buildings." World Health Organization Technical Report, World Health Organization, Geneva, Switzerland, 1975.
>
> "Optimizing the Benefits of Investments in Sewerage in Developing Countries," Proceedings, Workshop on Water Pollution Problems Arising from Development, International Association of Water Pollution Research, Stockholm, Sweden, 1978.

Ulric Gibson's best-selling *Water Well Manual* has been highly praised. One article that appears in the University of Minnesota, School of Public Health's *Advances* magazine reads, in part:

It's no exaggeration to say that the health of thousands of people worldwide can be traced back to one book, *Water Well Manual* ... Thanks to the book, for the first time families in developing countries could build their own source of clean drinking water. It became a key to both health and self-sufficiency .... Gibson went on to an illustrious career ... His water quality projects took him to places such as Guyana, the Caribbean, Argentina, Columbia, Israel, the Gambia, Senegal, Liberia, Russia, and the Ukraine ... More than a pioneer in water quality, Gibson was an early leader in global public health. "International work gave me the opportunity to use my expertise for the betterment of people around the world," he says.

Ulric is married to Rosemary Hazel of Kingston, Georgetown. She graduated from Enterprise High School and taught at Kingston Methodist School. Trained at the BBC, London, on its overseas broadcasters course, she has had a career at the Government Information Services (GIS) as a broadcasting officer, producing and voicing the Broadcast to Schools programs.

Rosemary was very active in the Guyana Theater Guild and played Mrs. Wharton (the villainous character) in Guyana's first radio soap opera. Rosemary completed her bachelor's and master's degrees from the University of Maryland University College. From 1976 to 1998, she was employed as executive secretary/executive staff assistant to the presidents of the Georgetown University Community Health Plan, and the Kaiser Permanente Mid-Atlantic States Health Maintenance Organization.

Ulric and Rosemary have a daughter, Laverne Gibson Mensah, born in Georgetown, British Guyana. She attended Bishops' High School (1973–1976) on a common entrance scholarship. Her education in the United States included attending Montgomery Blair High School (1976–1979); Massachusetts Institute of Technology (1979–1983), BS biology; Washington University, St Louis, Missouri (1983–1987), MD; Wayne State University, Detroit, Michigan (1988–1991), obstetrics and gynecology residency; Memorial Sloan-Kettering Cancer Center (1991–1994) gynecological oncology fellowship. She currently practices as a gynecologic/oncologic surgeon.

August 27, 2008

Dr. Ivelaw Lloyd Griffith

BSc, MA, MPhil, PhD
Provost, York College
The City University of New York

Dr. Ivelaw Lloyd Griffith is provost and senior vice president for academic affairs at York College of the City University of New York. He also holds the rank of professor of political science. He is a specialist on Caribbean and inter-American security, drugs, crime, and terrorism issues.

Dr. Griffith was associate dean for Budget and Facilities of the College of Arts and Sciences and later dean of the Honors College at Florida International University in Miami, Florida. He was provost at Radford University in Virginia.

He has been a consultant to Canada's Ministry of Foreign Affairs and International Trade, the Organization of American States, United States Agency for International Development, the Ministry of National Security of Jamaica, and other agencies.

A past president of the Caribbean Studies Association, Dr. Griffith was invited by the United States Congress to testify on Caribbean security issues. He presented testimony before the US Congress on the assessment of the Caribbean security situation and the prospects for the success of the security initiative of President Barack Obama.

Dr. Griffith has lectured at military and law enforcement colleges and agencies throughout the United States and the Caribbean and in Europe. He has been a visiting scholar at, among other places, the Royal Military College of Canada and the George Marshall European Center for Security Studies in Germany.

Ivelaw Lloyd Griffith was born and brought up in Georgetown, Guyana. He studied social sciences at the University of Guyana. He obtained his bachelor of social sciences degree (with distinction) in political science in 1980. He followed this with a Diploma in communication, from the University of Guyana in 1981. He emigrated to the United States and entered Long Island University, where he obtained his master's degree in 1984. He continued his quest for higher learning at the City University of New York and secured his MPhil in 1989 and his PhD in 1990.

His teaching and research interests include international and comparative politics—regional and hemispheric security; Caribbean politics and narcotics policy; hemispheric drug policy; international security and terrorism; and transnational crime.

Dr. Griffith has published seven books, including *Strategy and Security in the Caribbean* (Praeger, 1991), *Drugs and Security in the Caribbean* (Penn State University Press, 1997), and *Caribbean Security in the Age of Terror* (Ian Randle Publishers, 2004).

He also has written articles in many scholarly journals, including the *Journal of Inter-American Studies & World Affairs*, *Dickinson Journal of International Law*, *Journal of Commonwealth & Comparative Politics*, *University of Miami Law Review*, *Caribbean Perspectives*, *Low Intensity Conflict & Law Enforcement*, and *Social & Economic Studies*.

His research has been funded by the MacArthur Foundation, Florida International University, and the University of Miami's North-South Center, and he serves on the editorial board of the *Security and Defense Studies Review*, published by the Center for Hemispheric Defense Studies in Washington DC, and of the *Caribbean Journal of Criminology and Public Safety*, published in Trinidad.

Dr. Griffith has received numerous honors and awards, including:

Political Science Distinguished Alumnus Award for 2010, from the City University of New York Graduate School.

Award for Service. Florida International University Scholarships Awarding Global Excellence Inaugural Award for outstanding contributions to the pursuit of global excellence at Florida International University, 2006.

Starfish Award. Florida International University Friends of Disability Services, 2005, for outstanding support to disabled students and faculty.

FIU 2001 University Access and Equity Award for outstanding university service in the area of affirmative action and equal opportunity, 2002.

Award for Commitment to Caribbean Development and Education by the Caribbean Bar Association of South Florida, 2001.

Medal of Service from Caribbean Studies Association for scholarship, excellence, and leadership, 2001.

Excellence in Research Award, 1999, Florida International University.

Caribbean Studies Association Distinguished Service Award for Outstanding Leadership, Innovative Spirit, and Dedication to Promoting Caribbean Research and Scholarship, 1998.

Dr. Griffith is still an active scholar. His recent writings include the chapter "A New Conceptual Approach to Caribbean Security" in *The Caribbean Community in Transition* (2008) and an entry in *The Encyclopedia of Drugs, Alcohol, and Addictive Behavior*, 3rd edition (2009).

Source: website: http://www.york.cuny.edu/academics/academic-affairs/provost-bio.

October 5, 2010

Dr. Marva Gullins

BSc, MA, DMin
Medical Technologist
Christian Counselor

Marva has been a medical technologist in the federal government service for over thirty years. She received the Medal of Honor for exemplary service, signed by Secretary of State M. Albright. She specialized in parasitology and was assigned to the medical staff at various American embassies overseas.

A born-again Christian, Marva holds a master's degree in Christian counseling and a doctorate in biblical studies. She and her family are very active in their home church, in Suffolk, Virginia. Their son is a pastor, and she and her husband teach Bible studies.

Marva hails from Kitty, Georgetown. Born on September 30, 1939, at Gordon Street, the family subsequently moved to David Street when she was a year old. They lived there for fourteen years, then at Wismar, Demerara River, in the Christianburg area, until 1955, when they moved to the United States of America.

Her father was Samuel Parkinson. Her mother was Olga Haynes-Parkinson. Her father was a shoemaker, and her mother a housewife. Her siblings were Odel, Deryck, Regan, and Andrea. Marva was the second child.

She attended St. James-the-Less, an Anglican school in Kitty. Later, when the family moved to Wismar, she attended St. Aidens Wismar School. Her years of attending these two schools were from 1944 to 1955.

In December 1955, Marva left Guyana for Washington DC to live with her aunt, Mrs. Ena Dowridge. Upon arriving in Washington, she enrolled in Stewart Junior High School, and after graduating, she attended McKinley Senior High School, graduating in 1960.

While attending McKinley, Marva became interested in the medical technology field and in September 1960, she was accepted at Howard University, where she majored in zoology/allied sciences. This Washington DC university was a wonderful experience for her, and she dearly cherishes it. She graduated with a bachelor of science degree in zoology/allied sciences, and pursued further training to become a medical technologist.

In 1986, Marva decided to continue her education and graduated with a master's degree in counseling psychology from Bowie State University in Maryland. On a part-time basis, she was able to provide counseling to young adults, and this exposure enabled her to pursue Christian counseling.

In 1996, Marva and her husband were accepted at the state of Maryland's Maple Springs Bible College and Theological Seminary. They both graduated in 1999 and received graduate certificates in biblical studies. She continued on and received another master's degree in Christian counseling from a biblical perspective; this was very rewarding to her. In 2005, Marva enrolled in the Providence Bible College and Theological Seminary in Norfolk, Virginia, to pursue a doctorate of ministry, graduating in 2007.

After she graduated from Howard University, Marva started working in her chosen field of medical technology. Her first position as a medical technologist was with the George Washington University Medical Laboratory. She worked as an antibiotic research assistant, from 1965 to1968. From 1969 to 1971, she worked at General Hospital in Washington DC as a specialist in the field of microbiology.

In 1972, she was selected to become a foreign service officer with the Medical Division of the US State Department, in the capacity of medical technologist, specializing in the area of parasitology. In this position, she was assigned to the medical staff at various American embassies overseas. This was a very fulfilling experience for her. She retired in 1998 from the

US State Department after a combined US federal government service of thirty years.

Marva was an active member of two medical technology societies: the American Society of Medical Technologists and the International Society of Clinical Laboratory Technologists. She assisted in the annual preparation for the continuing education of all medical technologists who would be participating in the annual conferences. She was also a member of a national counseling organization.

Over her thirty years of federal government service as a medical technologist, Marva has been blessed with numerous awards and honors for excellent service in her field. However, two awards which she cherishes very much for outstanding service are the Medal of Honor/Exemplary Service, 1998; and the Retirement Certificate, Outstanding Service, 1998, both signed by Secretary of State M. Albright.

Marva has written two thesis papers for her graduate degrees. Her master's degree thesis was "The Effects of Positive Reinforcements for a Sense of Self-Worth." This was submitted to Bowie State University in 1986. For her doctorate of ministry, she wrote "Women of the Bible: Yesterday, Today, and Tomorrow." This was submitted to Providence Bible College and Theological Seminary in 2007.

As an achiever, Marva pays a tribute to her parents and her aunt:

> I feel that my father always encouraged his children to get a good education, and to become independent citizens wherever we lived. Also, my aunt Mrs. Ena Dowridge of Georgetown, Guyana, who had moved to Washington DC and [with whom] I stayed, inspired and nurtured me to study diligently in order to achieve my goals in life. My mother constantly kept me in her prayers for my achievements.

As to her abiding interest in counseling and service, she says: "I feel that I always had a servant's heart, and a gift of encouragement to others. I am happy to say that in the medical and counseling fields, I was able to provide those services."

Asked where she draws her inspiration from and what drives her to do well, she has responded:

> I feel that I have drawn initially my inspiration from my parents, my aunt Mrs. Ena Dowridge, my siblings, my husband, and

my two sons. However, most of all, my inspiration comes from my Lord and Savior, Jesus Christ. The inspiration that I have received from those mentioned has fulfilled my purpose as a person, which has enabled me to be a faithful servant to others.

Marva reflects with joy and satisfaction on her life. She feels she has been blessed over the last fifty-three years with many memorable and significant highlights. Some of those highlights include:

1. Coming to the United States of America from Guyana in December 1955 to live with her aunt Mrs. Ena Dowridge
2. Getting married to her husband, Earle R. Gullins Jr. and having two sons, Stephen and Brian Gullins, who together have given them seven grandchildren
3. Being selected to be a foreign service officer/medical technologist with the US Department of State and having the opportunity to serve overseas in various countries, such as Russia, Indonesia, Zaire, and Pakistan. While on assignment in these primary countries, her responsibilities took her to various regional countries as a medical technologist.

Marva and Earle R. Gullins Jr. met in 1959 and were married in June 1962. He is a former US Marine and has a master's degree in business/public administration and a graduate certificate in biblical studies. In 1992, he retired from the US Bureau of the Census as a branch chief, administrative services. He presently teaches American history at Old Dominion University, Norfolk, Virginia.

Their son Stephen has a degree in administrative justice. He and his wife, Margaret, have three children. Son Brian is a graduate of Regent University Graduate School. He is a pastor of his own church in Richmond, Virginia. He and his wife, Angeline, have four children.

Marva is very proud of her larger family and the family tree. Her Guyanese family tree consists of the McCrae-Haynes-Parkinson families. These families are now in the United States. They have held family reunions for over twenty years.

When asked about her most rewarding moments, Marva has replied:

> My husband and I are very active in our home church and in our son Pastor Brian Gullins's church. We also have an

active senior-citizens outreach ministry, whereby we teach Bible studies and have sing-a-long church hymns several times each week. These activities are very fulfilling for us, and we enjoy them very much.

My most memorable event in my life occurred on October 17, 1978, when I became a born-again Christian under the ministry of evangelist Archie Dennis. Subsequently, I am proud to say my entire family are now born-again Christians. This has been a life-changing experience for all of us. This special event for me occurred in Washington DC.

December 9, 2009

Sewack Gurdin

BCom, MBA
Accountant and Tax Consultant

Sewack Gurdin was the first of his family to have a university degree. A career civil servant, he was engaged in preparatory work for the creation of the Caribbean Development Bank and the Multilateral School System. In Canada he was director of tax appeals in the Ministry of Revenue and director of Business Systems in the Ministry of Finance of the government of Ontario.

Sewack Persaud Gurdin was born on November 30, 1941, at Salton, Corentyne, British Guiana. His parents, Gurdin and Sanichari, were mainly rice farmers, though during Sewack's early years they operated a rum shop at Golden Grove, West Coast Berbice. Sewack is an only child who has been blessed with numerous aunts, uncles, and cousins.

He attended Alness Anglican School on the Upper Corentyne and later transferred to Lachmansingh Canadian Mission School at Bush Lot, West Coast Berbice. The headteacher was Mr J.R. Ramlall. He received his secondary education first at Corentyne High School at Rosehall, Corentyne (now J. C. Chandisingh Secondary School), where he obtained the Cambridge Senior School certificate, and at the Indian Educational Institute in Georgetown, where he passed the London GCE O levels. Sewack then studied privately for the London GCE A levels. He passed in economics, British Constitution and economic history.

Sewack embarked on a career as a civil servant when he joined the Treasury Department in Georgetown in 1959, following high school.

His dream and that of his parents was he should obtain a university education. He left for Canada in 1963 and entered McGill University in Montreal, financed solely by his parents and his summer employment. In 1967 he graduated with a bachelor of commerce degree.

Following university graduation he returned to Guyana and joined the Ministry of Finance. During this time he was actively involved in creating the Guyana Economic Association as a forum for economic study and discussions.

Sewack returned to Canada in 1968 to pursue postgraduate studies in business administration. He believed at the time he would be better equipped to serve Guyana. In 1970 he obtained an MBA degree from the University of Toronto.

By 1970 the exodus from Guyana was well underway, so Sewack decided to remain in Canada. He secured an appointment as a tax auditor that year with the Ontario Ministry of Revenue and the Ministry of Finance. He qualified as a certified general accountant in 1972. He served the provincial government for twenty-eight years.

Sewack has held senior positions in the Ontario government at the director level. He is one of the first Guyanese to rise to that level in the Ontario government. His last positions prior to retirement were director of tax appeals in the Ministry of Revenue and Director of Business Systems in the Ministry of Finance. Ontario is the largest province in Canada and often leads the other provinces, so Sewack's work in promoting change and innovation in the field of taxation has had an impact not only in Ontario but in the other provinces.

Following retirement from the Ontario government, Sewack was engaged as a consultant working on projects financed by the Canadian International Development Agency. He was engaged in the reorganization of the tax departments of the eastern Caribbean countries, upgrading their legislation, administrative procedures, and tax systems.

His first name, Sewack, translates as "service," so he must have been destined to serve in some capacity in his life. He believes that "a good way of doing this is being of service to my fellow citizens. I have strongly believed that government should present a human face to the public, and I have tried to put this into practice. Government service has also given me the opportunity, in a small way, to influence policy and I hope for the public good."

Sewack's parents have been his mentors and the inspiration in his life. He says, "My parents have instilled in me the desire to always do my best and to overcome obstacles. That has helped me tremendously to succeed in a new country and to be a mentor to others who have followed me."

Sewack has been married to his wife, Florence, for thirty-seven years. She was born at Plantation Albion on the Corentyne. She also attended Corentyne High School. She obtained undergraduate degrees from Trent University, Peterborough, Ontario (BA with honors in sociology) and York University, Toronto (bachelor's in education), and a master's in education from Niagara University, New York, while at the same time being a wife and mother. A career schoolteacher, she has served with the Durham District School Board in Ontario for the last twenty years, and as of this writing, she is a principal.

Sadly, Sewack passed away on April 22, 2010. In addition to his loving wife, Florence, he is survived by their two sons: Mitra, a contract administrator on Ministry of Transportation highway contracts, and Rajendra, an auditor with the Canada Revenue Agency.

From a modest background, as indeed are most Guyanese, Sewack rose from his peasant-farmer background to civil service director in the government of Ontario and to tax and legislation consultant to the eastern Caribbean countries. He was well rewarded for his application to his work. One of the most memorable moments of his life was:

> When I returned to Guyana after qualifying with my bachelor's degree from McGill University in 1967and was greeted by my parents and family, the joy in their faces said it all. I was the first in the family to earn a university degree, and it was reward for their hard work and sacrifice as much as mine.

April 23, 2010

Peter Halder

Former High Commissioner to Canada

A man is not always defined by where he was born or the circumstances of his growing up. From walking barefoot and enduring depressed circumstances, Peter Halder ended up as high commissioner/ambassador to Canada. Before that, he was a journalist, administration officer, tax officer, and chief information officer in Guyana, and deputy ambassador in Washington DC. He later became a consultant to the government of Fiji and subsequently to its embassy in Washington DC, and then its permanent mission to the United Nations in New York. He met presidents and prime ministers. He received the Order of the Nile, Third Class from the government of Egypt. He visited over sixty countries in the world. He is now retired and has become a writer.

According to an ancient saying, "The winds of grace are always blowing, but you have to raise your sail." Peter Halder raised his sail to get where he did, from his very modest beginnings in Albouystown, Georgetown, Guyana.

He was born Burnett Alexander Halder (his pen name is Peter Halder) on November 17, 1936, on Non Pareil Street, a little-known street in

Albouystown, and grew up there. His father, Earshad Halder, came from India and sold cloth for a living. His mother, Jaitoon, a housewife, was from Essequibo. Peter was the third of five children, which included three brothers (Bonnie, Felix, and Vernon, all of whom have passed away) and one sister, Bernice.

Peter received his primary education at St. Stephen Church of Scotland School in Charlestown, Georgetown, and then proceeded on a scholarship to Enterprise High School. He graduated with Junior Cambridge and Senior Cambridge certificates.

His work career began in 1951 as manager of a drugstore, with the princely pay of four dollars per week. He subsequently became a journalist at the *Guiana Graphic* newspapers. He moved on to the accounts department of Sprostons Limited at Lombard and Broad streets. In 1955, he joined the then British Guiana Civil Service as a Class II officer; posted to the District Commissioner's Office for West Demerara at Vreed-en-Hoop and subsequently to the District Administration Office, Upper Demerara River, at Christianburg/Wismar, where he was a district administration officer. As the latter, he was appointed a Justice of the Peace, Commissioner of oaths to affidavits, mining warden, sub-protector of Amerindian rights and marriage officer. He was later posted to the License Revenue Office on Brickdam, Georgetown.

In 1961, Peter left for the United Kingdom to pursue tertiary education. He attended evening classes and studied public relations and commerce. He obtained a certificate in public relations from the Institute of Public Relations and became an associate member of the British Society of Commerce. He worked full time at the Department of Public Control, London County Council.

Peter returned to Guyana in 1964 and joined the Government Information Services, which later became the Ministry of Information and Culture. In 1968, on a scholarship, he attended the Institute of International Relations, University of the West Indies, at St. Augustine, Trinidad. He obtained a postgraduate diploma in international relations. His academic papers were "The Foreign Policy of Guyana"; "The Legal Aspects of Guyana/Venezuela Boundary Dispute"; "The Sino-Soviet Crisis"; and "Investment Incentives in the Caribbean."

Peter's career moved into top gear. He became Chief Information Officer in 1970 and pro tem executive director of Design and Graphics. He was a member of the board of directors of the Guyana Broadcasting Service and a member of the Guyana Film Censor Board. During 1972, he was director of Publicity and Public Relations for the Caribbean Festival of Creative Arts, held in Georgetown.

He joined the Ministry of Foreign Affairs as Director of Information and later became the director of North American and European Affairs.

In 1975, he was posted as a diplomatic officer to the Guyana embassy in Washington DC and later became deputy head of mission.

In 1980, he was appointed High Commissioner (ambassador) to Canada, based in Ottawa.

He resigned from the Guyana government service and accepted an assignment with the Commonwealth Secretariat in London as a media expert. He was assigned in 1985 to the Fiji Islands as press secretary to the prime minister of Fiji. He later became a consultant and was for a brief period advisor to the National Committee on TV in Fiji.

He and his family left Fiji in 1994 and returned to the United States, where he worked as a consultant on diplomatic affairs to the Fiji embassy in Washington DC and later as a consultant in international relations to the Fiji Permanent Mission to the United Nations in New York.

Peter was the recipient of the Order of the Nile (Third Class) from the government of Egypt in 1973, and in 1999, he received the Editor's Award, National Library of Poetry, Maryland.

Peter has written two adult supernatural fiction manuscripts set in Guyana; a Fable of the Forests; sixteen children's fairy tales, and a collection of eighty-four nursery *"Rhymes of the Times."* He has also written several nostalgias, one of which, *"On the Street Where I lived: Non Pareil Street, Albouystown,"* was published on the Internet and distributed widely. The excerpts below depict vividly the Albouystown of the late 1930s, 1940s, and very early 1950s, in which he had experiences as a child:

> I was born, grew up, and lived for many years on a virtually unknown street. It's name is Non Pareil Street and it's in Albouystown ... the long, narrow, southern suburb of Georgetown, often called a "slum area" due to its long ranges of one-room homes, thickly populated yards, and latrines for the use of both landlords and tenants ... The latrine was also used for baths, using a bucket of water and a small calabash ... "salt soap" ... and a dried nenwa was the wash sponge.
>
> In the third yard ... was the most beautiful girl on Non Pareil Street ... her sister, the only blonde ... folks organized a masquerade band every Christmas season ... I would

accompany them when they went masquerading ... I organized a youth group of my own and, using old sardine cans, Palm Tree salt-butter tins, bottles, and pieces of iron, we created our own music and dancing. We easily made $1 a night, not to mention free slices of cake and soft drinks ... American cream soda, Two-Glass Quencha, and Portello.

Towards the end, near the Punt Trench was a cow pen where I used to go to buy fresh cow's milk ... in the yard opposite ours was a Buxton spice mango tree, dunks tree, genip tree, guava tree, and calabash tree ... The Sussex Street trench .... was a real trench ... I used to fish in it for kassee, curass, hassar, and catchman prawns. ...

Across Sussex Street was the Le Repentir trench and burial ground. I walked through the burial ground daily ... to and from school. ...

At the corner of James and Curtis streets was ... a parlor and grocery ... I used to enjoy the sardine (Marshall's Tomato Sauce) and bread (penny loaf) and washed it down with a mauby or a pine drink. It sold the best custard blocks with raisin in them. In the middle of Curtis Street was a soap factory. We bought end scraps from it at a cheap price. We used it to bathe and wash dinner wares (enamel) and clothes.

His (the shopkeeper's) son and I attended Enterprise High School. [He] went to school each day with only one exercise book in his back pocket, but he was an expert in opera. He invited me some Sundays to listen to his LPs of Beniamini Gili, Enrico Caruso, and Richard Tauber.

The calypsos popular at the time were "Bring back the Saltfish" and "The More They Try to Do Me Bad Is the Better I Live in Trinidad." ...

The popular wines were Key and Gunboat. For rum, it was Cut and Drop and Dictator, sold in small, black lemonade bottles, called "cuttie" or "cut down." ... I [was] fascinated with the manner in which the men opened it. They shook it up and then slapped the bottom of the bottle with the palm of their hand and the cork eased out ...

A lonely woman, with a bottle lamp and a small wooden tray on a bench, sitting on a wooden bridge in front of a cottage, sold black pudding from a blue enamel pot on James Street opposite Buntan's Church on Friday and Saturday nights. ... Once a year, cumfa dancing was held ... I was always fascinated by the beat of the Congo drums, the dancing girls, and the strange language they spoke when they fell to the ground, foaming from the mouth.

Easter, a fair was held [at the ball park on Callendar Street] and one of the features was trying to walk across the "greasy pole," the round timber log across the Sussex Street trench laced with grease. The first across got a spanking-new green $5 bill. It was also an ideal area for flying kites.

My mother enrolled me at St. Stephen's Church of Scotland School at St. Stephen and Princess streets. Those were the days of slate and pencil ... until I was eight years old, I walked about barefoot. At that age, my teacher insisted I wear "yachting shoes."

The teacher of Lil ABC was Teacher Bessie, Big ABC was Miss Fletcher ... second standard was Miss Leitch, third was Miss Fox and Mr. Durant, fourth was Mr. Conrad Luke, fifth was Mrs. Cooke and sixth, Mr. Cooke. The headmaster was Charles B. Giddings. From third standard, I was elevated to scholarship class, run by Mr. Giddings ...

Being poor was not a crime nor was walking barefoot ... for lunch, I would buy a ticket from school for ten cents for five daily lunches at the Children's Breakfast Center ... At home, we ate from enamel plates, drank from enamel cups, and ate with our fingers ... There was no stove. My mother mixed mud with cow and donkey dung and made a fireside called chulha, with two holes at the top and one at the bottom for wood ... a large five-pound empty tin of Palm Tree salt butter was made into a pot to boil water. The only other cooking utensils were a frying pan, a large iron pot, a carahi, a tawa for making roti, and a large blue enamel pot for cooking pepper pot ... We didn't have toothbrush and toothpaste in our early years. We used black sage sticks.

My mother baked bread once weekly on Saturday. I would place each tin tray of the plaited bread dough on my head, take it to the bakery at the corner of Cooper Street ... collar, salara, butterflap, penny loaf, cottage roll, panbread, and doughboy were in fashion at that time.

In the second house on Albert Street ... the famous Texacan Steelband had its origin. It attracted a large crowd during practice sessions.

Cinema in Albouystown ... my parents took me there every Holy Thursday night to see the religious movie *Passion Play*. The wooden benches in pit and seats in house and balcony were more populated by bugs, Guyana kind, than by patrons. The cinema as a whole was an anathema to my mother, who was a devout Jehovah's Witness ... [she] permitted me to go to the Astor Cinema one Boxing Day morning to see two westerns ... I was not allowed to go in the dress circle because I was barefoot ... The pit was three cents, and if you sold an empty black lemonade bottle, you got a penny or an empty large rum bottle at Dictator Rumshop ... you got a bit-and-a-half or sixpence. ...

Problem was when the movie was on at night at the Empire Cinema on Middle Street ... The quickest way was through the burial ground. One night, when the serial *The Drums of Fu Manchu* was showing, I walked [through the] ... burial ground ... I was prepared for my return journey at midnight. As I climbed over the Princess Street gate, I took out fegs of garlic which I had in my pocket, threw them one by one over my head and whispered, "Pity, pity poor boy, sorry for me." I never saw a spirit but my mother believed in them, especially when dogs, looking into the burial ground howled mournfully..

There was no electricity. Homes were lit by kerosene lamps ... it was not easy reading and studying schoolwork under such lights.

My father had a old Victrola gramophone ... the only 78 records we had were two of Christmas carols and one was Indian, with songs sung by, if I recall, Lata Mangeshkar.

Biscuit [crackers] was a favorite breakfast item, eaten with Dutchman head cheese [Edam] or reddish salt-butter ... A drum of broken biscuits was cheaper and contained both salt and sweet biscuits, Edger Boy and Edger Girl. The factory was opposite "Count Orloff" Charles's wheelwright place. Charles built and repaired wheels for donkey and dray carts... There were quite a few drug stores in the 1940s Albouystown (at least four) on James Street. ...

Mr. Cozier walked around Albouystown with a push cart from which he sold shave ice in the shape of a heart, a diamond, or a club, lathered with thick red syrup. Sometimes he would put some Blue Cross sweetened condensed milk on top. He rang a bell constantly to let customers know he was around. ...

A great day ... was once a year when "bandin" opened. ... The residue of sugarcane crushing, locally called "lease water," dark in color and smelling of molasses, flowed into the Sussex Street trench, and fishes of all kinds, probably drunk from the odor or the water that reached their gills, floated on the surface. We filled our colorful mokra baskets ... with fresh fish that day. The biggest fish we got on one occasion was a cuffum.

That was Peter's world in which he grew up. He said of it, "Guyana in my young days was paradise and Non Pareil Street and Albouystown [were] incomparable."

August 31, 2010

Melanie Fiona Hallim

Rhythm & Blues Singer/Songwriter

Melanie Fiona Hallim was the winner of the Guyana Awards (Canada) 2010 Media & Culture Award. The citation of the award contains, in part, the following information:

Melanie Fiona Hallim rocketed to the limelight in less than a year after she released her debut album. She has been nominated for prestigious awards. She tours with celebrated musicians in the United States, Canada, the UK, and Europe.

Melanie Fiona was born on July 4, 1983, in Toronto, Ontario. Her parents emigrated from Guyana to Canada in the late 1970s. Her father worked as a janitor, then in finance, and her mother worked in banking.

Melanie Fiona was always interested in music. She would watch her father play guitar and listen to her mother's music collection, and she soon developed an amazing singing voice. She began writing songs at age sixteen.

Melanie Fiona's first single, "Give It to Me Right," was released in February 2009. It peaked at number 20 on Billboard's Canadian Hot 100 and number 41 on the UK Singles chart.

"The Bridge," her debut album, was released in June 2009. It peaked at number 4 on Billboard's R&B chart. It has remained on the chart for twenty-two weeks and secured an NAACP Image Award nomination for Outstanding New Artist. It was also nominated for a JUNO Award in the R&B Soul Recording of the Year category. This award is presented annually to Canadian musical artists by the Canadian Academy of Recording Arts and Sciences.

Beyond Race magazine ranked Fiona among the "50 Emerging Artists" of 2009.

Melanie Fiona's second single, "It Kills Me," has earned her internationally, critical acclaim. The song soared to number 1 on Billboard's R&B chart, stayed there for over five weeks, remained on the chart for thirty-four weeks—and earned Melanie Fiona a 2010 Grammy Award nomination for Best Female R&B Vocal Performance.

Among Melanie Fiona's other stellar achievements are:

- The single "Monday Morning" stood at number 1 on the Swiss charts for over six weeks.
- The single "Bang Bang" has been featured on episodes of the TV shows *Ugly Betty* and *Grey's Anatomy*.
- Melanie Fiona was invited to participate in the remake of "We Are the World" to benefit Haiti after the 2010 earthquake.
- She has made guest appearances on the *Ellen DeGeneres Show* (March 22, 2010), *Last Call with Carson Daly*, *Mo'Nique Show*, and *Jimmy Kimmel Live*, and she was featured on BET's "Rising Icon" segment.

She has toured with two of the biggest names in music: Kanye West and Alicia Keyes.

Sources:

Websites accessed May 27, 2010, on Guyana Consulate Toronto, Guyana Awards (Canada).

November 25, 2010

Harry Harakh

Harry Harakh was the winner of the Guyana Awards (Canada) 2008 Leadership Award. The citation of the award contains the following information, in part:

Harry Harakh is a founding member and managing director of the Guyana Burn and Health Care Foundation. He was instrumental in providing the leadership that resulted in Guyana having the first burn care unit in the Caribbean, having inspired a group of Guyanese-Canadians to devote energy and resources to see the project through to fruition.

The burn care unit was opened at the Georgetown Public Hospital on November 10, 2002, and provided specialized care to 210 patients in its first five years. The results were a clear improvement in mortality rates and a reduction in the average length of stay in the hospital.

A successful chartered accountant with a busy practice, Harry Harakh is described as "compassionate, with a genuine appreciation of people." That may explain why he has found the time to make substantial contributions of his services to numerous organizations, including:

- Secretary of the committee overseeing the establishment of the Canadian Museum of Hindu Civilization at the Vishnu

Mandir at Hwy 7 and Yonge Street in Richmond Hill, Ontario

- Member of the board of trustees of York Central Hospital, and on several of its committees

- Member of the York District Health Council Long-Term Care Redirection Committee

- A long-time member and contributor to Guyana Christian Charities, including voluntary service as the organization's accountant.

- Vice president of finance for the Voice of Vedas, and a director of Bharat Shivashram Sangha Canada Inc.

Sources:
Websites accessed May 27, 2010, on Guyana Consulate Toronto, Guyana Awards (Canada)

May 27, 2010

Dr. Mohamed N. Hassan

MD, FRCP, MPhil, PhD
Neurologist, Neuropharmacologist
Associate Professor
Specialist in Movement Disorders

"The winds of grace are always blowing, but you have to raise the sail."
—Ramakrisha

He came from Essequibo in Guyana. He grew up surrounded by deprivation. Yet Dr. Mohamed Noorudeen Hassan, infused with ambition, raised his sail, rose above the circumstances of his birth and childhood and achieved eminence.

Dragging himself up by his own bootstraps, he climbed the ladder of medical academic and professional heights with courage, determination, faith, hope, purpose, and the loving support of his wife, Sarah.

He jousted with the Fates and won. And when he did attain the topmost rung on the ladder of eminence, he never scorned the base degrees by which he did ascend, nor did he turn his face away from his family and friends. He never lost or sought to lose the common touch.

These words, taken from the foreword, of an autobiography of Dr. Hassan, are written by the accomplished author Peter Halder, renowned for his vivid writing. The foreword, headed "From Essequibo to Eminence," captures telling moments of a life of achievement against all odds. Peter Halder is an uncle of Dr. Hassan and former high commissioner for Guyana in Canada.

Dr. Mohamed N. Hassan is a board certified (Canada and USA) neurologist at Hartford Hospital and the University of Connecticut. He has over twenty-five years of clinical and research experience and also has a PhD in neuropharmacology. He was a former associate professor of neurology at the University of Ottawa and the founder/director of the Ottawa Parkinson's Disease Research Laboratory.

Mohamed Noorudeen Hassan was born on December 19, 1942, in the village of Middlesex, Essequibo, in the then-British Guiana. His father was Mohamed Sadique Hassan, a jeweler, farmer, and a self-taught engineer—he had no formal education. His mother was Bebe Jameeran. He had a brother who died in infancy. His mother, who also had no formal education, was a typical housewife who dedicated her life to her husband and her only child. She died when Noor was only eight years old.

Noor received his early education at Huist Dieren Primary School. In his first two years, his school was a single-story troolie [palm]-thatched roof building, which leaked when it rained. In the next two years, he moved into a revamped sugar barn built by the Dutch in the 1700s. In the next four years, he attended a modern school built on the site of the old troolie school

Peter Halder brilliantly sketched out a résumé of the doctor's story in the foreword to Dr. Hassan's autobiography, starting from his early years. He wrote, in part:

> Noor, as he was familiarly known, was born and grew up in the undeveloped rural village of Middlesex in the Cinderella County of Essequibo.
>
> The Hassan family did not enjoy the luxury of a kerosene oil or gas stove. His mother built a mud fireside (chulha) and the young Noor took great delight in trekking regularly to the nearby forest (backdam) to fetch dried wood for the fire.

> There was also no piped water, so it was the chore of the lad to fetch water from the village well for cooking and for drinking. The family stored water when it rained and that was used for bathing and washing dishes and clothes. There was no electricity. The family used kerosene oil lamps. When Noor attended primary school, he did his homework and read books beneath the low and flickering glow of such a lamp, pestered by mosquitoes.
>
> His primary education and books he read whetted his appetite to deeply engage himself in the pursuit of learning at higher levels and seek knowledge. At age fourteen, he graduated from grade school with the primary school certificate, as well as the gardening certificate. The delight he took in performing any menial task and his self-discipline under any condition, paved the path for that pursuit. And he chose the medical field as the destination on his journey of higher education. He proceeded to chart his destination. All that was left was to assiduously follow the chart.
>
> After primary school, the young, effervescent Noor, in pursuit of education and knowledge, elected to become a teacher. He obeyed his instinct and at the tender age of sixteen attained the Teacher's Appointment certificate and became a schoolteacher.

In 1958, just before his sixteenth birthday, he received the Guyana teacher's appointment certification. He then taught at his own school for the next six years. He taught history, geography, English language, English literature, and mathematics. Apart from formal teaching, he taught agriculture and carpentry after classes. This vocation opened the way for him to obtain a higher education.

Peter Halder continued:

> Noor never attended high school, as there was none in the entire county of Essequibo. During his teaching tenure, he studied privately, at home (through correspondence courses from England) and in 1963, sat the General Certificate of Education (University of London) examination as an external candidate. He passed in seven subjects (English language,

English literature, history, biology, mathematics, physics and chemistry), a unique achievement at that time in the then-British Guiana. He continued teaching until he was twenty-two years and rose to the rank of assistant headmaster at the very school where he had started in kindergarten ("Little ABC").

During Noor's teaching career, he was involved in farming, carpentry and engineering. He started as a member of the local 4-H club and became its president. He was also involved in the Young Farmers' Club. He had his students involved in many agricultural projects (e.g., gardening, cattle and poultry rearing, and fish farming). He was nominated by the Guyana government to run one of three national pilot projects and successfully did so in poultry rearing. The Henry Ford Foundation of America did a book documentary of agricultural activities in young people in Central and South America in 1960. Noor's fish-rearing project was the only item featured in this book for the British Guiana section.

Despite his busy teaching, studying and farming schedules, Noor found time to court the belle of his village and his next door neighbor, Sarah, to whom he became engaged just before leaving for England in 1964.

Noor's first step to gain admission to medical school was to pass the advanced level GCE in science subjects. For these, it was necessary to do "practicals," for which there were no facilities where he lived—indeed, anywhere in the country, except at a few colleges in Georgetown. He did the next best thing. He did all he could in Guyana and spent two years studying the theory parts of the science subjects before leaving for England.

In London, he enrolled at Tottenham Technical College, where he obtained the practical experience in zoology, chemistry and physics and passed the University of London GCE advanced level in these subjects in 1966. He also matriculated in the advanced English examination of the Joint Matriculation Board of the UK in the same year.

According to Peter Halder, Noor's "most important accomplishment that year was getting married to Sarah, who had now joined him in London. During 1966 and 1967, seeking to advance his medical learning and knowledge, Noor became a research assistant in electro-chemistry at

BEREC Research Laboratories in London and during 1967–1968, he was a research assistant in cancer pathology at St. Mary's Hospital in London. His research work expanded the horizon of his medical learning."

His professional training started with undergraduate studies in medicine and surgery at the University of Leeds, UK, 1968–1973, leading to his earning a MB ChB with honors. He pursued a postgraduate fellowship in epilepsy and stroke at the same university during 1974–1976, under the guidance of the internationally known Dr. Maurice J. Parsonage (of the Parsonage-Turner syndrome fame).

He obtained the Educational Commission for Foreign Medical Graduates certification in July 1974 and completed clinical residency in neurology at the University of Ottawa, Canada, 1976–1980, leading to Licentiate of the Medical Council of Canada (LMCC) in July 1978 and board certification, Fellow of the Royal College of Physicians of Canada -FRCP (C) in neurology in 1980. He then crossed the border and did postgraduate fellowship studies in movement disorders, under the tutelage of the world-renowned Dr. Stanley Fahn, as well as pharmacology at Columbia University, New York, 1980–1983. These studies led to the degrees MPhil (master's in pharmacology) in 1983 and PhD (doctorate in neuropharmacology) in 1984.

He obtained the diploma of the American Board of Psychiatry and Neurology in 2005. In 2009, he was honored with the Top Physicians in the USA award. His name was also entered as an honored member in Stanford's directory of *Who's Who*, which recognizes individuals for outstanding leadership or achievement in their industry, occupation, or profession. In January 2010, Dr. Hassan also received the Presidential Who's Who Membership Award, and a brief summary of his career/achievements will be lodged in the Library of Congress in Washington DC. In July 2010, he also received the Presidential Who's Who Neurologist of the Year award and his biography will be placed in the Library of Congress, Washington DC.

Dr. Hassan has held the following positions:

- Resident tenures in clinical neurology, neuropathology, electrophysiology, and general medicine at the University of Ottawa Teaching Hospitals
- Consultant neurologist, clinical pharmacologist, and clinical associate professor at the University of Ottawa, 1983–1999;

and Hartford Hospital and University of Connecticut, from 1999 to the present
- Founder/director of the Ottawa Parkinson's Disease Research Laboratory, 1983–1988, and the Movement Disorder Clinical and Research Facilities at the University of Connecticut, from 2000 to the present
- Principal investigator in movement disorder clinical research at the University of Connecticut and at Hartford Hospital, from 2000 to the present
- Served on the advisory panels of many international pharmaceutical companies regarding the development and laboratory/clinical testing of new drugs
- Trained speaker for many pharmaceutical companies with regard to clinical and pharmacological aspects of Parkinson's disease

He is currently consultant neurologist/principal investigator and associate professor at the University of Connecticut and Hartford Hospital, a position he's held since 1999. Dr. Hassan has the rare distinction of having served internationally as the Canadian member of neurological/Parkinson's delegations to China (1995) and Russia and Hungary (1997), and with his wife, as USA members of Gov. Bush's trade delegation to Canada (2004), regarding the pharmaceutical industry. He was clinical advisor to the government of Vietnam with regard to the construction of a new pharmaceutical plant in 1996–1997. He has been clinical advisor to the pharmaceutical industry, and physician education meeting moderator for Pfizer, Boehringer-Ingelheim, Glaxo-Smith-Klein, Novartis, and TEVA, from 1983 to the present.

His work includes writing for over one hundred publications in medical and scientific journals and books in Europe, Canada, and the United States, and over four hundred presentations at universities, hospitals, and scientific meetings in Canada, the United States, Europe, Asia, Africa, the Middle East, Central America, and the Caribbean.

Dr. Hassan has to his credit a number of audio-visual productions, including the videotapes *Promise for Parkinson's* (1981), *Current Research in Parkinson's Disease* (1983), and *Common Movement Disorders* (1993), as well as the audiotape *Clinical Management Review of Parkinson's Disease* (1992).

When asked how he decided to devote his life to medicine, Dr. Hassan has said:

> As a teenager, I had firmly made up my mind to study medicine. I was driven by the deaths of my brother in infancy, my mother in the prime of her life, when I was eight years old, an aunt in her twenties, and many children whom I had taught. I did not feel that sufficiently good reasons were given for these deaths, other than "their time had come." I vowed to try to make a difference. During my medical school days, I retrospectively diagnosed the causes of death in most cases, and realized that better medical knowledge and better medicines could have saved most of those who had died prematurely. I chose to specialize in neurology, as this field is logical, and diagnoses are made from facts and not just by "gut feeling."
>
> I drew my inspirations from my grandparents, parents, uncles, and aunts, school friends, students, my wife, my own children, and all the folks around me. In particular, my grandfather, Sheik Abdul Hamid, taught me to listen and learn from all the people who I deal with in everyday life. My father's cousin, Fizul Karim, distinguished himself as a flight lieutenant in the Royal Air Force during World War II. My father's brother, Dr. Mohamed Shahabuddeen, rapidly moved up from a practicing lawyer in Essequibo Coast to the attorney general of Guyana, and then on to become a judge at the International Court of Justice at the Hague. Dr. Shahabuddeen wrote *The Legal System of Guyana* and *Constitutional Development in Guyana*.
>
> I was also inspired by the discoveries of the giants in the field of medicine. For example, Louis Pasteur, the pasteurization of milk to prevent TB; Sir Alexander Fleming, the discoverer of penicillin—and I had the opportunity to work in the Wright-Fleming Institute at St. Mary's Hospital in London; Banting and Best, use of insulin in diabetes; Marie Curie's work, which led to the use of irradiation for the treatment of cancer; and Florence Nightingale, the start of modern nursing.

Dr. Hassan was also influenced by writers (Shakespeare, Milton, Byron), philosophers (Aristotle, Plato, Confucius), and freedom fighters (Gandhi,

Mandella, Martin Luther King). "These people all gave unselfishly of themselves to make the world a better and safer place for us to live in," he said. "I feel that we can pay tribute to these men and women by following in their footsteps."

Dr. Hassan has tried to live by following the opening lines of one of Prof. Rabindranath Tagore's poems:

> Where the mind is without fear
> And the head is held high
> Where knowledge is free

Dr. Hassan is driven by the belief that good health and knowledge were granted by a merciful God, not for personal gains but for the benefit of all humanity.

Among numerous highlights in his life, Dr. Hassan points to a "teaching career starting before I was sixteen years of age; marriage to Sarah, my childhood sweetheart and next-door neighbor; the birth of our two children; graduation from Leeds University with honors degrees; completion of my master's and PhD degrees at Columbia University in two years; the opportunities to be the founder of clinical and research facilities in Ottawa, Canada, and in Hartford, Connecticut, and the honor and privilege of being invited to lecture and teach and treat patients in so many parts of the world."

Proud of his teaching career, Dr. Hassan says, "Once a teacher, always a teacher." Many of the students he taught in Guyana have graduated from universities in the UK, Canada, and the United States. He has also trained dozens of neurology residents, and some are practicing in Canada or the United States, and many have returned to their own countries.

Dr. Hassan's wife, Sarah, studied at home and earned diplomas in economic history (UK) and business administration (UK, Canada, and USA). She is the president of her own company, United States Medical and Pharmaceutical Supplies Inc., which registers medical products manufactured in the United States, Canada, or overseas with the Food and Drug Administration of the United States. She had previously worked for sixteen years at Health Canada in Ottawa. Her company also obtains medical and surgical supplies for underdeveloped countries on a nonprofit basis.

Their two children are son Shareef and daughter Farah. Shareef has a bachelor's in international business and a master's in engineering technology. He lives and works in Nicaragua. Daughter Farah has a bachelor's in psychology and a master's in business administration. She lives and works in Escondido, California. Sarah and Dr. Hassan consider both children as God's supreme gifts.

Dr. Hassan has many hobbies, which he started in his teenage years in Guyana. He was a member, then president of the local 4-H Club. As a teacher, he realized that many of his students would not become academic but still needed to be taught skills that would be useful to them. He instituted self-help programs for carpentry and agriculture.

He taught modern methods and diversification in farming, after completing training himself at the Agricultural Station in Mon Repos, East Coast Demerara. He was nominated by the Guyana government to run a poultry project, which he had started as an example to Guyanese poultry rearers. He reached across the country with the weekly radio program *Farmers' Diary*.

He learned engineering from his father. Today, he uses all these skills. He does all the carpentry required in his home, and he does all necessary car repairs. He also has a large vegetable garden and six flower gardens around his house. Each flower garden is dedicated to someone who had made an impact in his life. He has also built gardens for relatives and friends in other parts of the United States, the Caribbean, and Central America.

Dr. Hassan completed a book of poetry during his teaching career in Guyana. He has also written a series of short stories and is in the process of writing his memoir. He and his wife are proud to say that they have never lost a friend around the world, other than through death.

Dr. Hassan has always reminded the younger generations that nothing is impossible and the sky is the limit. He has encouraged them to firmly set their goals and not to waver. These goals may be surrounded by many obstacles. Be persistent and chip away at them, and you get closer and closer to your goals. Mankind is imbued with tremendous potential, but first you have to find your own potential. Things which were previously considered impossible have been achieved: Hilary and Tensing climbed Mount Everest, Sir Francis Chichester sailed solo around the world in a small yacht, men journeyed to the moon, and single individuals have brought changes to entire nations and the world. They did not only dream, but they followed their dreams.

Peter Halder, in his conclusion to the foreword of Dr. Hassan's autobiography, writes:

> Dr. Hassan dreamed dreams as a lad growing up in Essequibo.
> He aspired to a distinguished career in the field of medicine.

But not in his wildest dreams did he conceive that he would achieve what he has achieved or attain the heights he has attained. And his ambitions are not yet finished. He has not retired. His sail is still raised. While there is a breath of life in him, he will continue to pursue the ultimate in his field in medicine for the benefit of mankind. The native son of the tiny village of Middlesex in Essequibo has achieved eminence and acclaim in the field of medicine in many parts of the world.

Based on his life's experience, Dr. Hassan has always taught his children and friends these simple sayings:

- Every day is a blessing.
- Life is for living.
- Turn adversity into an opportunity.
- The bigger the challenge, the greater the satisfaction.
- You can never find time; you simply have to make it.
- Freely give bread to the hungry; it will come back with butter and jam.
- What goes around, comes around.

August 22, 2010.

Dr. Arthur Ingram Hazlewood

BS, DDS, MPH
Dentist, Administrator, Consultant Educator

Dr, Hazlewood, a practicing dentist for over forty years, is chairman emeritus of the department of dentistry at Our Lady of Mercy Medical Center, the Bronx, New York. There, he developed new initiatives to enhance the delivery of dental care to the community. At that center Dr. Hazlewood was elected the first and only dentist to be awarded the title of Physician of the Year.

He has served at the highest echelons in his profession. Dr. Hazlewood has represented the best of dentistry, beyond the profession and in many areas of the world. He has devoted his entire professional career to bettering the lives of others.

Arthur Ingram Hazlewood was born on May 14, 1934, at New Amsterdam, Guyana. After successfully completing his education at Queen's College, Guyana, he entered Howard University to study dentistry. In 1957, he obtained his BS degree and in 1962, his DDS. This was followed by a one-year general dentistry internship, then a two-year prosthetic dentistry residency and the certificate in quality improvement process management. He obtained his residency training in prosthetic dentistry at Sea View Hospital in New York and the Jewish Chronic Disease Hospital in New York.

Dr. Hazlewood, a practicing dentist since 1962, is licensed to practice dentistry in the states of New York and Massachusetts. In 1965 he started his private dental practice and continued the practice until 1999.

In addition to his training in dentistry, he obtained a master's degree in public health, MPH from Columbia University in 1968 and has also completed course work for a master of science in international organization. Over the years he has pursued many continuing education courses, one of which culminated in 1986 in the advanced certificate for the chiefs of services at Harvard University School of Public Health.

Ever since he qualified as a dentist, he has sought to employ his knowledge and skills in the service of the wider community.

In 1968 Dr. Hazlewood accepted an appointment to serve as Assistant Commissioner of Health for the Nassau County Health Department.

He then went on to serve as director of the Bureau of Health Care Administration for Nassau County. In that position Dr. Hazlewood was instrumental in establishing the department's outreach programs. He initiated and implemented the conversion of the Health Department's preventive services to a program of comprehensive ambulatory care. He is to be recognized for his accomplishments and achievements in the area of ambulatory care services.

Serving as cochairman of the Nassau County Health Department's planning committee, he assisted with the development of the county's first neighborhood health center. The center's educational preventive and treatment programs were developed through his leadership.

The combination of timing and personal preparation has created the opportunity for his seminal participation in shaping a variety of important professional initiatives. For example, in the 1970s, there was the opportunity to be a member of the faculty that developed a branch of the New York Dental School and to play a leadership role in the development of contemporary ambulatory care facilities and services.

Dr. Hazlewood served as a member of the advisory task force to the governor of New York as the state attempted to solve access problems that beset the underserved population.

He has had the responsibility to direct and oversee staffing development for two major teaching hospitals in New York, as well as other major ambulatory facilities operated by the New York City Health and Hospitals Corporation.

In 1973, he was appointed Director of Program Planning and Development for the NYC Health and Hospitals Corp. There, he brought together several task forces on ambulatory care and successfully developed plans to save clinic programs in the New York City Municipal Hospital System from closure.

He was appointed by the NYC Health and Hospitals Corp. to coordinate the new facilities budget, which allocated funds to develop hospitals and neighborhood health centers. His contributions were seminal in the development of New York City Health Services under the NYC Health and Hospitals Corp.

In 1976 Dr. Hazlewood was also appointed the first Director of Dental Affairs for the NYC Health and Hospitals Corp. He held these two positions until 1978.

Among his most important accomplishments are his providing leadership in activities that maintained the presence and preserved the integrity of the hospital as a location for dental post-doctoral training and service.

From 1979 to 1983, Dr. Hazlewood served either as medical director or leader of the medical staff at Morrisania Family Care Center and Our Lady of Mercy Medical Center, the Bronx, NY, and director, Professional Affairs, Morrisania Neighborhood Family Care Center. At Misericordia/Morrisania NFCC, he was responsible for all professional services within the ambulatory center. From 1983 to 1999 he held the position of chairman, Department of Dentistry, Our Lady of Mercy Medical Center.

In 1999 Dr. Hazlewood retired as chairman of the Department of Dentistry from Our Lady of Mercy Medical Center and holds the title of doctor emeritus. He is attending dentist, Jamaica Hospital & Medical Center, a position he began in 2003. He now spends his energy in consulting. He uses his vast experience to advise and lead dental departments in program planning.

Dr. Hazlewood has taken a leading role in promoting education in the areas of health services and programs for inner cities in the United States and in other countries around the world, notably initiating the reform of the Guyana national dental plan in 1990.

He has served as consultant and educator at a wide range of organizations, which include the American Public Health Association, the Caribbean Women's Health Association, the Health Volunteers Overseas Steering Committee, and the United Nations Development Program for the Government of Guyana. He created a national oral health care plan for the government of Guyana. He also served as special advisor to the Minister of Health in the development of the Cheddi Jagan National Dental Center.

Dr. Hazlewood has lent his concern and energy to such organizations as Daytop Village Inc., an international therapeutic drug rehabilitation organization.

In academic areas, Dr. Hazlewood is an adjunct professor of community and preventive medicine at the New York Medical College and was a founding faculty member/lecturer at the State University of New York at Stony Brook. He was also a thesis advisor for Columbia University's School of Public Health. He is a passionate defender of education and the pursuit of education for all individuals and served on the Fellowship Council of the American Association of Hospital Dentists.

Dr. Hazlewood devotes a large portion of his time and energies to developing and implementing plans to advance teaching hospital programs and their residency programs. He has a long-standing interest in the continued growth and expansion of successful dental and residency programs nationwide. Within the confines of highly regarded teaching hospitals, Dr. Hazlewood directed and implemented action plans to develop all of the medical support and administrative programs for two new hospitals. He later created and established a formal hospital planning process for a major teaching hospital that included all control systems and documentation. Subsequently, as a member of American Dental Association Commission on Accreditation, he helped develop the accreditation standards and guidelines for hospital training programs.

He has served as consultant to the medical profession, the private business sector, and the government. Some of his independent consulting activities have included working with the US Department of Health and Human Services and the National Institutes of Health, focusing on the evaluation of administrative organization and structure in both the sickle cell and dental grant programs and, with the DHHS, in setting the guidelines for the AIDS dental reimbursement program.

Dr. Hazlewood served as consultant on dental care programs for the Robert Wood Johnson Foundation, evaluating the organization and administration of grantee hospitals. In 1979 he was appointed a member of the New York State Governor's Task Force on Dental Health Policy, which addressed the issues of access and which achieved changes in the state's Medicaid program.

He was also appointed US delegate at the African/African American Summit in the African nations of Senegal in 1995, Zimbabwe in 1997, and Ghana in 1999.

Since his retirement from Our Lady of Mercy Medical Center, he continues to be active in a number of areas, such as assisting hospitals prepare for accreditation and in program development; serving two years on the steering committee of the American Dental Association/Health Volunteers overseas; as well as being cochairman of the Dental Academy of the National Academies of Practice, a national interdisciplinary organization, and in assisting Columbia University School of Dental Medicine in its minority recruitment efforts.

He has served on the Committee of Fellowship of the American Association of Hospital Dentists and has recently been elected treasurer of the National Academies of Practice. Dr. Hazlewood also serves as an associate on the Council of Public Representatives, an advisory council to the director of the National Institutes of Health. Dr. Hazlewood's wide-ranging activities include service as a trustee of Daytop Village

Incorporated, an internationally famous drug treatment organization. As of this writing, he serves as the vice chairman of the board of trustees.

Dr. Hazlewood is a skilled writer, experienced in grant preparation, grant reviews, position papers, and other management report writing. He has authored a number of articles dealing with management issues, dating back to the first published dental article (1970) describing the dentist's role in child abuse detection.

Subsequently, he has authored articles on the topic of financial management and graduate medical education funding. He is a contributing author to the textbook *Hospital Dentistry Practice and Education* and has authored several general consultancy reports. He has also published articles on international programs, including the principles of volunteerism and on oral health in Cuba. Most recently, he authored a book titled *Handbook of Essential Information for Hospital Dental Leaders* (published by iUniverse, December 2007).

Dr. Hazlewood has been consultant to numerous governments and organizations, including the Guyana government's Ministry of Health, Government of Ghana Ministry of Health/Dental School, Government of Barbados Ministry of Health, Republic of Haiti Albert Schweitzer Hospital, New Jersey Jamaica Hospital, Queens New York Peninsula Hospital, Robert Wood Johnson Foundation, United Nations Development Program, and the Hamilton Dental Society Ontario, Canada.

His memberships in professional associations include the American Dental Association, the New York State Dental Association, the American Association of Hospital Dentists, the American College of Dentists, and the New York Academy of Dentistry. He is a past chairman of the New York section of the College of Dentistry and cochairman of the National Academies of Practice.

He has held high-level positions in the field of dentistry, including chairman of the board, American Association of Hospital Dentists; president, American Association of Hospital Dentists; regional vice president, American Association of Hospital Dentistry; member, Board of Governors, Special Care Organization in Dentistry; chairman, Medical Directors Committee, Our Lady of Mercy Hospital Center; member, American Dental Association, Health Volunteers Steering Committee; member, Executive Committee, Columbia University School of Public Health Alumni Association; chair, American College of Dentists, New York Section; member, Governing Council National Academies of Practice; cochairman, National Academy of Practice (Dental); member,

Fellowship Council, American Association of Hospital Dentists; special advisor, Ministry of Health (Guyana); advisor to private industry; member, Advisory Committee, Commission on Dental Accreditation, American Dental Association; treasurer, National Academies of Practice; and member, Governor's Advisory Task Force (NY).

Dr. Hazelwood's tireless efforts over the years attest to his commitment to serving health care needs and improving the lives of the less fortunate throughout the world. For his efforts, he received the Award of Distinction from the Academy of Dentistry International and the Distinguished Alumnus Award from Howard University College of Dentistry. The American Association of Hospital Dentists presented its highest award, the Lawrence Chasko Award for Distinguished Service in hospital dentistry, to Dr. Hazlewood. He also received the Distinguished Service Award from the American College of Dentists.

In 1996 he was inducted as a distinguished fellow in the National Academies of Practice, a national interdisciplinary organization. Having formerly served as treasurer, Dr. Hazlewood is president elect of that organization as of this writing. Other awards include honorary fellow, Academy of Dentistry International; fellow, New York Academy of Dentistry; Humanitarian and Service Award, Guyana Mission, Consulate, and Tristate Alliance; and several community service awards.

It is noteworthy that his broad knowledge of health affairs resulted in the privilege of serving as chairman of candidate Jimmy Carter's Health Affairs Committee during the primary election season in 1976.

Dr. Hazlewood has been a devoted fan of tennis and travels annually to one or other of the Grand Slams. His other hobbies are traveling, reading, and enjoying jazz music.

He is married to Paula Matthews Hazlewood. They live in Brooklyn, New York. The couple has two grown sons.

Dr. Arthur Ingram Hazlewood has given his all to his profession. He has used his education and personal achievements to make significant contributions to his profession, dentistry, and to the communities he has served.

He has reaped rich rewards personally and has bettered the life of many through the improvements he initiated wherever he served. He continues to serve at the highest levels, to better the practice of dentistry and dental care to people of all walks of life worldwide. His family and Guyanese all must feel great pride and celebrate his sterling achievements.

July 8, 2008

Paula Matthews Hazlewood

BA, MA
Educator and Artist

Paula Matthews Hazlewood was born in December 1933 in Georgetown, British Guiana. She is the daughter of the Rev. Patrick Alleyne Matthews and Una Inez Hendricks Matthews and sister of Marc Matthews.

Paula's earliest years were spent in Buxton, where her father was the pastor of Arundel Congregational Church. It is from her parents and the advantage of a privileged environment that Paula Hazlewood learned the tenets of her life. She learned that privilege carried responsibility, that the highest service one can render is to aid one's fellow human, and to follow the commandment of Jesus that we love one another.

Her earliest education was obtained in British Guiana. Paula attended Buxton Congregational School, Smith Church School, and Scott School, New Amsterdam, from which she received the Berbice scholarship to Bishops' High School, Georgetown. At Bishops's he completed her ordinary and advanced level certificates.

In 1953 her education continued in the United States at Wellesley College, Massachusetts, where in 1957 she earned a bachelor of arts (BA) degree, with a major in art history and studio. At Wellesley she participated in many clubs and served as chairman of the chapel organization. Being the first student to come from British Guiana (Guyana), she became an "ambassador," representing her country, its culture, and its history. She then attended Boston University Graduate School, Massachusetts, where she obtained a master of arts (MA) degree in 1958.

Having completed her graduate degree, Paula remained in the United States and became a US citizen. Believing that she could contribute best to society, Paula chose to be a teacher of early childhood and elementary children. Her choice was motivated by the desire to impart knowledge and influence young people to become productive, intelligent members of their communities. She joined the teaching staff in the New York City Public School System.

As a teacher her talents and skills were used to encourage students to express themselves through creative writing and art as they pursued their academic experiences. Paula holds certificates in many subject areas, including Spanish fluency, literary instruction, math enrichment, and art programming in elementary schools.

Paula retired after twenty-seven years, having served as elementary classroom teacher, teacher trainer, Title 1 specialist in reading and math, and parent-child instructor in the Even Start program, where she helped develop curriculum for enabling immigrant parents' participation in the education of children ages four through seven years.

In retirement, she was appointed assistant director, teacher trainer in a universal pre-kindergarten program at Bambi Day Care Center, Brooklyn, New York. Her responsibilities included program planning, teacher guidance, and parents' participation. Paula was also employed by the United Federation of Teachers Retired Teachers (Brooklyn Center) as instructor in painting. She is also facilitator of creative writing at Blenman Senior Center in Brooklyn, New York and Marble Collegiate Church in Manhattan.

Her most recent accomplishment is the completion and publication of *When We Grew Up in the Land of the Mighty Roraima*, published by Xlibris in 2007. It is coauthored with Claire Martin-Combs and is a compilation of memories culled from 1940s to 1950s. Its uniqueness lies in the structure of the memoir, which combines memories of Guyana's traditional holiday celebrations, culture, and cuisine related to them.

The book is meant to be a mirror of the past for young expatriates, as well as people wishing to learn about culture in the colonial period in Guyana. The authors have managed to give a genealogical study of their ancestry and issues surrounding their childhood. The authors hope that the memoir will also encourage others to record their own experiences and memories of their heritage.

Paula is a past president of Guyanese United Church Women in America (Brooklyn chapter), whose aim and mission is to help members adapt to life in the United States and to provide assistance (financial and spiritual) to the Guyanese Church Women chapter in Guyana. Their meetings provide an occasion to relax in a friendly ambience and share ideas and memories.

She was founder of the Bishops' High School (Guyana) New York Tri-State Alumni Chapter. Her hobbies are reading, traveling, painting, and writing. Her passion for art, which began in high school, remains with her. As an artist, she has exhibited in shows in the New York area.

She continues to serve her community through charitable contributions to organizations such as Christian Help in Park Slope (a Catholic welfare organization), the Salvation Army, and Meals on Wheels, organizations that strive to feed the hungry, clothe the naked, and provide shelter for the homeless. Paula is a public speaker whose topics include racism and its effect on community and biblical themes. She volunteers her time and talents at senior centers.

Paula Hazlewood says,
> Throughout my life I have been motivated by the wish to see others thrive. As an elementary school teacher, it was my joy to see students become enthusiastic and curious about subject matter. As a facilitator of art workshops, observing the gleam in participants' eyes when they completed their first painting gave me great pleasure and encouragement. As a writer myself, I find satisfaction in leading creative writing workshops and encouraging senior citizens to record their stories.
>
> Many persons influenced my career and life. My parents laid the foundation for my "growing up" and started me on my spiritual journey. The late Rev. Pat and Rev. Una Matthews supported all my endeavors. Rev. Pat Matthews (1900–1979) was a distinguished Congregational minister, orator, and missionary: He served the denomination until his passing in 1979 at Mission Chapel, New Amsterdam, Berbice.

Paula Matthews Hazlewood's mother, the Rev. Una Hendricks Matthews (1911–2000) combined a number of careers in her lifetime: helpmate to the Rev. Pat, social worker, radio announcer, and newspaper reporter. During her pastorate at Mission Chapel Congregational Church, New Amsterdam, Berbice, she served the Congregational Union as its first woman president.

Paula has said, "I share the artistic, creative temperament with my brother, Marc." Marc Matthews is a scholar, poet, educator, and actor. He was educated at Queen's College, Georgetown. He was the first winner of the Guyana Prize for Poetry. Marc Matthews's poetry is included in several Caribbean anthologies. Paula continues:

> In the professional field I owe a debt to my senior mentor teacher, Mrs. Glotherine Everrett, and my principal, the late Sophie Beller. To my ministers and church fellowship much thanks is due as I move along on my faith journey.

My husband, A. Ingram Hazlewood, DDS, supported my projects and gave constructive criticism over the years. He was a great influence—and continues to be—in my life; to him I am most deeply grateful.

Paula lives with her husband in Crown Heights, Brooklyn, New York. They have two grown sons.

August 31, 2010

Dr. Walter Hewick

BA, AphS, Med, MA, LittD, PhD
Psychology Professor

Dr. Walter Hewick, now a psychologist in private practice, was a principal and teacher at SDA Elementary Schools in Guyana in his early years. He was a CID officer in the Guyana Police Force, Special Branch. In the United States, he taught English and American literature at the American, Howard Universities, and Essex College and Prince George's Community College before finding his niche in the field of psychology, acquiring numerous higher degrees and playing a leading role in academia and many learned societies.

Walter was born on March 12, 1930, at Kiltern Village, Corentyne, Berbice, British Guiana, where he spent his formative years. He received his early education at Eversham Primary School and secondary education at Skeldon High School. Later, he emigrated to the United States to further his studies.

Walter was married twice. His first wife (now deceased) was Philomena D'Agrella, a Portuguese nurse-midwife, and his second wife's is Jaiseong

Cho, a South Korean medical doctor. Walter has four sons from his first marriage, all professional men.

Walter is one of ten siblings—six brothers and four sisters. Four brothers are businessmen and farmers; brother Norman, sister Sue, and Walter are college graduates.

Walter's father was Joseph Bhola, now deceased. Walter's mother was a homemaker. Joseph Bhola came to British Guiana in 1895 on the SS *Ganges*. He was a bookkeeper. Joseph was an Anglo-Indian, born in Malaka, in Allahabad, Uttar Pradesh, in North India. He was the son of John Edwin Hewick, and Gulbi, an Indian brahmin, of Malaka, Allahabad, India.

John Hewick, Walter's grandfather, was born in Calcutta, India, to English parents, who were merchants. He was educated in India and later went to London, where he finished high school and in 1887, he was admitted to Middle Temple, where he studied law and was called to the bar in 1880. Later, Queen Victoria sent him on several foreign assignments, to India, Singapore, Malaysia, and to British Guiana. In British Guiana he became the colony's first senior criminal puisne judge and then chief justice. He retired to Cliff Cottage, Dorset, England, in the 1920s.

Walter lectured and contributed widely as a consultant on psychology, counseling, psychopathology, personality and human behavior, child development, cognition and learning, human growth and development, and theories of marriage and family systems.

Walter has been steeped in academic work for most of his life and acquired a formidable list of academic and professional qualifications. Among these are: Fellow of the Royal Geographical Society, FRGS (London), Fellow of the Royal Geographical Society, FRGS (London),

- AA, Caribbean Training (now University of Southern Caribbean), specialty: elementary education, BA.
- Lincoln University, Pennsylvania, specialty: English
- APhS (London), specialty: philosophy
- MEd, the American University, specialty: educational administration. Thesis: "The Legislative Influences on Education in Guyana"
- MA, Howard University, specialty: English. Thesis: "An Analysis of Jack London's Naturalism"
- LittD, Stanton University (*Honoris Causa*), specialty: English literature

- PhD, California Coast University, California, specialty: clinical psychology. Dissertation: "The Incidence of Attention Deficit Disorder Symptoms in African American Inner City Children as Reported by Teachers and Parents"
- PhD, the American University, specialty: educational administration and supervision, minor: educational psychology, post-doctoral concentration: special education, post-doctoral: counseling psychology dissertation: "A Study to Compare the Effectiveness of the Differential Aptitude Tests and the Adapted Guyanese Tests for Identifying Aptitudes Among Students in Guyanese Secondary Schools."

The following are excerpts from his catalog of achievements:

Graduate and undergraduate courses taught:

English novel, poetry and prose, American realism, "Frontier in American Literature," "Structure of Present-Day English," Caroline & Jacobean literature, "Literary Research and American Romanticism."

Undergraduate English courses taken include English literature, seventeenth and eighteenth century literature, nineteenth century poetry and prose, American literature, Shakespeare.

Courses on special education include:
- Psychology of Exceptional Children
- Supervision of Student Teaching
- The Gifted, Child Development and Behavior
- Career Education for the Handicapped
- Classroom Management
- Learning Disabilities
- Mental Retardation
- Specific Learning Disabilities, Diagnostic and Prescriptive Teaching
- Survey of Exceptional Children.

He taught courses in education administration and supervision, including Children and Youth in the Urban Schools, School Law, Administrative Behavior in Schools, School Administration (Elem.), Educational Research, Statistics for Applied Research Design and Education, Politics in Higher Education, Higher Education and the

Courts, Education Policy and the Law, Finance and Economics in Higher Education, and Learning and Learning Theories.

Among graduate and undergraduate courses taught on psychology, counseling, and mental health are:
- Social Research
- Psychological Report Writing
- Interpretations of Psychological Tests
- Measurement and Evaluation
- General Psychology
- Psychopathology
- Personality and Human Behavior
- Group Counseling
- Family Counseling
- Child Development
- Cognition and Learning
- Practicum: Counseling and Mental Health
- Personality Adjustment
- Human Growth and Development
- Educational Psychology
- History and Systems of Psychology
- Personality Theory
- Abnormal Psychology
- Counseling Psychology
- Organizational Psychology
- Social Psychology
- Human Growth and Development
- Human Sexuality
- Theories of Marriage and Family Systems

Walter's professional career started in 1952 when he was Principal and teacher in Elementary Schools, in Guyana and from 1954 to1958 he was in the Criminal Investigation Department of the Guyana Police Force, Special Branch.

In the United States, from 1966 he was Instructor of English (part-time), at American University, Washington DC. He then moved on to Instructor of English, Howard University, Washington DC. In 1969 he was appointed Assistant professor of English, Essex Community College,

Essex, Maryland, then Assistant professor of English, (part-time), Towson Police Academy, Maryland.

His other appointments include the following:

Dean, Evening School Services, Federal City College, Washington DC.
Associate provost and vice president for Academic Affairs (acting), Federal City College, Washington DC.
Coordinator, secondary student teachers, Bowie State University, Maryland.
Chairman and professor, Department of Psychology and Special Education, District of Columbia Teachers College, Washington DC.
Lecturer of English, part-time, Prince George's Community College, Largo, Maryland.
Part-time chief counselor, Counseling and Psychotherapy Clinic, Bowie, Maryland
Adjunct professor, English and psychology, Prince George's Community College, Largo, Maryland. Adjunct professor, Union Graduate Institute.
Professor of Education and Human Ecology; Chairman and professor, Department of Human Resource Development, College of Education; and Professor, College of Arts and Sciences, University of the District of Columbia, Washington DC.

His Research work and Seminars include:

Research: "A Study to Compare the Effectiveness of the Differential Aptitude Tests and the Adapted Guyanese Tests for Identifying Aptitudes Among Students in Guyanese Secondary Schools."
Address: "The Cultural Background and Curriculum Development of the Caribbean Area," the National Association for Students' Affairs, Georgetown University.
Moderator: "Implementation of 504 Regulations for the Handicapped," Region III workshop, American Association for Affirmative Action, Washington DC.
Address: "Encouraging the Gifted and Talented in Our Schools," DC Association for Specialists in Group Work, Martin Luther King Library, Washington DC.

Research: "The Incidence of Attention Deficit Disorder Symptoms in African American Inner City Children as Reported by Teachers and Parents," Washington DC.

Walter's Publications include:

"Use of Behavior Modification in Exceptional Children's Needs." Mamie D. Lee Elementary School for the Handicapped, Washington DC. 1977.
"Is Your Child Gifted?" *Medical News*, Vol. 1, 73. 1997.
"Christ in Crisis." The American Academy of Crisis Interveners. 1990.
"It's Not Just the Child Who Suffers from Attention Deficit Disorder." *Medical News,* Vol. 1, L111. 1995.
Against the Odds. Xlibris, PA. 2002.
A Post-Slavery Nightmare. Author House. 2005.
Write On. Xlibris, PA, 2009.
A Village Chronicle. A collection of short stories (incidents).
In progress. Writing the Bhola-Hewick family history.

His membership of professional societies include:-

Fellow and Diplomate of the American Board of Medical Psychotherapists.
Fellow of the American Association of Integrative Medicine
Fellow of the American Board of Pain Management
Diplomate of the College of Mental Health
Diplomate of the American Academy of Crisis Interveners
Diplomate of the American Board of Forensic Examiners
Member of the American Psychological Association
Member of the Association for the Advancement of Behavior Therapy
Member, Maryland Association for Counseling and Development
Member, the American Board of Forensic Examiners.

Awards received include

1971. Award: Certificate of Merit for Distinguished Service in Education Proclaimed Throughout the World, London.
1973. Honored in 'Men of Achievement'.
1975. Award: Appeared in 'Community Leaders and Noteworthy Americans.

1976. Award: Appeared in *International Who's Who in North America*.
1980. From the Hon. Mayor Marion Barry, Washington DC: Certificate of Appreciation. Meritorious Public Service Award.
Proclamation for the Institute for the Gifted and Talented, Inc.
Awarded Certificate of Merit (London) proclaimed throughout the world for distinguished service in education and mentioned in the *International Biography*.

Walter's philosophy is "If you keep focused and work hard, you can accomplish your realistic goals in life. My parents played a significant role in my success and of course, a strong faith in God to help me through the hurdles. To emphasize: parental expectation was a driving force in my life."

Walter visited India in 2001, a vastly different world to the one of the days of British rule. That visit was very special for Walter. He has said:

> It was the most rewarding experience in my life. The people, the scenes, etc., were most exhilarating. To cap it off, I found my father's birthplace (in Allahabad) and what an emotional moment. It was beyond the senses and emotions. I walked where my father walked, and I walked where Nehru walked. I visited his home (in Allahabad) and walked also where Gandhi walked while visiting Nehru. Oh, I'll never forget those moments! I took about four hundred pictures, and they are a treasure in my library. Hope to visit again sometime soon.

November 4, 2010

Dr. Percy C. Hintzen

BSocSc, MA, MPhil, PhD
Professor, African American Studies
University of California, Berkeley

Dr. Percy Hintzen, professor of African Diaspora Studies at the University of California, Berkeley, holds a PhD from Yale University in comparative political sociology. In addition to his PhD, he also holds MPhil and MA degrees from Yale and an MA degree from Clark University in Worcester, Massachusetts, the latter in international urbanization and public policy. His MA thesis at Clark was a study of Guyana's four urban areas and the relationship between urbanization and racial integration.

One of his principal areas of research has been political and economic development of Guyana and Trinidad and the post-colonial political economy of the English-speaking Caribbean. He later added to this field of inquiry the study of West Indian immigrants to the United States. His current research engages with the role of race in the formulation modernity and the modern world through the lens of the African diaspora.

His services as a consultant and commentator are frequently requested on issues pertaining to Guyana, to the West Indies, and to the post-colonial political economies of countries of the global south by media (newspapers, television, and radio) where his commentaries appear.

He has served in a consulting capacity for many institutions in Guyana and the Caribbean. He has served as president of the Caribbean Studies Association, the premier and most important association for scholars working on the Caribbean (including Central and South America). He assumed the role as president of the organization in May 2006 after serving as vice president since May 2005. Prior to his election to this position, he served on two occasions as a member of its Executive Council. He also served as a member of the Executive Committee of the Cultural Studies Association (the international organization for cultural studies scholars) between 2008 and 2010.

Percy secured a place at the University of Guyana, and in 1973 he obtained his first degree, bachelor of social science (BSocSc). He then proceeded to study for his master's degree at Clark University, Worcester,

Massachusetts, and obtained his MA in international urbanization and public policy in 1975.

Percy then attended Yale University, New Haven, Connecticut. In 1977, he obtained another MA degree in sociology. In tandem with this degree, Percy studied for and was awarded the master of philosophy (MPhil) degree in comparative social change in the same year. Percy continued with higher studies and in 1981, he was awarded his PhD in political sociology and comparative social change from Yale.

After obtaining his BSocSc degree from the University of Guyana, Percy embarked on a teaching career while studying for higher degrees. He held the following teaching positions:

Spring 1974–Spring 1975. Teaching assistant, Department of Government and International Relations, Clark University.
Fall 1976. Teaching fellow, Department of Sociology, Yale University.
1977–1978. Lecturer, Department of Sociology, University of Guyana.
Spring 1979. Acting instructor, Department of Sociology, Yale University.
1977–1985. Assistant professor, Department of Afro-American Studies, University of California, Berkeley.
1985–2001. Associate professor with tenure, Department of African American Studies,
University of California, Berkeley.
1993–1994. Visiting professor, Faculty of Social Sciences, University of Guyana.
2002–present. Professor, Department of African American Studies. University of California, Berkeley.

Professor Hintzen authored what is considered to be one of the most significant and authoritative books on the racial politics in Guyana and Trinidad, titled *The Costs of Regime Survival: Racial mobilization, elite domination and control of the state in Guyana and Trinidad*. The book looks at the functioning of political elites and the strategies employed, such as racial mobilization, to gain and maintain control of the state in Guyana and Trinidad.

He also authored a book on West Indian immigrants to the United States, titled *West Indians in the West: Self-representations in an immigrant community*. The book deals significantly with West Indian immigrants of black and Asian descent, many of whom come from Guyana.

He edited a volume on black immigrants to the United States, titled *Problematizing Blackness: Self ethnographies by black immigrants to the United States.* Both volumes look at the way immigrants insert themselves into the United States and how they engage with issues of race.

He is coeditor of a recent volume, *Global Circuits of Blackness: Interrogating the African diaspora*, which engages with theoretical, conceptual, and analytical issues related to the African diasporic formations.

He has authored over forty articles in journals and chapters in edited volumes on the political economy of the Caribbean (with many focused on Guyana), on West Indian immigration to the United States, and on issues of race and ethnicity in the Caribbean, Africa, and the United States. He has presented close to one hundred papers at conferences and other forums on Guyana, the Caribbean, race and ethnicity, and political economy.

Percy has returned frequently to Guyana to conduct research, to teach at the University of Guyana, to present papers, to advise and consult, to visit family, and to conduct family business. He also occasionally publishes opinions pieces in the local media and participates in the country's radio and television programs. He maintains frequent contact with government officials, with officials from all the major parties, and with scholars and academics in the country. He also maintains contact with the Guyanese embassy in Washington DC.

In addition to his teaching positions, this distinguished, top-ranking academic has held numerous positions of high responsibility authority and influence.

His professional positions include: external examiner, Faculty of Social Sciences, University of Guyana; member, North American Consortium for the University of Namibia; member of board, National Council for Black Studies; president, Guyanese Association of Northern California, San Francisco, California; advisor, Guyanese Community Council, USA, New York; external examiner, University of the West Indies, Mona, Jamaica.

He was a consultant for Ford Foundation, African American Studies Survey; for Inter-American Dialogue, Washington DC and the United States Agency for International Development (Guyana) on Guyanese Immigrant Remittances. He was also a report respondent for the Academy for Educational Development, assessing proposals for US State Department Educational Partnership Program, Western Hemisphere.

In addition to his position as professor in the African American Studies Department, Percy has held several administrative positions at Berkeley.

These included chair of African American Studies (a position he held for a period of eight years), director of Peace and Conflict Studies, acting director of the Center for Race and Gender, and director of the Center for African Studies, as well as codirector of the Multi-Campus Research Group on Africa (that serves all of the ten campuses of the University of California).

Percy has amassed numerous awards, scholarships, and fellowships, including:
- Principal investigator, Ford Foundation, "African American Studies Strategic Planning Retreat"
- Principal investigator, Ford Foundation, "African Diaspora Studies in the Twenty-First Century: Developing the Discipline through Networks and Collaborations"
- Coprincipal investigator, "African Diaspora Studies, Multiculturalism and Identity Construction," Ford Foundation
- Coinvestigator, Institute of International Studies: Ford Foundation Crossing Borders Program. "Remapping Identities: The African American Diaspora and Pan Indian Movements"
- Project director, National Resource Center Grant Award for the Center for African Studies, University of California, Berkeley
- Project director, Foreign Language and Area Studies Program for African Centers, University of California, Berkeley (both from United States Department of Education International Education Programs)
- Coprincipal investigator, Multi-Campus Research in the Humanities Initiative Grant, University of California

He has been the recipient of a number of awards and grants, including:
- Center for Latin American Studies/Mellon Foundation Research Grant, University of California, Berkeley
- Ford Foundation Fellowship for Doctoral Candidates from the Caribbean Region
- Yale University Fellowship
- Clark University Scholarship
- Public Service Award Guyanese Council, USA

- Presidential Award for Overall Contribution to the Field of Black Studies. National Council for Black Studies
- American Cultures Faculty Fellowship. Center for the Teaching and Study of American Cultures, University of California at Berkeley
- Arnold and Caroline Rose Monograph Series, American Sociological Association, Manuscript, "The Costs of Regime Survival" accepted by series
- The Chancellor's Medal. University of Guyana, 1973. Awarded to the second-best graduating student
- The Board of Governor's Prize. University of Guyana. Awarded to the graduating student who has made the most outstanding contribution to university affairs, and the Milton Gregg Award, University of Guyana. Awarded to the most academically outstanding third-year sociology major

These various contributions are testament to his scholarship and a tremendous compliment to the primary role of this distinguished Guyanese professor of African American Studies, University of California, Berkeley.

August 30, 2010

George E. Hopkinson, PEng

TV Broadcast Engineer

"Whatever your goal, you can get there if you're willing to work."
—Oprah Winfrey

George Edison Hopkinson was born on March 6, 1928, in Diamond, a sugar plantation situated on the East Bank of Demerara in British Guyana. He was the second of four sons born to Rhoda (nee Wong) and Jonathan Protector Hopkinson, a foreman in the Mechanical Engineering Section (steam technology) of a sugar cane factory on the estate.

His parents were his role models, who, with their wisdom, foresight, and Christian values, gave him and his brothers guidance and direction and provided them with the strength to cope with any eventuality. They were an understanding and happy couple, and he felt their support, love, and care at all times. They endured tough times and never complained and by means of hard work, determination, and sacrifices provided all their sons with a sound secondary education.

He remembers one of his dad's favorite one-liners, "Hard work doesn't kill, son, worry kills!" George is a chip of that "old takuba" who had weathered turbulence for ninety-six years of his life.

In 1933 his dad was transferred to Ruimveldt, another sugar plantation, where George attended Elementary Public School. Those were his most difficult years. George was left-handed, and every morning when he wrote on his slate, he was systematically whipped on the knuckles of his left hand until he switched to his right hand. That incident left a lasting and painful memory.

He went on to attend Government Primary School in Georgetown, where Lugard Dolphin was the headmaster. He then attended Central High School where he obtained his Cambridge School Certificate. JC Luck was the Principal.

When George left high school in 1947, his dream was to become a customs officer in the government civil service, which at that time was considered a privileged position. Perhaps it was the uniform that held the attraction. He sent in an application but was rejected.

In British Guiana during that era, jobs were scarce. With no job prospects on the horizon, George reviewed his options: He could remain stuck in the mud, waddle in it, or get out. He chose to get out; he decided he would take the first job that was offered to him, whether he liked it or not.

After filling out numerous applications, he was offered his first job as a meter reader with the Demerara Electric Company (DEC) in Georgetown. Electricity scared him to death! He was aware that one mistake could be fatal, but he took that job and with that decision, left behind his dream of becoming a customs officer.

Along with twice-weekly meter readings, it was his responsibility to clean the stack of meters piled high in the workshop. Due to his perseverance and diligence, he acquired the technical knowledge needed to test the meters and was promoted to meter tester. He had conquered his fear of electricity and laid the ground work for his future career.

In 1949 he gained employment as a junior technician in the Telephone Exchange at Guyana Telecommunication Corporation (GTC) in Georgetown. He attended the Government Technical Institute in Georgetown from 1950 to 1952, where he obtained the Government Technical Institute certificates.

In June 1952, under the US Government Point Four Program, he was awarded a scholarship to attend the Metropolitan Vocational School in San Juan, Puerto Rico, where he obtained a diploma in radio mechanics. On his return to Guyana he was promoted to senior technician, working in the radio section. Staff shortages contributed to his challenge of maintaining and improving the performance of the radio equipment.

In 1955 the most important event of George's life took place: he met a shy and pretty girl named Juanita Smith. They both worked for GTC in the same building, but their paths had never crossed before that year. One year later, on June 30, they were married at St. George's Cathedral in Georgetown. A year later, their daughter was born.

In 1957 most of the senior professional positions were held by non-Guyanese. That same year the government was awarding conditional scholarships to enable Guyanese to qualify for appointment to senior professional positions in the public service. George now twenty-nine years old, applied. Although he faced strong competition from the young graduates of Queen's College and St. Stanislaus College, the top secondary schools in Guyana, he had a gut feeling that his on-the-job experience would give him the competitive edge to move him ahead of the pack. He was right; he was awarded one of the conditional scholarships.

In September 1957, George left British Guiana with his young family to pursue studies in electrical engineering at the Brighton College of Technology in Brighton, Sussex, England. That exposure to post-secondary education was one of his major career development opportunities.

In 1959 he received the Intermediate Certificate in Telecommunication Engineering of the City and Guilds of London Institute in England. In 1962 he secured his Diploma in Electrical Engineering specializing in electronics and telecommunication from the Brighton College of Technology. He was then offered postgraduate training with the British Post Office, engineering branch, from July 1962 to September 1964, where he received the practical experience necessary to complement his academic studies, which later qualified him for employment in his professional capacity.

On completion of postgraduate training in the UK, George and his growing family (he now had two daughters and a son) returned to Guyana in 1964. In that year he was among the first batch of local Guyanese senior technicians to be appointed to senior professional engineering positions in Guyana. George was appointed an assistant engineer in the radio and carrier section of the GTC.

On his return to Guyana, all the top professional positions in the civil service were now filled by Guyanese. The shortage was now a lack of technical skills at the technician level. In addition to his duties, George was drawn into teaching to assist in the technical training of the technicians at the GTC. There was a wide gap between the theoretical knowledge and its application to the practical environment.

His primary role was to ensure that the technicians were properly trained in order to support their supervisors in maintaining the radio and multiplex system effectively.

In bridging the theoretical and performance gap, George took the bull by the horns. He took the technicians through the basic stages, explaining the working of the radio and multiplex system. The basic radio and multiplex courses were designed in small modules comprising of frames or lessons. At the end of each lesson, tests were conducted to determine each technician's knowledge of the issues taught.

Soon the confidence and the skills of the technicians shot up. George stressed that however perfect was the telephone handset, if the radio and multiplex link was defective, the community would suffer. In that regard, he stressed to the technicians the importance of ensuring that communication standards be maintained at the highest level at all times.

In 1971 George received the necessary training in the Training School of GEC–AEI Telecommunications Limited in Coventry, England, as part of a multimillion dollar contract for modernizing Guyana Radio and Telephone System.

That same year in 1971, he was promoted executive Engineer of the multimillion-dollar microwave radio relay systems, a component of the telecommunications project that was known at that time as the Development Program.

From April 1972 until its completion in May 1973, he held full responsibility for the installation and acceptance testing of all the UHF radio and multiplex stations. George was also responsible for redeployment of all VHF radio and multiplex stations within the main direct distance dialing (DDD) network in the sparsely populated areas.

The outmoded, inefficient and non-cost-effective radio and telecommunication system was about to be replaced with a modern, cost-effective state-of-the-art telecommunication system, providing excellent service to its citizens and to the global community.

In 1973, he was promoted to senior executive engineer, head of the radio and multiplex section. In George's new role he managed the operations and maintenance of the VHF and UHF radio trunk and associated multiplex systems, HF and tropospheric scatter links, meteorological radio beacon, rural telecommunications and mobile radios. He was also secretary of GTC Consultative Committee, secretary of Guyana Frequency Assignment Committee, and acting senior executive engineer in telephone operations and maintenance.

In 1975 he was the first Guyanese responsible for the installation of a reliable international microwave link, which served and is still serving Guyana and Surinam via Benab and New Nickerie, respectively. When it was officially opened for twenty-four-hour service for public use, the Lands Telegraaf-en-Telefoondienst (LTT) authorities voiced their satisfaction with the significant part played by GTC personnel in engineering the Guyana-Surinam microwave link. Today, it is still providing a reliable service after thirty-five years in operation.

In early 1977 he was involved in acceptance testing of microwave equipment in a factory in Montreal, Quebec. He had ensured that all equipment was completely debugged before shipment to Guyana, which had ensured minimum trouble-shooting in the field.

All the while, he continued to teach unabated. He was part-time lecturer in radio and multiplex subjects at GTC, an evening lecturer in radio and telecommunications subjects at the Government Technical Institute (GTI), and an evening lecturer in microwave components and radio relay systems at the Department of Electrical Engineering, Faculty of Technology, University of Guyana. He was an assessor of the practical course work for the City and Guilds of London Institute 'Radio, Television and Electronics Servicing' at the Government Technical Institute in Georgetown and in New Amsterdam, respectively.

George is proud of his record of accomplishment and feels truly privileged to have served in the position as the senior executive engineer, head of the radio and multiplex section. The most memorable milestone of his engineering journey was the establishment of the international microwave radio link between Guyana and Surinam that has stood the test of time. Working with his GTC colleagues as a team, they were able to make a difference. They can all be proud of their outstanding contribution to GTC over those years.

"A pessimist is one who makes difficulties of his opportunities, and an optimist is one who makes opportunities of his difficulties." —Harry Truman

On Christmas Day 1977, George, his wife, Juanita, along with daughters Carolyn and Diane and son David, arrived in Toronto, Canada, and were met by his oldest daughter, Kathryn. The second chapter of his engineering career was about to begin.

One month later, he was in Ottawa, and his first priority was to find a job.

His compatriots informed him, "George, at your age, you are too old. The job market is not in good shape, and no one will employ you." His reply was: "Comrades, failure is not an option. I have more than thirty years of engineering expertise under my belt. I wouldn't let obstacles stand in my way of success."

On a bright, sunny, and freezing cold (-30°C) January morning in 1978, with lots of snow and ice on the ground, George arrived at 10:00 a.m. sharp at a downtown office in Ottawa for his first interview. He could hardly believe that exactly a month ago, he was in beautiful Georgetown, surrounded by flowers and green grass, and that it had been a bright, sunny, and hot day!

His expectations were shattered on that his first job interview. He had come from a developing society to a developed one, and his experience of that interview remains indelibly imprinted in his memory.

At the interview, he submitted his CV and after discussions, he was told that he was the man for the job; his qualifications and experience matched the job description. The interviewer told him there were other persons to be interviewed, and he would be informed by phone of the decision.

That same afternoon, the interviewer phoned to tell George that the "upper echelons" had advised that he did not meet the criteria set for the job. George asked, "What were the criteria?" The interviewer was reluctant to provide the information but gave the reasons as follows: They did not know where Guyana was situated and concluded that Guyana was a backward country with a backward communication system, and George had no Canadian experience.

George got the vivid impression that his case was not properly addressed and countered by telling them that if they did not know where Guyana was situated, they should take a course in geography. He pointed out that if Guyana's telecommunications system was backward, then he could conclude that the Canadian Telecommunications System was also backward, because Guyana was using a telecommunications system similar to that of Canada.

He further stated that Guyana and Canadian telecommunications systems were in compliance with the recommendations of the International Radio Consultative Committee (CCIR) and the International Telegraph and Telephone Consultative Committee (CCITT). For that reason, it was obvious that Guyanese could communicate with Canadians, and vice versa, with high-quality speech because both systems conformed to the same international standards.

Moreover, George said that he not only had Canadian experience, but he also had international experience. Guyana had bought Canadian equipment, and he had tested that equipment in Montreal, and he had installed that same equipment in Guyana.

He was promptly invited to return to the interviewer's office the next morning. Pay and health benefits were negotiated, and he got his first job in Canada.

On February 1, 1978, he started his job as a telecommunications consultant on a five-man team. He provided technical assistance in the development of the Canadian Employment and Immigration Commission (CEIC) telecommunications facilities, including analogue and digital facsimile systems.

From November 1978 to April 1982, he was employed as a technological specialist in the Thick Film Hybrid Facility, Digital Transmission Division, Northern Telecom Ltd., Aylmer, Quebec.

In April 1982, he was appointed by the Department of Communications as a broadcast engineer in broadcast applications engineering in the Broadcast Regulatory Branch. In later years, a major part of the work was to meld the Canadian DTV allotment plan with the United States's plan, taking into account the use of common spectrum near the border area.

The TV broadcast stations in the United States have been fully DTV-operational since 2009, and Canada will be DTV-operational by August 31, 2011. George is fully engaged in this activity.

In 2005, he was nominated a steward in the Professional Institute of the Public Service of Canada (PIPSC). He is also a PIPSC representative on the Occupational Health and Safety (OHS) Committee.

In April 2008, at a special ceremony, Kevin Lindsey, acting assistant deputy minister presented George with a Long Service Award certificate, in honor of his twenty-five years of distinguished service to the government of Canada, signed by the Right Honorable Stephen Harper, prime minister.

Also in 2008, he was nominated executive member on the PIPSC Place de Ville NR Sub-Group. In 2010, he served as member on the PIPSC Industry Canada National Consultation Team (ICNCT).

George's engineering work in radio, telecommunication and broadcasting in Guyana and Canada is a big part of his life. It has spanned more than sixty-two years. He continues to make a contribution to the broadcast engineering field in Canada.

Retirement for George is like playing the gentleman's game of cricket. He is "eighty-two not out" of the workforce and with "bat in hand," he continues to enjoy being productive.

His advice to the young and young-at-heart is to quote an ancient Chinese proverb:
"Failure is not falling down but refusing to get up."

Professional Status:
Member, Association of Professional Engineers, Ontario, Canada, 1979–present
Chartered engineer, Council of Engineering Institution, England, 1974–1982
Member, Institution of Electronic & Radio Engineers, England, 1970–1982
Member, Electrical Engineers, England, 1970–1982
Member, Guyana Association of Professional Engineers, Guyana, 1970–1982

Published Paper:
"A Public Radiotelephone System for a Developing Nation." This was published in the *Guyana Association of Professional Engineers* magazine, No. 4, June 1970.

Conferences, Conventions, and Seminars:
Seminar on "Technological Man," Delft, Holland, 1961
IFRB seminar on "Frequency Management," Geneva, Switzerland, 1966
ITU seminar on "Telephone Service," London, England, 1966
ITU seminar on "Progress in Microwave Systems and Techniques," Tokyo, Japan, 1968
ITU seminar on "Planning of Broadcasting Systems," San Paulo, Brazil, 1973
Conference on "RF Electrical Measurement Practice," University of Surrey, England, 1973
Second International Symposium on " Subscribers Loops and Services," London, England, 1976

Training seminar for "Meteorological Telecommunications Personnel," Buenos Aires, Argentina, 1977
Third International Colloquium on Advanced Television Systems: HDTV '87, Ottawa, Canada, 1987
Fourth International Colloquium on Advanced Television Systems: HDTV '90, Ottawa, Canada, 1990
Professional training course on principles of radio communications, Carlton University, Ottawa, Canada, 2000
Seminars on "ATSC PSIP Broadcast" and "2001 ITS Technology," Palm Springs, California, 2001
Central Canada Broadcast Engineers Convention, Barrie, Ontario, Canada, 2008

Voluntary Work:
Captain, sides person, St. Stephen's Church, Ottawa, 1986
Deputy warden, St. Stephen's Church, Ottawa, 1987
Member, parish council, Ottawa West, 1987–1989
Peoples' warden, St. Stephen's Church, Ottawa, 1988
Rector's Warden, St. Stephen's Church, Ottawa, 1989
Member, synod, diocese of Ottawa, 1989
Coordinator, parish bazaar, St. Stephen's Church, Ottawa, 1989–1991
Canvasser, Industry Canada Charitable Campaign, Ottawa, 2007

October 21, 2010

Dhaman Kissoon, LLB

Barrister, Lecturer
Community Worker

Dhaman Kissoon, barrister and law lecturer, is the consummate community worker. Among his many projects, he founded the Advocates for Etobicoke Youth, an organization that helps hundreds of underprivileged children.

Dhaman Persaud Kissoon was born on September 30, 1956, at Nootenzuil, East Coast Demerara, Guyana. He attended Ann's Grove Primary School. He then attended Golden Grove Secondary School, where he obtained his GCE O levels.

He emigrated to Canada in 1975 and obtained a bachelor's degree in economics (with honors) from Glendon College, York University, in 1985. He then went to the University of Kent, Canterbury, UK (Rutherford College), where he obtained a BA in law, 1987. He returned to Canada to complete his Ontario law degree, the LLB, at Queen's University, Kingston, Ontario, in 1989. Since 1991 he has been a member of the Law Society of Upper Canada.

Dhaman's career as a lawyer started in 1990, when he was appointed a prosecutor with the Metropolitan Toronto Legal Department. From 1991 to 1992, he was a lawyer with the Bay Street law firm of Danson, Recht, and Freedman. Between 1992 and 1994, he was a partner in the law firm Kissoon and Pachai, and from 1994 to the present, he's been a principal in the law firm of Kissoon and Associates. The firm specializes in criminal and immigration law.

From 1990 to the present, Dhaman has also been a sessional lecturer at Queen's University (Faculty of Law). He was one of the first lecturers in a law school in the Province of Ontario to tackle the thorny issue of "Race V and Law in the Canadian Context." Dhaman has used his law office as a training ground for many young lawyers from the community. He has been a mentor and teacher to these young lawyers. He is a member of the Canadian Law Teachers Association and a member of the International Criminal Defense Lawyers Association.

Dhaman is perhaps more widely known for community service. From the time he started his legal career, he has been involved in the work of numerous community organizations.

He was a former president of the Brampton Flower City Centennial Rotary Club. This club, which has made a significant impact in the Brampton community, has been involved with many projects, both locally and internationally, which focuses on literacy and the health of needy children. Dhaman's leadership of this club has contributed to its enhanced status as a pride of Brampton, Greater Toronto.

Dhaman is founder and cochair of the Advocates for Etobicoke Youth (AFEY). It is a nonprofit organization which touches the lives of over one thousand underprivileged children and disadvantaged at risk youths in the Etobicoke area. The organization has been instrumental in providing a forum for the young people and the law enforcement authorities to have a dialogue.

Dhaman has been organizing a Thanksgiving dinner on a yearly basis. This dinner provides meals and entertainment for more than 250 people from an old-aged home. Each year he also organizes a children's Christmas party. This event provides toys, meals, and entertainment for more than three hundred needy children.

In 1999, Dhaman organized an Annual Charitable Golf Tournament to raise funds for a community organization. To date, it has raised more than $100,000 for the Devi Mandir in Pickering, Ontario. The tournament was started in honor of Dhaman's father, Sugrim Kissoon. Dhaman is a skilled organizer, and he is enthusiastic about projects he works on. He makes an annual cash donation to students of the Mandir to assist its Heritage Music Program, which encourages children from parents of the Caribbean diaspora to integrate into the multicultural Canadian Society. His sponsorship also helps to promote youth activities on Vision Television, which provides the children with a sense of accomplishment and motivation.

Dhaman has established a scholarship for University of Guyana (UG) first-year law students. This scholarship was created in conjunction with the University of Guyana Guild of Ontario. The $500 scholarship, awarded annually for the next ten years, is named in honor of Dhaman's mother, Latchmin.

Dhaman said about the scholarship, "This is about rewarding excellence and ensuring that an aspiring law student gets the opportunity to pursue [his or her] studies. I know there are many young people out there with the potential who may just need that extra bit of financial help. Hopefully, this scholarship will be able to make a difference in some lives. Our family has been blessed, and we believe in giving back in whatever way we can to the community."

Dhaman is seen as a role model for the young. He is a mentor for a number of young lawyers in the community. He has been a regular contributor in the Indo-Caribbean newspaper in Toronto, and was former host of the *Law and You*, a legal affairs program on the ABC radio station; and a regular contributor of legal issues in the *In Pulse* magazine (a prominent Caribbean-based magazine published in Canada). He has authored *Racism and the Law in Canada*, soon to be published.

Among Dhaman's many other projects are:
From 1990 to 2000, he was cochair of the South Asian Consultative committee to the police chief of Toronto
2003 to present: member of the board of directors of the Etobicoke Sports Hall of Fame
2000 to present: chair of the advisory board of the Pickering Devi Mandir; legal advisor to the Devi Mandir and to the Pranav Cultural Center.
He is a former chair of the Legal Committee of the Canadian Cricket Association; former president of the Ontario Cricket Association; former vice president of the Toronto and District Cricket Association; former captain of Ontario Cricket team; former president and captain of the Cavaliers Cricket and Sports Club

He is a member of the Etobicoke Legal Aid Committee.

Over the years, Dhaman's work in the community has been duly recognized by a number of prestigious awards. These include:
2002: Queen's University Faculty of Law Teaching Award
2003: Winner of the Celebrity Chef competition organized by the United Achievers of Brampton, Ontario
2003: The Shabnam Radio "Man of the Year Award" for outstanding work in the community
2006: The Pranav Cultural Center: Award of Excellence for outstanding community work
2007: The Paul Harris Award from the Brampton Flower City Rotary Club

Dhaman is a recipient of the 2007 Toronto Arya Samaj/Vedic Cultural Center (VCC) Community Award. It was presented at a glittering ceremony, held at the VCC, and attended by over 350 guests, including people from government, the judicial service, and professionals. The citation accompanying the award described vividly Dhaman's numerous exemplary community activities. Accepting the award, Dhaman thanked the VCC and said he shared with most people strong feelings of responsibility to the youths to show them the right way and to encourage them to realize their potential.

Recently, the Law Society of Upper Canada, the body that regulates lawyers in Ontario, identified 278 minority lawyers from all parts of the world, who in the two-hundred-year history of the Law Society made a significant difference to the Canadian community. Dhaman Kissoon is the only Indo-Guyanese lawyer from the Caribbean to be on that list. In 2009 the law students from Queen's University voted Dhaman as the best visiting lecturer at the law school. This is the second time Dhaman captured this prestigious award.

Dhaman' s extensive community work has touched the lives of many Guyanese and Canadians. He reflected on his joys, sorrows, and satisfactions and what drives him to achieve more, commenting on what gives him the greatest satisfaction:

> The organization, Advocates for Etobicoke Youth (AFEY), that I founded continues to assist and mentor thousands of underprivileged children each year in Canada. Also, as

a lawyer the number of individuals I have prevented from being deported from Canada has given me tremendous satisfaction.

I was most inspired by Mahatma Gandhi—a small man with determination, who has brought about significant changes to the world. [I got the drive] from both my parents. I am motivated to do well because I want to be the best at what I do, and I want to make a positive impact in my community. Being told I did not have what was required to become a lawyer was the single most important thing that drove me over the years.

He was disappointed when, for unknown reasons, his application to the University of Guyana was rejected. Interestingly, in 2005 the Toronto chapter of the University of Guyana Guild invited him to be their keynote speaker. It was the year he established a scholarship in the name of his mother.

Dhaman's most unhappy day was when he heard that his father had died. The happiest days of his life were when his children were born. "When my father died and entrusted me with the responsibility of assisting my mother with the upbringing of my brothers and sisters, I could not fail him. I must congratulate my mother for the successes of my siblings. They are all successful, and my father must be smiling."

He has been successful in his legal career. Dhaman says his recipe for success is hard work and determination, time for play, time for God, and time for the family. In the right mix, that combination is the recipe for success. On what he would like people to think of him, he says, "He was a true friend."

What would be a good day for Dhaman? "A warm and sunny day on the golf course with good friends, very pleasurable and very relaxing. In the early mornings, the peace and quiet of the puja room is very good for the soul. At the end of the day, a glass of the best wine is very good for the heart."

August 31, 2010

Professor V. Chris Lakhan

PhD, FRGS, CEI, CES, CEC, GISP, LFIBA
Earth and Environmental Scientist

Dr. V. Chris Lakhan, a professor of earth and environmental sciences at the University of Windsor, is an internationally recognized and accomplished academic and educator who was cited in 2007 by the International Biographical Research Center, Cambridge, England, as one of the 2,000 outstanding scientists of the twenty-first century. This earned citation could be attributed to the fact that Prof. Lakhan belongs to an elite group of researchers who have demonstrated skills and expertise to conduct and publish both theoretical and empirical systems science research.

He specializes in the development of computer simulation models, and the use of geographical information systems (GIS) and remote sensing (RS) techniques to study and predict the dynamics at work in coastal and other natural environmental systems. Most of his models and techniques are applied to the study and management of coastal, environmental, and natural resources.

Dr. Lakhan (known as "Vish") is originally from Fyrish, Corentyne, Berbice, where his parents were shopkeepers. He and his eight brothers and sisters attended Fyrish Congregational School. He obtained his College of Preceptors certificate when he was only thirteen years old. He was among the first group of students in Guyana to have successfully obtained certificates in general education from the University of London while attending primary school. During his early education, Dr. Lakhan grasped the essential constructs of the Aristotelian tradition of philosophy and scholastic education. This provided some basis for his pursuit of higher education. He graduated from the University of Guyana, where he won the Sir John Bartholomew of Scotland Prize for being the best graduating student in geography. He subsequently won scholarships, including a Canadian Government Commonwealth Scholarship, to pursue graduate studies in Canada. In less than one year, he completed all the requirements for his master's degree at the University of Windsor, Ontario. He obtained his PhD in 1982 from the University of Toronto, where he was awarded open fellowships for academic excellence for four consecutive years.

A professor for over twenty-six years, Dr. Lakhan has won several merit and teaching awards in both the Faculty of Social Science and the Faculty of Science. From 2003 to 2006, he was a chairperson and member of the Ontario Graduate Scholarship Committee in Earth Sciences, Ontario Ministry of Colleges and Training. He also served as a member of the International Organizing Committee of Eurocoast. He participated in Eurocoast Littoral Conferences held in Aberdeen, Scotland, and Gdansk, Poland.

He has supervised, coread, and examined eighty-three undergraduate theses (eight focusing on Guyana) and fifty-one graduate theses (thirteen concentrating on Guyana). He has also officiated as an external examiner for doctoral theses done by students in Asia and the Middle East.

Dr. Lakhan's pioneering research in earth and environmental sciences has been published in more than thirty-three different international journals, including all of the world's major coastal journals. He is a recognized world authority for his publications on coastal modeling. He has edited three major publications on applications and advances in coastal modeling for the world's largest scientific publisher, and also published articles in the *Encyclopedia of Coastal Science*. In addition, he has authored eleven books and monographs on resources management and geographical information systems. His best-selling book on *Principles of Resource Management* is being translated into Urdu and Persian. Among his more than seventy-five peer-reviewed publications are several scientific publications focusing on research done in Guyana.

Prof. Lakhan's academic excellence, research skills, and intellect are highly recognized internationally, and his services are frequently sought for refereeing academic papers, speaking at conferences and professional associations, and collaborating with other researchers. Arising from his collaboration with other scholars—for example, with those at the noted Chinese Academy of Sciences—are innovative geospatial techniques and applications. He is also a member of several professional societies, among them the Coastal Education and Research Foundation, the Environmental Assessment Association, the Ontario Association of Remote Sensing, the Urban and Regional Information Systems Association, and the International Institute of Informatics and Systemics.

Dr. Lakhan serves as a member on the editorial board of the *Open Ocean Engineering Journal*. He is also the editor in chief of *the International Journal of Earth and Environmental Sciences* and editor in chief of the *Journal of Indo-Caribbean Research* (JICR). As editor of *JICR* he edited two special issue publications focusing on the life and legacy of President Cheddi Jagan, and selected contributions on the life of President Janet Jagan.

Prof. Lakhan has been a Fellow of the Royal Geographical Society (UK) for the past twenty-five years. He is also a certified environmental consultant, specialist and inspector who conducts geospatial and environmental research in Canada and several other countries. As a certified geographical information systems professional, he is a reviewer for the Geographical Information Systems Certification Institute (United States) and a consulting geoinformation scientist with International Computing Laboratories, Inc.

Dr. Lakhan was winner of Guyana Awards (Canada) 2007 Academic Excellence Award. He was also elected a life fellow of the International Biographical Association for his meritorious contributions on the application of systems science to elucidate the dynamics operating in complex coastal and environmental systems. In recognition of his outstanding interdisciplinary research, Prof. Lakhan was offered, but declined, numerous other awards and commendations, because he is of the conviction that certificates and medals are unwarranted for advancing the frontiers of knowledge for oneself and others.

Sources:

Websites accessed May 27, 2010, on Guyana Consulate Toronto, Guyana Awards (Canada), www.vclakhan.com

November 10, 2010

The Honorable Vibert A. R. Lampkin

LLB, LLM, LLD
Retired Judge, Ontario Court of Justice

Justice Vibert Lampkin, a friendly, easygoing, approachable man, avuncular to the young and a confidant to colleagues, is easily one of the best loved and most highly regarded judges in Canada. The quality of his early education and training, remarkable diligence in practice, and his boldness of spirit have earned him a place in the history books of Anglo-Canadian jurisprudence.

His legal mentor was the famous Lord Denning, Master of the Rolls of England, whose approach to law was Justice Lampkin's judicial philosophy, the essence of which is distilled in the noble Lord's comment in Packer v. Packer in 1954, thus:

> What is the argument on the other side? Only this: that no case has been found in which it has been done before. That argument does not appeal to me in the least. If we never do anything that has not been done before, we shall never get anywhere. The rest of the world will go on whilst the law stands still and that will be bad for both.

Denning was entreating those who deal in the law to be bold spirits and not timorous souls. Vibert Lampkin's bold spirit has been demonstrated on those many occasions on which he has done what had not been done before. One major example was he gave written reasons for his judgments long before it was a legal requirement for judges of his court to do so.

Vibert Arthur Ridley Lampkin was born on April 14, 1933, at Sandy Babb Street, Kitty, Georgetown, Guyana. He is the elder of the two children of David and Rosalie Lampkin. His parents were divorced before he was a teenager. After the separation of his parents Vibert and his sister, Doreen, lived with their mother and their grandparents. Vibert says that his grandmother had the greatest influence upon him during his formative years. Notwithstanding the separation, his parents remained on friendly terms and during his teenage years, when his father was headmaster at Hopetown Primary School, West Coast Berbice, Vibert looked forward to many an August holiday with him. His father later remarried Edith Andrews (a wedding which Vibert and his sister attended as teenagers) and started another family. His father was subsequently headmaster in Corentyne, Canje, and in Georgetown.

Vibert's father and his second family emigrated to Canada in 1965. His father taught in schools in some of the smaller towns in Ontario before his appointment as deputy headmaster of an elementary school in Scarborough, Ontario, a post he held up to the time of his retirement. His father died on December 31, 1987, half an hour after Vibert had visited him in hospital. Vibert's stepmother, Edith, died in Toronto on June 5, 2008.

Vibert's mother, Rosalie, was the eldest of the five children of Kemp and Gertrude Carter. There were four girls, followed by the baby of the family, who eventually became Uncle John to Vibert and all his friends. Vibert's mother emigrated to Canada in 1970 with her daughter, son-in-law, and their three young children. She joined that stalwart group of immigrant grandmothers who took care of babies and young grandchildren while their parents went out to work. She died in Toronto on March 9, 1988.

As Vibert relates it, his early years at school were unremarkable. He considered himself an average student until his mid-teens, when he suddenly transformed into a hard-working student, during which time he was a classmate of Rafiq Khan (later a Guyana radio broadcaster) at St. Stanislaus College. After obtaining his General Certificate of Education (advanced level) of the University of London, he taught Latin and mathematics at his alma mater to the middle school, beginning in September 1951. In 1952 he sat for the Guyana Scholarship. While he did not win the Guyana Scholarship, he was a runner-up and had the distinction of being placed first in the country in Latin and second in Pure Mathematics, one mark less that Sydney Jaikaran, the winner of the Guyana Scholarship.

Vibert continued as a teacher at St. Stanislaus College until September 1954 when he began the study of law and entered into Articles of Clerkship for five years with his uncle, John Carter, QC. Not only did he study for the English law examinations, but he made sure that he studied beyond the set curriculum, even covering the lives and careers of outstanding lawyers.

In 1957 he obtained the LLB degree of the University of London, by virtue of which the High Court reduced the period of his articles to four years, thus enabling him to write successfully the final examination of the Law Society of England in October 1958. In January 1959 he was admitted to the Roll of Solicitors in Guyana, where he practiced until 1967. During that time, in 1965, he was admitted to the Roll of Solicitors in England.

In 1961 Vibert married his teenage sweetheart, Lorna McArthur. He met her on the evening of April 13, 1951, and "tricked" her into going with him to the matinee the next afternoon. When he took her home from the cinema that Saturday evening, he revealed to her that it was his eighteenth birthday. That earned him a light peck on the cheek. She has been an integral part of his life for fifty-nine years, nearly 77 percent of his life. He attributes his success to his wife, Lorna, saying:

> None of the success I have achieved would have been possible without the love, understanding, and encouragement of my wife, Lorna. The month of April means much more to us than the month of my birth—we were married on April 30, 1961.

Vibert and Lorna emigrated to Canada in 1967, where their son Roger was born. In order to practice in Ontario, Vibert once again had to be articled to a firm of lawyers for twelve months and then complete the six-month bar admission course. He was called to the Ontario Bar and admitted as a solicitor in 1969 and was invited back to the firm of Rosenfeld, Schwartz and Brown, where he had been articled and was admitted into partnership in the firm in 1975. He continued to study and obtained the degree of master of laws of York University in 1977.

Vibert spent his entire professional life in Canada with his firm, up to the time of his appointment as a judge. Indeed, it was Alf Schwartz who first suggested to Vibert that he would be an excellent choice for the bench. In September 1982, Vibert was appointed a judge of the provincial court (criminal division), which was later renamed the Ontario Court of Justice. The bond between Vibert and his former partners remains to this day.

After more than twenty-five years, Justice Vibert Lampkin retired from the bench in mid-April 2008. A special "swearing out" ceremony on April 11 was the first such ceremony ever held in Canada. His address at the ceremony vividly reveals the fine attributes of the man. He spoke with humility:

> I am sure that my former teachers would not recognize the person of whom you have all spoken so eloquently. Two of them are here today—Mrs. Lawrence Ashby, whom I knew as Miss Rosie Zitman, introduced me to the three R's when I was about six or seven years old, at St. Winifred's Roman Catholic School in Newtown, Kitty. Mr. Compton Singh taught me math and English composition and literature when I was twelve and thirteen years old in third and lower fourth forms at St. Stanislaus College in Georgetown. He introduced me to Euclid and Pythagoras, Shakespeare and Thackeray. Both of them—as did my other teachers—had a hard time with me.
>
> I have been extraordinarily fortunate in my lifetime. I was fortunate to have been born into a family that nurtured me. Indeed, it was my uncle Sir John Carter, QC, who first encouraged me to study law, and it was to him that I was articled in Guyana. When I qualified as a solicitor, we practiced as partners for seven years until he took up a diplomatic post in 1966 as Guyana's first high commissioner to Canada, ambassador to the United States, and permanent representative to the United Nations.

In 1982, Honorable Roy McMurtry, QC, then attorney general of the province, recommended to Ontario Cabinet the appointment of Vibert Lampkin to be a judge on the Criminal Law Bench. The last twenty-five years have been the most dynamic period in the history of the court. The jurisdiction of the court has been increased beyond recognition.

Perhaps the greatest change is the delivery of reasons. In 1982, not many judges delivered written reasons. When Vibert Lampkin went on the bench and started to write reasons for judgment, one judge said to him: "You are not supposed to write reasons at our level. That is for the Court of Appeal and the Supreme Court of Canada." Vibert Lampkin ignored him. Today, reasoned reasons are mandated by the Court of Appeal and the Supreme Court of Canada. Vibert says, "Those who appear before us in the trial court, and society at large, are entitled to know why we agree or disagree with a particular version of the events that have brought them to court and the reason why a finding of guilt was made or an acquittal entered."

A gala dinner was held in Vibert's honor on May 8, 2008, at which the gathering of about three hundred included not only his colleagues and members of the wider legal community but also many of his friends and members of the Guyanese community. He received numerous glowing letters, cards, and e-mail tributes on his retirement. Excerpts from letters and e-mails below are just a sample:

Letter dated March 18, 2008, from Gavin MacKenzie, treasurer of the Law Society of Upper Canada:

> You have made enormous contributions to the administration of justice over the course of your judicial career and the Law Society and its 38,000 members are indebted to you.

Letter dated April 4, 2008, from Daniel Monteith, senior partner of Monteith, Baker, Johnston & Doodnauth professional corporation:

> It is with fondness that I remember my cases, which were heard by you. As you are retiring, you can be assured that I am not engaging in false flattery for my clients' gain.
>
> My recollection of my times in front of you are of a judge who was always courteous, dignified, interested, caring, thoughtful, hard-working, bright, and intellectually honest. Not once did I feel that my client or I was treated unfairly in your court.

Letter dated April 7, 2008, from Justice Michelle Fuerst of the Superior Court of Justice:

> I did want to congratulate you on a long, productive and distinguished career on the bench. You took the time and effort to think about and analyze issues at a time when many in your position did not. It was always a "win" to appear in

your courtroom, regardless of the actual outcome of the case, because at all times the parties could be assured of a fair and thoughtful decision. You were always a true gentleman, treating everyone who came before you with courtesy, regardless of gender, race, or background.'

Letter dated April 8, 2008, from Murray D. Segal, deputy attorney general of the province of Ontario:

Let me begin by applauding your contribution to the justice system. In your twenty-six years presiding as a judicial officer, you have heard an untold number of criminal cases. Your indelible contribution to the jurisprudence is undeniable given almost three hundred of your decisions being reported. Your thoughtful intellect is matched by an abiding compassion and respect for others. Everyone in your court is aware of your sense of respect and dignity: be they court staff, lawyers, accused, police, victims, and witnesses. At the end of such a long and distinguished career, thoughtful humanity has become your "brand."

As a supporter of diversity in the Ontario Public Service, I was pleased to be reminded that you were one of the first black judges to be appointed in Ontario. Not only were you a fine addition to the bench, you have served your community as well as a role model, inspiring young people to think about justice as a career.

E-mail dated April 10, 2008, from Honorable Justice Thomas P. Cleary of the Ontario Court of Justice:

Your judicial career was active, instructive, and of significant benefit to society. You gave a dignified air to your court and commanded respect by the appropriate solemnity. The participants were thus compelled to raise their standards. The advice I received, both in words and by example from you, in the first three months on the bench was a significant influence on my evolution into a judge. Sincere thanks for excellent work and examples to follow.

On April 10, 2008, Justice Lampkin received the gift of a book from Kelly Wright, then an assistant crown attorney at Newmarket, now a justice of the Ontario Court of Justice, which she inscribed as follows:

> Justice Lampkin, I give you this book not to inspire you but to remind you how much you have inspired others!

Letter dated April 11, 2008, from Honorable Warren Winkler, Chief Justice of Ontario:

> I understand that you will be retiring as a judge of the Ontario Court of Justice on April 14, 2008, following a distinguished twenty-six-year career. I know that you have been recognized by your community and by every level of the judiciary for your superior knowledge of the law, civility, and contribution to the body of criminal law through your most impressive list of 286 reported cases. You are truly a remarkable Canadian who has made a lasting contribution to Ontario, and you will leave a rich legacy to be shared by all Canadians.

E-mail dated April 11, 2008, from Honorable Mavin Wong of the Ontario Court of Justice:

> I send you heartfelt congratulations on a wonderful achievement. You have spent your career serving your community and being a mentor to so many young counsel and judges. I will always look back on the two years I was in Newmarket with fondness and with happy memories spending time with you.

Letter dated April 11, 2008, from William M. Trudell, chair (Toronto, Ontario), Canadian Council of Criminal Defense Lawyers:

> Your contribution to the important role of a justice in our precious criminal justice system has been exemplary. Your kind and principled approach to all who appeared before you was exactly as it should be, and you will be remembered for it.

E-mail dated April 11, 2008, from Ms. Michelle Rumble, assistant crown attorney, Newmarket:

> It didn't quite hit me until yesterday afternoon, as I sat in 201 Court, that you will no longer be presiding in our courthouse.

> Although we have been "bracing ourselves" for this moment, it is hard to actually envision our Ontario Court of Justice without its moral and intellectual leader.
>
> As I drove home yesterday after you rose from the bench for the last time, I remembered my days as a brand new crown. The nerves, the anxiety (and sometimes the dread) related to those first days on my feet will never be forgotten. But what I also remember is that I could always take some comfort in looking at the daily schedule and seeing that I had the good fortune of being in Justice Lampkin's court. Although I was always fearful of looking foolish in front of such a highly esteemed and respected jurist, I knew that I would be treated with kindness and patience. Every day in Your Honor's court was a tremendous learning experience.
>
> You have watched so many of us "grow up" in your courtroom. I fondly remember your kind wishes when I was married and had my children. And although it was far from pleasant at the time, I can now look back fondly at our longest trial (now under appeal), if only for the fact that it kept me in Your Honor's court.
>
> Thank you so very much for being our wise and patient teacher and role model. As expressed by so many of my colleagues, we will miss you enormously but wish you good health, happiness, and new adventures in the years ahead.

Letter dated April 11, 2008, from Tony Vanden Ende, assistant crown attorney, Newmarket:

> The reason that my face wears a curious look is because I am really wondering what the accused person is thinking as he is suddenly confronted with a quotation from Shakespeare or the Bible or with a Caribbean or Latin proverb. ... Will the prisoner start to repeat the lines from Shakespeare along with Your Honor, as Winston Churchill once did during a performance by Richard Burton? Will there be an equal but opposing response in Latin? ...

> That curious look of mine should have an element of hope mixed in with it. What is more to the point, however, is that the people who are being dealt with before Your Honor are, perhaps for the first time in their lives, being addressed by someone who is genuinely learned. And they are being invited to consider the possibility that they are important enough to be addressed in that way.
>
> All of which is to say, Sir, that I invariably find gratifying your fitting words and I will miss them upon your retirement.

Letter dated April 14, 2008, from Honorable Chris Bentley, attorney general of Ontario:

> You have made an enormous contribution to the York Region community, to the legal community, and to our justice system. For over a quarter century you have delivered judgments that have contributed considerably to the judicial landscape. You have always been known for your intellect. Your sense of decorum and civility in court sets a high standard for all. And now, at the end of your long and distinguished career as a judge, you leave a rich legacy of which everyone is proud.

Letter dated April 25, 2008, from Honorable Justice Brian Lennox, former chief justice of the Ontario Court of Justice:

> In a great many respects, your retirement represents a milestone not only at the Newmarket Court House, but also within the Ontario Court of Justice, a court which you have graced with your presence for so many years. Your twenty-five years of service encompasses a period which has seen fundamental change in the court's organization, structure, jurisdiction, and composition. Your interest and your commitment to the principles of justice and to the service of the public have not faltered over that time, and your passion for the law is known to everyone who has come into contact with you. Your personal relationship with Lord Denning and your connection to your home and to the broader commonwealth gave to our court a certain cachet which we will sorely miss. ...

> In addition to your obvious intellectual capacity, scholarship, dedication and humanity, there are two things that I will remember with pride and admiration. The first is your unfailing interest in communicating with your colleagues and your good humour in doing so. The second and the more significant is… (your) generous, gentle and genuine way,…both in private and in public, something which speaks volumes about the depth of your character, friendship and compassion.
>
> It has been a pleasure for me to have been your colleague, and I take great pleasure in having this opportunity to salute your many achievements.

Letter dated May 8, 2008, from Ms. Gemma Sang, assistant crown attorney, Newmarket:

> While sharing your mementos of Lord Denning with us one day, you shook your finger at us and told us to "pick a hero." I had already found one, long ago, in you. Thank you for all that you have taught us about the law and about life.

E-mail dated May 14, 2008, from Honorable Justice Bill Horkins of the Ontario Court of Justice, which he circulated to all the other justices throughout Ontario:

> Last week I drove up to Newmarket to attend a retirement dinner for Justice Vibert Lampkin. It was a wonderful evening of tribute and entertainment. Just scanning the crowd, you could tell that this is a judge we can all be proud to be associated with as one of our own. Friends, colleagues, and counsel from all areas of practice in York region were there to show their love and respect on both a personal and professional level.
>
> I first encountered Judge Lampkin as a young part-time crown attorney and defense counsel; he projected an unpretentious dignity in his court that engendered respect and confidence. Although I can't claim success in living up to the example he set, he was, and continues to be, a role model that we should all aspire to emulate.

> "Back in the day" Vibert was one of the few provincial court judges that actually gave full reasons for judgment. Win or lose, there was never any mystery as to the basis of his decision. His approach is now, of course, the form of reasons mandated by the appellate courts in order to provide a reviewable record. ... His approach not only recognized the concerns of the losing party before him but acknowledged the efforts of counsel.

Justice Horkins distributed a second e-mail, dated May 14, 2008, to the justices throughout Ontario, as follows:

> Steven Skurka, noted counsel, author, and legal pundit, has included this tribute to the recently retired Justice Lampkin in his online blog, and I thought I should share it with you:

> "One of the finest judges whom I ever had the privilege of appearing before as counsel, Vibert Lampkin, has retired from the bench. About three hundred of his judgments have been reported in various law reports, more than any other judge in the Ontario of Justice ...

> "In a moving letter to me after his retirement, Justice Lampkin expressed his view that Shakespeare was wrong when he had Marcus Antonius say at Caesar's funeral, 'The evil that men do lives after them. The good is oft interred with their bones.'

> "Justice Lampkin's virtuous legacy is sufficient evidence to refute Shakespeare's cynical claim."

E-mail dated May 16, 2008, from Aggrey King, a fellow Guyanese:

> I think that one of the greatest tributes any of us can achieve in any aspect of our lives is to be held up by our peers as an example of exemplary performance. This is a jewel to be prized almost above all others. You have clearly made a positive difference and impacted many in your distinguished career and for that, I salute you. You can justifiably be proud of what you have achieved.

E-mail dated May 16, 2008, from Bill Rosenfeld, QC, Justice Lampkin's former partner:

> It is obvious from the tributes which you have received that you have served as one of the best loved and most highly regarded of judges, not only in Canada, but perhaps throughout that world which has been shaped by English jurisprudence. I could not have been prouder or happier than I was upon attending your "swearing out" ceremony. It is one of my greatest achievements to be your friend. And Joe, I am sure, was smiling down on both of us.

A press release from the Law Society of Upper Canada contained the following news, in part:

> The Law Society of Upper Canada presented degrees of doctor of laws, *honoris causa* (LLD) to two distinguished persons who exemplify the values held in esteem by the legal profession. Recipients serve as inspirational keynote speakers for the graduating classes as they begin their careers. ...
>
> On June 20, an LLD was presented to former justice Lampkin for his service to the judiciary, the legal profession, and the wider community in Canada, as well as his native country, Guyana, with integrity and distinction for more than forty years.

The article contained a biography of Justice Lampkin, stating in part:

> The Honorable Vibert A. Lampkin is a recently retired judge of the Ontario Court of Justice. Throughout his career, he earned a reputation as a leader of the court, a trailblazer and a mentor to the many lawyers who appeared before him. ... Until his retirement this year, he served in Newmarket, where he was known for his knowledge of the law, civility, and contribution to the body of criminal law, with 286 reported cases. Everyone who appeared or worked in his court was aware of his respect and compassion for people.
>
> Mr. Lampkin was formerly a director of Oxfam (Canada) and is director emeritus of New Leaf: Living and Learning Together Inc. He is a supporter of many charitable organizations.

Justice Lampkin's address to the graduates at Roy Thomson Hall was a discourse on the values of integrity and assiduous application to detail, of which he is a shining example. He advised them to "read beyond the law reports" and to "follow the lives of the great lawyers through the ages: from Cicero to Sir Lionel Luckhoo, QC, from Denning to Laskin and Dickson. You are bound to find a hero among them that you can emulate." Reminding them of the comment of Denning ... that "if we never do anything which has not been done before, we shall never get anywhere," he said, "Be not afraid to put forward a novel argument if it is reasonable. The judge may accept your argument."

A renowned student of Shakespeare, Vibert closed his address, which was spiced with numerous gems from the bard, with the advice Polonius gave to his son Laertes, who was about to leave Denmark to complete his studies in France—time-honored words which, five centuries after they were written, still resonate in our lives today.

He concluded with his best wishes to the legal eagles, saying, "Now go forth and be the best lawyer you could be. And always remember that anything worth doing is worth doing well."

On June 24, 2009, Vibert was awarded a second honorary doctorate of laws by Osgoode Law School of York University. The announcement issued to the Osgoode Community by Patrick J. Monahan, Dean of Osgoode Hall Law School, read, in part, as follows:

> I am very pleased to report that the president has announced that Osgoode will have two distinguished honorary doctorate recipients at the upcoming spring convocation: the Honorable Justice Vibert Lampkin and our former colleague, Professor Emeritus Paul C. Weiler.

The announcement contained a biography of Justice Lampkin, similar to that set out above.

Graciously accepting the award, Vibert thanked the president and those responsible for conferring upon him the signal honor, regarded as the highest award granted by a university because it is recognition of a person's lifetime contribution to the advancement of knowledge. His acceptance speech continued with these words:

> Law has always been regarded in the British Commonwealth ... as a good foundation for other endeavors. Legal qualifications

are highly valued, not only for knowledge of the law but also for those transferable skills that come with the study of law.

I suspect that most of you will proceed to … the degree of a barrister at law and enrollment as a solicitor … some of you who have earned postgraduate degrees will become chancellors and presidents of universities, deans of law schools, professors and lecturers at universities. … Some of you may wish to go into politics … the very first prime minister of Canada, Sir John A. Macdonald, QC, was a lawyer. …

Some may think of entering the diplomatic service. Take a look at the career of Honorable R. Roy McMurtry, QC … he was one of the architects of the Canadian Charter of Rights and Freedoms …he was appointed as Canada's High Commissioner to the Court of St. James … he was appointed Chief Justice of the province in 1996 … Now he is Chancellor of this university. … Some of you may think of a career in business, where a legal background is always very useful. Paul Martin was a lawyer and a successful businessman long before he entered politics and became prime minister of Canada.

But whatever direction you take … remember always that deep in the hearts of each and every one of us, there is a common theme. We must each work for justice and peace because we are all one … There are certain tenets we can all observe. First and foremost you must be honest and truthful in all your dealings. Those with whom you have any dealings must always be able to rely on your word. Your reputation will depend not only on your ability as a lawyer, important as that is, but also on your good name.

You must treat everyone with courtesy, civility, and respect. You could disagree with the views of others without resorting to caricature …as another honouree recently said. Live by Newton's third law of motion: "To every action there is an equal and opposite reaction." That is as true of life as it is of mathematics.

Keep up-to-date. Your degree is the best evidence that at this time you possess certain knowledge. It is no evidence that five years hence you will be as knowledgeable. Look upon law as a living tree, constantly growing, changing, and developing by legislation and by decisions of the courts, to meet the challenges of the society that it serves.

Do harm to no one, either in word or deed. Remember the comment of that poet of the law, Lord Atkin ...in what is arguably the most important case in Anglo Canadian common law, Donoghue v Stephenson, the case of "the snail in the bottle". This is what he said: "The rule that you must love your neighbor becomes, in law, you must not injure your neighbor."

Once again congratulations to each and every one of you and your families. Good luck and best wishes to all of you.

September 15, 2010

Jolyon A. Lamwatt, DMD

Dentist

Florida-based dentist Jolyon Lamwatt is listed in the Consumers' Research Council of America's Guide to America's Top Dentists. The council is a Washington DC-based research organization, which provides consumer information guides for professional services throughout America. Its purpose is "to help educate and assist consumers in obtaining the finest professional services."

Jolyon is a member of the American Dental Association and the Florida Dental Association. An active member of American Mensa and Central Florida Mensa, he attends the annual gatherings of American Mensa and many of the regional gatherings around the nation. Mensa was originally founded in England in 1946 as a meeting place for intelligent people. Membership comprises people with diverse backgrounds, whose IQ is in the top 2 percent of the population. Its goals are "to identify and foster human intelligence for the benefit of humanity, to encourage research in the nature, characteristics, and uses of intelligence, and to promote stimulating intellectual and social opportunities for its members." There are currently about 100,000 Mensa members in one hundred countries around the world.

Jolyon was born at home on November 26, 1960, at South Road in Georgetown, Guyana. He is the youngest of four children. His father, Sydney Lamwatt, was a Businessman, a representative for F. W. Milling and Co. Ltd. He was born in British Guiana in April 1923. He died in Canada in 1987. Jolyon's mother is Enid Chung, homemaker, born in Canje, Berbice, Guyana, in 1927. She resides in Canada.

The eldest of Jolyon's siblings is his sister, Wanetta Cheung. She received a bachelor of arts degree with honors from the university of Toronto in 1971, followed by a bachelor's in education from Queens University in 1972. She is a retired high school English teacher. His older brother, Stanwick Lamwatt, a periodontist, holds the degrees of bachelor of science and doctor of dental science from the University of Toronto, and runs two practices. His other brother, Royden Lamwatt, holds a bachelor of arts and a bachelor's in education from the University of Toronto. He is the principal at Norway Elementary School, Toronto.

Jolyon received his early education at St. Ann's on Church Street before moving to Sacred Heart Primary School in Georgetown. He then went on to Queen's College, Georgetown, on a scholarship. The family moved to Toronto, Canada, in 1974, where he attended Erindale Secondary High School, in Mississauga. Jolyon worked for a few years before deciding to pursue higher education and follow in his brother's footsteps.

He did undergraduate studies at the University of Miami, Coral Gables, Florida. He was accepted at the University of Florida to study dentistry, and he graduated in 1991 with a doctorate in dental medicine (DDM). He is licensed to practice dentistry in the state of Florida.

Jolyon says, "My siblings have been my inspiration in their search for knowledge, and I decided to follow my older brother into dentistry."

Jolyon worked for a year with a dentist before buying his practice in 1992. The practice, with a staff of nine employees, is located in the Bay Hill area in Orlando, Florida, is in general dentistry, with his specialty being preventive and restorative dentistry.

Jolyon has diverse interests. He is active with many of the car associations in Central Florida—BMW, EVO, RSX, and Corvette. Members of these groups are all car aficionados who gather regularly to share their passion for speed. He has participated in several autocross races, and he takes a keen interest in Formula One racing. Other joys are photography, videography, the theater, and traveling. In sports, Jolyon was the under-thirteen track-and-field champion at Queen's College. He played badminton in the junior leagues in Toronto and still enjoys hitting a shuttlecock when his arm allows him that luxury.

Jolyon speaks with pride about his wife and two daughters. Wife Denise, also an achiever, holds the degree of bachelor of business administration from the University of Miami, Coral Gables, Florida. Her professional experience is in human resources in the banking and health care industries. She is a stay-at-home mom, party planner for the family, and enjoys scrapbooking, reading, the theater, and traveling. She also belly-dances several times a week. According to Jolyon, "She's the glue that holds our family together."

Of his two daughters, Jolyon says, "Chelsey is a smart young lady who can navigate her way through computers and technology and has her daddy's quick wit and love of all trivial and insignificant pieces of information. My younger daughter, Tiffany, is passionate about all forms of dance, with a heavy influence in classical ballet. I am particularly proud of her involvement with the dance therapy program as a mentor to kids with disabilities. Both girls are very intelligent and poised young ladies, and they bring a lot of joy to our life."

July 29, 2008

Vivian Lee

Broadcasting, Records, MC, Stage Shows
Advertising, Impresario, Icon

Vivian Lee has been a national celebrity in British Guiana since the 1950s; his was a household name. He was an entrepreneur in the enterprising world of entertainment, in broadcasting, stage shows, and advertising. He started Guyana's first record-producing company. He made the first locally produced film. Outstanding at soccer, he played for Guyana.

In Canada, at age seventy-five, he obtained a bachelor's degree in English, set up business ventures, and wrote an inspiring book *Super Seniors: Beyond 65 and fully alive,* about Canadian pace-setting seniors who live an exemplary lifestyle.

Vivian came from humble beginnings, but he was forever determined to forge his way through obstacles, not merely to do well but to break new ground, to create, and achieve. He set high benchmarks in Guyana in the fields of broadcasting and entertainment.

Vivian was born in Georgetown on August 27, 1919. His father, Lee Yew, came from China. His mother was Adelaide DeFreitas. The family was living in Albertown, Georgetown, when Vivian was born. They ran a laundry.

He attended St. Angela's Primary School in Church Street, Georgetown, then went to St. Mary's Roman Catholic School, and St. Stanislaus College, where he obtained his Cambridge Senior school certificate.

He got his first job with Andrew "Chunnie" James at BG Pawnbrokery in around 1936. Andrew James was a well-known name at the time, with businesses all over the country. Two years later, Vivian was offered a job in the civil service. This was something to celebrate, as it was much better than the prospect of being a laundryman. Indeed, according to most people, including Vivian's mother, the four top jobs were doctor, lawyer, working with Bookers—the biggest business enterprise in the colony—or working in the civil service, with good pay and conditions; a respectable job.

The war started soon after Vivian joined the civil service. He did well in the civil service, but he really did not like the job. He, like many young people of his time, longed to "see the world," to go abroad. He had a taste of travel when he went to Trinidad. He was enrolled in the military as a part-time auxiliary.

Not long after the war ended, Vivian made the brave decision to leave the civil service and seek his fortune in America. From steady pay and a reasonably secure future, he ventured into the unknown. But for many, America in those days, was the "land of opportunity." Vivian grabbed every opportunity that came his way. He worked and studied. He armed himself with know-how about broadcasting, script writing, commercials, and techniques for interviewing, and he returned to Guyana. The rest is history.

His son, Ron, has written a brief account of Vivian's achievements. Here it is in part:

Soccer:
Right-winger for a number of teams including Charlton Gunners (which he helped found) and British Guiana National Team, where he scored against Surinam in competition and was the first and possibly the only Guyanese to score against Brazil in a friendly match. His exploits on the football field were legendary.

Early radio shows:
During the late 1940s and early 1950s, Vivian was one of the pioneers of variety programming in Guyana. With programs such as *Ovaltine*

Kids (showcasing Guyanese kids' singing talent), *Mrs. Snodgrass* (a weekly comedy program that became a staple of the Guyanese radio audience), *Gypsy Caravan*, *Time Is Money* (a popular quiz show), and *The Gong Show* (a talent show where judges "gonged" acts that were deemed not good enough). Later on, he emceed two musical programs, *Let's Have A Party* and *XM Hit Parade*.

Vaudeville and variety stage shows:

During the 1960s Vivian Lee created many successful stage shows in Georgetown and then took the troupes on tour, up and down the east and west coast, going as far west as Mackenzie (Linden), at that time only accessible by boat, and as far east as Berbice and even crossing over to Surinam. His early stage shows featured his own skits and his then five-year-old son. The shows' stars included notable Guyanese Calypsonians such as Lord Canary, Fighter, Melody, and Mighty Intruder. The shows were a wonderful mix of song (both pop and calypso), comedy skits (which included Guyanese Sam Dopey and later, Habeeb Khan) and Guyanese characters, such as the Memory Man.

Advertising:

After returning from serving in the British Army (Trinidad), where he started, wrote, and published the *Infantry Star*, he opened the first independent advertising agency in Guyana.

ACE Records:

Perhaps his biggest contribution to the music industry was his founding of ACE Records, which included a record store at Robb and King streets. His "ACE" record label was ground-breaking. He was the first person to record the Mighty Sparrow—"Jean and Dinah." In 1958 he wrote, produced, and recorded "Princess Margaret," sung by Lord Canary. This hit was presented to the princess by Vivian during a public ceremony. Another one of his early hits and possibly his favorite was his composition "Down on the Bottom Floor," sung by Lord Canary. Other hits included "My Dear" by Fighter, and of course the many songs by Billy Moore and the Four Lords. He later recorded many hits with Eddie Hooper, including "Where Are Your Friends Now?" He then discovered, managed, and recorded Johnny Braff, debuting with "It Burns Inside."

ACE Records was the first label to ever record a masquerade band (which was also the first and only time an expletive was recorded on his label). This went unnoticed in the studio, production, and was even played on the radio for months before anyone (except the singers, of course) realized it. His "Let's Celebrate Guyana" album also included pop, calypso and Indian music.

Emcee:

Besides continuing to run a successful advertising agency (Ace Advertising), record store, recording company, and music concert tours, in 1972 Vivian agreed to organize, promote, produce, and emcee a week-long concert and show at the National Park at the first Carifesta. This grand task included organizing and programming acts from over thirty Caribbean countries.

Laffarama:

This was a series of shows and tours that included songs and dance and featured Guyanese comedian Habeeb Khan, with scripts written by Vivian. This successful project, like all his other projects, donated a large part of the proceeds to a variety of Guyanese charities.

Film:

Perhaps Vivian's most ambitious project was *If Wishes Were Horses*. For this film project, Vivian wrote, casted, scouted locations, produced, and directed this ground-breaking Guyanese endeavor. Besides writing the script, he also wrote most of the songs, including the title song. Except for the cameraman and soundman, the entire cast and crew were Guyanese.

Canadian education:

Vivian attended the University of BC and obtained his bachelor's in English language at the age of seventy-five.

Award

In 2001, he was awarded the Wordsworth McAndrew Award for Outstanding Contribution to Guyana's Culture and Heritage.

Business ventures in Canada:

In 1996, he developed, produced, and marketed "Flying High," a Canadian award-winning board game.

In 2005, his interest in keeping good health in mind, body, and spirit led him to write a book about Canadian pace-setting seniors who live an exemplary lifestyle: *Super Seniors: Beyond 65 and fully alive*. A press release on the book was issued in January 2005. It reads, in part:

His mission is to promote and encourage a new generation of Canadian women and men living actively in body, mind, and spirit.

Viv Lee, himself an eighty-five-year-old "youngster," wants to share his spirit of positive thinking and active living with Canadian women and men over fifty and especially those about to retire at sixty-five. These are the years of fun and freedom, according to him, and "the years that should bring freedom from a 9-to-5 job and lead to the fun of a lifestyle that's limited only by the sweep of one's own vision."

Viv declares that although, in later years, the physical body does tend to weaken, it is the mind and spirit that can remain dominant influences for positive ideas and assertive behavior. His own over-sixty-five activities attest to this success-oriented philosophy.

His current passion is the mission he has set himself, "getting seniors to believe in the power they possess and unafraid to stay young at heart." His self-published book … is an anthology of twenty-eight real-life stories of Canadian seniors living exemplary lives and written by fourteen authors, mostly members of the Professional Writers Association of Canada; Viv wrote seven of the stories …

His hopes are "that we've captured the essential qualities of these ordinary Canadians living extraordinary lives and, by their example, can influence our readers to see how satisfying it could be to follow their admirable lifestyles."

The editor of *Super Seniors*, Ms. Zoe Stronge, wishes that Viv Lee had included his own story in this 2005 edition. She writes: "If this anthology is to come under criticism for any one thing, it would be the obvious omission of the publisher, Viv Lee, as the subject of a story. He has been a *Super Senior* these past twenty years and has accomplished more in that time than many people do in a lifetime …

"He rose from humble beginnings to become one of Guyana's most prominent citizens … Upon arriving in Canada in 1985, at the age of sixty-six, he founded the Guyanese Canadian Association of British Columbia, a society with the objective of raising funds for Guyanese charities through social events ... He is now deeply ensconced in the world of *Super Seniors*, tirelessly working toward the success of this, his latest venture."

Vivian's family consists of seven children from two marriages—his youngest child, Mary, was born just weeks before his sixty-sixth birthday—ten grandchildren, and five great-grandchildren. Though he left Guyana thirty years ago, his homeland has never been far from his thoughts.

His favorite quote is from Norman Vincent Peale, and it summarizes well his approach to life: "You can precondition your mind to success. Always act as if it were impossible to fail!"

Sources:
Cane Ripples by Trev Sue-A-Quan. Published by Cane Press.

October 7, 2010

Geeta Leo

Geeta Leo

Indian Classical Odissi Dancer
Director of Geetika

Geeta Leo, the first—and so far, the only—Odissi dancer and dance teacher to emerge out of Guyana, was a dancer in the first Guyanese movie, *Anmol Bandhan*. She choreographed a play on the life of Mahatma Gandhi. She was creator of the Heritage Fashion Show "Retrospect," and she is a member of the Cultural Arts Advisory Committee, Town of Ajax, Ontario. She has performed at the first Caribana Inter-Faith Service in Toronto, and for Panorama India, the cultural arm of the Indian consulate in Toronto.

Odissi (pronounced "Orissi") is one of the main styles of Indian classical dance. It takes its name from the province of Orissa, in northeast India. Its special features are independent movements of head, chest, and hips. It is a sacred dance, a form of worship and meditation, with its origins in the great Jagannath Temple in the holy city of Puri.

Geeta Yindrawatie Leo was born on September, 28, 1949, to Jai Narain and Radhay Janki Singh of Alexander Village, Georgetown, Guyana.

Her father, known as "Uncle Gully," was head driver and later was appointed the first East Indian overseer for Ruimveldt sugar estate, in the then British Guiana. He was also president of the Headmen's Union. Her mother, popularly known as "Aunty Radhay," ran her own successful grocery store.

In addition to being successful in their respective careers, Geeta's parents were very committed to their religion, both being active members of the village temple. Her father was the president of the Alexander Village Mandir, and her mother was president of the Lakshmi Sabha. They were also members of the Sanatan Dharm Maha Sabha and the Balak Sahaita Mandalee, as well as community organizations such as the Dharam Shala, of which her father was president for several years, and the Guyana Red Cross. Her mother was a member of the Village Council and chairman of the board of Ruimveldt School. She also was quite well known for her beautiful singing.

Growing up in the village, the children lived a life that was the best of both worlds, with a proper Hindu upbringing with Hindi classes, instruction in Hinduism, and Hindi Sunday school, as well as attending the Christian Sunday school.

Geeta attended St. Andrew's School in Georgetown and Central High School. After the death of her father when Geeta was twelve years old, her mother became the guiding hand for the family and a strong role model for her children. Through her initiatives as a successful businesswoman, she was able to send her children to high school and later on to university and vocational school abroad.

Her mother was keen for her children to know more about their religion and culture, and they were able to meet visiting musicians and religious personages from abroad. One was Ma Yoga Shakti, with whom they had early morning and evening yoga and religious instruction, and Sant Keshavdas and Shri Chelaram and his wife, with their inspirational *bhajans*, who visited their home in Alexander Village. Her mother was also Geeta's first dance teacher, as she involved not only her children but many children of the village in performing on stage at the village temple fund-raising activities.

Geeta's eldest sister, Indranie, married Pandit Reepu Daman Persaud and that brought another major influence into their lives. They became more involved in the Maha Sabha, its youth group, and its activities, planning functions, baking, cooking, making handicraft for the Deepavali Melas, and other functions. All these activities led the family on a path of community involvement and service.

The Singh family were by now developing musical and dance skills. Brother Vickram was an excellent tabla player, and together with his brother, the late Onkar Singh, who played the sitar, he joined with the famous Guyanese singer Gobin Ram in radio and other performances. Her sister Ronica also started playing the drums and the harmonium. Sister Looma is now the singer of the family. From the early 1970s until Geeta left Guyana, their home was always full of the sound of music and dance by masters and students alike.

Geeta was the quiet one, neither a singer nor a dancer. She would never be included among the children to recite poems or any such things because she was just so quiet and shy. She was very good with her hands and became the baker, the one who would sew and embroider, fix saris for her mother, and later on sew costumes for the dancers. She much preferred to sit in a corner and read a book, oblivious to the world around.

She was sitting quietly reading one day when her younger sister ran into the room excitedly brandishing the newspaper. "Geeta, the Indian consulate will be opening a cultural center to teach dancing, and I am going to join up." Geeta listened with an indulgent smile. Her sister, Deviekha, was crazy about dancing.

The Indian Cultural Center (ICC) opened in January 1973, and Deviekha enrolled for Kathak dance classes. Their mother, who was a prominent singer in the community, registered for vocal lessons, and their brother for tabla classes. Once classes started, for three days a week, the house was very quiet for hours. Geeta would be the only one at home.

The classes at the ICC did not interest her at all. However, in February 1973, after some prompting from her sister, Geeta agreed to go with her for classes. Unfortunately, Deviekha's class was full, but her teacher recommended that Geeta try the new style of dance class. It was called Odissi. Geeta started classes in February 1973 and immediately excelled.

One month later, Geeta was involved in a car accident and sustained a serious head injury, with lacerations to her scalp and forehead that required stitches. Geeta remembers thinking, "So this is how I will die." Because of her injuries, Geeta did not return to dance classes for about two months. When she did return, she found that the class had grown from the original eight pupils to twenty-eight and split in two groups, one for new students, the other for the more advanced. Geeta was placed in the beginner group.

It was painful for Geeta, watching some of the students try to do the steps, and for weeks on end they kept doing the same thing over and over. Geeta was getting frustrated. She was not enjoying the classes and contemplated giving up. Her teacher noticed her frustration and moved her to the more advanced class.

Soon she was selected to perform an Odissi dance at the first concert to be staged by the ICC. When she was told that she was going to perform on stage, Geeta refused, saying that she had only joined to learn to dance; she did not want to perform on stage. Her teacher lost her temper and ordered Geeta out of the class. Her sister was mad at her, and her brothers laughed at her for being a scaredy cat, and Geeta realized she either had to give up dancing or overcome her inhibitions and get up on stage. The stage and dance won.

She learned a valuable lesson: "Encourage, not discourage. Never tell a person [he or she] cannot dance."

Geeta was one of a select group of students chosen to perform for the ICC. She performed a dance with this group in the local movie, *Anmol*

Bandhan. As far as she knows, she remains today the only Odissi dancer from Guyana.

From 1979 to 1985, she was the lead dancer and choreographer for the Guyana Hindu Dharmic Sabha, an organization launched by her brother-in-law, Pandit Reepu Daman Persaud, and she taught many young boys and girls to dance. Geeta was instrumental in bringing to the Guyanese audience a whole new level of creativity with her dance choreography.

Among several highlights as a dancer in Guyana, for Geeta the most memorable was when she choreographed the Shiv Tandav ballet to music composed by Dr. Sunil Satpatty of the ICC. On his recommendation, Geeta was offered a scholarship to India to train under the renowned Odissi guru, Kelucharan Mohapatra. She did not accept it because she was emigrating to Canada and did not think she would dance again.

As a student at the ICC, Geeta would occasionally conduct classes while her teacher was away in Trinidad or Suriname. That is how Nadira Shah, another prominent Guyanese dancer, who is still practicing her art, came to be taught by Geeta.

Geeta also collaborated with another dance teacher at the ICC, Girdhar Charan Chand, to choreograph the dance Makhan Chor to the song by Anup Jalota. Geeta represented Guyana at the International Festival of Youths and Students, held in Cuba in 1978.

Her services in Guyana were entirely voluntary, and among her students were her three nieces, Dr. Vindhya Vasini Persaud, Trishala Persaud, and Susan De Jesus. Vindhya and Trishala are now performers and choreographers in their own right, teaching dance in Georgetown and representing Guyana and the Guyana Hindu Dharmic Sabha, locally and overseas. Geeta has conducted Odissi workshops for students of the dance school in Guyana

Besides dancing, there were two other sides to Geeta's life. One was as a business administrator, the other was her involvement with the Maharishi Mahesh Yogi's Transcendental Meditation (TM) movement.

She joined the Maharishi's movement in 1977. When the advanced TM-Siddhis program, was offered in Guyana, Geeta was among the first group of participants, which included a number of prominent Guyanese. The TM-Siddhis program is said to awaken the eight *siddhis* —psychic powers achieved either naturally or by yogic practices—perfection in speech, speaking the truth, clairvoyance, clairaudience, ability to become invisible, astral travel, and ability to make oneself small or large.

The TM-Siddhis program brings the mind and body into a state of coherence for the practitioner to be able to perform yogic flying or levitation—the ability to lift the body off the ground and move above the ground. Geeta says she can levitate.

In 1979, Geeta was offered a scholarship to Medellin, Colombia, to take the TM teacher training program, but she again refused, not sure that it was what she wanted. She became the secretary of the TM movement in Guyana and ran the operations of the organization. She ran programs for teen meditators and offered lecture demonstrations on yoga to adults and students.

Geeta is married to David Leo of Mahaicony Creek. David was an auditor at Thomas Stoll Dias & Company in Georgetown. They met when their companies shared offices in the same premises. Geeta was working as the office manager/cocoordinator, working with three stalwarts of the Guyanese business community on a new venture, Management Services (Guyana) Limited. This organization which trained managers in Guyana, worked in collaboration with a Canadian company, the Foundation for International Training (FIT), and was funded by the Canadian government. All training was free to the managers.

Geeta and David moved to Canada in 1986 and currently live in Ajax, Ontario. David is the finance manager at the Oshawa Community Health Center. They have two children, Nicholas Rudranand and Premika. Geeta was employed at IBM Canada for five years. Within a year of joining the company, she became executive assistant to the legal and financial executives at the IBM Toronto Software Lab. This lab, at the time, was reputed to be the oldest of the Canadian labs and the largest software lab in Canada.

In Toronto, in April 1988, Geeta and her sister Deviekha, together with their nieces Kavita Doodnauth and Kirti Singh, performed the Jihagin dance, tracing a typical day in the life of the immigrant woman. This dance was conceived and choreographed by the sisters for the Association of Concerned Guyanese in Toronto and performed at York University. That was the sisters' first performance in Toronto and their first performance together since Deviekha left Guyana in 1979.

Because of her reputation as a dancer in Guyana, Geeta was approached by friends to start teaching dance in Canada. After discussions with her husband and her sister, Deviekha and Geeta decided to launch a dance school. The Tarana Dance School was set up to teach Kathak and Odissi dances; it would be two separate schools, operating under the one name: Tarana.

Geeta and Deviekha staged their first concert at the Ontario Science Center in 1989. Their cast comprised about five students and the rest were family and friends.

The sisters started their school in 1990. They brought to Toronto something that was not there before—a dance school that West Indians felt comfortable sending their children to, yet open to all. The sisters were kept busy with students and also performing for temples, Guyanese, and other organizations for which they received many volunteer and recognition awards, most notable the award from the Vedic Cultural Center for their contribution to Indian culture in Canada.

Geeta Leo and her students participated at the annual Guyana Day celebrations in Toronto until 1994. She has been actively involved in Indian Heritage Month from its inception, when she produced a fashion show tracing indentured women's fashion and jewelery through the years. They named it "Retrospect." In this fashion show, Geeta trained her students to model, adding a new element to the offerings of the Tarana Dance School. Six Canadian girls of Guyanese parentage proudly wore items of clothing similar to those worn by the early immigrant women from India, - the Gangri, Jhoola and Rumal, foot rings and nose rings, much like their great-grandmothers would have done. Gangri was a long full skirt decorated with at least 3 bands of contrasting material/ribbon at the bottom. Jhoola was the blouse, and Rumal was the headtie.

This was showcased at the first Indian Arrival Day celebrations in Toronto held in 1998 and has been repeated at Tarana Dance School's recital, the Guyana Day celebrations, and the Indo-Caribbean Golden Age Association's tenth anniversary celebrations. Many people praised the show for being extremely informative and said that it brought back memories of the ladies of Guyana in their rumal. Each year, Geeta choreographs new items specifically for Indian Heritage Month.

Geeta and her family moved from Scarborough to Ajax in the Durham region in 1999. She became the first Indo-Caribbean dance teacher in the Durham region, an area with a very small Indian population. She was, therefore, surprised at the response to her school, which grew rapidly in the first three years in Durham and continues to grow steadily.

In order to promote and reward the students who were focused on classical dance Geeta introduced a graduation exam and ceremony, at which certificates are awarded. Graduate students had to complete five

Odissi dances and be able to perform for one hour straight. Her first graduation ceremony took place in 2002 and to date, nineteen students have graduated.

Geeta has had the privilege of teaching Indian dance to Canadian ballerina Tania Hakkim, while Tania was preparing for her audition for a part in Andrew Lloyd Webber's Broadway production of *Bombay Dreams*. Tania got the part, appearing on Broadway from April 2004 to January 2005.

In July 2001, Geeta's sister Ronica Jaipershad, who lives in Tampa, Florida started a magazine, *We Indians*. After the first issue Ronica asked Geeta to become the layout editor. Geeta had absolutely no experience in magazine layout, picture enhancements, or sizing or anything else that goes into producing a magazine. She had to learn two software programs in order to put out the next issue. It was a steep learning curve, but she managed to get it done. The magazine was in operation for about three years and was circulated in the United States, Canada, England, Guyana, Trinidad, and Bahamas.

Geeta and her daughter collaborated with a jazz, tap, and ballet school in Ajax, teaching students in their Dance Intensive program to perform two Indian dances. They were all non-Indians, yet the language and the music did not bother them at all; in fact, they welcomed the opportunity to learn a new style. Within a few lessons they had completed and performed the dances.

In 2007, Geeta finally went to India, where she attended classes with Guru Durga Charan Ranbir. There she met another young dancer, Rahul Acharya, who, in addition to being a dancer, is a Vedic scholar and was her guide when she visited the famous Sun Temple in Konark and the Jagannath Temple in Puri, Orissa.

Geeta's visit to Jagannath Temple, considered one of the four places of pilgrimage for Hindus, was of special significance for her, as it was there that the Odissi dance of which Geeta is a humble exponent is said to have it origins, centuries ago.

In 2008 Geeta formally included her daughter, Premika, in the operation of the school and changed the name to Geetika, the Indian Dance Company. Their first performance as Geetika was for the town of Ajax in September 2008. Husband, David, and son, Rudra, always support Geeta and Premika in whatever way they can, whether it is making props or being the technical support at performances. The dance school has truly created a strong family bond.

Geeta calls her story one of "spinning straw into gold." You get a little bit of training but it is what you do with it, how much you use your initiative and share your knowledge. She was taught by her sister at home and became a top secretary in Guyana and in Canada, with her bosses amazed that she had received all her training in Guyana.

She received minimal training in dance but has trained hundreds, performed in front of large audiences, both local and international, produced quality performances, giving joy to many and made others proud. From a shy child afraid to speak, she transformed into someone who can stand and address a large audience.

Her students' performance of Odissi dance has been of a high order. The numerous requests from Indian organizations for her students to perform Odissi dance is praise enough. Perhaps her greatest compliment came from a Hindu priest in Canada, praising her for the work she has done teaching the children about their culture and religion.

According to Geeta, "It all starts with Geetika (a little song) or a piece of music from which a dance is created and a dancer emerges."

November 13, 2008

Ray Luck

CCH, FRCM, BMus(Hons), DMus
International Concert Pianist
Professor Emeritus

Ray Luck, an acclaimed concert pianist worldwide, the winner of numerous awards, is a music educator and music festival adjudicator, among many other of his achievements.

He has performed in concerts and recitals in several music capitals of the world. His performances in New York's Alice Tully Hall, in London's Queen Elizabeth and Royal Albert Halls, in Paris's Théâtre des Champs Elysées, and other major concert venues have won public and critical acclaim.

He has appeared as soloist with the Paris Conservatoire, Suisse Romande Orchestras, and the City of London Sinfonia. He has collaborated in chamber music performances with the New World and Lark String Quartets. His concert tours have extended through Eastern and Western Europe, North and South America, the Caribbean, Asia, and Australia.

Ray is an alumnus of Indiana University; Conservatoire National Superieur de Musique, Paris; University of London and Royal College of Music, London; Queen's College, Guyana; and Laureat du Concours International de Piano, Geneve. He is a master teacher, Music Teachers National Association, and an approved judge of the Florida State Music Teachers Association and a member of Greater Saint Petersburg Music Teachers Association.

Ray was born on November 18, 1942, at Georgetown. His father was A. E. (Cowie) Luck, a math teacher at Central High School. His mother, Claris, was the homemaker. He is their third of four children. The oldest is Desmond, followed by sister Beverley (Guyana Scholar, 1956), Ray, and sister Holly.

He attended Smith Church Congregational School, Hadfield Street, from 1948 to 53. He won a government county scholarship to attend Queen's College, where he studied until 1961.

Ray Luck's musical gifts were discovered very early. Early piano teachers in Guyana, Millicent Joseph and her sister, Ruby MacGregor, were his chief motivators. Participation in the biennial British Guiana Music Festival (founded in 1952 by Lynette Dolphin and Eleanor Kerry) throughout his childhood provided him and other young performers a platform to gain experience and confidence.

In Guyana, he studied and practiced and obtained the performing diplomas of licentiate and fellowship of the Royal Schools of Music and Trinity College, London.

He then proceeded to England, where he studied at the Royal College of Music in London, and later with Yvonne Lefébure at the Paris Conservatoire. He had the distinction of winning first prizes in piano and chamber music in his first year of study. His ability was rewarded with a scholarship from the Countess of Munster Musical Trust. This enabled Ray to specialize in music from the classical period with the British pianist Denis Matthews while gaining a bachelor of music degree, with honors, from London University.

Ray Luck then moved to the United States, where he entered the graduate program as a student of György Sebok at Indiana University and graduated with the doctor of music (DMus) degree, with high distinction. Ray thereafter launched himself fully into performing, along the way being showered with numerous awards, and he became sought after throughout the world.

He has conducted master classes at the National State Academy of Music in Sofia, Bulgaria; National Music Conservatory at Halandri, Athens; National University of Singapore; Kwassui Women's College, Nagasaki, Japan; Jamaica School of Music; St. Lucia School of Music; UWI Center for Creative and Festival Arts, Port of Spain, Trinidad; Barbados Piano Teachers Association; New Orleans Institute for the Performing Arts; Virginia Music Teachers Association State Convention; Brandon University, Manitoba; and the University of Manitoba, Winnipeg.

He has adjudicated at numerous music festivals, including the Trans-Canada Tour from Newfoundland to British Columbia for Canadian music competitions; Kiwanis Music Festivals in Ottawa, London, Calgary, and Edmonton; Brandon Festival of the Arts, Manitoba; Winnipeg Music Festival; Hong Kong Schools Music Festival; Guyana Music Festival; Antigua and Barbuda Music Festival; and Jamaica Music Festival.

Appointed professor emeritus, Ray Luck was the Charles A. Dana Professor of Music at Randolph College in Lynchburg, Virginia, until 2002. During his tenure he garnered a number of professional awards, including the Katherine Graves Davidson Distinguished Faculty Award, the master teacher certificate from the Music Teachers National Association, and three Senior Fulbright fellowships to the Caribbean, Greece, and Canada.

He has been a visiting professor at the Northeast London Polytechnic, UK; University of Maryland at College Park, MD; National Music Conservatory at Halandri, Athens; University of the West Indies at Cave Hill, Barbados; and St. Lucia School of Music, West Indies. Each July he conducts an annual international piano workshop at the St. Lucia School of Music.

Ray's musical accomplishments and service to music were deservedly recognized in 1992, when he was honored with the appointment as a Member of the Order of Service of Guyana and awarded the Cacique's Crown of Honor (CCH) for outstanding musical achievements.

June 25, 2008

The Honorable Judge Alli B. Majeed

Brevard County, Florida
From Cutlass and Grass Knife to Robe and Gavel

Over what mountains and hills, through what rivers and streams must his life have meandered from Anna Regina, Essequibo Coast, the son of rice farmers, with cutlass and grass knife the most familiar tools, way over the ocean to Brevard County/Space Coast Florida, to become a state judge with robe and gavel?

Before he became a judge in April 1993, Alli Baksh Majeed was a high school teacher, attorney in private practice, assistant public defender (Felony Division in Orlando, Florida), and assistant state attorney (Felony Division in Brevard County.)

He has a reputation as an energetic, engaging, and inspirational speaker. He has the nickname of "Mr. Patriotism" for delivering stirring patriotic speeches about the abundant opportunities America provides.

Judge Majeed is married and the father of three daughters—Faria, Allia, Amira—and a son, Noah. His wife, Yasmin, is the eldest child and only daughter of Mohamed Kamal and the late Shireen Kamal of Bloomfield, Corentyne, Guyana.

Alli Baksh Majeed, familiarly known as A. B., was born on June 30, 1947, at Anna Regina, Essequibo Coast, Guyana. He is the youngest of four brothers, followed by two sisters. His father had only one name, a common practice among Muslims, Majeed. His mother's name was Miriam. Both parents were rice farmers at a time when cutlass and grass knife were the principal agricultural tools. A. B. grew up learning the trade of "haaling Beyah"—shying the rice paddy by hand, cutting rice with a grass knife, weeding razor grass with cutlass, plowing and mashing rice with bulls.

He attended Anna Regina Government Primary School, where he passed his school leaving exams. He then attended the Anna Regina Government Secondary School, where he passed his GCE, O levels and became the very first student to pass one subject at the A level. Subsequently, he became the first student to become a teacher at the very high school where he attended for four years. During the years 1968–1969 he attended the University of Guyana at nights, at the Queen's College campus, and taught part-time at the Muslim Trust College/ High School in Brickdam, Georgetown.

In 1969, A. B. left Guyana for Howard University, Washington DC, where, in 1972 he earned a bachelor of arts degree, with the honors of *magna cum laude* and *phi beta kappa*. He then accepted a place at the Columbus School of Law/Catholic University, Washington DC, where he earned his juris doctor in law in 1975.

In 1979, he joined Community Legal Services, Philadelphia, Pennsylvania, where he served indigent clients and supervised staff. In 1982, he went into private practice in Delaware County, Pennsylvania, specializing in criminal defense work.

A. B. loved living and working in Philadelphia, but continued to suffer with very severe allergies, as he did while living in Guyana, from springtime pollen. He visited many dry regions, looking for a healthy climate in which to settle, which included the desert of Arizona and parts of California, before settling along the Atlantic Coast of Brevard County, Florida.

He served for a brief period as an assistant public defender in Orlando, where he defended indigent clients in felony cases. Living and working in Orlando provided a unique opportunity for A. B. to reconnect with one of his lost but not forgotten loves: the game of cricket. He was a first-choice opening batsman for the Caribbean Sports Club in Orlando, where he opened many an inning with former test star Faoud Bacchus.

In 1985 he accepted an appointment as assistant state attorney, Felony Division, Brevard County. Brevard County is known as the "Space Coast" because it is home to Cape Canaveral and the Kennedy Space Center. Brevard County has three rivers, the Indian River, the Banana River, and the Saint John's River and is situated along the Atlantic Coast. One of these rivers, the Saint John's attracts Guyanese from near and far, because it is a fertile breeding ground for the Guyana delicacy *hassa*. Word has spread from as far north as Toronto and as far south as Key West that…"nuff, nuff hassa dey a dah rivah.."

In April 1993, A. B. was chosen from a long list of applicants by the Honorable Governor Lawton Chiles to serve as a judge in the County Court Bench of Brevard County. Every six years he has been re-elected by the general voting population. In 2010, Judge Majeed was up for re-election, and no one opposed him. He was re-elected unopposed for the next 6 years beginning January 2011. Judge Majeed is the only man of a racial minority group to win a countywide election in Brevard County. In the entire state of Florida—and quite possibly the entire United States—A. B. Majeed is the only judge of Indo-Guyanese heritage.

Judge Majeed was elected president of the Conference of County Court Judges for the year 2004–05. In this capacity he served as president of all the county court judges in the state of Florida, bringing him in close contact not only with all the judges, but with the chief justice and elected officials in the Florida House and Senate in the state's capital of Tallahassee. He was elected by his fellow local judges as their administrative judge and also to oversee the fairness of the local elections by serving on the Canvassing Board of Brevard County.

He has served as faculty for the National Judicial College, Reno, Nevada, and as course instructor for the statewide Florida New County Judges Program. He was also selected as one of two judges from the United States to participate in a teaching program in the former Soviet Bloc country of Tajikistan.

A. B. is recipient of many awards, such as the Caribbean Bar Association Pioneer Award 2006, the Harvey Ford Award (the highest award given to any county judge in Florida), and the Silver and Bronze Good Citizenship Awards from the Sons of the American Revolution.

Judge Majeed's background in Guyana, his scholarship, patriotic verve, oratorical gifts, and zeal as an educator have been described in a glowing tribute written by Judge Peggy Gehl and was published in the *County*

Court Courier of Fall 2004. The occasion was his appointment as president of the Conference of County Court Judges for the year 2004–05.

In her article, Judge Gehl referred to Judge Majeed's nickname of "Mr. Patriotism" by noting, " acquired, for delivering stirring patriotic speeches about the abundant opportunities America provides… He has truly lived the American dream and come a long way from his humble beginnings in British Guyana, South America. His ancestors arrived in British Guyana from India as indentured servants, enduring a treacherous crossing over the *kala pani*, or black water, with the promise of a short journey and money to bring back home to India to their families."

At A. B.'s young age, Judge Gehl stated, he was determined to improve his economic and social position, — noting that persons better dressed working in offices were better off than his parents, who toiled in heat, mud, and sharp blades of razor grass.

During A. B.'s time, high school education was not free. His parents had to pay school fees of $22.50 per month, which was quite a financial burden for parents in Anna Regina at that time. His parents worked the fields while he and an older brother attended school. Two of his brothers were denied an equivalent education because the cost was too great. "For the first child to make it," AB said, "the other children would have to sacrifice, suffer, and be denied."

"Our new President AB Majeed enjoys a reputation as a dynamic public speaker. He has spoken for dozens of community, religious and educational groups in his own county, and enjoys every speaking invitation as an opportunity to promote his passionate patriotism, and beliefs in democracy, and Constitutional law."

In recent years the Department of Immigration has invited him to be the guest speaker at naturalization ceremonies, applying his personal experience to extend a welcome to new citizens.

Judge Gehl concluded, with these words: "A. B. epitomizes the American dream in every aspect of his professional and personal life. Becoming the leader of the Conference of County Court Judges creates another opportunity for him to enhance the image of the judiciary for all of us."

A. B. responded to his appointment, in part, with the following words:

> It is with great pride that I embark on the responsibility you have conferred on me as your president of your Conference of County Court Judges. I am grateful for this opportunity. I

> commit all my diligence, all my intellect, and all my industry toward promoting the welfare of each and every county judge. ...
>
> Education is the bedrock of our existence…At my first board meeting in July, I introduced a very special program to you entitled "For the Love of our Children." October 13 was set aside for County Judges throughout the State of Florida to read to students in our local schools. I am proud of all the County Judges who took advantage of this excellent opportunity to increase our community image while educating the public.
>
> As county judges we pride ourselves on being the "people's judge," presiding over the "people's court." ... Let us go forth in full force and give back to our neighbors' children in our neighborhood schools.

During his tenure, A. B. set and accomplished several lofty goals for his fellow judges, and he will be forever remembered for securing a very generous pay hike for all his fellow county judges from the Florida Legislature.

When he is not serving as a judge or engaging in stirring patriotic speeches, Judge Majeed finds time for tennis, golf, and his favorite sport, cricket. He was elected captain of the Brevard cricket team, where he acquired a just reputation as the slowest scoring batsman around. He was a fearless opening batsman and faced many a fast bowler. He was influential in persuading the county commissioners to allocate a beautiful plot of land for what is probably the best –entirely for- cricket field in Florida.. In 2009 the County Parks and Recreation Department dedicated, at a ceremony attended by the local Congressman, Mayor, County Commissioner, Guyana's Representative, and about 300 cricket fans, a lovely facility and named it the Judge Majeed Cricket Pavilion.

Judge Majeed never forgets his dear land of Guyana. He swears that he lived in heaven while growing up in Anna Regina:

"There were abundant streams, plentiful with fish. Nice trenches with sparkling water for swimming. Fruit trees galore—jamoon, dounce, guava, mangoes, coconuts, soursap, monkey apple, star apple, genips, fat pork, stink toes, and the unforgettable locus." He remembers the beautiful birds, gaily plumaged, and their sweet "whistles"—blue sackies, kiskadees, robin red breast, parakeets. "Every night a flock of noisy parakeets will bed down in our coconut trees."

He remembers the lovely flowers and healing plants such as black sage, sweet broom for tea, neem that heals anything, moco-moco that heals cutlass and grass knife wounds, and carrion crow bush, which "we used for scoring in cricket by tearing off a half leaf for every run. In the early mornings we did not need alarm clocks to wake us up because…foh day maanin cock a crow. I can still smell the 'green green grass of home', so ideal for cricket, and feel the prevailing Atlantic breezes.

"I used to have to sweep the fowl pen clean, for that was the ideal breezeless location to gather the gamma cherry and kite paper for Easter kite making. When Christmas comes, how can we ever forget Bad Cow and Laaang Lady? Not to mention hot Rotie, Doll Poorie, all kinds of mouth-watering curry, and ginger beer and freshly baked fruit cakes."

In the beginning there was Anna Regina, the rice fields, working with cutlass and grass knife, in mud and water, sun and rain. Now there is the Bench in Brevard County Courthouse, shade, air-conditioning, robe and gavel.

To what does Judge Majeed credit this dream-come-true journey? He does not hesitate: it was his godsend mother and father, unschooled but not uneducated. They daily demonstrated what hard work, discipline, and common sense economics meant. "My mother was the epitome of love and gentleness, and my father was a disciplined hard worker. He was full of *gyaan* (Hindi for wisdom). When asked to highlight one special gyaan that his father left with him, Judge Majeed recited this: "Nay Key Ka Reh Dar Yah May Dal". Do good, then throw it in the river and never mention it again."

Judge Majeed's mother entered into an arranged marriage with his father. She was thirteen and he was twenty-three. They immediately set about the task of forging a living and raising a family. Although they were denied many of life's luxuries, they lived long enough to see many of their dreams realized through the accomplishments of their children and their grandchildren. Their first born is a graduate of the University of Glasgow Medical School. Another is a lance corporal in the Guyana Defense Force, and another son is a Hajji. They also have two dedicated and lovely daughters, one of whom has a master's degree from the University of Maryland.

Among their many grandchildren, one served in the United States Navy, one served in the United States Air Force, and one great-grandson recently completed a stint in the United States Marines.

Judge Majeed is emphatic in his belief that the entire Majeed family, children, grand-children, great-grand-children, daily are influenced and blessed by the works and teachings of his beloved father, Majeed, and mother, Miriam. For all of his personal and professional accomplishments, he gives thanks to his God and to his beloved parents.

He has said, "MAJEED and MIRIAM now Rest in Peace in Fort Linclon Cemetery, Maryland, USA. May Almighty God Bless them with eternal Peace and everlasting Rest. May they forever bask in God's special Rose Garden, FIRDOUSH.

"I have been blessed to visit many historic and beautiful places in the world, in the United States, Alaska, Hawaii, Puerto Rico, Europe, India, the Caribbean, England, Wales, and Ireland, but I never ever forget Guyana.'is whe me navel string berry.'"

>Oh dear land of Guyana from you we can never be free.
>Home you are, and home you shall always be.
>Dear land of Guyana, I love you so.
>Pack up me grip and lemme go.
>Me ah go back ah Essequibo.

Sources:
Websites accessed April 6.2010.
www.flcourts18.org/bio_majeed_bre.
www.countyJudges.com/courier/Fall04.
www.flcourts18.org/PDF/BIO.

November 4, 2010

A. Shakoor Manraj, QC

BA, LLB
Barrister/Attorney at Law, Diploma of Jurisprudence
Broadcaster and International Consultant

Shakoor Manraj, QC, a brilliant criminal defense attorney with success at 330 murder trials, has practiced in over thirty-five different jurisdictions, in the Caribbean Islands, Europe, Asia, the United States, and Canada. He successfully defended a Guyanese seaman in Venezuela charged with murder. He has appeared before the Privy Council in England. In Canada he was a crown attorney.

He was a broadcaster on the BBC and Radio Demerara. He lectured at Imperial College in London. He studied law in the United States, England, France, and Canada. An ace debater, he won his USA University prize for oratory. His father was a detective sergeant in the British Guiana Police Force. His maternal uncle became a barrister at law in 1925.

Abdool Shakoor Manraj was born on July 25, 1925, in Georgetown, British Guiana, at Lamaha and Albert Streets in a house that his grandfather originally built at Mahaica, East Coast Demerara—he had it removed and re-erected when he decided to come to Georgetown to take up residence in Lamaha Street.

Shakoor's father, Azeez Rahamat Manraj, was the eldest son of Indian immigrant Manraj who had estates on the East Coast, Demerara. Azeez wanted to become a surgeon but Grandfather Manraj wanted him to go into the family business. Azeez eventually decided to join the British Guiana Police Force as a detective and he attained the rank of sergeant. After he retired from the police force, he ran a small business. When Shakoor returned to Guyana to practice his profession, his father joined him in his law office. For this, Shakoor was very happy, as his father had tremendous experience about police investigations and court practice.

His dear mother, born Jane Makbulan Bunyadi, bore his father eight children—four boys and four girls. Shakoor is the fifth child. His mother's brother, P. M. Benson, was an East Indian Guyanese, who studied law in England, became a barrister at law and was called to the bar of the Honorable Society of the Middle Temple Law School in 1925, the same year Shakoor was born. As long as he can remember Shakoor always wanted to study law although his father wanted him to become a surgeon.

He was educated at the Houston Methodist School, East Bank, Demerara. Miss Mildred Millington, the headmistress, a very dedicated and motherly lady, guided him through primary school. He went to Enterprise High School, which had as its founder principal that very outstanding educator, the late R. B. O. Hart, then on to Central High School under J. C. Luck, and then on to Queen's College. He was very impressed by Mr. H. A. M. Beckles, a qualified barrister at law who was head of the French Department at Queen's.

Shakoor then proceeded on to Lincoln University in Chester County, Pennsylvania, where he earned the BA (with honors) degree in English. While at Lincoln University, he displayed a natural gift for oratory. He was the prize winner of the university oratorical contest and in 1947, he was a member of the Lincoln University debating team, which debated with England's Oxford University in New York. Later, when he went to England, he had the pleasure of meeting both members of the Oxford team in London and Oxford.

From Lincoln University, Shakoor went to Columbia University in New York, where in 1948 he obtained the diploma of international law. He then left for England to continue his law studies at the Middle Temple in London. During this time, from 1951 to 1953, Shakoor took up an appointment as lecturer at the Imperial Institute, Kensington, London.

Having completed the bar finals, he was called to the bar at the Honorable Society of the Middle Temple, London, on February 9, 1954.

While studying and lecturing law, Shakoor added broadcasting to his career. He was a broadcaster at the BBC in London.

On January 23, 1954, Shakoor married Gladys May Goodway of Wimbledon, England.

Shakoor has studied in the United States, England, France, and Canada, and he eventually practiced in New York after being specially admitted to appear there, to defend a Guyanese charged with several serious criminal offences.

Returning to Guyana he soon made a name for himself as a criminal defense lawyer, in particular, remarkable success of acquittals in murder trials.

While in the legal practice in Guyana, Shakoor took on other public duties. In 1960, he had the privilege of being the leader of the Progressive Liberal Party in Guyana, but only for a short term, as he was very committed to his law practice and not politics.

In 1960, he was appointed as the independent member of the Building Trade Commission of Enquiry. In 1961 he was appointed chairman of the Quarry Workers Advisory Committee and held meetings in the relevant areas in Guyana involving quarry workers.

Also in 1961, he appeared before the Privy Council in the celebrated Mahaica Creek Murder Case Trial. The Privy Council was presided over by the brilliant jurist, the late Lord Denning. When he visited Guyana in 1974, accompanied by Lady Denning, Shakoor had the pleasure of meeting him again at various functions.

In 1965 Shakoor appeared before the three-man International Commission of Jurists, which came to British Guiana to investigate and report on the inter-relationship, economic, educational, social, and political conditions of the six races of British Guiana. At the conclusion of his submissions and representations, he felt a glow of complete satisfaction. Each member of the commission, in a flow of ornate language, thanked him for his "useful and in-depth arguments and presentation," which all the members emphatically stated would "help them immensely in formulating their report."

Shakoor presided as the judge in the final round of the Patrick Dargan Debating Shield Contest, held in Georgetown, Guyana, in 1967. The shield was presented to commemorate the memory of Patrick Dargan, and the debates were held in Georgetown on a "knock-out" system, which eventually recognized the finalists of the debating contests.

On December 31, 1969, Barrister Shakoor Manraj achieved his greatest ambition. He was appointed Queen's Counsel by Her Majesty, the queen, for "his distinguished and meritorious service to the legal profession and the public."

Broadcasting, Shakoor's other career, also flourished, although the law was his main commitment. "It wasn't law all the time. Since my student days, I was assiduously connected with radio and broadcasting." In Guyana, he delivered commentaries over the radio. The most popular program he aired over Radio Demerara was the morning program called *Analysis*. It was recommended by many schools as required listening. The subscribing schools had students write their views on his Radio Demerara morning *Analysis* program.

He was also a member of the panel on the *Stump the Panel* program in 1969, heard every Tuesday night on Radio Demerara. Continuing his radio commitments, he hosted the Saturday night radio show *Off the Record*. "This was a one-hour radio program that I hosted and played the records I liked and the music, which I identified with places I visited, along with reasons for my selections," states Shakoor in his memoirs, *In Pursuit of Justice*.

> I also found time to enjoy some relaxation. I was always a member of the Georgetown Cricket Club and my professional body, the Guyana Bar Association and the Guyana Motor Racing Club. My recreation is still motoring, walking, and reading. I am an avid reader and that keeps me superbly informed of the many developments that are taking place in our social, economic, academic and educational affairs.

On December 14, 1976, his dear wife, Gladys, passed away after a short illness. He and his children decided to go back to England, where the maternal grandparents of his children resided. However, in England the memories were still very much alive with them, so they all decided to find a new life in a new country.

In 1978, Shakoor and children emigrated to Canada, which he said was "a very lovely and hospitable country." In 1979, he joined the Ministry of the Attorney General as crown attorney in the then new Provincial Offenses Appeal Court in Ontario.

The attorney general of Ontario at the time was Mr. R. Roy McMurtry, QC, "a very fine and learned gentleman." They became great friends. Mr. McMurtry was attorney general of Ontario from 1975 to 1985. On April 30, 1985, he was appointed Canadian High Commissioner to the United Kingdom. Shortly after his return from London, he was appointed Chief Justice of Ontario.

In his long career, Shakoor has written numerous articles on important aspects of the law. During his appointment as crown attorney in Ontario, he completed the book, *The Law on Speeding and Radar*, coauthored with his colleague and friend Dr. Paul D. Haines. Although the offense of speeding is perhaps the most prevalent offense before our courts, the law in this particular area is anything but simple. This book sought to set out the law relating to the offense of speeding. It provides a convenient and useful source book for all persons dealing with speeding cases—defendants, lawyers, police officers, and judicial officers. Today, that book is in its third edition as *The Law on Speeding and Speed Detection Devices.* The three editions of this book examine the law regarding speeding and detection of speeding by radar and other speed detection devices. Dr. Paul D. Haines is a brilliant senior consultant in remote systems, and his present work involves guidance and control systems for both the Canadian and U.S. peace-keeping forces.

Shakoor, who enjoyed being defense counsel, resigned his position with the Ministry of the Attorney General in July 1988 to return to private practice after an absence from practicing bar of nine years. On his resignation from the Ministry of the Attorney General, his colleagues presented him with a lovely plaque and this beautiful inscription:

SHAKOOR

A lawyer named Shakoor had many degrees
He made prosecuting seem like such a breeze
The courtroom was his favorite place to be
Arguing and sentencing were his cup of tea
In his spare time a book he did write
On speeding, he knew he could shed some light
Now on his own again, off he will go
But back to the courtroom for a different kind of show.

Despite his deep commitment to the practice of the law, Shakoor squeezed some time out during 2004 to write his fifth book, *In Pursuit of Justice.* This book has been acclaimed as an informative work. It is not a textbook on the law; it contains his memoirs and experiences in the courts in which he practiced his profession—events to illustrate the courage it takes to stand up with courtesy and professional rectitude to obstinate and sometimes uninformed judges, in order to achieve justice for his clients. His constant vigil to protect the rights and liberties of his clients exemplifies his approach to the law—"only appear in your cases after full preparation of the facts and the relevant legal principles. Justice is what we all want and expect. Justice is sometimes considered to be what is fair, correct, morally right, and acceptable. Justice is very often regarded as an illusory goal. … In this book … the author … provides … a very straightforward and unpretentious account of his experiences, courtroom dramas, and other encounters while in pursuit of justice. The aims and objective of any criminal defense attorney must be to ensure always, at all times that 'Justice must not only be done but must be seen to be done.'"

Coauthor Paul D. Haines. PhD, penned a very forceful endorsement of the contents of *In Pursuit of Justice.* It reads as follows:

> Many people will enjoy reading the memoirs of A. Shakoor Manraj, QC, a competent, and highly successful criminal defense attorney, who has been in practice for over fifty years. I sincerely recommend this book to the entire reading public, including all professionals. It is a well-written and engrossing book about justice and the attainment of justice, with all the inclusive ingredients of humor, courtroom dramas, and the role of experienced counsel in our criminal justice system.

Janet Naidu, poet, writer, and equal rights award-winning educator, wrote a perceptive review of *In Pursuit of Justice.* It reads, in part:

> With admirable clarity, the book is well put together with sixteen chapters each progressively moving the reader into many decades of Mr. Manraj's experiences in some extraordinary cases. Chapter one begins with the question, "What is justice?" While many will have different answers, the general discourse that Mr. Manraj brings, makes a person who is not familiar with the "law" become aware of its applications in a general sense … a most scholarly written chapter on his appearance before "The Three-Man International Commission of Jurists"

in 1965. The book wonderfully concludes with an epilogue: "The Evolution of Justice," which reveals a humbling person who, with all his accomplishments, expresses himself in a genuine way for the betterment of humanity.

Guyana Journal of December 2005 featured another article on *In Pursuit of Justice*. It reported on the glittering event of the book launch in New York. Albert Baldeo, former prosecutor and magistrate in Guyana and a legal practitioner in New York, wrote this stirringly brilliant tribute of Mr. Shakoor Manraj, which reads in part,

> Icons like Shakoor Manraj and other great Guyanese have inspired the younger generation like myself to strive to emulate their achievements. Queen's Counsel and attorney at law Mr. Shakoor Manraj … one of Guyana's leading luminaries … and others of that golden era in the jurisprudential history of Guyana, gave an insight into his remarkable life at his book launch recently. … Such a presentation was more befitting an academic forum. … His book … encapsulates his life's work with vivid glimpses of his stellar legal career. … Mr. Manraj earned the respect of the entire profession in the many places he practiced, to wit, thirty-five different countries, each with its own unique legal system, which may be another record of itself. … Readers will find this book a must-read book, written by an accomplished and legendary lawyer, a man whose contribution to the development of jurisprudence and to the legal profession is second to none.

In the course of his practice, he had the privilege and pleasure of presenting the petition of thirty-two freshly qualified barristers for admission to practice their profession in the courts of their respective residences. The petitions included two female barristers. At that time, female members of the bar were rare gems that adorned the legal profession. They were a refreshing and stabilizing infusion to the hitherto predominantly male bar. They brought a new spirit to the Guyana bar and a welcome competence reminiscent of the Shakespearean Portia in *The Merchant of Venice*.

During his fifty-plus years at the bar, Shakoor has practiced in over thirty-five different jurisdictions in the various Caribbean Islands, Europe, Asia, the United States. and Canada. In all, he has completed 330 murder trials without any convictions. These were all tried in different jurisdictions. He also successfully defended a Guyanese seaman in Venezuela charged with the offense of murder.

Ever since he practiced in Guyana and later while he was in Canada, he received many offers to accept an appointment to the judicial bench. He "never had the disposition to ascend the judicial bench." As a matter of fact, Shakoor states in his book *In Pursuit of Justice*, "I saw myself as a gladiator, fighting sometimes against overwhelming odds to get justice for my clients, who put their trust and confidence in me."

Why is the law so great a part of his life and why has he specialized in jury trials? Now in his fifty-fourth year as a barrister at law, Shakoor said:

> I derived my inspiration to be a lawyer from my maternal uncle. I attended the same law school (Middle Temple) where my maternal uncle P. M. Benson studied law in the 1920s.
>
> Law was not my only field. I drew inspiration from disseminating knowledge and sharing my experiences, but the law was and is my first love, and practice of the law gives me a feeling of fulfillment. I hold the view that if I am going to do anything, I must give it all the energy and sincerity and dedication I have.
>
> I am grateful to God for his help, guidance, and blessings of health, which he gave to me to achieve my goals as a practicing lawyer. I am happiest when I am at the bar table in any court in any jurisdiction appearing for any litigant, be it a civil or criminal matter.
>
> One cannot be forced to pursue an occupation in life for which one is not suited or has no desire to become involved. Each individual has his or her own preferences when it comes to life's calling, and no one should be pressurized into going into a profession or pursuing a particular line of activity for which one is not suited or has no interest to be part of that profession, occupation, or calling.

Gladys, who passed away in 1976, had borne Shakoor four children—Michael, Anne, Andrew, and Sorayah. Michael Manraj is now an airline captain in Canada. He is married to Esther, and they have two children and live in Canada. Anne is an employee of the US Federal Government. She is the mother of two daughters. They all live in Florida. His second son, Andrew, his wife, Anabela, and two sons live in Canada; his specialty is computers. His other daughter, Sorayah, and her husband, Ken, live in Vancouver Island. She is the mother of two girls. She has a master's degree and specializes in child psychology.

Barrister, broadcaster, lecturer and author Shakoor Manraj, QC, says, "I saw all my children safely settled in their respective matrimonial life. Eventually, on October 26, 1990, I married my present wife, Bonita Mangal. Her father, the late Dr. Krishna Mangal, and her late mother, Muriel Mangal, who was the only daughter of the late Dr. Jairam Bissessar, lived in Vlissengen Road, Georgetown. Bonita brought into my life her young daughter, Marcina, who became Marcina Manraj, my fifth child, who is now a registered nurse in Florida."

Shakoor Manraj tells of the humor in court. He writes in his book *In Pursuit of Justice*:

> Appearances in court have their rewards and exposure to the many humorous events that occur in court. Without formerly entering appearances and informing the judge who was appearing for which party in the civil action, the two young lawyers embarked upon their opening speeches; the two lawyers abused each other violently, one calling his adversary a rogue, a scamp, and a charlatan, while his opponent retorted that his so-called learned friend was deceitful, dishonest, and a masquerade who has a smattering knowledge of the law.
>
> The learned judge, very much annoyed at this exhibition of unprofessional behavior, then intervened and, addressing the two lawyers said, "Now that you two so-called gentlemen have been fully and properly identified by each other, let us get on with the case. Which one of you two misfits is appearing for the plaintiff and which one is appearing for the defendant?" The effect was devastating. Justice is a "many splendored thing." It is a lofty but understandable concept and functions best when the rules relating to its achievement are observed and respected.

October 30, 2008

Heytram Maraj

Barrister at Law
Former Member, Immigration and
Refugee Board, Canada.

Heytram Maraj was a teacher, then a civil servant. He studied privately while working to become a lawyer. As a barrister, he became assistant registrar, magistrate, rent assessor, and permanent secretary. In Canada, he was appointed a member of the Immigration and Refugee Board.

Heytram was born on July 16, 1931. His father, a farmer and money lender, was Subedar Maraj of Bachelor's Adventure, East Coast Demerara, Guyana. His mother was Dhanrajie Maraj (nee Singh). He was the eldest of his siblings, followed by sister Leelawatie (deceased), brother Morari Lall, sister Mohanie, brother Nandram, and sister Satie.

He attended St. Mark's Anglican, at Paradise, East Coast Demerara from 1937 to 1944. The Headmaster was Mr. S.E. Persico. His secondary schools were Modern High School from 1944 to 1946, under Principal Mr C.A. Yensen, then Enterprise High School from 1946 to1947, under Principal Mr. H.C. Humphreys, and Cardiff High School from 1947 to 1949. The Principal was Mr C.A. Viera. At Enterprise High School, he was successful at the Junior Cambridge examination, and he came second in class of about 125 successes. At Cardiff High School, he passed the Senior Cambridge Examination with exemption from the London matriculation examination. He was first in the class of about fifty successes. Due to this achievement, he was awarded a two-year scholarship to study for the Higher Cambridge School Certificate.

In 1950, Heytram started work as a teacher at International High School. In June 1951, he secured employment in the civil service as a magistrate's clerk. He worked there until 1958, when he was promoted to a Class I Clerk position. He was transferred to the Supreme Court Registry and worked there in different capacities, including clerk to the chief justice. While at work, he studied privately to become a barrister at law.

He passed the Intermediate Examination in law (Inter LLB) of the University of London in 1960. He was accepted as an external student in 1961 by Lincoln's Inn, London, England, to read for the bar examination. His Inter LLB gave him exemption from two subjects of the bar examination. He passed the remaining three subjects and obtained second-class honors in criminal law, regarded as an achievement for an external student.

Heytram left Guyana in September 1963 for part II of the bar examination (the finals), on study leave without pay for one year. He attended lectures at the Council of Legal Education and passed the part II bar finals in June 1964. To satisfy a condition of obtaining no-pay leave, he attended a three-month course of study at the Royal Courts of Justice, London, England, to observe the practice and procedure there and method of filing records.

He then attended post-final practical training as a barrister. This was a three-month course of practical training conducted by practicing members of the bar in England. Heytram was called to the bar in May 1965. He was then initiated as a barrister by signing the Roll of Barristers, and formally introduced to the masters of the bench and senior barristers.

He returned to Guyana in June 1965, and his career as a barrister started as a judicial officer from June 1965. In June 1966 he was appointed clerk of the Chancellor of the Court of Appeal, and in 1969, he became Assistant Registrar, Court of Appeal.

As clerk to the Chancellor and Assistant Registrar, he was engaged in preparing summaries of appeal records for the use of the justices of appeal. He also had to prepare draft judgments for the court when required. He was a state prosecutor, temporarily, while in the Court of Appeal and prosecuted about twenty criminal cases in the High Court.

Heytram also acted as magistrate for six months while he was Assistant Registrar. He was appointed a rent assessor on a part-time basis. He used to preside in the evenings. This lasted for about five years. He was appointed Deputy Registrar of the Supreme Court in 1973 and held this post for three years.

In 1976, President L. F. S. Burnham called him while at work as Deputy Registrar. He invited him to his office that evening. The president offered him a position as Permanent Secretary. He had to respond within two days and accepted after a great deal of reflection.

From June 1976 to April 1979, he was Permanent Secretary, Economic Development. His minister was H. D. Hoyte, who later became president of Guyana. This was a coordinating ministry dealing with foreign aid and agreements of an international nature. The Technical Assistant Unit, Statistical Bureau, and Economic Planning Departments fell under this ministry.

Heytram was Permanent Secretary, Ministry of Labor, Social Security and Housing from 1979 to 1983. The minister was Hamilton Greene. Heytram was instrumental in obtaining double the increase of payment for old-age security recipients. He brought about, with the approval of his minister, payment of social assistance: old-age pension through the post office throughout the country; an innovation of immense assistance to the recipients, thereby avoiding the grave hardship they experienced when paid by social security officers.

Heytram Maraj emigrated to Canada and started on a new career. His qualification as a barrister was not recognized in Canada. He had to obtain accreditation. He was told that he was exempted for two years from the LLB degree and required one year of university training to obtain the equivalent. There he had to take the Canada Bar examination. He started to attend Osgood Law School at York University. After three weeks, he received an offer of employment as a law clerk. He grasped the opportunity because of financial necessity and domestic responsibility with a wife and five young children.

His career in Canada started. He was law clerk (1983–1986) with a major legal firm, Cassels Brock; then law clerk (1986–1988) at Borden and Elliot, another major legal firm.

Heytram was then appointed a member of the Immigration and Refugee Board in 1988. It is an administrative tribunal with great legal emphasis, and a federal governmental appointment. He wrote many decisions. Some were subjected to appeal to the Federal Court of Appeal, but his decisions were upheld in nearly all the appeals. His legal background and administrative experience helped him in obtaining this position. He retired in 1998.

Away from work, Heytram was a keen sportsman. He played cricket; was a left-arm bowler and a right-handed batsman. He was a member of the Lions Club of the East Demerara branch, Guyana. He was also instrumental in obtaining and supervising the running of water pipelines in Courbane Park, East Coast Demerara. As a founding member of the Gandhi Youth Organization in Guyana, Heytram served as assistant secretary for a number of years.

He was married in 1955 to Leila, the daughter of Pandit Dowlat Ram Chowbay. The couple has seven children. Eldest child Indira is married with two children; second child Kamini is married with two children; third child Subhas is married with three children; fourth child Geeta, born in England, is married with two children; fifth child Heytram Dev Anand is married with four children (two sets of twins); sixth and seventh children are twin girls, Sunita and Savita, both married and both with three children. Heytram and Leila are now proud grandparents of nineteen grandchildren and great-grandparents of one.

What has motivated Heytram in his career? He has said, "I was inspired to study law because of my experience both in the Magistrate's Court and Supreme Court. The advocacy of some lawyers had made a great impression on me."

November 16, 2010

Wordsworth McAndrew

Folklorist

Wordsworth McAndrew is featured on the Guyana Consulate website 2008 awards magazine under the heading "Legacy of Excellence." The citation of the award contains the following information, in part:

He is one of the most influential folklorists in Guyanese history. Wordsworth McAndrew dedicated his life to the collection, preservation, and celebration of Guyanese folk life. His impact on Guyanese language, literature, and culture is indelible.

Wordsworth McAndrew was born in 1936 in Georgetown, British Guiana, and died April 25, 2008 in New Jersey. Over his life, he distinguished himself as newspaper columnist, radio broadcaster, poet, and legendary folklorist. In almost anything that involved the artful use of words, Wordsworth excelled, living up to his name.

He attended "Teacha Marshall's" prep school, Christ Church Primary School, and Queen's College, but his greatest teachers were the ordinary men, women, and children of every race and creed in his native land, who became his folk teachers.

Wordsworth was editor and columnist with both the *Guyana Graphic* and *Daily Chronicle* newspapers, and information officer at the Guyana

Information Service. As broadcaster and program director at the Guyana Broadcasting Service for eleven years, Wordsworth created popular radio programs like *What Else* and *Proverb for Today* that allowed him to educate hundreds of thousands in the intricacies and joys of our native "culchuh".

Wordsworth McAndrew was also an accomplished poet. Most Guyanese are familiar with his famous poem "Ole Higue," which begins:

> *Ol' woman wid de wrinkled skin, leh de ol' higue wuk begin.*
> *Put on yuh fiery disguise. Ol' woman wid de weary eyes,*
> *Shed yuh swizzly skin.*

But he also published other notable poems, like "To a Carrion Crow," which ends:

> *I long to have you say a De Profundis for me when I die,*
> *And I wonder: Was yours a punishment, or a purification?*

Wordsworth moved to the United States in 1980. The creation of the Wordsworth McAndrew Awards at the 2002 Guyana Folk Festival in New York recognizes him as a "Guyanese national treasure."

Sources:
Websites accessed May 27, 2010, on Guyana Consulate Toronto, Guyana Awards (Canada).

May 27, 2010

Clifton Ancel H. McDonald, MA

Headmaster

Clifton McDonald grew up in a sugar estate. At sixteen he was a pupil teacher; at twenty-three he entered the Government Teachers Training College. He was a primary school headmaster and a high school principal. Two of his students won the Guyana Scholarship.

His colleagues regard him as a "thoughtful Titan," endowed with succinct eloquence, impressive diction, superb command of the English language, and of profound intellect. He is thought to be a colossus as an educator.

He was a district scoutmaster and won medals for scouting. He was a community leader. He is a deeply religious man in the way he lived his life and in his love and genuine concern for others. He inspires people to reach for the stars. He has set very high standards for those who follow him.

Clifton Ancel H. McDonald was born on October 11, 1922, at Plantation Bath on the West Coast of Berbice, British Guiana. He is the fifth of seven children born to Joseph and Ethel McDonald. His father was employed at the sugar estate as a mechanic, and his mother was a hard-working faithful housewife, who augmented the family's income by baking and selling pastries.

Theirs was a close-knit family in a home where order prevailed. Every child had his or her chore to perform and suffered the consequence for neglecting it or for being tardy, so Clifton learned at an early age to manage his time efficiently. His morning assignments were filling a large container with water by making several trips to a nearby canal, sweeping the sheep pen adjacent to his home, and running errands—all done before he could swim and bathe in the punt trench. He would then have breakfast and be at school by nine o'clock or be flogged by the headmaster, with the cane in his hand, waiting for latecomers. He was never among them.

Clifton's formal education began at age six when he was enrolled in the preparatory division of St. Uriel's Anglican School, located very close to his home in Bath Estate. Aunt Rhoda, his father's sister, was his teacher, and Mr. L. B. Obermuller, his father's good friend and neighbor, was the headmaster, so Clifton was under very watchful eyes. Clifton liked school. Every year he was awarded a certificate for regular attendance. He was always among the three top students in his class.

Early in the 1930s the cramped, dilapidated red schoolhouse was replaced by a new, bright, well-ventilated building furnished with solid dual desks and benches, a library, hat racks, and cupboards. These were an upgrade in amenities previously provided. The school was named St. Nicholas Anglican, and Mr. C. O. Patterson, a Class 1 teacher, was appointed headmaster. He recruited some excellent and caring teachers who motivated their students to excel. Encouraged by his eldest sister, Ruth, Clifton read the small collection of Brodie books in the school library, and looked forward to the weekly *Junior Chronicle* of which he was a member and contributor. Imagine his joy one Sunday when he realized that the bold-print headline "Berbice Reader Wins First Prize" was referring to him for his essay "Kindness to Animals"!

His thirst for academic excellence was rewarded in April 1938 when he was successful at the country's Pupil Teachers' Appointment examination with the distinction of placing second, the first place having gone to a classmate. In March 1939 he was appointed a pupil teacher at his home school, St. Nicholas Anglican. Over the next four years, he moved up the ladder of professional development by passing the first year, second year, third year, and fourth year pupil teacher examinations administered by the Ministry of Education of Guyana.

Around his eighteenth birthday, the popular "Teacher Clifton" acceded to the request of a small group of boys to form a Boy Scout group under the supervision of Mr. Bywater, an English scouter and overseer at Bath Estate.

They learned quickly, gained several proficiency badges, looked smart in uniform, did their good turns, held campfires, attended national scouting rallies, and raised money to defray camping expenses by holding fund-raising concerts. They were the pride of Bathians. Clifton availed himself of training and received his scoutmaster certificate in 1942, but he did not let popularity and scouting affect his studies toward his career choice.

Having been successful at the highly competitive entrance academic examination as well as the interview and medical physical examination that followed, Clifton was among the ten other men and nine women who, in September 1945, entered the reputable Government Teachers Training College located in Georgetown, Guyana, for a two-year course in pedagogy. The men were housed in a dormitory about half a mile away from the women's dormitory and lecture halls. Besides an intensive course in the principles of teaching, child psychology, methodology, and teaching practice under the critical eyes of the lecturers and second-year students, the new students covered a comprehensive examinable course in English language and literature, mathematics, biology, geography, history, child psychology, principles of teaching, speech training, theory of music, home economics (women only), and woodwork (men only). The non-examinable courses were religion and physical education.

In July 1947 Clifton graduated third in his class with a Class 1 Trained Teacher certificate. He was assigned to the Christianburg Scots School, located about sixty miles up the Demerara River, and he was instructed to report for duties on the first day of the new school year in September.

His concern regarding the availability of suitable accommodation was allayed by the Demerara Bauxite Company providing him with a furnished room with running water and electricity in one of its living quarters for bachelors at the incredibly low monthly fee of four dollars—and the stern warning that women were not permitted in the building. He knew of no one who was so displaced. Most of the men were young teachers who came from the coastlands after graduating from high school. There were periods of fun and laughter and times for serious study and lesson preparation. Clifton volunteered his services to those who requested his help.

To get to his school, Clifton boarded a small paddleboat with his bicycle as a boatman took him from the right bank of the river to the left bank. He then bicycled about a mile to his school.

He was assigned to teach children aged ten to twelve years in what was officially the middle division of a primary school, but which was better known as Standards III and IV.[1] The students were a good representation of the ethnic composition of Guyana's population: Amerindian, Negro, Chinese, East Indian, and mixed race. They were a joy to teach—clean, neatly dressed, well disciplined, eager to learn, and very cooperative. Clifton and his pupils enjoyed their days in school as well as on the playground. The commendable report given to the middle division by the visiting inspector of schools was well deserved and resulted in an increment in Clifton's salary at the beginning of the new school year. During the August vacation of 1948 he attended a Boy Scout leaders' training course in Trinidad and returned to Christianburg School in September to complete his two-year assignment there.

In September 1949 Teacher McDonald reported for duty at St. Michael's Anglican School, Hopetown, which was only three miles away from his home. Again he taught students in the middle division and agriculture to those in the upper division. He obtained great cooperation from the headmaster, David Lampkin, all members of the staff, the pupils and their parents, who cooperated fully in erecting a fence for the school garden, which was very productive and a valuable practical teaching medium. Several senior students received certificates for passing agriculture in the Primary School Leaving Examination. During this period he was awarded the Gillwell Medal for Scouting; he was appointed district scoutmaster for West Berbice; he started new Boy Scout groups and he organized training sessions for their leaders.

In June 1952 Clifton was promoted to senior master, second only to the headmaster, at St. Jude's Anglican School, Lichfield, West Coast Berbice. Besides his duties as the Standard IV class teacher, he was responsible for the discipline and instruction in all the other classes in the open school (i.e., a school without any walls to separate the different classes). He had a pupil teacher who assisted in the marking of students' work and kept the class occupied and in control for the short time he might be called away. Most of the staff had years of teaching experience but were not graduates

---

1 In his day, compulsory elementary education began at age six and ended at age twelve, but free education was available to age sixteen for those who so desired. In primary school, children were admitted at age six to the infant classes (also popularly known as ABC classes, Prep A, and Prep B), after which they advanced to Standards I to VI. In Standards V and VI, students took the Primary School Leaving Certificate Examination, then left school to find work or attend high school.

of the Teachers Training College, so as senior master he suggested and/or demonstrated updated methodology to those teachers.

A new experience for him at that school was his instructing a group of senior boys in woodwork. The Ministry of Education provided the tools, workbenches, and lumber. Years afterwards, on a street in Brooklyn, New York, a carpenter greeted him warmly and thanked him for introducing woodworking to him.

In 1955 Clifton was awarded the Bain Gray Gold Medal of Merit in recognition of his excellent service to the school and community. Three years later, his unquestionable dedication to duty earned him his first principal promotion to St. John's Anglican School, Suddie, Essequibo. This was a failing school and quite a challenge, even to an experienced headmaster. His reputation as an excellent educator preceded him, so when he arrived there in March 1958 to take up the principalship, his first few months on the job were observed with keen interest by all concerned. Clifton wasted no time in providing evidence, by way of his performance, that he was, indeed, a proficient, efficient, conscientious, and a very caring leader and teacher. His impact on the school and the community reverberated. There was soon talk about his engaging management skills and his knowledge and understanding of the art of teaching. The obvious outcomes included a recommitted and highly motivated teaching staff and a school population that was thoroughly equipped with the necessary academic and social skills.

The status and the popularity of a school are partly determined by the quality of the students, and the results at external examinations. Over the five years that Clifton remained at St. John's Anglican School, the results produced by the school at the Secondary Schools Entrance Examination, the Pupil Teachers' Appointment Examination, and the Primary School Leaving Certificate Examination were astounding. The first two examinations named were very competitive. Student successes were determined by how well the students did in relation to the performances of all the other students in the county.[2] Clifton's students always obtained the coveted scores and results. In 1962, a record was created in Essequibo when the children at St. John's secured four passes at the Government County Scholarship examination.

Clifton also paid a significant amount of attention to the extra-curricular activities of the school. Before arriving in Essequibo he had

---

2   Guyana has three counties: Demerara, Essequibo, and Berbice.

served as a district scout master. He soon started a scout troop but did not limit membership only to his school students. Boys from other schools in the area were allowed to join the troop. In this way Clifton reached out beyond his immediate community and influenced the character building and adventurism of many teenage boys.

Additionally, no one who was in close contact with Clifton could miss the fact that he was a deeply religious man. This was not only evident in his active membership of the church, but also in the way he lived his life, and in his love and genuine concern for others.

Clifton's success in transforming St. John's made him popular for promotion. He turned down an offer to a grade B school, accepted moving to the grade A, Providence Government School at East Bank Demerara, then consented to return to the Essequibo Coast as acting education officer. That caused a stir among some senior members of the Guyana Teachers Association, of which he was a very active member up to that time; but that did not deter him. Instead, he maintained his usual composure and efficiency.

In September 1964 Clifton was awarded an American International Development (AID) Scholarship to Kent State University, Ohio. He graduated with a bachelor of science degree in 1966. On his return to Guyana he took up his substantive post as graduate headmaster at Providence Government School before moving on to the headship of Christ Church Secondary School in Georgetown in March 1968.

He transformed that school physically, psychologically, and academically. In the spirit of the existing government self-help program, he mobilized the teachers, the students, their parents, and others in the city in effecting a much needed extension of the building to accommodate more students and such facilities as science laboratories and classrooms for home economics, technical drawing, and woodwork. School spirit was high, and academic results showed marked improvement. The Guyana government recognized his work, and the late President Burnham spoke glowingly of Clifton's achievements at the official opening of the new addition to the building.

Many of the graduates from Christ Church Secondary School left with impressive numbers of passes at the London General Certificate of Education (GCE), Ordinary Level Examination. Some of these graduates gained places in senior secondary schools to pursue studies for the advanced level GCE examinations. A significant number of the other graduates gained immediate employment in the public service. Even to this day, teachers who served with Clifton at Christ Church Secondary attest to his qualities of leadership, and his ability to inspire and motivate. Many of them testify that their stint at that school was the most satisfying and enjoyable of their careers.

With the resignation of Mr. Siegfried Luyken as principal of Mackenzie High School (MHS), Clifton applied successfully to fill that vacancy. Mackenzie, renamed Linden, is the bauxite mining town up the Demerara River. Clifton assumed duties on November 1, 1972, in a not too friendly environment. Some senior students exhibited a belligerent attitude toward him for several months and the breakdown in discipline affected academic performance that year. However, he worked assiduously to build confidence. After a period of observation, and when the 1973 GCE O level results revealed that twenty-two of the ninety-one students failed to gain a pass in a single subject, Clifton recognized that the traditional grammar school type of education was quite unsuited to the students' needs, aptitudes, and abilities.

With the parents' approval, Clifton and his staff embarked cautiously upon some curriculum improvement at MHS. Business education (including typewriting and accounting), technical drawing, agriculture, and home economics were introduced. To add variety to school life, and to provide avenues for enrichment, enlightenment, character development, and recreation, music, dance, and art were promoted and the following organizations were started: a Boy Scout Troop in 1974, a Cadet Corps in 1975, and a branch of the Young Socialist Movement (YSM) in 1976. The long-established Bible Club became even more popular, as did the weekly school assembly which provided opportunity for the development of latent talent and admirable school spirit.

Recognizing the need for more classrooms, Clifton, in his dual role of principal and secretary of the school board, undertook the building of the Linden Concert Hall and School (LICHAS). The Guyana Mining Enterprise (Guymine) supplied the steel frame, some of Guymine's engineers volunteered their drafting and supervisory services, and the Parent Teacher Association carried out successfully massive fund-raising drives. The goal was achieved. Built largely by self-help, LICHAS became a valuable learning experience for the students, the parents, and the teachers who participated physically, financially, and emotionally in the project. Besides accommodating classrooms on the top floor, LICHAS became the center for cultural activities in Linden.

Results at the external examinations—GCE[3] and CXC[4]—improved with the years, and MHS secured its first two Guyana Scholars Alfie Collins in 1974 and James Kranenburg in 1981.

Forty years of loyal and devoted service to his lovely native Guyana came to an end when, in September 1983, Clifton accepted a teaching assignment at St. Mark's Day School in Brooklyn, New York. Along with other Guyanese, Caribbean, and American teachers, he provided a sound academic and great moral education to hundreds of boys and girls. He earned his master's degree at Brooklyn College and secured employment in the New York City Public Schools, where he left his footprints.

A colleague who worked closely with Clifton during his tenure at Middle School (MS) 394 in Brooklyn, New York, made this observation of him:

> A healthy respect for genuine Guyanese parlance compels me to declare that Clifton is no "Mack." From the time I first met him in September 1988 to this day, he has been "A Man for All Seasons," and I think this is a limited assessment of this "thoughtful Titan."
>
> If you have not been spellbound by his succinct eloquence, or his impressive diction, or his overall superb command of the English language, surely you were the beneficiary of his incisive reasoning, his wisdom or his profound intellect. If you ever met Mr. McDonald, you would not have walked away without knowing that he is a man who relishes doing whatever is appropriate for the uplift of the spirit, or the betterment of the human condition.
>
> Here is a man whose light has shone brightly. Here is a man who has done "good works" for uncounted numbers of students, teachers, parents, administrators, and the teaching profession in general. During the years we shared together at MS 394, it is impossible to recall an instance when he was approached by a student in need of assistance or a teacher on

---

3   London General Certificate of Education

4   Caribbean Examination Council Secondary Education Certificate (first administered in 1979)

the throes of uncertainty that he did not respond with calm assurance and appropriate information.

Mr. McDonald was the person to whom his colleagues turned for effective teaching strategies and workable approaches to the very often challenging situations that seemed to be the daily fare of the Crown Heights[5] experience. Every administrator valued his counsel. Sometimes it could have meant either bringing home the bacon, or being out in the cold. His innate understanding of the value and dignity of work always led him to advocate on behalf of the assumedly errant but serving breadwinner.

Even though he epitomized enviable dignity, professional integrity and abundant self assuredness, he was not puffed up. There was no one with whom he didn't find a way to get along. He holds in high esteem those of us who have distinguished ourselves in some field of endeavor, yet he does not spurn or demean the man or woman who may have encountered misfortune and who is trying to make ends meet.

It seems to me that "Bro Mac" knew more of the human condition than most of the people who have made this phenomenon a study. I once asked him the rationale for working at his then age. After all he was unquestionably entitled to the joys and comforts that come with retirement at fifty-five. He told me of his many colleagues who, on so doing, relegated themselves to the brink of senility stemming from the under-use of a once active and fertile brain.

Mr. McDonald always found ways to extend himself to the people in his world. It was a privilege and a pleasure to share with him and his family on the many occasions when his home was an oasis of comfort from the stresses of work and the scars of worry. On those occasions one was treated to the

---

5 Crown Heights is a predominantly Jewish and West Indian neighborhood in Brooklyn, New York. It is subject to periodic racial tension, which included a riot in August 1991 after a vehicle driven by a Hasidic Jew struck and killed a young black child.

dignified support of his lovely wife and the respectfulness of his adorable children.

Mr. McDonald is an amiable man. He is a colossus in his own right. He inspires you to take the high road. You cannot mistake the footprints he has left on the marches of time.

Clifton McDonald, as an educator and as a person, has created high standards for those who follow to emulate. Through all of his many successes and achievements, he remains a humble and humane person, an admirable husband and father, and a true and trusted friend. He wishes to leave readers with a verse from "To a Louse" by Robert Burns:

> O wad some Pow'r the giftie gie us
> To see oursels as others see us
> It wad frae monie a blunder free us
> An' foolish notion
> What airs in dress an' gait wad lea' us
> An' ev'n Devotion
>
> Translated it reads:
> Oh, That God would give us the very smallest of gifts
> To be able to see ourselves as others see us
> It would save us from many mistakes
> And foolish thoughts
> We would change the way we look and gesture
> And to how and what we apply our time and attention.

April 11, 2009.

Shirley McDonald

Educator

Clifton's story would be incomplete if it did not include the sterling part played by his bright, beautiful, and beloved wife, Shirley, who has been his inspiration, his great motivator, his wise advisor, and his steadfast companion for the past fifty years.

Shirley was born on December 1, 1926, in Georgetown, Guyana, where her parents, Thomas A. McLean and his wife, Ivy, resided. Her father was a businessman and her mother was a stay-at-home housewife. At the age of six years, Shirley started her primary school education at Comenius Moravian School in Queenstown, Georgetown. Four years later, she sought and received a transfer to the very classy Broad Street Government School with its spacious classrooms and the most modern equipment of the time. Some of Guyana's best teachers were on the staff, so their examination results were excellent.

At the age of sixteen, Shirley passed the Pupil Teachers' Examination but could not find employment, so she began attending Central High School. While a student there, she was offered an appointment as a pupil teacher at Broad St. Government School and opted to accept it, as teaching was her first love. She remained on the staff of Broad Street Government

School until she was admitted to the Government Teachers' Training College in 1949. After graduating from Teachers' Training College in 1951, Shirley was assigned to St. Thomas Anglican School, West Bank Demerara. Thereafter, she accepted an appointment at Freeburg (subsequently St. Cyril's Anglican School) in Georgetown. The headmaster was Mr. C. C. Lewis, who was also the Commissioner of the Boy Scout movement in Guyana. In addition to her teaching duties at St. Cyril's, Shirley was also a Cub Scout mistress.

It is ironic that although Clifton spent at least forty Monday afternoons at the Broad Street School observing teachers in training, he did not see Shirley while she was teaching there. She told him years afterwards that he couldn't because his eyes were elsewhere. However, when he did see her during a business visit to the Commissioner, it was love at first sight. He was elated later when she responded in the affirmative to his question, "Will you marry me?" His prayers were answered when their wedding was solemnized at Christ Church Anglican Church, in Georgetown, on the afternoon of April 4, 1959.

Giving up the glamour and bright lights of the city, Shirley took up residence with Clifton at Johanna Cecilia, on the Essequibo coast. Being only a stone's throw away from a beach, and having a backyard with coconut and some fruit trees compensated for the ride lost to Bourda Market and the Seawall in Georgetown. Instead, for one year Shirley rode past Clifton's school, St. John's, Suddie, for hers (Riverstown Government School), two miles away until she was transferred to St. John's, where she joined him. Working as a team they improved the quality of instruction and learning.

Shirley, a dedicated educator in her own right, conducted special training classes not only for the young inexperienced teachers on the St. John's staff but also for others from neighboring schools. Their appreciation of the service she rendered them is reflected in the very cordial relationship they have maintained with her to this day. Years later in Linden she still had the energy and drive to run very successfully two schools: Regma Primary School[6], followed by McKenzie All-Age School.

Shirley retired in 1981, emigrated to the United States and continued her good work at a private elementary school until 1996, when she retired finally.

---

6   Regma was a private school that had been founded by Reginald Hoyte and his wife Maude Hoyte, hence the name Regma. It later became a government school.

Their very happy marriage is blessed with five loving and dutiful children, three girls and twin boys, born within a span of ten years. They also have six grandchildren.

Shirley and Clifton are octogenarians. They have this to say about their richly rewarding life:

> Ours has been a long journey spanning the three Guyana counties and the Atlantic Ocean. We are satisfied that we served the country of our birth long and honorably, and that we impacted positively on the lives of many not only in our native Guyana but also in our adopted city, New York. We are most thankful to our Lord and Savior who answered our prayers, showed us the way, and gave us the strength and courage to persevere and overcome difficulties on the way. Our recipe for success is simple: set your goal, work prayerfully and assiduously toward it, and persevere until you achieve your dream.

April 11, 2009.

Chris Mohan

Owner, Manufacturing Company

Chris Mohan is the president and owner of Maple Leaf Wheelchair, Mississauga, Ontario.

Born in 1955 to Mike and Betty Mohan at No 47 Village, Corentyne, Chris Mohan received his education at Skeldon Lutheran High School while living with his aunt Doreen and uncle Jamna Persaud (overseer) at Crab Wood Creek. He immigrated to Canada in 1974. He continued his education at York University where he obtained his BSc degree. After graduating from university, he held several management positions in the plastics industry.

Chris Mohan started Maple Leaf Wheelchair Inc. in 1993. He focused on creating unique designs, and building mobility and seating devices for the elderly and disabled population. Some of these devices include manual and motorized wheelchairs, recliners, geriatric chairs, tilts, commodes, platform lifts, and walkers. The business has grown, with multimillion dollar sales and a staff of more than sixty. It is the largest Canadian-owned wheelchair manufacturing company in Canada.

Chris has served on the board of many associations dedicated to improving the quality of life of our seniors and disabled people, including the

Canadian Assistive Devices Association and the Canadian Manufacturing Association.

Chris is a consistent supporter of many charitable organizations including Three Rivers Kids Foundation, the Caribbean Children Foundation, Canadian Spinal Cord Research, Canadian March of Dimes, and the United Order of Solomon Chapter 12, which has donated medical equipment including wheelchairs to over one hundred countries around the world.

He is always very grateful to his mother, Betty Mohan, who has been both a mother and father to him, his two brothers, and sister since their father died in 1976. He claims that his mother's love, determination, and commitment has been his inspiration for success.

Chris lives in Georgetown, Ontario, with his wife, Angela. His daughter, Alaana, who as of this writing is attending Ryerson University, lives in nearby Mississauga, while his son, Jason, and his wife, who are both involved in the business, live in nearby Milton, Ontario, with their two children.

Chris Mohan was winner of Guyana Awards (Canada) 2009 Business Excellence Award.

Sources:
Websites accessed May 27, 2010, on Guyana Consulate Toronto, Guyana Awards (Canada).

November 11, 2010

Janet Naidu, BA

Poet, Writer, Author
Diversity, Equity, and Inclusion Champion

Janet Naidu is the manager of Diversity Management and Ombuds Office at the Liquor Control Board of Ontario (LCBO).

She oversees two major areas of responsibility where she oversees and promotes policies and programs in relation to workplace diversity, equity, and inclusion as a viable business imperative; and directs and oversees an employee complaint handling process and investigations into human rights and non-human rights allegations of discrimination, harassment, bullying, and threats that could lead to workplace violence.

She started working with the LCBO in a management capacity in 1986. In 1991, she was promoted to her current position, where she commenced the introduction of strategic change management plans to demonstrate the value of diversity, equity and inclusion in a working environment. Her major accomplishments include overseeing and specializing in the strategic leadership and promotion of an organization-wide diversity plan that impacts over five thousand employees in a retail, public sector, and unionized environment. Janet works to engage senior management's commitment; to influence middle-management as well as employees; and to secure the notion of diversity, equity, and inclusion as a core business value. In this role, she has shown the recognition of a long-term vision with strategic goals and takes the corporate climate into consideration in her recommendations for progressive change.

Overseeing a comprehensive barrier elimination strategy that allows for the creation of open communication channels, Janet continues to be an advocate of progressive change, encouraging ambassadors for the broader understanding of diversity, and leading educational programs to foster diversity and inclusion in employment. In addition to her role in promoting an inclusive workplace, Janet has initiated a policy and video-based educational program on workplace intimidation and violence prevention. She has received recognition awards for video-based educational programs.

She played a leadership role in the *Working in Diversity* video-based educational program on valuing diversity in the area of gender, race, and ethnicity, and disability.

Other employers sought out the video to show employees in their workplaces. In addition, Janet directed the development and production of the acclaimed video on *Zero Tolerance*, a policy and educational program on workplace intimidation and violence prevention. She oversees the Policies and Educational Program on Harassment and Discrimination Prevention; Preventing Racial Profiling; and Intimidation and Violence Prevention.

Janet started several diversity awareness initiatives to progressively engage employees in the consciousness awareness that she believes is a valuable approach to foster workplace harmony. She is the architect of the LCBO's annual Workplace Diversity Calendar, which was created in 2000 in order to raise diversity awareness. It showcases national holidays, religious observances, national and international dates, as well as information on workplace issues. In late November and early December, a time for reflection on violence against women, she promotes awareness of the White Ribbon as a symbol for employee awareness of violence against women.

During the Christmas season, when there is a Christmas tree in the lobby of the main building, she also introduces the "Peace Tree," which is decorated with symbols of different religious and cultural observances as well as other identities. It aims to demonstrative the inclusiveness of December as a festive season for employees. In addition, she held lunch-

and-learn sessions of a "Peace Tree" film, an aim to enhance the value of embracing differences and foster an inclusive work environment.

Believing in continuous awareness of the wholeness that people bring to the workplace, Janet introduced a new initiative in 2008: Discover Diversity Day, an annual festival event, celebrating cultural heritage as well as diversity inclusion, with the vision to engage employees' awareness of the diversity among employees. Employees are involved in the creation of pavilions to celebrate their culture heritage and to raise awareness of other dimensions of diversity.

Janet Naidu is a regular speaker at conferences on workplace diversity, equity, investigations and workplace violence prevention. Janet is cochair of the Union/Management Sub-Committee on Employment Equity and Diversity. She is chair of a number of steering committees and consulting teams in the engagement of new policies and program initiatives. She represents the LCBO as a speaker at external conferences in these related fields.

Janet has lived in Canada since 1975. She has a BA in political science and Caribbean studies from the University of Toronto. She is a certified investigator and life-skills coach. She has skills in mediation, human rights and leadership in the development of diversity strategies. She is a strong advocate for inclusion and fairness in the workplace and has acquired extensive experience in the development of visionary and strategic approaches to incorporate these in organizational development and growth.

Janet is a member of the Human Resources Professional Association (HRPAO), the Urban Alliance on Race Relations, and she is a former president of the Toronto Employment Equity Practitioners Association.

In addition to her high-profile role in the workplace, Janet Naidu is a poet, writer, author, and social activist. She has three collections of poems and has written and published in the *Guyana Journal* in New York, short stories, profiles of elderly Guyanese living in Toronto, essays on the Indian women of Guyana, and "The Transculturation of Hinduism in the Caribbean."

Born in 1953 in Guyana at Covent Garden on the East Bank of Demerara, Janet comes from humble beginnings. Her father was a cane cutter and her mother sold greens in the village and the market. Her grandparents came to Guyana in 1915 from Tamil Nadu, India. She is the seventh of eight children, so one can imagine their struggles. They were hard-working people and also high achievers in their own way.

She has been involved in the Guyanese community in Toronto in many capacities. She has been a member of the Association of Concerned Guyanese in Toronto, which agitated for the return to democracy and fair and free elections in Guyana. Janet was the cochair of the 1998 Guyana Independence Festival and was instrumental in the creation of the first event to have expanded activities such as a cultural extravaganza, first cricket games of celebrated Guyanese cricketers, softball, and other activities. She coordinated the videotaping of the event.

Her first collection of poems, Winged Heart (1999), was short-listed for the Guyana Prize for Literature, poetry category.

Her second collection, Rainwater, published in 2005, contains fifty-one poems that shape and deepen an understanding of uprooted movements, nostalgic memories, and haunting moments of resettlement elsewhere. Many of the poems also trace ancestral origins and grounding for cultural identity.

In Janet Naidu's third collection, Sacred Silence (2009), the poems capture many moods of silence in the heart of one's journey, exploring the mysteries of despair and endurance, attachment and departure, longing and fulfillment. In spite of life's baffling moments, the presence of peace and healing dwell at the core of one's being, bringing new reflections.

Being a community activist, Janet initiated the formation of a literary group in 2005, Pakaraima (Guyanese Canadian Writers and Artists Association), where prominent writers come together to share their works, experiences, and to support each other in the literary and writing environment. The group holds annual events to raise awareness, to inspire new writers, and to share their works with the public.

Here is an excerpt from the poem "The Whole Yard Awakens" from the collection *Rainwater* (2005).

> *Today, I come to this place again*
> *to find the ground*
> *not so fathomless;*
> *I come to gather wrapped up years*
> *still at the grindstone.*
> *I see my father's old shirt waiting*
> *on the door handle,*
> *holding the scent of rainforest*

October 31, 2010

Dr. Suresh Narine

BSc, MSc, PhD

    Physics and chemistry professor Dr. Suresh Narine is an internationally renowned expert in biomaterials and a world leader in the field of agro-energy. He is the founding director of the Center for the Study of Biomaterials at Trent University in Peterborough, Ontario. His work focuses on the utilization of plant oils to create environmentally friendly materials such as polymers, lubricants, adhesives and drug delivery matrices for everyday use. He has written two seminal textbooks in the area of lipid crystallization and coauthored numerous scientific publications and patents.

    The author of Guyana's Agro-Energy Strategy, Professor Narine spends a significant amount of time in Guyana assisting in the science and technology sector, having accepted a presidential appointment as director of Guyana's Institute of Applied Science and Technology in 2005. He boosted the country's economic development by establishing a commercially viable biodiesel production facility in the Northwest District of Guyana that employs 180 people. He was recognized by the Guyanese diaspora in Canada with a Special Achievement Award in 2007.

    Suresh Narine was born in 1971 in the small village of Herstelling in Guyana. His father worked for the Guyana Sugar Corporation, and his mother was a tailor and housewife. He has three older sisters. He attended Providence Primary School and Queen's College, where he was the captain of Moulder House, a member of the Prefect Council body, and a competitor in debating and elocution. He emigrated to Canada in 1991 to attend Trent University, where he completed a BSc in physics and chemistry in 1995 and an MSc in condensed matter physics in 1997. He went on to complete his PhD in food science/material physics at the University of Guelph in 2000.

After working as a research scientist with M&M Mars in New Jersey, Dr. Narine was recruited to the University of Alberta as an associate professor at the age of twenty-seven, where he became one of four Alberta Value Added Corporation research chairs. He founded the Alberta Lipid Utilization Research Program, focused on the utilization of fats and oils for the production of industrial materials, high-value edible applications, and drug delivery polymers. In 2005, he was named Professor of the Year with the Department of Agricultural, Food and Nutritional Science and also received the University of Alberta's prestigious Student Union Award for Leadership in Undergraduate Teaching. That same year, he was awarded the Growing Alberta Leadership Award for Innovation.

In the fall of 2009, Prof. Narine was recruited from Alberta to Ontario to lead the new Biomaterials Research Program at Trent University, his alma mater, who awarded him with a Distinguished Alumni Award in 2006. He continues his work as a full professor of chemistry and physics and astronomy at Trent University. In 2010, at the age of thirty-eight, he was awarded an Ontario research chair in green chemistry and engineering and a senior industrial research chair from the Natural Sciences and Engineering Research Council of Canada (NSERC). This is an unusual level of accolade and achievement for someone still below the age of forty.

He was lauded by Guyana's president, His Excellency Bharrat Jagdeo, who attended, as a special guest, the launch of Trent University's Biomaterials Research Program and the Center of Knowledge in the Environment in October, 2010. "One of my proudest accomplishments," said Prof. Narine "has been to share a speaking platform and to work closely with President Jagdeo, a man whom I greatly admire."

In his current position at Trent University as the director of the Biomaterials Research Program, Prof. Narine's work involves the research and commercialization of green chemistry and engineering and building networks with other researchers and research bodies in Canada and abroad, including industry and non-governmental organizations. He contributes to public understanding and policy development in the area of toxics reduction and trains highly qualified personnel, while teaching undergraduate and graduate students.

Maintaining a connection with his native Guyana, Prof. Narine writes and performs Guyanese dialect poetry and plays Indian drums (tabla and dholak). He is compiling a dictionary of Guyanese Creole, and continues his volunteer work in Guyana as the director of their National Institute of Applied Science and Technology. In Peterborough you may see him exploring the back roads on his Honda VTX 1300 motorcycle, on which he travels across Canada every year.

In response to being named a Guyanese Achiever, Prof. Narine says that "the reverence with which our Guyanese people hold educational accomplishment is a great source of inspiration for me. I tell my students to be relentless in the pursuit of excellence. As a person from the third world, I take very seriously the role that a scientist can play in the development of a country. It is a privilege to be in a position to unravel the mysteries of this world, to ensure a better future for our children, and to be in charge of the development of young minds."

On a more personal note, Prof. Narine shares how his mother inspired him as a child. "She is an amazingly strong woman, who taught me to question authority, to think for myself, and to reach for the stars. She said that you are the only one who can limit yourself and that a disciplined tongue can sweeten the entire world." He speaks also about his strong connection to his late father, whom he describes as a gentle man who taught him the necessity and value of humility.

Suresh is the proud father of triplets, Vandana, Rudra, and Geetanjali, who, at the age of ten, believe that, "Dad is cool," and "what Dad does is good for the world."

November 5, 2010

Richard Outram

FCCA, CPA, CFE
Financial Executive

He has twenty-five years of strategic financial management and executive leadership within major public and private companies around the globe. He has an outstanding record of building companies and navigating them through various growth cycles.

Richard is 47 years old. He was born and raised in London, England. His father, Umrao Patrick Outram, was a very talented government welfare officer in Guyana who was responsible for various aspects of community well-being. He left Guyana after political unrest and joined the UK Post Office. He was courageous and determined to make a better life for his family, albeit sacrificing his own career and personal aspirations. His priority goals were to raise and educate all of his children in England and give them the best opportunities possible. Richard's mother, Kamaldai (Doris) Outram, was a school helper and full-time mother of six children. She set goals to ensure all the family members were nurtured and happy in a loving, supportive home and successful in their individual ways.

Brother Jerry is the eldest sibling, followed by sisters Nalini, Marlene, and Indira. Richard was number five, before Pamela, the youngest of the family.

He received his early education at Brockwell Primary in South London. He then attended Beaufoy Secondary. Richard loved school and in that setting, he realized the power of teamwork, strong relationships, and courage. Fiercely competitive academically and in the sports arena—he played and excelled in several sports, where he captained and represented school and district sports, especially in soccer and cricket. He was also an excellent artist and spent much time in art and design for school exhibitions and competitions. He always set out to be the best he could be in all his endeavors. With this focus and attitude, he received many sports, art, and academic awards.

Richard proceeded to North London University, where he qualified with first-time passes in the Association of Certified Accountants (ACCA) examinations in 1984, and fellowship in 1993. He became a member of the American Certified Public Accountants (CPA) in 1993 and Certified Fraud Examiners (CFE) in 2003.

Richard's professional experience and key achievements started in 1985 when he joined a London-based management consulting firm and then progressed to the audit profession at "Big Four" firms PricewaterhouseCoopers and Deloitte Touche. In the period from 1985 to 1992, he was responsible for many diversified audit, investigations, and accounting engagements in London, and Nassau Bahamas, primarily within investment banking and retail sectors. He also conducted numerous promotional seminars in accounting, taxation, and raising finance. He was also lecturer in various professional and business management courses at the London Business School of Education.

He then joined Burger King Corporation global headquarters (US) in 1992, as senior accounting analyst. He was responsible for the UK, United States, and international GAAP, (Generally Accepted Accounting Principles), interpretations and international consolidated financial statements, including cash flow and treasury reporting. He compiled and implemented a worldwide accounting and internal control policy manual.

In 1995, he joined the specialty retail firm Sunglass Hut International. As senior manager of International Finance, he built and integrated international finance and operations functions for fifteen countries across the globe, and recruited local staff and managed hub offices in the

United Kingdom, Australia, Mexico, the Caribbean, and Singapore to service local business and global regulatory requirements. He established and coordinated foreign currency hedge, risk management, trademark, and global treasury strategies. He was chairperson for the international committee responsible for the successful coordination and execution of necessary functions during a 250-store expansion overseas.

Richard was then recruited for managing director and chief financial officer of KC (USA) Inc. He built up and integrated US start-up operations of the Belgian international apparel chain. He restructured corporate entities and financing and changed strategic focus from owned stores to department store distribution to ensure long-term survival of brand. His expanded management responsibilities also included human resources, operations, legal, marketing, traffic, real estate and construction and management information systems.

From 1998 to 2007, Richard progressed very quickly up the executive ranks to executive vice president and chief financial officer of a major global public company, PRC LLC, before successfully spearheading the sale of the company to a private equity investment firm. During this tenure he navigated the financial turnaround of the company to significant consecutive profit growth as well as reengineering and building financial infrastructure, processes, and talent to support revenue growth from $175 million to $475 million. He developed the business strategy for offshore businesses and negotiated outsourced contracts in the Philippines, India, and the United Kingdom, which resulted in 80 percent revenue growth and triple US operating margins. Richard instituted functional best practices, negotiations, and managed business acquisitions that have yielded value and savings of over $25 million per annum.

Richard was then hired in 2008 by a large private equity firm as executive vice president and chief financial officer of Heritage Brands Inc., a global beverages distribution company, where he executed a significant turnaround by restructuring subsidiary operations in ninety days, increasing profitability by 230 percent over the prior year. In a short space of time he established effective start-up internal control and reporting infrastructure for private equity, and he has been a key contributor on global finance and operational initiatives, such as transfer pricing, currency hedging, and global corporate restructuring.

As of this writing, Richard is executive vice president and chief financial officer of Signature Consultants LLC, a fast-growth top-information technology staffing company in the United States. He was brought on to guide the company through the next significant phases of growth.

Richard's extensive accomplishments and competencies in his professional field are summarized as follows: He is recognized in local, national, and international business communities as a high performance CFO with a visionary, team-building, and motivational management style; he builds an effective execution culture and has an outstanding record in setting corporate strategy and linking strategic, operational, and capital planning process to increase shareholder value; he naturally establishes, builds, and integrates effective investor, banks, credit agencies, industry analysts, and internal and external business partnerships; he is an ethical and highly effective leader in strategic management, performance management, treasury, human resources, and risk and cost management.

He has extensive experience in international business and diverse intercultural sensitivity. He is proficient in United States, UK and international GAAP, SEC reporting, and Sarbanes-Oxley regulations. He has highly developed communication skills and is a presenter of choice for executive, media coverage, investor, and business development communications.

Richard is a member of these professional organizations:
- American Institute of Certified Public Accountants (1992)
- Fellow Chartered Certified Accountant, United Kingdom (1993)
- Certified Fraud Examiners (2003)
- Financial Executives International (2003)
- CFO Summit and CFO Pulse (2006)
- ACCA International Financial Reporting Certificate (2008)
- Society of Human Resources Management (2007)
- Chief Learning Officer BI Committee (2008)
- American Society of Training and Development (2008)
- CEO & president of Financial Acumen, Inc., Corporate Financial Executive Services and Financial Literacy Specialists (2007). This organization is dedicated to educating people on managing money effectively.

He has authored a first book in a series of children's financial literacy, *The Adventures of ExoKid and the Teachings of Money* (2008).

Richard has received numerous awards in recognition of achievements in his work and hobbies, including corporate financial presentation and business community awards; sports awards; and art exhibition awards. He also led a team to design and paint a mural in 1980–81 to commemorate the famous Lambeth Walk in London.

Richard is immensely proud of the values his parents instilled in him. They supported and encouraged a balance with academia and all extracurricular activities that interested him. These gave him a broad perspective and developed his leadership skills from an early age. His family life instilled trust, integrity, fun, happiness, strong friendships, and loyalty. These have all contributed to his career success and from which he gets his satisfaction. He explains:

> Executive leadership positions still boil down to the very basics my parents raised us to have: trust, passion, integrity, strong relationships, and in doing the right thing. I truly believe that these traits enabled me to excel in leading companies and teams to get to the next levels of growth. It's so much a part of my DNA because I enjoy leading, molding teams, and bringing out the best in people. I learned this strength at any early childhood stage with my family, relatives and friends.
>
> I chose this career path because it had the potential to broaden into other disciplines and functions and was in demand throughout the world. I was very interested in exploring other parts of the world, and this career gave me the keys to experience that. Over the years, my leadership skills and competitive edge catapulted me into senior executive positions.

Of his parents, he says:

> Never forgetting where I came from and seizing the opportunities my parents worked so hard and unconditionally to give me. I always strive to be the best I can be. I love to have fun and always look for the positive in all situations. I continually look for ways to expand my circle of positive influence and to give back. I think that I was blessed to inherit the individual and combined strengths of my mother and father in courage, determination, compassion, and a big heart.

> My brother, who is a wonderful example to us as the eldest sibling, points out that our family cherishes our endearing relationships rather than individual accomplishments. Our dear parents deserve all the credit in the world for giving us the inspiration and individual opportunity to serve. They were examples which provided the inspiration to "dream big" and change lives along the way. All of my sisters are also such wonderful, kind, and thoughtful individuals, who were all such a significant positive influence in my life. They cared and nurtured me throughout my youth, and I'll always cherish the fun and endearing times we had together, when we were growing up. My brother and sisters will always be my best friends for life.

Among the sad and happy moments in Richard's life so far, these are uppermost in his mind:

> The passing of my dear mother was a life-changing event for me. It taught me about the fragility of life and the need to live every moment in the present. Her legacy of unconditional love, honesty, and humility will live on for many generations to come. She was the best leader that I knew and impacted so many people's lives in such a great way. Her life example and teachings continue to expand the circle of influence through each of us, every single day.

> Meeting my wife, Naseema, was a calling. I know I dreamed her beforehand, and I guess karmic forces took hold for me to leave my close-knit home. She's my soul mate and has been a significant factor in many of our personal, family, and professional successes.

> I cherish the first time I saw my sons at birth. It was a surreal experience. They make my life complete and have taught me so much about myself. They are my best buddies for life!

> I still tingle when I think of the excitement and adventure of going to live in another country to experience and appreciate different cultural perspectives in the Bahamas. I wanted to understand how my parents lived in a Caribbean culture and embracing all the wonderful aspects of island life. It was also

> a catapult for understanding my own independence, strength, resilience, and edge.
>
> My career hit a pinnacle when I was promoted to the top chief financial officer position of a major US company in the most competitive markets in the world. I knew that I had grown up in my "executive thinking" and business acumen at the highest organizational level through the "school of hard knocks." I saw several business cycles and changes in the US fiduciary environment and rose to the top because of the simple traits my parents instilled in us but seem to be missing in the fast corporate environment—passion, integrity, trust, and strong relationships. Given the significantly low probability of anyone's reaching a CFO spot in the United States, I felt really proud because I was not from the States, nor was I trained there, so I had much ground to make up in a short space of time. I truly believe that my humble beginnings, leadership skills, work ethic, and spousal support account for whatever career success I have achieved.

In his spare time, Richard likes reading (spiritual, business, world news); sports (he'll watch or play cricket anywhere; football—Arsenal); and world traveling. He loves to come "home" to England to see family and friends.

Richard's wife, Naseema, is a registered nurse and a legal medical consultant. They have two sons, Ishan (twelve) and Kiran (nine), who are both school students and recipients of many sporting, art, and music awards for their young ages.

> My wife and I have the same goals and objectives of our parents and want to carry on that legacy—a loving, happy, and fun home with a key emphasis on giving our sons the best opportunity for them to progress in the future. Naseema stays at home with Ishan and Kiran to ensure the work/family balance is effective. This home understanding and simple living has created much positive momentum and energy in our lives. Ishan and Kiran are loving, intelligent, spiritual kids with a great sense of humor.

We both recognize the utmost importance of mental, physical, and spiritual balance, and we are constantly trying to improve and build these aspects of our family life. I believe that this balance has also been the foundation of my personal, familial, and career success.

October 5, 2010

Michael Anthony Patterson

BSc, MSc, PEng

Michael Patterson is a geoscientist. His MSc is in engineering geology. His career of over thirty-five years has taken him all over the world, from Quebec to the Gold Mines in Guyana, to hydroelectric projects in Nepal, Costa Rica, and Saskatchewan. He has worked with leaders of the northern Manitoba and Nunavut communities on a roadway link through those remote areas.

Long before the first brick is laid for a building, the engineering geologist investigates the structure of the ground, whether it is soft soil or rock, its strength, wetness, if it is on a water course or an earthquake fault line. These are just a few of many factors investigated to avoid collapse, even loss of life. They affect a building structure, be it an office block, bridge, airport, dam, and levee. The engineering geologist is the unsung hero of large building structures throughout the world. Michael is one of these professionals.

Michael and family have lived in Canada since 1973. They recently moved to live in Fort Erie, Ontario. Before that, they lived in Edmonton, Alberta, and Winnipeg, Manitoba.

Born in Charlestown, Georgetown, British Guiana, on December 9, 1946, Michael is the eldest son of the late Joseph and Miriam Patterson. Joseph was an accountant and Miriam a schoolteacher.

He attended St. Stephen's Primary School in Charlestown, Georgetown. From there in 1957, he won a Government County Scholarship to Queen's College. Michael attended Queen's College from 1957 to1965, passed his GCE O and A levels, and was awarded a conditional scholarship, which enabled him to pursue studies in geology to obtain a BSc at McGill University in Quebec.

He returned to Guyana in 1971 and worked with the Geological Survey Department until 1973, when he returned to pursue his MSc in engineering geology. He obtained his MSc from McGill University, in 1975.

In 1996, he studied for the IQA, an intensive one-week course pertaining to quality and excellence, and passed the exam to be a certified lead assessor, on the IQA, International Register of Certified Auditors. This is not related to accounting and financial auditing. It is strictly related to workplace quality systems.

Michael started his professional career in Guyana. As geologist on Geological Surveys of Guyana, he worked on investigations in areas of gold mineralization and supervised geological mapping exploration and in-situ testing for the proposed Upper Mazaruni Hydropower Development. He was responsible for geotechnical engineering for a phase of the Omai Gold Mines in Guyana. In Canada, he was senior assistant geologist, Quebec Ministry of Natural Resources.

In order to optimize his work experience, Michael accepted a position in 1975 with SNC Lavalin Inc., one of the leading companies in the field of engineering and geology. His work assignments offered many challenges, creating and improving infrastructure to communities worldwide in Guyana, Costa Rica, Nepal, Vietnam, Canadian provinces, and others.

His work covers all phases of project development, from conceptual studies through detailed engineering and construction in tropical, temperate, and cold regions. He has acquired a sound knowledge of the hydropower, transportation, irrigation, mining, and petrochemical industry sectors.

As total loss management manager at SNC–Lavalin Inc., he prepared and analyzed quality statistics and provided stewardship for managers and contractors during design and construction on Petro-Canada's

Desulphurization Tank Farm 2 Relocation and Refinery Conversion Projects.

He was quality assurance and quality coordinator for Bell Canada on the Alberta SuperNet Project. He prepared quality plan and held major responsibility for ensuring that the acceptance tests for the broadband fiber-optic network facilities were successfully performed.

As geotechnical environmental specialist, he managed geotechnical site investigations. He provided specialist advice to diverse engineering projects in the hydropower, irrigation, municipal, mining and petrochemical industries, including:

- The 12000 Megawatt Chisapani Hydroelectric Project and 200 Megawatt Upper Karnali Hydroelectric Project, in Nepal, financed by the World Bank;
- Boruca 1520 Megawatt Hydroelectric Project, Costa Rica;
- Riverhurst Irrigation Project, Saskatchewan;
- Hydroelectric Feasibility Study on Great Bear River and Tazin Lake Dam, Northwest Territories;
- Wreck Cove Hydroelectric Project, Nova Scotia;
- Island Falls Hydroelectric Expansion, SaskPower, Cutarm Creek, Saskatchewan;
- Gas processing facilities in the province Alberta;
- 210,000 barrel tank and related infrastructure, Husky Tank Farm Expansion, Hardisty, Alberta;
- Wood Treatment Plant, Elizabeth Metis Settlement, Alberta;
- Solid Waste Transfer Station Site Investigation, Whitecourt, Alberta;
- LPG pipeline, PetroVietnam, Vietnam Gas Utilization Project, Vung Tau, Vietnam;
- Facilities for disposal of fly ash and bottom ash from the 4000 Megawatt Paiton Steam Generation Plant, Indonesia;
- Golden Star Resources: Omai Gold Mine, Guyana;
- Major expansion of the existing terminal and shipping facilities, Shell Forcadas Integrated Projects, Nigeria;
- Diavik Diamond Mines Inc., Calgary, Alberta;
- Pipeline between the Suncor and Syncrude Plants Suncor-Syncrude Pipeline, Fort McMurray, Alberta;
- Oil Pumping Stations, Alberta;

- CFB Cold Lake: Wastewater Treatment Plant Headworks Facility, Alberta;
- Military aircraft facility Yellowknife Forward Operating Location, Northwest Territories, Canada.

In Red Deer, Alberta, he was a member of the Dickson Dam Team, which facilitated potable water supply for the residents.

In the period 2005–2007, he served as manager, Geotechnical Department, at SNC–Lavalin Inc., Winnipeg, Manitoba, with project responsibilities for design, analysis, site investigations and construction supervision. His projects included:

- The Red River Floodway Expansion;
- Detailed Design and Contract Administration for Manitoba Floodway Authority, Winnipeg, Manitoba;
- Hydroelectric Projects, James Smith Cree Nation, Fort a la Corne, Saskatchewan, Canada;
- Concept level study for 200 megawatt hydropower development on the Saskatchewan River.

Michael served on a Feasibility Study Team to determine the construction of a road to Nunavut. The team conducted reviews with the leaders of the Northern Manitoba and Nunavut communities to review their concerns and receive their input to determine the best possible route for a direct roadway link through those remote areas. This link will significantly improve the lives of native residents, as it will allow better access and distribution services.

He retired from SNC–Lavalin Inc., on Feb 27, 2008. Michael is a field guy. For this reason, he has started Ajomi Geoscience Consulting so that, as president, he could continue to be of service, employing his knowledge and experience, wherever and whenever required.

Michael is a member of the Association of Professional Engineers and Geoscientists of Manitoba; Association of Professional Engineers, Geologists and Geophysicists of Alberta; Engineering Institute of Canada; and the Canadian Geotechnical Society.

He was awarded the Geosynthetics '91 Award of Excellence in Geogrid Technology, North American Geosynthetics Society, Atlanta, Georgia. He has also received multiple recognition awards throughout his career from various project sponsors.

In addition to his professional associations, Michael has served in various capacities for charitable organizations, including the United Way (Canada) through employer's participation. He was active as a member of the Sickle Cell Society of Alberta and served as its president from 1997 to 2003.

Michael enjoys the arts and was featured in various stage productions including *HMS Pinafore*, *Pirates of Penzance*, and *Schooldays Can be Fun* during his years at Queen's College. He enjoys traveling, dancing, and all types of music but most especially jazz.

Reflecting on his life and career, Michael's most memorable events include the camaraderie/interaction with fellow students while at McGill University and spending summer vacations in New York. Visiting Mount Rushmore is one of his most interesting trips, and he continues to revisit at each opportunity.

Michael believes in doing his best; letting wisdom and integrity be his guide; and rising above mediocrity. In his life, his most unhappy occasions were the deaths of his parents and three of his siblings.

He comes from a family of achievers. Youngest brother, Peter, is a PhD in chemical engineering in Wisconsin. Younger sister, Verna, is a choreographer and owns her own dance studio. She teaches various types of dance. Youngest sister, Barbara (wife of retired brigadier general Michael Atherly—Guyana), is currently with UNICEF in Mozambique The family is driven by hard work and ambition, like most high achievers.

Michael's wife, Joan M. Leow Patterson, is vice president of Ajomi Geoscience Consulting. She is in charge of the administration of the business, as this is in keeping with her studies at York University and University of Toronto. She retired from IBM Canada Ltd. headquarters after a twenty-three-year career. Her last position was business analyst, and she was responsible for the incentive compensation for more than 1,100 sales/marketing personnel across Canada. During her tenure at IBM, Joan received several Achievement Awards for her high standards of job performance and commitment to excellence.

Michael has two daughters, Abiona, a schoolteacher, and Michelle, a real estate professional. His elder sister, Mrs. Patricia Barrow, lives in London, England. She has three daughters, Grace, Deidre, and Selena. Grace is a proud mother of three. Deidre is a pastor, along with her husband, Joseph; Selena attended Oxford University and is a high school teacher.

Michael's special pleasure is being with his family, taking charge of the barbecue. His cooking motto, in Guyanese lingo, is "When it bun, it done." He also enjoys bike rides with wife, Joan, in their Fort Erie neighborhood.

Many people maintain a low profile, but they have made significant and outstanding contributions in their respective fields. Michael Anthony Patterson is this type of person. He thoroughly enjoys engineering/geology and often risked life and limb to offer his professional skills. Michael's contributions through infrastructure work have helped to improve the lives of many people worldwide, and to make their world a better place.

September 23, 2010

Birendra (Don) Persaud

BSc (Chemistry), BSc (Chem. Engineering)
Chemical Engineer

Birendra (Don/Luxie) Persaud is the chief pipeline engineer for the province of New Brunswick in Canada.

He was born in New Amsterdam, Berbice, Guyana, on March 18, 1956. His father, Soomnauth Persaud, was a sanitary health inspector in the county of Berbice. He died in 1966. Soomnauth was the son of Durga Persaud of Number 60 Village, Berbice, Guyana. Don's mother, Khilwatteedaby, also known as Aunty Gago, was a teacher at New Market Elementary School. She is the daughter of Pandit and Mrs Brijbassi, a well-known landowner and rice miller of 64 Village, Upper Corentyne, Berbice, Guyana. Gago, long since retired, lives with Don and his family.

Birendra has two sisters. Sunita Evans is a teacher in Calgary, Alberta, and Vidyotama (Rosanna) Sehmbi is a nurse manager in London, England. One older brother, Rajendra (Brudsie) Persaud, died in 1977.

Birendra attended Messiah Primary School, then Skeldon Lutheran High School and Indian Educational Trust College in Georgetown. He passed his GCE examinations in ten subjects (1972–1973). He also passed his advanced level in biology, chemistry, and physics in 1975.

He emigrated to Canada in 1975. He attended the University of Prince Edward Island and graduated from there with a bachelor of science degree in chemistry in 1979. He then attended the University of New Brunswick and graduated from there with a bachelor of science degree in chemical engineering in 1981.

Birendra was married in 1981 to Sheila Herring, a registered nurse working at the veteran's hospital in Fredericton, New Brunswick.

He has worked as project engineer for Gulf Canada Resources, Calgary, 1981–1992. He worked as a project engineer at the Strachan Gas Plant in Rocky Mountain House and later in the main Gulf Canada Office in Calgary. During this period, he was involved in numerous gas and oil pipeline projects dealing with the design, construction, and commissioning of oil/gas pipeline facilities.

In 1992, he moved to Fredericton, New Brunswick, and has been working for the New Brunswick Provincial Government as a senior pipeline engineer. He has been involved in introducing natural gas in the province and has been actively involved in numerous projects dealing specifically with oil and gas. He was involved in assisting the government with the major Maritime and North Pipeline project in New Brunswick and again with the development of Enbridge Gas Pipeline distribution system in the province. In addition, he has been involved in writing the New Oil/Gas Pipeline Act and Regulations for the province.

Birendra is a cricketer, too. He plays regularly and is the main wicketkeeper for the only cricket team in the New Brunswick Cricket League. Typically, the three neighbouring provinces New Brunswick, Nova Scotia and Prince Edward Island engage in an annual cricket tournament. On many occasions, he has won the best batsmen/wicketkeeper's award.

His other interests include church, squash, jogging, movies, reading, and traveling abroad.

He is also involved in humanitarian work. He visited and sponsored a child from Malawi Africa in 2006. In addition, he has sponsored two families to Canada.

Birendra and Sheila have two children, Andrew and Melissa. Melissa is now a practicing physician in Winnipeg, and Andrew will complete his medical degree in 2011.

Birendra believes in hard work and determination. He has faced many challenges in his life, and has always worked diligently to overcome these.

He is inspired by the legacy and motto left by the great Mahatma Gandhi: nonviolence and peace will ultimately triumph over evil.

Today, he is still working to make a difference. He is very active in his local community and, in memory of his dear brother Brudsie, with the suicide and prevention team in New Brunswick. He wants to one day return to his native Guyana and extend this mission to help reduce suicide in our world. In 2010, he visited his homeland for the first time in thirty years and was quite impressed with the development. He is planning a missionary trip next year to build a center for suicide prevention in his village.

September 17, 2010

Dwarka Persaud

Industrialist

Dwarka Persaud was born in Unity Village, ECD, Guyana on June 2, 1948, and is the second child of Mr. and Mrs. Ganesh Persaud of Supply Mahaica.

He attended Supply Methodist School as well as Helena Presbyterian Primary School before attending Indian Education Trust and Muslim College in Georgetown for his secondary education.

Dwarka worked with the government of Guyana for two years before emigrating to Canada in 1969, where he studied electronics and attended University of Waterloo.

In 1972 Dwarka married Koomarie. In 1974, just prior to the birth of their first child, Latchmin Laura, Dwarka lost his younger brother, Gobin, who died after a very short illness. A year later, their son Tribuwan was born.

While working for Butler Metal Products Cambridge Ontario, a tier one automotive supplier, in 1974, he was offered a management position as a shift supervisor. Encouraged by his new friends in management, he became very motivated and in a few years was made the plant superintendent responsible for production, safety, and labor relations and sat on various planning and production teams. In 1978, when Ontario introduced Occupational Health and Safety legislation, Dwarka was selected from among thirty-eight other management personnel to become the firm's in-house specialist.

In 1987, after being overlooked for two promotions, Dwarka decided to accept an offer to become a 50 percent business partner in Norwich Recycling Woodstock Ontario. In 1993, along with his business partner and friend, Bill Gosse, they started Norwich Plastics, a complete industrial plastic recycling and reprocessing business with operations in the United States and Canada. They developed the operations by bringing together employees, relatives, and friends as business partners.

In 2003, they recycled over 140 million pounds of plastic, of which a significant amount would have gone to landfill, had it not been for their unique processing capabilities. Their final product is used in automotive sound attenuation, and garden and industrial hoses, as well as many flooring applications. More recently, they have used their expertise in assisting manufacturers to reuse their scrap, as well as post-consumer scrap, as part of the growing trend to be "green."

Throughout his life Dwarka Persaud has always given back to the community by sponsoring fund-raising activities and donations to various charitable organizations, including the Cancer Society and the Red Cross. In the late 1980s he became involved with a group of friends and started Radha Krishna Mandir, a Hindu temple in Cambridge, Ontario. He was its first president, a position he held off and on for almost fourteen years.

In 1999, he was a founding member of the Federation of Hindu Temples of Canada. In 2005, he became the president, and he is currently in charge of membership. In 1996 he chaired a province-wide program to increase the awareness of the Indo-Canadian population to get involved with blood donation and the Bone Marrow Registry, as there was poor participation by the community, and there was a growing need for both. In early 2002, he became involved with SEWA Canada, an organization that helps the less fortunate in India.

With his friends, he began to raise the awareness of one-teacher schools in tribal villages in India, health care clinics, and orphanages. They have seen success, such as sponsored children becoming doctors and engineers returning to be full-time providers in their community. Dwarka took the initiative to help SEWA Canada raise and send almost $125,000 (Canadian) to Guyana for various charitable organizations.

He also has become involved in Three Rivers Kids Foundation, another Canadian charity that takes children with serious medical ailments overseas, mostly to India, for treatment. Currently, he is working with Dr. Budhendra Doobay of Vishnu Mandir to set up a renal clinic in Guyana. This clinic, like the Three Rivers Kids Foundation, will be funded from charity events in which Dwarka will be involved in years to come.

Dwarka is president of Agri Solutions Technologies and has been producing biodiesel in Region 1 Guyana, where it is consumed by the local electrical authority to produce electricity to the citizens of Region 1.

In May 2008, he was presented with the Guyana Award for Business Excellence.

Over the years Dwarka has made and maintained many friends, and he is very committed to his family. He enjoys family reunions and socializing and often remarks how lucky he is to be surrounded by good people. His parents and grandparents, as well as growing up in Guyana, have taught him many valuable lessons, including his obligations to help the less fortunate without expectation of rewards.

He enjoys golf and continues to play to improve his game. He enjoys being with his grandson, Sachin, and he is looking forward to his new grandson expected in 2011.

More than anything else, Dwarka would love to see a world of peace and contentment, with everyone doing his or her part for others and for the environment. Dwarka is a proud Hindu who believes that the world will be a better pace if we loved and served all selflessly.

November 30, 2010

Dr. Kavita Persaud

MB, BCh, BAO (UK), FGM, MD
Physician (Geriatrics)
Broadcaster, Literacy Advancement Volunteer

Dr. Kavita Persaud runs her own practice, Carolina Geriatrics, which provides medical care to elderly people. She has been medical director of Britthaven Northchase Skilled Nursing Facility, a nursing home with 130 beds. She is medical director of Hermitage House, an assisted living community, and of Wellcare Home Health, a home health care agency. She is a weekly guest on radio, speaking on senior health issues and on health care reform.

Kavita Persaud was born in 1964 in Georgetown, Guyana. Her parents are Maharanee Persaud and Dr. Krishna Persaud. Her father, a physician, was educated at the University of the West Indies. Her mother graduated with a BSc (with honors) degree in sociology from the University of London.

Kavita started school at St. Gabriel's, a private primary school in Georgetown, Guyana. She was seven years old when her parents immigrated to Canada. Most of her school years were at the Bishop Strachan School in

Toronto, Canada. She graduated in 1982, winning the Governor General's Medal, placing as top student in her graduating class. Her major extracurricular involvement was debating, and she participated in tournament debate for many years, winning several Best Speaker prizes, including winning city of Toronto championships.

She attended the University of Western Ontario, 1982–1984. She then went to the Queen's University of Belfast in Northern Ireland and attended medical school from 1984 to 1989. She won several awards in medical school, including awards in oncology and pharmacology. During those years she enjoyed traveling in England, Ireland, Europe, and Africa. She graduated with her medical degree, MB, BCh, BAO, in 1989 and was licensed by the General Medical Council in the UK.

After graduating from medical school, she was junior house officer in 1989–1990 at the Royal Victoria Hospital, rotating in medicine and surgery. In 1990 she began her internal medicine residency program through the State University of New York at Buffalo. She completed the residency in internal medicine in 1993. Her education and practice continued from 1993 until 1995, with a postgraduate fellowship in geriatric medicine, also at the State University of New York at Buffalo. During her residency and fellowship, she took a keen interest in biomedical ethics and engaged in many activities, including teaching, community education, and projects for the betterment of patient care and physician involvement.

In 1993 she was board certified in internal medicine through the American Board of Internal Medicine. She has since recertified. In 1996 she was board certified in geriatric medicine through the American Board of Internal Medicine. She has since recertified.

In 1996 she began her medical career in Indiana as director of senior health services for Lutheran Hospital of Indiana. Her time was spent with clinical work and administrative duties. During her time in Fort Wayne, Indiana, she served on the board of directors of the Fort Wayne Alzheimer's Support Group and as medical director of a local hospice. She held a teaching position through Indiana University and taught medical residents. She was active at the hospital and served on the Pharmacology and Therapeutics Committee for many years.

In 2001, she moved to North Carolina. She started her work there as an employed physician in a private geriatric medical practice, caring for elders in the community in home and nursing home settings. She opened her own medical practice in 2006, Carolina Geriatrics, and it is now a busy clinic, providing medical care to community patients. She has chosen to remain in solo practice and be the direct caregiver for her patients.

She is a regular weekly radio guest with Marty Shirah on *Talk on the Town* on 980 WAAV Radio in Wilmington, North Carolina. On Monday mornings she speaks on health topics with a focus on senior health issues. Sometimes, she tackles controversial issues regarding health care reform taking a committed stance as an advocate for senior patients.

Kavita has been active as a volunteer since 2002 with the Cape Fear Literacy Council. She has served for the past four years on the executive committee of that board as secretary. She chaired one of their major fundraisers, the CFLC Annual Spelling Bee, from 2006 to 2009. She has a passion for advancing literacy in the community for those who are unable to read and do basic math and helping those individuals and families. Her inspiration for these endeavors was her maternal grandmother, Dookhni Persaud, who could not read or write but was an enthusiastic champion of education and very respected by her large family of children and grandchildren.

Kavita also volunteers at her daughter's school. Although her daughter is in the elementary school, Kavita volunteers as the sponsor and coach of their Speech and Debate team for the high school grades, leading a dedicated group of high school students. She is still thrilled with having students eager to learn and thankful for the guidance and mentoring. To be involved in debating again has made this a true pleasure for Kavita.

Kavita has been married to Dr. Sunil Arora since 1995. He was born and raised in India and has traveled the world, and they reside in Wilmington, North Carolina. He is a pain management physician, trained originally in anesthesiology; he completed his interventional pain management fellowship at the Cleveland Clinic in Ohio. He is board certified by the American Board of Anesthesiology in anesthesia and pain management. He is now a physician and partner at Center for Pain Management in Wilmington and practices exclusively in pain management.

They have one child, a daughter, Maya Arora, born in 2002 in Wilmington, North Carolina. She attends school at Cape Fear Academy in Wilmington. She is an active child, busy with her own activities such as Chess Club, Girl Scouts, and piano lessons and weekend sports of tennis, golf, and roller skating. During Maya's first four years, Kavita was involved in the local La Leche League and participating in mother-to-mother support among breast-feeding mothers. She nursed Maya for four years. This was a traditional approach to child feeding and nurture and led to a philosophy of attachment parenting that they pursue to this day.

Kavita was raised by parents who lived a way of life that incorporated always doing your best, doing the right thing, serving others, and giving to your community. Competition with others has always been a method to meet individual potential and has been a driving force in her own life. Being aware of all the sacrifices her parents made for her education, including emigrating from Guyana and starting over in life, was a reminder that she had a huge responsibility to move forward and do even more for herself and others.

Mistakes serve as the most valuable learning experiences for her. Each has humbled her and made sure she took next steps more carefully. Never much of risk-taker, she still regrets her inability to be a visionary, leading more by example as a hard worker with keen analytical and organizational skills, but certainly never stepping out as a radical thinker.

For Kavita, the most meaningful part of life is a happy and close family. The support of her personal dreams by a loving husband, the opportunity to share values and goals with a husband who is a true partner, and the gift of a child who is in her heart and thoughts every moment of every day—these things come to mind as the core of living a wonderful life every day. Her parents have continued to offer encouragement and counsel to their grown-up child. Every grown-up child still needs that gentle, wise parental hand to advise and support, and the constant feeling of unconditional parental love lends a confidence that cannot be surpassed. To this day, Kavita is made happiest if she sees her mother smile.

As to the future, Kavita feels the future is to nurture the next generation. She wants to raise a child that is kind and courageous, innovative and hard-working, proud of her heritage and culture and confident to take her place in the world and make her community and society a better place.

October 17, 2010

Dr. Parmanand (George) Poonai

MB, BS, FRCS (Edinburgh), FRCS G (Glasgow)

Parmanand Poonai studied medicine in India. He later obtained fellowships as both physician and surgeon in Scotland and lectured at the University of the West Indies. He also is an accomplished singer of Indian classical music.

Parmanand, familiarly known as George, is the youngest brother of Premsukh, the agriculturist, and Niranjan Oudho and Premnath, both solicitors.

Soon after high school George set sail for Mumbai, India. He passed his pre-medical examinations and entered Grant Medical College, graduating in December 1960. In 1967, he became a Fellow of the Royal College of Surgeons of Edinburgh (FRCS Ed) and a Fellow of the Royal College of Physicians and Surgeons of Glasgow (FRCS G).

George practiced as a general surgeon until retirement in 2005. He worked in several countries, including Guyana and England. He spent some time as a lecturer in surgery and a consultant general surgeon at the University of the West Indies, Kingston, Jamaica.

In 1973, he moved to the United States and has been living at Port St. Joe, Florida, since 1976.

His research, publications and prizes include:

1. *A New Technique for the Repair of Inguinal Hernias.* WI med Journal, Sept. 1972 (vol. XXI. No 3) Parmanand Vijay Poonai FRCS Ed.,FRCS G.

2. *A case of widespread endometriosis and the review of the literature.* WI Med.Journal.1972 XXI 105. Dr. Anila P.V.Poonai. DRCOG Lond., MRCOG Lond.

3. *The effects of estrogens on the activity of carbonic anhydrase in human and canine gastric mucosa. The role of carbonic anhydrase inhibitors in the treatment of peptic ulcers.* By Drs. P. V. Poonai & Anila Poonai. Presented at the seventeenth scientific meeting off the Standing Advisory Committee for Medical Research in the British Caribbean on the April 21,1972, at Nassau Beach Hotel, Bahamas.

4. *Upper massive gastrointestinal tract hemorrhage from jejunal diverticula.* Report of a case and review of the literature. Presented at the Association of Surgeons of Jamaica Meeting, Oct. 1971.

5. Presentation at the 18th Scientific Meeting of the Standing Advisory Committee for Medical Research in the British Caribbean held at the Pegasus Hotel, Georgetown, Guyana, June 1973:
(a) *Hemodynamic Studies in Eleven Patients Before and During Peritoneoscopy.* By Dr. S. Sivapragasm & Dr. P. V. Poonai.
(b) *Alterations in Secretion and Fine Structure (Electron Microscopy) of histamine stimulated stomach mucosa following administration of estrogen.* By Dr. B. R. Sparke, Dr. P. V. Poonai & Dr. D. Morris.

6. *Color Infra Red Versus Conventional Color and Black and White Photomicrography.* Won 2nd Prize in Competition of the Society of Pathologist, sponsored by and held at the Cleveland Clinic, Ohio, November 1974.

7. *The Histochemistry of the Human Breast in various Pathological Conditions.* Won 1st Prize in Resident Papers Competition in May 1975, at St. Alexis Hospital, Cleveland, Ohio.

8. *Relation Between Glucose, Insulin, and Growth Hormone in the Fetus During Labor and at De*livery. Journal of Obstetrics and Gynecology (Green Journal), Vol. 45, No 2, February 1975. Dr. Anila P. V. Poonai, Dr. K. Tang, Dr. P. V. Poonai.

George married Dr. Anila C. Jhaveri during their internship in Mumbai. She is a Gujrati Jain by religion and was born in Mumbai. It is understood that the Jains form 10 percent of the population in India. Anila also graduated in the same year as George from GS Medical College, Mumbai. While in England, she did her DRCOG and MRCOG, (Diploma and membership respectively, of the Royal College of Obstetricians and Gynaecologists).

While studying medicine at Grant Medical College, George simultaneously studied Indian classical vocal music at the Professor Deodhar School of Music.

George says that his brothers Sunny, Oudho, and Premsukh were his role models. "Prembhaia (the suffix 'bhaia' is Hindi for 'respected brother') was the one who first suggested that I should go and study in India so as to get some Indian culture in me."

September 15, 2010

Dr. Premsukh Poonai

AICTA, FRSS, MD, PhD
Economic Botanist, Linguist, Scholar
Doctor of Medicine

One of the brightest people one could ever meet is Guyanese international scholar, linguist, economic botanist, and doctor of medicine, Dr. Premsukh Poonai. He was one of the early graduates of the renowned Imperial College of Tropical Agriculture in Trinidad. An agricultural scientist, he became a doctor of medicine in his later years and a college professor in Florida. Before he passed away, he published his book, *Origin of Civilization and Language.*

Dr. Poonai was the son of the distinguished Poonai family of the Upper Corentyne coast of Berbice in Guyana. In his early years, he was a high school teacher and later a chemist and researcher in the Department of Agriculture in the days of British Guiana. An unassuming man, he was invariably seen in his agriculturist "uniform" of khaki shirt and trousers and a safari hat.

Premsukh was born on December 15, 1919, at Number 56 Village, Upper Corentyne, Berbice. His father was Aditya Poonai and mother,

Mahadei Poonai. They both died within months of one another—his mother in April 1945, and his father in August 1945. They were farmers.

Premsukh was the fourth of eleven children. His younger brother Niranjan Oudho, a solicitor, had a long established practice with offices in Charlotte Street, facing the rear grounds of the Victoria Law Courts, the main law courts of Guyana. He was better known in the 1940s and 1950s as a regular columnist on cultural issues in the Sunday newspapers, along with another well known writer of the day, Peter Rohoman. The widely read Oudho took time off his practice in his later years to obtain an MSc degree in zoology at Cornell University, Ithaca, New York, and produced a book on the flora and fauna of British Guiana.

Another younger brother Premnath (Sonny), qualified as a solicitor and had a successful practice in Georgetown. He is now retired and lives in Toronto. Youngest brother Parmanand (George) is a doctor of medicine. He studied at Grant Medical College in Mumbai, India. He practiced in Guyana and then moved to the United States. After having a successful practice, he is now retired and lives in Florida.

The four brothers have an abiding interest in Indian music and culture. Premnath plays the Indian flute -the Basuri. Parmanand is an accomplished Indian classical singer.

Premsukh received his early education at Number 56 Canadian Mission Primary School. He then attended Berbice High School for Boys from 1932 to1936. At that time, very few people sent their children to high school. The Principal was Rev. James Dunn. Other well known teachers were Mr J.A. Rodway and Mr J.J. Niles. Mr Niles later went to teach science at Queen's College. Premsukh's contemporaries at high school were Justice Dan Jhappan, Justice Aubrey Fraser, and Senator Vernon Nunes.

At Berbice High School, Premsukh won several prizes. For Best All-Round Boy in the Fifth Form (1935 to1936), his prize was the *Complete Works of William Shakespeare*, and for Highest Average in the Fifth Form (1935 to 1936) his prize was the *American Oxford Dictionary*. (His younger brother now has these books.) He was an outstanding athlete and cricketer and won many trophies in athletics for Berbice High School.

From 1937 to 1939 he was a primary school teacher at Massiah Canadian Mission (CM) School and at Molson Creek CM School, both in Upper Corentyne, Berbice.

He then attended the Imperial College of Tropical Agriculture in Trinidad, the premier institution in the British empire at the time for the study of tropical agriculture. He studied there from 1939 to 1942 and qualified with the Diploma, Imperial College of Tropical Agriculture, -DICTA.

From 1942 to 1944, Premsukh worked for the Grow More Food Campaign in Trinidad.

From 1944 to 1945. he was a teacher of physics, chemistry, biology, and French at Berbice High School.

Premsukh then secured employment in 1945 at the Department of Agriculture, British Guiana. He worked as a chemist and economic botanist at the Rice Experiment Station, Mahaicony Abary Rice Re-Development Scheme (MARDS), and at Mon Repos. In 1951 he was awarded associateship, Associate of the Imperial College of Tropical Agriculture -AICTA.

In 1954, in recognition for his work in the field of statistics, Premsukh was awarded the certificate of FRSS—Fellow of the Royal Statistical Society. His work in agriculture was of a high order and in 1957, he was awarded the Diplome Botanique, University of Strasbourg, France.

He studied for a doctorate in agriculture, and he obtained his PhD in agricultural sciences from Louisiana State University in 1965.

In 1966, Doctor Poonai emigrated to the United States. He secured an appointment as university professor, Bethune Cookman College, Florida. In the course of his work, he decided he would study medicine. He obtained his MD degree and qualified as a doctor of medicine in 1979. He retired in 1995.

In 1994 Dr. Poonai published a unique book, a well-researched Indo-Vedic text, *Origin of Civilization and Language.* He wrote it with the youths of Guyana in mind. From early days he was fascinated with scientific research and linguistics, and equally with Hindu philosophy and Indian culture. He was also proficient in several languages—French, German, Spanish, Sanskrit, and Hindi—and he had a working knowledge of some ancient languages. The book is, in a way, the distillate of his wide knowledge and interests.

The notes on the back cover of the book include the following:

> Premsukh Poonai MD, PhD, served for a period of about twenty years in the British Commonwealth as plant breeder and geneticist, economic botanist and analytical chemist before coming to the United States. ... During that service he was awarded the Associateship of the Imperial College

of Tropical Agriculture for a very high standard of research, by the Governing Body under the Patronship of his Majesty King George VI. He was also awarded the Diplome d'Etudes Superieures "avec la mention tres bien" by the University of Strasbourg for research in physiology.

The author is an international scholar and research worker. … In the present work he has convincingly proven the unicentric origin of race, language, culture, and civilization by using mainly linguistic and archaeological data.

The concept of unicentricity of origin is not merely an important fundamental principle in its own right. It goes further and provides a pillar for building mutual respect and cooperation between peoples and nations. It behooves the world leaders to direct its unifying forces to create and consolidate a genuinely international world order.

Rampersaud (Ram) Tiwari, former permanent secretary in several ministries in Guyana, wrote a review of the book. He had worked with Premsukh and Dr. Giglioli in the experimental station at MARDS in the early '50s. Premsukh was then an agronomist who bred new varieties of paddy.

In the review, Ram stated, in part:

Using mainly linguistic and archaeological data with incisive analytical skill, the author … discusses the unicentric origin of language and culture in a very scholarly manner.

Dr. Poonai … recognized for his distinguished achievements in the Commonwealth, in the United States of America and in France … one of the early graduates of the Imperial College of Tropical Agriculture … promoted the "Grow More Food" campaign during the painful years of World War II.

Dr. Poonai … geneticist and an agricultural scientist, his greatest gift to Guyana, his homeland, is perhaps, the D79, D110, and Rustic varieties of paddy which enriched the agrarian culture and economy of the country for many years.

Dr. Poonai was a president of Arya Samaj in British Guiana in his younger years and in the early years of the organization.

Premsukh was an active member of Arya Samaj in Guyana and Trinidad. He was president of the Guyana Arya Samaj, formally known as the American Aryan League in 1954 to 1955. *Arya Samaj* is Sanskrit for "Noble Society." The organization was founded by Swami Dayanand in 1875 in India, in its early preindependence period. The purpose of the Arya Samaj has been to adhere to the teachings of the Vedas and its goal is *Krinvanto Vishvam Aryam'* ("Make This World Noble").

Ram's review continued:

> Students and scholars of language, history, archaeology, anthropology, and related studies will find this book very useful in advancing their academic and professional interests. It will be highly beneficial to … anyone with special interests in the origin and migration of the Indo-Aryans of the Himalayan-Gangetic region, and the influence of Sanskrit and the Vedic culture on civilization and language in other parts of the world.

Premsukh wrote many scientific papers on rice research while at the British Guiana Department of Agriculture.

Not a flamboyant personality, not much known outside of scientific circles, Premsukh Poonai was a great inspiration to his students, many of whom went on to higher learning in their own right.

His greatest inspiration was his love for learning. He combined his academic studies with field work and was a tireless student all his life. He died in Florida, March 1996. He is survived by his wife, Savitri; their daughter, Shanti; son Vish Poonai, a chiropractor in Georgia; and son Vikram, a medical practitioner in Maryland.

September 9, 2008

CCH Pounder

Hollywood Actress

CCH Pounder has starred in the films *Avatar, Orphan,* and *Bagdad Café*, and has appeared in many other successful films and mini-series.

She first appeared in TV guest roles on *Hill Street Blues* and *Cagney & Lacey,* then landed recurring roles on *ER, Miami Vice, LA Law, The X-Files, Living Single,* and *Quantum Leap,* and made guest appearances on *The Practice, Law & Order,* and *The West Wing,* among others.

CCH Pounder was featured in the Guyana Consulate 2008 Awards under the heading "Legacy of Excellence." The citation of the award contains the following information, in part:

> CCH (Carol Christine Hilaria) was born on Christmas Day 1952 in British Guiana. Her father is Ronald, and her mother is Betsy. She spent part of her childhood on a sugar plantation until her parents moved to the United States.
>
> She and her sister, Shelley, were sent to a convent boarding school in Britain where they studied art and the classics. In 1970, CCH moved back to the States to attend Ithaca College

in New York, where she earned a bachelor of fine arts in drama.

After her feature debut as a nurse in Bob Fosse's award-winning musical *All That Jazz* in 1979, she moved to Los Angeles in 1981, and landed more film and television roles, including one opposite the noted 1970s actress Jill Clayburgh in *I'm Dancing as Fast as I Can* in 1982. Back in New York, she appeared with Morgan Freeman in *The Mighty Gents* at the New York Shakespeare Festival, and she made an impressive Broadway debut at the Music Box Theater in a production of Shirley Lauro's two-act drama, *Open Admissions* in 1984.

In the critically acclaimed FX series *The Shield,* CCH was nominated for two NAACP Image Awards for Best Actress in a Drama Series, and she received her second Satellite Award for Performance by an Actress in a Series, Drama.

Other accolades include an Emmy nomination for Best Supporting Actress for her role as Dr. Angela Hicks on the NBC series ER, and an Emmy nomination for Outstanding Guest Actress in a Drama Series for her role in Fox's *The X-Files.* CCH also received a Grammy Award nomination for Best Spoken Word Album for *Grow Old Along With Me.*

Recent credits include the films Avatar, December 18, 2009; and Orphan, July 24, 2009. She has won an AUDI, the Audio Publishers Association's top honor for *Women in the Material World.*

Sources:

Websites accessed May 27, 2010, on Guyana Consulate Toronto, Guyana Awards (Canada)

November 25, 2010

Lisa Punit

BCom (Hon.), MBA

Lisa Punit was winner of Guyana Awards (Canada) 2010 Youth Award. The citation of the award contains the following information, in part:

> Lisa Punit was a volunteer manager for the 2009 World Junior Hockey Championships in Ottawa. She is employed with the federal government and was a senior member of the Vancouver Olympics team for her employer. She played a key role in developing a student internship program between her employer and the University of Ottawa.
>
> She also holds an Honors BCom degree, majoring in international management, from the Telfer School of Management, University of Ottawa.
>
> At the age of twenty-four, Lisa completed her master of business administration (MBA) from Queen's University while gaining valuable work experience. She was the youngest graduate in her year. After completing the program, she was appointed

by her peers to become a senior member of the Board of Representatives for the class of 2009.

Lisa believes in giving back and helping others. Throughout university she was involved in creating a number of clubs dedicated to helping others, such as the University of Ottawa Public Speaking Development Club.

She is director of finance for Global Partnership for Literacy: SchoolNet Guyana—an organization dedicated to bridging the digital divide between developing and developed nations.

A regular volunteer for the Guyana Independence Festival during her teenage years, Lisa was also a recipient of the IODE (International Order of Daughters of the Empire) Award for outstanding contributions to the community.

She strongly believes that "there are many opportunities to achieve great things if I work hard and set achievable goals for myself."

Sources:

Websites accessed May 27, 2010, on Guyana Consulate Toronto, Guyana Awards (Canada)

May 27, 2010

Gloria Rajkumar

Business CEO

Gloria Rajkumar was winner of Guyana Awards (Canada) 2010 Business Excellence Award. The citation of the award contains the following information, in part:

> Gloria Rajkumar is CEO of SIMAC—Superior Independent Medical Assessment Centers—a firm she founded in 2001.
>
> SIMAC, regarded as an industry leader, has three locations, twenty-two full-time staff, and affiliations with more than 250 respected medical professionals.
>
> Gloria had worked her way through a variety of positions in the insurance industry, over a period of eighteen years, continually upgrading her skills through credit courses and on-the-job learning. As her industry knowledge and expertise grew, she recognized a need for improvements in the way the industry's medical assessment needs were being met. In 2001, that she made the bold move to leave her successful sales

position in the insurance industry , risk her life savings, and start her own company—SIMAC.

She was born in Mahaica, the seventh of eight children.

Gloria is highly committed to her social and community responsibilities. A champion of environmental preservation she is fiercely committed to supporting "green" initiatives. She is civic-minded and philanthropic and supports many charitable causes and community fund-raising activities.

Her dedication to quality service, ethical standards, her contributions to the community, and the respect she has gained from her colleagues have all been recognized and celebrated when she was the proud recipient of the 2010 Business Achievement Award from the Richmond Hill Chamber of Commerce.

Gloria's entrepreneurial success is a testament to the fact that humble beginnings do not have to lead to mediocrity in life. She believes that "it is a content of character to want to be something better and that with drive and determination, anyone can accomplish their goals."

Sources:

Websites accessed May 27, 2010, on Guyana Consulate Toronto, Guyana Awards (Canada)

May 27, 2010

Dr. Vivian Rambihar

BSc, MD, FRCPC, FACC, FACP
Consultant Cardiologist

Dr. Rambihar, a 1969 Guyana Scholar, and recipient of numerous awards, is renowned as a cardiologist and a pioneer in "chaos and complexity"—considered by Stephen Hawking to be the science for the twenty-first century. Dr. Rambihar has also been a pioneer in ethnicity and health and disparities in health, being the first in North America to raise awareness of high rates of premature heart disease and diabetes in South Asians and other populations. He is currently working on global grassroots engagement for change in all populations using a complexity approach and across the South Asian diaspora, and wrote a landmark editorial on this for the *American Heart Journal* in January 2010.

He has virtually coined the phrase "chaos and complexity science." He sees chaos and complexity everywhere in the world, mirrored in the workings of the human heart and cardiovascular system as well as in the physical world and human relations and thus applicable to human affairs and complex world problems. He has focused his energies in developing this new field, proposing the use of complexity ideas in global issues, including peace, health, development, and poverty reduction.

Vivian Srinivas Rambihar was born in 1951 at Beterverwagting, East Coast Demerara, but lived in different parts of Essequibo and Demerara, then mostly in Prashad Nagar, Georgetown. He attended Queen's College 1962–69, was the deputy head prefect in his final year, and in 1969 won the Guyana Scholarship, which entitles the winner to study for a profession, free of all fees and ancillary expenses. He taught mathematics at QC for a year, then, uncertain of a career choice, went to Canada to study math and physics while considering medicine, receiving additional UN and University of Toronto Admission scholarships.

He entered the University of Toronto in 1970, obtaining his BSc degree in two years, then a medical degree after three years at the innovative McMaster University Medical School in Hamilton, Canada, by the age of twenty-three. He stayed on at McMaster, completing specialist training in internal medicine and cardiology, following this with sub-specialist training in the new field of echocardiography at Toronto General Hospital and Hospital for Sick Children.

He progressed rapidly in his profession and soon held the position of president of the medical staff, member of the Board of Governors and Medical Advisory Committee at Scarborough General Hospital, and was extensively involved in research, teaching, organization, community outreach, and development and diversity and health issues.

Dr. Rambihar focused on preventing premature heart disease, especially in the South Asian and ethnic communities, and in reducing disparities in health identified in his research. He has authored the book *South Asian Heart: Preventing heart disease*, published in 1995. On this subject, he lectures widely, and he is actively involved in the community. He convened the first conference in North America on this subject, with OSSICC (Ontario Society for Services to Indo-Caribbean Canadians) at York University in Toronto in 1990 and the first South Asian Heart Health Fair, among many other initiatives. He is credited with the development of a specialist field of study—ethnicity and heart disease in Canada, lecturing, writing, and holding conferences on the subject internationally. He is the author of four books, two of which relate to chaos and complexity science in medicine and health, and one to a global approach to the use of complexity.

His publications include:

Race, Ethnicity and Heart Disease: A challenge for cardiology for the 21st century. Editorial in the *American Heart Journal,* January 2010, with Dr. Sherryn Rambihar and Vanessa Rambihar.

Ethnocultural Heart: Another challenge for an emerging diversity. VS Rambihar & DG Jagdeo. Commentary: Can J Cardiology 1995.

Jurassic Heart: From the heart to the edge of chaos. Commentary: Can J Cardiology 1993.

CAD and South Asians. Letter. Can J Cardiology 1996.

Science, Evidence, and the Use of the Word Scientific. Letter, Lancet 2000.

Complexity: The science for medicine and the human story. Letter, Lancet 2010.

Complexity may help in defining health. Letter, BMJ 2009.

Heart Disease in South Asians Fifty Years Later: A time for change. Letter, HEART 2010.

Tsunami, Chaos and Global Heart: Using complexity science to rethink and make a better world. Vashna, Toronto 2005. Available free at femmefractal.com or by Googling words from the title.

South Asian Heart: Preventing Heart Disease. Vashna, Toronto 1995.

Chaos 2000: A New Art, Science and Philosophy of Medicine, Health ... and everything else. Vashna, Toronto 1996 and 2000.

A New Chaos-based Medicine beyond 2000: *The Response to Evidence.* Vashna, Toronto 1999.

Dr. Rambihar's exemplary work in the field of cardiology is prominently featured in his alma mater's website, headed "Profiles of the Founders of McMaster Cardiology." The entry, which includes an outline of his background and early education, reads, in part:

> Along with Dr. Eric Stanton, he was one of two inaugural cardiology fellows at McMaster in 1978. He continued his studies with Dr. Rakowksi in the early days of echo at the

Toronto General Hospital. Early in his career, Dr. Rambihar explored the role of ethnicity in health, particularly the increased and premature burden of coronary disease in South Asian and other populations. Currently, he uses chaos and complexity science to understand the complex interactions of ethnic heritage, culture, customs, family history, gender, genes, environment, and social dynamics that lead to health and disease, and has spoken on the need for the health community to adopt a broader outlook on health, prevention, and health promotion.

Dr. Rambihar was awarded the prestigious CCS (Canadian Cardiovascular Society) 2007 Dr. Harold N. Segall Award of Merit for his "significant contribution to the prevention of cardiovascular disease or to the promotion of cardiovascular health in Canadians." The Canadian Cardiovascular Society provides the following information on their annual awards:

> Each year the Canadian Cardiovascular Society recognizes the outstanding achievements of individual Canadians and Canadian organizations that contribute to cardiovascular health and care. CCS Awards are granted for excellence in research, teaching, exemplary care, prevention of cardiovascular diseases and overall career contribution.

At the Guyana Awards Gala held on May 26, 2007, Dr. Rambihar was honored with the Community Service Award. He was among ten winners, recognized for their "special contributions ... toward the promotion and development of Guyana, Guyana's heritage and culture, as well as acknowledging the achievement of excellence by Guyanese individuals and community." The citation accompanying the award reads, in part:

> With more than twenty-five years of cardiology practice in Toronto, Dr. Rambihar has been actively involved in research and community health promotion throughout his career. His research suggests that as immigrants, we are at increased risk for health problems and need to be proactive now. Recognized around the world for his pioneering health and health promotion ideas and practice, and a dedicated activist for the health rights of ethnic and mainstream communities,

Dr. Rambihar created an innovative grassroots community program to reduce health risks in vulnerable communities.

In 1993 he implemented a multicultural cardiology project to address the excess risk of heart disease in South Asians and other ethnic communities. He has also pioneered the concept of ethnicity and health, particularly heart disease and diabetes and inspired diversity and health initiatives across Canada.

Returning to his roots in mathematics and the developing world, Dr. Rambihar introduced the new ideas of chaos and complexity science to medicine, peace, health, and development, the first in the world to do so, and initiated a global heart project. His innovative ideas are contained in his book *Tsunami, Chaos and Global Heart— Using chaos and complexity science to rethink and make a better world.*

Dr. Rambihar has served as an executive member of community organizations including OSSICC (Ontario Society for Services to Indo-Caribbean Canadians) and … actively supports Guyanese community organizations and events, tirelessly advocating the use of social occasions for health promotion.

Dr. Rambihar was among the first recipients of the Newcomer Champion Award presented by the government of Ontario, Ministry of Citizenship and Immigration. The awardees were named on Canadian Multiculturalism Day. A news release of June 27, 2007, by the Ministry of Citizenship and Immigration, stated, in part:

> The Newcomer Champion Awards program … honors persons who have made significant contributions in areas such as cultural outreach, cultural celebration and connecting and integrating newcomers to communities … Dr. Rambihar was honored for "his involvement in the social, cultural and health needs of newcomers for twenty-five years." Dr. Rambihar is a passionate activist for the health rights of newcomers.

The Indo-Canada Chamber of Commerce (ICCC) honored Dr. Rambihar with the award of Humanitarian of the Year. The presentation was made at the ICCC Annual Gala held on Saturday June 14, 2008, in the presence of distinguished guests and members totaling around a thousand. The award was presented on behalf of the chamber by India's Minister of Science, Technology and Earth Science, Hon. Kapil Sibal, and Canada's Minister of Human Resource and Skills Development, Hon. Monte Solberg.

The *Indo Caribbean World*, June 18, 2008, reported Dr. Rambihar's "two important paradigm shifts, seeing the heath and societal needs of Indo-Canadians differently and rethinking our perspective of the world and how things change, both with tremendous implications globally. From research in 1990, he started and sustained the movement in North America to describe and change the heart health risks of South Asians with ideas and experiences transferable to all people of Indian origin."

The report continued:

> Dr. Rambihar's notable achievements include being the founder of the Heart Health of South Asians movement in North America. He has also done groundbreaking work introducing the concept of ethnicity and health to Canadian cardiology. He is also a pioneer in the field of chaos and complexity science, being the first in the world to apply it to medicine and health, including using health promotion in Indo-Canadians.
>
> Dr. Rambihar has independently discovered and developed this idea and is now extending it to society as a new science for poverty reduction, peace, health and development. His contributions have been particularly valuable to the Indo-Canadian and South Asian community, and his ideas will most likely be pivotal in dealing with the increasing complex health and other issues facing people of Indian origin across the diaspora, as well as all humanity.

At the Twentieth Anniversary Convention of Global Organization of People of Indian Origin (GOPIO), held in New York in August 2009, Dr. Rambihar, a guest speaker at one of the sessions, gave a warning that South Asians are at risk if they do not address their health problems now. The *ML Brampton Guardian* of September 23, 2009, carried a report on the doctor's speech, reprinted across the world and in *Pravasi Today* in New

Delhi. The excellent report, headed "Health Threatens Economic Future of South Asian Diaspora," reads, in part:

> Toronto cardiologist Dr. Vivian Rambihar, and University of Toronto medical student Vanessa Rambihar warn the tremendous economic success of India and the South Asian diaspora is at risk if we do not address urgent health concerns now. …
>
> Showing evidence of high and rising rates of diabetes and premature heart disease in India and across the South Asian diaspora, related mostly to stress, diet and lifestyle changes, which are preventable, they advanced this as a challenge and an opportunity for change.
>
> Their warning comes on the fiftieth anniversary of the first report of excess and premature deaths of Indians settling abroad, which has gotten worse all across the diaspora since. The two underlined the World Health Organization predictions of most of the world's heart disease and diabetes in India by 2015, affecting young people in the prime of their lives. This will cause $237 billion (US) in lost productivity in India over the next ten years, proportionately similar across the South Asian diaspora.
>
> Dr. Rambihar and Vanessa proposed health as the next big challenge. "Put simply, we need to eat more healthy, eat less if overweight, exercise more, reduce stress, keep as flat an abdomen as possible, and start early to check and reduce our risks, which are often underestimated. It's much more complex, however, with everyone and each community different, with unique and changing challenges."

What drives Dr. Rambihar to do better? It is an abiding interest in helping to make a better world. He lists his father as his source of inspiration. A teacher, headmaster and education officer in Guyana, he worked tirelessly for education and community development, while pursuing his own educational goals, graduating as a mature student in the first class of the University of Guyana. Other inspiration was taken from Dr. Rudranath Capildeo, from Trinidad, a physicist and politician, and numerous others in widely different fields, who taught him the value of passion and transformative ideas in changing the world.

An example of such transformative ideas is the proposal by Dr. Rambihar and his daughter Vanessa Rambihar for a Valentine's Day Global Heart Hour, similar to Earth Hour, to stimulate and sustain humanitarianism. They use the term "heart" for both heart disease and helping the world and invite everyone to join them in this novel mass collaboration to rethink and make a better world.

Sources:

Websites accessed August 6, 2008:
www.guyanaconsulate.com. Posted May 24, 2007. Guyana Awards (Canada) 2007
www.columbia.edu/cu/lweb/data/indiv/area/idsas/RAMBIHAR,Vivian.

Websites accessed January18, 2010
http://www.femmefractal.com/tsunami.htm
http://www.ccs.ca/awards/index_e.aspx.
http://fhs.mcmaster.ca/cardiology/history/profiles.html.
   Profiles of the Founders of McMaster Cardiology.
www.citizenship.gov.on.ca/english/news/2007/n20070627.
http://www.indocaribbeanworld.com/archives/2007/may_16_2007/community.htm
http://www.indocaribbeanworld.com/archives/2008/june_18_2008/june_18_2008.htm
http://zoominlocal.com/ml-brampton-guardian/2009/09/23/s1/#?article=549998

October 11, 2010

Dr. Bram Ramjiawan

BSc, MSc, PhD
Biomedical Scientist

Dr. Bram Ramjiawan was a winner of Guyana Awards (Canada) 2010 Academic Excellence Award. The citation of the award contains the following information, in part:

> Dr. Bram Ramjiawan is a seasoned biomedical scientist. He is director of Research, Innovation and Regulatory Affairs at St. Boniface General Hospital and Research Center in Winnipeg, Manitoba. He is also an adjunct professor of the Faculty of Pharmacology and Therapeutics at the University of Manitoba.
>
> Bram Ramjiawan came to Canada at the age of fourteen. He entered the University of Winnipeg, where he obtained his bachelor of science degree. He then proceeded to the University of Manitoba and completed a master of science degree with a focus on cardiovascular sciences, and his

doctorate in pharmacology and therapeutics at the Faculty of Medicine, University of Manitoba.

Bram has worked with the government of Canada (National Research Council) as a scientist, as well as an advisor who specialized in life sciences and biomedical technologies. He has published more than twenty peer-reviewed articles and is the author of two books and an encyclopedia chapter.

He has been an invited speaker to numerous events around the world and has served on many national and international organizations who seek out his expertise.

Dr. Ramjiawan is on the steering committee of the Canadian Standards Association on Medical Technology and Health Care, and the National Research Council Ethics Board.

Internationally, his role has been as a reviewer for the United States National Institute of Health and is a current member and chair of the European Union Commission on Health Science and Ethics. He sits on the editorial board of an international journal in London, England—*Journal of Pharmacoeconomics and Outcomes Research*, and has received numerous national and international awards.

Sources:
Websites accessed May 27, 2010, on Guyana Consulate Toronto, Guyana Awards (Canada)

May 27, 2010

Harry Ramkhelawan

Founder, Publisher, Editor
Indo-Caribbean World Newspaper

Harry Ramkhelawan was the winner of Guyana Awards (Canada) 2009 Media and Culture Award. The citation of the award contains the following information, in part:

> Harry Ramkhelawan, founder, publisher and editor of *Indo-Caribbean World* (ICW), is a pioneer of the Guyanese and Caribbean print media in Toronto.
>
> For the last twenty-six years *Indo-Caribbean World* has made a significant and permanent contribution to the history and development of ethnic journalism and multiculturalism in Canada by providing an important voice for immigrants from Guyana and the Caribbean. *ICW* has also kept the diaspora informed of developments in Guyana and the Caribbean through articles and thoughtful analysis on politics, religion, culture, economics, music, entertainment and sports.

Harry Ramkhelawan is a graduate of the University of Guyana with a BA in English.

A practicing Hindu priest and a dedicated member of the Hindu community in Toronto, Harry Ramkhelawan is also a talented Indian musician and music teacher. His ability to spot talent has helped many aspiring musicians to achieve their full potential.

Harry has quietly inspired and supported many charitable organizations. He is an ardent promoter of Guyanese causes and a key supporter of Guyanese businesses.

Sources:
Websites accessed May 27, 2010, on Guyana Consulate Toronto, Guyana Awards (Canada)

May 27, 2010

Pandit Ramlall

BA, DipEd
Vedic Scholar

Pandit Ramlall is a well known Vedic scholar and founder of the Arya Spiritual Center in New York. He is a well-loved doyen among Guyanese religious and political leaders, a legend as one of the most influential leaders of the Hindu faith of Guyanese heritage.

From an early age, he had a passion for learning all about Hindu religion and culture, and with equal verve, fighting to better the lot of fellow Guyanese. These have forged in this humble and affectionate Guyanese, commitment, vigor, and boundless energy to be a fearless leader in the fight for freedom from injustice under colonial rule in British Guiana, and a learned exponent of Hindu Vedic thought, an accomplished scholar of Sanskrit and Hindi.

He was born on February 28, 1928, in British Guiana. He was orphaned at an early age, only age four when his father died and age seven when he lost his mother. His father had come from India, indentured to Port Mourant, then went to Skeldon. He was raised in a Hindi-speaking environment of his uncle's home.

Ramlall had a rough childhood. He worked in his uncle Goberdhan's bakery business as a child from as early as he can remember. He had no opportunity to go to school. He had to find work instead. He was only nine when he was helping out men building the road, for which he was given a pittance. He fetched water to give to the men to soak burned bricks before they pounded them into smaller bits to make up the red brick road. He was one of a number of young boys who worked in the Creole gang in the fields at the sugar estate. Their job was to fetch water and earth to make up the beds where they grew sugar cane. Their boss was a fierce man who didn't spare the whip when he didn't get his way.

A better job came when Ramlall, finding himself near the tennis courts where the white overseers played, picked up tennis balls outside the courts. For this he got six cents a day.

One kind overseer, Mr. Shultz, then gave him the job of housekeeper. It was a decent job, a servant to the overseer, to do errands and minor chores in the house. For this he had to look tidy and wear clean shirt and pants. This led to a better job in the estate porter gang. Mr. Shultz then found him an opening in sugar boiling, where he could learn sugar boiling and be a chemist. He was getting on well there, until the chief chemist fired him. The man was an Orthodox Hindu. He learned that Ramlall was from an Arya Samajist family, regarded then as religious upstarts. Despite protest from fellow workers, the boss had his way.

Another white overseer, Mr. Scargall, came to Ramlall's rescue. Scargall was the welfare officer at the sugar estate. Ramlall was given work in the mechanical section operating the lawn mowers in the estate.

By this time, Ramlall had developed his knowledge of Hindi and Hindu religious ceremonies. He also sang well. There was a public meeting at which Skeldon Pandit Deodat presided. Scargall suggested to Ramlall that he could attend the meeting also and conduct the Hindu prayers. This he did, and his abilities were acknowledged. There was also a fund-raising event at Albion Sugar Estate, where Ramlall contributed with his singing. At the same time, through the guidance of Mr. Scargall, he secured a steady job as a mailman in the sugar estate. He did this job for over ten years.

From very early in life he was active in the Arya Samaj and became a practicing pandit of the Arya Samaj at age nineteen.

The Arya Samaj, a Hindu reformation and intellectual movement, was founded in 1875 in preindependence India by Swami Dayananda. Its purpose was to adhere to the teachings of the Vedas, summarized in the Sanskrit words "Krinvanto Vishvam Aryam" (Make the Whole World

Noble). It was active in education and social reform in the early years of the India's struggle for independence from colonial rule.

From his youth, Ramlall fervently promoted the tenets of Arya Samaj. He seized every opportunity to learn from the Arya Samaj (Vedic) missionaries who came to British Guiana from India, including Pandit Ayodhya Prasad, Professor Bhaskaranand, Pandit Narayan Dutta, Shrimati Janki Devi, Pandit Bhesh Pati Sinha, and Pandit Usharbudh Arya.

In addition to being a Hindu priest and a postman, he was also a good Hindi teacher. In the early 1950s he played a leading role in the Hindi Schools Convention. This annual event, organized by the American Aryan League in British Guiana, was a showcase for students of Hindi schools throughout the country. Top students were brought by their teachers to display their learning and talent in speaking Hindi, reading shlokas (verses) from the Vedas, Ramayan, and Gita, singing bhajans (Hindu hymns), and group performances.

At the Hindi Schools Convention, a panel of judges from among the senior pandits in the country adjudicated. The best students were suitably awarded prizes by the chief guest. The chief guest, a prominent person in the country, included among others in British Guiana the acting governor, the mayor of Georgetown, and the district commissioner, Upper Corentyne.

Ramlall's knowledge of Hindu scriptures and philosophy, coupled with his grasp of the essentials of the ancient and sacred language Sanskrit and his excellent command in speaking Hindi, made him stand out among contemporaries. He did so over years of hard work, self-study, and dedication.

Under the guidance of Pandit Usharbudh Arya (now Swami Veda Bharati), Pandit Ramlall became a leader in the youth movement known as the Arya Veer Dal. This was in the late 1950s. He excelled in the Arya Veer Dal, which provided a combination of yoga exercises and meditation. This youth movement, which began in Arya Samaj of India and was known to be associated with the India independence struggle, provided Pandit Ramlall a formidable training ground for strict spiritual discipline and physical training.

He has dedicated his life to freedom and justice. He was an indomitable leader in the fight for human rights and was a stalwart in the campaign for an independent Guyana under the leadership of Dr. Cheddi Jagan. Because of his activism, he was jailed with others in 1964 by the British government. During his incarceration at the Sibley Hall Detention Center, he taught many of the other inmates to read and speak Hindi and educated them in Vedic philosophy.

He was a teacher at the Tagore Memorial High School, Corentyne, Berbice, Guyana. There he was the head of Hindi classes for seventeen years, and he taught other subjects as well.

In 1974, Pandit Ramlall was awarded a two-year scholarship by the government of India for intensive studies in Hindi at the Kendriya Hindi Sansthan, New Delhi, India.

In 1979, Pandit Ramlall emigrated to New York, where he obtained employment and also enrolled at Roshell College. He completed his bachelor's degree in psychology and subsequently, the DipEd (diploma in education). He was employed at New York County Health and Hospital Corporation as hospital care investigator. He was also a union representative for the Local 371 Civil Service Union.

Pandit Ramlall's commitment to his passion for learning and sharing his knowledge of Vedic philosophy and culture, combined with his scholarly accomplishments in the Hindi and Sanskrit languages, propelled him on to more significant roles on the world stage in the United States, in Canada, Europe, the Caribbean, and India.

He is the founder and spiritual head of the Arya Spiritual Center, a pioneering institution of its kind, at Queens, New York. He is a patron of the Arya Pratinidhi Sabha of New York. He is the founder of the Cultural Center in East Coast Demerara, Guyana.

He has gained international recognition for his missionary work. He regularly travels to Surinam, Guyana, Netherlands, Europe, the United States, Canada, and India, where he lectures on Hinduism. He is a motivational speaker, a spiritual guide, and religious counselor. He has authored many books, and articles on Hinduism.

Pandit Ramlall was the special guest of the Vedic Cultural Center in Markham, Toronto, on March 8, 2008, where a prayer service was held to honor him on his eightieth birthday.

Adit Kumar, distinguished journalist, wrote an illuminating report on the event, for *Indo-Caribbean World*'s March 19, 2008 issue of *Community News*. He described the celebration, noted the many other events held to honor Panditji on his special birthday, and traced his remarkable life story from his childhood. Adit Kumar wrote, in part:

> The occasion was used to recognize the esteemed religious personality for his outstanding contribution toward the spread of Vedic philosophy worldwide. He was presented a plaque by the presidents of Toronto Arya Samaj and Arya

> Samaj Markham, Mr. Anand Rupnarain and Pt. Amar Erry, respectively.
>
> Among those who extended their personal good wishes to Pt. Ramlall were many of his long-standing friends and coreligionists that included Dr. Ganraj Kumar and Dr. Krishna Persaud …
>
> This was only one of many similar celebrations to mark Pt. Ramlall's attainment of the status of an octogenarian. He was likewise felicitated at the Central Vedic Mandir in Georgetown, Guyana, as well as at the Vedic Mandir in Nickerie, Surinam, on February 28, his actual birth date. In New York, where Pt. Ramlall is domiciled, celebrations were held at the Trimurthi Sanatan Dharm Mandir, the Arya Spiritual Center and at the Fair Field Pavilion in Richmond Hill.

Kenneth Persaud, esteemed writer, a former headmaster and university lecturer, in a reverential biography of Pandit Ramlall, paid homage to this exemplary Guyanese religious and political leader. Pointing to the pandit's role in Guyana's fight for independence, he stated, in part:

> Pandit Ramlall is one of Guyana's distinguished sons. He has been in the forefront for Guyana's independence since the middle of the last century. For resistance to the British Raj, in his fight for freedom for all Guyanese, he suffered imprisonment by the British in 1964. He was granted a pardon and released on Independence Day, May 26, 1966.
>
> This freedom fighter continued to dedicate his life to freedom, justice and the protection of children … by dint of selfless duty to his people, he continued to support and influence the youths of Guyana and the United States.
>
> Pandit Ramlall … has been a leading light in his work with inter-faith groups both in New York and elsewhere around the world. He says that his sole aim is to engender peace and harmony among religious faiths and especially among the Indian community …

He initiated the Phagwah festival in New York, which has become highly respected with the colorful attendance of thousands of participants, including elected officials ...

Most recently recognizing the plight of children and the great need for housing and care facilities in Guyana, Pt. Ramlall has built an orphanage in the Corentyne, Guyana, he himself an orphan. It is testimony to his strength of character and perseverance that he has risen to become one of the most respected pandits and revered persons both in the United States and at home ...

He has also published the *Vedavandana* and produced an English version. It is a book of prayers and contains spiritual and healing songs as well. He also wrote three Hindi textbooks.

Panditji's accomplishments have received recognition at the highest levels.

In 1975, in the presence of Indira Gandhi, prime minister of India, and Dr. Sewsagar Ramgulam, prime minister of Mauritius, at the first Vishwa Hindi Sammelan (World Hindi Conference) in Nagpur, India, he was presented with a prestigious literary award.

On the occasion of Dr. Shyam Sundar Das centenary celebration organized by Nagri Pracharini Sabha, he was, among thirty-two other literary scholars, presented with an award by the vice president of India, Shri BB Jatti.

He was a guest of honor at the 16th International Ramayan Conference in India, which was attended by intellectuals and academics from twelve different countries around the world. He has attended every Ramayana Conference since its inception in 1984 and represented Guyana and the United States in different locations in the world. In 1984 he received the Vishwa Hindi Darshan Award.

He was also nominated as chief delegate representing the Vishwa Sahita Sanskriti Sansthan (Institute of World Literature and Culture) to the Tenth International Ramayana Conference in India, in 1993. Pt. Ramlall was awarded the honor of chief guest at the Kanya Kumari Seventh International Hindi Seminar in 1997.

In 2002, the National Arya Samaj Award was presented to him and the Vedic Cultural Center Award at their Annual Dinner and Awards Program.

On the occasion of Phagwah celebrations in New York in 2003, Ms. Helen Marshall, Queens borough president, declared March 23 as Pandit Ramlall Day, he being the founder of an important ingredient in the cultural fabric of the city. The citation of the county's Declaration of Honor says, in part:

> This declaration acknowledges Pandit Ramlall on the occasion of the Hindu festival of Phagwah … A priest, scholar, and a leader for Guyana's struggle for independence, Pandit Ramlall has continued to live by his humanitarian ideals in New York, as a union representative, as the founder of the Arya Spiritual Center, and as a pioneer of the Phagwah Festival Parade in Queens. Through his interfaith work and his special concern for children, he lights the way for all people.

The prestigious Bharat Gaurav (Pride of India) Award was bestowed on him on January 8, 2005, by the India International Friendship Society (IIFS) for sterling community service at home and abroad, for "your fight in life and your worthy example to inspire others to a certain remarkable achievement." The IIFS is an organization of international repute and influence. Some of the past recipients of this coveted award include Her Holiness Mother Theresa; a former vice president of India, movie stars, and the famous cricket star Sunil Gavaskar.

In 2006, the International Arya Samaj presented Panditji with the International Service Award.

Pandit Ramlall is now a retired social worker from the Cumberland Hospital and Woodhall Hospital, Brooklyn, New York. He has been appointed commissioner of deeds for the state of New York and also voluntary chaplin of NY Transit Authority.

He continues to serve and lead the way to make real those values of his faith, "Make the whole world noble," lecturing around the world and writing on Vedic philosophy.

Sources:
Biography of Pandit Ramlall by K. Persaud. August 27, 2008.
Website accessed January 6, 2009: www.indocaribbeanworld.com/archives/march 19.2008/community.

January 6, 2009

Mohabir L. Ramnarine

BSc Ed, Cert Ed
Headmaster, Education Officer

He was a headmaster and education officer in Guyana and a teacher in New York. He started school when they used slate and pencil, walked barefoot, and the school uniform was khaki shirt and trousers. When he was a schoolboy, the cane was the staple instrument that teachers used to encourage their pupils to learn.

Mohabir Lakhram Ramnarine was born in Crabwood Creek, Corentyne, Berbice, British Guiana, on June 2, 1930. His father, Ramnarine, was a rice farmer and shopkeeper. His mother, Nemrajie, was a housewife who never attended any school, who could not read or write but was able to add up various amounts and give correct change in the grocery store. Mohabir is the third among nine children, three boys and six girls.

His brother, Jai Moolprashad Ramnarine, who holds an MSc in education administration, an MSc in instructional technology, and a BSc in economics, served as head of the Math Department in a junior high school in the Bronx. He is now mentor in District 8 of the New York Board of Education. Brother Seeram Ramnarine is a successful rice farmer and taxi driver. His sisters are all housewives. Hemwattie had passed her Pupil Teachers' Appointment Examination. Soamwatttie had taught for a couple of years until her marriage.

Mohabir was educated at Massiah Canadian Mission (CM) School from 1936 to 1943. The head teacher, Mr. J.R.Lachmansingh, commanded respect from both teachers and parents. Children feared him as he believed in the old adage "Spare the rod and spoil the child." They used slate and pencil but in higher classes wrote in exercise books with hand pens dipped in ink. Ink pots were imbedded in their desks. Blotting paper was used to dry the ink.

At Tagore Memorial High School, from 1943 to 1947, he passed the Cambridge Junior Certificate exam in1946, and Cambridge School Certificate in1947. The Principal was Mr. S.S. Chandra. The school, a private institution, was housed in the upper flat of a residential building. They concentrated only on academic subjects: English, English literature, math, history of the British empire, religious knowledge, geography, hygiene and physiology, and Latin. The cane was widely in use, even at this level. Mohabir hated high school.

Mohabir's professional career began in 1949 when he was appointed a pupil teacher at Crabwood Creek CM School and an assistant master in 1950 at the same school. He attended Government Teachers' Training College (GTTC) from 1960 to 1961. There he addressed the student body on race relations, a time when politics played an ugly role resulting in a huge division between the two major races in British Guiana. He was elected president of the Photography Club, and photography became his main hobby. He graduated with a First Class Trained Teachers Certificate.

He was awarded a Teachers Scholarship to study at the University of the West Indies, Jamaica in 1962. He graduated with a professional certificate in education in1963. On his return to Guyana, he served as lecturer at the In-Service Teacher Training Program. During this time he was appointed senior master, 1964, and acting deputy headmaster, 1965, at Crabwood Creek Government School. In 1967, Mohabir was promoted to the position of headmaster, Orealla Government School, and later headmaster at Number 43 Government School, 1968 to 1976.

In 1970 the country became the Cooperative Republic of Guyana. That year, Mohabir left for Kent State University, Ohio. He was admitted in senior standing and graduated with a bachelor of science in education (BScEd). He served in the student judiciary board. He earned an award for High Academic Achievement and won an International Student Scholarship. He was admitted to graduate school where he worked toward a master's degree in education administration and supervision. In the midst of his postgraduate studies, he received a cablegram from the permanent secretary, Ministry of Education, offering him a better position. He returned home.

Mohabir joined the Ministry of Education as education supervisor (1977–79) and was appointed education officer, a position similar to that of superintendent of schools, in 1980. He served on the Corentyne, East Coast, and East Bank Demerara, Linden District, and West Bank Demerara.

He retired in 1985, at 'the grand old age' of fifty-five, the official retirement age for government employees at that time in Guyana. He then took up employment as personnel manager and training officer with a private firm in Georgetown, Gafsons Industries Ltd.

He emigrated to the United States in 1989 and served as a teacher in the city of New York from 1989 to 1998. He taught at St. Matthew Lutheran School in Upper Manhattan.

Mohabir was chairman of the Recreation Committee in the Crabwood Creek Community Development Program, librarian at the Crabwood Creek Library, and member of the Lions Club, a charitable organization, and a member of the Student Judiciary Board of Kent State University, Ohio, USA.

He authored "The Dyslexic Child," an article published in a magazine produced by the Upper Corentyne Branch of the Guyana Teachers Association (GTA). He wrote a paper titled "The Impact of the Cuisnaire/Gattegno Method in the Teaching of Mathematics." His published memoir is *Beyond the Blackboard*.

Mohabir was nominated and accepted for a 2010 Citizens Awards Arts Acclaim achievement. In her letter to Mohabir, the Mayor wrote, "It is members of our community such as yourself that make Brampton the great city that it is!"

What made teaching such an important part of his life? Mohabir reveals, "I love challenges, and teaching was a challenge. I fought tooth and nail to work and study to reach the top. I also believed that whatever is worth doing is worth doing well. I always loved what I did, no matter how small or how great a task it was. I put my heart and soul into it and gave it my best shot. I got a kick out of teaching particularly when children grasped the concept of a topic. My school motto, 'Do it with thy might,' left an indelible impression in me."

His parents were his main source of inspiration. "I was inspired by my parents who wanted their son to become a teacher. They provided all the means to achieve my ambition. My teachers in primary school, instructors in teachers college, and professors in the universities who all nurtured me, were unwittingly great sources of inspiration. I also drew my inspiration from educators, some of whom I have not met but only read of their study and their findings, and who have become authorities on the subject of teaching. Educators, Dr. Edualino, a member of the UNESCO team in Guyana, Dr. Bacchus of the Ministry of Education, Dr. Gordon and Dr. Ramsey of Kent State University, Dr. Elsa Walters, and others have all inspired me."

Some memorable highlights in his life tell of his strength of character and determination to turn failure into success. He says, "Failure breeds success. Having failed my first examination in high school, I thought I was a complete failure, but I was encouraged to go on, resulting in a series of successes until I reached the top rung of the ladder of my professional career. Do not allow failure to daunt you. At one point in my career, I felt like chucking it up. In Guyana, during a strike by cane cutters for better wages which they rightly deserved, we were forced to work as scabs. I swallowed my pride and continued with the job I loved. Like many things you care for in your life you stick to it in spite of the storms and tornadoes. I lost two of my closest and most loved members of my family during crucial periods of my life, yet I moved on. Do not allow anything in your life to keep you away from your dream."

Mohabir's wife is Beverly, sister of Dr. Milton Sankar, the late Dr. Kennard Sankar, Arnold Sankar, field supervisor, and Morris Sankar, accountant. Mohabir and Beverly were married in 1954 when they were both teachers at Crabwood Creek Government School. Beverly is a first-class trained teacher and a trained home economics teacher. She holds a BSc in education, a diploma in early childhood education, and a certificate in communication in management.

Beverly served as assistant mistress at Crabwood Creek Government School, and senior mistress at Skeldon Government School. She was then admitted to Kent State University, where she graduated with a BScEd. She returned to Guyana, as she badly wanted to serve her country. She was later appointed nursery supervisor in the Corentyne District. Her transfer to the Ministry of Education at Brickdam preceded her promotion to the position of District Education Supervisor of Nursery, Primary, and Secondary Schools in Georgetown. She went on early retirement in 1986 and accompanied her husband to New York.

Beverly served another ten years as a teacher in New York and two years as a librarian. She first taught at Grace Lutheran School in the Bronx, where she was awarded a plaque in appreciation for her commitment to quality education. She later worked at the Mt. Vernon Library in the Westchester County, New York. She is now retired.

Their son, Nimrod Ramnarine, is a computer network coordinator. He graduated with a BSc from the University of Guyana, worked in the public service, and later joined a private firm. He emigrated to the United States and upgraded his skill in computer science. He now lives with his family in Canada.

Mohabir says this about making a dream a reality: "I guess every one of us has a dream. I would urge all young people, in particular, no matter what the odds, to stick to their dream. Go all-out, give it your best shot, and change it into reality."

January 31, 2011

Professor Dindial Ramotar

BSc, MSc, PhD
Cancer Specialist

Prof. Dindial Ramotar is a world-renowned scientist whose cancer research has led to the discovery of a new drug transporter that allows the entry of anti-cancer agents into cancer cells. These findings, reported on March 25, 2010, may change the way doctors treat cancer patients.

He was born on February 28, 1960, at Bath Settlement, West Coast Berbice. His father was Byron Ramotar and his mother was Champadia Ramotar. They owned a grocery and hardware store. He has four siblings: Chatram, Hardial, Ramdial, and Devi.

Dindial was educated at Bath Settlement Elementary School, then at Bush-Lot Secondary School. He left Guyana in 1977 to study in Canada, obtaining a BSc from McGill University in 1982, MSc from Concordia University in 1984, PhD from McGill University in 1989, and postdoctoral training at Harvard Medical School in 1992.

In 1992, he was appointed associate professor at Laval University in Quebec. In 1996, he was recruited by the University of Montreal as an assistant professor. Dr. Ramotar is now a full professor at the Université de Montréal Faculty of Medicine and a scientist at the affiliated Maisonneuve-Rosemont Hospital.

Dr. Ramotar began testing his theory a full decade ago using baker's yeast, which is remarkably similar to human cells. He explained the process and the discovery, thus:

"Our discovery went from that model system to human cells and will soon reach the bedside through translational therapy. We are on the brink of testing patients … We found a gateway, which is present in all humans, that allows anti-cancer agents … to enter the body so they may reach and attack leukemia cells."

Dindial has received several awards and served on the Canadian Institute of Health Research, National Cancer Institute of Canada, and National Institute of Health (US) panels to decide on which grants get funds throughout Canada and the United States.

Active in a number of community organizations, he was a founding member of the Centennial Cricket Sports Club and is past vice president of the Guyana Cultural Association in Montreal.

He was winner of Guyana Awards (Canada) 2010 Special Achievement Award.

Sources:

Includes websites accessed May 27, 2010, on Guyana Consulate Toronto, Guyana Awards (Canada)

November 22, 2010

Ashook Ramsaran

BSEE, MSEE
Business Chief Executive
Public Service Leader, New York and Globally

Ashook Kumar Ramsaran is chief executive officer of his own electronics communication manufacturing business in New York. However, he is more widely known for his public service in New York and worldwide.

He is the very active vice president of GOPIO International, the Global Organization of People of Indian Origin. He leads in the Tracing Our Roots drive to enable persons of Indian origin to trace their roots back to their ancestral villages of India.

In New York, St. John's University has established an annual scholarship to deserving students for Caribbean and Latin American studies to honor his contributions to education and community service. He was honored as the Outstanding Immigrant by New York City Council in 2004, and he was the recipient of the highly acclaimed 2010 Asian Heritage Award in New York.

Guyana Journal featured him in the article, "An Immigrant Success Story: From the Village of Letter Kenny (Guyana) to the City of New York."

He serves annually as Principal for the Day' in New York City Public School System.

In a *Global Indian* publication, he was featured as one of Top Twenty-Five Indian Luminaries in the World.

Born February 26, 1948, in the farming village of Letter Kenny in the Corentyne district of coastal Guyana, he is the third generation of Indians who came to the former British colony as indentured laborers. He is the third of ten children (six brothers, four sisters). His father, Ramsaran Ramlochan, and grandfather were born in British Guiana, and they both worked in the nearby sugar plantation.

Ashook attended Auchlyne Primary School, Corentyne, Berbice, from 1953 to 1959. He was awarded a Bookers Sugar Estates Scholarship from Port Mourant District to attend high school and matriculated in 1964 from Corentyne High School, with certificates from the University of Cambridge (1963) and University of London (1964). Due to his young age at the time of high school graduation, he worked as a pupil teacher at Yakusari Primary School for nine months. He subsequently joined the civil service and was employed in the magistrate's courts in New Amsterdam and Whim, in the Corentyne.

On January 7, 1967 Ashook married Camille Parvati (nee Ramgadoo), also of Guyana. They have two sons. Their first was born in Guyana.

Ashook decided to go abroad to pursue higher education and in February1968, he headed for the United States. His first preference was the United Kingdom, but due to lack of funds, being from a very poor family, he decided to go the United States, where opportunities were known to be available to work and study.

He came to the United States with his wife and baby son, Arnold Mahendra. Their second son, Gerald Rajendra, was born in the United States in 1970. In January 2005 Ashook and Camille were blessed with two wonderful grandsons, Jaden Ashook and Gavin Laskhsman, two delightful additions to the family.

Upon arrival in the United States, Ashook set to work on higher education. While engaged in his studies, he was working full time and on multiple jobs to finance his education and support his family of wife and two young children. He studied electronic engineering at the Polytechnic University in New York and obtained his bachelor's and master's degrees (BSEE and MSEE).

After graduation from university in 1974, Ashook worked in the United States, in industry as electronics communications design engineer, and progressed to become vice president of engineering for a large-sized US national corporation.

He had acquired considerable experience, and in 1968, with his own funds, he established his own electronics design and manufacturing business, Ramex, Inc., in College Point, New York. He is the CEO of Ramex, Inc. Ramex designs and manufactures intercommunication and signaling systems for the health care, transportation, and penitentiary marketplace. Its services include engineering, special fabrication, manufacturing and repairs.

Ramex is the recipient of many large-sized contracts, including the passenger emergency call system at all Washington DC Metropolitan Authority Transit Systems and the emergency public address systems at New York City's Department of Corrections. Ramex has been a phenomenal success and has been named among the Top 100 Indian-Owned Businesses in the United States for eight consecutive years.

Ashook's success in his business is testament to his drive, abundant energy, superb intellect, and managerial prowess. His innate talent and abilities also found a much larger stage: public service, in which he has played numerous rewarding roles. His passion for public service is boundless, surpassed only by his limitless energy to focus on issues that are meaningful and with relevance.

This powerhouse of talent deployed every available moment of his time and skills towards enriching the life of his community locally in New York, addressing issues of concern of fellow Guyanese, the Indian diaspora globally, the downtrodden and the unfortunate.

He has lived in the United States for over forty years and he has made his home in the United States. Enormously appreciative of the many wonderful opportunities afforded him, in the United States, he is a proud and active community minded citizen and determined to use acquired skills, time, talent, and available resources to make a positive difference in the lives of others.

He is proud to be a person of Indian origin, the recipient of a rich and enduring culture, with a deep sense of cultural bond and belonging that has provided personal sustenance, motivation, and focus even under adverse conditions, while not diminishing valued national loyalty to his adopted homeland. He is an ardent advocate of the preservation and promotion of Indian culture throughout the Indian diaspora and bringing more awareness among non-Indians as well.

Some of his high-profile roles and the organizations in which he is actively involved include the Global Organization of People of Indian Origin (GOPIO), and as executive vice president of GOPIO, and chairperson of

GOPIO's Tracing Our Roots Committee, as well as chairman of the Kolkata Memorial Committee.

He has been a driving force in GOPIO for many years. Prior to election as executive vice president, he was GOPIO's secretary general. In this role, Ashook Ramsaran injected his considerable expertise and management skills to enhance the structure and functioning of the organization on many fronts to establish guidelines and procedures for many of the activities and councils of GOPIO.

He developed the mission objectives and operational policy guidelines for GOPIO's nine councils, two committees, and chapter by-laws. A very active proponent of human rights, he developed the complete mission and organizational structure of GOPIO's Human Rights Council.

On GOPIO By-Laws Committee and Academic Council, he contributed significant organizational improvements to achieve clear and concise understanding of responsibilities and operations from local to international levels and for the development of chapter and council reporting formats.

He developed the complete awards criteria for GOPIO's Annual Community Service Awards (CSA). This provides the guidelines and procedures for nomination and selection of suitably qualified persons for GOPIO CSA awards.

He planned and managed GOPIO's 2004 Human Rights Conference held at St. John's University in New York. The event was a huge success with delegates from all over the world in attendance. He was the convener of GOPIO's highly successful 20th Anniversary Convention, 2009, in New York.

The chairperson pro-tem of GOPIO's Tracing Our Roots committee, he established the committee in 2006 to collaborate the efforts of GOPIO, working in conjunction with various persons of Indian origin (PIO) governments and India's Ministry of Overseas Indian Affairs, to enable persons of Indian origin to trace their roots back to their ancestral villages of India.

He organized GOPIO Symposia in the Caribbean on the subject: "India's Emergence as an Economic Power and the Mutual Benefits of Increased Bilateral Trade in the Caribbean." The venues were Trinidad, Suriname, and Guyana.

The three symposia were held in conjunction with the visit of India's Minister of Overseas Indian Affairs, Vayalar Ravi, and staff to attend Indian Arrivals Days celebrations in several PIO countries in the Caribbean. That high level trip to the region brought greater awareness of the Caribbean PIO community of the work of the Indian government, Ministry of Overseas Indian Affairs, and mobilized more GOPIO chapters.

To enhance the efforts of people of the Indian diaspora, worldwide, Ashook developed a summary proposal in 2006, titled "The Global Indian Diaspora: A Blueprint for the 21st Century," and submitted this to the Indian Ministry of Overseas Indian Affairs (MOIA).

The Proposal contained ideas, suggestions, and recommendations, which included holding more regional conferences and seminars on Indian diaspora issues; for example, holding mini Pravasi Bharatiya Divas (PBDs). He cited the example of the successful PBD held in New York on September 23, 2007. Many of the recommendations contained in Ashook's proposal have been adopted.

Pravasi Bharatiya Divas which means Non-Resident Indians Day, is the name given to mark the important day when Mahatma Gandhi returned to India from South Africa. PBD events celebrate the Indian diaspora, share experiences, and honor diaspora members for their contributions to society.

Ashook is an ardent advocate of the lawful rights of all persons, with emphasis on Indians living in adopted countries, the land of their birth around the world. He assisted with drafting of GOPIO resolutions of Fiji, Guyana, Malaysia, and others.

On the matter of non-resident Indian (NRI) issues, he was instrumental in the very successful GOPIO large-scale global petition to the government of India that resulted in a reversal of the decision on excessive fees and procedures for surrender of Indian passports.

He is prominently featured in the *Global Indian* 2010 publication of "Top 25 Indian Luminaries of the World," a globally distributed volume with foreword by MOIA Minister Vayalar Ravi.

Ashook has written several acclaimed articles on topics related to the Indian diaspora and actively responds to current events. He is actively sought by the media for commentaries on local community and global Indian diaspora issues. He is on the editorial board of *GOPIO Newsletter* and the *Bharatiya Jo*urnal. He is coeditor of GOPIO's semi-monthly newsletter publication, which reaches over 65,000.

Ashook is an advisory board member of St. John's University's Center for Caribbean and Latin American Studies in New York. In collaboration with St. John's University, he has developed and coordinated these global conferences on Indian issues:

- "Coping In America: Caribbean East Indians in the USA" (1999).
- "Human Rights Experiences of Indians" (2004).
- "Regional Community Dialogue" held in Georgetown, Guyana, in May 2009 in commemoration of the 171st anniversary of the first arrival of Indians as indentured laborers from India. This included participation from the English, Dutch, French, and Spanish speaking countries of the Caribbean region. Ashook was the international coordinator of this conference.

He is a contributing writer and coordinator of the widely distributed book developed from the 1999 conference, titled *Coping in America: The Case of Caribbean East Indians in the USA*, on the issues of interest and concern among PIOs from the Caribbean living in the United States.

He initiated the idea and theme for conferences in the autumn of 2009, in conjunction with St. John's University on these subjects: "The Indian Diaspora: Its Contributions and Responsibilities in a Multi-Ethnic Society," and "The Plight of Persons of Indian Origin in the Indian Diaspora."

Ashook Ramsaran is a prominent elder of the First Presbyterian Church of Flushing in New York City. He is chair of its Centennial Celebration, and chair of its Finance and Budget Committee.

He is an active member of the NRI/PIO (Non-Resident Indian/Person of Indian Origin) community in the New York tri-state region. He works assiduously on analyses of current issues of interest and concern and on deploying appropriate acquired resources to worthwhile and needy causes as well as emergency needs of the Indian diaspora. He has initiated regular GOPIO community meetings worldwide that discuss issues of interest and concern among the Indian community with feedback to the respective governments.

In collaboration with New York City's Mayor's Office of Immigrant Affairs, he has developed and coordinated these global conferences on Indian issues:

- "Caribbean East Indians in New York: The Journey Continues," held as part of New York City Immigrant Week, April 16–20, 2007.
- "Community Dialogue among Caribbean and Latin American Immigrants in New York City," held on April 19, 2008, as part

of New York City Immigrant Week 2008 and continuing annually.

He collaborates with the New York City Mayor's Office of Immigrant Affairs on annual events on immigrant experiences in New York City. Among many other activities he is:

- An executive on the board of directors of Fresh Meadows Civic Association. He is a member of the Queens New York City Democratic Party and participates in New York City community board activities on issues of interest and concern to the community.

- He is very active in neighborhood community affairs and preservation of the quality of life in partnership with New York City Public School, PS 90, Horace Mann Elementary School and in his local New York community's civic, cultural, and religious groups and contributes generously to causes on behalf of the needy.

- He is an initiator and provider of substantial annual US Savings Bonds for improving the lot of deserving students of Indian origin graduating from New York City elementary, middle, and high schools, in neighborhoods where the majority of Indians from the Caribbean currently reside.

- He is a board member of several other United States-based civic organizations.

Ashook's personal yearning for finding his own roots in the ancestral villages of India has provided the motivation and desire to develop and establish a global database system as the means to meet the needs of millions of the Indian diaspora in their quest on a global scale.

The following is a list of his efforts:

- Initiated and chaired the first "Tracing Our Roots" session at Pravasi Bharatiya Divas (PBD) on January 8, 2005, in Mumbai, on the introduction of a global Indian diaspora database to trace one's ancestors who left India for other lands.

- Is an integral part of a team, requested by India's Ministry of Overseas Indian Affairs, to document and organize a global database of Persons of Indian Origin (PIOs) from around the globe beginning with migration in 1820.

- Has engaged Guyana's Ministry of Culture to preserve the frail Indian indentured immigrant documents in the archives.

- Was a speaker on "Engaging PIOs in India's Development" at the January PBD 2007 in New Delhi. He presented a statement on "Issues of Interest and Concern of the Caribbean PIO Community" at the Government of India Ministry of Overseas Indian Affairs, PBD on September 23, 2007, in New York. He was a speaker on the January 8, 2008, PBD panel session titled, "The Americas" on "Engaging the Diaspora: The Way Forward." He was chairperson of PBD 2009 Regional Session "Caribbean" with the overall theme "Engaging the Diaspora" and speaker at PBD 2010 in New Delhi.

- Works in close collaboration with India's Ministry of Overseas Indian Affairs (MOIA) on issues of interest and concern to the global Indian diaspora and on PBD sessions.

Ashook Ramsaran also spearheaded the international effort by the Global Indian Diaspora Heritage Society (GIDHS) for an emigration memorial and museum/resource center (the Kolkata Memorial) at a Kolkata site where Indian indentured laborers were housed and processed prior to assignment and shipment to plantations in various British colonies from 1834 through 1920. He has worked in close collaboration with India's Ministry of Overseas Indian Affairs (MOIA), PIO country governments, and other agencies to make this a reality.

Ashook's unquenching thirst to do community service has made him very well known as an ardent community supporter and global Indian diaspora advocate. He steps forward and takes the lead in numerous initiatives. The following are some of his efforts:

- Cofounder and director of the Guyanese East Indian Civic Association (GEICA), established in the United States in 1998 to monitor and address matters of adaptation and assimilation in the United States by persons of Indian origin (PIOs) from the Caribbean region.

- Cofounder and director general of the Caribbean Indian Business Development Center (CIBDC), a New York-based business advocacy group that fosters improvement of bilateral business development and trade between countries of the Caribbean region and India.

- Planned, organized, and coordinated several reunions of PIOs from Guyana, including Yakusari Teachers Alumni.

- Is an ardent supporter and advisor to Corentyne High School Alumni and 2006 Reunion event in Toronto, Canada. He was chairman of the highly acclaimed and successful 70th Anniversary and Reunion 2008.

- Initiated, coordinated, supported, and implemented a massive July 31, 2006, protest rally at the United Nations in New York against the blatant abuse of rule of law, violation of constitutional due process, and targeting PIOs by the government of Trinidad and Tobago. It was successful and resulted in a favorable decision by the Privy Council.

- Actively supported and promoted the recently signed India/USA nuclear treaty on both the United States congressional and local community levels. He was the global coordinator of the November 2008 conference "Regional Community Dialogue" in Georgetown, Guyana.

- Presented a paper titled "Peaceful Co-Existence of South Asian Communities in Multi-Ethnic Societies: The Caribbean Experience" at the conference South Asian Diaspora Communities Between Mainstream and Multiple Identities, held in Kunming, China, in April, 2009.

- Works in close collaboration with the government of India, Ministry of Overseas Indian Affairs, and other agencies on development, analyses, and actions on relevant and meaningful PIO issues of interest for the promotion of civic, economic, and cultural benefits.

- Is a board member of *Bharatiya Journal*; patron of the *Guyana Journal*, a monthly NYC and Caribbean news magazine; and contributor to *Caribbean New Yorker*.

- Arranged, coordinated, and supported fund-raisers for victims of the cyclone in Fiji, mostly people of Indian origin. He supported and participated in many other fund-raisers such as tsunami, Guyana floods, Gujarat earthquake, and several others.

- Is the initiator, advocate and supporter of regional collaboration, networking, and unity among persons of Indian origin in the Caribbean region for cultural, academic, economic, and political achievement.

Ashook has been profiled in the following publications:

Guyana Journal magazine of New York, December 2007 issue, as "An Immigrant Success Story—from the Village of Letter Kenny (Guyana) to the City of New York." He received numerous global messages of congratulations and acknowledgement of a journey from the rice fields of Guyana to one of high levels of achievement and civic contribution on the local, regional and global levels.

Global Indian online magazine, March 2008 issue: "Ashook Ramsaran—Embracing the Roots of Heritage," profiling his life as a prominent person of Indian origin whose achievements rank among the most outstanding.

India Empire, January 2009 issue:, with the title "Diaspora Duke."

India Empire, August 2010 issue ,on the Kolkata Memorial, with the title "New PIO Site."

Ashook Ramsaran is the recipient of numerous awards and citations for his contributions of time, talent, and resources to local community service work, as well as global Indian diaspora issues. He has received GOPIO International Awards and United States Census Bureau, civic, cultural, and community organization awards. Among many others are the following:

In November 2007, he was given a special citation of recognition by New York St. John's University's Center for Caribbean and Latin American Studies.

On October 22, 2009, the Council of the City of New York bestowed a signal honor on Ashook with a proclamation for "his outstanding service and contributions to New York City." The occasion was New York City's Deepavali celebrations. The citation read, in part:

> The Council of the city of New York is proud to honor Ashook Kumar Ramsaran … for his outstanding contributions to the community …
>
> Ashook Kumar Ramsaran is the executive vice president of the Global Organization of People of Indian Origin (GOPIO) and chairperson of GOPIO's Tracing our Roots Committee. He is also the cofounder and director of the Guyanese East Indian Civic Association (GEICA) and director of the Caribbean Business Council (CBC).
>
> He is an ardent advocate of universal human rights and observance of the rule of law in the Indian diaspora and collaboration with St. Johns University's Committee on Caribbean and Latin American Studies…on a continuing series of seminars and conferences. On November 15, 2007, St. John's University recognized his work with their creation of the Ashook Ramsaran Scholarship.
>
> Mr. Ramsaran also collaborates with the New York City Mayor's Office on Immigration Affairs on annual events on immigrant experiences in New York City. He has been honored as the Outstanding Immigrant for New York City Council and served as a Principal for the Day in the New York Public School System.
>
> He is very active in his local New York community civic, political, and cultural groups, contributes generously to causes on behalf of the needy, and has worked extensively on issues of interest and concern affecting people of Indian origin in the global Indian diaspora …
>
> Ashook Kumar Ramsaran's life in New York is a testament to the vitality of the American dream and his generosity, dedication, and creativity have earned him the esteem of all New Yorkers …

> Be it known that the Council of the city of New York most gratefully honors Ashook Kumar Ramsaran for his outstanding service and contributions to New York City.
> (Signed)
>
> Christine C. Quinn. Speaker for the Entire Council.
> John C. Liu. Council Member, 20th District, Queens
> With council members Alan J. Gerson, Gale Brewer, Helen Sears, David I. Weprin

This Guyanese has made giant steps in achievement, both in his business and in public service. It is a source of pride for all Guyanese.

What is Ashook's guiding light and principles of his life? It is revealed in his personal statement:

> Life should also be measured by the events, places, and people that take our breath away, more so than by the number of breaths we take in our lifetime; by the steps we take and the tracks we make; by how much we give to others in need than how much we keep for ourselves; by how much we care for those less fortunate more so than how much we desire; by how much we need than how much we want; by the generosity of the heart rather than the size of the pockets. Life should be measured by the difference we make than the difference we take.

Ashook is keen to institute his proposal for global Indian diaspora leadership training, civic, economic, and political. Leadership among the global Indian diaspora is severely lacking in organization, planning, succession, discipline, and accountability. These deficiencies hamper progress on several fronts. He would like to see his efforts succeed in establishing the Kolkotta Memorial. His other ambition is to continue to have a happy family and to continue to nurture good values and civic responsibility among them so that he can leave a legacy of gratitude and goodness.

October 12, 2010

John R. Rickford

BA, MA, PhD
Professor of Linguistics, Stanford University, California

John R. Rickford is the J.E. Wallace Sterling Professor of Linguistics and the Humanities, and Pritzker University Fellow in Undergraduate Education at Stanford University, California. He also has a courtesy appointment there as Professor of Education. Among other things, he has been chair of the Faculty Senate of the Academic Council at Stanford; director, Stanford Overseas Studies Summer Focus Program, Oxford; vice chair, Department of Linguistics, Stanford; and the holder of the Martin Luther King Jr. Centennial Chair at Stanford.

He was assistant dean in the Faculty of Arts, University of Guyana, and external examiner for linguistics courses, MA and PhD theses, at the University of the West Indies and the University of Guyana. His prodigious output of writing and lecturing on linguistics across United States and Canada is second to none.

John Rickford was born on September 16, 1949, in Georgetown, Guyana. He grew up for the first ten years at 118 Cowan Street, Kingston.

He spent many a day fishing in the "forty foot" trench—hooking cuirass and catching cheriga crabs.

His father was Russell Howell Rickford, an accountant who used to work for BG Consolidated Goldfields in the "bush"—Potaro, especially around the Mahdia/Tumatumari Falls. He later worked for Panell Fitzpatrick in Georgetown and started Guyana Travel Tours, chartering Guyana Airways planes and otherwise organizing trips for locals and visitors to see Kaieteur Fall, Orindiuk, and elsewhere in Guyana's interior, which he loved. John's mother, Eula Rickford (nee Wade, and known as "Baby Wade," as she was the youngest of her mother's fourteen children), was a homemaker and mother of ten children, nine of whom grew to adulthood: Edward, June, Dawn, Peter, George, Elizabeth, Pat, Nancy, and John. He was the youngest.

John went to Sacred Heart Roman Catholic (RC) school (although he was an Anglican, not a Catholic). This is his account of his schooling:

> The headmistress for a while was Sister Mary Joseph. My most memorable teachers were Miss Ogle (patient, soft-hearted) in first or second standard, Miss Philadelphia (tough lady, third standard or so; used to roll a baton over your knuckles on the desk as punishment), Mr. Hing (fifth standard; used to cane all sixty to seventy students in the class if he "heard a noise"), and, most of all, Mr. Arokium (sixth standard; prepared me superbly for the Common Entrance exam, in part through private lessons at his home in Kingston). I won a scholarship to Queen's College on the basis of my Common Entrance exam performance, thanks in no small measure to him.
>
> At QC, I was "head boy" (head prefect) in my final year (66–67), and during my time there (1960–67) I was also president of the Literary and Debating Society, editor of the school newspaper (*QC Lictor*), president of the Junior Debating Society, and a member of the school magazine production/editorial staff. I won the prize for best results at the GCE ordinary level exams in 1965, and gained a distinction in English literature, a credit in history, and a "C" pass in French at the GCE advanced level exams in 1967. I won the Wishart Memorial Prize for my distinction in English.

John taught at QC for a year and worked part-time as features writer for the *Guyana Graphic* newspaper before winning a US scholarship/Institute for International Education Scholarship and a Fulbright-Hays travel grant to study at the University of California, Santa Cruz (UCSC).

John studied at UCSC from 1968 to 1971, initially in literature and then in sociolinguistics (a self-designed major drawing on linguistics, sociology, and anthropology). In 1970 he secured first prize at the Stevenson College oratory competition, UCSC, and in 1971 he obtained his first degree, BA, Sociolinguistics, with highest honors from UCSC, as well as Stevenson College honors. He also won a Danforth Graduate Fellowship, which allowed him to go on to pursue a PhD.

He went on to the University of Pennsylvania, where he studied for higher degrees beginning in 1971. In 1973 he obtained his MA in linguistics, and he was awarded the Linguistic Society of America (LSA) Institute Fellowship.

During the period 1970 to 1973, while at university, John did other studies during the summer: in 1970 at the Sociolinguistics Institute, Stanford; in 1971 at the California Linguistics Institute, UCSC; and in 1973 at the LSA Linguistic Institute, University of Michigan.

John then secured an appointment as lecturer, Linguistics, at the University of Guyana. He worked there from 1974 to 1980. In 1974 John secured a National Science Foundation Doctoral Dissertation Grant, and while at UG in 1979 he obtained his doctorate, a PhD in linguistics, University of Pennsylvania. His dissertation, supervised by Professor William Labov, examined variation in Guyanese pronouns and its implications for the quantitative and implicational approaches to the analysis of variation in linguistics. In the same year he also took a University Teaching Methods course, taught at University of Guyana, by visiting University of London Teaching Methods unit staff, and he credits that with helping him win teaching methods awards at Stanford in the 1980s and 1990s. In fall 1979 he also worked as visiting assistant professor, Anthropology, Johns Hopkins University.

Dr. John Rickford was then appointed assistant dean, Faculty of Arts, University of Guyana, in 1979, and in 1980 he was promoted to reader, linguistics (intermediate between associate and full professor), with tenure, University of Guyana.

After receiving a tenure track offer from the University of California, Los Angeles, and a visiting assistant professorship from Stanford University, John accepted the latter offer, and emigrated to the United States in 1980.

In 1981 he was offered a regular tenure-track position as assistant professor of linguistics at Stanford, and in 1986, he was promoted to associate professor of linguistics, there, with tenure. In 1990 he was promoted to full professor, and in 2009 he was honored with an honorary endowed chair, the J. E. Wallace Sterling Professorship in the Humanities, which honors one of Stanford's most distinguished presidents. In that year he also won the Distinguished Alumni Award at UCSC, and in 2010 he was invited to give the commencement speech to graduating students at his alma mater, Stevenson College, UCSC.

In the years between his first university appointment as a lecturer at UG in 1974 and his endowed professorship, John established himself as an authority on sociolinguistic variation and change in Creole and vernacular varieties of English (including African American vernacular English) in the Caribbean and the United States. He used every opportunity to extend and employ his knowledge and experience to the full at Stanford University, at Oxford, and in New Zealand, Guyana, and the West Indies.

Here is a brief résumé of his employment.

From 1982 to '86 he was external examiner for linguistics courses, MA and PhD theses, University of the West Indies (Mona, Cave Hill, and St. Augustine campuses), and at the University of Guyana. From 1986 to '90 he was associate professor, with tenure, linguistics, Stanford; in the summer of 1987 instructor, LSA Linguistics Institute, Stanford; in 1988–90 he was Associate professor, by courtesy, education, Stanford; 1990 professor, with tenure, linguistics, Stanford; 1990 professor, by courtesy, education, Stanford; 1990 director, Stanford Overseas Studies Summer Focus Program, Oxford; 1993 instructor, LSA Linguistics Institute, Ohio State University, summer; 1996 vice chair, Department of Linguistics, Stanford.

From 1998 to 2005, John held the position of director, Program in African and African American Studies, Stanford, and holder of the Martin Luther King Jr. Centennial Chair. He taught in Sophomore College, Stanford ("Spoken Soul in American Comedy") in the summer. In 2001 he taught in Sophomore College, Stanford ("Ebonics and Other Vernaculars in Schools and Society" course). In 2002 he was Erskine Professor, Department of Linguistics, University of Canterbury, New Zealand (he taught two courses and delivered two university/department lectures, in July and August).

In 2003 at the LSA Linguistic Institute, Michigan State U, summer, he held the Herman and Clara Collitz Professorship in historical linguistics, taught one course, and delivered a plenary forum lecture. In 2004 he taught in Sophomore College, Stanford ("Language in the USA" course).

In 2005 John was team leader, External Quality Assurance Review of the Linguistics program, University of the West Indies, Mona, Jamaica, October; and in 2006, he was team leader, External Quality Assurance Reviews of the Linguistics programs, University of the West Indies, Cave Hill, Barbados (February) and St. Augustine, Trinidad (March); in 2006 visiting professor, University of the West Indies, Mona, Jamaica (taught Linguistics 620, "Language Variation," under the auspices of a Fulbright Fellowship).

In July 2007 he was instructor, "Stylistic Variation" course, U Southern California, LSA Linguistic Institute, Stanford; in September 2007, taught Sophomore College course ("Ebonics, Creoles, and Standard English in Education"). In 2008 he was elected president of the Society for Caribbean Linguistics (SCL), and in August 2010, at the SCL's biennial meeting in Barbados, he delivered the presidential address, focusing on relativizer omission in Guyanese, Barbadian, Jamaican, Appalachian and African American vernacular English, and its theoretical implications.

John Rickford, the promising, bright Guyana County Scholarship winner, and Queen's College scholar, who continued on to university and to a dazzlingly brilliant career as a university don, did not sit on the laurels of past achievements. That was not John's way. At every stage he was extremely energetic and innovative.

Ever since he was a student at Queen's College, he found the time for extra studies and for writing (for instance, he was a founding contributor to *Expression* magazine in Georgetown in the 1960s, along with John Agard, Brian Chan, and others who went on to distinguished literary careers). He was also active, from high school and beyond, in many extra-curricular activities, like debating and student government, and voluntary community work. He has packed into a few decades a long list of activities.

The scholarships and academic honors John has won, include Queen's College prize for best results at London University General Certificate of Education (GCE) ordinary level exams; Wishart Memorial Prize for distinction in English at London University GCE advanced level exams; Fulbright/IIE Grant for undergraduate study in the United States; at university, first prize, Stevenson College oratory competition, UCSC; as a lecturer the Dean's Award for Distinguished Teaching, Stanford; the

Bing Fellowship for Excellence in Teaching, Stanford; Martin Luther King Centennial Professorship, Stanford; American Book Award (for *Spoken Soul*) from the Before Columbus Foundation; elected chair of the Stanford University Faculty Senate for 2001–02; Anthropology and the Media Award (American Anthropology Association); Linguistics, Language, and the Public Award (Linguistic Society of America); Collitz Professorship, LSA Institute, Michigan State; Wordsworth McAndrew Award for outstanding contributions to Guyana's cultural life; Pritzker University Fellowship in Undergraduate Education, Stanford.

This distinguished professor of linguistics has secured numerous research grants and fellowships including: Danforth Graduate Fellowship; LSA Institute Fellowship; National Science Foundation Doctoral Dissertation Grant and research grant; Fellowship, Center for Advanced Study in the Behavioral Sciences, Stanford; Ellen Andrews Wright Fellowship; Fulbright Fellowship (for teaching and research in Jamaica; Visiting Erskine Fellowship (teaching), University of Canterbury, New Zealand.

His post-degree honors and awards include:

Research and Publications Grant, University of Guyana; Rockefeller Humanities Fellowship (for research on adequacy of pidgins and Creoles); Center for Urban Studies Fellowship (for research on divergence of black and white vernaculars in East Palo Alto); Ellen Andrews Wright Fellowship, Stanford Humanities Center; seed money from the Stanford President's Fund, to lead African and African American Studies Learning Expeditions (thirty to fifty students, staff, and faculty) to the South Carolina and Georgia Sea Islands (1999), Jamaica (2000), and Ghana (2001), over spring break; ward from associate dean, Humanities and Sciences, to lead an African and African American Studies Learning Expedition (thirty-plus students, staff, and faculty) to Belize over spring break.

Aside from his teaching commitments, John Rickford takes a keen interest in public service. In Santa Cruz, California, from 1968 to '71, he was a teaching volunteer, tutorial program; president, Black Students Association; member, Drama Society: acted in *The Tempest*, *Julius Caesar*, and *An Evening of Leonard Cohen*, and directed *An Evening of Black Poetry and Song*, and *People Get Ready* evening (the latter while participating in a quarter-long extramural community service program on Daufuskie Island, South Carolina, which included work as a tutor in the elementary school and other community responsibilities).

He was educational vice president, Toastmasters Early Risers Club, Palo Alto; Cub Scout leader, Juana Briones school; soccer coach, American Youth Soccer Organization; designer/director (with Christine Theberge) of a lecture program on "Rapping, Reading, and Writing" for Costaño School sixth graders, East Palo Alto; guest lecturer, Gunn High School; classroom volunteer, Costaño School, East Palo Alto.

He has been editor, the *Carrier Pidgin* newsletter; associate editor, the *Carrier Pidgin* newsletter; guest editor, issue 71, *International Journal of the Sociology of Language* ("Sociolinguistics and Pidgin-Creole Studies"); referee for *Language, Language in Society, Studies in Second Language Acquisition*, National Science Foundation.

He is on the editorial board of twelve publications, including: *21st Century Perspectives on Language, Ethnicity, and Education* series, *Language and Identity and Education, Journal of Pidgin and Creole Languages.* He is also on the board of consulting editors of other journals.

His membership in professional societies includes cofounder and chair (with Susan Ervin-Tripp), Bay Area Sociolinguistics Association; member, American Anthropological Association, American Dialect Society, International Sociolinguistics Association, Linguistic Society of America, Society for Caribbean Linguistics, Society for Linguistic Anthropology, the Society for Pidgin and Creole Linguistics; vice president, president and immediate past president, Society for Pidgin and Creole Linguistics; Selection Committee member, Linguistics, Language and the Public Award, Linguistic Society of America (2004, 2008) and vice president (2006), and president elect (2008), Society for Caribbean Linguistics.

His activities in conference, organization, and program directorship include:

Coordinator, Festival of Guyanese Words Colloquium, U Guyana; co-organizer, with P. Eckert and C. A. Ferguson, conference on "The Social Context of Language Change," LSA Institute, Stanford; co-organizer, student conference in Linguistics 73 "Black English" course; director, Stanford Overseas Studies Oxford Summer Focus Program, "Britain in the Third World; the Third World in Britain"; co-organizer (with Vera Grant and Sarita Ocon, of the Program in African and African American Studies, Stanford) of a national workshop on "Black Studies Curriculum and Pedagogy," Stanford.

John Rickford has delivered numerous lectures and made research/conference presentations. His invited lectures were delivered at universities across the United States from Washington to Los Angeles, from New York to Florida, and in Canada, Guyana, Barbados, Jamaica, Germany- Kiel, Freiburg and Berlin, Puerto Rico, New Zealand, and Cayenne, French Guiana,

In 1997 he delivered numerous talks on Ebonics, in response to public interest and controversy following the Oakland School Board's December 1996 decision to recognize the vernacular of their African American students and use it in the teaching of standard English. His talks focused, among other things, on the structure and history of Ebonics or African American vernacular English and its potential for improving the success of inner-city African American students in reading, writing, and the language arts, as demonstrated in studies of contrastive analysis and dialect readers in the United States and Europe.

His talks were given, sometimes as part of panels or symposia, at Stanford University (several sites), and other venues, including universities in the United States, the Standard English Proficiency conference of the California State Department of Education, the Oakland Alliance of Black Educators, and the National Black Association of Speech, Language and Hearing Practitioners. He also gave a talk on "Ebonics Humor" at the Stanford Humanities Center.

John was also interviewed about Ebonics by reporters/broadcasters from a variety of local and national news media, including ABC, CBS, *Nickelodeon News*, *The News Hour with Jim Lehrer*, the *New York Times*, the *Washington Post*, the *Chicago Tribune*, the *Chronicle of Higher Education*, the *Los Angeles Times*, *Education Newsday*, WOR, KALW, KKUP, the Education Forum (public access TV, Palo Alto), *Charleston Post and Courier*, the *Stanford Daily*, *Education Daily*, *Education Week*, the *Christian Science Monitor*, *USA Today*, *Newsweek*, KQED (*Talk of the Nation*, *Forum*, and *To the Best of Our Knowledge* shows), *US News and World Report*, the *Detroit News*, *Psychiatric Times*, *San Francisco Chronicle*, *San Jose Mercury News*, *Oakland Tribune*, and *Toronto Star*.

He also drafted the resolutions of the Linguistic Society of America on Ebonics, which were approved, with minor revisions, at their January 1997 annual meeting in Chicago. In 1998: "Language Diversity and Academic Achievement in the Education of African American Students: An Overview of the Issues." He delivered the opening address at the Conference on Language Diversity and Academic Achievement in the Education of African American Students, organized by the Center for Applied Linguistics and Howard University, held after the Linguistic Society of America's annual meeting, New York.

John has authored numerous books and edited works, including:
- *A Festival of Guyanese Words.* Georgetown: University of Guyana. 1976. Second edition, revised and expanded, 1978.
- *African American English*, ed. by Salikoko S. Mufwene, John R. Rickford, Guy Bailey and John Baugh. London: Routledge. 1998.
- *African American Vernacular English: Features and Use, Evolution, and Educational Implications.* Oxford: Blackwell. 1999.
- *Creole Genesis, Attitudes and Discourse: Studies Celebrating Charlene Sato*, ed. (with Suzanne Romaine). Amsterdam: John Benjamins . 1999.
- *Spoken Soul: The Story of Black English.* (With Russell J. Rickford) New York: John Wiley. 2000. [Winner of a 2000 American Book Award].
- *Style and Sociolinguistic Variation,* ed. (with Penelope Eckert). Cambridge: Cambridge University Press. 2002.
- *Language in the USA: Themes for the 21st Century*, co-ed. with Ed. Finegan, Cambridge: Cambridge University Press. 2004.

His published articles include:
- (with Angela E. Rickford). "Cut-Eye and Suck-Teeth: African Words and Gestures in New World Guise." *Journal of American Folklore*, 89 (353): 194-309. 1976. Reprinted 1978 in *Readings in American Folklore*, ed. J. H. Brunvand, 355-73. New York: W. W. Norton and Co., Inc., Also reprinted 1980 in *Perspectives on American English*, ed. J. Dillard, 347–66. The Hague: Mouton.
- (With Barbara Greaves). "Non-Standard Words and Expressions in the Writing of Guyanese School-Children." In *A Festival of Guyanese Words,* ed. J. R. Rickford, 25-45. Georgetown: University of Guyana. 1976. Reprinted in second edition, 1978: 40-56.
- "Me Tarzan, You Jane: Cognition, Expression and the Creole Speaker." *Journal of Linguistics* 22.2:281–310. 1986.
- "The Haves and Have Nots: Sociolinguistic Surveys and the Assessment of Speaker Competence." *Language in Society* 16.2: 149–77. 1987.

- "Rappin on the Copula Coffin: Theoretical and Methodological Issues in the Analysis of Copula Variation in African American Vernacular English." (with A. Ball, R. Blake, R. Jackson and N. Martin.) *Language Variation and Change.* 1991.
- "Syntactic Variation and Change in Progress: Loss of the Verbal Coda in Topic-Restricting As far As Constructions." *Language* 71.1:102–131 (with Tom Wasow, Norma Mendoza-Denton, and Juli Espinoza). 1995.
- "The Creole Origins of African American Vernacular English: Evidence from Copula Absence." In *African American English*, ed. by Salikoko S. Mufwene, John R. Rickford, Guy Bailey and John Baugh, 154-200. London: Routledge.1998.
- "Using the Vernacular to Teach the Standard." In *Ebonics in the Urban Education Debate*, ed. by David Ramirez, Terrence Wiley, Gerda de Klerk, and Enid Lee. Long Beach: Center for Language Minority Education and Research, California State University, Long Beach. 1999.
- "The Living Language." Introductory essay, and Living Language notes, in the fourth edition of *The American Heritage Dictionary*. Boston. Houghton Mifflin, 2000.
- "Implicational Scales." In *The Handbook of Language Variation and Change*, ed. by James K. Chambers, Peter Trudgill & Natalie Schilling-Estes, 142–67. Oxford: Blackwell. 2002
- "African American Vernacular English." In the *Oxford Encyclopedia of Linguistics*, second edition. Oxford University Press. 2003.
- "Pidgins and Creoles." In the *Oxford Encyclopedia of Linguistics*, second edition. Oxford University Press. 2003.
- "Spoken Soul: The Beloved, Belittled Language of Black America." In *Sociolinguistic Variation: Critical Reflections* (Carmen Fought, ed.). New York. Oxford U Press. 2004.
- "Intensive and Quotative ALL: Something old, something new." (Lead author, with Isabelle Buchstaller, Tom Wasow, and Arnold Zwicky.) *American Speech* 82.1:3–31. 2007.

John Rickford is married to Angela (nee Marshall) of Georgetown, Guyana. She went to Bishops' High School (she was deputy head girl), and they started dating in high school. Angela won a Guyana Conditional

Scholarship to study English at University of the West Indies, Mona, Jamaica. They married in 1971 in California.

Angela earned her master's in education at the University of Pennsylvania, and later a diploma in education at the University of Guyana, and a PhD in education with a minor in psychology at Stanford University, in 1996, before joining the Faculty of Education at San Jose State University, where she is now full professor. Angela is an achiever of distinction in her own right.

They have four children: Shiyama, Russell, Anakela, and Luke, and (as of this writing) four grandchildren: Nyla, Lance, Anaya, and Kai.

August 30, 2010

Shyraz Riyasat

Dip. Electronic Eng
Publisher

Shyraz Riyasat is owner of the Victoria Bookbinding Company and Firstchoice Books, a publishing company, located in Victoria, British Columbia.

Shy, as he is familiarly known, was born in May 1951 at Skeldon, Berbice, Guyana. His mother is Zaitun, a homemaker, and his father, Sattaur, was employed as a supervisor for cane cutters at Skeldon Sugar Estate. He has three sisters and five brothers, and he is the fourth youngest. His older brother, older sister, and youngest brother (a doctor) are still in Guyana. There is a brother and a sister in the United States and a brother and a sister in Toronto, Canada.

He received his early education at Skeldon Scots School and Skeldon Lutheran High School, in Guyana.

After his GCEs, he obtained the teaching certificate in Guyana, and started work as a high school teacher in Guyana in 1969.

In 1970 he emigrated to Canada, attending George Brown College in Canada after a short stint with the University of Toronto, where he did not have sufficient funds to continue. With no friends or family to support him, he managed a college degree in electronics but could not find work in that field at that time. Not being a Canadian citizen, it became a struggle to find suitable employment.

While attending college, he managed to secure full-time work in the printing department of a large manufacturing company, where he quickly moved up to a print production manager position. Now, with some solid experience and a college degree, he moved from Toronto to Calgary where he met his wife, Angel, and adopted two beautiful children.

After ten years in Calgary, and a downturn in the Alberta economy, he made a bold move to beautiful Victoria without his family for a three-month period. Loving the city, but concerned about his low wages, he decided to mortgage his home to start a small business. While developing the business he had two children of his own, Rachad and Lisa, in British Columbia. His wife used to take their newborn baby to work amid the noisy machinery.

Shy started the Victoria Bookbinding Company in 1988 without any knowledge in the bookbinding industry. All he saw was a need for a bindery company on Vancouver Island since most jobs were going to mainland Vancouver. After many trials and errors and customer complaints, he persisted and the company continued to grow.

With many years of success, there appeared to be a change (downturn) in the printing industry when computers and publishing programs were becoming more prevalent and easy to use. Shy then had to make a very difficult decision: continue servicing the print industry and go down the path with them or move to the new trend of on-demand self-published books. It was an easy change since he knew a lot about binding books. So Firstchoicebooks.ca, his new publishing company was born.

Shy endured a lot of struggles during his career and owning a small business. But focus and persistence always won in the end.

He is an avid golfer and takes an active interest in community affairs. He is a member of the Lions Club, Chamber of Commerce, Craftsman Club (printing member) and the Local Organizing Community to beautify the town where he lives.

Shy's achievements have been duly recognized. In his own field of printing and publishing, Shy was awarded the Craftsman Club PI Award (Excellence in Printing). He has been St. Andrews High School track coach for three years and holds the Canadian Track-and-Field Coach certificate.

Shy published *A Self-Publishing Guide for Publishers*. His website, firstchoicebooks.ca, contains a lot of publishing information. Shy wrote many articles on publishing, bookbinding, textbook rebinding, and trade bookbinding. He has produced many books of all genres through his three websites: firstchoicebooks.ca, selfpublishingbc.com, and victoriabindery.com.

As insight into Shy's success, he said:

> Do not be afraid of change.
>
> After many years in the printing industry, and the changes that were occurring, a difficult decision had to be made to find an easier way to make a living. While jogging on a lonely road -memories of my youth, like those famous lone, long distance runners, I had to determine what I know best and whether there is a future demand for it. Book publishing was one option. I had extensive knowledge on creating, binding and even rebinding books. All I had to do was hire someone who is a graphic artist and buy printing equipment to manufacture books in-house. The only question was where I would get customers to support my new venture. Finally, it hit me. The Internet! ...
>
> With many sleepless nights, I had to learn the secrets of Google Adwords and Adsense and made my site informative and appealing to prospective clients.
>
> With new technological advances in computers, programs and information on the Web, authors were empowered to produce their own labels. I thought of the traditional publishing houses. What happens with all the manuscripts rejected by them? Further investigations assured me that over 80 percent of authors do not conform to their restrictive genres.
>
> A few on-demand publishing companies were already ahead of me, and that's when I decided to purchase equipment and hire professional people to help create this new venture. Our clients are very happy when they receive their books and that makes us happy.

Highlights of Shy's life include
- A high school teacher in Guyana
- Moving to Canada
- Moving from Calgary to Victoria, BC
- Starting his own company
- Children and grandson.
- His small contributions to Canadian society (paying taxes, helping charities and athletic coaching)
- Helping his brother develop a farm in Linden, Guyana.

If he has regrets, they would be:

- Not spending enough time with his kids while growing the business
- Not surrounding himself with positive people earlier in life
- Putting on the golf course.

His story, in his own words, is as follows:

> I am very fortunate to be alive today considering my early childhood. My mother died when I was about nine years old. Raised by older brothers and sisters, I was left alone most of the time and had to fend for myself. I was reluctant to go to school and spent most of my time in the sugar cane fields and pastures shooting birds with slingshots to have a meal.
>
> I swam with alligators and snakes and jumped into moving cane punts from high bridges.
>
> Chased by security people for trying to pick sugar cane, I had to jump through barbed wire fences to escape them. I was slashed with a cutlass for picking a coconut and dumped into a trench when I could not swim.
>
> Going hungry in the afternoon, I was faced with a meal of curried squash (*nenwah*) or pumpkin, both of which I hated. We lived on salt, oil, and bare rice. A chicken meal was a real treat.
>
> Doing well in school was a priority. I worked and studied hard and was rewarded with success. I became the first educated

> one in my family. I studied Islam and Christianity with the hope of increasing memory retention by reciting chapters and verses.
>
> Being a teacher was a proud time for me in Guyana. I had many offers of marriage.
>
> I left Guyana in 1970 with only about $500 (Canadian) and came to Canada without knowing anyone. It was a severe struggle. ...
>
> Through sheer determination and a willingness to embrace a new society, I had to make the best of what little I had. ...
>
> I am proud to have sponsored my brother and sister to Canada. I learned to integrate in this wonderful, tolerant Canadian society where opportunities are abundant.

About his inspiration, he has said:

> I am inspired by people who work hard and make what they do seem easy—Mohammed Ali, Tiger Woods, Barack Obama, my staff, my brother, a doctor, farmer and everything else.
>
> Believe in yourself. Do not be afraid of rejection. "No" is just another word. Be aware, not everyone will like you or what you do. Do your research. Set goals and if only half is achieved, then be happy. Take up a sport that challenges you, golf. Be cool about taxes and speeding tickets; it is only money. Achieving a few is better than none. There are dreamers and doers. Be a doer.
>
> Here is a simple philosophy that I go by: create a vision of what you want and take incremental steps to achieve it. If you decide to run a mile in ten minutes and you are out of shape, then try to run one minute at a time for ten times.

September 12, 2010

Mayor John Rodriguez

Teacher and Ontario MP

Mayor John Rodriguez was winner of Guyana Awards (Canada) 2009 Lifetime Achievement Award. The citation of the award contains the following information, in part:

> John Rodriguez received his elementary and high school education in Guyana and emigrated to Canada in 1956.
>
> He attended Teachers College in Toronto, and started his teaching career in St. Catharines, Ontario. He moved to the town of Coniston in 1962, where he assumed the role of principal of St. Paul School.
>
> His leadership abilities and passion for community eventually led him to political life, first as a member of Municipal Council in Coniston and later as member of Parliament for the riding of Nickel Belt.

During his eighteen years in federal politics, John worked to improve the economic well-being of the Sudbury area and the quality of life of its citizens. A vibrant and respected politician, he served on numerous standing committees, including Finance; Trade and Economic Affairs; Labor; Employment and Immigration; Regional Development; Indian Affairs and Northern Development; Single Industry Communities and Regional Economic Expansion.

In 2006, John Rodriguez re-entered the local political arena when he was elected mayor of the city of Greater Sudbury—an office that oversees the trillion-dollar Sudbury Basin, the richest mining district in North America. A strong advocate for community growth and development, he has worked diligently to shape the community's strategy for growth in areas such as mining and mining research, health care, arts and culture, and recreation.

John Rodriguez is a former member of the Board of Governors of the Ontario Teachers Federation, past president of both the local and provincial Catholic Teachers Unions.

John holds a bachelor of arts degree in English and Spanish literature from Laurentian University. He is a long-time volleyball coach. He and his wife, Bertilla, have five sons and five grandchildren.

Sources:

Websites accessed May 27, 2010, on Guyana Consulate Toronto, Guyana Awards (Canada)

May 27, 2010

Hugh Sam

Composer

Hugh Sam is a composer and pianist who has written over two hundred compositions in various mediums. In Guyana he was associated with music for the theater, steel bands, and jazz ensembles. He was a part of the piano and theory faculties at two music schools in New York and has given several recitals during his tenure. His main goal as a composer was incorporating Guyanese and Caribbean folk songs into formal classical compositions, much in the same manner as was done by composers such as Chopin, Brahms, Tchaikovsky, and Bartok.

Early influences in his piano arrangements were the pianists Don Shirley and Peter Nero, who both used classical pieces as the framework for their arrangement of popular songs. Hugh has also written five Caribbean rhapsodies and numerous arrangements of popular tunes.

Born in Guyana in 1934, Hugh Sam received his formative musical education in piano, theory, and harmony from Guyanese music teachers, Mildred Joseph, the sister of New Amsterdam music teacher, Ruby McGregor and Berle Marshall. As a child, he showed an attraction for music, often interrupting his brother's piano practicing by trying to play on the keys with him. At about seven, his father tried to give him violin lessons, but stopped after it seemed that Hugh wanted a new lesson every day! He nearly missed out on going for piano lessons at Mrs. Joseph's because his mother felt that although his two siblings were sent to lessons, they did not appear to be very interested. She therefore decided that she would not waste money by sending Hugh; he was about fifteen years of age then. Luckily, his Aunt Edna stepped in and offered to pay for his lessons. Later, his mother relented and took over payment of the fees.

Hugh's father played the violin and was the leader of the second violins section of the BG. Philharmonic Orchestra. His mother played the piano and often accompanied his father. Soon that function was given to Hugh. He was the last of three children. There were Friday night get-togethers at which all three children were accompanied by their mother, playing from a song book of old English and American songs.

His brother Rev. Eric L. Sam served as a priest at All Saints Anglican Church in New Amsterdam and in the Bahamas. He died in Florida in 1992. Rev. Sam also took piano lessons and passed the associated board examinations up to the Grade VII level. His sister, Nathalie, who is widowed, has two children who now live in Toronto. Hugh's wife, Patricia, is an accomplished pianist who has an LRSM diploma and taught piano both in Guyana and in New York.

Hugh was self-taught in composition and produced a number of piano pieces while in Guyana. The earliest was his "Little Suite" for piano which was written in 1952. He subsequently performed this in March 2007 at a faculty recital at Third Street Music School Settlement in Manhattan. His method of studying was to analyze the piano compositions that he was learning and see how the composers notated their work. He played the popular songs of the day in his own arrangements and was an admirer of the Guyanese pianist Ignatius Quail whose modern harmonies were interesting to Hugh. Later he appeared on a weekly fifteen-minute radio program on Radio Demerara where he played popular songs.

At the 1952 Guyana Music Festival, he was awarded third prize in the under-eighteen piano solo division. In 1954 his "Idyll" won him the first prize in composition. He had only entered the festival at the urging of Joan McDavid, a fine Guyanese pianist and her fiancée, Michael Gilkes, who persuaded him that his work merited being presented. They were proved correct! During the 1958 Guyana Music Festival, his composition "Caribbean Seascape" (which won the second prize) was chosen by the adjudicator to be performed in Trinidad by the English concert pianist Kendall Taylor. This took place at the Public Library in Trinidad on March 11, 1958.

Hugh was a member and arranger of the steel band, Symphonia, which rehearsed under the famous Taitt residence in Murray Street (now Quamina Street). Members included Ronnie Savory, Arthur Henry, Joan McDavid, and Patsy Jackson. He also arranged and wrote the music for the Invader's Steel Band when their music was to be featured in a documentary film about the bauxite industry. The location for most of the band's rehearsals was Federation Yard in Regent Street, a locale that was regarded as not the best of places for most well-regarded citizens!

After hearing the Englishman Arthur Benjamin's arrangement of the Jamaican folk song "Linstead Market" and some other Jamaican folksongs for two pianos, Hugh decided that someone from the Caribbean should be doing what the Englishman had done. He then made it his life's work to arrange many of the folk songs of Guyana and some of the Caribbean Islands. These included Jamaica, Trinidad, Barbados, and St. Lucia. These compositions appear in both piano solo and piano duet versions. The first of these, "Fantasia on Three Guyanese Folk Songs," won first prize at the Department of History and Culture competition in 1959. Dr. Ray Luck, the Guyanese pianist, has premiered many of Hugh's works in this genre, including the 2010 Caribbean Music Educator's Conference in St. Lucia, where he held a piano workshop. He performed Hugh's arrangement of two Trinidadian folk songs.

Hugh was also associated with the musical play *Amalivaca* when it was performed in Guyana. This musical dealt with the myth surrounding a legendary Guyanese god. His short ballet *Legend of the Carrion Crow* was performed by the dancer, Patricia Evan-Wong, and a small dance troupe at Queen's College Auditorium in Guyana. It is interesting to note that Hugh was also the pianist for Helen Taitt's School of Dance. In this capacity he often had to improvise music to the dance steps. Hugh remembers his various visits to the Taitt establishment with fondness and recalls that Clairmonte Taitt, Helen's brother, always had in his possession recordings of the latest twentieth century music. It was there that Hugh first heard Benjamin Britten's "War Requiem."

The daily radio program *Birthday Requests* often featured classical selections. It was here that Hugh heard many classical pieces played by great pianists including Iturbi, Horowitz, and Paderewski.

While listening to BBC Radio on his father's floor-length Atwater Kent radio, he also heard performances not only by European pianists, but also by Caribbean pianists, like Guyanese Billy Pilgrim and Jamaican

Marjorie Few. Of course, this was done while he was supposed to be doing homework.

In 1956 it was decided to bring together artists from various sections of the art and form Theater 13. Members included Helen Taitt, Ken Corsbie, and Clairmonte Taitt (dance), Cecil Barker, Anne Greenidge and Lawrence Taitt (décor and costumes), Cecile Nobrega and Barbara Osman (drama), Vincent DeAbreu (conductor of the BG Militia Band), Michael Gilkes, and Hugh Sam (music) and Ricardo Smith (publicity). These meetings took place at the Taitt residence.

Their first and only production was *Stabroek Fantasy*. Helen Taitt had suggested that as Hugh had already written a composition titled "Stabroek Market," the work would revolve around life in the market and related areas. It was also decided to use a number of piano compositions that Hugh had already written and convert them to vocal pieces. The Symphonia Steel Band was conducted by Ron Savory. The overture, which was written for two pianos, was performed by Hugh and his wife, Patricia. The show proved very popular, no doubt in part because much of the dialogue was in Creolese.

In 1965, the American musical *The Fantasticks* was at the height of its popularity in the United States. Somehow, the Theater Guild of Guyana was given permission to produce it in Guyana. Hugh remembers the evening when he was approached by the organist and choir director, Reggie McDavid, and asked if he would be willing to be the musical director. After hearing the LP, Hugh remarked, "That music sounds just as if I had written it!" However, the score given to him was only for voices and solo piano. The recording he had received featured two pianos. Hugh then set about arranging the solo piano part for two pianos and sought out Colin Forde as the second pianist.

The Fantasticks was a big hit and was performed in Georgetown, Berbice, and McKenzie (now Linden).

In Guyana, his two choral works, "Land of Our Birth" and "River Song," were performed by the Bishops' High School Choir, conducted by the late Edith Pieters. These were written around 1960 and the words were respectively by A. J. Seymour and Edgar Mortimer Duke; one, a Guyanese writer and the other, an educator. One of these compositions was chosen as a set piece for a subsequent Music Festival.

At the 1967 Music Festival, Hugh was awarded the Trinidad Music Association Cup for the Most Outstanding Performance. He was the winner in two composition classes.

In addition to being a classical musician, Hugh Sam is also a jazz pianist and arranger. In 1965 he recorded a jazz album, *A Saxful of Harry*, with legendary Guyanese saxophonist Harry Whittaker, drummer Art Broomes, and bassist Maurice Watson. They were known as the 560 Quartet (taking the name from the frequency of the local radio station). He was also the arranger of the Guyanese folk songs that were sung by the Police Male Voice Choir (when they participated at Expo '67 in Montreal) and also their accompanist.

Hugh emigrated soon after Expo '67 and took up residence in England. He pursued piano and harmony studies in London at the Guildhall School of Music, and in 1968 he left England for the United States. In 1973 he graduated in composition from the Manhattan School of Music. This was no small task as he was working full-time, including in the evening, at a stock brokerage firm at which overtime was compulsory. There were a few occasions when he missed classes because his manager refused to release him from the job. Postgraduate studies in composition were done at Brooklyn College under the distinguished American composer Robert Starer. In 1975, Hugh's ballet *Metempsychosis* was commissioned and performed by a graduate dance student and her group at the suggestion of Professor Starer.

He joined the Theory Faculty of Turtle Bay Music School in 1976, and after performing in a concert at the school he was invited to join the Piano Faculty. He remained there for almost eighteen years. During his tenure he performed at several drawing room concerts, which were given to bring attention to the school. His selections consisted mainly of popular tunes arranged in the style of classical composers.

Hugh also formed a family jazz group, Starlite, with his sons Gregory and Andre when they were approximately eleven and seven years old. They played tunes mainly from television and a couple jazz standards. They were featured on a New Jersey television station at this time.

In 1981 Hugh took part in one of many yearly Yuletide concerts held at the Cramton Auditorium at Howard University. These concerts were organized by Dr. Frank Beckles and were on behalf of the Guyana Assistance Project. Several Guyanese performers were featured. Proceeds were to be relayed for hospital supplies in Guyana.

For a 1988 concert commemorating the 150th anniversary of the abolition of slavery in Guyana and billed as "A Grand Reunion," Hugh wrote a Festival Overture and a Festival dance for piano. Both compositions quoted a few Guyanese folksongs and the "Festival Dance" featured stylized African, Portuguese, and East Indian melodies and rhythm.

On a subsequent visit to Guyana, he was also reunited with drummer Art Broomes in a choral performance of a jazz version of "The Creation" by David Bobrowitz, which was conducted by Edith Pieters.

In July 1994 Hugh was invited to give a piano recital at the National Cultural Center as part of the 150th anniversary of the establishment of Queen's College, one of the premier secondary schools. There was a moment of levity at this concert as the television crew who were filming on stage was deemed too disruptive and was asked to leave by the management of the Cultural Center. In addition the piano was not secured from bangers during the period between Hugh's rehearsal and performance and as a result there was one note stridently out of tune during the entire performance. In addition to some classical standards, he also performed his arrangement of the QC school song "Laude Gratemur Scholae" and some of his Guyanese folk song arrangements.

In the summer of 1994 he also gave a recital at a music summer camp called Summerkeys in Lubec, Maine. He later returned there in 2005 to give another recital.

Hugh's four Caribbean rhapsodies (Guyana, Barbados, Jamaica, Trinidad) written for piano and orchestra, and a St. Lucian rhapsody for two pianos and orchestra are all based on folk songs of the respective countries. In 2002, the Guyana rhapsody, called "A Folksong Concertino," was performed with a prerecorded orchestral part in Ottawa at the invitation of a Guyanese association there. One of these compositions features a steel orchestra and piano. This was done at the suggestion of Ray Luck, who was planning a solo recital in Trinidad. He was scheduled to play a Mozart concerto with the University of West Indies Steel Ensemble and asked Hugh if he could rearrange the orchestral part in his Trinidadian rhapsody for steel ensemble. This composition, "A Trinidadian Rhapsody," which fused some Trinidadian folk songs together, was performed in Trinidad at Queen's Hall by the University of West Indies Steel Orchestra and Guyanese pianist Ray Luck in October 2004. The steel ensemble was conducted by Jessel Murray. Hugh stated that this event was the highlight of his musical career.

As a result of the intervention of a friend who was a conductor, Hugh was commissioned to arrange some Christmas songs for the New York Housing Authority Symphony Orchestra in December 2002. This was his first orchestral assignment.

In 2003 he was invited to give a recital at the Savannah suite of the Pegasus hotel in Guyana. The concert was part of a "Music from Around the World" series arranged by Gems Theater Productions. As a result of the theme, Hugh played music by Latin American, Spanish, Italian, and Polish composers and of course, his arrangement of Guyanese folk songs. His arrangement of "Missi Los' She Gol' Ring" was performed by violinist Ghislaine Benabdullah, a violinist in the Paris Opera Orchestra and also the wife of the manager of the Pegasus Hotel.

Over the past thirty years while Hugh Sam was serving on the faculties of the Turtle Bay Music School and Third Street Music School Settlement in New York City, he was also working full-time at the stockbrokerage firm at Merrill Lynch.

In 2005, his composition, "A Tale of Two Rivers," for small orchestra was performed in Bulgaria under the direction of the young Afro-American conductor Marlon Daniels. It received a brief review in the Russian newspaper, *Pravda*.

A presentation of Hugh's music for various mediums (piano, voice, flute, cello, and two pianos) was featured by the Third Street Music School Settlement in March 2007. It was billed as "A Celebration of the Music of Hugh Sam" and featured performances by faculty members of the school and Hugh.

He has been giving faculty recitals at Third Street Music School Settlement from the inception of his employment in 1990. His recitals usually have a theme: children, nature, folk songs of Latin America. On several occasions he has been called upon to write music for specific events at the school. These included the retirement of a director and the fortieth anniversary of the tenure of two teachers at the school. Some of these arrangements have featured two performers at each of two pianos. He also did an arrangement of the famous ice cream truck song for six hands. This was played by three adults, presenting a bit of a space logistic at the one piano.

Hugh was one of the recipients of a Sunshine Award in 2007, given to those who made significant contributions to Caribbean culture. Other awardees that year included Rex Nettleford, the Jamaican scholar and choreographer, and Monty Alexander, the Jamaican jazz pianist.

Hugh Sam continues to give recitals at Third Street Music School Settlement, often featuring members of the faculty performing his compositions and arrangements and, on some occasions, using his sons, Gregory and Andre, as participants.

September 2010

Terry B. Sawh

President and Owner
Topnotch Group of Companies

Terry landed in Canada with just twenty-four dollars in his pocket and a burning ambition to succeed. He had a tremendous amount of enthusiasm and hope for a better future.

In 1992, he launched his company, Topnotch Employment Services Inc., which employs eight full-time employees, and manages more than three hundred contract staff—many of whom are visible minorities and members of aboriginal communities—through its spin-offs, like Prime Time Plus and Topnotch Executive Staffing.

Terry is active in business associations, local charities, service clubs, and the Guyanese community. He is also a certified supplier and chair of the Supply Committee of CAMSC (Canadian Aboriginal and Minority Supplier Council), which helps minority-owned businesses connect with large and medium-sized Canadian companies.

He sits on boards of various cultural and religious organizations, and he serves as a mentor to other newcomers.

Terry was one of the winners of the Top 25 Canadian Immigrants 2009 Award. This is an annual award presented by *Canadian Immigrant* magazine. The award recipients were honored at ceremonies held in Toronto and in Vancouver. This awards program celebrates the untold stories and remarkable achievements of outstanding Canadian immigrants, who have all contributed to Canada in a big way. The winners come from all the six provinces of Canada.

Terry believes that Canada offers tremendous opportunities to anyone who decides to call it home, but he stresses:

> You must seek out your own path and create your own niche. That's what I did after arriving from Guyana. As an immigrant myself, it is my sincerest desire to share my thirty-three years of experience in Canada with recent and prospective immigrants to Canada, with the hope and expectation that I can make life easier for those who arrive after me.

> Looking back at my humble beginnings, my experience has ever since been an inspiration to me. If I can succeed from a state of deprivation, it is inspiring to think of what more I can achieve today with the resources, knowledge, support, and experience now at my disposal.

Orrin Benn, president, Canadian Aboriginal and Minority Supplier Council, has stated, "Terry remains motivated to be a coach, mentor and barrier breaker for immigrants trying to find employment in the Canadian workplace."

Sources:
Website accessed November 17, 2010
http://www.canadianimmigrant.ca/TerrySawh
http://www.canadianimmigrantbook.com/aboutauthor.html

November 17, 2010

Captain Joseph Schuler

Airline Pilot

Captain Joseph Schuler has been a pilot with Air Canada for thirty-five years. He flew the Jumbo, the Airbus and other aircraft.

Joseph Schuler was born in Georgetown, Guyana, in 1948.

He attended the Convent of the Good Shepherd and Main Street Catholic Primary Schools. He left in year two at St. Stanislaus College for Canada. He completed high school in Montreal, Quebec.

He completed flying school at Laurentide Aviation in Montreal, Quebec. He flew for Lariviere Service in Schefferville, Quebec in 1971.

Joseph returned to Guyana and flew there for Klavair Ltd. in 1972, and transferred to Wings Ltd. in St. Lucia in 1972. Both companies were owned by Anthony "Bungles" Clavier.

He started a charter airline service, Tropical Air Services Ltd., in Barbados in 1973. He was hired by Air Canada in 1973. He trained on and flew Lockheed L-1011, Boeing B-727, B-767, B-747/400, Airbus A-320, A-330, A-340 aircraft.

Joseph retired in 2008 and presently resides in Vancouver with his wife and family.

April 19, 2010

Gail S. Seeram

Immigration Attorney

Gail S. Seeram is an experienced immigration attorney who represents and advises corporate and individual clients on all aspects of immigration matters, worldwide. Her law offices are headquartered in Orlando, Florida.

Gail was born on September 9,1974 in New Amsterdam, Berbice, Guyana. Her father, Ralph Seeram, is a retired business owner and computer technician. Her mother, Bibi Seeram, was a seamstress and ran a housekeeping business. Her brother, Calvin Seeram, is a director and instructor in computer engineering.

She grew up in New York and as a naturalized US citizen can appreciate the personal and legal challenges faced by those seeking to call the United States home. She received her early education at the elementary school PS 100 in Richmond Hill, New York, attended junior high school in Ozone Park, New York, and attended Ridgewood High School in New Port Richey in Florida.

Gail attended Hofstra University in New York, graduating in 1996 with a bachelor of business administration in accounting degree. Following college, she attended Hofstra University School of Law, graduating in 1999 with a juris doctorate degree. She continued her legal studies at New York University School of Law and attained a LLM in taxation in 2003. She was admitted to the Connecticut Bar in May 1999 and the New York State Bar in June 2000.

She was a senior associate with PricewaterhouseCoopers, law clerk with the Hon. Stan Bernstein at the US Bankruptcy Court, EDNY, and adjunct professor at Queen's College in New York. In early 2003 Gail decided to leave the corporate sector and focus on establishing her own law firm, the Law Offices of Gail S. Seeram. After handling a variety of legal cases, she decided to dedicate her practice of law exclusively to immigration and nationality law. She has extensive experience in all aspects of family-based immigration, employment-based immigration, deportation defense, criminal waivers, and citizenship. She has successfully litigated deportation defense cases in Immigration Court and before the Board of Immigration Appeals.

Gail is serving her second term as executive vice chair for the Central Florida American Immigration Lawyers Association. Further, she is the former chair of the Orange County Children and Families Services Board and serves on an advisory committee to Orange County Sheriff Jerry Demings. She is a frequent writer and lecturer on immigration law and has been quoted over ten times in the *Orlando Sentinel* newspaper.

Her professional membership include:
- Secretary, American Immigration Lawyers Association, Central Florida Chapter, 2008–2009
- Member, American Immigration Lawyers Association, Central Florida Chapter, 2004–present
- Member, New York State Bar Association, 2000–present
- Associate member, Orange County Bar Association, –present

Gail's community leadership roles include:
- Chair, Orange County Children & Family Services Board, 2008–2010.
- Vice President (2006-2009), Secretary/Treasurer (2005–2006) Caribbean Bar Association Central Florida Chapter.
- Chair, Guyanese American Cultural Association of Central Florida Board of Directors, 2005–2006.

- Member, Florida Immigrant Coalition, 2008–present.
- Council Member, St. Stephen Lutheran Church 2008–2011.
- Panelist, American Civil Liberties Union, Orlando, FL, "Know Your Rights" Forum, 2008.
- Panelist, Caribbean American Business Expo, Orlando, FL, 2006.
- Volunteer, Homeless Coalition, Orlando, FL 2007–Present.
- Panelist, Florida Caribbean Student Association 33rd Bi-Annual Conference, University of Central Florida, 2007.
- Coordinator, Caribbean Bar Association Central FL Chapter Community Citizenship Drive, 4/2007, 8/2006.

Her publications include:
- Immigration columnist, *Caribbean Sun* Newspaper, 2004–present.
- Immigration columnist, *Khaas Baat*, 2007–2010.
- Immigration columnist, *Karibbean Under One*, 2008–present.
- *Journal of Multistate Taxation and Incentives*, "Can Local Tax Authorities Make Adjustments to Income in a Federally Tax-Free Reorganization," September 2003.

Gail has received media recognition as follows:
Orlando Sentinel, September 29, 2008: Quoted on advice she would give clients about the adjustment of status interview.
Orlando Sentinel, August 10, 2007: Quoted on her view of the expanding practice of immigration law.
Orlando Sentinel, June 17, 2007: Interviewed, photographed and quoted on her background and experience in immigration law.
Orlando Sentinel, May 30, 2007: Quoted on the proposed immigration fee increase effective July 30, 2007.
Orlando Sentinel, March 10, 2006: Quoted on her view of the immigration backlog.
Orlando Sentinel, February 27, 2005: Quoted on her involvement in a town hall meeting with the Caricom Consul Generals of Florida.
She draws her inspiration from her parents, saying, "My inspiration to excel and help those in need was learned from my mother and father. I've heard

stories about my forefathers and their struggles and these stories have been life lessons that I apply to my own life."

Her husband is Raymond Ali, a corporate paralegal. They were married in 2002.

September 7, 2009

Ishwar Sharma

BA, LLB (Kent), LLB(Ont)
Barrister, Solicitor, and Community Activist

Ishwar is actively involved in community legal clinics providing pro bono legal services in Greater Toronto, and in charitable organizations, including the Caribbean Children's Foundation, the Canada Hindu Organization, and the Gayatri Mandir. Ishwar received his early education in Canada, then studied law at York University, Toronto, and at the University of Kent in Canterbury, England.

Ishwar Sharma born in Georgetown, Guyana, emigrated to Canada with his family in 1970 at the young age of four. Ishwar completed most of his education in Canada, culminating in a bachelor of arts degree in law and society from York University in 1988. He was also the proud recipient of a bachelor of law with honors from the University of Kent in Canterbury, England.

As if this was not enough, Ishwar went on to graduate with his second bachelor of law degree from the University of Windsor, Ontario, in 1999. His educational and professional background was cited when he was called to the Ontario bar through the Law Society of Upper Canada as a barrister and solicitor in 2001.

Ishwar has successfully argued cases at the Immigration Appeal Board, the Immigration and Refugee Board, and the Federal Court of Canada in the area of Immigration law. He has successfully argued cases in the Ontario Court of Justice in the area of criminal law. He has been featured in several national and community newspapers, writing on topics of interest (both cultural and religious) for the Caribbean community.

Ishwar has always believed that the underprivileged of society should have access to justice. His volunteer legal work through community-based organizations and legal clinics has enabled him to assist those who ordinarily could not gain legal remedies because of their socio-economic status. He describes his greatest success and fulfillment as being able to assist minorities in his community.

He draws his inspiration from world leaders and freedom fighters, both men and women who have dedicated their lives to make this world a fair, tolerable and just place to live. Persons like Mahatma Gandhi, Martin Luther King Jr., Nelson Mandela, and Indira Gandhi, just to name a few, are those that have changed the world to be a better place and have inspired this young lawyer.

He is presently partner in the law firm of Sharma and Sharma with his main focus in immigration law and criminal law. He is married to Kirtanna Sharma who was born in Guyana and holds a bachelor of arts degree from the University of Toronto in political science. She is the senior legal secretary and manager of the family's law firm.

Ishwar's father, Roop Narine Sharma, has been and continues to be a constant source of inspiration both in his son's personal and professional life. It was his father who also inspired Ishwar's uncles, cousins, nieces, and nephews to pursue the noble profession as a barrister and solicitor to fight for the right of individuals in society.

September 15, 2010.

Roop Narine Sharma, LLB (Ont.)

Barrister and Solicitor
Lecturer, Hindu Religion and Philosophy

Roop Sharma was the youngest person in his day to qualify as a sworn clerk and notary public in Guyana. He was a crown prosecutor. In Toronto, he played a lead role in forming the Canada Hindu Organization, Inc. He made legal history by being the first Canadian lawyer to win refugee status for a client from Guyana. He has acted as chairman of the Police Complaints Commission. He has received many awards for community service.

Born in humble circumstances in Sparta, a small village located on the Essequibo Coast in Guyana, Roop Sharma, the quintessential lawyer and humanitarian, is known for his humility and accessibility. Today one of the most successful lawyers of Guyanese heritage to have practiced in Canada, Roop Sharma's devotion to his fellow Caribbean men and women reaches far beyond the courtroom or his law office in Toronto.

You will find Roop Sharma equally at home in front of some of Canada's most powerful judges and lawmakers, as with fellow devotees at the Hindu temple he frequents.

Roop is the son of Pandit Ramachal Sharma, an accountant by profession, and Phulmattie Maraj. Roop's father, like his father before him, was a Hindu priest, a calling Roop quickly adopted as he grew up.

He attended the St. Agnes Primary School at Danielstown, Essequibo, and on graduating from Standard 6, obtained a scholarship to Standard High School in Georgetown. From there he graduated with Cambridge Senior School certificate with exemptions from London matriculation.

He began his lifelong affair with law on gaining his first job in Guyana's Supreme Court Deeds Registry, where he would admire lawyers dressed in their robes, attending court to ensure the wheels of the country's justice system were moving smoothly.

He moved on to become the youngest person then, to qualify as a sworn clerk and notary public in the Deeds Registry, under the guidance of the late R. S. Persaud, registrar.

In 1960, Roop met the love of his life, Dhani, at a Hindu temple in Georgetown. It was a case of love at first sight, and they entered into a marriage that would last an entire lifetime. From that union there were five children, one son and four daughters, all of whom are now university graduates and professionals, with his son, Ishwar, following in his father's footsteps as an attorney.

In 1961, Roop and Dhani packed up and left Guyana for London, England, where he had gained entry at the prestigious Middle Temple Law School in London, chosen because one of his idols, Mahatma Gandhi, had graduated from there.

In short order, Roop began his collection of a lifetime of awards, his first being a gold medal in public speaking from the London Academy of Music and Dramatic Art.

In 1964, he was awarded a diploma of associate from the London Academy of Music and Dramatic Art. Later that same year, he graduated from Middle Temple as a Barrister at law.

Anxious to return to his homeland to put his new skills in law to use for the betterment of the country, Roop returned home shortly after graduation, and immediately joined the prestigious law firm of R. H. Luckhoo, whose brother was the then chief justice of Guyana, J. A. Luckhoo.

At that time there was a regulation that lawyers had to have three years experience before they could join the government legal service. However, within three months of joining the Luckhoo firm, Roop was asked by the then Solicitor General Sir Gonsalves Sabola to join the attorney general's office; thus, history was created as the regulation had to be amended by an Act of Parliament to facilitate the appointment.

After two years, Roop was appointed in the Office of the Director of Public Prosecutions. There he was one of the crown prosecutors in the famous Rupununi murder case. While a prosecutor at the DPP's chamber, he had the distinction of having 100 percent convictions.

With his law career soaring, Roop did not forget his duty to serve his community. He spent a great deal of time as president of the Gandhi Youth Organization, a group that worked primarily with young people to propagate and foster the Hindu religion and culture. He and the late Dr. Balwant Singh, who was then secretary of the Gandhi Youth Organization, played a key role in Guyana's Hindu community to the point of establishing a Hindu school within the organization. Roop, meanwhile, conducted weekly radio programs on Hindu religion and culture.

By 1970, now the parents of five young children, Roop and Dhani had to make the difficult decision to leave their beloved Guyana. Because they felt, the country offered little hope for a bright future for the young Sharmas, and although it meant starting over for Roop, they made the sacrifice and left for Toronto, Canada, where he went back to law school as per the requirements of Canadian law at the time.

In 1974, Roop graduated with an LLB degree from the University of Windsor Law School, and was offered articleship with the Ministry of the Attorney General in Ontario.

Roop qualified in Canada as a barrister and solicitor in 1977, and, as the saying goes, hung out his shingle at a historic building where the prestigious law firm of Sharma and Sharma still stands today. The building itself once housed a major branch for the Canadian Bank of Commerce at a time when the area of east Toronto was being developed. Over one hundred years old, it is an historic building, and Roop's law firm has preserved its original architecture, down to an ancient bank vault, which can still be seen inside the building.

Although he was busy going back to law school and raising a family, Roop once again found the time to serve his community.

Immediately on arrival in Toronto, as a newcomer, he discovered there was a great need for Hindus in the city to unite under one roof, and he went on to form the Canada Hindu Organization, Inc., the country's first incorporated Hindu group, which began, humbly, in the auditorium of a school. Eventually, the organization grew to the point where it bought its own building, now known as the Gayatri Mandir. Roop still remains the president of the group.

He then went on to form the Canada Hindu Parishad (Council of Hindu Priests), which remains the only one of its kind in Canada. Roop still serves as the chairman of the Parishad.

His religious contributions did not keep Roop from creating other types of history in Canada. In the early 1990s, while representing a Guyanese client in a criminal matter, he found himself stymied by the Canadian Immigration, which refused visas to defense witnesses to come to Canada to give evidence.

He petitioned the Canadian High Court and obtained an order for the federal government to send a prosecutor to Guyana, and a Guyanese court was convened under the jurisdiction of a Guyanese judge to take evidence from those witnesses which was then presented at the trial in Canada. It was a legal precedent, as no foreign court had ever been set up in such a way to receive evidence in a Canadian matter.

Roop also made a name for himself in immigration law, winning success after success—some of them unprecedented—in that area of practice.

One such case involved a Nigerian visitor to Toronto who was detained on arrival after being granted a visitor's visa in Nigeria by the federal government. The client spent a month in detention, and Roop won his release after arguing that his stay at the detention center was an "imprisonment imposed by officials of the same ministry which had granted him a visa to enter Canada."

He then repeated the feat for a client from Bangladesh, and since then he has won similar precedent-setting cases for clients from India, Africa, Fiji, and several Caribbean nations. Roop's success at blazing legal trails in Canada, as well as the reputation he left in Guyana, won him notice at the highest levels.

In 1992, shortly after the elections in Guyana, Roop was invited by the country's new president, Dr. Cheddi Jagan, to serve Guyana as a judge in the country's High Court. After thinking long and hard about the offer, Roop had to weigh once again the welfare of his family over the opportunity of self-advancement, and opted to remain in his practice in

Canada. The offer was repeated in 1997 and turned down yet again for the same reason. The decision served him well.

Roop has done Guyanese proud in the many positions of leadership and honor he has, both as a legal eagle and servant of the community. He was appointed by the attorney general of Ontario as member, and acted as chairman of the Police Complaints Commission for three years. He is founding member and legal advisor, the Caribbean Children Foundation, and counsel, Agincourt Legal Community Center.

He is the recipient of numerous awards, including Certificate of Appreciation, Ministry of Citizenship and Culture for Volunteerism in the Community; Adyatam Sadhak Award, New Delhi, for selfless contribution in propagating Hindu religion and culture overseas; Dharm Ratna, presented by the Canada Hindu Organization; Dharm Bhushan, presented by the Guyana Pandits Council. He is the "anointed, dean of Caribbean lawyers in Canada" by the Canadian media.

In 2001, Roop and Dhani stood proudly in the Convocation Hall in Toronto as their son Ishwar was called to the Ontario Bar. Ishwar was not the first family member to follow in Roop's footsteps, as his only brother Chetram Sharma is also a lawyer, as are Roop's nephew and nieces, all of whom cite Roop as their inspiration.

Ishwar's becoming a lawyer, however, was the moment Roop had worked so hard for all of his life. Now he could pass the torch and a life's work, not to mention a valuable inheritance—a name and reputation that has stood proudly for more than four decades in law, and which has been enshrined in the history books of two countries.

September 15, 2010

Dr. Shakir Sheikh, MD

Psychiatrist, Physician, Pharmacist
Muslim Teacher and Poet

Dr. Shakir Sheikh was awarded the certificate of accomplishment for his original paper on antibiotics from the Biological Society, Royal College, Ireland, in 1966.

He was recipient of these awards: the Correctional Service Canada Interfaith Committee Appreciation Award 2000; Ottawa Muslim Association, President Award 2000; Guyana Caribbean Muslim Association, President Award 2004; Equity and Diversity Committee Award, 2001, by the mayor of Ottawa; International Conference of Islamic Scholars, Certificate for Participation in Global Justice and Peace, Jakarta, Indonesia.

He performed Hajj -Pilgrimage twice. On his second Hajj, Dr. Sheikh was guest of the Saudi government.

Shakir Ullah Husain Sheikh was born on May 4, 1930, at Adelphi, Canje, Berbice, British Guiana. His father, John Sheikh, was a pharmacist, religious scholar, and imam. He was a news correspondent for the *Daily Argosy,* a national newspaper in British Guiana. His mother was a housewife and businesswoman, loving and caring. Shakir is the eldest of five children, three sons and two daughters. Both parents and two daughters have passed away. May their souls rest in peace.

Dr. Sheikh attended Canje Rosehall Anglican School, where prayers were said in the morning and midday. He also attended Rosignol Government School, where he was an ardent cricketer. Upon passing his Primary School Leaving Certificate, he attended Berbice High School, in New Amsterdam, where he obtained his Cambridge School Certificate.

He taught Latin and English at the Berbice Educational Institute, New Amsterdam, then studied pharmacy and qualified in 1955. Shortly after, he went to England, to pursue higher studies, accompanied by his family.

In London, Shakir worked as a pharmacist at St. Giles Hospital, Camberwell, and at Lewisham Hospital. He then entered medical school in Dublin, Ireland, in 1962. He qualified in 1968 from the Royal College of Physician and Surgeons, Dublin, as a medical doctor.

Shortly after qualifying, Dr. Sheikh left for Canada to do his internship at Civic Hospital in Ottawa. Here he did his postgraduate diploma in psychiatry at the University Hospitals. He did subspecialty in mental retardation at the Rideau Regional Center, affiliated with Queen's and Ottawa University. During his tenure there he was chairman of the medical staff. He is now a retired psychiatrist, physician, and pharmacist.

Dr. Sheikh's religious activities started from an early age. At age five, he gave Azan, or "Call to Prayer" at the mosque built by his great-grand mother at Adelphi, Canje, Berbice, Islamic teachings and behavior were enshrined at this early age by his parents and home environment. While in med school, he periodically led prayers and gave the Friday sermon.

In 1968 when Dr. Sheikh came to Canada, he became a member of the Ottawa Muslim Association (OMA). From that time onward he held many different positions in the OMA, as follows: He was member of its board of directors; trustee; vice president; president; first chairman of the OMA's Think Tank, under the auspices of the late Imam Dr. Taufiq Shamin, Al Azhar University, Cairo; chairman of the Education Committee; and principal and teacher of the OMA School for ten years.

He worked as a Muslim leader in the wider community also. He was president of the Guyana Caribbean Muslim Association, in Ottawa for two years. In 1974 he became a registered Muslim officer with the Ontario government, enabling him to perform civil marriages. In the past ten years he has been participating in Parliamentary Breakfast Seminars held in the Federal Parliament Ottawa, and presented a paper on "Unity in Diversity."

On other occasions he read his poems. He has been a volunteer Muslim chaplin consultant at Correctional Services, Canada, and a member of the Inter-Faith Committee for Muslim Inmates in Canada Prisons.

Dr. Sheikh has traveled widely in Europe, Africa, the Middle East, Asia, and the Far East.

His outstanding contribution towards the betterment of the larger community of Ontario, where he has made his home has been duly recognized at the highest levels, and he has received many commendations.

Dr. Sheikh received a letter in 2003 from the Department of Foreign Affairs and International Trade, Secretary of State (Asia-Pacific) Ottawa, Canada. The Honorable David Kilgour, PC, MP, wrote: "Dear Shakir, A little note to say how very thankful the organizers were for your great work on the Diversity and Islam Conference. It would have not been as great a success without your help and support and that of everybody that was part of it."

The premier of Ontario, Dalton McGuinty, honored Dr. Sheikh on his eightieth birthday with a formal printed citation, which read:

> On behalf of the government of Ontario, I am delighted to extend warm congratulations to Dr. Shakir Sheikh on the occasion of his eightieth birthday, May 7, 2010. Dr. Sheikh, I am very pleased to join in the tributes being paid to you as you mark this special milestone.
>
> Today is an ideal opportunity to recognize your countless contributions to your community, and to the province you are proud to call your home, including your achievements as a psychiatrist, pharmacist, imam, Muslim marriage officer, and conflict resolution mediator, and educator. Your hard work, professionalism, and community spirit have done much to benefit our society.
>
> And this is also a date on which those you hold most dear are given the chance to express their affection for you and to let you know how much they admire, respect and care for you.
>
> As you take time to reflect on eight decades of living life fully and joyfully, please accept my best wishes for a most

enjoyable day. May you continue to enjoy, a rich measure of life's blessings.

Shakir has also acquired a reputation as a poet in recent years. His poems have been published in books, magazines, newsletters, and on the Internet. He reads his poems at public, private, and social events, in Canada and internationally. The bard, Dr. Sheikh published this poem in May 2009:-

King and the Beggar

King poised in his palace, drinking wine from his chalice.
Beggar in his mud hut, thinking to escape his shut.

Beggar came to palace gate, singing the mighty king's fate.
Be kind to the people, before you become inevitably feeble.

King and beggar both die, in mausoleum king does lie.
No more petroleum to sell, abandoning wealth as he fell.

Beggar in muddy grave lies, king and beggar sever ties.
No more sighs or moans, no more loans or groans.

This is the end of all life, be it in contentment or strife.
The event has taken place, no more competitive human race

What drives him in his professional career and in his work in the community? What has been his inspiration? Dr. Sheikh has no doubts, saying, "Quest for psychic and spiritual knowledge to understand self-expression and service to humanity by academic achievement. My father instilled in my early ethics the following: 'He who aims at the sky hits the tallest tree. He who aims at the tallest tree will fall to the ground.' This drove me to higher studies and success."

Of his most memorable experiences in his life, Dr. Sheikh lists the following: "At primary school, my headmaster, Mr. J. A. Henry, challenged me while I was playing inter-school cricket. He said he would give me one shilling if I hit a four. I did." Other highlights in his life were visiting the Taj Mahal, Pyramids, Leaning Tower of Pisa, sailing down the Bosphorous under the bridge joining two continents, visiting Hiroshima ground zero, where the atom bomb was dropped, the African safari, and Cape Horn, where two great oceans, Atlantic and Pacific, meet.

An act of mercy that he is pleased to remember was when he gave timely advice to a captain at sea. A man at the steering wheel was bleeding from the temporal artery. The captain heeded the advice and immediately rushed the man to Georgetown hospital with the pilot tugboat.

October 7, 2010

Joy Simon, BA

Educator, Community Leader, Youth Worker

Joy Simon was winner of Guyana Awards (Canada) 2009 Community Service (Individual) Award. The citation of the award contains the following information, in part:

> Joy Simon believes in giving back to her community and has been doing so for over twenty years, promoting educational, spiritual, and cultural growth in the many communities in which she has worked. She is a former elementary schoolteacher, child and youth advocate, and counselor.
>
> Mrs. Simon is president of the Guyanese Canadian Community Center; vice president of the Alliance of Guyanese Canadian Organizations (AGCO); executive board member of the Guyana Ex-Police Association of Canada; chapter president of the Scarborough North Spelling Bee of Canada; and vice president and fund-raising director of Malvern Onyx Lions Club.

A York University psychology graduate, she is a member of the Toronto District School Board Safe Schools Work Group, which deals with issues such as confrontational and cyber-bullying, cultural competence, reviewing alternatives to suspension, denial of access (procedure and clarification), and more.

For the past five years Mrs. Simon has been facilitating the Saturday Mentoring Program for AGCO, along with a team of qualified teachers, educators, and volunteers. This program provides additional educational assistance to youth ages five to eighteen.

Joy Simon is a life member on the board of the Catholic Children's Aid Society, where she does volunteer work with child abuse agencies in and around the GTA, counseling abused women, mentoring young teenage mothers in areas such as crisis intervention, single families in crisis, and at-risk youths. She conducts workshops in parenting skills, anger management, job skills, and personal grooming.

A grassroots community leader with a passion for guiding and nurturing young people to reach their full potential, Joy Simon is the founder/owner of Bourda Green Nutrition and the proud mother of three children.

Sources:
Websites accessed May 27, 2010, on Guyana Consulate Toronto, Guyana Awards (Canada)

May 27, 2010

Chet Singh

Human Rights Activist, Dub Poet.

    Chet Singh is a human rights activist, college professor, and dub poet. His work as an artist and educator was influenced by his formative years in the Caribbean, where he was struck by the deeply entrenched racial, gender, and class hierarchies of these societies. The anti-colonial/liberation movements of the 1970s, along with cultural developments such as reggae deeply influenced his worldview.

    Dub poetry, a form of performance poetry over reggae rhythms, is mostly concerned with politics and social justice. After Jamaica, Toronto is said to have the second highest concentration of dub poets, followed by England. Chet is one of the early pioneers of dub poetry in Canada. Chet is also a founding member of Canada's Dub Poets Collective and has served as the organization's creative director. The collective is regarded as a major contributor to the development of Caribbean culture and arts in Canada, hosting a number of international festivals and conferences since its inception. Chet was artistic director for the International Dub Poetry Festival 2010.

    Chet's parents are Guyanese—accountant Samuel Singh and Thansari Singh—though he was raised primarily by his stepmother, the late Farida (nee McDoom). He was born in Jamaica, and because of his father's job, he was raised in a number of countries, including Guyana, Barbados, St. Kitts, St. Lucia, Grenada, Fiji, and Canada.

As a student activist in the 1980s Chet organized public education events as well as directed political action on international and local issues. He fronted the reggae/Latin/punk fusion band One Mind. Noted for its uncompromising stand against racism, sexism, and international oppression, the band was popular with university students and activists. His undergraduate thesis on the state's response to racist assaults in Peterborough was awarded the Symons's Award for Canadian Studies.

Chet has worked at all levels of the educational system, within government and community organizations, developing and implementing human rights policies and educational programs aimed at transforming Eurocentric/patriarchal/heterosexist educational ideologies and organizational structures.

As a community development worker he founded the youth group MYA (Malton Youth Alliance) to pressure a Toronto area school board to develop and implement a human rights policy, and stop the practice of streaming black youth into dead-end academic programs. Working inside the system, he developed innovative anti-discriminatory educational programs under the guidance of renowned anti-racist theorist and educator Enid Lee. He organized dozens of student and teacher equity conferences using the arts (theater, dub poetry, music, film, and video) to challenge the public school system to be more inclusive of the communities they served. He brought many emerging artists as well as established artists, social activists, community leaders, and academics into the school system to perform and work with teachers and students. An important aspect of this work was bringing together artists, activists, and educators to develop curriculum that addressed many of the contemporary issues associated with Canadian society.

As senior advisor at York University's Center for Race and Ethic Relations, he played a pivotal role developing access programs and curriculum transformation initiatives along with a broad coalition of human rights groups. His work in this area led to a number of provincial government appointments, including advisor on post-secondary human rights policy implementation with the Ministry of Colleges and Universities, human rights advisor to the Toronto Arts Council, and board member of the Ontario Arts Council.

He is one of the contributing editors to the college textbook *Global Citizenship: From Social Analysis to Social Action* (2009). He has also written articles and manuals on education equity. Chet continues to present papers and workshops at national and international conferences, addressing issues of human rights and equity in the educational system.

Over the years he has been nominated for a number of awards including the Hubbard Award for his work on human rights; the Governor General's Gold Medal Award for his graduate thesis, "Human Rights Organizational Change"; Centennial College's President's Award for Excellence for his work on education equity; and the Wicken's Award for Teaching Excellence.

After a sixteen-year hiatus, he was coaxed into the recording studios by Greg Roy of the Dub Trinity Band. Their 2004 release received critical acclaim in international reggae magazines and topped the reggae charts at several campus radio stations. These creative endeavors also coalesced with his cofounding of the Peterborough Anti-Racist/Anti-Oppression collective, where local academics, teachers, administrators, citizens, and grassroots community organizations worked collaboratively to address local issues related to human rights and the environment.

At the 2007 International Dub Festival, he launched the hip-hop-influenced Darkness of Daylight, a collaborative effort with electro acoustic musician, Jarret Prescott; hip hop producers, the Workhouse Boyz; and Dub Trinity. Also making an appearance on this album was Canadian cultural icon Lillian Allen and multi-award winning jazz artist Nick "Brownman" Ali. In 2010 he released the neo-dub electronic influenced *Recessionary Revolutionaries* backed by Jarret Prescott, and LAL's Nicholas Murray and Rosina Kazi.

His recordings include *Unity Music Revolution*, One Mind, 1983; *One People, One Planet, One Mind,* One Mind, 1984; *Dub Trinity and Chet Singh,* 2004; *Darkness of Daylight*, 2007; and *Recessionary Revolutionaries*, 2010.

Chet has performed in numerous events over the years at various venues, including:
- Re-Frame International Film Festival, Peterborough. 2010
- Trans Canada Institute Performance Poetry Colloquium, Guelph University. 2009.
- Aboriginal Day Celebrations, Saugeen First Nations Reservation, Sauble Beach. 2008.

- Canadian Association for the Prevention of Harassment and Discrimination in Higher Education Conference, Ottawa. 2008
- Beyond the Margins, Ontario College of Art and Design. 2008
- In Resistance to War. The Gordon Best Theater. 2007.
- Peace and Justice Fair. Sanford Fleming College, Sept. 21, 2006.
- The Peterborough Folk Festival. Turtle Island Park, 2005.
- In support of the seven-year squatters and OPIRG. Ottawa, 2004.
- Irie Music Festival. Nathan Philips Square, Toronto, 2004
- Benefit for Independent Media. Babylon Night Club, Ottawa, 2004
- Benefit for Greenpeace. Toronto, 2003.
- Mayworks Festival of Working People and the Arts, 2003
- Symposium on Accessible Education in Canada. Guelph University, 2003.

October 11, 2010

Chetram Singh

FIHM (Fellow Institute of Health-care Management, UK)
CHE (Member of the Canadian College of
Health Service Executives)
Hospital Administrator

Chetram Singh, a formidable name in hospital administration, has added prestige to the job. From junior clerk at Georgetown Public Hospital, he won a British Government Scholarship to study hospital administration in London. He passed his finals with distinction in every subject and topped the entire British Isles.

In Guyana he managed all five hospitals in the county of Berbice. He assisted in the restructure of Guyana's health care system. In Canada, he worked as senior hospital administration consultant with the Ontario Ministry of Health.

As secretary of the Mahatma Gandhi Organization in Georgetown, Guyana, with Dr. Balwant Singh as president, they built the current Gandhi Bhawan in Thomas Lands. A leader of the Hindu community in London, Ontario, he spearheaded the building of a mandir and cultural center.

Chetram Singh was born on June 21, 1930, at Ogle Sugar Estate, seven miles from Georgetown, British Guiana. Ogle was then a grinding estate; it had a sugar factory.

His father was Dallu Singh; his mother was Budhnie Singh. They were married in 1929, when Dallu was age eighteen and Budhnie, from Triumph Village on the East Coast of Demerara, was seventeen. Dallu started work at age seventeen as a junior clerk at Ogle Estate.

Chetram's paternal grandfather was Raghunandan Singh. He was a head driver of Ogle Sugar Estate. He came to British Guiana from India at age ten, with his parents Jhundoo Singh and Bitania.

Chetram's great-grandfather Jhundoo Singh was thirty-five and his great-grandmother Bitania was twenty-five when they arrived in British Guiana on the Foyle on November 25, 1887. They were accompanied by three sons: Raghunandan, ten years old; Rutton, seven years old; and Rewti, six months old. They came from the province of Uttar Pradesh, in northern India, from the district of Khiri, also known as Lakhimpur, in the town of Nighasan, and from the village of Barontha, respectively. These are located near the border with Nepal.

Chetram is the eldest of nine siblings, six boys and three girls. His father did not have the benefit of a secondary education and swore that his children would not suffer from the same fate. Although they could not afford to give their children a university education, three first sons were able to get their university degrees through scholarships.

Chetram and his second brother, Dr. Sobharam Singh, a geologist, won British Government Scholarships. Third brother, Dr. Yudistir Singh, agriculturalist, won a Bookers Scholarship.

Brother Dr. Durjodhan Raj Singh is a very successful dental surgeon in Toronto, and brother Dr. Rudra Dallu Singh is a very respected chiropractor in Toronto. Their eldest sister, Jasmine Singh, now retired, was a cosmetologist in London, England, where she still lives. Their second sister still lives in Guyana, and the last one, Leila Daljit, is a real estate professional in Oakville, Ontario.

Chetram attended the Ogle Canadian Presbyterian School and later Modern Academy, a small high school in Georgetown. He rode a pushbike for the fourteen miles round trip from Ogle to Georgetown. At Modern Academy, the principal was initially Mr. Sugrim Singh, his uncle, who later sold and left for England to study law.

In 1945 Chetram passed the Cambridge Junior Examination and in 1946 the Cambridge Senior Examination. He started on his first job, in 1946, teaching the pre-junior form of sixty-seven students at Modern Academy. He found this very difficult especially because he was required to teach seven subjects.

In 1948, he found another job as junior clerk at the Public Hospital Georgetown. He took this job pending a job in the public service, but he never got in. In those days, jobs were scarce and for jobs in the civil service, there was discrimination against sections of the population. In 1951 he completed the London Matriculation of the University of London, by private study. In 1953, he was married, and in 1954 Chetram won a scholarship to study abroad.

The scholarship was granted by the British Government under the Commonwealth Development and Welfare Scheme, and this one was for the study of hospital administration. Chetram won the scholarship against stiff competition. He and 230 other qualified Guyanese candidates applied in 1954 for that scholarship. In May 1954, he received a formal letter notifying him that he was awarded a four-year British Government Scholarship to study hospital administration in Britain and that he must be prepared to leave for England by September 1954 to take his place at the college. The whole family was overjoyed, and there were celebrations with thanksgiving prayers.

Chetram studied at the City of London College, London, from 1954 to1957. He completed the four-year scholarship program in three years, with honors. At the final examination he got a distinction in every subject and placed first in the entire British Isles. For this he was awarded the coveted Edward and Adelaide Hardinge Medal by the institute for being the most outstanding final year student in 1957. He was told he was the only overseas student to have accomplished this as at 1957.

On his return to Guyana on October 7, 1957, he embarked on his career in hospital administration. He was appointed assistant hospital administrator, Georgetown Hospital, and in 1960 he was promoted to hospital administrator of all of the hospitals in the county of Berbice, Guyana. These included the New Amsterdam Hospital, the Mental Hospital, Port Mourant, and Skeldon Hospitals. The hospitals had 250, 750, 40, and 60 beds, respectively, a total of over a thousand beds. He served in this capacity until 1966.

Chetram resigned from the government service in 1970 and took a job as administrator with ALCAN to manage their hospital and hotel in the mining town of Mackenzie. After the company was nationalized in 1974, he emigrated with his family to Canada.

In 1974, Chetram secured an appointment as senior consultant in hospital administration, with responsibility for funding, monitoring, and advising the forty-two public hospitals in southwestern Ontario. In 1980 he was chief operating Officer of the St. Joseph's Health Center, located in London, Ontario. This is a teaching hospital for doctors and other health professionals. He left that post in 1990 and formed his own consulting company, Chet Singh & Associates, and served as consultant to three Catholic hospitals in Ontario.

In the periods 1993 to 1996 and 1999 to 2000 he was recruited by the Inter-American Development Bank to assist the government of Guyana restructure its health care system. From 1993 to 1996 he supervised the construction of the new $32 million Ambulatory Care, Diagnostic and Surgical Center at the Georgetown Public Hospital and from 1999 he has participated in the preparation of a strategic plan titled Vision 2000 for Heath Care in Guyana. In 2000 he participated in the development of plans for new Georgetown, New Amsterdam and Bartica Hospitals and a new obstetrical suite at the Suddie Hospital.

Aside from his career of achievements, he was very active in community work and in Hindu religious and cultural activities.

In 1958 he was elected secretary of the Mahatma Gandhi Organization in Georgetown, while Dr. Balwant Singh was the president. They converted the land into a cricket ground and raised funds to build the current Gandhi Bhawan in Thomas Land. In 1960 when he served as hospital administrator in the county of Berbice, he was elected chairman of the Berbice Regional Committee of the Guyana Sanatan Dharma Maha Sabha and invested considerable time and effort in organizing the Hindu community of that county.

While in Berbice County, among his initiatives to contribute to inter-religious harmony, he promoted joint appeals with the Muslim leaders to the government for Hindus and Muslims to be given national holidays, as Christians had. From 1960 to 1966 he organized programs for visiting swamis and Indian Playback Singers Manna Dey, Rafi, Mukesh, and Hemant Kumar to the county of Berbice. In 1964–65 he served as secretary of the Berbice Cricket Board of Control and as a Berbice Cricket Selector. In 1970 he served as chairman of the Guyana Personnel Officer's Association.

On May 7, 1966 Chetram was presented with the Ashok Chakra Gold Medal by Mr. Harding, the United Nations representative in Guyana, on behalf of the Berbice Bharati Sewah Sangha, for his "selfless voluntary service for our people, you have been selected as the most outstanding social, cultural and humanitarian worker in the county of Berbice for the years, 1964 to1966."

In Canada in 1975 he chaired the Provincial Laboratory Committee of the Ontario Ministry of Health for five years. In 1988 while working as chief operating officer of St. Joseph's Hospital in London, Ontario, he was elected president of the Hindu Cultural Center of London, Ontario. He was able to weld the small Hindu community into a cohesive group and within three years they were able to build a mandir and cultural center that can accommodate four hundred people. At its opening, it was fully paid for.

Chetram was elected chairman of the Finance Advisory Committee of the Ontario Hospital Association in 1999. His committee, working in collaboration with the Ontario Ministry of Health, designed a system for equitably funding hospitals in Ontario, based on diagnosis-related groups.

He has contributed much to achieve significant improvements in his field of work, in the Caribbean and in Canada. In 1974 he presented a paper at the Caribbean Medical Congress held in Jamaica on the role of hospital administration in the health care industry.

In Canada, in 1975, at the request of the Ministry of Health of Ontario, he conducted a study of the occupants of the psychiatric hospitals in Ontario. He designed a system for the medical superintendent and nursing director of each psychiatric hospital to evaluate each patient using a form which he designed. The forms were returned to him, and when he collated the information, he was able to demonstrate to the Ministry that for a large proportion of the patients there were community residential facilities, better suited to their needs.

The Ministry next asked him, in the same year to review the provincial laboratories in the province to determine whether they could be better utilized. He demonstrated to the Ministry that the volume of laboratory work that the province of Ontario generated could be adequately performed by fewer laboratories with the use of couriers to move specimens from one area to another. The Cabinet approved and implemented his recommendations which resulted in savings of millions per year.

In 1976, he prepared a correspondence course in hospital administration for administrators of small hospitals in Ontario who did not complete the master's program but needed academic help. It was very well received. In 1999 he published a paper on case mix groupings, a system to fund public hospitals in Ontario on the basis of the complexities of the patients they treated, instead of just the days they spent in hospitals. This has contributed to more equitably funding hospitals in Ontario by the government.

Why does he feel so passionate about hospital administration? It is a job which he has found rewarding beyond measure. Chetram has said:

> The field that I am in provides ample opportunity for me to help people in need. When a person arrives at a hospital, he is not usually in his best frame of mind, either because he is sick or he has a relative or friend who is sick. The average person is very fearful of the hospital. To be able to help people allay any fears and to put their minds at ease is extremely satisfying to me.
>
> At age seventeen, I wanted to do dentistry so I applied to Howard University in Washington and was admitted to their dental school. I soon discovered that my parents could not afford the fees. So I took a job at the Georgetown Hospital as a clerk where I had numerous opportunities to help sick people, especially those from the area where I lived. I was enjoying it very much and so when the government advertised the scholarship in hospital administration, I applied for it. I was told that there were over two hundred applicants for this scholarship, but in the end I got it.
>
> When I look back and think of the improvements that I have been able to make for the benefit of the patients at the mental and leprosy hospitals in Guyana, I tell myself that my job provides me with the opportunity to practice Karma yoga (work with no expectation of reward) and I truly enjoy this. What better way to serve God than to help those who cannot help themselves?
>
> I draw my inspiration from helping people in need. My planning and organizational skills help me to make meaningful contributions to voluntary and charitable organizations that I serve in. I am a people person and enjoy the company of people.

Chetram feels particularly blessed with a wonderful family.

In 1953 I married Hemrajie Singh, daughter of Patraj Singh a well-known businessman of Georgetown. I was working as a clerk at the Georgetown Hospital. I was twenty-three years of age at the time, and she was seventeen. She bore me six sons. One passed away in Berbice.

Our eldest son Rabindra works in the information technology field. He is married to the former Roma Mungol who is a lawyer in Canada. Our second, Narendra, and his wife, Shirley, are both pediatricians in Toronto. Our third son, Mahendra, completed his MBA and MHA and is operating walk-in medical clinics in Toronto. His wife, Lalita, is a hospital pharmacist. Our fourth son, Mukesh, is in information technology. He lives in New Jersey and works with IBM. Ramendra, our last son, is a doctor who lives and works in Trinidad, in emergency medicine, at the St. Augustine Private Hospital. His wife, Neesha, is in human resources development.

I have always believed in a good education followed by observance of the teachings of our Hindu Scriptures. As the eldest member of the family alive today, I am very proud of the accomplishments of my brothers, sisters, and my sons. I gauge success not by how rich a person is, but by how educated he is (and this does not mean only book learning), his way of life and humility.

September 9, 2010

Cyril Patraj Singh

Entrepreneur Businessman
Politician, Community Leader,
TV and Radio Broadcaster

Cyril Patraj Singh was an entrepreneur all his life. Energetic and extroverted, he was, in his early years, a familiar figure in Georgetown in business, in Hindu religious affairs, and in politics. In Canada he was a household name as a TV and radio broadcaster.

For his untiring work for the community, he was honored at the annual Indo-Caribbean Music, Culture and Community Award gala for 2008. Given for selfless service and the appreciation of the community, a plaque was presented to Cyril at the function, which was held in Toronto on January 24, 2009.

The *Indo-Caribbean Times* of February 2009 featured a report on the generally popular event. The report stated, in part:

> Within the Indo-Caribbean communities of three countries, Guyana, Canada, and the United States, Cyril Patraj Singh was a renowned entrepreneur who had served his country and

community, both politically and in the sphere of religious work. Cyril migrated to the United States and in 1973 to Canada. In those early years, there were few Caribbean ethnic activities, and Cyril set to work on the task of bringing together small groups of people from Guyana and Trinidad in order to have religious services in Hindu homes, including his own. With the growth of the Hindu community, he formed the Canadian Vedic Sabha and sought to obtain permission from the city of Scarborough to hold religious functions and activities.

[At the time] current Hindi movies were played in schools and community centers. There were Diwali and Holi celebrations, fashion shows, Diwali Beauty Contests and Melas among the events that were organized by Cyril Patraj Singh. In a bid to make the new home country comfortable for the immigrants from the Caribbean, Cyril's vision included means by which Hindus could worship and practice within a nurturing environment. He was instrumental in sponsoring priests for emigration to Canada and engaging the services of musicians from Guyana and Trinidad.

In 1977, Cyril collaborated with Dr. Budhendra Doobay and Harry Panday to found the Voice of the Vedas Society. This organization was responsible for the first Hindu television program on which Cyril was host and Dr. Doobay the officiating priest. That organization evolved into what we know today as the Vishnu Mandir.

A stalwart in the promotion of Hindu Dharma, Cyril Patraj Singh was the founder of the "Voice of Dharma," Again, the initiator of a television production, the organization also started a group known as Ramayan Gole. Until recently, they have performed at many religious events and temples.

Through the medium of radio, Cyril promoted Hindu Dharma. One of the best known of these programs was *Indian Memory Album* on CHIN Radio and was aired on various radio stations for twenty-five years. During this time, he also produced the

Indian Memory Album magazine and the *MegaCity Gazette* both promoting Hindu culture and tradition.

Sadly, Cyril Patraj Singh passed away on the morning of February 25, 2009. On Saturday, March 13, 2009, the 13th Day Shraad rituals were held in his home where he lived in Scarborough, Ontario.

Rampersaud (Ram) Tiwari, a well-known and highly respected retired senior Guyana public (civil) servant was a very good friend of Cyril's from their early years. He orated his own reflections of Cyril, the man he knew. In his eulogy, he said, in part:

> During the many years of our acquaintance and friendship, I knew that Cyril Patraj Singh was a strong voice for democracy, the rule of law, reform, and refinement in all that he did in his various activities in culture and media in respect of Hinduism and Hindu rituals and festivals, the performing arts, the cinema, the media, commerce, and politics.
>
> Although Cyril did not have the benefit of formal higher education at the secondary or tertiary levels, this was no handicap as he pursued his interests in commerce, the cinema, and in religion and culture with informed intelligence, dignity, and decorum. These interests were inculcated in him by his father who was a leading personality in the Guyanese mercantile/business community.
>
> Cyril was an avid reader on all aspects of the philosophy, history, and culture of Hinduism and a regular researcher on matters relating to the rituals and the oral traditions and customs of Hindus. He also kept himself informed on all aspects of local, regional, and international affairs in politics, government, and governance and diplomacy. These defined him as the intelligent, liberal, sensible, and sensitive person he was ever since he was young and adventurous in his homeland in the 1940s, the 1950s, and the 1960s and cautious and careful person he was in later years both in Guyana and in Canada.
>
> In Guyana, following in the footsteps of his late respected father, Patraj Singh, he emerged as a leading member of the

Guyana Sanatan Dharma Maha Sabha; and through the Sabha, he was able to relate and interact with members of the Guyana Pandits Council and with pandits who were not members of the council.

Cyril initiated a number of changes when he served as general secretary of the Sabha during the presidency of Dharma Acharya Pandit Ramsahoye Doobay, of revered memory. Cyril was probably the youngest general secretary of the Maha Sabha at the time. He made his contribution to effecting significant changes in, and elevation of the two Hindu festivals of Holi and Diwali to the status of national celebratory events in Guyana in 1966. His many messages on behalf of the Maha Sabha were relayed by voice on the airwaves and in print in the local media to almost every community in Guyana, and visual expressions of his work were seen in the Diwali Melas and beauty contests that he had organized from time to time.

Cyril received much committed support for his mission and his efforts from his family and friends and from two successful businesses, in which he was a principal player: the two Patraj Singh Cinemas, the Strand Cinema (formally named Olympic Cinema) on Lombard Street in Georgetown, and the Gemini Cinema on the public road in the village of Mahaicony on the east coast of Demerara, and in the Patraj Singh family commercial enterprises in Georgetown.

Cyril also owned and operated three other cinemas: the Realto Cinema on Vlissingen Road, Georgetown; Starlite Cinema in Vreed en Hoop, on the West Bank; and the Lotus Cinema in Whim, Corentyne, Berbice.

Cyril's public ventures in Guyana also included work in politics. His intense nationalist feelings for orderly liberal changes in political affairs led him to help in forming the United Force (UF), a political party, with the late Peter d'Aguiar and crafting the political ideology, mission and programs of the party and to enable it to contest in the August 1961 general election in the country. He was selected for nomination as the UF candidate in Electoral District Number 11, Mahaica on the East Coast of Demerara.

Cyril Patraj Singh contested in the 1961 general election as Cyril Puran Singh, the name he was given at birth. I was privileged to hear what Cyril had to say, both informally as a friend and functionally as a public servant when I was assigned to promote the 1961 "How to Vote" campaign in film and print. This required me, in part, to attend campaign meetings of candidates and assess voter reaction. I was at the time an administrative cadet (ADC) on secondment to the Government Information Services (GIS), an autonomous department of the chief secretary's office. Without any feelings of fear, favor, bias, or influence, I am pleased even now, to say that I was impressed, and I remain impressed with many of Cyril's expressions of strong feelings for social justice, human development, and freedom in Guyana. Cyril was defeated at the election but his messages for forward-looking social changes in government and governance were not lost to many who attended his campaign meetings.

Cyril Patraj Singh was a modest man, a distinguished Guyanese, and a dynamic individual whose work in culture and media instilled in people a sense of belonging and to say to them that Guyanese and Caribbean Hindu cultural values were as good as those of any other culture in the world. He has always appealed to Guyanese Hindus not to lose their collective sense of identity and, through their common historical experiences with other groups, strive to promote communal harmony, national unity, regional co-operation, and international friendship.

Cyril was a man of great principle and his contribution to Guyanese culture in his homeland and overseas is inestimable. The qualities of his generosity, graciousness and humane character should not be lost to the present and succeeding generations.

Born on November 25, 1929, he was blessed with a full and productive life of seventy-nine years of great achievement, as an enterprising entrepreneur businessman, community leader, outstanding media practitioner in television and radio and a good, warm-hearted human being.

Ram Tiwari concluded his tribute thus:

> Cyril Patraj Singh has completed his mission of legacy of service to his family, his faith, his community, Guyana, his country of domicile, and Canada, his country of residence. Memories of his good work and service will live with all who knew him. He was a good man who will be truly missed.

Sources:

Cyril's biography provided by his son Ken Singh to Shabnam Radio.
Indo-Caribbean Times of February 2009. Report titled "Thirteen receive Indo-Caribbean Music Culture and Community Awards."
Rampersaud Tiwari's reflections on the life of Cyril Patraj Singh, March 2009.

October 28, 2010

Ken Singh

BA (UG), BA (York), CITT, MCIT
Businessman, International Cargo Transportation

Ken (Kanhai) Singh is head of his own international cargo transportation company. He is president and owner of Atlas International Freight Forwarding Inc., Canadian Customs Brokers Inc., and other companies.

Atlas International's head office is in Toronto, Ontario, and branch agencies are in Calgary, Edmonton, Montreal, and Vancouver. The Atlas group of companies and affiliations have offices in the United States, United Kingdom, France, and Germany. It plans further expansion in several other countries.

Ken was presented with the 2005 Businessman of the Year Award, at a gala dinner reception on May 28, 2005, in the presence of His Excellency Mr. Rajnarine Singh, high commissioner for Guyana, and Jim Karygiannis, MP, Ottawa.

He has received numerous other awards and certificates of recognition for significant contributions to industry, trade and charitable organizations, including Service Award from Singapore: chairman 1996–2000; Service

Award from CICA; Service Award from CPPS Mission Projects, Tanzania; and Seal to the State of Florida.

Ken comes from Strangroen, East Coast Demerara, Guyana. He was an Easter baby, born in 1949. He attended De Hoop Canadian Mission School. There, he had two excellent teachers, of whom he still speaks today: Teacher Roy (Mr. James Singh) and Teacher Georgie (Mrs. Georgie Thomas), a strict disciplinarian.

He realized very early in his life the value of a good education. He helped his parents tending their cattle and attending to the garden plot while still at primary school, an experience in the real world which he valued, but he felt he would do better with higher education. He therefore persuaded his parents to send him to Tutorial High School in Georgetown, and subsequently to the University of Guyana. There, in 1976, he obtained a degree in sociology and psychology.

From his early years Ken had dreams of working in the travel industry. The opportunity came later. Before that, Ken secured a good position as the regional sales manager for Germany's Berger Paints in Guyana. He then moved to a job closer to his dream job, with British Airways, from where he received training in England. He worked with British Airways from 1972 to 1976, then moved to Canada.

In an interview for the *Life Illustrated* publication, featuring "Meet the Immigrant Ken Singh —a success story," Ken looks back at the early days in Canada as periods of "trials and tribulations." He soon discovered that in spite of the experience and training while working for British Airways, he could not find employment in the field. Like many newcomers, he discovered that the training through British Airways in England was of little help. Also, the fact that he was regional manager for Germany's Berger Paints in Guyana did not open doors for him. The article goes on to say:

> Eventually, Ken was hired by Border Brokers, now Livingston International Freight, where he worked for nine years and left while he was international development manager, before establishing Atlas International in 1986 from the basement in his home in Scarborough. Today, Atlas owns and occupies several very spacious offices and accommodating warehouses.

Ken realized upon arriving in Canada, that more education would certainly give him an advantage, that being more qualified than his colleagues would place him in a strategic position over his colleagues in securing a job. York University then was the next source of this education. There he earned two bachelor's degrees, one in 1979 in sociology and psychology; the other in 1981 in business administration.

He pursued further professional studies, which included a three-year program, and graduated from the Canadian Institute of Traffic and Transportation (CITT): cargo insurance in Scotland, claims and legal liability in New York, project management, negotiation techniques, sales & marketing management and many more training courses in Canada. In addition to the CITT, Ken is a member of the Chartered Institute of Transport (MCIT); the International Federation of Freight Forwarders Association, Switzerland (FIATA);Indo Canada Chamber of Commerce (Life Member); Cool Chain Logistics—Luxemburg; Aviation Logistics Network—Germany; and Cargo Partners Network Inc, a worldwide freight network association.

Ken says of the business, "Freight forwarding is a very competitive industry so the entrepreneur has to muster all the knowledge, skills, and technology and carefully synchronize them in order to be successful. … The international transportation industry is dominated by large multinational corporations. This puts a squeeze and tremendous pressure on independent companies to succeed internationally.'

To counter the dominance of the multinationals, Ken founded a world cargo association, Cargo Partners Network Inc. This association selects and appoints prominent independently owned freight companies in countries to serve as a global network and currently has seventy-five representative countries with membership in this association. Today, each of these independent companies can now claim presence in every major city around the globe.

Ken sees his company Atlas as a microcosm of the population of Canada, as there are employees from many of the groups of immigrants living in this country. Employees in Canada include people originating from various parts of the world, including Hong Kong, China, United Kingdom, India, Pakistan, Guyana, Bulgaria, Trinidad, South Africa, Sri Lanka, Mexico, Columbia, France, and the Netherlands.

He believes that business has an important social role to play. He says, "Business and owners of businesses … being a segment of the community, ought to work hand-in-hand with the community in times of need. Business people should offer their expertise to help community organizations grow."

On globalization, Ken said, "Globalization should focus on raising the standards of living around the world. People in every nation should have work and food. As production spreads to other countries, the standard of living in those countries will be raised."

Ken finds the time to actively assist his local community and many other social causes worldwide. The *Life Illustrated* magazine article continues: "He volunteers with the CPPS, a Catholic mission project that works on projects to provide health care and clean water in Africa. The Central American arm of World Vision; Bosnian Children Foundation; CODE, which is involved in education in Africa, and the Chinese Cultural Heritage Center are all beneficiaries of his efforts to contribute to the various communities."

He has contributed for over twenty years toward humanitarian and charitable relief to many countries: Guatemala, India, Bangladesh, Bosnia, Serbia, Guyana, Jamaica, El Salvador, Brazil, Tanzania, Uganda, Angola, Senegal, among others; books and education materials worldwide for twenty-six years for many organizations; the Samaritans Purse (Operations Christmas Child) since 1988; and recent flood relief efforts in Asia and South America.

Amid Ken's involvement in his business as well as the various communities and missions, his other business-related activities are endless. Ken served on the Advisory Board of Indo-Canada Chambers of Commerce. Presently, he serves on Faculty of Arts at York University.

Ken's other voluntary contributions include:
- William Osler Health Center Ambassador—current as of this writing
- 2008 Guyana Awards Judge
- Guest Speaker (Canada): From 1980, Livingston Consulting Group, Educational Seminar Series-Transportation, Sir Sanford Fleming College, International Transportation, George Brown College International Transportation
- Guest Speaker (globally) Venezuela, China, Australia, Austria, UAE, UK, USA, Singapore, Thailand, Spain, Brazil, Mexico, Germany, Finland
- Conducted lectures worldwide on transportation, security, customs and trade issues
- Advisory Board: Indo-Canada Chamber of Commerce (served two terms)

- Advisory Council: York University, Faculty of Arts Advisory (2002 present)
- Humber College Advisory Council, addressing the feasibility of implementing a degree program in international trade and logistics.

Reflecting on his experience in business, Ken says, "When I was a child my main goal was to have a phone and to wear a tie. I think I have achieved that goal. I always wanted to be the best in what I did. I enjoy this business tremendously. I have surpassed, by far, all the objectives I set for myself."

For him, his job is very much like a hobby. "I enjoy every moment when I am at work and equally reap the rewards. This business requires extensive travelling overseas to personally meet with my overseas colleagues and partners as well as clients. In addition, I have the flexibility to spend time with my wife."

Ken believes "immigrants contribute immensely to the growth of the Canadian economy by owning and operating small businesses: Our [small business] contribution is at its greatest right now. People who immigrate from overseas have a great desire to achieve and the propensity to produce. There is an eagerness and desire driving them to reach for better standards of living."

Ken credits his mother with bringing him up to be open-minded and tolerant of all, irrespective of race, religion, or creed. He is a Hindu, attended a Canadian Mission School, worshipped at Baptist, Catholic, and Presbyterian churches and to this day, he says, he "attends the Presbyterian Church at Christmas, Easter, and other special occasions." He believes in fostering good community relations.

Ken's immediate family is a big contributing part of his success in life. Ken, along with Jessie, his wife, and their four children, Darren, Justin, Shaun, and Stacey, continue to pool together their strengths to solidify the Atlas group of companies.

Jessie, an ex-senior banker who holds a BA degree as well as a professional freight forwarder certificate awarded by CIFFA, manages the operations in the group of the companies. Darren, their eldest son and a business graduate of York University, is actively involved in handling the Cool Chain Logistics at Atlas.

Justin's goal is to become a medical doctor and is currently enrolled in the Global Scholars Program of St. George's University School of Medicine and Northumbria University School of Applied Science, UK. Amidst his hectic schedule, Justin finds the time to monitor and assist with the IT and Web services of Atlas, CCB, and CPN. Shaun, a recent IBBA graduate from Schulich School of International Business, is exploring the marketing and international business opportunities at Atlas.

Stacey, his only daughter, apple of his eye, and his baby at heart is also a York business student. Stacey enjoys participating at Atlas on a part-time basis during her vacation breaks, but she clearly tells her dad that she is willing to take over her mom's job only for the travel benefits. Ken's hope is that one, if not all of his children will find the same joy and excitement in keeping Atlas alive for many years.

Ken strongly believes "I must do my duty here and now and not wait for sometime in the future, because the future may never come. Success is achieved through smart work, dedication, and commitment to a cause and to provide superior customer service. I like meeting people and of particular pleasure and benefit are my many international trips meeting people from all walks of life." For the past thirty years of his life, Ken has had the luxury to travel extensively, reaching all corners of the globe.

July 7, 2008

Onkar Singh

Onkar Singh

BSc (Agri), MA
Sitarist, Musician, Finance Consultant

Onkar Singh was an accomplished tabla player, sitarist performer, teacher of Indian classical music, and philanthropist. He founded the Shastriya Sangeet Group of Vishnu Mandir in Toronto. He was also a finance expert and was a senior officer in the Commercial Real Estate Lending Department of the Bank of Nova Scotia.

Onkar Romeash Chandra Singh was born on September 8, 1948. He is the son of Radhay Janki Singh and Jai Narain Singh of 65 Cross Street, Alexander Village, Guyana.

His mother, affectionately known as "Aunty Radhay," took a great deal of interest in the arts and instilled a strong value for Indian culture in all her children. The family home was a wonderful staging ground for her children's achievements in Indian music and dance. Onkar's eldest sister, Indra, has focused on promoting Indian culture through the work of the Guyana Hindu Dharmic Sabha. Sisters Geeta and Deviekha are accomplished performers and teachers of Indian classical dance. Sister Looma is a reputable singer of bhajans and kirtans, and sister Ronica is a skilled keyboard player.

Brother Vikram is an ace tabla player who won several competitions in Guyana. Onkar and Vickram were part of the Radio Demerara radio program called *Local Indian Performers*, a popular radio show that aired every Sunday on Radio Demerara. Onkar was the programming director and lead musician of the show. The brothers were also part of the Gemini Orchestra. They accompanied many of Guyana's top singers in competitions and performances.

Onkar's musical experience spans over forty years and touched lives all across the world. In his early years, he found a passion for learning the harmonium and tabla. It was the legendary V. Balsara who came to Guyana from India and first set Onkar's hand on the keyboard. Balsara's message to Onkar was that the study of scales and paltas (basic exercises) would lead to proficiency over all melodies. Onkar noted that and dedicated countless hours to the study of the Sargam (the Indian scale system sa, re, ga, ma, pa, dha, ne, sa).

When it came to tabla, Onkar had the good fortune of spending a great deal of time with Pandit Sudarshan Adhikari of the Mumbai Film Industry. Sudarshan's lessons to Onkar helped him to create a crisp and distinct tonality on the tabla, which was a trademark easily recognized in his tabla playing throughout his life.

In addition, Onkar was an integral part of yagnas led by his brother-in-law, the Hon. Pandit Reepu Daman Persaud. Onkar and Pandit Reepu have performed crowd-inspiring yagnas all across the country. He carefully orchestrated all the instrumental pieces of a film song into the singing of the glorious exploits of Lord Raam. This was a huge success, and many people today use this same technique to contemporize the musical traditions of a Hindu Sat Sangha (religious meeting).

Onkar's musical journey took a different path in the 1960s. He was introduced to the sound of the sitar, via a 45 rpm record titled "India's Master Musician" and featuring Pandit Ravi Shankar. Captivated by Ravi Shankar's command of the Raag-Ragini system of north India, Onkar began on a life journey to master the sitar.

When he immigrated to Toronto, he continued his study of the sitar. Key musicians Prof. Adesh and Randev Pandit helped Onkar along his musical education and his next guru for sitar was Steven Oda, who is a senior disciple of Ustad Ali Akbar Khan. The Ustad (master teacher) is of the Maihar-Baba Allaudin Khansahib Gharana (school or lineage) of music. This Gharana has produced many of the biggest names in Hindustani classical music. Onkar spent over ten years with Steve Oda as guru, learning some of the most famous gats and compositions of this Gharana.

In 1998, Onkar met Partha Bose, an up-and-coming young master sitarist from Kolkata. Their music was a close bond between them. This has led Onkar to make yearly trips to Kolkata, to further his expertise on the sitar, and in 2006, he attended the Dover Lane Music Conference in Kolkata with Partha and his wife, Esha Bandyopahdyay. On Onkar's last visit to Kolkata, Partha presented his friend with a special gift: a sitar handcrafted by a master craftsman, the famed sitar maker Hemen Babu.

Onkar has performed in over one hundred programs, including in the National Guyana Auditorium, the University of Toronto, the Markham Theater, the Haborfront Center, the Minkler Auditorium and the Roy Thompson Hall. His proficiency on the sitar showcased a maturity and resonance that was charming and captivating. Some of the organizations who have hosted Onkar's performances include the Vishnu Mandir, the

Tarana Dance Center, Ontario Society for Studies in Indo Caribbean Culture, the Hospital for Sick Children, and the government of Ontario.

Beyond studies and performance, Onkar has devoted countless hours every week to teaching students of all ages the art of Indian classical music. His first student, his daughter Kirti, who was put onto a rigorous training schedule at an early age, found a deep passion for the art of Kathak dance. She often shared discussions with her father on how Kathak (one of the principal classical Indian dance styles) is applied to tabla rhythm. Kirti is an accomplished Kathak dancer.

Onkar's son Ravi is an accomplished musician in his own right. Onkar initiated Ravi from the age of five into classical music by introducing him to harmonium and tabla. He set Ravi's hand on the tabla and showed him the basic bols (hand strokes) of the pair of drums. He took Ravi to be a disciple of and to study with the legendary Pandit Sharda Sahai of Benares Gharana. Ravi's musical achievements have been rewarded with tours across the world and a busy teaching and performance schedule.

Onkar has shared his music with over fifty other students, many of whom are excellent singers and instrumentalists in their own right playing tabla, harmonium, and sitar.

His philanthropic efforts led him to organize and promote Indian classical music through concerts under the umbrella of the Vishnu Mandir, in Toronto. Onkar founded the Shastriya Sangeet Group of Vishnu Mandir. This group has hosted several top Indian classical musicians.

Onkar's efforts to promote these concerts have been rewarded with tremendous success with jam packed audiences being exposed to the rich cultural tradition that has been so close to his own heart. At the Vishnu Mandir, Onkar was named the first principal of the Sangeet Academy. His own son, Ravi, was the first tabla teacher at the academy, and now the institution is fully equipped with a roster of teachers from India, contributing to the musical growth of youngsters in Canada.

Onkar's remarkable passion for music is matched by his achievements as a finance expert, following academic distinction and professional success.

Upon graduating from Central High School in Georgetown, Guyana, he met and later married the girl of his dreams, Sita. However, he understood that in order to provide for his sweetheart and to succeed in life, he needed to further his education, and he went on to study at the Guyana School of Agriculture in Mon Repot, Guyana.

At Mon Repot he excelled in the studies of agronomy and biology so much that he gained admission to study in the Bachelor of Science in Agriculture Program at Louisiana State University in Baton Rouge. This was a huge accomplishment for Onkar. He had left his new bride, Sita, to begin his studies in a foreign land with no family or friends.

He was able to quickly adjust to the situation, and he learned what it took to stand on his two feet. The United States' Deep South in the 1970s was a place that was marked by racial tension and ignorance toward non-whites and non-blacks. He succeeded in befriending people of both major races as well as many foreign students. When Sita joined him in his second term, they faced the challenges of a new country together and enjoyed life's simple pleasures, and their marriage unfolded like a storybook romance.

Onkar was a practical man and upon his graduation with his bachelor's degree, he decided that he would pursue a field that was growing rapidly. With no prior foundations, he made a 180-degree change in fields and pursued a career in finance. It was a huge accomplishment for him in 1976 when he earned the degree of master's in finance. His thesis defense was a grueling six-hour sitting with a panel of the most reputable men in his field. Question after question was answered in depth with phenomenal accuracy and skill. The session ended with the panel leader saying to a young Onkar, "So now that you have this degree … what's next?" As tears partially filled his eyes, Onkar replied, "I will be starting a life in Canada."

Like many Guyanese who came to Canada in the late 1970s, the promises for a Utopian order according to the then Prime Minister Pierre Trudeau seemed like a wonderful opportunity.

In 1980, Onkar was the only Indian working on the executive floor of the Bank of Nova Scotia. At this time, the financial district of King and Bay was not the multicultural mosaic it is now and in fact, many a time, security would follow Onkar to his office curious to see how he had reached such a position!

Onkar's ascent in the bank continued for years. He spent ten years working in the Commercial Real Estate Lending Department of the bank with a portfolio in the hundreds of millions of dollars. He then moved to take up a senior post with the firm of United Lands, a development company based out of Oakville, Ontario. He assumed the role of treasurer for United Lands in 1989 and became their chief financial officer in 1990.

In 1998 after an exhausting recessive real estate market, Onkar rejoined Bank of Nova Scotia and began another climb up the corporate ladder.

He then moved to work in the area of special loans and insolvency under the umbrella of Dennis Belcher and Jameel Sethi. He was in a high-paced environment where he was instrumental in managing the debts of some of the largest companies in Canada. He had acquired special skills in keen negotiation and financial management.

His professional career was split equally between real estate banking and insolvency. As of this writing, his two children are involved in each industry. Kirti is working on her trustee's license to become a qualified member of the Canadian Association of Insolvency and Restructuring Professionals, and Ravi leads a successful career as a top producing realtor with Re/Max Vision Realty Inc.

Onkar's passion for the arts, Indian culture, and music is coupled with strong emphasis on academic and professional achievement and a balance of family and spiritual life. His accomplishments in the Hindustani classical tradition of northern India is of the highest order.

The most interesting remarks Onkar's colleagues share are less about his work and more about the character of man he was, his values, and ethic. Onkar is reputed to have shaped many lives by the positive impact he has made on people. He exemplified the lineage of hard working, industrious Guyanese that came before him.

Just like the generations before him, who had come from India to the then British Guiana, Onkar had to blaze new trails for the betterment of his family. As he came abroad to Canada he was able to assimilate without losing his own cultural identity, and the community has benefited by what he has passed on. His rich skills were only matched by his pleasant nature and deep warmth. He died on March 19, 2008. The example he has set continues to inspire, and the work he has done has created a better Canada for those following in his footsteps.

November 7, 2008

Ramraj Singh

AA, BA, MA
Minnesota Educator

Ramraj built a career in community education and rose to become director of Community Education in his district in Minnesota. He was a member of the Minnesota Board of School Administrators, and commissioner, Burnsville/Eagan Telecommunications Commission. Among awards received, Ramraj was State Community Educator of the Year, 2002.

Ramraj, familiarly known as Ram, was born and raised at Belmonte, Mahaica, East Coast Demerara, Guyana. He taught at Helena Government School, Mahaica, and at Enmore-Hope Government School, Enmore, East Coast Demerara.

After teaching, Ram served as probation and welfare officer, district information officer, and public relations assistant in Guyana. He was a member of the Mahaica–Unity District Council and was chairman for four terms. Ramraj was also active in the National Road Safety Association as secretary, and in the East Demerara Union of Local Authorities.

In 1974, Ram and his wife moved to the United States and settled in Minnesota.

Ram's first priority was education. He obtained an associate of arts degree from Minneapolis Community College in June 1976 and a bachelor of arts degree in public administration from Minnesota Metropolitan State University the same year, December 1976. Ram graduated with a master's degree in administration of community education from the University of St. Thomas, Minnesota, in December 1977. He topped the graduation class with a 4.00 GPA.

In July, 1980, Ram started his community education career in the Minneapolis Public Schools as a community education coordinator and later, as manager. He was credited with expanding the school-age care program to every elementary school in Minneapolis.

After fourteen years in Minneapolis, Ram accepted the director of community education position in the Rosemont–Apple Valley–Eagan School District (District 196) in February 1994. He served with distinction, leading his staff of over six hundred (including licensed teachers) to achieve unparalleled results in all areas. During Ram's leadership, School District 196 Community Education Department received more state and national awards than any other department in all of Minnesota. Ram retired from his position as director in June 2008.

As an educator in Minnesota, Ram played an active role in many organizations promoting life-long learning, adult literacy, and diversity. He has been recognized locally and nationally for his outstanding contribution to education and community development.

He has held these positions:
- Member, board of directors, Minnesota Community Education Association, 1987–88
- Member, board of management, Blaisdell YMCA, Minneapolis, 1985–88
- Charter member, Apple Valley Optimist Club, 1994
- Member, National Community Education Association, 1980–2008
- Member and chair, Dakota County Family Services Collaborative, 1995–08
- Member, Dakota County Juvenile Detention Alternative Initiative Committee, 2005–08

- Member, Minnesota Board of School Administrators, 2004–09, appointed by Minnesota governor Tim Pawlenty
- Commissioner, secretary and chair, Burnsville/Eagan Telecommunications Commission, 2005–08, appointed by Burnsville City Council
- Commissioner, City of Burnsville Planning Commission, 2009–10
- President, Guyanese Association of Minnesota, 2010

He has received these awards:
- Certificate of Commendation, Minnesota Governor, Rudy Perpich, 1990
- State Leadership Development Award, MN Community Education Association, 1993
- National Multicultural Leadership Award, National Community Education Association, 1994
- State Community Educator of the Year, Minnesota Community Education Association, 2002
- Asian Pacific Leadership Award, MN State Asian Pacific Islanders Association, 2006
- Outstanding Service Award, Rosemont,–Apple Valley–Eagan School District, 2006
- Good Neighbor Award, WCCO Radio, Minnesota.

Ram has been married for over forty-six years to Rukhmin (Ruth), a nurse educator with the Minneapolis Veterans Home, Minnesota. They have two children, Dr. Andrea Devi Singh (husband, Rajesh), a pediatrician at Park Nicollet Clinic, St. Louis Park, Minnesota; and David Ramraj Singh (wife, Shabana), a corporate litigator with the law firm of Weil Gotshal and Manges in Manhattan, New York. They have two winsome grandchildren, Ajay Singh and Avishan Singh.

He is keeping busy in his retirement, heading up the Guyanese Association of Minnesota.

October 23, 2010

Samuel Sewpersad Singh

BSc (Econ), FCA, FCMA, JDipMA, FBIM (UK) CA
CLU (Canada), FLMI (USA)

Samuel is a chartered accountant and one of few Guyanese to hold the JDip MA—a joint diploma in management accounting. He holds the FLMI diploma, Fellow of the Life Management Institute of the United States. He was vice president and director of administration of CALICO (the Caribbean Atlantic Life Insurance Company) and vice president of the Travelers Life Insurance Company, Miami, Florida. He was deputy director of the Caribbean Development Bank, and a finance advisor to many developing countries.

Samuel (Sam), the son of a laborer (watchman) at a sugar estate, rose to the position—by the age of thirty-six—of chief internal auditor of the Booker Group of Companies in Guyana, which owned/managed all but two of the sugar estates in Guyana.

Sam was born on the West Coast of Berbice, Guyana, at Bath Estate on the December 29, 1932, the fourth of seven children of Raghunath and Sukhdaya. His father died when he was not yet twelve, yet he was the only one of his brothers and sisters who had the opportunity to continue his education beyond primary school level.

Progress toward his present position was slow but steady. It followed a carefully thought-out plan, influenced, in part, by other sons of Bath, most notable among them, the late Victor Jeet Gangadin, a brilliant student, who came from a family of modest means but who worked hard, became an accountant, and rose to the position of tax commissioner for Guyana.

During his early years, Sam did not enjoy good health, and his father was determined to ensure he had a good education. He was sent away from Bath to Bush Lot to prepare for the Government County Scholarship Examination. He won a free place at Berbice High School in 1944, but his father's death prevented him from taking up the scholarship until January 1946.

Every Saturday night when he took his father's dinner, they sat and talked and his father repeated the difficulties he had experienced in life. Despite the fact that his father could not read or write, he taught Sam, in simple words, two significant behavior traits:

1. As you go through life, you will "stub your toe" and fall. When this happens, forget who notices you, get up, and continue walking.

2. Live your life so that you can always walk on the road with your head up and face those you pass with a smile and a friendly greeting.

In December 1948 Sammy passed his Cambridge School Certificate examination with exemptions from London Matriculation. Very few in his day achieved that exemption. Sam was a good student. That was the beginning of his process of education that saw him undertake three apprentice training programs.

Between the completion of his examinations in December 1948 and the publication of results, Sam worked first as an ashes boy in the sugar estate's drainage pumping station and then as a stores clerk in the Blairmont Sugar Factory.

In September 1949, the first apprenticeship began with his appointment as a pupil teacher at Lachmansingh Memorial Canadian Mission School at Bush Lot. This appointment ended in 1957, at which time Sam decided that primary school teaching should not be his ultimate goal. By that time he was a first-class trained teacher and was acting headmaster of a small school at Wash Clothes, Mahaicony.

To ensure university entrance, Sam initiated studies for the GCE A levels and to this end, moved to Georgetown. By 1958 he had completed five A level passes and did not have difficulty in gaining admission to the University College of the West Indies to be one of their first batch of economics graduates.

A significant fact to note is that although admission was secured, no thought was given to financing of the studies. Applications for funding were all rejected, and private resources could have only paid for the first term's fees. But Sam's prayers were answered. A loan from the Government Students Loan Scheme was arranged on the basis that government's contribution was to be used for the second and third terms of each year.

University training was the beginning of the second phase of apprenticeship. During this period the idea of him becoming a chartered accountant was born. Just before the end of the second year university examinations, an officer from the Booker Group of Companies visited Jamaica to recruit accountancy cadets. After a meeting with Sam he was awarded a Booker cadetship in 1962 and articleship to Mellors, Basden and Mellors of Nottingham, England.

Sam qualified as a chartered accountant in November 1965. He returned home and continued his professional development by qualifying first as a management accountant (CMA) and then completed the joint diploma in management accounting (JDipMA). At that time, Sam was one of only two Guyanese with that designation.

From ashes boy in the sugar estate to chartered accountant, Sam now tasted the fruits of his hard work and dedication to study. In 1966, he was appointed senior accountant, Booker Shipping; a year later he was promoted to chief accountant, Booker Shipping; and in 1968 to be chief internal auditor, Booker Central Services.

Sam, on the lookout for greater opportunities for professional development, then ventured out of Guyana. He was appointed accountant to the Caribbean Development Bank, based in Barbados from 1970 to 1972, and from there he was appointed chief accountant and secretary, St. Kitts (Basseterre) Sugar Factory, from 1972 to 1974.

In 1974 Sam emigrated to Canada. Despite his professional and academic qualifications, he found it difficult to find employment partly because of his lack of Canadian experience, but more so, because employers were concerned he was overqualified. This prompted his decision to practice as a consultant, and he registered as a sole practitioner with two organizations: the Foundation for International Training (FIT), a not-for-profit organization mainly funded by CIDA; and the Commonwealth

Fund for Technical Cooperation (CFTC), an international group, of which Canada is a member.

While in Canada, in 1974, still a practicing accountant, working on his own, he was induced out of accountancy into the insurance industry. Although he entered the industry at a senior level, director of administration, he felt obliged to learn as much as possible in the shortest possible time and devoted his spare time to his educational uplift. During this third period of his apprenticeship, he passed both the Fellowship of the Life Management Institute (FLMI) and the Chartered Life Underwriters (CLU) examinations, completing each in a period of one year.

The Travelers Life Insurance Company, which employed him at their regional head office in Jamaica recognized Sam's contribution and made him a vice president before extending his contract for a further three years. Travelers then decided to transfer their regional office to Miami, Florida.

He was director of administration, Caribbean Atlantic Life Insurance Co. (CALICO), 1974–1975, and vice president and director of administration, CALICO, 1975–1977.

While at CALICO, Sam expressed his availability to CFTC. Within months he received his first assignment from CFTC. This was followed by many more from 1977 to 1999. The assignments were variously advisory and management roles in a number of countries. The first set included:

- Antigua, finance advisor. Antigua Marketing Corporation (three months). 1977
- St. Kitts, finance advisor. St. Kitts Marketing Corporation (six months). 1977–78
- Barbados, assistant director (loan supervision), Caribbean Development Bank. 1978–1980
- St. Lucia. management accounting advisor (CFTC). Attached to Caribbean Development Bank. 1978 (nine months)
- Barbados, deputy director and head of industry, Tourism and DFC's Division, Caribbean Development Bank. 1980–1984
- Fiji -University of the South Pacific. Fellow, attached to The Institue of Social and Administrative Studies.Training, all levels of Management, in Fiji and other Territories from Kiribati to the Cook Islands. 1984–1987

In 1987, Sam lost his wife and had to return to Canada to be with his younger son who was in second year at York University. This gave him the opportunity to complete the requirements for registration as a licensed chartered accountant in Ontario in 1991.

Sam went back to Guyana on an appointment as advisor to the Minister of Finance, Guyana. from 1992 to 1993. In the period 1994–1996, he took up an assignment in the Maldives, Maldives Institute of Management Administration (MIMA), as finance management expert CFFC, and later, in 1997–1999 in Maldives, as finance advisor to the chairman, Villa Shipping and Trading.

In addition to the CFTC assignments, he also undertook these special consultancy assignments:

USAID funded study. (three months in 1984). Analysis of the performance of state-owned enterprises with recommendations on future ownership and management.

APDC (Asia Pacific Development Center) and SPEC (South Pacific Economic Commission) from January to April 1987. Headed a team of consultants conducting an investigation into joint venture potential between public/private sectors of Association of South East Asian Nations (ASEAN) and SPEC.

CDI (EEC) (October 1986) Review of the performance of resource-based industries in the South Pacific.

FIT. Foundation for International Training.1983. Development of a training manual for use in Workshop on Public Enterprise Management. Member of a monitoring mission to revise the implementation of a CIDA Small Business Program in Lesotho (Africa). Member of a two-man team conducting two workshops in joint venture negotiations, one in Jakarta (Indonesia) and other in Manila (Philippines).

Despite his very successful career in his field at the highest levels in various countries Sam never allowed his employment obligations to detract him from his passion, from his very early years, to contribute whatever he could to better the community where he grew up and the communities where he worked worldwide.

As a school teacher, he served in various capacities on the local branch of the Teachers Association: assistant secretary, secretary and was also representative on the central executive of the then Guyana Teachers Association.

He was a scout and was one of the first two Queen Scouts in his troop, 15 Bath Estate. He later became a scout master at Bath, Bush Lot, and Novar, in Guyana. He participated and held office, including that of president in various youth groups and young people's associations.

He served as member of various service clubs: Nottingham Round Table (1962–1965) and the Rotary Club of St. Kitts (1972–1974). He was a member of the student council while at university serving as treasurer of the Students Union.

As an accountant he served as a member of the Management Committee of the Guyana Association of Accountants and was its vice president and chairman of the Education Committee in 1970. During this time he started the institute's first formal training program for accountants in Guyana. Before he left in 1970, the program had seen at least twelve people through Part 1 and enrolled six through the Part II examinations. The twelve enrolled, which began classes under his house in 1968, rose to sixty by the time he left, at which time the classes were being conducted at the Government Technical Institute.

Sam also taught at the University of Guyana on a part-time basis, between 1968 and 1970, with responsibility for the studies in management accounting and financial accounting.

His love for teaching continued in Jamaica, where he did part-time teaching for both the Institute of Chartered Accountants and the Insurance Institute; in St. Kitts where he taught at the Extra Mural Center of the University of the West Indies; and in Barbados where he directed his attention to the preparation of training materials for management of small businesses.

In Fiji, he worked closely with the Fiji National Training Council and was a contributor in their training workshops. He worked with Fiji government corporations (Fiji Broadcasting Corporation, the Ports Authority, and Fiji Forest Industries) in the development of their work plans and budget. In addition he was appointed by the prime minister to conduct a review of the pricing practice of the petroleum distributors in Fiji to ascertain the fairness of the prices charged in Fiji vis-à-vis prices charged in the other South Pacific Islands.

In the Maldives, when needed, he made himself available to any government department that required his services and worked with the Ministry of Finance, the Tourism Ministry, the Ministry of Education, and the Government Audit Department.

Sam's career commenced as an educator. He perceives his whole life as that of an educator. He became an accountant because the salaries for teachers in Guyana were low. While executing his management duties he repeatedly prepared others to replace him or to perform their duties more productively.

His frequent change of jobs evidences his strategy of moving on to greater challenges. His educator's role widened from primary school, secondary school, colleges, universities, professional training, management training, to training of his clients to exercise their duties and responsibilities with due regard to their accountability obligations.

Sam's students and those who worked with him all considered him a "hard man." A common note frequently received from them can be summarized in a statement: "I want to thank you for all you have taught me over the years. Though I may have resisted, I now understand the value and wisdom of your words and actions."

Sam's weakness was that he never accepted mediocrity; he persistently expected excellence. He warned his students and colleagues not to rest on their laurels but to continue to maintain the high standards expected of them.

Sam's chosen career as an educator has been an enjoyable one and the happiness he experiences when his former colleagues, students, and workshop participants record their gratitude continues to make him proud of the role he lived. His educational achievements were reached in the course of his professional development during his working life, demonstrating his acceptance of the need for professional development.

He saw the stumbling blocks on his path as challenges and faced them with courage, determination, faith, and trust in the Creator.

Sam's thoughts, which he is happy to share with the future generations, are "Success is a succession of small efforts. Success is assured when an individual does what he enjoys doing and does it well. Each individual has a latent skill which can be used to advantage. Seek diligently to ascertain your particular strength and having found it, use it to advantage. Satisfy yourself that you have done your best and take pride in your work."

Sam believes the "greatest happiness one can experience is that which flows from the satisfaction of doing things of which one is proud and with which one is happy to be associated."

September 7, 2010

Dr. Vernon Singhroy

Earth Science Professor and Space Scientist

Dr. Vernon Singhroy is the chief scientist at the Canada Center for Remote Sensing in Ottawa, a government of Canada Center of Excellence in Space Application and Research. He has achieved the highest scientific level in the government of Canada. He is also professor of earth observation at the International Space University in Strasbourg, France, and adjunct professor in planetary and earth sciences at McMaster University and the University of New Brunswick in Canada.

Born at Number 30 Village, West Coast Berbice, and a graduate of Berbice High School, Dr. Singhroy pursued studies in Canada and the United States in the areas of earth sciences and environmental and resource engineering, ultimately achieving a PhD in environmental and resource engineering.

He has published four books and over three hundred papers in scientific journals, proceedings and books. He was the editor in chief for the *Canadian Journal of Remote Sensing* for seven years. He served on the editorial boards of several prestigious international journals in space sciences and a member of the editorial board for the *Encyclopedia of Remote Sensing*. He is an advisor to the Canadian Space Agency on space exploration and earth observation programs and the principal scientist of the Canadian Space Agency RADARSAT Constellation Mission. Dr. Singhroy is a member of the RAVEN science team of NASA-proposed mission to Venus.

Dr. Singhroy is well known in Canada and internationally for his expertise in satellite technology for environmental and resource mapping and disaster management. This has made him a much-sought-after expert, providing advice to the Canadian and other international space agencies and to over thirty countries (including Guyana and Venezuela) where he applied satellite technology to assist in mapping of their mineral and hydrocarbon resources and climate change adaptation issues.

Satellite monitoring of global high-risk regions affected by volcanoes, landslides, earthquakes, and floods is also an important component of his recent research. He recently applied satellite imaging technology in assisting the Haiti reconstruction efforts.

Dr. Vernon Singhroy is a worthy example of a country boy from Guyana who, through diligent study, hard work, and imaginative innovation has made it to the very top in the area of Canadian and international scientific studies and administration.

Dr. Singhroy was winner of Guyana Awards (Canada) 2008 Special Achievement Award. He lives in Ottawa with his wife and four children: Diane, Celine, Eric, and Richard.

Sources:

Websites accessed May 27, 2010, on Guyana Consulate Toronto, Guyana Awards (Canada)

November 15, 2010

George Subraj

President, Zara Luxury Apartments and Homes NYC
Philanthropist

George Subraj and his brothers are owners of Zara Luxury Apartments and Homes NYC and proprietor of over two thousand apartments in New York City. He is the president and CEO. George also provided financial assistance and was the prime mover in a history making first kidney transplant operation in Guyana and the West Indies on July 12, 2008.

George Subraj, a member of 'Guyana Watch' (a charitable non-profit organization), who has provided assistance of various kinds over many years to the needy of his home country, Guyana, decided that he would respond to the call for assistance when the case of young eighteen-year-old Guyanese, Munesh Mangal, who had lost the services of both his kidneys reached George's desk.

In March 2008, George Subraj, together with Dr. Jindal and some other friends, went to Guyana to discuss their plans with the Minister of Health, stating that they were interested in using the lab at the Georgetown Hospital to conduct the first kidney transplant and to ascertain whether it could be done there. After he was told that the kidney transplant could be done there, he planned to take a team of specialists to Guyana to carry out the operation. He would bear all the expenses and would initiate a program of providing assistance to the local specialists so that in future other patients could receive help in the country.

George had spoken about his plans earlier to Jerry Adler, a celebrated writer, who reported on George's extraordinary generosity in his article for *Newsweek* magazine, published on May 26, 2008. George, confirming his earlier promises for continued support, had said, "I do not want this to be the end of our assistance. I have made many trips to Guyana for the past fifteen years in an individual capacity and several times with Guyana Watch. Now I have introduced my son Tony to this humanitarian concept. If for some reason I cannot be there, I hope he will be, to assist when required."

So said, so done. The operation was carried out. It was a major success. This news was published in all the local newspapers: *Guyana Chronicle*, *Stabroek News*, *Kaieteur News*, *United States Southern Command*.

Kaieteur News reported on this first kidney transplant operation, stating, "After nearly six hours of intense and intricate medical procedures, the first kidney transplant in Guyana, hosted by the Georgetown Public Hospital Corporation, was completed ... with claims from the operating team that it was a major success."

The report stated, in part, that, the initiative to have the operation done in Guyana was spearheaded by New York-based Guyanese George Subraj, president and founder of Zara Luxury Apartments and Homes, after he saw a flyer, which was being circulated for financial assistance. After some investigation, George solicited the assistance of Dr. Jindal, who in turn organized the medical team of renowned experts.

The report continued:

> With no financial assistance from anyone, Mr. Subraj sought the assistance of Caribbean Airlines, which sponsored the tickets for the team; the owner of Buddy's International Hotel, who accommodated the team at a reduced rate; and a few others who have helped in the area of providing meals for the team since their arrival here in Guyana.
>
> The medical operation, which was spearheaded by Indian-born Dr. Rahul Jindal, saw 18-year-old Munesh Mangal, of Lusignan, East Coast Demerara, who has for many years

suffered from renal failure, receiving a kidney from his mother, 41-year-old Leelkumarie Nirananjan Mangal. ... In addition to Dr. Jindal, an attending general surgeon at the Brookdale University Hospital, the team consisted of Dr. Edward M. Falta (transplant surgeon of the Walter Reed Army Medical Center, Washington); Dr. Melenie Guerero (pulmonary care physician); Laura Owens (transplant coordinator); and Dr. Arthur L. Womble, attached to the Athens-Limestone Hospital, Athens, Alabama.

Members of the local supporting team included Dr. Ravi Purohit (surgeon), Dr. Ramsundar Doobay (consultant, internal medicine), Dr. Anita Florendo (registrar, internal medicine), Dr. Vivienne Amata (anesthesiologist), Dr. Pheona Mohamed-Rambaran (laboratory director), Mr. Delon France (medical technologist), and Dr. Wilson (radiologist).

Distinguished journalist Iana Seales of Stabroek News paid a glowing compliment to George when she wrote:

> Were it not for the persistence of George Subraj, Guyana's first kidney transplant surgery might still be months away or longer. However, the only thing the overseas-based businessman took credit for was getting involved and seeing things through to the end of what he said was an incredible journey.

She stated that though he emphasized teamwork, Subraj made the phone calls, met the doctors, coordinated the earlier and recent visits here, and handled the fund-raising. He called it "merely some of the work," but others summed it up as the work that essentially made everything happen.

At a press briefing hours after the historic surgery was completed at the Georgetown Public Hospital, George described briefly early struggles in New York to find his feet and eventually to establish the business for which he is well known. Though he was well known in Queens, New York, as president of Zara Luxury Apartments, very few there knew anything of his roots as the son of a rice farmer who started working in the fields from age ten. "I saw an opportunity to help a young man who was ailing and I did. I am sure there are many others out there but it requires a certain amount of collaboration and funds as well," Subraj told the media.

Iana continued in her report:

> He recalled that it all started after he responded to an e-mail one of his brothers had sent him about the "boy in Guyana who needed a kidney." Subraj said Munesh Mangal's story compelled him to act and to seek the support of his family and closest friends.
>
> Shortly after, the name Dr. Rahul Jindal started floating around. Subraj subsequently met Dr. Jindal and the Indian-born transplant surgeon who had never been to Guyana or the Caribbean immediately agreed to visit the young Lusignan boy. According to Subraj, the rest is history.
>
> What actually happened was a continuous flow of e-mails, phone calls, and meetings, coupled with planning and coordinating both in the United States and in Guyana. Though he still speaks of the surgery with pride, he cannot finish a sentence without mentioning the name of a friend or relative who worked tirelessly along with him to see it happen. However, his major praises are repeatedly sounded for the medical team. "Munesh's case was unique in that through him, I hope to open the door to help others who are confronted with a similar situation or having to find huge amounts of cash for overseas medical emergencies," Subraj said.
>
> His opportunity to help others came immediately after Mangal had the surgery for Dr. Jindal spoke of at least two other local patients he had evaluated who were also suffering from end-stage renal failure and were candidates for transplants. Subraj told reporters that he would fund a minimum of five more surgeries.
>
> Subraj said while the need was there he would try to assist by bringing the best teams and working in collaboration with the Ministry of Health and the Georgetown Public Hospital. He made mention of working in collaboration with the Guyana Medical Watch team for close to fifteen years and giving back to Guyana but pointed out that the surgery was a tremendous achievement to be a part of.

At the time they were in Guyana, the team also did surgery on another patient. In addition, George Subraj and Zara Luxury Apartments and Homes have donated the following equipment: Page Writer III all options, two EKG 1200 Pagewriter, four deluxe wheelchairs, ear/nose/throat machine, ophthalmoscope, and sale thermometer.

In 1971, George Subraj left Guyana with $850 (US), which he had borrowed and journeyed to the United States in search of a better life. His life in Guyana was fairly good at the time, given that his family's paddy operation had expanded into a harvesting and milling business, but he had dreams of doing much more for the business.

He arrived in the States to find an environment where more working hours were demanded of him, and one where courses in agriculture were few and far between. Subraj shifted to business studies while working in the clothing business and eventually worked his way up. He now runs the Zara Luxury Apartments, which is an empire of twenty-three apartment complexes in Queens, Long Island, and Florida

George said he provides clean, safe and affordable housing for his clients. He said that when he came to United States, it was very difficult to find housing; if it was affordable, it was not safe, and if it was safe, it was not affordable. Now he is providing both safe and affordable housing for his clients.

In a full-feature article that appeared in the *Hibiscus* magazine (a publication in Queens), he recalled that his first night in the United States was a cold and lonely one as he waited for hours until a friend returned home to accept him. He also recalled how difficult it was in those early years. "I would put my milk on the window ledge in the cold to keep it from spoiling and used the warm water from the tap to make my tea and soup." But he pointed out that dedication, discipline, and determination were his anthems.

On the day he married his wife, Gloria, they were both working, and after the civil ceremony they went back to work. The two later feasted on a meal she prepared: dhall, rice, and potato.

Through business ventures with his brothers, he was able to rise up and today, his family is known for providing excellent accommodation to hundreds of families. Subraj still has tenants from 1981, when he made his first purchase.

Zara Realty was started in 1982 with just one building; now there are twenty-three, 90 percent of which are located in New York's most diverse and sought-after borough, Queens.

George said they went into the rental end of apartment business because they saw a need, as people are moving every three to five years. What does Zara offer to potential residents? George said he feels top of the list of people's needs are clean, safe, affordable accommodations, near to shops. Each of their sites is within access to transportation, highways, airports, shopping, and entertainment, and in respect of the New York sites, Long Island's famous beaches, golf courses, parks, lakes, race tracks, and ball fields are easily reached, most with one-fare public transportation.

The company has expanded in the past year by relocating their headquarters to accommodate growing staff numbers. They want to be at the cutting edge of the business, constantly updating with current technology. Zara is expanding to Long Island and Florida, providing homes to more than two thousand residents.

April 15 2008.

Ken Subraj

CEng, MI.MechE, MI.Prod.E

Ken Subraj is a chartered engineer, mainly involved in construction plant maintenance, the arch road builder, often referred to as "king of the road" by his boss in Muscat. Before age forty-three, he had completed one of the longest roads (780 km, over 500 miles) in the Middle East, the Nizwa-Thamarit Highway that connects the north and south of Oman. This highway was twice the distance of all the paved roads in Guyana.

Ken was born in Guyana in 1941. Now he sits in his New York office, having traveled to and worked in London, Oman, Greece, Saudi Arabia, Kuwait, Bahrain, Abu Dhabi, Qatar, India, Pakistan, Philippines, Canada, and of course his homeland.

Since he left school at age twelve, Ken has blazed a trail of achievement that took him from finding firewood in the mornings for the family kitchen to cleaning the workshop floor to heading a division in the Ministry of Works, Guyana, and eventually to managing contractors and operators of gigantic machinery, in mines and in the building of roads, oil refinery, bridges, and pipelines in the Middle East.

Ken attended the St. Mary's Lutheran School in Bel-Air, East Coast Demerara, up to his twelfth birthday. He helped his parents in their rice farming. His dad told him he would not get anywhere with the plough in the rice field, and he should be a trade person. He went to study at the Government Technical Institute (GTI) in Georgetown in 1956 for half of the week, and the other half he worked in various welding, fabricating, motor vehicle, and turning shops. His first job was at Bookers Garage, Water Street, Georgetown. His first wage: a token of $3.50 per week. He then got a job at the Ogle Estate, East Coast Demerara, at a wage of $8.50. There, his supervisor restricted him initially to only cleaning the workshop floor.

But Mr. Woods, an engineer from England, told him how he could better himself. In 1958 Ken returned to GTI and wrote exams for his City and Guild of London Certificate. He was successful, and he immediately went off to join the Ministry of Works, Hydraulics Division. There, he met Mr. White a mechanical engineer, chartered status, from Great Britain. Mr. White saw that Ken got the full minimum wage of $17.50, as opposed to the $13.50 proposed earlier by the Ministry of Labor Exchange.

Ken was married in January 1961 to Shirley of Kitty, Georgetown, and then flew off to England in June 1961. There, only twenty years old and his wife still in Guyana, he worked at a motor vehicle repair shop, and studied for the Ordinary National Certificate. Armed with that, he gained entrance to full-time university, had qualified for a grant, a Major County Award, and studied for the polytechnic diploma in mechanical and production engineering. He graduated at the top of the class 1967. This was the equivalent of an engineering degree. Immediately he got a job as a trainee engineer to assemble huge steam-generated turbines but stayed for only a year and in 1968, returned home to Guyana.

Back home, Ken Subraj started working with the Ministry of Works and Hydraulics and was offered a lucrative contract. He was given the job of his former boss, Mr. White. He had come full circle.

Ken had by now acquired a taste for working with big machinery. That was his calling: bigger collection of machinery; the larger they were, the better. In 1970 he went on to work with the Demerara Bauxite Company (DEMBA) in the Primary Stripping Department in Guyana's mining town, Mackenzie, now Linden. He was there for over four years, then returned to England.

Ken Subraj had achieved the status of a chartered engineer in 1973. His dream of getting to this distinguished academic landmark was finally realized at the age of thirty-two years.

In England, looking for a job, he completed an application form for a job as a plant manager. There was one little hiccup—the job was all the way in the Middle East.

In spite of difficult times, Ken was still able to place a 10 percent down payment on a house in London and then flew to Beirut, Lebanon, for his orientation in the new job as a construction plant manager.

His first task was to undertake the development and maintenance of the very large fleet of equipment used for housing, road, and sea defense projects in Muscat, Oman. That was in 1975. At the age of thirty-four, Ken Subraj, the mechanical engineer, chartered status, began his historic twenty-year stopover in the Middle East.

He stayed on these projects for eighteen months and was then transferred to the head office in Athens, Greece, from where he coordinated and visited the operations in several other surrounding Middle Eastern countries, which included Saudi Arabia, Kuwait, Abu Dhabi, Dubai, and Muscat.

During these productive years of Ken's life, tragedy struck. In May 1979, on one brief holiday in the United States, he stopped to celebrate his dad's fifty-sixth birthday. Just ten days after that his dad passed away.

This was a shock to him, but from this agonizing moment of loss was born one the more magnificent of Ken's projects: the Nizwa-Thamarit Highway of Oman.

He recalled the moments, saying, "I flew to Athens and then to Muscat to begin one of the most ambitious tasks in my lifetime which was quite simply dubbed the 'Longest Road.' This road was going to connect the main pipelines from the north to the south. It was an incredible distance, like driving from Queens, New York to Toronto, Canada. We had a work force of over 3000 with 350 directly under me and about $35 million of equipment, including 250 trucks, dozens of compressors, drill machines, asphalt and crushing plants, and lots of caterpillars, wheel-loaders, dozers, and scrapers, plus lots of power plants."

Upon completion of the road project, Ken was transferred to Kuwait in 1983 and worked eight months there, before he was sent back to Oman to oversee several smaller projects. He had been on the road for almost a decade and felt it was time to quit.

Ken's bosses had other plans. "I approached my boss, Yousaf Shammas. He said they needed me to travel urgently to Saudi Arabia. We had to build an 1100km (740 mile) pipeline from the east to the west of the country—a massive project that would take oil from the major refineries to the central depot and then pump it to Yanbu for export overseas by tankers. The trench for the fifty-six-inch diameter line had to be over ten feet deep, then padded for the pipe, refilled, and covered like a roof on a house."

Ken completed his project and despite attractive offers from his bosses, he made his decision and finally took the plane back home.

In 1984 when Ken's only daughter, Dinah, was born, to join his three sons, he thought he would take things easy and settle down with his brothers in the apartment rental business in New York.

Ken recalls: "Our office initially was in the boiler room of our first building in 144 Street, Jamaica. We then moved to a room on the ground floor. My brothers, George and Jay, and George's daughter, Sandy, all put in six days a week of work and looked at every opportunity to expand the business by way of upgrading the buildings that we already had and looking to purchase more."

Soon after they purchased building number five and upgrading was completed, Ken got the itch again for the road. After the first Gulf War in 1990, his previous employers called on him. They had a contract to build an impressive gas train in the gulf of Arabia, 180 km offshore for Abu Dhabi, National Oil Company, which he completed in 1994. He was then rushed off to Kuwait, and he started on the construction of a pipeline and ethylene plant immediately. He stayed on this job and in late 1995 he quit again, said it was time to go home, and returned to the family business in Queens, New York.

Ken Subraj has played a significant role in the development and success of Zara Luxury Apartments and Homes.

In an interview for *Hibiscus* published in 2008, Ken spoke to Richard Mahesh, who writes that Ken is very proud of the Guyanese community. Asked if he felt any pressure, being the eldest brother in such a large family, Ken said, "No. Our parents guided us equally and that respect for each other remains." When asked about religion, Ken replied, "I know God exists, and I do visit mandirs but not very often. I actually prefer the Indian way of worship: individualized as opposed to congregational."

Ken spoke of the Guyanese community. "I am extremely proud of the Guyanese success here. We are independent, hard-working people and given the right environment and opportunities, we can make a decent living. Many have forged ahead in the various specialist fields like I did.

Keep climbing, guys; it is only through positive actions, both mental and physical, that the world honors you."

Sources:

E-mail from George Subraj dated July 23, 2008
Websites accessed on August 12. 2008
www.zararealty.com/video
www.kaieteur.com
www.stabroeknews.com
Jerry Adler's article in the May 26, 2008, edition of *Newsweek* magazine.

August 15, 2008

Trev Sue-A-Quan

BSc, PhD
Fossil Fuels Research Engineer
Author

Trevelyan A. Sue-A-Quan was born in November 1943 in Georgetown, Guyana. He is the great-grandson of Soo A-cheong an indentured laborer from China, who had embarked on the ship *Corona* at Canton with his wife and son, Soo Sam-kuan. They arrived at Georgetown in February 1874 after seventy-eight days at sea. The family was allotted to La Grange Sugar Cane Plantation on the West Bank of the Demerara River. In the process of cultural assimilation Soo Sam-kuan's name became transformed into Sue-A-Quan, thus initiating the distinctive family surname.

After completing their service of indenture, the Chinese typically ventured into shopkeeping and were thereby able to provide the financial means for subsequent generations to become trained professionals. Trev Sue-A-Quan's generation was the one that typified that transition to the professions based on higher education. Trev attended Queen's College in Georgetown and attained BSc and PhD degrees in chemical engineering at the University of Birmingham, England. His brother and sister both graduated from Edinburgh, Scotland, and became chief surgeon and mathematician/computer specialist, respectively.

Trev immigrated to Canada in 1969. He seized upon a career opportunity with Amoco Oil (now BP) in Chicago, where he was engaged in research in petroleum processing and fossil fuel utilization. In one of his research projects he developed a novel catalyst for refining petroleum, for which he was granted patents in the United States and Europe. Eight years later, Trev headed to Beijing, China, becoming senior research engineer at the Coal Science Research Center. He spent five years in China, and in 1984 returned to Canada with his wife and son. They now make their home in Vancouver.

Trev has long been curious about the circumstances that caused his great-grandfather to leave his native land. This curiosity became more intense in the years he lived and worked in China. He has since had an abiding interest in learning all about his family history and that of Chinese immigrants to Guyana. In 1979 he obtained a copy of his great-grandfather's contract of indenture. Trev then applied his training in analytical research to delve into the circumstances and conditions that caused Chinese to emigrate as laborers to a distant land in the nineteenth century. He uncovered a history that was previously unknown to him, and he realized that it would also be unfamiliar to many Guyanese of Chinese ancestry. From the materials he researched he was able to compile a comprehensive account of the experiences of the first Chinese immigrants in Guyana.

Trev is regarded as the foremost authority on the subject of early Chinese immigration to Guyana. He has authored two books on the subject. These two best-sellers are significant contributions to the history of the unique Guyanese multi-ethnic and multi-cultural diaspora.

His first book, *Cane Reapers*, is "the story about the Chinese who were procured to replace the emancipated slaves on the sugar plantations of Guyana (then British Guiana)."

> Following China's defeat by Britain in the Opium Wars in the 1840s, the European powers, and Spain in particular, began a recruitment drive to obtain Chinese laborers for their colonies.
>
> This was executed using all manner of methods, ranging from subtle inducement to kidnapping. Numerous abuses arose from this trade in human cargo and Britain later set up local

emigration depots aimed at enlisting willing emigrants, with some degree of success. Between 1853 and 1879, a total of 13,541 indentured laborers arrived in British Guiana from China, but by 1900 the resident Chinese population was down to 3,000, mainly because only 15 percent of the Chinese immigrants were females.

The Chinese endured many tribulations both in the journey and after arrival in the new land. In the process of assimilation into Western culture some unique names have evolved for Chinese families, creating both a mystery and a topic of fascination for their descendants and for genealogists.

Cane Reapers, 2nd revised edition (2003), has 352 pages, including thirty-six pages of illustrations, and is published by Cane Press. There are ten chapters. The chapter headings and summaries give a taste of the interesting contents of this book on the fascinating background and circumstances in the life of Chinese immigrants into British Guiana.

Included in the chapter headings and summaries to Cane Reapers are these words and phrases that tell the story: The End of Slavery, Massa Day Done, Orientals from the West, The Opium Trade, Crimping Methods, Coolie Trade at Macao, Demerara Bound, Visions in the Hot Sun, Pursuing Chinese Women, First Ladies, Arrival of the Corona, The Last Shipment, Working on the Plantation, Odd Men Out, Slow Boat to China, Plantains, Other Dishes, Class Conflict, Cream Collar Crime, Respected Citizens, Becoming Creole, Opium and Gambling, Social Interactions, Christian Influences, The Shepherd and Hopetown, Becoming Free, Getting Down to Business, Country Shops, Property Purchases, Gaining a Higher Education, Name Calling, Chinese Characters, Anglicized Names, Lineage Charts, Going International.

Cane Ripples, the second book, is a sequel to *Cane Reapers*. In this, Trev describes "the experiences of the Chinese in Guyana, presented in the form of short stories about individuals and families in their working and recreational lives. *Cane Ripples* is a 352-page book with eighty-five illustrations, published by Cane Press'

Dr. Vibert C. Cambridge, the distinguished Guyanese chair of the Department of African American Studies at Ohio University, has written this:

> *Cane Ripples* is an integrated work that expresses the joy and pains experienced by a vital sector of Guyanese society during the twentieth century. ... It uses oral histories, personal recollections, photographs, and archival materials to illuminate an important aspect of Guyana's complex history. ... We can see the names and the faces that influenced Guyana's social, economic, political, cultural, and scientific life. Contributors take us into their homes, share family histories, and tell us about the creation of some of Guyana's most successful institutions and enterprises. ... Dr. Trev Sue-A-Quan must be congratulated for a most valuable and accessible contribution.

The contributors to *Cane Ripples* include well-known household names and those not so well known of the Guyanese Chinese community who have all made significant contributions to building Guyana.

The thirty-nine stories in *Cane Ripples* provide firsthand accounts about the many facets of the indentured Chinese laborers and their descendants, their enterprise, drive, and achievements. The contents include these subjects: Entrepreneurial Spirit, Mixed Marriage, Path to Education, Dry Goods Shop, Baker's Man, Hand Laundry, Bee Queen, Rice Milling, Dental Practice, Chinese Merchant, Broadcasting Ace, Chinese Lessons, Drug Store, Rice Grader, Laws and Lows, Sound Effects, Commission Agent and Hairdresser, Cookshop, Cakeshop, Country Doctor, Good Sport, Community Spirit, Family Jewels, Overseer, District Commissioner, Life on the Plantation.

Trev launched a website that provides information about the Chinese in Guyana, beginning with their introduction to Guyana (then called British Guiana) as indentured immigrants between 1853 and 1879. It is titled "Chinese in Guyana: Their Roots." It provides information under key headings (routes), with a brief outline of what you will encounter depending on the route you choose, as follows:

> The History route gives a brief overview of the reasons for and results of Chinese immigration. The Contract route shows a typical contract of indenture used in 1873 for the Chinese laborers. Details of the travels of the thirty-nine immigrant ships can be found on the Voyage route. Examine the Passengers route for statistical data about the people who embarked in China and landed in Georgetown. Names of immigrants

and their descendants to four generations are listed based on the boats on which they arrived. The locations to where the immigrants were allotted are shown in the Distribution route. Go "rooting" to trace your ancestral ties and share your stories.

Further, there is the opportunity to take part in a search for relatives along the Reach Out route, and Frequently asked questions are answered via the FAQ route.

Trev was a winner of the Wordsworth McAndrew Award at the Guyana Folk Festival in 2003 for outstanding contributions to Guyana's culture and heritage. His citation reads:

> Trev Sue-A-Quan: An outstanding and unselfish historian. A North American-based scientist, he has published the important history, *Cane Reapers*, on Chinese indentureship in British Guiana.

Sources:

Websites
http://www.rootsweb.ancestry.com/~guycigtr. Accessed Jan. 28, 2010
http://www.guyfolkfest.org/awards2003.htm. Accessed February 27, 2010

March 25, 2010

Dr. Margaret S. D. Sukhram

EdD, MA, MPH, BS, NP
Nursing Professor and Nurse Practitioner

Dr. Margaret Sukhram's professional career spans over thirty years as a professor of nursing, health education, clinician, and administrator. She is in health care with a specialty in women's health, as well as a health consultant to a variety of international and national organizations. Her extensive national and international experience includes health program needs assessment, health planning, education, and evaluation, as well as in policy development

She has also presented at national and international conferences, has published, and was a major contributor to a Caribbean Family Planning Training Guide published by the International Planned Parenthood Federation/Western Hemisphere Region (IPPF/WHR). She has mentored nursing and medical students, medical residents, and other health professionals.

Her work in the health disparities field began in the 1990s with Long Island Minority AIDS Coalition (LIMAC) —Coalition to Eliminate Health Care Disparities, as well as with the Nassau County Minority Task

Force. With positions as the associate director of the Office of Minority Health, Suffolk County Department of Health Services, and director of Women's Services in Nassau County Department of Health Services, she was instrumental in pioneering many health programs with the community, schools, and universities before going to SUNY College at Old Westbury full time, where she had served part-time for over twenty years.

Over the years she has worked closely with underserved communities and utilizes her knowledge and skills to help increase health care access for racial and ethnic minorities. She collaborates with community and faith-based organizations and other agencies to increase awareness about existing health care disparities, improve on cultural competency, and implement health promotion and education programs to eliminate identified disparities. Dr. Sukhram is a community leader and an avid consumer advocate.

In addition, Dr. Sukhram has done extensive work in the field of reproductive health, including HIV/AIDS, sexuality, and peer education. She has extensive experience as an international health consultant for various agencies including the United States Agency for International Development (USAID), the Caribbean Family Planning Affiliation (CFPA), the Commonwealth Fund, the American Egyptian Cooperation Foundation (AECF), Millennium Sistahs, Deskan Institute, Caribbean American Medical & Scientific Association Inc., (CAMSA), Caribbean American Organization Association Inc., NYS AIDS Institute, and Faith-Based Common Ground.

Dr. Sukhram is a founding member of several organizations including CAMSA and LIMAC's Coalition to Eliminate Health Disparities. She serves on several advisory boards and committees. She has been a member of the Nassau Suffolk HIV Health Services Planning Council for over three years, and serves on the Executive Committee and Strategic Planning Committee. She volunteers for the American Red Cross. Recently, she was appointed by the Suffolk county commissioner of health as vice chair of the Nassau–Suffolk HIV Health Services Planning Council. She has been appointed to the New York State HIV Prevention Planning Group, Women's Committee.

A women's health nurse practitioner, her academic qualifications include a doctorate in education (EdD) and a master of arts in education (MA), both from Teachers College, Columbia University, and a master of public health (MPH) from the Columbia University School of Public Health.

Margaret Sukhram was born on December 28, 1946, at 64 Village, Upper Corentyne, British Guiana. Her father was a heavy equipment operator. He worked with the government in many areas of Guyana, and Sookram's Cross in Corentyne was named after him. Her mother was a businesswoman and primary caregiver of the family. She owned rice lands. Margaret is the fifth child with two brothers and four sisters.

She attended New Market Anglican Primary School at Number 63 Village, and Tagore High School in Guyana. She emigrated to London, England in 1964. She finished high school in London. She was an athlete and loved volley ball and table tennis.

Margaret qualified as a registered professional nurse in New York State in 1974. She studied further and graduated in 1978 with a bachelor of science degree from St. Joseph's College, New York. In 1980 she obtained the degree of master of public health from Mailman School of Public Health, Columbia University, New York, and in 1990 she became a certified nurse practitioner women's health in the state of New York. She followed this up in 2001 with a master of arts degree obtained from Teachers College, Columbia University, New York and in 2003 from the same college her doctorate, doctor of education.

Her professional experience extending for over thirty-five years is summarized as follows:

1981–1984: Assistant professor of nursing, SUNY Stony Brook, LI, NY. She lectured and supervised students in a various clinical specialties in a variety of health care organizations.

1983 to the present: health consultant, international and national, with a variety of organizations.

1984–1987: Director of nursing, Home Care America, Mineola, NY. She directed the operations of the nursing department.

1986–1988: Assistant professor of nursing, adjunct, SUNY Farmingdale, New York

1985–1988: Assistant professor of nursing, adjunct, Suffolk Community College, NY

1988 to the present: Nurse practitioner, women's health (part time), Student Health Services, SUNY, College at Old Westbury.

9/05–5/08: Suffolk County Department of Health Services (SCDHS), Long Island, New York (LI, NY), Health planning coordinator (associate director/Office Minority Health; nurse practitioner).

4/88–9/05: Nassau County Department of Health/Community Health Centers (NCDOH/CHCs) LI, NY.

9/99: Transferred to Nassau Health Care Corporation/Community Health Centers (NHCC/CHCs)

She is a major contributing author, 1991 to date, to the IPPF Publication, *Caribbean Family Planning Guide: A Self Instructional Manual for Health Professionals*. She has also contributed in the September 1984 issue of the *Journal of American Association of Occupational Health Nursing*. (Sukhram) Cheddie, M. & Dri E "Substance Abuse and the Prenatal Employee: A Nursing Diagnosis Perspective"

Her professional presentations have been ongoing at national and international levels. Major highlights among these are:

1988. Coauthor: Paper presented at American Public Health Association. "Issues in Family Planning Training." Easter Caribbean.

1995. Paper presented at an international conference, Counseling and Treating People of Color: Barbados. "Issues in HIV Counseling and Treatment in people of color."

1998. Paper presented at a regional conference, Sexual Pleasure/Sexual Health: HIV/AIDS Prevention: Trinidad. "Achieving a satisfactory sex life: A counseling role for nurses."

2001. Variety of presentations on health topics

2004: Keynote Speaker on HIV AIDS: Guyana Conference

2005. Keynote Speaker, Jack & Jill of America Inc. SC Chapter: Theme: "Taking Control, Body and Soul: Nutrition, life balance and health choices to enhance lives of children."

2006. Keynote speaker at SCCC at ESL Graduation. Presentation: NC Perinatal Services Network Conference. "The Hand that Rocks the Cradle." Presentation: Conference, SNAP, LI. "Dismantling Racism, Eliminating Disparities in Adolescent Health."

2007. Presentation, Cultural Competency, Focus on HIV/AIDS, Nassau/Suffolk Ryan White Planning Council. Presentation: "Disparities in Health Care–Focus on African American Women." 100 Black Women of Long Island Conference.

2008. Presentation: "Disparities in Health Care–Focus on HIV/AIDS," NUMC 19th Annual HIV Symposium.

About her choice of nursing as a career, Margaret says this:

> It goes way back to my great-grandmother who hailed from India lived to be 117. I assisted my mother to take care of her, as she was bedridden. From there on I decided that I wanted to take care of the sick and wanted to be a nurse. I still love to do what I do educating and helping all especially women who do not always have the opportunity to advocate for themselves.
>
> I draw my inspiration from my early experience. As a child, I realized that educational emphasis was placed primarily on sons, and I have strived for excellence to show that women can do just as well if not better and should be treated equally.
>
> The early years away from family can be depressing, but you have to keep your focus on the goals. Never let anyone hinder your progress. Stand up for what you think is right and learn from failure. Set higher goals.

Margaret married in London in 1968. Her first daughter, Nadia, was born in London. She emigrated to New York in 1973. A son, Nigel, and another daughter, Nicole, were born in New York. Also she is a proud grandmother of Ashaa Mohana. Her children are college educated. Margaret has been a single parent since 1984 and continues to work full time in her profession, provide volunteer services, and be the primary caregiver of her family.

November 12, 2010

Pandit Satyanand Sukul

Pandit Satyanand Sukul has followed in the footsteps of his father in becoming a Hindu priest. He worked in London, England, in Holland, and in Toronto. He is the Hindu priest at the Lakshmi Mandir at Mississauga, Ontario.

Under his father's training from the age of four, Satyanand was happy memorizing mantras and pujas (hindu religious service). While schooling, his training continued rigorously. At age fifteen Satyanand Sukul performed his first puja in the public at Pouderoyen, West Bank Demerara. The training continued and he kept practicing as a part-time priest of the Hindu religion.

Satyanand Sukul was born on May 18, 1939, at La Grange Village, West Bank Demerara, British Guiana. His father was the celebrated Pandit Lalman Sukul. His mother was Jagwanti, who passed away when he was twelve years old, leaving six children for his father to look after. Pandit Lalman Sukul had all the wisdom and a big heart, and he was ambitious for his family. He died at the age of seventy-seven and even at that age he was always writing and reading.

Satyanand attended Central High School for two years. Later, when his father became ill and could not afford the financial demands of his family,

Satyanand, being the eldest son, was forced to leave school. However, he continued his education through private lessons and evening classes.

After obtaining O level passes in English literature, English, and British Constitution, Satyanand started working at the Argosy (newspaper) Company in Georgetown. He also attended accounting training under the tutorship of the late Victor Gangadin and reached the intermediate stage of the examinations of the London Chamber of Commerce of the United Kingdom.

In 1957 Satyanand left the Argosy Co. and joined the team of Sir Lindsay Parkinson & Co. on the Boeraserie Extension Project at their head office at Bagotville, West Bank Demerara. He worked in the chief engineer's office as a clerk, analyzing progress on various sites and preparing payment claims from government representatives who checked the accuracy of works being done on the sites.

In his spare time, he contributed to the work of the Maha Sabha (then known as the British Guiana Sanatan Dharma Maha Sabha) as assistant secretary. His father Pandit Lalman Sukul was a founding member, along with the late Dr. J. B. Singh and other stalwarts of the Hindu community.

In 1962 he emigrated to London, England, where he continued working and studying. He attended the Chiswick Polytechnic while he worked in the field of accountancy and practiced as a part-time Hindu priest. He passed the GCE advanced level in Hindi and accounting in 1968.

Satyanand encouraged his other siblings to leave the shores of Guyana and take up residence in London. His father also joined them in London but maintained his connections with his followers and devotees in Guyana, Suriname, Trinidad, and Holland.

In 1974 England suffered a semi-recession. The miners strike went on for quite a few months causing lots of unemployment, and Satyanand was laid off during the winter months. This forced him to seek employment in Holland, where it was not too difficult to obtain work permits because England was a member of the European Economic Community.

Within one month of his arrival in Holland in 1975, he secured a good accounting position with an English-speaking company in Amsterdam. His father also joined him in Holland, though he continued to travel to the various places as needed. Satyanand lived and worked in Holland for five years, then decided to emigrate to Canada.

He entered Canada in June 1980 and settled finally in Mississauga, Ontario. He worked as a bookkeeper for Sound Waves, and Supersound Car

Radio Ltd., simultaneously. He was offered a partnership with Supersound Car Radio, which he accepted in October 1980.

With the passing away of his father in 1981, Satyanand realized that his calling to the priesthood was imminent. His father was the main inspiration in his life. He was his idol.

Being a partner with Supersound Car Radio, he was able to take time off for functions. This led him to seriously consider the career as a Hindu priest. He felt a calling in this path, through which he could serve and give back to the community part of that rich cultural legacy he had inherited from his late father. In 1990 Supersound Car Radio Ltd. suffered severe financial losses and the directors decided to sell the business, releasing Satyanand for his priesthood career.

He decided to serve the community as a full time Hindu priest. It was very important for him that the values his father taught him should live on and be preserved.

In January 1992, with the encouragement of many disciples and followers of the Hindu community, Pandit Satyanand Sukul started the Lakshmi Mandir movement from the school hall of Floradale Public School in Mississauga. Within one year, with the backing and encouragement of followers, Lakshmi Mandir purchased the property at 588, Needham Lane, Mississauga. The property had two free-standing small buildings. One was used as an auditorium, with kitchen facilities, and the other was converted into a place of worship. A modern temple has now been constructed on the site at a cost of over one million dollars.

The mandir has provided a means of giving something back to the community and brought many people from various places together. Over the years, Pandit Sukul has tried to preserve Sanatan Dharma, which was brought to Guyana by his forefathers from India. He has taught Hindi to children of Canadian birth, who now read the Ramayan fluently. He also taught and trained Hindu priests in Canada, who are now practicing pandits in the community.

As a full-time Hindu priest and registered marriage officer in Ontario, Pandit Sukul serves the needs of the temple's congregation and continues to serve the Hindu community in religious and cultural activities, not only in Canada and the United States but also in Guyana, Trinidad, Barbados, and Bermuda. He is well established and accepted in the community as a leading Hindu priest.

On his calling to the priesthood, Panditji says:

> I see the necessity for this "call," and I am happy and very satisfied to follow in the footsteps of my father to serve the needs of mankind in this manner. The satisfaction I gain cannot be described. I am proud of my son Satish, who now understudies me in the priesthood career. He is quite capable, and I am sure that this legacy, which dates back to four generations of priesthood, will continue to be practiced with authority and accuracy.

Panditji has been honored for his praiseworthy work in the community. He has received awards locally from the Canadian community in respect to the Spiritual Retreat and Youth Camp at Lakshmi Mandir. He was honored in January 1995, at a special function for Dedication and Relentless Service in spreading the teachings of Sanatan Dharma. From Surya Narayan Mandir in New York City, he has been honored twice: in November 1997 and June 2003, for promoting and preserving the Hindu religion and culture for over four decades.

Of success and service, he has said, "The recipe for success in life rests with honesty and dedication. I just want to be remembered as a humble individual helping and counseling others in reaching their goals."

November 19, 2008

Albert Sweetnam

BSc, FCSCE, Diploma Business Administration, Executive Vice President, Nuclear New Build, OPG

Albert Sweetnam was winner of Guyana Awards (Canada) 2010 Leadership Award. The citation of the award contains the following information, in part:

> Albert Sweetnam is executive vice president, Nuclear New Build, at Ontario Power Generation Inc. (OPG), whose principal business is the generation and sale of electricity in Ontario.
>
> Albert Sweetnam is responsible for the design, construction, licensing, and commissioning of the Nuclear New Build project ($20 billion), including developing the organizational capability to operate the facility, managing senior level stakeholder relations, and overseeing the completion of the request for proposal (RFP) process currently underway with Infrastructure Ontario. He also has responsibility for the Deep

Geological Repository ($1 billion) which, when completed, will store Ontario's low and intermediate nuclear waste.

Prior to OPG, he was a senior vice president with SNC Lavalin, Canada's largest engineering construction company, where he was project director of the $4.1 billion (US) Ambatovy Project in Madagascar. Prior to this, he managed SNC Lavalin's Infrastructure, Construction, Engineering, and Environment Divisions in Ontario, Manitoba, and several offshore locations. Ontario projects include Highway 407 and the Air Rail Link between Union Station and the Toronto Airport. His wide-ranging worldwide experience includes managing SNC Lavalin's engineering and construction operations in West Africa for thirteen years, and executing projects in Africa, Asia, Guyana, and South America.

Albert Sweetnam holds an honors degree from the University of Waterloo and a diploma in business administration from Ryerson University. He is a fellow of the Canadian Society for Civil Engineering, a member of various professional engineering organizations in Canada, the United States, and Africa, and has sat on the boards of four professional organizations. He is also recognized as a Gold Seal project and construction manager by the Canadian Construction Association, and has been consulted as a water expert by the World Bank in West Africa.

An active member of his community, Albert is involved in fund-raising for cancer and is on the board of the Community Share Food Bank. He is recognized as an international sailor, having held a national title for three consecutive years.

Sources:
Websites accessed May 27, 2010, on Guyana Consulate Toronto, Guyana Awards (Canada)

May 27, 2010

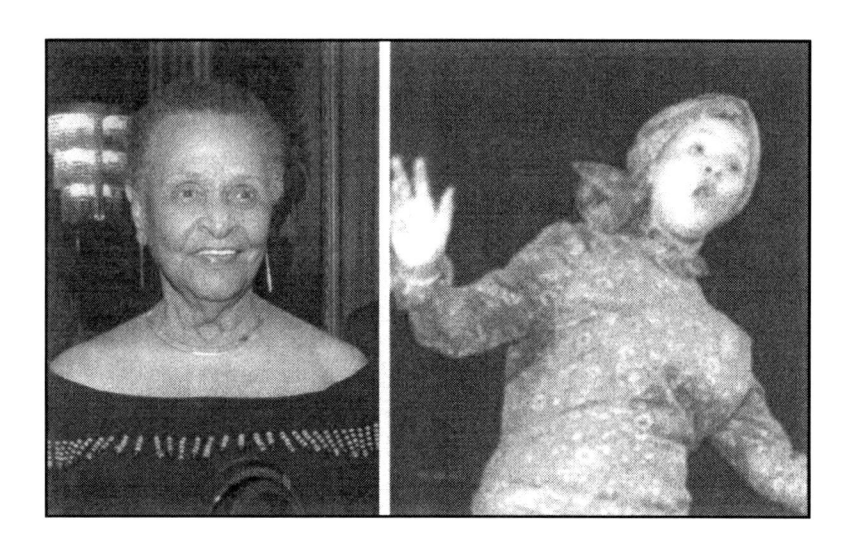

Pauline Thomas BA

"Auntie Comesee"

Pauline Thomas, "Auntie Comesee" was winner of Guyana Awards (Canada) 2008 Media and Culture Award. The citation of the award contains the following information, in part:

> Auntie Comesee had her formal "coming out" at a Theater Guild Christmas party in 1968 in Georgetown. After that, Auntie Comesee appeared many times all over Guyana until 1980, when her creator, Pauline Thomas, emigrated to Canada, where she continued to perform and promote Guyanese culture throughout the diaspora.
>
> Considering that as a teacher she would always speak formal English, Pauline's performances as Auntie Comesee would be even more striking. Her use of Creolese was born of her conviction that Guyanese should "know their folklore and respect it," and that Creolese should be kept alive.
>
> Pauline Thomas started her performing career when she was three years old. Her early tutelage in singing and reciting came

from her mother. Formal voice, stage, piano, and dance lessons followed, as did a career in teaching.

An accomplished singer, Pauline Thomas won several prizes at music festivals in Guyana, was a member of the Woodside Choir, and regularly performed classical and semi-classical song recitals on Guyanese radio stations for over twenty years.

Sustaining the character of Auntie Comesee on stage and radio for four decades is a testimony to her dedication and love of learning. Pauline Thomas entered the University of Toronto and graduated in 1999 with a BA degree at the age of seventy-eight. Since then, she has continued as a student of music at the Royal Conservatory in Toronto and, at eighty-seven, sings with two choirs at the Conservatory as well as with Caribbean Chorale.

Like her creator, Auntie Comesee continues to perform and promote Guyanese culture and folklore to appreciative audiences of all ages in North America.

Sources.
Websites accessed May 27, 2010, on Guyana Consulate Toronto, Guyana Awards (Canada)

May 27, 2010

Rampersaud Tiwari

Distinguished Indo-Guyanese Public (Civil) Servant
Canadian Imperial Bank of Commerce (CIBC) Ambassador
Recipient of the 2008 Guyana Lifetime
Achievement Award

Rampersaud Tiwari served with distinction in the public (civil) service of colonial and independent Guyana from 1953 to 1983. His first appointment was to the position of a junior Class II clerk in the Magistrate's Department in May 1953. He moved progressively on promotion from a Class II clerk to administrative cadet (ADC), then to administrative assistant and on to assistant secretary to the Council of Ministers (de facto the Cabinet/Privy Council of the Government of Guyana), and ultimately to the level of permanent secretary. He retired from the public service in December 1983.

For his extensive accumulated experience in public and community service he is regarded as a "walking encyclopedia" on matters of government and governance and public administration in Guyana. He is also a source of much information on the oral traditions and customs mainly of East Indians and Africans of Guyana.

His work in Canada is wide-ranging in the corporate and community sectors. He is an ambassador of the Canadian Imperial Bank of Commerce (CIBC) in Canada and an ad hoc interpreter of the Guyanese Creole dialect and culture at hearings of the Federal Immigration and Refugee Board and other municipal, provincial, and federal legal and administrative institutions and agencies and a director of the Canada Guyana Forum.

Ram, as he is familiarly known, was born in Buxton Village on November 27, 1932. His paternal (Aja and Ajee) and maternal grandparents (Nana and Nanee) were indentured immigrants from Uttar Pradesh in undivided India. His aja was from Kanpur and his ajee was from Varanasi. They were indentured on Plantation Non Pariel. His nana was from Bharatpur and his nanee was from Gorakhpur. They were indentured on Plantation Enmore.

Ram's father was Shiwprashad, a small-scale peasant farmer in the Buxton backlands and a sugar worker at Non Pariel and Lusignan Sugar Estates. These estates were near to Buxton where he lived with his family. Ram's mother, Dhanraji (nee Sukhan Singh) was an ideal Hindu spouse, mother, grandmother, a diligent traditional homemaker and a small-scale seamstress. She was a native of Bachelors Adventure, East Coast, Demerara. Ram was the eldest of nine children: six girls and three boys. He and his family were part of a large traditional Hindu family unit in Buxton from 1932 to 1964 and later in nearby Annandale, from 1964 to 1985.

Ram attended Arundel Congregational School in Buxton from 1936 to 1944. Ram won scholarships and proceeded to higher secondary education in Georgetown, first at Wortmanville Educational Institute from 1943 to1944, then at Alleyne High School from 1945 to 1946, and finally at Wray High School from 1947 to 1950. He passed the Junior Cambridge Examination in 1947 and the Senior Cambridge Examination in 1949 with high credits and distinctions. These were external examinations of Cambridge University in England.

After working in certain short-term high school teaching assignments and then in a few junior/apprentice level clerical and technical jobs in surveying, drafting, agriculture, and in social work of the Sugar Industry Labor Welfare Fund (SILWF) at Lusignan Sugar Estate, Ram joined the clerical service of the British Guiana Civil Service as a Class II clerk in the Magistrate's Department in May 1953. He was posted to the East Demerara Judicial District Office at Vigilance, a village that was near to his home in Buxton. There he remained as a clerk for eight years to the presiding magistrates of the District Courts.

Ram was also clerk to the magistrates who were appointed revising officers for the voters lists for the 1957 general election in the Central Demerara electoral district and for the 1961 general election in the East Demerara electoral district. He coordinated preparation and publication of the final lists of voters for the general elections in these two electoral districts. When the magistrates later appointed returning officers for these elections, Ram continued as their clerk. He was as well a supervisor of the polls in two Buxton Village polling stations of the Central Demerara electoral district, one in 1957 and the other in 1961. Ram also served on an ad hoc basis as clerk to the coroners and chairmen of the Cinematograph and Liquor Licensing Boards. The coroners and chairmen were also serving magistrates in the East Demerara judicial district.

While in the Magistrate's Department, Ram took the highly competitive 1961 in-service Public Service Commission (PSC) Examination for administrative cadets, junior administrators in training. He was successful at the examination and at the PSC interview that followed and was selected and posted initially to the Government Information Services (GIS), a specialist public relations and education extension services department of the government, where he served for six months. The GIS was at the time a semi-autonomous department within the portfolio of the chief secretary to His Excellency the Governor. After August 1961 and abolition of the Office of Chief Secretary, GIS was included in the portfolio of the premier and Minister of Development and Planning.

While at GIS, Rams's most memorable experiences were working with a team of GIS senior officers on the preparation, publication and distribution of a booklet titled "Patterns of Progress," a record of the achievements of the 1957–1961 government, participating in the Schools Broadcasts Program of the Ministry of Education, and participating in scripting and acting in a documentary that was produced by the Films Division of GIS. The film was titled *How to Vote* and it was widely projected in open-air community sessions, with poster displays in many urban, rural, and hinterland electoral constituencies by the district information officer of each region in the country. The information officers were accompanied by Ram and other officials, as resource persons who explained the voter education messages in the film and in the posters. The film was also projected in cinemas as a trailer, before the main feature films. After his tour of duty at the GIS ended in December 1961, Ram was posted to the Ministry of Communications for six months.

The purpose of his posting to the Ministry of Communications and to certain other government ministries and departments was to understudy some of the more experienced senior civil servants in the techniques and procedures of ministerial management, as British Guiana had become a progressive internally self-governing nation that was on its way to independence. Ram's main duties in the Ministry involved traveling with the Minister of Communications, the Honorable Mr. Earl Maxwell Gladstone Wilson, MLA, to several coastal and hinterland communities. The purpose of the minister's visits was to review public and privately owned and operated transportation services and the level of citizen satisfaction, considering improvements that were made by the government between 1957 and 1961.

When his tour of duty ended in the Ministry of Communications in June 1962, Ram was posted to the Office of the Premier and Ministry of Development and Planning. There he served as the assistant secretary to the Council of Ministers (the Cabinet) and to the premier, Dr. the Honorable Cheddi Jagan, BSc., DDS, MLA, and the premier, the Honorable Mr. L. F. S. Burnham, QC, MLA, from January 1963 June 1965, when he was transferred on promotion to the newly established Ministry of Foreign Affairs where he served as head of the administration division of the Ministry until November 1969.

During his tour of duty in the Office of the Premier, Ram was sent overseas to pursue special postgraduate level studies and training at the School of Public Administration, University of Rio Piedras in Puerto Rico, with attachments to the planning board of the government of Puerto Rico from July 1962 to December 1962. Later in 1967, when he was serving as assistant secretary in the Ministry of Foreign Affairs, Ram was sent to pursue special advanced postgraduate level studies in public administration and international relations at the Faculty of Government and Politics of Carleton University in Ottawa, Ontario, with attachments in the Department of External Affairs and in certain other departments of the government of Canada. These special academic courses and training sessions were sponsored by the government of Guyana and generously funded from external aid programs of the government of Puerto Rico in 1962 and the government of Canada in 1967.

Ram moved progressively on to higher senior executive career levels in the service through normal promotional opportunities in the Ministry of Foreign Affairs, the Public Service Ministry, the Ministry of Education and Social Development, the Ministry of Transport, and the Ministry of Works and Housing, from which he retired in December 1983.

In addition to his normal public service duties, Ram was assigned additional duties between 1964 and 1975. He was secretary to the 1964 Indian Immigration and Repatriation Fund Committee with Attorney at Law Mr. Sase Narain, OR, (later Speaker of Parliament) as chairman; secretary to the 1964 Displaced Persons Relief and Rehabilitation Committee with Sir Stanley Gomes, a retired chief justice of the West Indian Court of Appeal as chairman; member of the 1973 Labor Code Commission; facilitator for the 1974 Commonwealth Secretariat's Seminar/Workshop on Education Administration; advisor to the Minister of Education at the 1974 Meeting of CARICOM Ministers of Education and University Representatives; member of the 1975 Guyana Air Transport Advisory Board; Guyana's representative on shipping at the West Indies Shipping Corporation and the Caribbean Development Bank (CDB) in 1977. He was Guyana's representative at the 1978 Standing Committee of CARICOM Ministers, responsible for transportation, and secretary to the Guyana National Transport Advisory Commission in 1984. He also served as a trustee of the Buxton Scholarship Fund from 1963 to 1973.

Ram became a permanent secretary in 1978. The *Guyana Chronicle* newspaper of April 26, 1978, featured the news. There was a photograph in the newspaper of Ram signing the oath of office in the presence of the president of Guyana, His Excellency Mr. Arthur Chung. The article stated, in part:

> Tiwari, who is in the public service for twenty-five years, worked in various government departments, starting as a magistrate's clerk. He did courses in public administration and international relations at the University of Puerto Rico and Carlton University in Canada. He did the course while he was attached to the Ministry of Foreign Affairs where he served for more than five years. He also served as assistant secretary to the Cabinet between 1961 and 1964, in the Public Service Ministry and acted as permanent secretary in the Ministry of Education.

From 1983, as the age of optional retirement approached, Ram was assigned special responsibilities as legal services advisor to the Construction Management Combine, a government holding company for other companies that were concerned with construction and maintenance of public projects including heritage buildings and monuments and the Demerara Harbor Bridge.

Between March and May 1985, after retirement, he served as a member of the Guyana Commemoration Commission under the distinguished chairmanship of Sir Edward Victor Luckhoo, QC., retired chancellor of the judiciary. The Commemoration Commission was tasked with responsibility to advise the government on matters of national unity through study of the cultural heritage of the Guyanese people with special reference to written history, folklore, customs, and traditions. Ram also served on a National Crematorium Committee that was appointed by the president, His Excellency Mr. L. F. S. Burnham. This committee was established to advise the government on a crematorium either by the open pyre system or by any other system. For his public services to Guyana, the senior vice president and Minister of Works and Housing wrote to Ram in 1985 expressing the government's "appreciation for the outstanding service he had given to the state over the past thirty years."

In June 1985, Ram went to join his family and siblings in Toronto, Canada. There he secured employment with the Canadian Imperial Bank of Commerce (CIBC), first in the Visa Department and then in the Mortgage Servicing Department of the bank. As a customer service officer at CIBC, he interacted on a daily basis with numerous customers on matters of consumer credit, housing and small business loans, and mortgages.

A very high percentage of these customers were Guyanese, West Indians, Latin Americans, Asians, and Africans, who were earlier residents in Canada or new immigrants to Canada. He also performed ad hoc human resources functions in respect of performance and reward incentives. He retired from the bank in December 1996 and was designated a CIBC ambassador for life.

Ram's extensive experience as a public servant in Guyana, under several administrations, including colonial ones, makes him a font of knowledge on matters of government and governance in the country. His knowledge of the history of Guyana and the culture of its multiethnic population makes talking with him an enriching experience. Many students engaged in higher studies, writers, journalists, and others who wish to learn more about Guyana invariably seek him out as a profound and wise resource with invaluable information.

Ram is a founder director of the Canada–Guyana Forum (CGF), which was formed in 1987. The forum is a Canadian/Guyanese non-governmental organization (NGO) in Toronto. Its founder and president is Dr. Hazel Campayne, a sister of the Holy Order of the Ursulines. The organization promotes social justice for Guyanese in Guyana and in Canada. CGF, deeply concerned at the upsurge of terrorism and violence and flagrant violations of the rule of law and challenges to government and governance, benefits greatly from Ram's views and analyses on efforts to protect citizens rights and to promote conditions for peace and security.

The forum is also committed to promoting the richness of the history, culture, and folklore of Guyana. Ram has been its senior resource person, consultant, and advisor. Drawing on his vast knowledge and understanding of the diverse aspects of Guyana's history, the country's culture and folklore, his contribution to the forum's mission and work has been truly valuable. Equally invaluable has been Ram's work with the forum in securing greater cooperation between Canada and Guyana on constitutional and human rights and on human and structural development in the country.

While serving at CIBC, Ram was retained through the good offices of Dr. Hazel Campayne by the Canadian Council of Churches to be an election observer with the Canadian/Guyanese Election Watch Committee at the October 1992 Guyana general and regional elections. He played a significant role as a coleader of this observer mission with Dr. Campayne in monitoring the elections. For this important task, he was released by CIBC with full pay for two weeks to travel to Guyana to observe and report on the conduct of the elections.

Among the forum's projects on which Ram was a leading voice are the Guyana Eldorado Series and the presentation on the history and culture of Buxton, Ram's native village in Guyana. With significant help from the Ministry of Education in Guyana, the forum implemented an Education Renewal Project in 1994 that established an educational program for youths in the Tiger Bay community of Georgetown.

Ram has been serving as an interpreter of the Guyanese Creole dialect and culture at hearings of the Canadian Federal Immigration and Refugee Board since 1995. He is also engaged by the Interpreters Group, a private quasi-legal group in Canada that requires his help from time to time in interpreting the Guyanese Creole dialect and culture at administrative and/or legal hearings that involve Guyanese, especially those of the country's rural communities.

While in retirement, considering his expertise in electoral and election matters, Ram was retained by the Guyana Elections Commission under the chairmanship of Mr. Doodnauth Singh, SC, with funding support from the United Nations Development Program and the National Democratic Institute of the United States to be its voter education consultant from August 1997 to February 1998.

The commission also took advantage of his education and training in diplomacy and election observation to assign to him the duties and responsibilities of facilitator for the:1997 International Election Observers of the Organization of American States (OAS), International Foundation for Electoral Systems, Commonwealth Secretariat, European Union, and designated diplomatic representatives of certain commonwealth and other countries who were accredited emissaries to Guyana. His election and electoral experiences earned him pride of place as an observer with the OAS Electoral Observation Mission to Suriname for that country's 2000 general election. He was selected by the head of the Unit for Democracy of the OAS in Washington DC.

Ram has consistently sought to serve Guyana and fellow Guyanese in whatever way he could, wherever the opportunity arose. He has occasionally extended pro bono services to Guyana's high commissioner to Canada, who was based in Ottawa and to the consulate general in Toronto. Former high commissioner, His Excellency Mr. Brindley Horatio Benn paid this compliment to Ram: "As high commissioner, I frequently sought [Ram's] advice on certain matters bearing on his accumulated knowledge of government and public affairs in Guyana." Ram was also one of three judges for the 2004 Guyana Awards in Canada. The other two judges were the Honorable Justice Vibert Lampkin and Honorary Consul General Thakur (Danny) Doobay.

Ram's knowledge and experience of government and governance and Guyana's history and culture is matched by his knowledge of the Hindu faith, traditions, and customs. He acquired this learning from his parents and from his grandfather (Aja), his father's father, and other elders of the Indian indentured community in Guyana. His aja was a closely bonded brother in faith of Pandit Latchman Persaud, who lived in Buxton.

Pandit Latchman Persaud was a Sanskrit scholar and Hindu priest of Kashmiri heritage. Ram's aja and Pandit Latchman were among a small but significant community of Hindus and Muslims of Kashmiri heritage in Buxton and in Guyana. It is of note that Pandit Jawaharlal Nehru was the most outstanding Kashmiri pandit of his time.

Ram has also done considerable self-study and is often addressed as Pandit Tiwari. In his case, "pandit" is used not in its everyday sense of a Hindu priest but in its other specific meaning: "erudite/learned/scholarly," thus honoring him by addressing him as pandit, as it was used to address Pandit Jawaharlal Nehru.

Pandit Nehru was one of India's independence leaders and the country's first prime minister. He was the father of Indira Gandhi, India's assassinated prime minister. Here it is necessary to place on record that Ram was a protocol officer to Mrs. Gandhi when she was on her state visit to Guyana in 1969.

Mrs. Gandhi earned an abiding respect and affection of the Guyanese people during her historic visit to the Guyana. This high esteem and respect for Mrs. Gandhi as a person, prime minister, and international scholar and humanist was matched only by the personal high admiration of her graceful and erudite qualities by the Honorable Mr. L. F. S. Burnham, SC, MLA, the prime minister of Guyana and other eminent persons in the country

In Ram's wide-ranging work in the Guyanese community overseas, he is seen and respected for his strong Hindu heritage values, while he is deeply respectful of the values of other religious and cultural groups in the wider community. He has promoted and devoted much time and energy to achieve genuine cooperation and understanding in relationships between the various ethnic groups.

What made Ram decide on a career in the civil service? After completing the higher secondary levels of his studies, Ram believed it was his duty to help his parents to provide for the education, welfare, and security of his siblings. In view of this commitment, and the knowledge that his parents were too poor to send him to pursue higher studies in institutions of higher learning overseas, he dedicated himself to securing gainful career employment in the British Guiana Civil Service. The civil service was at the time the goal of almost every educated young person from the working poor families, especially in communities in the rural areas of the country.

Throughout his career, he has drawn from the expectations, counseling, and encouragement from many respected family and community elders and from certain special friends of his father and grandfather who were concerned with central and local government affairs and with religious, spiritual, and community matters.

Among the memorable enriching experiences in his life, Ram cites his exposure to competitive cricket at school in Georgetown, as a prefect and captain of the Wray High School Cricket Team in the 1948 secondary schools Chin Cup Competition, exposure to debating skills as a member of the Government Information Services (GIS) team in the 1961 debates for the Patrick Dargan Shield, and exposure to the game of volleyball and public speaking skills as a member of the Luther League of the Holy Trinity Lutheran Church in Buxton. These rich experiences, including his selfless contribution with his elders, Sydney King, Balram Singh Rai, and Albert Ogle to the election of Dr. Cheddi Jagan, the young, handsome, and forward-looking politician to the Legislative Council in 1947, have all helped to mold his strong personal and civic values, as well as his wider community outreach relationships in Guyana and elsewhere.

In his everyday relationships with others, Ram, in a genuine spirit of humility, is always open to learning. This way, he has shown that contemplation and action are best realized through dialogue and listening and collaborating with others. His humanity and generosity of spirit demonstrates what is required if we are to find instructive ways to address the difficult situations we face wherever we are.

Ram is a proud Guyanese nationalist, consistent practitioner of the Hindu faith, loyal Buxtonian, distinguished public servant, outstanding Canadian citizen, and accomplished employee in the private sector. He is a person who straddles multiple boundaries with grace, dignity, and humility. He is constantly urging Guyanese to aspire to the highest standards of excellence in performance, in all spheres of life and living. These are attributes any Guyanese would be truly proud to possess.

October 28, 2010

Professor Alissa Trotz

BA, MPhil, PhD

Dr. Alissa Trotz was awarded the University of Guyana Pro-Chancellor's Medal and University of the West Indies Book Prize for the most outstanding first-year law student in the Caribbean. She was a Cambridge Commonwealth Scholar, and the winner of the award for distinguished contribution to graduate teaching at the Ontario Institute for Studies in Education, University of Toronto. She edits a weekly column in the *Stabroek News* titled "In the Diaspora."

Alissa Trotz was educated at St. Margaret's Primary School and then, from 1978 to1985, at Queen's College, where she took A levels in history, literature, and economics. She then completed the first year of the LLB Program of UG/UWI Faculty of Law in 1985 and proceeded to study for her degree. In 1989 she obtained her BA (with honors),York, in political science/Latin American and Caribbean studies. This was quickly followed by the master's (Cambridge) in international relations in 1990 and her PhD (Cambridge) in social and political sciences in 1995.

Her career in lecturing at university started in 1994 when she was appointed affiliate lecturer, social and political science, at Cambridge, then research fellow, Latin American studies. She moved quickly up the academic ladder and from 1996 to1997; she was director of studies (social and political sciences) Trinity College, Cambridge. From 1997 to 1999, she was assistant professor at Queen's University, women's studies, Queen's National Scholar; 1999 to date, assistant professor, sociology/equity studies women's studies and gender studies, Ontario Institute of Social Education, University of Toronto; and in 2006, director, Caribbean Studies, New College. She has been the principal supervisor of two doctoral theses and fourteen master's theses.

Dr. Trotz has packed into just over twenty years a vast body of work, including awards.

Honors and Awards include:

1986. Awarded UG Pro-Chancellor's Medal, UWI Book Prize, for most outstanding first-year law student in the Caribbean.
1989. Cambridge Commonwealth Scholar
1995. Appointed Junior Research Fellow (non-stipendiary), Wolfson College, Cambridge
1997. Queen's National Scholar appointment, Queen's University.
2004. Dean's Merit Award, Faculty of Arts and Science.
2005. Nominated for a teaching award, Faculty of Arts and Sciences.
Dean's Merit Award, Faculty of Arts and Science.
2007. Dean's Merit Award, Faculty of Arts and Science.
Award for distinguished contribution to graduate teaching, Ontario Institute for Studies in Education, University of Toronto. University of Toronto Students Union/Association of Part-Time Undergraduate Students Undergraduate Teaching Award.

Editorial Positions include:

2007: Aaron Kamugisha & Alissa Trotz (eds) (2007) Special Issue on Caribbean trajectories: 200 years after, to commemorate 200th anniversary of the abolition of the British Slave Trade for *Race and Class*, October

2004: Guest coeditor (with Darcy Ballantyne, Sylvia D. Hamilton, Katharine McKittrick, Andrea Medovarski, Leslie Sanders, Esther Tharao-Lyaruu, Njoki N. Wane). Special issue on women and the black diaspora for *Canadian Woman Studies*, 23:2

2004: Associate editor, *Wadabagei: A Journal of the Caribbean and Its Diaspora*

July 2002: Guest coeditor (with Marilyn Porter). Special issue of *Atlantis: A Women's Studies Journal*, "Gender and Globalization."

Coeditor (with Andaiye and Sara Abraham), "Woman's Eye View," *Stabroek Daily News*, Guyana (1998-1999).

Invited Talks (selected):

"Violence in the Caribbean: Gender and Political Conflict in Guyana," invited panelist, Violence in the Caribbean, Africana Studies, University of Pennsylvania, March 27, 2008.

"Gender, Generation and Memory: Remembering a Future Caribbean," invited keynote speaker, Dame Nita Barrow Annual Memorial Lecture (Women Catalysts for Change), Bridgetown, Barbados, November 16, 2007 (broadcast live to St. Vincent and the Grenadines and on the Web).

"Counting Women's Work," invited public lecture, Critchlow Labor College, Guyana, July 2007.

"Transnationalizing the Curriculum: Perspectives from Women's Studies," Canadian Adult Education Association Annual Conference, Victoria, May 2004.

"From Invisibility to Inclusion: Gender and the Politics of Marginality," Conflict Resolution Conference, Guyana, February 2004.

Publications include:

Linda Peake and Alissa Trotz (1999) *Gender, Ethnicity and Place: Women and Identities in Guyana*, London: Routledge.

Chapters in Books include:

D. Alissa Trotz (2008) "Feminisms and Feminist Issues in the South," Vandana Desai & Rob Potter (eds.) for reprint of *Companion to Development Studies*, London: Hodder Arnold (previously a coauthored entry, rewritten and resubmitted as single author).

D. Alissa Trotz (2004) "Engendering Democracy: Challenges and Response." in Jayant Lele and Fahim Quadir (eds.), *Globalization,*

Democracy, and Civil Society in Asia, London: Palgrave Macmillan, 107–129.

Alissa Trotz (2002), "At what cost sustainable communities?" An interview with Sister Susan Mika, in Eichler, M., Larkin, J. & Neysmith, S. (eds.), *Feminist Utopias: Redesigning Our Futures*. Toronto: Inanna Publications, pp. 66–76.

D. Alissa Trotz (2002), "Gender, Ethnicity and Familial Ideology: Household structure and Female Labor Force Participation Reconsidered," in P. Mohammed(ed) *Gendered Realities: An Anthology of Essays in Caribbean Feminist Thought*, Kingston, Jamaica, the University of the West Indies Press, pp. 249–276.

Alissa Trotz and Linda Peake (2001), "Feminisms and Feminist Issues in the South," in V. Desai & R. Potter (eds), *A Companion to Development Studies*, London: Arnold Publishers, pp. 334–337.

D. Alissa Trotz and Linda Peake on behalf of Red Thread (1999), "'Givin' lil bit fuh lil bit': Sex Work and Sex Workers in Guyana." in Kempadoo, Kamala (ed) *Sun, Sex and Gold: Tourism and Sex Work in the Caribbean*, Rowman & Littlefield, 1999, pp. 263–290.

D. Alissa Trotz (1998), "Guardians of our homes, guards of yours? Economic crisis, gender stereotyping, and the restructuring of the private security industry in Georgetown, Guyana," in Barrow, C. (ed.) *Caribbean Portraits: Essays on Gender Ideologies and Identities,* Kingston, Jamaica: Ian Randle Publishers, 1998, pp. 28–54.

Articles In Refereed Journals include:

D. Alissa Trotz (2007) "Red Thread: The Politics of Hope," *Race and Class*.

D. Alissa Trotz (2007) "Going global? Transnationality, Women/ Gender Studies, and lessons from the Caribbean," the inaugural issue of the *Caribbean Review of Gender Studies* (online journal, CGDS, University of the West Indies), April.

D. Alissa Trotz, (2006) "Rethinking Caribbean transnational connections: Conceptual itineraries," *Global Networks*, January 2006, 6 (1): 41–60.

D. Alissa Trotz (2004) "Between despair and hope: Towards an analysis of women and violence in contemporary Guyana," *Small Axe: A Journal of Criticism* 15: 1–25.

D. Alissa Trotz (2003) "Behind the banner of culture? Gender, race, and the family in Guyana," *New West Indian Guide/Nieuwe West Indische Gids* 77 1&2 (July 2003): 5–29.

Ena Dua and Alissa Trotz, 2002, "Transnational Pedagogy: Doing Political Work in Women's Studies: An Interview with Chandra Talpade Mohanty," in *Atlantis: A Women's Studies Journal*, 26,2: 66–77.

Alissa Trotz and Linda Peake (2001), "Family, work and organizing: an overview of the contemporary economic, social and political roles of women in Guyana," *Social and Economic Studies,* 50:2, pp. 67–101.

D. Alissa Trotz (1996) "Gender, ethnicity and familial ideology in Georgetown, Guyana: household structure and female labor force participation reconsidered," in *European Journal of Development Research*, 8:1, June 1996, pp. 177–99.

Editorial Positions (Special Issues):

2007: Aaron Kamugisha & Alissa Trotz (eds) (2007) Special issue on Caribbean trajectories: 200 years after, to commemorate 200th anniversary of the abolition of the British Slave Trade for *Race and Class*, October.

2004: Guest coeditor (with Darcy Ballantyne, Sylvia D. Hamilton, Katharine McKittrick, Andrea Medovarski, Leslie Sanders, Esther Tharao-Lyaruu, Njoki N. Wane) Special issue on women and the black diaspora for *Canadian Woman Studies*, 23:2.

July 2002: Guest coeditor (with Marilyn Porter), Special issue of *Atlantis: A Women's Studies Journal*, Gender and Globalization.

Abstracts and/or Papers Read (selected)

The Politics of Representation and the Representation of Politics: Race and Caribbean Feminisms, paper presented at Latin American and Caribbean Studies, Montreal, September 2007.

Organizer and chair of panel, "The poverty of politics, the politics of poverty in the Caribbean," Caribbean Studies Association, Trinidad & Tobago, June 2006.

"Migrancy, Mobility and Livelihoods: Caribbean Realities," Association of Caribbean Economists, Port-Au-Prince, Haiti, November 2003.

"Mapping the Nation: Gendered Practices, Guyanese Identities," CERLAC International Migration in the Americas, York University, May 2–3, 2003.

"Making a living, making a home: Remapping Caribbean gendered identities," Canadian Association of Geographers, Toronto, May 31, 2002.

"Race, Culture and Violence: Feminist Reflections," paper presented at the Caribbean Feminisms Workshop: Recentering Caribbean Feminism. University of the West Indies, Cave Hill Campus, June 17–18, 2002.

"Gender, 'race' and culture in Caribbean familial narratives," Conference on the Humanities, Bridgetown, Barbados, June 5–7, 2001.

"Behind the banner of culture: Gender, 'race' and politics in Guyana," presented at Conference, Engaging Walter Rodney's Legacies: Historiography, Social Movements and African Diaspora, SUNY Binghamton, Nov. 6–8 1998.

"'Givin' lil bit fuh lil bit': Sex work and sex workers in Guyana," paper presented with Linda Peake and Karen de Souza at Tourism and the Sex Trade Conference, July 16–18 1998, Kingston, Jamaica.

"Gender and Ethnicity in Guyana," presented at Canadian Association of Latin American and Caribbean Studies, Vancouver, BC, March 1998.

"Gender, 'race' and nation," Seminar series, Women in Society, Faculty of Social and Political Sciences, Cambridge University, January 16, 1997.

"Representations of Indian femininity in colonial discourse in Guiana," paper presented at Cambridge/Tulane University joint symposium on slavery and the Atlantic World, New Orleans, November 1996.

"Laborer to housewife: The colonial state and constructions of Indian femininity under indentureship in Guyana," Commonwealth History Seminar, Oxford University, December 1995.

"Of households, familial ideology and income-earning: Reflections from Guyana," Seminar series, Institute of Commonwealth Studies, University of London, November 13, 1995.

Popular Articles:

"A Disservice to the Caribbean, indeed," *Stabroek Daily News*, Guyana, April 21, 2008.

"Marching for Peace in Jamaica," *Stabroek Daily News*, Guyana, March 3, 2008.

"The Revolutionary Promise of Courtesy," *Stabroek Daily News*, Guyana, Feb. 4, 2008.

"Time for Action?", *Stabroek Daily News*, Guyana, Jan. 27, 2008.

"Responding to the EPA," *Stabroek Daily News*, Guyana, Jan. 21, 2008.

"Tell Tara and Tara tell Tara: Rumor, fact, truth and history," *Stabroek Daily News*, Guyana, Oct. 1, 2007.

"Haitian human rights activist disappears: A call for support," *Stabroek Daily News*, Guyana, September 24, 2007.

"Remittances," *Stabroek Daily News*, Guyana, January 25, 2007.

"Overseas Guyanese: What kind of tribe are we?", *Stabroek Daily News*, Guyana, January 11, 2007.

Alissa Trotz and Sara Abraham, "Misconceptions, missing history, missing people, and misplaced loyalty," Woman's Eye View, *Stabroek Daily News*, Guyana, 12-6-98.

"Mothering … at what cost?" Woman's Eye View, *Stabroek Daily News*, Guyana, 07-02-99.

August 11, 2008

Belle Patricia Tyndall

BA, MA, PhD
Associate Professor Emeritus
George Washington University

At a moment in the history of education in the English-speaking Caribbean, Belle Tyndall was one of the agents of change responsible for developing the Caribbean Examinations Council (CXC) syllabus for Secondary Schools English Examination that replaced the British GCE.

She taught at all levels in Guyana: at primary school, high school, the Teachers College, the Technical Institute, and the University of Guyana. In the United States, she taught English at Howard University, and English as a foreign language, as well as linguistics, at George Washington University.

In Guyana, she was chief examiner for English at the Teachers Colleges. She set the language aspects of the entrance test for the University of Guyana. In the United States, she was involved in assessing the oral proficiency of international students applying for teaching assistantships, as well as the written proficiency of MA and DSc candidates.

At the University of Guyana, she was head of the Department of Curriculum Development, and dean of the Faculty of Education. She also served as chair of the Committee of Deans and acted as vice chancellor, University of Guyana. At George Washington University in the United States, she was chair of the Department of English as a Foreign Language. She was one the first commissioners to be elected to the Commission on English Language Program Accreditation, the only specialized accrediting agency for English language programs in institutions in the United States and schools outside the United States.

Belle Patricia Tyndall was born on September 13, 1934, in Bent Street, Wortmanville, Georgetown, Guyana. Her father, Clement Thorne, was an engineer. Her mother, Sheffield Mansfield, was a seamstress.

Belle attended Smith Church Congregational Primary School and won a Government County Scholarship in 1945, which secured for her a free place at Bishops' High School, in Georgetown, the top secondary school for girls in Guyana. In 1953, after passing the advanced level, London General Certificate of Education Examination, she embarked on a career in teaching. She attended the Government Training College for Teachers, Georgetown, Guyana, where she obtained, the Trained Teachers Certificate (First Class) in 1955.

At university level, Belle first secured a diploma in the teaching of English overseas (English as a second language) from the University of Manchester, England. She followed that with a BA, University of London,England; and MA, language and literature in education (English as a foreign language), University of London Institute of Education. She obtained her PhD in linguistics from Georgetown University, Washington DC. Later, she obtained the professional development certificate in distance education from the University of Wisconsin–Madison, School of Education Graduate Program in Continuing and Vocational Education.

From a modest job as primary school teacher, Belle's career in education developed into a force for educational reform, first in Guyana then in the Caribbean and the United States. Her remarkable intellectual ability matched in equal measure with drive, propelled her to leading positions in the field of education. Catalogued below is a summary of Belle's achievements, her employment history, advisory, and reviewer roles, university service, professional development activities, publications, and presentations and awards she has received.

Employment. Positions held in Guyana:

1955–1963: Grade school teacher, Ministry of Education, Georgetown, Guyana.
1963–1971: Lecturer, Government Training College for Teachers, Georgetown, Guyana.

The following positions at the University of Guyana, Georgetown, Guyana:
Jan.–Sept.1972: Language research fellow, Carnegie Research Unit, Faculty of Education.
1972–1978: Lecturer (assistant professor) in language education, Faculty of Education.
1974–1978: Head, Department of Curriculum Development & Carnegie Research Unit, Faculty of Education. (Research unit funded by the Carnegie Corporation of New York), responsible for administering the first MA program offered by the Faculty of Education.
Sept. 1978: Appointment with tenure, Faculty of Education.
Sept. 1979: Senior lecturer (associate professor), Faculty of Education.
1980–1983: Dean, Faculty of Education. During this period was chair of the Committee of Deans, and when the vice chancellor was away, acted as vice chancellor.

Employment positions held in the United States:

1989–1991: Adjunct professor, School for Summer and Continuing Education, Georgetown University, Washington DC.
1989-1990: Assistant professor, English, Department of English, Howard University, Washington DC.

The following positions at the George Washington University, Washington DC.,- Columbian College of Arts and Sciences:
1989 (Fall): Assistant professorial lecturer, English as a Foreign Language.
1990–1992: Assistant professor, English as a Foreign Language..
1992–1998: Chair, Department of English as a Foreign Language. During the period of chairmanship, the department served approximately 800 international students per year.

2000 (March-June): Interim Chair, Department of English as a Foreign Language..
1993–2004: Chair, Linguistics Program.
1992–2004: Associate Professor, English as a Foreign Language..
2004. Associate professor emeritus.

Other appointments held:

1980-1983: External examiner, Applied Linguistics, Department of English, Faculty of Arts, University of Guyana.
1980-1983: Chief examiner, English Language and Literature, Teachers Colleges, Guyana.
1981: Assistant chief examiner, English Literature (secondary schools examination for thirteen Caribbean countries) Caribbean Examinations Council. Barbados, West Indies.
1986: External examiner, English Curriculum Research Study, Faculty of Education, University of Guyana.
2004–2006: Commissioner, Commission on English Language Program Accreditation, Alexandria, Virginia (Accredits English language programs in institutions in the United States and schools outside the United States).

Advisor/Reviewer.

1972-1978: Consultant, University of Guyana Open Entrance Examination. Prepared multiple-choice-type reading comprehension tests. Developed a test of written English.
1977-1980: Advisor to Longman Group Limited, British Publishers, in connection with the publication of "New World English," a series of text books for secondary schools in the Caribbean, by Dennis Craig and Grace Walker Gordon.
1978–1983: Advisor to the Guyana Reading Project, Ministry of Education, Georgetown.
1995: Member, Editorial Committee, Journal of Education and Research in the Caribbean (ERICA), University of Guyana.
1995: External examiner for Jean Bovell's PhD (education) thesis: *"The Effects of a Reading Program on Reading Skills and Self-Concept."* University of the West Indies, Mona, Jamaica.

1997: Outside reviewer of papers and publications for Susan Grace re: promotion to assistant specialist in the Applied English Center, University of Kansas.

1998: Member of the Dissertation Committee for Marnie Lynn Johnson's PhD: "The Attribute-Value Distinction: How Commonalities can be Positively and Negatively Related to Alignable Differences." Columbian College of Arts and Sciences, the George Washington University.

2001: Outside Reviewer of papers and publications for Christine Jensen re: promotion to associate language specialist in the Applied English Center, University of Kansas.

2008: External reader for Andrea Christine Todd's EdD dissertation: *"English as a second language instructional approaches for college-level coursework and academic writing: A survey of program directors in institutions of higher education in the United States."* Graduate School of Education and Human Development, the George Washington University.

University service:

At the University of Guyana:
1974: Member, Academic Board
1980: Member, Finance and General Services Committee; member, Appointments Committee; member, Admissions Committee; member, University Council.
1983: Chairman, Committee of Deans; Chairman, Research and Publications Committee.

At the George Washington University:
1991–2000: Conducted oral proficiency interviews for international teaching assistants, and candidates for the DSc in engineering management.
1992–1998: Responsible for reviewing and administering the English Tool Examinations set for Elliott School of International Affairs (ESIA) and the Dept. of Engineering Management (SEAS).
1992: Cochair, New Directions in Testing & Evaluation Colloquium on Foreign Language Teaching, open to universities in the Washington area, held on April 10.
1992–1995: Member of the University Council on International Programs (appointed by the university president).
1994: Member, Search Committee, University Librarian (appointed by the vice president for Academic Affairs).

1995–2000: Responsible for developing, administering and evaluating the written English Tool Test for DSc candidates in the Department of Engineering Management.
1995: Interviewer for selection of 1996 Colonial (Student) Cabinet.
1996: Member, interview panel for director of International Services.
1997–1998: Member, Strategic Planning Project, Students and Academic Support Services.
2000–2001: Member, Search Committee, Romance Languages Department.
2002–2003: Chair, Testing Committee, Department of English as a Foreign Language.

Other Professional Development Activities:
Reader Training Workshop for TOEFL Test of Written English (TWE), sponsored by the Education Testing Service.
Oral Proficiency Interview Tester Training, organized by American Council on the Teaching of Foreign Languages (ACTFL) Washington DC.
Course in the Organization of In-Service Education, University of Leeds, Leeds, England.
Course in textbook development conducted in Port of Spain, Trinidad and Tobago, by the Commonwealth Secretariat, London.
Test Development Workshop (item writing) conducted in Barbados, West Indies, by the Educational Testing Service, Princeton, for the Caribbean Examinations Council (CXC).

Memberships
Guyana and the Caribbean:
1974–1983: Member, National Education Committee, Ministry of Education, Guyana.
1975–1981: Guyana's representative on the English Syllabus Panel appointed to develop a syllabus for the new Secondary School Leaving Examinations for Caribbean countries. Caribbean Examinations Council (CXC), Barbados.
1976–1988: Member, Society for Caribbean Linguistics.
1980–1983: University of Guyana's Representative on the CXC, Barbados.
1980–1983: Member, Schools Examination Committee, CXC, Barbados.

1982–1983: Member, Administrative and Finance Committee, CXC, Barbados.

Professional Societies in the United States:
1985–1989: Member, Washington Linguistics Society.
1989–2004: Member, TESOL (Teaching of English to Speakers of Other Languages).
1990–1998: Member, National Council of Teachers of English.
1992–2000: Member, American Association of Applied Linguistics.
1992–2000: Member, International Language Testing Association.
1992–present: Member, NAFSA: (National Association for Foreign Student Advisers,now Association of International Educators),1994–1995: elected to NAFSA's ATESL (Administrators and Teachers of English as a Second Language) Nominations Committee.
1997–1999: Appointed ATESL Representative for NAFSA Region VIII (NAFSA membership is divided into eleven geographical regions).
2002: Chair, NAFSA Region VIII (Delaware, District of Columbia, Maryland, Pennsylvania, Virginia, West Virginia).
2004 to present: American Association of University Women.

Publications include:

1978: English Language Curriculum: BV and Lodge Experimental Projects. Georgetown, Faculty of Education, University of Guyana. Teachers manuals and students booklets covering thirteen units of work for classes equivalent to US grades 7 to 9, requested by the Ministry of Education for use in all community high schools in Guyana.
1982: "The Language of Instruction. Do we need a Policy?" *Journal of Education*. Vol.1:1. University of Guyana.
1986: Review of "Communicative Competence Approaches to Language Proficiency Assessment." ed. by Charlene Rivera. *Language*, Vol.62:1.
1989: "What influences raters' judgment of student writing?" *Linguistics and Education,* 3, 191-202 Norwood, NJ: Ablex.
1996: with Dorry Keynon, "Validation of a New Holistic Rating Scale Using Rasch Multi-Faceted Analysis." *Validation in Language Testing. Selected papers from the 14th Annual Language Testing Research Colloquium.* Eds. Alister Cumming and Richard Berwick. eds. Avon: Multilingual Matters.

1999: "Tense marking in the writing of Caribbean Students." *Language in Action: New Studies of Language in Society.* Eds. Joy Kreeft Peyton, Peg Griffin, Walt Wolfram, and Ralph Fasold. Cresskell, N.J: Hampton Press, Inc.

Awards:

1954: The Arthur Seymour Cup for first place in the Verse Speaking Competition in the British Guiana Music Festival
1978 – 1979:   British Government Postgraduate Award.
1984 – 1987:   Graduate Fellowship, Graduate School, Georgetown University.
1987 – 1988:   Writing Center Fellow, Department of English, Georgetown University.
1999: Cyril Potter College of Education Award in appreciation of dedicated service to the education of teachers in Guyana
2003: NAFSA Award in recognition of service to NAFSA and the field of international education and exchange.
2006: Commission on English Language Program Accreditation Award for dedication to quality English language instruction and administration.

Belle has lectured on the teaching of English, both at the Teachers College and at the University of Guyana, and supervised teachers in schools. In the United States she taught English at Howard University, and English as a Foreign Language, as well as linguistics, at the George Washington University.

She has been involved in large-scale curriculum/syllabus development, both in Guyana and in the Caribbean. In Guyana, she was responsible for developing an English language curriculum for community high schools. The program was piloted first in two schools, expanded to twenty-six schools, and eventually extended to five hundred schools in Guyana. She conducted workshops for teachers in several areas of Guyana in connection with this project.

> With regard to the Caribbean, I was a member of a small team of Caribbean educators charged with the development of a syllabus for the English language examination offered by the newly formed Caribbean Examinations Council (CXC).

> The examinations were developed to replace the British examinations taken by high school students in all of the English-speaking territories in the Caribbean.
>
> Language testing was an important part of my responsibilities in Guyana, and the Caribbean, and continued to be important at the George Washington University. In Guyana, I was chief examiner for English at the Teachers Colleges, and was, for many years, responsible for setting the language aspects of the entrance test for the University of Guyana. I was trained by the Education Testing Service (USA) and Oxford & Cambridge Joint Board Examining Bodies in item writing and was later appointed by the Caribbean Examinations Council as assistant chief examiner for English literature.

On her early thoughts of becoming a teacher, Belle's reflections touched on the interesting issue of the influence of Creole on her students' work in English.

> I knew that I wanted to be a teacher from the time I was in primary school. When I completed secondary school, I thought I would specialize in history. However, when I became a teacher after graduating from the Teachers Training College, I encountered a problem that intrigued me. Why was it that my students would make grammatical errors in writing English compositions, but when I drew the errors to their attention they would be able to make the correction almost without hesitation? I became aware of the influence of Creole on their ability to produce standard English. The study of linguistics at the University of Manchester in 1964 helped me to understand the problem, and on my return to Guyana, I adapted some of the techniques of teaching English as a Second Language to the situation in Guyana.
>
> I continued to study the teaching of English as a Foreign Language at the University of London, and, after completing the PhD in linguistics at Georgetown University, I opted to teach in the Department of English as a Foreign Language at the George Washington University. I derived the greatest satisfaction from helping non-English speaking foreign

students at both undergraduate and graduate levels to develop the ability to communicate in English in both speech and writing.

Who inspired her?

> My inspiration comes from my mother. She wanted to be a teacher herself but was denied the opportunity. She taught me to read, and instilled in me the importance of education. She encouraged me to settle for nothing but the best but, at the same time, never ceased to remind me of the virtue of humility. As I progressed in my career, I always had the unswerving support of my husband.

Belle says her greatest satisfaction comes from being one of the agents of a history-making change in education in Guyana and the Caribbean.

> I have been fortunate to have had the opportunity to serve Guyana in the field of education in several different capacities. One of the areas that stands out is my involvement in the Caribbean Examinations Council (CXC), an examination body established in 1972 by the Caribbean Free Trade Association (CARIFTA, the predecessor to CARICOM) to replace the British examination bodies and to offer examinations more finely tuned to the needs of the Caribbean.
>
> I was selected by the Ministry of Education to be Guyana's representative on the committee of Caribbean educators responsible for developing the syllabus for the secondary schools English examination that replaced the British General Certificate of Education examination. My involvement, not only with the other committee members, representatives of the English-speaking Caribbean countries but also with the secondary school teachers throughout these countries, as we introduced the syllabus to each of the countries, was truly stimulating and exciting. We were all aware of the fact that we were agents of change and gave of our best.'

Belle is married to Joseph A. Tyndall, AA, CCH, economist and former government minister. He holds the degrees of BA in Philosophy (with honors), BSc (Econ.), London, and the advanced diploma in public administration, University of Exeter, England. From his early days as a primary school teacher, he moved on to senior positions in the Guyana Public Service and regional and international organizations. Among the leading roles and positions he has held, Joseph was the secretary and chief administrative officer of the Bank of Guyana; chairman of the Working Party for the establishment of the Caribbean Free Trade Association (CARIFTA); chief economist, CARIFTA; director, Trade and Integration Division, CARIFTA, and deputy secretary general of CARICOM, ending his service with the organization as Secretary General Ag (1977–1978). He was Minister of Trade, and later Minister of Agriculture, Guyana; executive director, Inter-American Development Bank (Washington DC); special representative for trade and investments, government of Guyana, based in Washington DC; and the first chairman of the Guyana Public Utilities Commission.

Their three children are themselves distinguished achievers. Daughter Irma Alison Tyndall BSc. (Hons), FIA, was a 1978 Guyana Scholar. She is a graduate of the London School of Economics, and actuarial consultant in the firm of Towers Watson, London, United Kingdom. Son Joseph Adrian Tyndall, MD, MPH, FACEP, is associate professor and chair of the Department of Emergency Medicine, University of Florida, Gainesville, Florida. Daughter Althea Patricia Tyndall-Smith, MS, MD, is a board-certified family physician in York, Pennsylvania.

September 14, 2010

Michael Van Cooten

Founder, Publisher, Editor Pride News Magazine

Michael Van Cooten was winner of Guyana Awards (Canada) 2007 Media Award. The citation of the award contains the following information, in part:

> Michael Van Cooten is the founder, publisher, and editor of *Pride* news magazine, Canada's foremost ethnic newspaper serving the African Guyanese and Caribbean community in Canada.
>
> The newspaper has been at the forefront of providing high quality coverage of news and events relevant to the Afro-Caribbean community and has effectively served to promote the special interests and culture of the community. The inaugural edition was published in January 1983 as *Caribbean Life* magazine, later changed to *Pride* news magazine.
>
> Born in Guyana, Michael Van Cooten migrated to Canada in 1972. He is a seasoned entrepreneur and journalist who held

management positions at the *Globe and Mail* and the *Toronto Sun* and has established many small businesses.

The vision of *Pride* is "to act as a catalyst for the advancement, empowerment and happiness of peoples of Caribbean and African heritage" by providing positive, inspiring stories about the successes, achievements and accomplishments of its target communities. *Pride* provides a significant link for the Guyana and Caribbean diaspora to news and views from back home, and often acts as a watchdog and social conscience to protect the rights of community members.

In addition to nurturing many young, promising journalists who later progressed to highly successful careers, *Pride* donates thousands of dollars in sponsorships to deserving non-profit organizations and has been generous in providing free advertising and coverage for community organizations which could not afford the costs.

Pride has been the recipient of several awards since its inception, including awards from the United Way, the Jamaican Canadian Association, and the Toronto Bathurst Lions Club.

Michael Van Cooten initiated the African Canadian Achievement Awards in 1985, described by the *Toronto Star* in February 2007 as "one of the country's most prestigious award events." These awards pay tribute to the exemplary contributions of members of the African Caribbean and Canadian community and foster a sense of pride and dignity within these communities.

Sources:

Websites accessed May 27, 2010, on Guyana Consulate Toronto, Guyana Awards (Canada)

May 27, 2010

Dr. Ivan G. Van Sertima

January 26, 1935–May 25, 2009

By Jacqueline Van Sertima

They Came Before Columbus, the *Journal of African Civilizations*, and *Early America Revisited* have created a different historical perspective within which to view the ancestor of the African American, as well as the potential and achievement of contemporary black people the world over.

Focus is on the heartland rather than on the periphery of African civilizations. Therefore, both categories of past and present, remove the "primitive" from the center stage it has occupied in Eurocentric histories and anthropologies of the African. Each publication is dedicated to the celebration of black genius, to a revision of the role of the African in the world's great civilizations, and to the contribution of Africa to the achievement of man in the arts and sciences.

Concisely, *They Came Before Columbus*, the *Journal of African Civilizations*, and *Early America Revisited* emphasize what blacks have given to the world, not what they have lost.

Excerpts From Ivan Van Sertima's Mission Statement:

> All through my life, from my boyhood in the jungles of Guyana, where my father was superintendent of Road and River Transport over an area as large as Scotland and Wales put together, my dream was of a world where the dark races of man would be seen as equals.
>
> When I left the jungle area and came to the main city of Georgetown, it was even harder to believe in the essential equality of man. My [mother's] Christian upbringing, however, saved me from any racial prejudice though it could not cloud my eyes from the often secret and sometimes public and naked agony of many of my friends and members of my family.
>
> Thus was born a sense of what was to become the mission of my life.
>
> It became my dream in life to rescue my people—all people—from myths of the African race.

Ivan Gladstone Van Sertima was born to Clara Smith Van Sertima and Frank Obermueller Van Sertima, where the foundation of who he was to become also was given birth in Kitty Village Guyana, South America on January 26, 1935.

After primary schooling in the counties of Essequibo and Demerara, Ivan Van Sertima attended Central High School, Georgetown (September 1947 to December 1953). In 1952 he became president of the Central High School Literary and Debating Society, secretary of the Prefect Body, and editor of the Central High School magazine.

From 1957 to 1959, he served as press and broadcasting officer in the Guyana Information Services. During the decade of the 1960s he broadcasted weekly from Britain to Africa and the Caribbean.

Ivan Van Sertima completed his undergraduate studies in African languages and literature at the School of Oriental and African Studies at the University of London in 1969, where he graduated with honors.

In 1970 Ivan immigrated to the United States. He began graduate studies at Rutgers University, New Brunswick, New Jersey.

In 1984 he was awarded an honorary doctorate of humane letters from Sojourner Douglass College.

His teaching career of over thirty years at Rutgers University began in 1972. In 1977 he received his master's degree in anthropology and began his teaching career as an associate professor, eventually promoted to full professor of African studies in the Department of Africana Studies. He served as visiting professor at Princeton University for several semesters during his tenure at Rutgers University.

He has earned numerous additional awards and recognition for his outstanding scholarship, commitment to intellectual excellence, courage, and relentless research. He was an anthropologist, historian, literary critic, linguist, activist, poet, essayist, and made a name in all aforementioned fields.

As an Anthropologist and Historian

In 1976, his first celebrated classic, *They Came Before Columbus* (subtitled "The African Presence in Ancient America") was published by Random House. It is presently in its thirty-first printing and was also published in French in 1981. In the same year, he was awarded the Clarence L. Holte Prize, a prize awarded every two years "for a work of excellence in literature and the humanities relating to the cultural heritage of Africa and the African diaspora." This groundbreaking book deals with a number of contacts, both planned and accidental, between Africans and Americans in different historical periods. With his considerable scholarship, Dr. Van Sertima examines the facts of navigation and shipbuilding, the sources of latitudinal and longitudinal coordinates, the scores of cultural analogies found nowhere else except in America and Africa, African languages, and the transportation of plants, cloth and animals from Africa to the Americas. And from the diaries, letters and journals of the explorers themselves; from Carbon-14 dated sculptures found in the Americas; from Arabic documents, charts, maps; from the recorded tales of the griots to the kings of Mali; from the dated skeletons found as recently as 1975, Dr. Van Sertima builds his pyramid of evidence. In addition to a scholar's fastidiousness, Van Sertima used the skill of a novelist to create some of the most powerful scenes history has to offer.

Clement A. Price—professor of history and founder/director of the Rutgers Institute on Ethnicity, Culture and the Modern Experience—wrote:

> *They Came Before Columbus* dared to challenge one of the largest mythologies of Western civilization; Africans' incapability to make contributions in the area of science, global migration,

etc. This book has inspired African scholars worldwide, people who wanted to know what smart black scholars were thinking about. It is the book on everybody's bookshelf. The book is seminal.

Toni Morrison, Nobel Prize and Pulitzer Prize-winning novelist, editor, and Princeton professor, wrote. "Dr. Van Sertima's work is one of the most important contributions to African scholarship."

Journal of African Civilizations, Ltd., Inc.

In 1979, as editor, contributor, and founder, Dr. Van Sertima established the *Journal of African Civilizations*, Ltd., Inc. as specialized periodicals, primarily requested by public and private libraries. In response to an overwhelming demand by institutions of higher education, in 1980, he and then Jacqueline L. Patten began to expand the journals to widely recognized books made available to schools and educators of all levels, hospitals, businesses, laymen, etc., worldwide. Abundant and respectful credit is due to the many scholarly and dedicated researchers, administrators, translator, webmaster, and cover designer/art consultant, and supporters who made the *Journal of African Civilizations*, Ltd., Inc. possible. All books presently continue to be published, expanded, newly created and distributed by Mrs. Jacqueline L. Van Sertima in honor of the outstanding scholarship and fortitude provided by all participants.

Alphabetical List of Anthologies *(Journal of African Civilizations Ltd., Inc.)*:

African Presence in Early America
African Presence in the Art of the Americas
African Presence in Early Asia (Coedited with Runoko Rashidi)
African Presence in Early Europe
Blacks in Science: Ancient and Modern
Black Women in Antiquity
Egypt: Child of Africa (presently including original Nile Valley Civilizations* publication)
Egypt Revisited
Golden Age of the Moor
Great African Thinkers: Cheikh Anta Diop (Coedited with Larry Obadele Williams)
Great Black Leaders: Ancient and Modern

Nile Valley Civilizations*

Juanita Millender-McDonald, member of Congress, wrote, "Your works have nurtured a nation and laid the foundation for the global rebirth of a people."

Manu Ampim, historian, primary research director, wrote:

> Whereas *They Came Before Columbus* is, indeed, seminal, I believe the *Journal of African Civilizations* has made, yet, an even greater impact on the institution of academia and the world, at large. The journals are being read and used, internationally, by educators of all grades and in every field, of higher learning institutions, and the general public. Being a great visionary and scholar, Dr. Van Sertima brought together a community of researchers and scholars to further study the role of the African in the world's great civilizations. We found that, historically, Africans were at the apex of civilization, not on the periphery. Thus, we witnessed and were a part of a great moment in historiography. And so, the *Journal of African Civilizations* was born in celebration of black genius. Collectively, we forced the world to put on the table, an African reality that had been ignored, and might still be, if it weren't for Dr. Van Sertima's courage, scholarship, commitment and broad appreciation for the true legacy of our people. We are left with a deep appreciation for his body of work and scholarly nourishment that will be the springboard for future generations.

Cheikh Anta Diop, Directeur du Laboratoire du Radiocarbone Ifan Universite, Dakar, Senegal; physicist, historian, linguist, wrote these words:

> In my works titled "L'Afrique Noire Pre-Coloniale" (Pre-Colonial Black Africa) and Antiquite Africaine par l'image" (African Antiquity through Images), I dealt with the possibilities of pre-Columbian contacts between Africa and America, but it was only a working hypothesis. Thus you can imagine how much pleasure your discoveries gave me, because

of the conclusive evidence they constitute for historical science. All my congratulations!

Early America Revisited. Twenty years after the publication of *They Came Before Columbus*, Dr. Van Sertima presented, in his new book *Early America Revisited* a number of new facts that were not known during his writing of *They Came Before Columbus. Early America Revisited* was forged out of the desire to update previous information. This book is a carefully balanced case for an African presence in America, before Columbus's voyages, by Africans from the Mandingo Empire of Mali, as well as for an Egypto-Nubian presence in both Central and South America before the Christian era. At the same time, this work is, in no way, a denial of the importance of Columbus's voyages in opening up the New World to Europe and, hence, changing the economic and political map of the world for all time.

The critical cutting edge of this book is that there is an anthropological and ethnographic dimension to the process of discovery; one in which black Africans of non-European origins played a central role. Dr. Van Sertima marshals the literary and pictorial evidence, showing its authenticity to be beyond question. The pre-Columbian period is not just a matter of dating, but of discovery. The impact of these early discoveries are of far more than historical interest. They serve as a basis to examine, anew, the study of cultural contacts between civilizations. And in so doing, offer a serious base to a multifaceted re-examination of earlier hypotheses of influences in both directions. This publication has been of wide interest to historians, social scientists, and all those for whom the question of race and culture is a central facet of their own work and lives.

Runoko Rashidi, writer, activist, essayist, "the Global African Community", had this to say:

> With absolute certainty it can be stated that, due to Dr. Van Sertima's consistent and unrelenting scholarship over the past twenty-five years in the rewriting of African history and the reconstruction of the African's place in world history, particularly in the field of the African presence in ancient America, he has cemented his position as one of our greatest [living] scholars. Indeed, during this turbulent and exciting

period, he has been at the vanguard of those scholars fighting to place African history in a new light.

As a Literary Critic

Dr. Van Sertima was the author of several major literary reviews published in Denmark, India, Britain, and the United States. He was honored for his work in this field by being asked by the Nobel Committee of the Swedish Academy to nominate candidates for the Nobel Prize in Literature from 1976 to 1980. He was also honored as an historian of world repute by being asked to join UNESCO's International Commission for Rewriting the Scientific and Cultural History of Mankind.

As a Linguist

As a linguist, Dr. Van Sertima published essays on the dialect of the Sea Islands off the Georgia Coast. He was also the compiler of the *Swahili Dictionary of Legal Terms*, based on his field work in Tanzania, East Africa, in 1967.

As a Poet and Essayist

As an acclaimed poet, in 1958, a collection of his poems were published in *River and the Wall*. Poems translated into German appear in an *Anthology of African and African-American Writers*, Schwarzer Orpheus, in 1964. He also wrote *Poetry from the Negro World*, 1967.

Caribbean Writers, a collection of critical essays were commissioned by the Foreign Office for Dakar through the auspices of the Central Office of Information, London. They were broadcast largely in French to French West Africa and French-speaking Canada. Later the English version was sent out to scores of radio stations in the commonwealth and used by the British Council on the occasion of the independence of the various Caribbean territories, 1968.

As an essayist, his major pieces were published in *Talk That Talk* (Introduction by Henry Louis Gates Jr.), 1989. In 1986 he was published in *Future Directions for African and African-American Content in the School Curriculum, Enigma of Values* in 1975, and *Black Life and Culture in the United States* in 1971.

As an Outstanding Scholar, Lecturer and Activist

In addition to his professorship at Rutgers and Princeton Universities, he lectured to more than one hundred universities in the United States, Canada, the Caribbean, South America and Europe. He also defended his highly controversial thesis on the African presence in pre-Columbian America before the Smithsonian Institution, which published his address in 1994.

On July 7, 1987, Dr. Van Sertima, single-handedly made a landmark appearance before a Congressional Committee to challenge the Columbus myth. It was stunningly illuminating and brilliantly presented in the name of all peoples of color across the world.

Colleagues, Comrades and Friendship

Out of the many contributors to the *Journal* whom Dr. Van Sertima also considered friends, there are three who have been in the struggle, side by side with him since before he ever set foot on the shores of North America. The three are Jan Carew, Wilson Harris, and Edward Scobie. There are no words that can adequately describe the constant emotional support, friendship and inspiration that weaved an unbroken brotherhood, other than the warm and understanding relationship that each maintained and nurtured throughout the years.

Jan Carew and Van Sertima's friendship began in their homeland, Guyana, South America. They never questioned their commitment to the cause or to each other. And so, in their own ways, and with their own specialized scholarship, they worked together in spirit to achieve a more just world; a world of parity between races, always seizing the moment to provide an honorable and truthful, free-flowing education and dialogue with all whom they crossed paths with.

Prof. Carew, though born in British Guiana in 1920, spent most of his life abroad. He still leads a rich and varied life as writer, educator, artist, philosopher, and has also served as advisor to several nation states. After his initial education in British Guiana (now Guyana), he studied at universities in the United States, Czechoslovakia, and France.

Books by Carew include *Black Midas, The Wild Coast, Ghosts in our Blood: with Malcolm X in Africa, England and the Caribbean, The Sisters and Manco's Stories, Rape of Paradise: Columbus and the Birth of Racism in* the Americas, Gentle Revolutionary: Essays in Honor of Jan Carew, and The Guyanese Wanderer.

Prof. Jan Carew, emeritus professor, Northwestern University, wrote:

> There was a huge popular demonstration—probably the first major anti-colonial demonstration in which all the anti-colonial movements in the country joined forces to show their solidarity. And there was a particular incident which happened at the grave site during Ivan's father's funeral. The priest who was presiding over the burial ceremony had objected to the union flags that were unfurled at the gravesite. Van, who was willing to take risks for his beliefs from an early age, got hold of one of the flags and insisted that it be unfurled over his father's grave. He was in his teens at the time and he declared in a loud voice that all who wanted to unfurl red flags should do so, because, he said, that is what his father would have wanted. That was Van's first public, political statement.

Prof. Wilson Harris, also a fellow countryman, was granted knighthood by the queen of England in 2010. Van Sertima and Harris shared the love of literature and relished in the fruits of their labors. Harris provided a constant ear, encouragement, and cultural consciousness with Van Sertima throughout his young adult years, and that bond remained until the very end. It was a privilege and honor for Van Sertima to appraise Wilson Harris's novel *Tumatumari* under the title "The Sleeping Rocks" in *Enigma of Values*, 1975. Both delighted in the commonality of thought and analysis, as well as in the success of their literary creativity.

Among Harris's twenty-seven novels are *Palace of the Peacock* (1960), *The Secret Ladder* (1963), *Heartland* (1964), *The Waiting Room* (1967), *Black Marsden* (1972), and *Companions of the Day and Night* (1975). His short stories include "The Sleepers of Roraima" (1970) and "The Age of the Rainmakers" (1971).He is also the author of a volume of critical essays, *Tradition, The Writer and Society* (1967).

"Only a dialogue with the past can produce originality."

Sir Theodore Wilson Harris, novelist, essayist, poet, lecturer, wrote the following in 1978:

> Dear Ivan, I will be giving four lectures at the University of Guyana. In one of my public lectures I shall speak of your book, *They Came Before Columbus*. I have been re-reading it and would like to congratulate you again, Ivan, on the courageous and significant way you have pursued the themes of pre-Columbian presences. I am struck again by the style of the book which is excellent.

Prof. Edward Scobie distinguished professor, City College of New York, wrote regarding the *Journal of African Civilizations*. "A major work of scholarship ... It will have its permanent place in the rich cultural history of Africa."

Dr. Van Sertima concluded each lecture with the words of the great poet Aimé Césaire:

> Let me say in closing, it is not out of envy or hatred of any race that we seek to proclaim the great achievements of our own. We do this because we know that no race has a monopoly of intelligence, enterprise, or genius ... because we know that the race of man is far from finished, there is a great deal left to be done in the world. The race of man is only just beginning, and there is room for all of us at the rendezvous of history.

He is survived by his wife, Jacqueline L. P. Van Sertima, four adult children (in order of age) LaCheun, LaSarah, Lawrence, and Michael. He is also survived by siblings, Carlton, Maureen, Phyllis, Geoffrey, and brother-in-law, Ronald, a host of nieces and nephews and his longtime friends, Jan and Wilson.

Credits:

Webmaster for the *Journal of African Civilizations, Ltd.*, Inc. at www.journalofafricancivilizations.com: LaCheun L. Patten

Photographer: ©2008–2010 Jacqueline L. P. Van Sertima, photographer. Permission granted for one-time use in *Guyanese Achievers USA & Canada*.

Excerpt from Mission Statement:
Permission granted for one-time use in publication, *Guyanese Achievers USA & Canada*.

Jacqueline L.P. Van Sertima

November 15, 2010

Jennifer Welshman

Administrator and Community Worker

Jennifer Welshman is chief of staff to Ontario's Minister of Health Promotion. She is a past president member and current director of St. Rose's High School Alumni Association, Toronto chapter. She trained in Guyana as a stenographer and secretary.

She is a very active member of the Guyanese-Canadian community in Toronto. She has also acquired a good reputation for her commitment and dedication to excellence in management, community, and individual development which extend beyond the Guyanese community to the province of Ontario and beyond.

Her passion for helping and interacting with people and the countless hours given to numerous community projects throughout the years are all legendary.

Jennifer was born on April 27, 1947, in Georgetown, British Guiana, and lived first on Middle Street, then Robb Street, Dowding Street, Kitty, and South Ruimveldt Gardens, Greater Georgetown.

Her father was Joseph Christopher Dummett. He worked as a clerk at Weiting & Richter in Georgetown. Her mother, Edith May Dummett (nee Webber), was a housewife and administrator. Jennifer was the third child. The eldest was brother Maurice Albert Raymond Dummett, who was deputy controller of Customs in Guyana. Her sister Patricia Anne Dummett/McWatt/Castanheiro was a banker.

Jennifer's grandfather was A. R. F. Webber, a politician and journalist/writer in the then British Guiana during the 1920s and early 1930s. He was born in Tobago in 1880 and moved to British Guiana in 1899. He was editor of the *Daily Chronicle* from 1919 to1925 and editor of the *New Daily Chronicle* from 1925 to 1930. He became an elected official in 1921 and, in 1926, he and some other colleagues formed the first political party in the West Indies, the Popular Party. It preceded Marcus Garvey's People's Popular Party by two years. He represented the British Guiana Labor Union at various conferences in the United Kingdom. He was a poet and author of *Those That Be in Bondage: A Tale of Indian Indentures and Sunlit Western Waters* (1917) and *Centenary History and Handbook of British Guiana*. He died in 1932.

Jennifer was educated at the Ursuline Convent in Georgetown, St. Agnes (for primary education) and St. Rose's High School up to fifth form and obtained her GCE O levels. From St. Rose's she went to the Government Technical Institute in Georgetown where she attended a commercial course (shorthand, typing, business practice). Jennifer was a stenographer for a number of years; shorthand (an almost dead art now) eventually fell by the wayside.

Jennifer embarked on her secretarial/administrative career in Guyana, first as secretary to the general manager, First Federation Life Insurance Company in 1965. In 1975 she moved to the American Life Insurance Company, where she was secretary to the agency manager, up to 1978, and secretary to the general manager, IBM.

In November 1979, she moved to Canada. She secured appointment at the Bank of Montreal in 1980, and worked as executive assistant to various executives. She retired from the Bank in 2007 after twenty-seven years service with them.

In 2008, she was recruited as executive assistant and office manager to then newly elected member of Provincial Parliament for Scarborough-Guildwood, Honorable Margarett Best, who also held the portfolio of the Minister of Health Promotion. In 2009, Jennifer was promoted to chief of staff in the minister's office at the Ministry of Health Promotion.

Apart from her day job, Jennifer's life has always been filled with voluntary work, ever since her early years in Guyana. While in Georgetown she was associated with various organizations related to St. George's Cathedral. In Canada she served on the committee of St. Rose's Alumni

Association (Toronto). She is a past president and continues to serve on that committee.

She is one of the founding members of the highly successful Last Lap Lime and was assistant project manager for over three years up to 2008. In 2009 and 2010 she was a volunteer at the events. Last Lap Lime has grown at a rapid pace throughout the past fifteen years.

Jennifer is associate of the Guyana Burn & Healthcare Charitable Foundation and a member of the Executive Committee of the Scarborough-Guildwood Provincial Liberal Association (political association).

Jennifer's commitment, high standards of excellence, and willingness to develop innovative strategies and management practices is said to go a far way toward helping the province of Ontario to lead in health promotion within Canada and internationally.

What made Jennifer decide on the field of work in which she obviously has excelled? She says:

> Not being an academic, the "field" I am in chose me more than I chose it. The University of Life is a great teaching institution and one thing I think I have learned is that it is essential to do your best at whatever it is that you do. It is important to focus on the goal and keep moving forward without letting any surrounding negatives distract or detract from that goal. You have to keep moving forward. The unofficial name of one of Guyana's national songs (known to every school child) is "Onwards, Upwards." Very simple but a true goal. I was brought up in a home where moving "onwards and upwards" was expected of you, coupled with the grounding received at school.

When asked if there was anything significant in her early life that was a source of inspiration, she answered:

> The only thing I can think of as significant (and maybe something which contributed to some sort of political awareness) is attending a political meeting at Bourda Green as a teenager. While standing there not totally engaged in what the speaker, Sir Lionel Luckhoo, was saying, suddenly some of his words attracted me. The words were that one of the first socialists he ever met was A. R. F. Webber. That

sentence stopped me in my tracks for A. R. F. Webber was my grandfather. I didn't know a lot about him, having been born some thirty-five years after his death, and certainly did not know that he was a socialist. I think those few words set me on a different path; not an immediate 90 degree turn, but it did get me interested in who and what *he* was and, more importantly, who *I* am.

Jennifer has been married to Howard Anthony Welshman for forty-three years. They were married in September 30, 1967. He is a mechanical engineer. They have three children, Trevor, Roger, and Nicole, from whom they have four grandchildren, Mikayla, Adrianna, Naomi, and Ryan.

She was winner of Guyana Awards (Canada) 2010 Community Service Award.

Sources:

Websites accessed May 27, 2010, on Guyana Consulate Toronto, Guyana Awards (Canada)

November 3, 2010

Leslie Wight

Cricketer
British Guiana and Canada

Leslie Wight was a formidable opening batsman for British Guiana in the early 1950s. In Canada he played for Ontario and in 1959, he represented Canada against the MCC.

George Leslie Wight was born on May 28, 1929, in Georgetown, British Guiana. He died on January 4, 2004, in Toronto, Canada.

His father was Henry Delisle Wight, and his mother was Mary. Henry Wight was office manager at Percy Wight & Co., a well-known business in Georgetown. His mother was a housewife. Leslie was the sixth in the family of eight siblings. Older sisters Dorothy, Joyce, and Winnie are deceased; brothers Arnold, Norman, Peter, and Darwin are still alive.

Leslie attended the Ursuline Convent Primary School, then St. Stanislaus College in Georgetown, where he excelled at cricket and football.

His first and only job in British Guiana was with Bookers Sports Department. He emigrated to Canada in 1953 and secured employment at the Workmen's Compensation Board, where he worked until his illness in 1984 and subsequent retirement.

Leslie, Les to his friends, joined the Georgetown Cricket Club upon leaving St. Stanislaus College and followed the footsteps of his illustrious uncles Vibart Wight and Oscar Wight and brothers Arnold and Norman, all of whom represented British Guiana at cricket.

Norman was a British Guiana spin bowler for many years. Younger brother, Peter, also represented British Guiana at cricket before emigrating to the UK when he became a professional with Somerset. The youngest of the clan, Darwin, represented the colony at tennis.

Les was selected to play for the West Indies in the fourth test match against the touring India team at Bourda, his home ground, March 11 to 17 in 1953. The match ended in a draw and in his only inning he scored 21, batting at the number six spot in the order. This was unusual because he was an opening batsman.

Cricket was his life and love. He took great pride in representing his country and the West Indies at cricket and practiced assiduously. He possessed great powers of concentration and patience and these coupled with excellent technique made him into a formidable opening batsman. Evidence of this came in 1951 when he scored 262 not out in a total of 692 against Barbados at Bourda. The opening partnership of 390 with Glendon Gibbs (216) stood for many years. Les was on the field of play for the entire duration of match.

Les first represented British Guiana in 1950 against Barbados at Bridgetown in what were virtually trials for the West Indies Team to tour England later that year. His first class career spanned four years, during which he amassed 1171 runs at a very good average of 68.9. Shortly after representing the West Indies in 1953, Les emigrated to Canada. He settled in Toronto and continued to play cricket, representing Ontario on several occasions and Canada in 1959 against the visiting MCC team

In domestic cricket in Toronto, Les was a member of several clubs, including Dovercourt, Yorkshire, Victoria Park, Scarborough Colts, and Milliken Sports Club.

In 1984, Les was diagnosed with cancer of the spine, and doctors informed him that he would never walk again and that he had played his last cricket match. The doctors would not have known of the man's indomitable spirit and courage. He not only walked again but in a few years, he was back playing cricket, albeit of the "friendly" variety. He continued playing cricket up to three years before his passing in 2004.

Les married Elaine da Silva in 1953 in Toronto. The union produced four sons: Marvin, Jamie, Scott, and Andrew, who are all married and living in Toronto.

Leslie Wight was a laid-back, placid individual who lived for his wife and cricket. He had many friends in the cricketing world.

Source:
Joe Castanheiro, October 16, 2008

October 21, 2008

Colonel Geoffrey E. Woo-Ming.

MBBS, MSc, FScPH

Colonel Geoffrey Woo-Ming was one of two Open Scholars in Medicine for the University College of the West Indies in 1957, graduating with the degree of MBBS (Lond.) in 1964.

He did his internship at the UCWI University Hospital, then two years of pediatric training at the Hospital for Sick Children in Toronto, followed by a master's in public health and fellowship at the School of Public Health at the University of California, Berkeley.

His first US job was as an assistant professor of pediatrics at the Ohio State University School of Medicine for four years; then he moved to San Francisco to be the medical director of the largest neighborhood health center serving Asians in the United States, a position he held for another four years.

After that he was the chief medical officer of the Indian Health Service in California for nearly ten years, providing health services to 75,000 American Indians with a $130 million budget. He was also trained as a flight surgeon in the US Air Force Reserve, later transferring to the California Army National Guard, and then the US Army Reserve, where he was made a colonel focusing on bioterrorism.

In 1990 Geoffrey was admitted to the University of California, Davis, Law School, based on his LSAT (Law School Admission Test) score, which placed him in the 94th percentile of those taking the law school admission exam that year. In order to keep his benefits he tried to go to full-time law school and work as a part-time state physician, but he never graduated.

However, later that year he started a two-year racial discrimination lawsuit against the authorities for trying to prevent him from becoming a general. He argued this himself before the Ninth Circuit Court of Appeals, one step below the US Supreme Court.

August 7, 2008

Professor Michael O. Woo-Ming

MBBS (Lond.), FRCS (Edin.), FRCS (Eng.), FACS

Michael Ovid Woo-Ming was the only Guyanese in the original class of thirty-three medical students who started at the University College of the West Indies (UCWI), an overseas extension of the University of London, at Mona, Jamaica in 1948. Not only was he the first UCWI graduate professor of cardiothoracic surgery, but he developed the first open-heart surgical team in the British Caribbean in 1967, which is still operational in Jamaica and still the only one.

At age fifty, Professor Woo-Ming emigrated to the United States because of the violence in Jamaica, and practiced as a chest and vascular surgeon in Vero Beach, Florida, for twenty-three years.

Michael Ovid Woo-Ming was born on May 31, 1927, at Buxton, East Coast Demerara, British Guiana. His father ran a small business, and his mother was a homemaker. He is the third of four brothers and four sisters.

Eldest brother Winston, a brilliant student, gained six distinctions out of seven subjects in the Cambridge Senior School Certificate Examination and was persuaded by their aunt to help her husband run his wholesale grocery business in New Amsterdam. Brother Rex was a science graduate from UCWI, who obtained his PhD (London) before returning to Guyana to be the government analyst. Fourth brother Geoffrey was also a medical graduate from the newly independent University of the West Indies (UWI) in 1964. He did postgraduate studies in Canada and the United States, specializing in public health.

Sister Elsie was the first in the family to go overseas to get a BA (Toronto). She specialized in librarianship and was a librarian at the UCWI when it started in 1948. Bernice, a successful homemaker remained in Guyana to be with their parents while the rest of the siblings were overseas. Pat, also a successful homemaker, was the first of the family to emigrate to the United States. Norma, an arts graduate of UCWI, is the only one of the family still living in the West Indies, in Trinidad.

Michael attended St. Stephen's Scots School in Georgetown from 1938 to 1940, then went on to Central High School in Smyth Street, Georgetown, from where he passed the Senior Cambridge Certificate in 1943. He proceeded to St. Stanislaus College to study for the Cambridge Higher School Certificate. He passed this in 1945, and in 1946 he was runner-up for the Guyana Scholar. He took subjects Latin, and Pure and Applied Mathematics.

Keen to do medicine, he had to study from scratch the science subjects physics, chemistry, and biology to the Cambridge Higher School Certificate level. For this, Michael studied at home for one year, taking private tuition by Jerry Niles (physics and chemistry) and Bevis (biology), who were teachers at Queen's College. He passed those subjects, obtaining exemption from the intermediate BA (London) in 1947.

He was admitted to study medicine at the University College of the West Indies in 1948. Michael was the only Guyanese in the thirty-three students selected from 800 applicants from the English-speaking Caribbean Islands. They were the first batch of students to enter the brand new University College, and Michael, with fourteen others, graduated with the degree of MBBS (London) in 1954.

Michael did his internship and surgical residency at University Hospital of the West Indies in Jamaica from 1955 to 1958, then obtained postgraduate surgical qualifications: FRCS (Edinburgh) 1959, FRCS (England) in 1960, and FACS (USA) in 1983.

For his further training as a surgeon, Michael was surgical registrar at Middlesex Hospital, one of the leading London teaching hospitals. In 1960 until 1962, he was surgical resident and chief resident, London Chest Hospital, training in heart and lung surgery. Here, one of his teachers was the famous Sir Thomas Holmes Sellors, who did the first open heart operation in Great Britain.

He returned to the University of the West Indies (UWI) in 1962 to take up an appointment as lecturer in surgery and consultant surgeon at the University Hospital. In 1968, he was promoted to senior lecturer in surgery and senior consultant surgeon, University Hospital and National Chest Hospital. In 1971, the title of "reader in surgery" was conferred on Michael as a mark of distinction for his performance in open heart surgery. Finally, a new professorship in cardiothoracic surgery was created for him in 1976 for his pioneering work in open heart surgery.

Michael's greatest accomplishment was starting the cardiac surgery unit in Jamaica in 1967 after three years of preparation. At this time, open heart surgery was just coming out of its infancy, and there were rapidly changing developments in cardiac diagnosis, surgical techniques, surgical equipment, and patient care. As to be expected, operative mortality was quite high. In order to update himself, Michael spent three months visiting cardiac surgical units in London, Denmark, Sweden, and the United States; one month was spent with world famous heart surgeons Cooley and Debakey in Houston, and Kirklin at the Mayo Clinic.

He then had to use limited funds to buy the updated equipment and train a team for over a year in the animal laboratory before undertaking the first open heart operation in the British West Indies. His first twenty-six patients with congenital heart disease (seven were complex cyanotic Tetralogy of Fallot) had no operative mortality, at a time when even at the best cardiac centers the operative mortality was about 10 percent.

Michael was particularly gratified when he was approached in the United States by a healthy looking thirty-five-year old man who was working full time with an airline in the Bahamas, on whom he had done a total correction of a Tetralogy of Fallot, thirty years earlier in Jamaica.

The story of that history-making open heart surgery at UWI is told by Michael's recollection of these highlights of the exciting and challenging activities in his role as a lead surgeon in the teaching, practice, and development of open heart and lung surgery:

> Promote and teach this topic as a separate major specialty. This message had to be delivered to medical students, graduate doctors aspiring to be surgeons, all medical staff members (surgeons and non-surgeons), administrative staff of the

hospital, administrative staff of the university, doctors outside the university, and the general public.

The message was delivered through lectures, meetings, personal contacts, and performance of the surgery. Key members of the various committees, especially those controlling funds had to be convinced to support development of this "new" specialty in the presence of competition from all the other established specialties for the same available, and always inadequate, funds.

This rapidly advancing specialty demanded visits to the most reputable centers to update our surgical practice, especially in relation to open heart surgery, which required expensive equipment and a large team of trained personnel to start the program.

The experimental laboratory had to be equipped and organized for regular training visits by members of the team. Support to the cardiologists to get expensive equipment for a cardiac catheterization laboratory to investigate and select patients for surgery.

Costly expansion of the intensive care unit also had to be supported. Careful preoperative planning, good surgery, and excellent postoperative care by the team provided the necessary data for promotion of the specialty. Small mortality and minimal complications after surgery were essential to get continued support in the poor financial setting.

Development of a joint cardiothoracic surgical unit between the university and the Jamaica Government National Chest Hospital to help accommodate the resulting expansion of all these services.

The *West Indian Medical Journal* publication of December 1980 contained a supplement, that featured articles by the leading participants in that moment of history. Titled "A Decade of Open Heart Surgery 1968–1978: at the University Hospital of the West Indies, Kingston, Jamaica," the supplement recorded the first open heart surgery operations performed in the English-speaking Caribbean.

Sir Harry Annamunthodo, professor of surgery, wrote in the foreword, in part:

> The two outstanding milestones in the development of the Department of Surgery, University of the West Indies (UWI), were the establishment of neurosurgical and cardiothoracic units.
>
> In the early 1960s the expanded University Hospital became functional. The University Hospital had been operational for nearly ten years … At about this time, two members of our first graduating class, Mr. M. O. Woo-Ming, who was trained in cardiac surgery, and Dr. D. Christian, who had acquired training in cardiac investigation, including cardiac catheterization, joined the staff.
>
> The need for a cardiac surgery unit in the West Indies was undeniable. A few patients could go abroad for treatment, but the majority here were denied the opportunity of consultation and adequate investigation. The start of a unit, however, presented enormous problems in attracting suitable personnel, to train and weld them into a team and, of course, there was the cost to be considered in a developing community. It was realized that to start this project in a small insular community with early failures could set back the entire program indefinitely.
>
> Against this background it was decided to embark on an intensive animal laboratory study, and to select the team carefully and train members locally. Because of limited funds, ingenuity and improvisation were essential. Over the period of a year in the laboratory, technicians, including heart-lung machine operators, were trained by the anesthetist, Dr. Sivapragasam. Operative techniques were improved upon and a research project was conducted. During this year, the UWI cardiologists prepared a waiting list of fully investigated patients for open heart surgery. The support of voluntary bodies to ensure an adequate supply of fresh blood was elicited.
>
> The first open heart surgical operation at the University Hospital was successfully performed on April 9, 1968. The

> first twenty-six operations, with the aid of cardiopulmonary bypass for congenital heart defects, were performed without an operative death.
>
> The next stage was valve surgery. It was felt that homograft replacement would be most suitable for Jamaica because of the low cost involved and decreased incidence of thromboembolism. These valves had to be collected and prepared by the unit. The co-operation of other departments, especially pathology, and the enthusiasm of the technicians made this project feasible. …
>
> The University of the West Indies has shown that it is possible to establish a modest open heart surgery unit with limited funds supplemented with a great deal of dedication and enthusiasm. Incidentally, I know of no other similar unit which became functional with such meager funds. In spite of this, few units can boast of equal initial success. The unit has provided treatment to patients from the entire Caribbean area.

Professor of Anesthesia, John W. Sandison, in the foreword, added, in part:

> Twelve years ago, no open heart surgery was performed in Jamaica or elsewhere in the English-speaking Caribbean … The ensuing ten years saw the introduction and development of a successful open heart surgical unit at the University Hospital of the West Indies … The fundamental achievement of this project was that within a ten-year period, cardiac surgical care of a standard found in an advanced medical community had been made available to nearly two million inhabitants of Jamaica …
>
> Professor Michael Woo-Ming directed the unit through its first few years. Although he steadfastly maintained that credit must be directed to the "team" and not to him, he was the leader of the group. He was uniquely involved in the concept, growth and function of the project. He had an unswerving determination to succeed and despite all financial, bureaucratic and administrative difficulties, his steady optimism positively

> influenced his colleagues to sustain their efforts. He was a careful planner. Only after a prolonged period of preparation based on visits abroad by the physicians involved and a lengthy period of experience in the experimental surgery laboratory did he cautiously institute the program. He was indeed fortunate in having Dr. Sivapragasam in anesthesia and Dr. Christian in cardiology as his associates from the earliest days of the project ... The relationship between the senior surgeon and anesthetist was a model one, based on trust, respect, and recognition of each other's ability.
>
> Professor Woo-Ming clearly recognized the need to train surgical personnel for this area ... Two striking memories remain. One was the intense level of personal contribution shown by the team ... Second was the evident satisfaction, pleasure, and enjoyment shown by the participants. It was an exciting time in the University Hospital of the West Indies. A significant advance in the medical services of the community was underway.

Michael's contribution to the foreword was, in part:

> The day arrived for the first operation. This had to be successful if the program were to survive! I well remember the morning of April 9, 1968, when, just before making the skin incision, the thought flashed through my mind that one small air bubble to the brain could mean the end of all our previous efforts. Thanks to good team work, the operation was a success and the team went on to correct its first twenty-six congenital cardiac defects (seven were cases with cyanotic Tetralogy of Fallot) without an operative mortality, quite an achievement in those early days ...
>
> The main cardiac surgical problems which were of economic importance were congenital and rheumatic heart disease. To obviate the disadvantages of prosthetic valve replacement—high cost and post-operative systemic anticoagulation—a homograft valve replacement program was developed ... From this arose a method of mitral valve replacement in small

> children that could well turn out to be a major contribution of international significance.
>
> In the early years, there were periods lasting from weeks to months when open heart surgery could not be performed because of some "unavoidable" reason ... These periods of inactivity could have seriously interfered with the development of the necessary intra-operative expertise, had it not been for the extraordinary efforts by the team, especially in the area of pre-operative preparation and planning.
>
> Full credit must be given to those who participated and supported the program especially the nurses, technicians, and medical personnel, all of whom frequently performed well beyond their line of duty. One of our chief surgical residents, Mr. H. Spencer, deserves special mention for his performance ... Sir Harry Annamunthodo, the head of the Department of Surgery during those early years, was outstanding in his support. There were many others who freely gave of their time and expertise; and to them a special word of thanks. And to those who were with me for most of the decade—Professor J. W. Sandison, doctors Sivapragasam, Don Christian, James Ling, Keith McKenzie, Colin Miller, and Gerry Humphries—congratulations to you, the pioneers of open heart surgery in the West Indies, for a difficult job well done! From outside Jamaica, assistance came from many world-renowned surgeons, including Magdi Yacoub and Mark Baimbridge.
>
> The survival of open heart surgery at the University Hospital is certain as the foundation has been well laid. With recent advances, particularly with improving myo-cardial preservation, I am confident that the salvage rate will be even higher amongst those patients with "sick" hearts.

Dr. S. Sivapragasam, Department of Anesthetics and Intensive Care, University of the West Indies Kingston, Jamaica, wrote in the preface to the supplement, in part:

> It has been a pleasure and a privilege working with professors Woo-Ming and Sandison, the two pioneers of open heart surgery at the University Hospital. Their contribution to the

program set an example to all the other members of the team, including myself.

In 1979 Michael resigned from the Chair of Professor of Cardiothoracic Surgery because of the severe social unrest in Jamaica.

In the United States, Prof. Michael Woo-Ming, pioneer open heart surgeon, had to start all over again. He found that the American cardiac surgery programs only needed their own residents to complete training, not professors who had run their own program, and particularly since he had no formal American training. So he worked as an emergency room physician at the Indian River Memorial Hospital (IRMH), in Vero Beach, Florida, while he looked for an opening in cardiothoracic surgery.

One night a man was admitted. He had been shot in the chest by the police, creating a hole in the main airway going to the right lung. He needed emergency chest surgery. Michael stood behind the general surgeons and instructed them how to use a muscle flap from the chest wall to repair the very serious injury, and the man survived. Later, the general surgeons invited Michael to join their group as a chest surgeon after they monitored and approved him for operating privileges. After a critical analysis of the requisite number of surgical operations, he was made a Fellow of the American College of Surgeons, without having to take an examination, on the recommendation of several established American surgical peers.

From 1980 to '85, he was the first thoracic surgeon in Vero Beach, Florida, in private practice, with a group of four general surgeons. There was a community need here. From 1986 to 2003 he was the thoracic and vascular surgeon in solo private practice, at the Indian River Memorial Hospital (IRMH), Vero Beach. He retired in 2003 at age seventy-six. For his twenty-four years service at Indian River Memorial Hospital, he was feted at a rare and magnificent farewell party by the staff (medical and non-medical) of the hospital—a fitting good-bye to a man who had made a special place in the hearts of all at IRMH.

Michael's exceptional gifts have been marked from his early years by significant awards. In 1946, he was runner-up, Guyana Scholar. In 1951 he received the Clinical Introductory Course Prize for medical students; in 1954 Obstetrics & Gynecology Prize in the final medical graduation examination; in 1958, Leverhulme Fellowship for two years further postgraduate surgical training in England, the award based on his performance as a trainee surgeon at the University Hospital the previous three years.

He was recipient in 1969 of the Kingston Jaycees Award for Outstanding Service to the People of Jamaica, mainly for developing and making open heart surgery available to the people of Jamaica.

In 1976 he was president of the Association of Surgeons in Jamaica. He took a sabbatical (to update himself on the surgery of blocked arteries of the heart), as visiting professor, Division of Thoracic and Cardiovascular Surgery (Research), University of Miami School of Medicine, Miami, Florida, and research fellow, Miami Heart Institute. In 1977 he received the Princess Alice Award.

In August 1978, Sir Harry Annamunthodo, FRCS, professor of Clinical Surgery at the UWI, in a letter of introduction, paid this tribute to Michael, in part:

> From his early years as a junior doctor in the University Hospital, he showed an aptitude for surgery. He was meticulous, reliable, and good with his hands. He always placed the interest or his patients and their family first. He was always able to create enthusiasm among his professional colleagues and other members of the health team, even when he makes great demands or them ...
>
> He then set about organizing a cardiothoracic service in Jamaica ... Woo-Ming, with very little funds, set about training the entire team required. He had to improvise much of the equipment ... After two years of hard work in the laboratory, he started an open heart service. I was myself pleasantly surprised at our high success rate...The university has recognized the contribution of Woo-Ming in development of cardiac surgery by creating a professorship in the discipline, to which he was appointed.

In the United States, he was in 1983 elected a Fellow of the American College of Surgeons without having to sit an examination, to acknowledge his performance in heart and lung surgery.

Michael's community work in Florida was recognized. In 1997 the Florida Medical Association presented a Certificate of Recognition, in appreciation for educational and professional services donated to children, teenagers, the homeless, the indigent elderly, and the medically indigent.

On the occasion of its fiftieth anniversary, in 1998, Michael was named distinguished graduate of the University of the West Indies.

In November 2001 Michael received the University of the West Indies Medical Alumni Award. The citation, read by Henry S. Fraser, at the glittering event held at St. Kitts/Nevis, gave glimpses of Mike's special gifts as a surgeon, his leading role in the groundbreaking developments in open heart surgery, and the warm person he is. The citation stated in part:

> He entered the very first class and the very first medical class in 1948…He was the only Guyanese…He soon met a beautiful Jamaican, Prudence Lue Sang, and Mike Woo wooed Prue Lue, Sang his way to her heart, and carried her off on the pillion of a memorable motorbike, which he bought, behind his father's back…But romance did not hinder his other academic goals…and he started an epidemic of UWI Woo-Mings, arriving at the same time as his oldest sister, Elsie, to be followed by Rex in 1954 and Geoffrey in 57; sixteen years of Woo-Ming undergraduates and many more of Woo-Ming contributions at the highest level.
>
> After graduating …his fame for single-minded pursuit of knowledge was exceeded only by his notorious alcohol intolerance - he was reputed to get drunk just standing among drinkers! In 1958 he won a Leverhulme Fellowship to pursue postgraduate training in Edinburgh and London…He was the role model…being the first UWI graduate appointed lecturer and consultant…his good humor, wit, enthusiasm, mimicable mannerisms and unique laughter made him a great favorite with students.
>
> We all recall the trauma of crime and harassment at that time in Jamaica … that drove some 60,000 Jamaicans to the United States. Mike was a victim of threats, and some of his family were attacked, and sadly, Jamaica lost a dedicated adopted son. But starting again at fifty-two is not easy, (but he did so) with inimitable Woo-Ming flair and distinction … Mike Woo-Ming was a West Indian pioneer and a vintage product of our alma mater - actively associated with UWI for thirty years.

What has motivated Michael, who has coauthored and authored over twenty-seven publications? He says:

> Looking back, I believe it all started with my parents. From early childhood, encouraging me to go to school and do my best in whatever I did. All my teachers also always encouraged me in various ways to do my best.
>
> Specific motivating factors developed along the way. After passing the Senior Cambridge Exam, it struck me that a university education would better qualify me to be a useful member of the community. My parents did not have the financial means and so the only way to do this was to win the Guyana Scholarship. I therefore competed for this in 1946, but missed it as the runner-up. This failure seemed to have spurred me on to being someone really useful in the community. At this time I was beginning to appreciate that physicians were among the most highly regarded members of the community because of their great help to the sick. This idea of becoming a physician was made possible by the financial assistance from my older brother Winston and my aunt Keturah Sam.
>
> Thereafter, my progress was influenced by opportunities as they occurred. During the early years after graduating, I was encouraged to become a surgeon by one of my teachers, a renowned Guyanese, Sir Harry Annamunthodo, who was the chairman of the Department of Surgery. This led to my winning a Leverhulme Fellowship to go to Great Britain for two further years surgical training and obtain the necessary higher surgical qualifications. During this training, I also passed both of the coveted Scottish and English surgical fellowship examinations. Sir Harry Annamunthodo then asked me to spend two additional years training in heart and lung surgery, as there was a great need for such a surgeon at the University and in the West Indies. That's how I became the surgeon to develop heart surgery at the University of the West Indies.

When asked if he has any advice for young people, he summarizes it thus:

> As you progress through high school, try to develop a general overall plan to do things which will make you and those around you happy. This plan will be modified as you mature and will get more specific as time goes by. Do a job of your choice. This makes you happy and able to work tirelessly to achieve your goals. Do your best in whatever you do. Do not give up if any of your plans fail. Use any failure to achieve greater heights. Seek guidance and help when you cannot solve any problem. Freely acknowledge this assistance. Help others whenever you can. Do not stop at any achievement. There is always something better or something new. Be honest in whatever you do.

Michael's wife, Prudence, is the daughter of Thompson and Lucy Lue Sang, and was born in Kingston, Jamaica, on May 30, 1931. She is the fourth of ten children. Her father was born in Southern China and emigrated to Jamaica in 1925. He was a scholar, read and wrote Mandarin, and was fluent in several Chinese dialects. He ran a small business with the technical expertise to repair watches, clocks, and firearms, including automatic weapons. Her mother was the daughter of a Scottish landowner and a native Jamaican. Her eldest sister Ena Lue Sang-Allen (now deceased) was the first female judge to be appointed to the Supreme Court in Jamaica in 1973.

Prudence was a bright student. In 1951she passed the Higher School Certificate; in English language, English literature, Spanish, and history. She took this exam after one year's study and came first in her class. In 1961 she became an associate of the Chartered Institute of Secretaries, London, England, winning the award for the best woman candidate. In 1966 she obtained her BA (Hons) UWI, in English, economics and sociology. She has coauthored a publication titled "Aspects of fertility control in Jamaica."

After the family emigrated to the United States in 1978, Prudence was Michael's office manager for seventeen years until they both retired in 2003. She had to learn to establish and run a physician's office, dealing with all the complex non-medical aspects of patient care, but Prudence's main job during the fifty-five years of their marriage has been as codeveloper and provider of their home as Michael moved to different jobs.

Their only child, Ann Marie, is a physician specializing in psychiatry. She is married to Henry Park, also a physician, who has specialized as a dermatologist. They have three daughters.

September 23, 2010

Map of Guyana

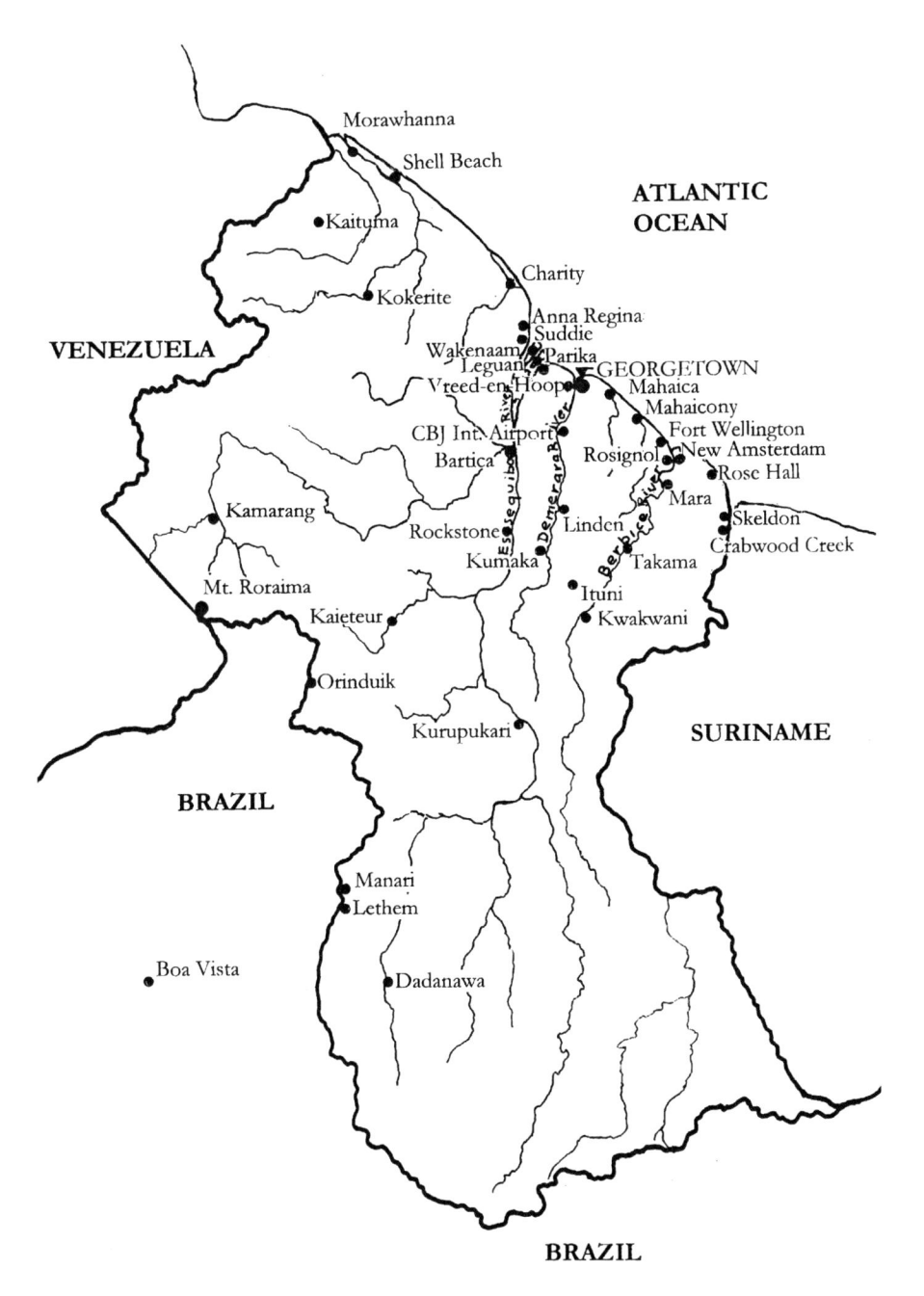